Conversations With Alice Paul

The Bancroft Library   University of California/Berkeley
Regional Oral History Office

Suffragists Oral History Project

CONVERSATIONS WITH ALICE PAUL:
WOMAN SUFFRAGE AND THE EQUAL RIGHTS AMENDMENT

An Interview Conducted by
Amelia R. Fry

Copy No. 1

Alice Paul in 1917 (left) and today: A lifetime crusade

TABLE OF CONTENTS -- Alice Paul

Conversations of November 24-26, 1972

SECTION II: THE USA SUFFRAGE CAMPAIGN

THE NATURE AND ROLE OF WOMEN   401

PREFACE

    The Suffragists Oral History Project was designed to tape
record interviews with the leaders of the woman's suffrage
movement in order to document their activities in behalf of
passage of the Nineteenth Amendment and their continuing
careers as leaders of movements for welfare and labor reform,
world peace, and the passage of the Equal Rights Amendment.
Because the existing documentation of the suffrage struggle
indicates a need for additional material on the campaign of
the National Woman's Party, the contribution of this small
but highly active group has been the major focus of the series.

    The project, underwritten by a grant from the Rockefeller
Foundation, enabled the Regional Oral History Office to record
first-hand accounts of this early period in the development
of women's rights with twelve women representing both the
leadership and the rank and file of the movement. Five held
important positions in the National Woman's Party. They are
Sara Bard Field, Burnita Shelton Matthews, Alice Paul,
Rebecca Hourwich Reyher, and Mabel Vernon. Seven interviews
are with women who campaigned for suffrage at state and local
levels, working with other suffrage organizations. Among
this group is Jeannette Rankin, who capped a successful
campaign for suffrage in Montana with election to the House
of Representatives, the first woman to achieve this distinction.
Others are Valeska Bary, Jessie Haver Butler, Miriam Allen
de Ford, Ernestine Kettler, Laura Ellsworth Seiler, and
Sylvie Thygeson.

    Planning for the Suffragists Project and some preliminary
interviews had been undertaken prior to receipt of the grant.
The age of the women--74 to 104--was a compelling motivation.
A number of these interviews were conducted by Sherna Gluck,
Director of the Feminist History Research Project in Los
Angeles, who has been recording interviews with women active
in the suffrage campaigns and the early labor movement.
Jacqueline Parker, who was doing post-doctoral research on
the history of the social welfare movement, taped interviews
with Valeska Bary. A small grant from a local donor permitted
Malca Chall to record four sessions with Jeannette Rankin. Both
Valeska Bary and Jeannette Rankin died within a few months of
their last interviewing session.

The grant request submitted to the Rockefeller Foundation covered funding both to complete these already-recorded interviews and to broaden the scope and enrich the value of the project by the inclusion of several women not part of the leadership. The grant, made in April, 1973, also provided for the deposit of all the completed interviews in five major manuscript repositories which collect women's history materials.

In the process of research, a conference with Anita Politzer (who served more than three decades in the highest offices of the National Woman's Party, but was not well enough to tape record that story) produced the entire series of Equal Rights and those volumes of the Suffragist missing from Alice Paul's collection; negotiations are currently underway so that these in-party organs can be available to scholars everywhere.

The Suffragists Project as conceived by the Regional Oral History Office is to be the first unit in a series on women in politics. Unit two will focus on interviews with politically active and successful women during the years 1920-1970; and unit three, interviews with women who are incumbents in elective office today.

The Regional Oral History Office was established to tape record autobiographical interviews with persons prominent in the history of the West and the nation. The Office is under the administrative supervision of James D. Hart, Director of The Bancroft Library.

Malca Chall, Director
Suffragists Oral History Project

Amelia Fry, Interviewer-Editor

Willa Baum, Department Head
Regional Oral History Office

2 January 1974
Regional Oral History Office
486 The Bancroft Library
University of California at Berkeley

SUFFRAGISTS ORAL HISTORY PROJECT

BARY, Helen Valeska. Labor Administration and Social Security: A Woman's Life. 1974

MATTHEWS, Burnita Shelton. Pathfinder in the Legal Aspects of Women. 1975

PAUL, Alice. Conversations with Alice Paul: Woman Suffrage and the Equal Rights Amendment. 1976

RANKIN, Jeannette. Activist for World Peace, Women's Rights, and Democratic Government. 1974

REYHER, Rebecca Hourwich. Working for Women's Equality. In process

THE SUFFRAGISTS: FROM TEA-PARTIES TO PRISON. 1975

    Thygeson, Sylvie, "In the Parlor"
    Butler, Jessie Haver, "On the Platform"
    deFord, Miriam Allen, "In the Streets"
    Seiler, Laura Ellsworth, "On the Soapbox"
    Kettler, Ernestine, "Behind Bars"

VERNON, Mabel. The Suffrage Campaign, Peace and International Relations. 1976

INTERVIEW HISTORY

Alice Paul was the leader of the more militant suffrage
and equal rights organization called the National Woman's
Party. After campaigning in England with Mrs. Pankhurst,
the young Quaker returned to this country, finished a Ph.D.,
and in 1912 became the head of the congressional committee
of the National American Woman Suffrage Association. Her
group soon spun off from the mother organization, rejecting
the state-by-state referenda as a method of achieving equal
suffrage and evolving into the National Woman's Party, which
worked for suffrage by constitutional amendment. The ener-
getic militants soon became known for their central political
strategies: make suffrage a mainstream issue through public
demonstrations and protests, and increase political clout by
holding the party in power responsible in elections in western
states where women already had the vote.

The actual tape recording of Alice Paul's memoir was
preceded by a half dozen years of intermittent and fruitless
negotiations between this indomitable leader and myself. I
first met her when I came to research the archives of the
National Woman's Party headquarters at the Alva-Belmont House
in Washington and to read the party's papers in the Library
of Congress.

Each trip east thereafter I stayed at the Alva-Belmont
House, where Alice lived and where women writers, doctors,
lawyers, and long-time Woman's Party members frequently so-
journed. There Alice and I had long conversations at night
about the past. While these increased our friendship, they
did little to get Alice's own story preserved for posterity:
she objected to tape or notebook, and explained more than once
that it was unthinkable to embark on a taping project when
the ERA still needed everyone's assistance in Congress. It
was not long before I was sporadically lobbying House Judiciary Subcommittee members for passage of the ERA whenever I
was in Washington, or when Alice called me and I could arrange
my work to go.

I had jokingly struck a bargain with Alice: I would lobby
if she would agree to tape record after ERA passed Congress.
While my lobbying held undetermined value for the ERA, it
was an indispensable apprenticeship for historical inquiry
into political processes. I am indebted to Alice and to the
National Woman's Party for making this experience possible.

It was Alice's departure from Washington after the passage of the ERA in Congress in 1972 that set the stage for our interviews. Although she continued to nurse ratification through state after state from her telephone in her lakeside cottage in Ridgefield, Connecticut, she has never returned to headquarters. The abrupt change in leadership in the National Woman's Party which occurred at that time is a fertile subject for theses of the future.

Regardless of her continuing work on ratification, Alice recognized that she could make time to tape her memoirs, and she invited me to come to Ridgefield.

Our first interview sessions were held November 24 to 26, 1972, with neither of us knowing whether there would ever be adequate funding for transcribing, correcting, and retyping. The following spring Rockefeller Foundation made possible the processing of that session's tapes and a much-needed second session, which we held May 10 to 12, 1973. Both were three-day marathons.* The second session circles back to expand on some of the material we had covered during the first because the arrival of the grant made possible additional research in other collections and, therefore, different questions.

Among sources which proved most helpful were the National Woman's Party's The Suffragist, a weekly publication which became Equal Rights in 1923, Inez Haynes Irwin's Story of the Woman's Party (Harcourt, Brace & World, New York, 1921), and Doris Stevens, Jailed for Freedom (New York, 1920). Many papers relating to the Woman's Party and Alice Paul were found in several cross-referenced collections in Radcliffe College's Schlesinger Library and in the Anne Martin-Mable Vernon papers in The Bancroft Library at the University of California, Berkeley. Because at the time of the interview the National Woman's Party was denying most people, including myself, access to Paul's papers and other materials in the headquarter's library, the ample footnotes in the thesis of Loretta Ellen Zimmerman, who earlier had had access to the Paul correspondence, were of unique value. (See "Alice Paul and the National Woman's Party, 1912-1920;" thesis, Tulane University, Ph.D., 1964.)

Among difficult-to-locate books that Alice made available at her cottage was one whose careful documentation made it especially helpful: Carolyn Katzenstein's "Lifting the Curtain," written from her notes at the time of the campaigns; although

---

*See the more detailed account, "Interviewer's Impressions," dictated December 30, 1972, which follows.

it is from the vantage point of the Pennsylvania chapter of
the Woman's Party it sheds a great deal of light on the national
scene. The classic six-volume history of suffrage from the
view of the National American Woman Suffrage Association is
probably familiar to anyone who reads Alice Paul's transcript;
volumes V and VI, edited by Ida Husted Harper and published
in New York in 1922, provided the first steps in my preparation. So also did the ground-breaking history, Century of
Struggle, written by Eleanor Flexner in 1959 for Harvard University Press; chapters XX to XXIV of my paperback copy (Atheneum
Press) were well-thumbed by the time Alice agreed to tape
record. Other more recent books on suffrage and on the broader
struggle for women's rights (like William L. O'Neill's Everyone Was Brave, Quadrangle, Chicago, 1969) were used and are
referred to in the interview text.

Alice was still working on ratification of the ERA in
Connecticut and other states when I sent her the rough-edited
version of the first two chapters of our transcript. As could
be predicted, they lay on her desk while she organized supporters via her telephone, and while her next door neighbor
and close friend, "Scotty" Reynolds, and I carried on a lively
correspondence about how to get Alice to check through it.
Among other obstacles, Alice was plagued by poor vision and
would not take the time to get new glasses.

Then, one day in March, 1974, Alice fell. Ultimately she
was taken to a New York hospital, then transferred shortly
to a nursing home in Ridgefield. Diagnoses had progressed
from "just bruises" to a concussion to a mild stroke. Her
period of residence at the nursing home drew more protracted,
and in November I was granted the rare privilege of visiting
her. She was eager to know how the ERA campaign was progres-
sing and anxious to get to Washington so she could properly
organize her papers for deposit in an archive. Although our
discussion was as lucid as old times, an anxiety to return to
her cottage underlay her customary serenity, probably because
she still was denied newspapers, TV news, letters, phone calls
and visitors. We agreed that her transcript should be issued
as soon as possible, that this office would finish it in its
verbatim form and edit any ambiguities in the text with
notations in footnotes and brackets.

Her nephew, Donald Paul, proofread the manuscript and
added notations about the family, which are in brackets and
footnotes and attributed to him.

At this writing, the current legal efforts on Alice's
behalf have removed some of the restrictions on her, two
years after she was placed in the convalescent home. Hopes
are high that she may indeed move back into her cottage. It

should be noted that her indomitable spirit and powerful mind
may well lend her determination enough to live to see the ERA
through to ratification and to establish her long-cherished
plan for a world-wide equal rights organization. The wise
research historian using this manuscript would be well-advised
to check for a post-memoir career for Alice Paul.

> Amelia R. Fry
> Interviewer/Editor

5 January, 1976
Regional Oral History Office
486 The Bancroft Library
University of California, Berkeley

THE INTERVIEWER'S IMPRESSIONS OF ALICE PAUL

Dictated on December 30, 1972 after the interview sessions of
November 24-26, 1972; edited, December 23, 1975.

    Alice Paul and I met about six years before the interview,
when I had gone to Washington searching for material about Sara
Bard Field's 1915 automobile campaign for suffrage. National
Woman's Party headquarters, in the elegant and ancient Alva-
Belmont mansion, housed a veritable goldmine of suffrage material in its library. When I met Alice Paul to get her permis-
sion to use it, she wondered aloud how anyone in good conscience
could spend research time on the long-gone suffrage campaign
when so much effort was currently needed to pass the Equal
Rights Amendment. I pondered silently how anyone could continue
to make history and remain insensitive to the historical impera-
tive.

    After that first stalemate, I usually took one of the rooms
at the elegant Alva-Belmont House whenever I was in Washington.
There, after dinner in the garden in the warmer months, or with
trays in the living room if it was winter, Alice would tell
me some of the history of the Equal Rights Amendment. When our
talks stretched into the evening hours, she would even go into
her recollections of the suffrage struggle, and often our sessions would not break up until the early hours of morning.
But she would never let me turn on a tape recorder, and if I
pulled out a pencil to take notes she would say, "Oh, don't
take notes on this. This isn't really worthwhile," or "Everything we have is either in the Library of Congress or right
here."

    In 1972 the Equal Rights Amendment passed Congress. It
was yet to be ratified, but she had moved to Connecticut because
there were some drastic changes taking place at the Alva-Belmont
House. At the same time an article had appeared on her in a
popular history magazine which she felt was unsatisfactory.
These two factors created hope that she might finally respond
to the constant overtures to tape record her life history.
Perhaps Alice realized that because she had never produced a
memoir she was going to have more inaccurate articles appearing
about her, but that if she could record a fairly complete oral
history, writers would have access to her account of her life
which they could use without bothering her.

    It was November and I was in Washington when I called Alice
in Connecticut to make arrangements to begin an interview. We
decided that she would see me the Monday before Thanksgiving.
However, there were difficulties in my getting access to the

library in the Alva-Belmont House, so that pre-interview research was slowed as I searched out substitute sources in Washington and New York. We postponed our date to Thanksgiving Day itself.

I was to meet her in her cottage in Ridgefield, Connecticut. She was fretting and apologetic over the fact that she could not provide her usual level of hospitality because she had just moved in. One hostessing problem was that she had not found anyone to cook for us. I remembered that at Belmont House, she always had a cook come in to prepare breakfast and dinner. I assured her that I was happy and able to do the cooking or anything else domestic; but she wouldn't hear of that. Further evidence of her hospitality was her insistence on having me met at the train some fifteen miles away at the Stamford station. Lacking a driver and a car, she arranged for a taxi driver to watch for me at the train and take me to Ridgefield.

Inadvertently, I was delivered to Alice's little white frame cottage about thirty minutes earlier than expected. I knocked. A dismayed Alice Paul opened the door; she had not yet dressed for the day, and her handyman's wife was still running the vacuum cleaner. (She introduced her not as her handyman's wife but as "a friend and neighbor.") For Alice's peace of mind, I wanted to back out the door and re-enter in twenty minutes. But she soon reappeared in a dress of brilliant turquoise sparkling with bead trim. A long string of pearls was further accented with a star-shaped pin of gold netting with a pearl at its center, which I suddenly realized had almost become a symbol of Alice Paul to me. She had worn it frequently in Washington, and, regrettably, I never asked her where it came from.

The little white cottage had been owned jointly by her and her late brother since the middle thirties, and although she had lived here in the forties while she worked with the United Nations at Lake Success, she was now converting it for permanent living. It was rustic, built by some early day Thoreau and his daughter on the edge of a small, wooded lake which Alice Paul also owned. The house itself still had the wide, wide planks that the early builders had hewn by hand. Ax marks still lined the rough logs that formed the ceiling beams. A great fireplace dominated the main room, which was a rather modest-sized living room with a windowed bay which, lined with blooming plants, served as a dining area. The other rooms had been added long before. There are now two bedrooms, a bath, and a study off the living room. In the study was a beautifully preserved rosewood desk that had belonged to Susan B. Anthony. Beyond is another addition, an airy sunroom windowed on three sides over the lake. There is a small kitchen,

and adjacent to it a built-on informal breakfast room of
brick and wood and tile; behind that was what Alice called the
"back kitchen," which holds pantries, a small coal bin, and
a place where the handyman stored the logs that he cut for the
fireplace. The basement apartment below was being made into
a year-round flat, and a young woman had rented it, a potter.

    The period furniture was comfortable overstuffed, carved,
and dark-stained. There were no graphics, paintings (except
family portraits), objets d'art, or sound systems for music,
unless one counts the small radio on the kitchen table--used
mainly for news while I was there.

    Throughout the house, particularly in the bedroom I was
assigned, were portraits of members of her family, all of whom
were Quakers, going back to the time the first Quakers arrived
on the American continent. Alice carefully identified each
one as she showed me around. Over the fireplace was a beautiful portrait in oil of a woman whom I think she said was two
generations ahead of her, a close relative of William Penn.
(I think she had Penn in her name.) Alice's family had been
in New Jersey and Pennsylvania for many, many generations and
had been Quaker even before the first one came to America.
Her grandfather had helped establish Swarthmore College, where
her mother attended. This strong Quaker tradition comes out
in the interview.

    Alice's relatively simple housekeeping needs were met by
neighbors who were also close friends. "Scotty"(A.S.) Reynolds,
who lived next door in a house also owned by Alice, was a
competent, witty woman retired from Life magazine (she had been
a photography editor) and a dear friend of Alice's. It was
she who cooked and brought over Thanksgiving dinner for us.

    The day I arrived was crisp and cold. Ice edged the lake,
and Alice had given a local carpenter the task of fitting
storm windows. After her handyman laid a fire in the fireplace,
Alice said to me, "Now I will make you Captain of the Fireplace."
The title was never fully earned, but I shoveled and poked
assiduously, and Alice assured me that I was a marvelous fire-
builder.

    She's very good at thanking people--a trait I noticed with
some surprise when lobbying for her. Inez Haynes Irwin had
written in 1921, "...it never occurred to [Alice Paul] to thank
anybody..."* Yet often, in response to a task performed by

_____

*Irwin, Inez Haynes, Up Hill With Banners Flying, reprinted
1964, Traversity Press, Penobscot, Main, p. 25. Formerly
The Story of the Woman's Party, Harcourt, Brace & World, New
York, 192?

the handyman, or Scotty, or the carpenter, she would say, "Oh, that's so wonderful you were able to do that, and do such a good job, and do it with such dispatch. I don't know what I would do without you."

The same concern for people close to her showed in her attitude toward the young woman who had taken the apartment downstairs. The tenant frequently complained that she was cold, and she probably was. Alice would then request that I turn up the thermostat, thus making it too hot upstairs so that the basement would be habitable. To put an end to this untenable situation Alice had ordered a new furnace installed in the small apartment. In the meantime she frequently asked the handyman or the carpenter (they were always coming in and out) to check to see if the tenant was comfortable. When she invariably said that she was still cold, Alice, very concerned, would say, "She always says it's cold." Although a little annoyed, she was going to great expense to make the apartment comfortable.

To prepare for our interview sessions, Alice had assembled in the study her complete set of The Suffragist (the weekly National Woman's Party magazine for the suffrage movement) and other papers. By this time, I had drafted three different interview outlines--one in Berkeley, one in Washington, and now a third was developing from the additional records; I was frantically trying to get these combined before she was ready to record. After our Thanksgiving dinner we talked at length about the scope of the history and what it should include. As we talked, her sense of scholarship expanded her role from respondant to co-worker.

A few days before, contrary to her life-long policy, she had agreed to a long journalism interview. The lucky writer was Robert S. Gallagher from American Heritage magazine.* While she felt that this young man was perfectly able and most charming, she was having grave second thoughts because of qualms that she had limited unduly her answers to his questions and omitted some vital material.

At that point, we agreed that in our interview I would ask questions, that we would cover the subject year by year chronologically, and that she would tell everything of relevance that she could think of, whether I asked her or not; whenever I felt she was leaving out something, I would ask. This is pretty much the way the interview developed, although

---

*Gallagher, Robert S., "'I Was Arrested, Of Course,'" an interview, American Heritage, February, 1974, pp. 17-24, 92-94.

we had to review this procedure two or three times before we really got a firm agreement that was clear to both of us.

Alice was eighty-seven at this time and she was in fragile physical condition. Trying to keep a balance between her strong mental and intellectual health and her precarious physical health presented a challenge for which, as an interviewer, I was scarcely prepared. About six months before, in May, one of Alice's friends in Washington sensing some deterioration in her general health had whisked her to a New York hospital. Although they both told me what happened, it still is not clear to me. It seems that after the amendment passed Congress, Alice had what she called a "tired heart." In the hospital her pulse rate was very low, she was given digitalis, and after a few days she returned to Connecticut.

She discussed this in quite cavalier fashion, partly because she has only airy disdain for any physical discomfort and thus refuses to dignify ill health by catering to it, or even admitting it exists. Alice told me of the Christian Science influence on her by her brother, who after his marriage had become a Christian Scientist, and of his widow who was still living in Connecticut.

During the intervening six months since her hospitalization, Alice saw no doctor, but a local "visiting nurse" regularly came to see her. That was her only contact with the medical world. Since her own doctor in New York was too far away to be of assistance even should Alice have needed her, it was necessary to maintain a careful and continual check on Alice's health, in order to be aware of significant changes that might require immediate attention.

Scotty, having had some first aid training, came over daily, and listened to Alice's heartbeats with a stethoscope, kept a daily log of her heart rate, and checked to see whether her ankles were swollen. That was the extent of Alice's medical care.

Planning to start the interview the following day, we stayed up rather late that first night. I worked even later in my own room in order to complete my research. Alice awoke very early the next morning and, noticing that the furnace was off, hauled the logs from the back kitchen into the living room and built a fire. By the time I finally got up, probably two hours later, the house was still very, very cold.

As I began to make breakfast for us, I noticed that Alice looked rather gray; she obviously was not well. My first impulse was to dash to the phone and call Scotty, but I didn't know either her phone number or her whole name. I wrestled with

the stethoscope but couldn't distinguish Alice's heartbeat.
Finally, I counted her wrist pulse--47 and very irregular.
Even with no medical background, I knew that she was a sick
woman. She accepted the idea that she had better lie down--
a big concession. She was very chilled.

Scotty was due to come by some time that morning. In
the meantime the handyman came and, as the only person who
knew the cottage's electrical system, was able to hook up the
heating pad. We piled blankets and hot water bottles on her.
I was feeling somewhat panicked. Here was Alice needing
medical attention and there was none at close hand. Because
it was the Thanksgiving weekend, I knew that even a call to
a New York hospital would not produce a doctor. Although
we were close to the biggest concentration of medical facilities in the world, we might as well have been in the Australian
bush. The irony could be tragic.

Scotty appeared in a few minutes. We had a hurried conference. Alice protested. She would not hear of our even
calling the visiting nurse. She said she would be quite fine,
we were not to worry, nor, clearly, were we to worry her. She
got so anxious about our calling in some medical help on a
Thanksgiving weekend that we felt we were making matters worse
by discussing it. She asked to be left alone.

I took some of the suffrage literature from her library
and sat by her bedroom doorway where I could ostensibly study,
but where I really could watch her closely by looking in at
her sideways. I knew she would object if she caught me watching.
Scotty gave me her phone number so I could call if Alice's
condition seriously changed.

So the day passed with me sitting at her doorway, doing
whatever research I could, and surreptitiously watching her.
The carpenter was in and out building stormwindows, and Alice
actually roused enough to give him directions, then went back
to sleep.

Alice got up about seven or eight o'clock that evening,
astonished at the incredible fact that she had slept all day.
I tried to take her pulse; I tried to hear her heart. Again
I could not find her heart with the stethoscope, and our
efforts dissolved into giggles that mercifully released the
tension of the day. When I counted three widely varying rates
for her pulse, we concluded that all we had to go on was the
way she felt. Her color was much better, she was warm, and
much of her energy had returned, but the prognosis was still
quite obscure.

Then she called her Christian Scientist sister-in-law.
I remember Alice saying, "No, I don't really need you to come
over; I just wanted you to know that--that I feel this way,
that this is going on--because I thought that would help."
She said this very matter of factly, and, after a little conversation, she hung up. She retired for the night confident
that she was going to be all right, and the next morning she
was.

I was careful to leave my door open in order to get up
when she did, and thereby prevent her from hauling wood, or
in any other way exerting herself, although the problems of
the day before had been resolved at least temporarily. The
oil company, which had inadvertently let Alice run out of oil,
finally filled the tank and the furnace was started again.
Coal and a large bag of wood had been hauled in by the fireplace. Scotty came over, took her pulse, and found it had
much improved. After breakfast we began the taping, but we
agreed that, having lost a day, we would only have time to talk
about Alice's life up through the suffrage period.

The world outside now was a deep freeze with the lake
a solid crystal plain. During a break, Alice stood at the
window and showed me where she and her brother had sold a number of lots around the shore. Some beautiful homes are tucked
back in the woods. A large piece of land was saved around her
cottage. She told me that the lake had become quite a worry
to her because one million dollars a year in insurance was
required to cover liability for almost anything that could
happen on the lakeshore. She was beginning to think of selling
the lake to the city of Ridgefield, which wanted to buy it.

While I prepared a lunch for us that day, Alice was looking
pink and bright-eyed. I mentioned this to her, and she said,
"I thought I would, after I called my sister-in-law." (In
fact, she looked stronger than I felt after the perils of the
day before.)

Her diet was meatless. "Alice, when did you become vegetarian?", I asked. I think she said it was just after the
suffrage campaign. She laughed and said, "I didn't have much
time to think about such things until then. It occurred to
me that I just didn't see how I could go ahead and continue
to eat meat. It just seemed so--cannibalistic to me. And so,"
she said, "I'm a vegetarian, and I have been ever since."
Perhaps Alice's experiences of hunger strikes in the prisons,
both in England and in this country, may have had an effect
on her attitude about food in general. Two or three times
she has said to me, "Food simply isn't important to me; they're
always bringing in these things," referring to her refrigerator
which was stacked will ⌐ ⌐⌐⌐⌐ ⌐⌐ ⌐⌐⌐⌐⌐⌐⌐⌐⌐⌐⌐ with all kinds

of health food. It was another proof that "taking care" of
Alice requires some very adroit chicanery.

A corollary to this was Alice's sincere inability to
recall past physical discomfort. Our interview starts out
with a discussion of whether she really did spend some time
in a rain storm on the roof of a building in England during
a suffrage protest. To the American Heritage writer, she
had denied this had ever happened. I was puzzled by her
denial, and the interview opens by my showing her both the
Pankhurst and the Inez Haynes Irwin accounts of this.* One
says she spent the whole night on the roof in the rain; the
other only that she was up there for quite a time. Alice
was perplexed and amazed that this actually had happened.
Another instance was a scuffle during the picketing of the
White House in which, I believe, a sailor was reported to have
knocked Alice down and dragged her across the sidewalk. She
said she doesn't ever remember being manhandled.

She also insisted that the account of that first parade
of the Woman's Party, in March, 1912, during which the U.S.
Cavalry and police were called in, was not a "riot," nor that
anyone got roughed up; the reports she claimed have been
exaggerated. I'm inclined to accept this because reports of
mass actions inevitably tend to become exaggerated.

This lack of concern about her physical condition probably
accounts for the fact that she simply cannot recall hunger
strikes in prison (or even being hungry). Nor can she remember
what must have been extreme physical discomfort, or much of
anything concerning her treatment there. Thus the interview
is lacking some of the more brutal details about the prison
experiences, but that would hardly be the major value of an
interview with Alice Paul.

Her ability to set strategy rapidly and unerringly is
one of the most astounding things about her. About two years
before the interview Alice had asked me to come to Washington
to do a week of lobbying for the Equal Rights Amendment in
Congress. I happily agreed. First of all, J believed in the
cause. I also wanted to see what it was like to work under
Alice Paul.

———————————

*Pankhurst, Estelle Sylvia, The Suffragette; the history of the
women's militant suffrage movement, 1905-1910. New York, Sturgis
& Walton Company, 1911.

Alice, then age eighty-five, had a running record in her
head of every congressman. She knew almost anything that she
needed to know about his past actions on the ERA and his
operations with other congressmen. She usually knew the attitudes of wives, secretaries, and administrative assistants.
She knew that Mrs. Alan Cranston had her hair coiffed in a
particular place where Alice sometimes went. (Belmont House
was across the parking lot from the Senate Office Building.)
Thus had she become acquainted with Mrs. Cranston, and it was
through Mrs. Cranston that she had been working to get Senator
Cranston's approval of the Equal Rights Amendment.

Her knowledge of the connections in Washington as well
as out in the states was amazing. It was clear that in the
campaign for the Equal Rights Amendment, as it wore on through
the decades, she had utilized a small nucleus of women, maybe
only one or two women per state, who in turn knew how to contact those persons most influential with the key senators and
with certain congressmen. In more recent years she had been
concerned with the members of the judiciary committees, since
the struggle came to focus there. The result was a very com-
pact campaign. There was only a little of the big, scattergun
grass roots approach to create support which in turn would
bring pressure on the Congress in general. Before I went back
to California, I found myself appointed Northern California
chairman for the ERA (much as I was appointed Captain of the
Fireplace) and I understood why I had few troops to command.

In lobbying, I learned to apply caution after talking to
Alice. When she would tell me what a congressman had once
done for the ERA, it could have been several congresses ago.
I had to check before I went to talk to him to be certain that
the last time he had helped on the Equal Rights Amendment was
indeed recent enough to form a basis for current action. This
same trait enabled Alice Paul to put two and two together to
make a vote. Finding the two and two often required complete
recall, and she carried the chess board of maybe thirty Congresses and political manueverings thereof in her head, and
from that formulated her own successful strategy.

Alice Paul's executive ability included an uncanny way
to utilize whatever manpower was within her range. Irwin has
written about this at length, and in the seventies it was still
true. I witnessed one coup about 1970 that she brought off
when a young woman from Los Angeles came with her sociologist
husband to do some research on the woman's movement. They
asked to use the library in Belmont House, one of the best
women's political history libraries at that time. They needed
access to some as-yet-uncatalogued, unorganized papers that
were sitting in boxes in the old, old, rambling two-story
carriag h use, re f tw buildings behind Belmont House.

(This building has since been torn down for a Senate parking
lot.) The sociologist appeared to be apolitical and intent
on doing his research while his meager budget for travel
expenses lasted; he could stay only a very limited number of
days. I met both of them and commiserated over the fact that
he would probably never get in to see those papers because of
Alice's belief that the ERA work should have top priority with
everyone.

Later that day Alice mentioned to me, "You know, Chita,
he's from Los Angeles. I wonder if he knows Congressman
Danielson? He probably could go speak to him as a constituent."
Doubting that the scholar would submit to a lobbying assignment,
I murmured that it was unlikely he would be from Danielson's
district. Danielson was the lone urban Democrat in the subcommittee who had voted against the ERA, causing a tie vote.
Neither Don Edwards, the subcommittee chairman, nor anyone
else, could figure out why. I had talked to the solon twice
and had received only a "Well, maybe I'll vote to bring it up
again," but that had been as far as I could get with him.

Alice found that although the sociologist himself did not
come from the congressman's district, he volunteered to Alice
that his students had done some research in that district and
had found that the young Mexican-Americans were very much for
equal rights for women, whereas the older Mexican-American
women couldn't have cared less. Alice said matter-of-factly
to him, "I want you to go to Congressman Danielson and tell
him that his district is changing, and that he'll be put out
of office because of these changes of the young Mexican-Americans that are now of voting age in his district." The professor, disgruntled at the prospect of spending his limited
research time lobbying, protested that he didn't have the money
or the time to go over and try to see Danielson. Sometimes
hours, even days were required to get in to talk with a congressman not from one's own district.

Shortly Alice told me that he did talk to Danielson. And
Danielson, as a matter of fact, did request that the ERA be
voted on again in the subcommittee, at which point it was voted
out for a full committee vote.

At the end of my first week's lobbying, my notes of June 29,
1971, read, "...I marvel at her [Alice's] obsession. By the
third day, I was delirious to have a break from the continuous
pressure of advocacy. It was like living with a single beam
of strong light piercing my world constantly. I accepted a
lunch appointment with a single-tax expert--mainly to have an
hour's reprieve. It was almost a holy moment, like stepping
off a race track for a time. And I knew that a mile away was

Alice, in the 180th day of the forty-ninth year of telephoning, assigning tasks, getting advocate statements written, and running her small army. At times I doubt that she ever notices the news about Viet Nam or the ghetto riots..."

Alice's campaign, in fact her whole life, was a one-issue affair: women's rights. Moving to the drum beat of her commitment, she is a person whose tremendous intellectual energy is put behind that commitment, with no tangents allowed.

But there were times when other issues almost intervened. It required fortitude, but Alice would not let the Viet Nam war issue in the late sixties interfere with or become related to the Equal Rights Amendment issue, just as she had refused to allow World War I to slow the suffrage campaign. One weekend when I was in Washington, women were gathering for a women's peace march on Washington that was led by Alice's old friend, Jeannette Rankin. Jeannette Rankin was staying at the Alva-Belmont House, as were some of the other so-called "Rankin File" marchers. Alice was anxious that their presence at the National Woman's Party headquarters have no relationship to the events of that weekend. She mentioned to me that evening how NBC and CBS network men and reporters from Life and Time had been trying to get interviews with the leaders of the march there at the house, but how she feared a background of the National Woman's Party headquarters would connect the ERA with the anti-Viet Nam marchers. She singlehandedly held off what sounded like the entire national news media--and quite successfully too.

There is another aspect to Alice's personality that one has to keep in mind: her background of aristocracy. Her family was cultured and well-to-do. They were also highly respected leaders in the Quaker community. These two worlds--her family and the Society of Friends--were the only worlds she knew until after she was graduated from Swarthmore. Her contact with other socio-economic classes was limited to the maids who worked for them, and the fact that the maids went dancing and behaved differently was excused because they were "that class" of people. Her class consciousness is still something that one from a different generation senses now and then. While she always denied that the women's movement she has led has been made up primarily of the higher socio-economic classes, the actual proportion of upper middle class educated women who participated in successive phases of the campaign might be the subject of further research.

The attention to class carries over into her campaign. For instance, when I was working for her in the ERA campaign, I would come in to report after lobbying on the Hill. Regarding a certain congressman, "What is he?" she would ask. Her question always baffled me. She meant, was his name Irish, Italian, or what? Alice was well aware of the strength of political ties between members of an ethnic group, particularly in the East.

The Alva-Belmont House in Washington now is in a high-crime neighborhood--with the Senate Office Building adjacent, however, and the U.S. Supreme Court on an adjoining block. It was such a dangerous neighborhood when I was there that we could never carry our purses with us when we went out at night because of the probability of provoking attack. Most of the women there had been mugged at least once. Alva-Belmont House itself had been broken into two or three times. This was all laid at the door of the blacks. It is true that the neighborhood was nearly all black, but whether the crime had a racial cause or something else (drugs, for instance) was a question in my mind.

This attitude of Alice's however, seemed to be less a classical color prejudice than a consciousness of class that is almost benevolent with her, coupled with generalizing about people who, as she grew up, had been outside of her experience. Her close work with women from ethnic minorities is a matter of record.

Alice held other attitudes which colored her political outlook; at least they were her attitudes by the time I came to know her. She was non-partisan; personally, however, she seemed to trust Republicans in Congress more than Democrats. This probably began or was reinforced in the suffrage struggle when Woodrow Wilson, a Democratic and recalcitrant president, became the object of her attack in "holding the party in power responsible" for defeats of the suffrage amendment. She also had a great fear of the machinations of communism and how it might manipulate her cause. She felt further that government was doing too much to help people who did not work; she deplored the welfare system--a view which is shared by many people of both parties, of course. Her views of these and many other social issues, however, seemed not to concern her unless they were related to the issue of the Equal Rights Amendment. While she had opinions about them, they held a low priority with her, and she did not spend time analyzing their causes and effects as broad societal manifestations. For instance, when we watched the television news in the living room at Belmont House, with our dinner trays brought in by the cook, Alice rarely commented on any news item unless it was of a senator or a congressman who had recently done something concerning the ERA. (Or more likely who had not so recently done something.)

Alice talks rather fast and her voice is very even in tone, thus feeling and emotion come through muted. Her mannerisms in talking show an efficient energy at work at all times. There are no "uhs" or "ahs" in her speech. While she gropes for a word, she's absolutely silent. When a problem is presented to

her, she simply sits silently for a minute; you wonder if she
heard you. ("She has the quiet of a spinning top," wrote Irwin.)
Then she will lay out maybe eight or ten relevant points and
conclude with a statement on the major focus.

Yet I have seen her upset about the twists and turns of
the Equal Rights Amendment. She has a short laugh which seems
on occasion to cover up despair. It might be considered a "bitter
little laugh," except that Alice Paul doesn't sound bitter. She
will laugh about things as though she sees the irony in a sudden
twist of fate that has led to the wrong congressman getting on
a committee, or a public issue like abortion suddenly coupled
with the ERA in the press. A set-back in support brings from
her a pause, then, "Well, then, here is what we must do." Frus-
trations seemed to lead to increased persistence and determination.

In Ridgefield, once we began recording, Alice had the
same commitment to getting this story on tape that she had to the
suffrage and ERA campaigns. She worked and worked and worked.
Usually several attempts would be made before I could get her to
take a break for lunch. By the second day, I had added two
extension cords to the tape recorder to that her words could be
captured at the dining table as well as in the study.

Finally, I stayed an additional day in order to finish--
but Alice felt another was needed. Since another change in my
schedule was impossible, we continued to work so that by nightfall
we had wrapped up what we expected to be our last session. The
recorder was turned off. Conversation came around to her genealogy. She mused on my maiden name, Roberts, and was certain that
this signified a relation between herself and myself because she
had a Roberts on her Quaker family tree. I was touched that she
wanted to send me back to California with information on her forebears so that I could check records to confirm her conviction.
But little did I suspect what this meant. The next morning Alice
mentioned (in an off-hand way) that she had finally found the
genealogy chart she was looking for, even though she had to hunt
for it until four o'clock in the morning. This was alarming
news in view of the health crisis of three days before. As I
prepared to leave, the phone rang. A reporter wanted an interview on the ERA. Alice agreed. I knew she was going to go
strong all day. As Scotty drove me to the airport, I extracted
a promise. "For heaven's sake, Scotty, please let me know if
Alice doesn't make it through the day." But we both knew she would.

From Equal Rights, August 18, 1923

STRIKING PEN-PICTURE OF ALICE PAUL

CRYSTAL EASTMAN, under the caption, "Personalities and Powers," draws a striking pen-portrait of Alice Paul in the July 20th issue of *Time and Tide*, Lady Rhondda's interesting periodical which we are glad to have come regularly to our desk. Miss Eastman writes:

History has known delicate souls from the beginning men and women whose every waking moment is devoted to an impersonal end, leaders of a "cause" who are really at any moment quite simple to do for it. But it is rare to find in one human being this passion for service and sacrifice combined first with the shrewd calculating mind of a born political leader, and second with the ruthless driving force, sure judgment and phenomenal grasp of detail that characterize a great entrepreneur.

"It is no exaggeration to say that these qualities are united in Alice Paul the woman who inspired, organized and led to victory the militant suffrage movement in America and is now head of the Woman's Party, a strong group of conscious feminists who have set out to end the subjection of women in all its forms.

Alice Paul comes of Quaker stock and there is in her bearing that powerful serenity so characteristic of the successful Quaker. Like many another famous general, she is well under five foot six, a slender, dark woman with a pale, often haggard face and great earnest, childlike eyes that seem to seize you and hold you to her purpose despite your own desires and intentions. During that seven-year suffrage campaign she worked so continuously, ate so little and slept so little that she always seemed to be wasting away before our eyes. Once in the early years, when she was housed in a basement—the Woman's Party, then the Congressional Union, was housed in a basement impossible to ventilate, she seemed so near to collapse that she was taken, under protest, to a nearby hospital to rest. But she had a telephone put in by her bed, and went right on with the campaign, forgetting, as usual, to eat and sleep. After a few weeks of this she got up and packed her bag and came back to the foul air and artificial light of that crowded basement headquarters. And nothing more was said about a breakdown. The truth is of course that she looks frail, as anyone would who was subjected to constant overwork, and under nourishment but actually she possesses a bodily constitution of extraordinary strength and a power of physical endurance that quite matches her indomitable spirit. * * *

"Rebecca West once said, 'The American struggle for the vote was so much more difficult than the English for the simple reason that it was much

more easy.' And that is profoundly true. Indifference is harder to fight than hostility, and there is nothing that kills an agitation like having everybody admit that it is fundamentally right. If you can so frame your issue or so change your method of attack as to precipitate discussion and difference of opinion among honest men, so that all your followers become passionate explainers you have put life into a movement. Alice Paul knows this and she is a master at training a mighty issue. As I look back over that seven-year struggle I sometimes suspect that many bold strategies were employed more to revive the followers than to confound the enemy.

"The very concentration of the Woman's Party on the Federal amendment created a new issue. States' rights is an important political concern in America, and the agitation in Washington had barely started before the milder suffragists began to declare, 'I am in favor of women voting, but I am against the Federal amendment. I believe the States should decide.' This gave the movement something to feel on, it gave delegate orators something to talk about besides 'liberty' and 'equality.'

"It is almost never a mistake to create a situation which divides the polite and timid advocates of a measure of justice from those who are really determined to get it. And every move that Alice Paul made had this effect. Organizing the women voters of the suffrage States to defeat democratic candidates, picketing the White House, the hunger strike, burning the President's war speeches—each of these policies was begun under a storm of protest from within and without the movement. Yet each proved in the end good political strategy, and at the same time had an enormous re-enlivening influence on the suffrage movement. Those who stood by suffered so from the almost universal criticism that they gained the power and faith of crusaders. And the more conservative suffragists who opposed these policies were stimulated to more and more effective action along their own lines from a sense of rivalry. And so the movement grew and grew from the mighty dissension in its ranks.

"Alice Paul's active leadership in the American feminist movement was almost an accident. She was a student at an English university intending to pursue the career of a scholar when she was caught up in the English militant movement and served a brief apprenticeship in jail. It was during this experience that she began to plan what she would do for woman suffrage in America. American women owe much to the English militants, but this above all."

SECTION I: FAMILY AND EDUCATION

FOREBEARS: QUAKER

Prelude: Memory Discrepancy About the Rooftop Episode

[Tape 1, Side A]

Paul: You ask questions. I'll answer, you see. Just the way
the [American] Heritage man did [last week].* Whatever
you wish.

Fry: I just want you to be Alice Paul, like we've always
talked, that's all. But this time I want to get it down
for the record.

Paul: No but I mean you'll want to guide the questions.

Fry: Yes.

Paul: So you guide the questions that would be useful to you.
I will try to just answer those. If you want me to
elaborate, you can say so. I didn't dare elaborate
with [the man from American Heritage]. I was so--my
first interview--I was so humble [laughter], so I think
he would have had a better interview if I had elaborated,
but I didn't.

Fry: It's different, too, when you are being interviewed for
publication, compared to this kind of interview, which
isn't necessarily going to be published. If it's
published, it'll be just as one part of someone else's
research, so that ours can be a lot looser.

Paul: I'd like to know, before we begin, just what did Sylvia
Pankhurst say on this episode on the [roof]top. Because

---

*Gallagher, Robert S., "'I Was Arrested, Of Course,'"
an interview, American Heritage, February, 1974, pp.17-24,
9 - ? .

Paul: I just have to write to the man [Robert Gallagher] and tell him what it was because I said I can't remember a thing about it.

Fry: Well, according to the outline that's in my head, we'll probably get to that in about twenty minutes.

Paul: Well, couldn't you just tell me about that now? Where was the place?

Fry: I think what I'll do is read it to you.

Paul: He read it in Mrs. [Inez Haynes] Irwin's book* and said it was in Glasgow. I said, "I know I never was on a roof in Glasgow but for one meeting when I was probably arrested and didn't have time to get up on the roof." [Laughter.]

Fry: Sylvia Pankhurst** puts you on a roof, too, Alice.

Paul: I know, but I want to know where the roof was. Sylvia spoke also at the meeting. She was the principal speaker at this meeting in Glasgow. There were all of us at this meeting and so she knows whether I was on a roof in Glasgow.

Fry: [thumbing through the Pankhurst book] All right, here we are. It says:

> "On August 20th, when Lord Crewe spoke at the great Saint Andrew's Hall, Glasgow, Miss Alice Paul succeeded in climbing to the roof, and, in the hope of being able to speak to the Cabinet Minister from this point, she lay there concealed for many hours in spite of a downpour of rain. When she was discovered and forced to descend she was heartily cheered for her pluck by a crowd of workmen, one of whom came forward and apologised for having told a policeman of her presence..."

Paul: [Laughter.]

Fry: "...saying that he had thought that she was in

---

*Irwin, Inez Haynes, Up Hill With Banners Flying, pp.11-12.
**Pankhurst, Sylvia, ibid., pp. 416-17.

Fry: need of help."

Paul: Well, then, that was really bad. I don't remember one
         thing about it.

Fry: Well, then "later"--I guess it means later in the day--

         "when the women attempted to force their way
         into the building, the people needed no urging
         to lend their aid, and the police who were
         guarding the entrance were obliged to use
         their truncheons to beat them back. When the
         officers of the law attempted to make arrests,
         women were rescued from their clutches again
         and again. Eventually Adela Pankhurst, Lucy
         Burns, Alice Paul and Margaret Smith were
         taken into custody..."

Paul: Who was the first one?

Fry: [mispronouncing] Adela Pankhurst.

Paul: Adela, we call her. She was Mrs. Pankhurst's youngest
         daughter.

Fry: And Lucy Burns, and you, and Margaret Smith.

Paul: And Margaret Smith was the niece of the Lord Mayor of
         Glasgow. I remember that.

Fry: Oh she was?

Paul: Yes. Which gave us a little standing. [Laughter.]

         Then I guess it's true about the roof, but isn't it
         strange that I can't remember one single thing about
         that!

Fry: You don't remember the rain on the roof? Well,

         "...even when the gates of the police station
         were closed upon them, the authorities feared
         that they would not be able to hold their
         prisoners for the crowd shouted vociferously
         for their release and twisted the strong iron
         gates. It was only when the women themselves
         appealed to them that they consented to refrain
         from further violence."

Paul: Well does she say what happened?

Fry: I will read you one more paragraph.

>   "When Lord Crewe had safely left the town,
>   friends of the women were allowed to bail
>   them out on the understanding that they would
>   appear at the police court at nine o'clock
>   the following morning. Nevertheless though
>   they arrived before the appointed time, there
>   was no one to show them the Court room, and
>   whilst they wandered about in the passages,
>   trying to find their way, the case was disposed
>   of behind locked doors and with the public
>   excluded. The bail was escheated and a warrant
>   was issued for their arrest before five minutes
>   past nine. At this Mr. Thomas Kerr--

Paul: Oh it was another arrest all over again?

Fry: You were bailed out and now you are coming back for
        your court appearance.

Paul: But then when we came back they dismissed the case.
        And what was it, we were arrested again?

Fry: Yes, a warrant was issued for your arrest, but at this
        point Mr. Thomas Kerr, one of the bailies,

>   "rose to protest and asked two minutes' leave
>   to find the defaulting prisoners, saying he
>   was sure they were already in the building,
>   but he was abruptly told that the court was
>   closed. So he went outside and immediately
>   met the ladies and brought them in before
>   Bailie Hunter, who presided, had left the
>   bench, but though the Bailie saw them, he
>   hurried away whilst the Fiscal tried to put
>   all the blame upon him." (The Fiscal is the
>   officer who prosecutes.) "The bail was never
>   refunded, and the women never answered to
>   the warrants, so the matter was dropped."

Paul: I knew it was dropped, but I didn't remember all these
        things. Isn't memory a strange thing. You know that
        it's so many years since I would ever even turn my
        thoughts to England and so on. But you wouldn't think
        you would ever forget [laughing] spending a night on
        the roof!

Fry: Well, this was 1909, on August 20th--

Paul: That's right.

Fry: --so that's a long time ago.

Paul: That's the last summer I was in England, you see.

Fry: And you had gone through so many episodes. I can see why you wouldn't remember just one.

Paul: Well, anyway, now I can tell him what really happened.

Fry: Okay. You think you must have spent a night on the roof then if--

Paul: But I denied it! I didn't want to deny something I had really done, but I didn't think [laughing] I ever had been on a roof. Now let's begin with you.

Fry: I thought that we might spend the first few minutes talking about your own biography.

Paul: All right. You ask the questions and I'll answer. I want you to get everything you need before you leave [on Sunday]. Now you tell me what you want to know.

Fry: I will. What I need to know is some of your genealogy, particularly going back to the Penns. If you have this written down somewhere, I could just use that.

Father and Mother

Paul: Yes, I will go and get my chart, so let's skip that for the minute.

Fry: Okay, fine. Where were you born?

Paul: I was born in Moorestown, New Jersey. That's a little Quaker village in Burlington County, and it's about nine miles out of Philadelphia.

Fry: And let's see, your birthday is in January?

Paul: January 11, 1885.

Fry: I saw the pictures in the guest room of your mother's family. They were Quakers. Was your family Quaker on both your mother's and your father's side?

Paul: From the beginning of the Quaker movement, yes. In England. They all came [to this country]. My first Paul ancestor was imprisoned in England as a Quaker and came to this country for that reason, I mean not to escape prison but because he was such a strong opponent of the government in every possible way. You know I told you, this little village was named after him, the town of Paulsboro in New Jersey which is now quite a big place. His original home is there, and I think I have a photograph of it which I could show you.

Fry: Okay.

Paul: And on my mother's side they were all Quakers. I have practically no ancestor who wasn't a Quaker. I don't know whether I had any who wasn't a Quaker. My father and mother were, and their fathers and mothers were.

Fry: Why don't you give me a picture of your immediate family, then? What did your father do?

Paul: He was a banker. And he was president [one of the founders.- Donald Paul] of the Burlington County Trust Company, which was the principal bank in Burlington County. And he was a director of other companies and so on.

Fry: [calling out] Come in.

Paul: Who's that?

Fry: Your carpenter.

We had gotten to your father being president of Burlington County Trust Company and on other boards. Could you give me some idea of your mother's education?

Paul: Well, I told you, she was one of the first girls who ever went to Swarthmore (I think I told you that) because her father collected the money with this little committee and founded Swarthmore. And he sent his daughter there and other women members of the family. My mother's first cousins went there and they were there with her. Anyway, she had an education the same as I did in a little Friends school, Quaker school, in a town called Cinnaminson, New Jersey, where she lived and was brought up.

Fry: Called what?

Paul: [spelling] Cinnaminson, I guess they still call it that.

Paul: And I have something here which I will just give to you to read. It is the anniversary quite recently of the founding of Cinnaminson. And in it they give a photograph of my grandfather's home. He was the judge of that community and had probably one of the biggest homes, with enormous grounds around it and so on, which was recently bought by Campbell's Soup. It is so pitiful, you know, that you can't keep these old homes. My grandfather's son, oldest son, inherited this property and died shortly after. His widow, not knowing anything I guess about business at all, was induced to sell it for a large sum to the Campbell Soup. So then they demolished this whole beautiful old building.

That was my mother's education. She went to a Friends school and then went to Swarthmore and then married her year she would have graduated, but she didn't finish.

Fry: But she almost finished?

Paul: Well, I don't know if she almost did or not. I don't know how long before she graduated she married, but I know she married the year she could have graduated. I believe it was the year.

Fry: Where did your father go to school?

Paul: He went to--I guess probably but I don't know--probably to the same Friends school because my father's father died before he was born, and so I never saw him and my father never saw him. And so he was brought up in the home of a, I presume a relative, another Quaker family. (We always called them "uncle" and so on because my father was brought up [by them], and I suppose they were, but I don't know how close a relative.) It was in the same section where my mother was born, very close to it, so he probably went to the same school, but I never asked him where he went. He died in my life before I was interested in where people went to school. I was just a freshman at Swarthmore. I was sixteen when he died. So I didn't know very much about--I never cared to ask him where he went to school. I just never thought of it.

Fry: Did he die very suddenly? Unexpectedly?

Paul: No, he went to Florida with my mother, to get away from the cold I suppose, and I don't know, stayed maybe two weeks. He was extremely busy, terribly busy, so he came back pretty ~~~~~~~~~~~~~~~~~~~~~~~~~~ible cold

Paul: at once when he came back and died very quickly from pneumonia.

Fry: Oh, for goodness sakes.

Paul: So.

Fry: That must have been a blow to you, just at that age.

Paul: Well, I was too young for it to be much of a blow to me. Life went on just the same. Of course it was a great blow, I presume, to my mother, who was left with four young children and all of this responsibility.

Fry: Who took over all of his banking interests and financial things? Your mother?

Paul: Well, he was the president. I suppose the vice-president became the president. I don't remember.

Fry: I meant, did your mother then supervise the investments and so forth?

Paul: No she didn't, and she wouldn't have known enough. [She had had no experience. - Donald Paul] But her brother was one of the board of directors of the same bank. I remember vividly, oh, I remember so vividly, every week when there was a meeting of the board of directors of the bank, my uncle came up and had dinner with us in the middle of the day (or lunch, or whatever it was). He would come out after their bank meeting, and then went back to the bank meeting. So he more or less took charge of all the investing in things. And then the man who was elected to succeed--I presume the vice-president--took over; I don't know [for sure] about that. But soon they had an election of the board of trustees, and they elected a president who was a cousin of ours and who lived very, very close to us and he--

My father also had a very big farm, not as big as [in] the West, though, but about three hundred acres, and my mother hadn't the faintest idea I'm sure how to run the farm. My father did it with no difficulty at all. He had a superintendent and he gave him orders in the morning and off he went. Certainly my mother had no idea how to run a farm or anything else. [She was a very wise woman who turned to experts for advice on many matters and prospered. - Donald Paul] This cousin, who was made president of the bank, whom we saw every day, I should say, he came in every day and rode

Paul: around the farm and saw that everything was all right and gave directions. So everything went on all right. We didn't have any great [hardships].

None of this is of any importance, but I only tell you because you asked me.

Fry: I am interested in it.

Sister

Fry: Alice, I am still confused, though, on your brothers and sisters. I know you had one sister who, much later, would come and live with you here in the cottage in Ridgefield, Connecticut.

Paul: I had one sister [Helen] who graduated at Wellesley, and while at Wellesley she became what they call a "student volunteer," if you know what that is.

Fry: No.

Paul: It's an organization that had students volunteer to go to the foreign mission fields. [to carpenter] Charlie, may I speak to you a minute?

Ch.: I will be right there.

Paul: And she was very prominent in that movement at Wellesley, and when she graduated and wanted to go with the missionaries to China, they said she was too young; they had an age limit. She wasn't old enough. So she went to the University of Pennsylvania, after she graduated from Wellesley, for graduate studies in Chinese, thinking she would prepare herself to know the language and so on. And while there she became suddenly interested in Christian Science, and deeply interested. So interested that--

Charlie, I wanted to ask, how you are getting on [with the storm windows]?

Ch.: Oh, I'm doing good. I'm working out on the back door.

Paul: Can you put them up again, or do you want Mrs. _____ to put them in?

Ch.: Oh no, I put them in. I take them out and paint them and then I put them right back.

Paul: You can do it?

Ch.: Oh sure.

Paul: Good. Good for you.

[to Fry] So she then founded a Christian Science Church in our little village of Moorestown, and they built a little Christian Science church building, and she was sort of the soul [an active member. - Donald Paul] of this little church, though she was very young.

That made her stop wanting to go to China because the Christian Scientists don't send missionaries. So she changed her whole life from that moment on and devoted practically her whole life to Christian Science. And then she studied in what they call "the classes," which they give to all the people who want to be students and then, through her teacher (who was named Mr. Johns and lived in New York; she came up and studied in New York) he told her of this little cottage which he owned out here, this very little cottage. (This is of no importance to your study but I will just tell you.) He owned other territory [property - Donald Paul] out here, and in this little cottage was one of his assistants. He had, I guess, rented it to him and he was living here. This porch wasn't on and this [sun] room wasn't on. It was just a very little house. So she had become so deeply interested in Christian Science that he told her the great need of having camps for Christian Science children, so she opened a little Christian Science camp right here in this little cottage. And that was her purpose in taking the cottage.

Fry: And that's when the lake and everything around here was bought, is that right?

Paul: Yes, we bought the whole territory. She bought it; I didn't buy it. I was over in Europe at this time and I remember writing to her and saying, "Now please don't undertake anything that is going to involve you in too much expense," and so on, and she wrote back and said she would certainly be careful not to. But this little camp turned out to be a great expense. People wouldn't pay enough and didn't want to pay enough.

So finally she felt it was costing her more than she

Paul: could justify in doing, so she gave up the little camp.
In the meantime I returned from Geneva, where I had
been, and I came up to see her here in her little
camp. I had bought almost a similar little one up in
Vermont when I had gone up--I had finally decided that
I couldn't live any longer in New Jersey with the
enormous taxes on your real estate, which were simply
wiping everybody out, and so--

Fry: Was that at your old family home in New Jersey?

Paul: No. We had divided up our family homes. One brother
took one and one brother took the other. And then my
sister took our home in the town; they had three houses
there. I took one that was the least desirable because
I thought I would be the least able to look after these
places. I didn't want to live in this little place and
I didn't want to pay the taxes which were so enormous.
So I thought, "I'll find a little home for myself, and
I'd like to go far away from everybody and go up into
the most remote place I can get, where we'll have some
American people left, and so on." And so I went up to
Vermont.

Fry: And this was for summertime living?

Paul: There's a painting of it.

Fry: Oh, the watercolor?

Paul: Yes. One of my cousins who came up to visit me
painted that while she was there.

Fry: That's a lovely house.

Paul: It's called Echo Lake and the reason that I got to know
about it was through the [Porter Hineman] Dales--who
gave me the dishes you had for breakfast this morning--
so well because we [the National Woman's Party] had
bought our headquarters in Washington from Senator Dale
when we moved over from the old brick Capitol. So I got
to know Senator Dale and his wife pretty well in that
transaction.

So Mrs. Dale invited me to come up and visit her in
Vermont, and I drove up to Vermont with a friend of mine
from Holland, who had come over and married an American
man who was a cousin of mine. So we drove up together
to visit Mrs. Dale. And while I was there she showed
me this enchanting little, (I thought) this very old,

Paul: old house just across the lake from her. And so I
bought the little house, for a very small sum. I lived
there I guess, off and on, maybe ten years or so. And
my sister came up and stayed with me a good deal. But
I was trying then to work with the United Nations, and
it took so long to come down from this little far away
lake in Vermont to New York to go up to the United
Nations that finally I sold it. And then I came down
to live with her all the time [here in Connecticut].

Fry: When you were at the United Nations, did you try to
commute on weekends to Vermont?

Paul: Not on weekends. When I was here (up until this time,
because this is the only time I haven't had Elsie Hill
here with me) we always drove in together. First when
it [U.N.] was out on Long Island, Hunter's College,
whatever the place was called--Lake Success wasn't it
called? That's very close to here. So I had my car
and she had her car, so in one car or the other we
drove down together every day to Lake Success the whole
time that anything connected with the woman question
was up. And then when they [U.N.] moved into New York,
we drove into New York every morning.

Fry: Did your sister marry?

Paul: No, she never married.

Brothers

Fry: And what about your two brothers: where did they go to
school and what were they interested in?

Paul: Well this brother whose photograph I showed you over
there (in fact this little painting here in the living
room is when he was a child; it's right over the desk)
his name was Parry Haines Paul. Parry after my mother's
family and Haines after one of our families. He went to
the same little Quaker school and graduated, and then
he went to the University of Wisconsin and graduated
in engineering, and he then joined the Friends Service
Committee to teach the use of tractors and so on to
the Russians.

I remember he told me many times how he would get

Paul: short season in which he could teach them. All day
long he would go over the fields with them showing them
how to use tractors and so on. That he did for about a
year.

Then he came home and married this Jean Dagget, who
is my sister-in-law now.* She was a very devout Christian
Scientist, and she wouldn't marry anybody who wasn't a
Christian Scientist. So between the influence of my
sister, (who was such a Christian Scientist, who had
put him in touch with Jean Daggett; she was a very
great friend of this Jean Daggett's, and so they got
married) my young brother then became not only a
Christian Scientist, but a very convinced one, I guess.
He became the treasurer of the church out in Haverford,
and the rest of his life he lived as an engineer and a
consultant engineer to--I think it is called the Mac
Company**which manufactures trucks. So he was there
until he died a few years ago.

Now my older brother went to the same Friends high
school, and then he went up to Rutgers College because
he wanted to become a farmer. Did you ever hear of
Rutgers?

Fry: Oh yes, I have heard of Rutgers, but I didn't know that
it was an agricultural school.

Paul: Well it is mainly that. At least it <u>was</u> mainly that.
I always thought it was mainly that. (My mother's
father) I think my grandfather was chairman of the
board of trustees, or at least he was <u>on</u> the board of
trustees of Rutgers, so my brother went there. I
presume he graduated. I don't remember whether he did
or not, but I imagine. And then he went on to Cornell
and studied in the Cornell School of Agriculture.

He inherited this family farm of my father's you
see. So he was trying to equip himself to take care of

---

*She was from a suburb of Chicago--and was supervisor
of music in the Moorestown schools and high school at
this time. - Donald Paul.
**The White Motors Company, Autocar Division. (They had
one son, Donald Daggett Paul, and when Donald was very
small they moved from Moorestown, N.J. to Haverford,
Pennsylvania when Parry joined the Autocar Division of
White Motors.) So he was there until he died a few
years ago. Donald Paul.

Paul: it all right. Then he turned and he was made the vice-
president of the bank [He served on the board of
directors of the bank. - Donald Paul] which my father--
no, I'm not sure. Don't say vice-president because
maybe he wasn't, maybe he wasn't--I think he was.
Anyway, he was put on the board of directors, and he was
on the board of directors until his death, which was
quite a short time ago. He continued quite prominent--I
won't say quite prominent but fairly prominent--in the
Quaker meeting in Moorestown.

Fry: So he didn't turn Christian Scientist like the others
did. Where do you fit in this line-up of children?

Paul: I was the first. Then came my brother William, the one
that became the agricultural one. Then came my sister.

Fry: What's her name?

Paul: Helen. And then came my younger brother. My first
brother was named William Mickle Paul. Mickle is one
of our family names. Parry was my mother's name.
[spelling] Mickle I guess. I could look it up in the
family Bible and make sure, but I think that's what it
is.

Fry: Is Perry's name spelled Perry?

Paul: [spelling] Parry. That was my mother's name. And her
mother was Alice Stokes, the one I was named after.

Fry: And you went to this private Friends school in
Cinnaminson?

Paul: No, no, no. In Moorestown. That's the one we all went
to. My mother went to--

Fry: Your mother went to Cinnaminson?

Paul: I think she must have. I don't know that she did, but
I know that she went to a Friends school, and that's
the only one that I can conceive of that was near her
home. Her mother and her father were almost, I would
say, the heads of the Friends Meeting there, so I'm
sure she would have gone to a Quaker school. She never
told me anything about it. She told me a good deal
about going to Swarthmore, but she never told me about
the school. But I'm sure she had to go to that school.

Childhood

Fry: What sort of Quaker life did you practice in your home? Some of the Friends I know don't have a lot of formalized practice in their homes and others do, and I wonder what kind yours was.

Paul: Well, of course, I never met anybody who wasn't a Quaker, and I never heard of anybody who wasn't a Quaker except that the maids we had were always Irish Catholics, always; we never had anybody but Irish Catholics. But I never met anybody who wasn't a Quaker, and I don't know, I suppose it was like all Quaker homes.

Fry: Did you have a lot of prohibitions?

Paul: Prohibitions of what?

Fry: Prohibitions of anything, that sprung from Quaker beliefs.

Paul: What kind of things?

Fry: Let's see. Some Quakers would prohibit music.

Paul: Oh yes, we never had any music at all. I never <u>heard</u> anything musical in the beginning of my childhood. Later on when I went to Swarthmore was the first time I ever heard, I guess, a hymn or <u>anything</u> like that, any music. But gradually after my father's death my mother--of course that was so early in my life--I remember my mother buying a piano and engaging a teacher for my sister. I was off [at school] and I didn't have any time to be taught, I guess, or to practice or to do anything, but my sister was. So finally we had music introduced.

Fry: I see. Did Quakers have any dancing in social events?

Paul: Quakers change quite a good deal. At Swarthmore for instance we did have musical instruments and we had, although it was purely Quaker when I went there, we had hymns every Sunday night. We had hymns in some kind of a general assembly of all the students. But I never heard a hymn until I went to Swarthmore; [laughter] I never knew there was such a thing as a hymn.

Fry: You'd never sung any songs?

Paul: I guess not. I don't believe so. Maybe we had, maybe we tried to; [laughing] I don't remember. You didn't regard it as oppressive, you know, you didn't know there was such a thing. You just knew all these gay maids we had were going off to dances and had a different life than we did. We just felt that was a sort of common people who did these things.

Fry: The lower classes.

Paul: Yes, the lower classes did these things [laughing].

Fry: What did you do for recreation, then, when you were at home?

Paul: Well, we played tennis. I showed you this photograph of our house, this little painting of our house. Well, the whole grounds in front, where you look, that was a great porch around the whole building and in front was a lawn, a very great lawn, so we had a tennis court there, and that is the only game I think that we played at home. And we played all the little things that people play, checkers and such things; I don't remember what we did.

And I read just endlessly, ceaselessly, almost every book it seems! We had a Friends library there in the meeting house, and I took out every book in the library. Also a great part of these books here [indicating several bookcases] were those that I had in my home, that I grew up with, any number of them. There is a whole set of Dickens right in there I have to put away. I remember reading every single line of Dickens as a child over and over and over and over again. So we just read whatever books there were, and there was pretty nearly everything I can remember. It's a wonder.

COLLEGE AND SOCIAL WORK

<u>To Swarthmore in 1901</u>

Fry: You must have been a pretty well-educated little girl
         by the time you entered Swarthmore.

Paul: Well I knew that when I went there you had to decide
         what to be your major, you know. You had to decide.
         You did there anyway. And I thought well, most of the
         girls were taking English and Latin and things like
         that.

         So I thought, "I already know these things pretty
         well." I said, "I don't think there would be much use
         in my doing this because whether I studied or not I
         will always read." So I said, "The one thing I don't
         know anything about and I never would read and I can't
         understand it or comprehend it or have any interest in
         it are all the things in the field of science."

         So I decided to make biology, which I knew nothing
         about, my major. I thought, "This is the only way I
         will ever learn about biology." And then I had
         chemistry and physics and higher mathematics and all
         these things that normally [laughing] I would never have
         known anything about. I don't think I did too well in
         them because it was not very native to my disposition,
         but anyway these classes were almost all the young men
         students because they were all studying to be engineers
         and took it very seriously.

Fry: And doctors--

Paul: No, not doctors. I can't remember if we had anything
         like premedical there. But in this biology course we
         even had dissection of human beings you see. [This is
         doubtful. It may have been animals. - Donald Paul]

Paul: And it was maybe pre-med from that point of view. That
was my major, the subject I am still most ignorant of in
the whole world! [laughter] I can see when I talk to
my doctor and she tells me these things about [my]
heart, I think, "What on earth are these things, why
don't I remember some of these things?"

Fry: Did you intend to do anything with your biology training?

Paul: Well, I never <u>thought</u> then about <u>doing</u> anything.

Fry: You didn't foresee a career for yourself then?

Paul: If I did I don't remember. But I did think by the time
I got to graduate that I'd like to become a teacher.
When I was in the senior year--not by any effort on
my part--but I was awarded by the college, a fellowship,
or scholarship, if that's what you would call it, by
the College Settlement Association of America. It was
a time when the college settlements and all the settlements started by Miss Jane Addams were becoming rather
common through the country, and so they had formed an
association and they gave these scholarships or fellow-
ships (I don't remember what they called them) every
year to certain colleges. One was Smith, one was
Swarthmore, one was Vassar. I don't know whether there
were any others, but I remember these colleges. One was
Wellesley. And it was awarded by the college to the
person that was most probably interested in that field
of thought.

I had a Professor Robert Brooks, who came I think
the last year I was there. He became a quite famous
professor at Swarthmore and he started courses in
political science and economics, which I had never
studied, and immediately I seemed to have a great joy
in them. He evidently thought I was very good, so he
had this fellowship given to me. (I don't think it was
called a fellowship but this grant; scholarship may be
the word.) That was to [allow me to] go into some
settlement for one year and help. This was to pay all
my expenses you see, or part of my expenses.

To New York School of Philanthropy

Paul: I went up to College Settlement in New York. I could go
to any one I wanted to.

Fry: Where was that?

Paul: 95 Rivington Street.

Fry: In the city?

Paul: Yes. It is in the Jewish section, next door to the
        synagogue. We were in the Jewish and the Italian section.
        So I spent that year there, and the same time I went to
        the School of Philanthropy. I graduated in 1905 from
        Swarthmore, then I graduated from the School of
        Philanthropy in New York in 1906; that's now called
        the School of Social Work under Columbia University.
        It's been incorporated into Columbia. And so I am an
        alumna member of Columbia; I get their bulletins--I
        think I got one today--asking for money and so on, or
        giving reports about what they are doing in the School
        of Social Work, while I never went to it: I went to it
        under its previous name.

Fry: What sort of training did they give then?

Paul: I guess they give the same as the do now. They just had
        lectures, authorities in one field after another field,
        in what you call social work, and then they took you of
        course to visit all kinds of institutions. I remember
        the head of Bedford Reformatory for Women coming in
        and lecturing us, and Miss Lillian [pause] what is her
        name, let's see--the nurse's settlement, Lillian Wald,
        but I don't think that she--

        Dr. Edward Devine was the president of it when I
        was there. It was an extremely good school and had a
        very good reputation, and most of the people who went
        there wanted to become professional social workers
        because that's what they were being trained for, you see.

Fry: And is that what you had decided on for a career at this
        time?

Paul: No, I had never decided to be a [social worker]. By
        the time I had been there a while, I knew I didn't
        want to be a social worker, whatever else I was. Are
        you taking this down now?

Fry: Yes, I am.

Paul: I will have to be more careful what I say!

Fry: Well, Alice, we will type it up for you and send it back

Fry: to you, the whole thing, so you can look at it.

Paul: I can put in what I really felt. I can cut it out then.

       I knew in a very short time I was never going to be a social worker, because I could see that social workers were not doing much good in the world. That's what I thought anyway. I still think so. So to spend all your life doing something that--you knew you couldn't <u>change</u> the situation by social work.

Fry: Yes. There wasn't any real reform taking place to prevent these unfortunate situations from occurring.

Paul: No, I didn't think so. I thought the work we'd be asked to do--

Charity Organization Society, Summer of 1906

Paul: Now the next summer, after I graduated, I was asked by, I suppose, somebody in the School of Social Work--I'm not quite sure who asked me--to join the force of the Charity Organization Society. Did you ever hear of that? The Charity Organization Society, COS, they called it. And at that time I think in every city in the United States there was a COS. One of the lectures we had had--probably somebody in the lecture course that asked me to come. <u>Somebody</u> did.

       So I spent all that summer working in New York for the Charity Organization Society. We were paid the tiniest little sum of money, perhaps enough just to pay your lodging, hardly anything at all. I worked in the office in my own section when I was living in the College Settlement. I kept on living at the College Settlement all summer although my scholarship was up, and I had this little salary from the Charity Organization Society. It was just a marvelous experience. I was assistant to an exceedingly experienced social worker, and I was just sent to this family and that family and the other family to see what their troubles were.

       You see, then they couldn't get welfare [payments]; they couldn't get <u>anything</u>. The only thing anybody could get would maybe to get a church to help her or

Paul: help him, or go to the Charity Organization Society, which was organizing all the existing welfare groups. They were all independent you see. Church groups and civic groups and any group that was organized to help people in distress were all federated in this Charity Organization Society. So you would be sent to somebody who was needing medical attention and then you would try to call up the hospitals and so on that she might be eligible for and get her in and get it for her. Just all day long. So you got to know the city of New York in places which were sort of the underground places--not underground, but the under layer of people who were up against it. So all that summer I stayed there.

To the University of Pennsylvania, Fall of 1906

Paul: Then I decided that I didn't know very much. I was thoroughly convinced of that [laughter]. I had learned enough to know that I didn't know anything about this field, the political and economic field which, if I had known it existed in the beginning, I think I would have majored in always because that just was what I really was interested in. So I went to the University of Pennsylvania and enrolled as a graduate student.

Fry: That must have been the fall of 1906. Is that right?

Paul: Yes, because I graduated the School of Social Work in 1906 in the spring. And I'd had a certificate from it and all the things you get, you know. So I could have become a social worker, but I am certainly glad I never did that.

Then at the school of economics I took as my major, sociology and as my minor, political science and economics. And I kept on with those minors and majors until I finally took my doctorate degree, but I didn't start to take any degree excepting a master's degree, which I got the following spring, which was 1907.

Fry: Did you have to write a thesis?

Paul: Yes.

Fry: What did you write it on?

Paul: It was called "Toward Equality" and it was on the subject

Paul: of equality for women in Pennsylvania.

Fry: Was that the first time you had picked up this subject?

Paul: [pause] I was wondering. I'm not quite sure whether I
         took my master's degree. I could look it up in one of
         the old Who's Who. It has to be an old one because I
         suddenly began to get questionnaires from Who's Who and
         I filled them out for quite a number of years and then
         I decided that I didn't think much of this idea of Who's
         Who so I stopped sending any replies.

Fry: That's why I can't find you in any recent Who's Who.

Paul: Well, I didn't send anymore. I just didn't see why it
         was anybody's business, all these questions they ask
         you; there wasn't any conceivable reason for it. So I
         just didn't fill them out anymore. But I do have some
         old ones probably, and then I would remember what year
         I took my master's degree.

Fry: Well, I can check that out. Let me just make a note
         here to myself to see an old Who's Who.*

         [Tape 1, Side B]

Paul: You asked me if I had written a thesis. I don't think
         I wrote a thesis that first year, is what made me
         suddenly pause. But of course I wouldn't remember very
         well about my thesis. Anyway, whether I took a degree
         or not, I took the courses anyway and passed all the
         examinations and everything, and felt just great joy in
         it. Especially this Professor Patton I felt was a
         great, great, great teacher. Simon Patton made a
         profound impression upon me.

Fry: Was he in economics?

Paul: Economics, yes.

         Anyway at the end of the year I was given a
         scholarship--I suppose you call them, I really don't
         know what they call these things, or a fellowship--to
         someplace called Woodbrook in England. Now this College

---

*The 1922-23 Edition of Who's Who shows that the M.A.
was awarded from the University of Pennsylvania, 1907.

Paul: Settlement one that [had] come to me, I hadn't known about it even and I hadn't asked for it; I was just awarded it. And it was more or less the same I think to Woodbrook. Because I don't know that I ever knew there _was_ a place called Woodbrook in England. Woodbrook was a central training school for young Quakers in the field of public service and theology, and young Quakers, a very few of them, were selected in different countries to go there, and they gave you this quite liberal fellowship there. They paid all your expenses while you were living over there in the school. It was a one-year fellowship or scholarship, whatever the thing was called. So I received this just toward the end of my first year at the University of Pennsylvania.

I was very happy to go. [I left] the day, I think, of commencement or right immediately afterwards. Now at that time there were almost no women students at the University of Pennsylvania except in graduate school, and there were very few graduate students.

Fry: So you were kind of a rarity there?

Paul: Well, I was in the graduate school, and you weren't conscious of it there because the few girls that were there were in those classes and we got to know each other very well. It was a splendid, splendid group of young women whom I have kept in touch with nearly all my life.

More About Friends and Activities at Swarthmore

Fry: That is one of the things that I wanted to ask you: Who were the friendships that you formed at Swarthmore and at the University of Pennsylvania who meant the most to you, that you kept up with later in your life? I know Mabel Vernon was at Swarthmore. Were there any others who later on were active in the women's equality work with you?

Paul: Amelia Walker was. Her name was Amelia Himes when I knew her, a Swarthmore girl. She married a Robert Walker. She was a Quaker of course. She was a senior when I was a freshman and the loveliest person. I remember being in a Shakespearean play--by that time we were having these things at Swarthmore--and she was Ophelia, and I still can remember her being so beautiful

Paul: and such a lovely voice and singing so wonderfully. So
when we went to Washington, she was one of the people
who had married over in Baltimore, and she joined in our
committee and later became our national chairman, I
believe, of the Women's Party.

I think those were the two who I continued to know
the most just because they went into our own campaign.

Fry: Anyone at the University of Pennsylvania?

Paul: At the University of Pennsylvania? I just kept up with
them [Mabel Vernon and Amelia Himes] more or less because
that time I was so absorbed I couldn't take the time to
really keep in touch with any more people, which I would
have liked to have done. I was always so awfully busy
after I got in the suffrage movement. I remember one
person I knew the best was named Clara Louise Thompson,
from St. Louis, and I roomed with her for a time in the
graduate school. You see we had no graduate building
or anything like that and we had to live in little
pensiones around the University. She became a great
Latin authority in the field of Latin and Sanskrit and
went down to teach in a college in Georgia. I think
she has been teaching there ever since and I have
occasionally crossed her path. For a few months she
came to Washington and helped us in our campaign and
stayed there helping the first year I was in Washington.

Fry: I have two other little things to pick up at Swarthmore:
One is Mabel told me that she met you when you and she
were on a debating team, so I figured from that you
must have done some debating at Swarthmore.

Paul: I'm sure if I did I was the worst possible debater. I
guess they were teaching us how to debate probably.
But I remember Mabel being probably the most eloquent
and best public speaker in Swarthmore. She was a year
older than I was but for some reason or other (I don't
know why; she was later in getting to Swarthmore) she
graduated the year after I did. I remember we were in
a Latin class together--it is the only class I can
remember being in, studying the poems of Horace--I can
remember that very well. I was named what they called
the Ivy Poet at Swarthmore. Every year they had what
they called the Ivy Stone; another stone was put by a
class into the building. And they had an outdoor
ceremony at commencement with all the alumni present
and all the college present and they had somebody--a
boy always--who made the speech and presented the stone,

Paul: and then they always had an Ivy Poet. So suddenly I was told that I was the Ivy Poet, to my great horror and amazement. I remember being oh, so troubled by that, terrible. [Laughter.]

Fry: What did you have to do?

Paul: I had to write the poem.

Fry: Oh, write it; not just select one and say it.

Paul: No, you had to write it. You had to compose, and a boy had to compose a proper speech connected with the placing of the stone, and the Ivy Poet had to sort of set the atmosphere.

It was a great tragedy when this happened to me. I had once written a little sort of jingle which was published in the college paper and I guess that gave me the reputation of being a poet, probably [inaudible]. I remember I struggled away and I struggled away and I wrote a little poem and took it to our English professor and asked him if it would pass as a poem. He thought it was a very good little poem.

So then I thought, "Well, I've done all I can on composing, and now the awful problem, with my complete lack of oratorical knowledge or any oratorical power, how will I deliver it outdoors to all these people?" So then I went to Mabel Vernon. [Laughter.] Maybe she told you this.

Fry: No, she didn't.

Paul: And I said, "Now will you train me so I can deliver my poem?" So she undertook very religiously to have me practice and practice and practice my poem. So when the day came--I think she had gotten me up to a point where probably people could hear me--and this great audience [was there, and] I gave my little Ivy Poem. I wish I could remember a word or two of it. I'd have to think about it to see if I could. [pause] Oh well, it doesn't matter. Since it was my first poem, I think about it once in a while.

Fry: Had you written much poetry or been encouraged in that in your Quaker household?

Paul: No, I never thought of writing anything. Anything of

Fry: After you had this initiation into the world of being a poet, did you ever write any more?

Paul: No, never wrote one more. I'll see if I can think of it. But anyway, I remember my aunt, my father's sister, who was, well, her whole mind more or less was devoted to the world of books and such. I remember telling my mother that she thought it was a very good poem, so I got some little support for it. [Laughter.] I'll see if I can think of it. I hope I can.

Fry: I hope you can. You think of it and write it down.

The other thing was, Mabel said you were in sports at Swarthmore.

Paul: Oh yes, I was.

Fry: Did you follow up on your tennis?

Paul: Everything that happened I took part in, or tried to at Swarthmore. And I naturally was, I don't think I was very good but I think that I had the championship in tennis. (I am not quite sure. I believe I did among the women tennis players.) And then I played basketball; everybody had to play basketball, so I played. I played with great happiness. I was very happy in playing it. And I played hockey. All the things that the girls played there.

Fry: Was there a lot of difference then between what girls played and what boys played? For instance, was baseball on the campus?

Paul: I don't know; the boys may have played baseball, but I don't remember ever hearing of it. I remember that they played football and lacrosse. And the girls had an instructor, a person we all liked very much, in athletics, and so it was just every afternoon, it was part of the regular routine you see.

You had breakfast at a certain hour and all the students were together you know. At the long table at the head of the room sat the dean of the college, the woman dean. She presided just as though it were her own private dining room. It was great decorum and at each table was a certain number of girls, a certain number of boys and one professor. Maybe there were not enough professors to go around, but generally there was

Paul: a professor. You all came in together, you all sat
       down together; they all had grace together, then the
       boys arose and went out and brought in the food and
       placed it on the table.

       The professor at the head of that little table, she
       just saw that everything was done with the greatest
       attention to proper form. Some of the people came from
       homes, you know, which they hadn't perhaps known very
       much about how to serve food and so on, so she was there
       to see that her table was perfect. . Then the boys came
       in and sat down, and we all had breakfast or lunch or
       dinner. Three times a day we had this. Probably Mabel
       has told you all this so--

Fry: No, she hasn't told me any of it.

Paul: So then the boys cleared the table, took everything off,
       and came down and sat down, and then the dean arose
       and with great ceremony walked away from the table and
       out, and all the students arose and with great ceremony
       walked out behind her. It was a very dignified and a
       very lovely regime that she--it was her own, of course,
       ideas and thought; she was from, oh, just a very dis-
       tinguished family, a Quaker family, and was a very
       distinguished person herself. She had an enormous
       influence, I think, on the whole sort of good breeding,
       of this college.

Fry: What was her name?

Paul: Elizabeth Powell Barnes [Bond?].

Fry: Did she teach classes?

Paul: No, she did nothing but be dean.

Fry: Did you personally get to know her?

Paul: Oh, of course. You know there were only four hundred
       students altogether. I can't say exactly four hundred,
       but it was about four hundred. They weren't allowed to
       have any more. There must have been about two hundred
       girls. Well naturally, she knew every girl. She made
       it her business to know every girl personally, and I
       guess she made it her business to know every boy
       personally.

       Then they had a director of athletics who was
       another big figure in the college, a man who was very

Paul: much admired I think by all the young boys there. He had entire charge of all the athletic life of the college. She had entire charge of all the social life of the college.

The president lived in the president's house with his wife and he presided at important gatherings. I think he presided every morning in the college collection.

Fry: That was a chapel service, wasn't it?

Paul: Yes, but it was also what they called "collection." Every student <u>had</u> to go there. You <u>had</u> to attend this collection unless you were ill or something like that. And you were seated alphabetically, I guess by class, but anyway alphabetically. Every person had his own seat, always, from the first year to the last that I was there at Swarthmore. So the president I think presided there.

Every Sunday we went to the Quaker meeting which was on the grounds. I think the president and the dean and everybody else, I guess all the professors, always went there and stood up in the benches facing you know to the students.

Fry: What other social life did you have besides that?

Paul: Well, every night after the dinner (or supper is what we called it; I don't know what we called it but everything was very simple) everybody was invited always (but not a formal invitation, just in the beginning you were <u>invited</u>) to go into the social hour. You went or not, as you wanted; most of the students went. This was held in quite a large room on the main floor presided over by the dean. And there was a piano, and some people would go to the piano and sit down and play, and some people would sing, and some people would sit down and talk to each other. It was just a [inaudible] of students, I guess, everybody always went. It was a way to get to know each other.

Fry: Did you have the temptations that your mother had before you, of getting married at the end of your college year?

Paul: No, no such temptations at all, no such at all. And I don't think many of the students did there then. Of
.tside;

Paul: my father wasn't at Swarthmore, you see.

Fry: You mean students in your generation were getting married later in life?

Paul: Well, they might have, but I never heard of any student being engaged at Swarthmore.

Fry: That surprises me.

Paul: You see they were quite young. I went there when I was sixteen and I was out at twenty. Some of them were maybe out at twenty-one or twenty-two, but certainly nobody older than that.

   Let's see, Amelia Walker for instance married Robert Walker who was in her class at Swarthmore. You know you didn't get to know the older people, the older class people very well. I knew Amelia mainly by sight, seeing her as Ophelia and things like that. She married some years later. I don't think anybody at Swarthmore ever dreamed that they would get married.

   It was sort of a generation--I think maybe people are marrying in colleges now much more than they were then. I never _heard_ of a person being married or being engaged at Swarthmore.

Fry: This kind of goes up and down in the generations, it seems. There for a while in the '50s, there were a lot of marriages at the ages of nineteen and twenty, and college marriages then.

Paul: See, now, I don't know at Swarthmore, but up here in Ridgefield, I heard them over the television (I'm not sure if it's reporting Ridgefield, maybe it's reporting all of Connecticut or maybe it's reporting New York state) where they are considering at their boards of education what to do about the large portion of the senior class and junior class girls who are pregnant. You see, you never _heard_ of these things at Swarthmore. And the boys had one dormitory and the girls another dormitory. The only time that you ever were totally together would be at the meals, and that's only at your own table. And the one little social hour which was probably an hour long.

Fry: Could you go out somewhere together after the social hour with a boy you liked?

Paul: Oh, no, no. You couldn't. You couldn't do anything. You went then to--then everybody dispersed to their dormitory. Girls went to the girls' dormitory, boys to the boys' dormitory. I never saw or heard of anybody-- of course I suppose you could have surreptitiously, but nobody ever seemed to do anything that was against the rules.

Fry: It's that Quaker conscience, I guess.

Paul: Well, it was just the rule of the college. I never heard of-- So I think people got to be good friends, just as Amelia Walker got to be a good friend of Robert Walker, sitting at the table with him for maybe four years, and then they probably continued to see each other afterwards, and I remember when she was married everybody was very much surprised. We hadn't any idea [laughter] that she was thinking of being married. I have continued to know her a little bit. I don't remember anybody else at Swarthmore with me that married a Swarthmore person; there must have been some others.

Fry: I wonder, in the Friends' education of devoting yourself to a cause, would this have made a number of girls feel that they really don't want to tie themselves up with a marriage because they have more important and higher things to do? Was this a part of the feeling at all, that you know of, at Swarthmore?

Paul: No, I don't think so.

Fry: It wasn't seen as one or the other? Was it mutually exclusive, marriage or work?

Paul: Oh, no, no. As far as I can recall, the general impression that I had among the men students was that they were all preparing to sort of succeed their fathers in taking care of their families, and having a family, and most of them that I can remember were specializing in engineering. It was not any cause; it was just what they were preparing to do.

The girls were--I remember in my class, there was one young man who came from the same school that I did in Moorestown, the same Friends meeting, and his father was president of some very large dairy firm in Philadelphia. And as a young boy I remember, while there was no college in the summer, he would go in ～～～ ～～～～～, ～～～ ～～～～～ ～～ ～～～～～～, ～～～r the

Paul: direction of his father to help with this business.
And he was growing up wanting to succeed his father, and
he did. But he wasn't seeking any particular preparation
in college, but most of them were.

All the girls planned to start in and support
themselves--and you know it wasn't so general then for
girls to support themselves. If their families were
able to, they didn't give it a thought. They just
supposed they'd go home, live at home and maybe they
would marry; they didn't think much about anything but
finishing college, I guess. But the girls who did
think that they were going to begin to earn some money
to help support their families, were all, every one
(I never heard of one who wasn't; I heard of one only,
in the years I was there) all were going to be teachers,
they hoped. And in the last years they were all taking
courses in the things they would teach, and writing to
different schools, mainly Friends schools, asking if
there would be any vacancy.

Mabel Vernon, for instance, was preparing to be a
teacher, and she became a teacher of German, I think.
Her father was an editor and I presume that she was
really trying to help meet the expenses of her own
college work and so on.

Then one girl I remember wanted to be a physician,
and I think after maybe two years she left and went
into a women's medical college to prepare herself. But
I don't remember anybody else ever going into a profession
of any kind.

Fry: Was there a lot of social work type of things gone into
by the young women who did not have to support themselves?

Paul: No, nobody. Nobody went into it, did anything at
college. You see I told you how this professor came,
Professor Brooks, the last year I was there and started
this interest in social work. We never heard of it; we
never knew there was such a thing as social work.

The University of Birmingham and Woodbrook, England, 1907

Fry: Well, Alice, how did you get interested in the idea of
political reform? Was it that year after college?

Paul: In suffrage, you mean?

Fry: Yes. How did you come around to it? Was it through your work in England?

Paul: Well, you see the year that I went to--First of all, I never heard of the idea of anybody being <u>opposed</u> to the idea of [suffrage or equality]; I just knew women didn't vote. I know my father believed and my mother believed in and supported the suffrage movement, and I remember my mother taking me to suffrage meetings held in the home of a Quaker family that lived not far from us. It was just--I just never thought about there being any problem about it. It was one thing that had to be <u>done</u>, [laughing] I guess that's how I thought.

So then when I went to England, this Quaker school, this place at Woodbrook, I remember one day when I was one of the students there, I went into the University of Birmingham as soon as I went there because I wanted to go on with what I had started at the University of Pennsylvania, in the same field. So I enrolled in a few courses there, maybe three times a week or something like that. I rode in on a bicycle, I remember, through the <u>deep</u> fog; the main thing I can always remember is riding through this terrible fog in England on a bicycle into Birmingham and going up to the University of Birmingham. And there I went, I studied more or less the same fields I had been studying at the University of Pennsylvania and went on with it.

Fry: Did you do that while you were at Woodbrook?

Paul: Yes, I was living in Woodbrook and I was taking the courses <u>they</u> had, and then they were very glad to have students go into the University of Birmingham and take special courses on any field that they wanted to. So I studied economics there in that department, mainly economics.

Then I went in, I don't know how many times a week, to the settlement house because I had lived in a settlement in New York City, you see, and knew about them. So I went into, it was called Summer Lane Settlement in Birmingham. The head of that was a well-known, very prominent Quaker woman, and they welcomed me, and immediately--every day I had lunch with them there, I remember, every day that I went in; I don't know how many days a week--So then because I just knew exactly

Paul: New York City, they would send me to this house and that
       house and the other house, where people were appealing
       there for help. I thought I got a very _thorough_ idea
       of the poverty situation in a big city.

       I know when the head of the settlement came out to
       give a lecture at Woodbrook. They were always having
       people come and lecture on all the things that they
       thought the students ought to know about. An absolutely
       wonderful, wonderful place this Woodbrook; I couldn't
       possibly say enough in admiration of it. Later on my
       sister went there, and one of my first cousins went
       there. And gradually from all over the world young
       Quakers came. When I was there there were for instance
       two from Holland, who still have been lifelong friends
       of mine. And there were [some] from Ireland, I remember.
       Of course from England. And from Norway. And from
       India. I've forgotten these places.

       It was a small little settlement. You couldn't
       have very many people. They had one little house just
       for the women students. There weren't so very _many_,
       but the teachers were superb, I thought.

       And this one night, or one afternoon I guess it was,
       there was a meeting at the University of Birmingham to
       which all students were invited to all these public
       meetings. Sir Oliver Lodge was then the head of it, if
       you have ever heard of him. He is a great scientist and
       a great name in English history. He was the president,
       I guess you'd call it, the head, of the University of
       Birmingham.

       Under his auspices they would have these distinguished
       or undistinguished people coming on all sorts of subjects.
       So one day they were having one on votes for women. You
       didn't go unless you wanted to. I wanted very much to
       go to this one, so I went to his public meeting--after
       school hours you see. It was Christabel Pankhurst. I
       don't know that I'd ever heard of her name before.
       [She] was the principal speaker, and she had a little
       group of two or three women with her. She was Mrs.
       Pankhurst's daughter. (You know who Christabel
       Pankhurst was probably, because she ended her life in
       California.)

Fry: I didn't know--

Paul: All the last years of her life she spent down there. I
       am so sorry I didn't take advantage-- So many regrets

Paul: when I begin to tell you all these things that I think
I ought to have done, and should have done and wanted
to do. I did get up maybe two meetings for her. She
was absolutely wonderful whenever she got up to speak.

Fry: Where was she in California?

Paul: She was down near Santa Monica, somewhere down there.
And she died about a year ago, I guess.

Anyway she was a very young girl and a young
lawyer, one of the few women that had ever studied law
I guess in England at that time. Quite entrancing and
delightful person, really very beautiful I thought. So
she started to speak. And the students started to yell
and shout, and I don't believe anybody heard <u>one single
word</u> that Christabel said. So she kept on anyway for
her whole speech. She was completely shouted down.

So I just became from that moment very anxious to
help in this movement. You know if you feel some group
that's your group is the underdog you want to try to
help; it's natural I guess for everybody. When I had
gone to the suffrage meetings in this country there was
no oppositions at the meetings, everybody was in
accord, all the Quakers were in accord. This had been
one of their principles since Quakerism was started,
you know: equality of the sexes. This is the only
group I ever heard of that had it in their <u>first
principles</u>, first enunciated back in 1684. It wasn't a
subject for discussion. You just knew that there were
many things in which the world hadn't come along and
this was one that had to come along sometime. But here,
when I saw this outbreak of hostility, I thought, "That's
one group now I want to throw in all the strength I can
give to help."

I went back to Woodbrook, and then I learned that
Sir Oliver Lodge, who hadn't been at this meeting, was
very aroused when he heard of this rowdyism in his
college. (You see they had a totally different attitude
than they have in this college here of giving way to all
the rowdyism, which I think is a great mistake.) Anyway
over there Sir Oliver Lodge didn't have any patience
with it. He wasn't going to say, "Well, we want to give
the students all the right to express themselves."
[Laughter.] Not at all. He said, "This is a great
disgrace to the University of Birmingham. I call a
meeting and all students--" I guess they were all
ᵣ . . . . , wᵗ ⁱ w ᵗᵢ ᵗ. conducted

Paul: under his supervision. And it was. He was there and
he was a great figure in English life, supposedly a
most distinguished man. Christabel Pankhurst and her
friends were invited to present their case, with many
apologies from him to them, as to the unforgivable
spectacle that the college had witnessed. I can tell
you that no student would have dared to open his mouth
at this meeting.

Well, then I understood everything about what the
English militants were trying to do. She and the other
young women who spoke with her--they were all three
young girls--they had anyway one heart and soul
convert--I don't know how many others they had. That
was myself. The meeting was over, very decorous indeed,
and that was all there was to it.

Social Work in the Dalston District, 1908

Paul: So then when I finished at Woodbrook, my one year, which
is what you all went for--[pause]

While I was at Woodbrook one of the leaders of the
charity organizations in London came to speak and visit
Woodbrook. Quakers came from everywhere, you see, if
they were authorities in any field. It seems that this
Quaker head of the settlement in Birmingham felt that
I had been doing quite good work, I guess, because she
was invited to make a speech too, and people began to
ask questions. She said, "Well I am going to ask"--
she referred to me; she wanted me to answer the
questions. She said to the group, "I think Miss Paul"
(I don't suppose they called you Miss in those days) "I
think this young girl Alice Paul knows more about these
points than I do." So I got to have quite a good
feeling it seemed to me toward my own little efforts
in social work. So this lady who came down from London
began to talk to me, and she said, "I need an assistant
in the charity organization work. I am in charge of a
certain district, the Dalston, northeast district of
London."

Fry: The what?

Paul: It's just a district of London up in the northeast,
and a very poor section. So she said, "I want to
invite you to come up and be my assistant. We will pay

Paul: a very tiny sum to you which would maybe cover your
expenses. There is nobody there but one man who is
assisting me, and you." So I said I would like <u>very</u>
much to do it, so right then and there we made that
arrangement.

Cycling in France

Paul: Then I went over first to visit France for a little
while and I took my bicycle along with one of these
Dutch girls whom I came to know exceedingly well. (We
became friends for all our lives, and she married
ultimately one of the boys from Woodbrook who happened
to be a distant cousin of mine.) Anyway we went together
all through the north of France, Normandy and--

Fry: This was that summer I guess.

Paul: Yes, summer.

Fry: What fun. And you just bicycled?

Paul: I did. She didn't. She went by train or something.
We would always meet and then spend the night in some
little pension and then we would go and see everything
together. Then I would go on my bicycle to the next
place and she would get there whatever way she wanted
to use.

Fry: What did you do when you had flats on your bike and
things like that?

Paul: Well, I can't remember that detail.

Fry: Wasn't it unusual for a girl to tour France on her
bicycle in that period? This was 1908.

Paul: I don't know. If it was it didn't seem to me unusual.
Seemed to me a very normal thing. You see, everybody
in England always went everywhere on their bicycles,
you know--any place you <u>could</u> go. I remember many
bicycle trips that we took there from Woodbrook, with
some of the boy students and girl students, maybe five
or six, to this famous castle and this famous place in
history and so on. All nearby England we went to this
way. That's when I bought my bicycle over there, because
I ___ I _____ _ __. __ __ __ __ bicycle.

Paul: Then having gotten it, I just naturally took it over with me to France.

So then I think she had another term at Woodbrook because there were two terms and I think I came at the beginning of one and she came at the beginning of the next one. I think so. And I believe she went back to Woodbrook [to finish]. I went on to Paris.

And I remember arriving in Paris on my bicycle. The great city of Paris [laughing]. And I had the address of some students' house conducted by English and Americans for students with an enormous wall around the garden. I remember not knowing very much French--very very little, although I had studied it all through Swarthmore but still I didn't know very much about speaking it. Still I managed somehow finally, because very many people spoke English, to find out where the house was. And I landed there and saw this great wall, and went in. Everything was so lovely from then on. So I stayed in Paris quite a little while at this very lovely students' place. I suppose it was for American and English students. It was a student's hostel anyway, conducted by English and American people who wanted to have assurance their daughters were in a safe place in Paris. And certainly it couldn't have been a lovelier place.

Then I went back by myself to London and went up to this place up in Dalston, this very poor spot. This lady had arranged for me to live in the little house that she lived in which was the headquarters for the whole charity organization movement there. So it was very nice. She had a housekeeper and you got all your meals there. You were right in the office. Then my bicycle became precious to me because I had to ride all over. Everybody else was doing it; it was nothing unusual certainly in London to be riding on a bicycle. I rode all over my district.

This was [still] in the summer. I stayed there maybe a year; I'm not sure how long. While I was there, when I first began, Miss Lucy Gardner was the person I went to assist; she was a high-up person in the charity organization work. She needed an assistant very much because she didn't have anybody excepting this one man. She couldn't possibly cope with it.

She couldn't possibly have been a nicer person to work with and be under. So she wanted me to be trained

Paul: in the way that people did in England. She knew I knew
how we did it in America, and that is one reason I guess
why she wanted me. Because I chose by this time to be
a trained social worker. I had graduated from the
foremost school for social work in the country, which
was this New York one. That's really the reason that I
went to New York with my scholarship that year.

Well, so she asked the head of the neighboring
district if she would let me go there and work maybe a
month, without any pay at all, to be trained. And this
was an equally splended person, I thought, that I
worked under. But in addition, she was a fervent
member of the Woman's Social and Political Union.

SUFFRAGE WORK IN GREAT BRITAIN

The First Suffrage Procession

Paul: I won't say it was the Woman's Social and Political
Union; that was Mrs. Pankhurst's. But she was a fervent
member of some suffrage society. They were having a
great procession through the streets of London, otherwise
I might never have known about it. So I signed up to
walk in this big procession, as it turned out. From all
over England people came for this procession, and
probably you will find a lot about it in Sylvia Pankhurst's
book. Enormous procession. I guess I would never have
gone if this hadn't happened, to suddenly meet this lady
who knew all about it and made the arrangements so I
could go.

   Well, I was put in a section anyway, and marched in
that section--and we marched down to Hyde Park where it
was to end. And my particular section was the section
that was led by Lady Pethick-Lawrence; she was then Mrs.
Pethick-Lawrence.

Fry: Oh, that's where you met her?

Paul: Well, I didn't <u>meet</u> her. I was just one of many marchers,
and she was the very great figure. And when we got
there, here were these great--platforms (I don't know
what they were [called]; I don't know how they put them
up, the great platforms from which they were speaking.
She was the principal speaker at this place. I was
standing there right at her feet. Just by chance. I
didn't know where I was going. I just walked where I
was sent. And it was right down to this platform--we
were all sent down to this platform, surrounding this
particular platform. The other people were surrounding
another platform, just by chance I had her platform.
And I was <u>thrilled</u> beyond <u>words</u> by this <u>marvelous</u> speech.

Paul: She was a great, great speaker I thought. And so I
became sort of again linked with what I had heard of in
the University of Birmingham.

Do you want me to tell you all these things?

Fry: This is just what I want. Perfect.

Paul: You see, when I had this man [here from the magazine
last week] he was so different. He just would say--and
I didn't put any of this in because none of his questions
could possibly have related to it. The only question
was whether I spent the night on the roof; that's all he
wanted to know about England!

[Tape 2, Side A]

Paul: Following or just preceding, anyway on this occasion,
I became a member of the Women's Social and Political
Union. You became a member by signing an application
blank and giving 25¢. I still remember my thrill at
getting a letter from Mrs. Mabel Touk, the national
treasurer I think she was, of the organization, a
beautiful letter welcoming me into their ranks and
thanking me for my 25¢ and so on. I was just so extremely
happy to really be a part of it. Then I began to go to
all their meetings. They had brief meetings every week
in a big hall in London. The meetings were all oh, so
enthusiastic.

So all this time then that I continued working for
the charity organization (to finish that part) I took
this period of training and then I went back to the
original place I was to go, Mrs. Gardner's. I did I
guess just about everything there was to be done there,
everything that you could do. I learned again a great
deal about a very poor working class section of London
and what their lives were. I was again more and more
and more convinced that I didn't want to be a social
worker, but that I wanted to learn what life was like,
as many aspects as I could. At the same time the
Quakers had a headquarters in London for their own
social work at a place called Clerkenwell.

Fry: How do you spell that?

Paul: I guess it was Clerkenwell. It was one of the very
poorest sections of London. There was a little Quaker
meeting there.

Paul: Anyway, after a time of working here at this Charity
Organization Society, this chairman decided to resign.
I don't know what she was going to do, I've forgotten.
To travel or something.

Fry: Oh, that's Lucy Gardner.

Paul: Yes, the head of my place. And so she proposed to the
board, her board of directors (whatever they had) that
I be engaged in her place. She said that I knew now
all about the work and all about the district and all
about how to raise money for it, and there was nobody
else she wanted to propose.

So then they considered and they said would I agree
to stay on. I said no, I was going back to America
probably next year. So then they said, "Well, we can't
have a person take this excepting undertaking it for
some period of time." I said well then I would stay
and help the new person they got, help her get started
all right because this other lady, whatever it was that
she had to do, she had to go to pretty soon. So I did.

They finally found someone whom I liked very much,
who came down from somewhere up in the Midlands. I
thought she was a <u>splendid</u> person. So we worked together
for maybe a month or two, until she got on to the ropes.
She was the daughter of a clergyman and such a spiritual
type of a person and so consecrated really in her work.

Then I thought that I didn't want to keep on, I
<u>couldn't</u> keep on as head of it because of the fact that
I wouldn't stay [more than] a little while. She took
it over and I know everything was all right.

Then I thought I'd go up to the School of Economics
in London and learn a little more; I still knew I didn't
know very much. I went up and stayed at the Friends'
Quaker hostel that they had in London. That's one
wonderful thing that Quakers have done; they've had
these places for students. Every place I went I found
some hostel, not <u>always</u> for Quakers but some hostel for
students. And this one in London was run by Miss Anna
Littleboy, I remember.

Fry: Littleboy?

Paul: Littleboy. That was one of the most outstanding Quaker
families in England. One word. Happened to be her name.
Her brother had been the head of Woodbrook before I went

Paul: there. He was no longer head of Woodbrook, but he had it for a few years. People who were the heads of Woodbrook--it was an unpaid, honorary position. They would take leading Quakers, always a husband and wife, who would, say, take it for a year or two years, or three years. The year I was there, a Mr. and Mrs. Braithwaite [?] were what they called the wardens.

Anyway, this Mr. Littleboy's sister was in charge of this hostel which took in students. So I became one of her students, one of her group anyway, and went up to the School of Economics in London.

London School of Economics and the Pankhurst Movement

Paul: I went there for two years. That's part of the University of London, you know. I didn't try to take any degree. I wanted to go back and take it at the University of Pennsylvania; I thought it would be more useful in my own country. But I took all the courses as though I were studying for a degree.

I remember taking a course in the history of human marriage by a professor named Westermark, from Denmark, and he was at that time, I suppose, the greatest authority-- certainly in England, maybe in the world--on the question of forms of human marriage. I remember while I was there he would depart for, say, half a year and go down to some new tribe that he had never visited in some very remote place (we'll say Africa, I don't know where these places were) and sink himself into the community and learn the marriage systems. Then he would come back and teach us, and then he would go back to another place. It was a perfectly wonderful course, I must say. You got familiar with every possible variety of human marriage [laughing] that there was. It makes you have a very good idea too, and you don't get too excited when people want to have some other form of marriage.

Fry: You at least know that--

Paul: You know that it exists there, and exists there and exists there; whatever they think of, it is always something that you had known about.

So I took courses like that that I couldn't get

Fry: What was the School of Economics like then? Was this a
       fairly "radical" school?

Paul: No, it has become very much so, but it wasn't then. It
       was neither radical nor non-radical. The head of it
       was a Mr. Pember Reeves [sp?] from New Zealand, and I
       would say it was a very scholarly school. Just like
       this Westermark. He wasn't advocating any extreme form
       of marriage you see, but he was making you really know
       all the forms that mankind had been able to think of.
       And doing it in a very scholarly way. And he's written
       a book, The History of Human Marriage, which we all
       studied, and I think I still have it here.

       Then there was Sydney Webb, did you ever hear of
       him?

Fry: What was he?

Paul: He was a great--and Mrs. Sydney Webb--they were great
       authorities in the field of economics, but really more
       in its practical application to the life of England
       For instance there was a great study being made while
       I was there, a study of unemployment. Mrs. Sydney
       Webb and I guess Sydney Webb too, were people who were
       very prominent in making that study. They were known
       to every person in England, the Sydney Webbs. Well,
       he was one of the professors there.

       You had people, these outranking, just marvelous,
       marvelous professors. I never heard of anybody advocat-
       ing anything either radical or not radical, it was so
       purely scholarly.

Fry: It was an inquiry without any advocacy--

Paul: Well, they were teaching people whatever subject you
       were taking, the basic agreed-upon facts in that field,
       I thought. I know now whenever I say to people I have
       been to the School of Economics they look with somewhat
       suspicion.

Fry: I have in my notes that you were there at the School of
       Economics for 1908 and '09.

Paul: I guess so. I graduated, let me see, the School of
       Social Work in New York in 1906. Then I finished my
       first degree at the University of Pennsylvania, whether
       I took my master's now, I can't remember, in 1907.
       Then I went in the spring of 1907, about June, to

Paul: Germany. Oh, I spent my first summer over there, by the way, in Germany.

Fry: Oh, in 1907.

Paul: Yes. When I went over I went first to Germany because I had this scholarship for Woodbrook but I didn't wait till Woodbrook opened in the autumn. I went the first boat I could get and landed at Antwerp. Then went down through Germany to Berlin, and spent the summer in Berlin. I studied German all summer.

Fry: In Berlin, that was primarily for language?

Paul: Primarily to see something of the world, I guess. Being there I wanted of course to try to learn as much as I could. So from the day I started almost I got somebody to teach me German by talking to me. I went to a hostel there, students' hostel. I learned about that on the boat over. Somebody told me how she had spent so many months or so at this students' hostel. So I went to it. It was again a place I never shall forget. It was so excellent, oh delightful in every way, delightful. And I learned really quite a little German. I remember every morning we had a sort of church service and we had the Lord's Prayer and everything was in German. I think I can still say the Lord's Prayer in German, because by saying them every day you learned a good deal.

I was given a roommate. She was a teacher of German, so I let her teach me German. Then after a little while I met, I guess an American who had been to Swarthmore with me, I'm not sure. I met somebody. Maybe it was somebody crossing in the boat with me. Somebody over there. She told me she was staying in a German family and she thought I would perhaps learn more there. So I went the rest of the summer and lived in this German family.

Fry: Did you like that?

Paul: Yes. Very much. Liked them all. Very, very much.

Fry: Alice, what sort of things did you visit and seek out when you were in France and in Germany. For instance, architectural examples, or did you go a lot to art museums?

Paul: No, I don't think I ever went to one. I went to the

Fry: The German family?

Paul: Yes, the German family place because they had young
men in their--little what you called there a pension,
you know. The loveliest woman was the head of it. Her
business in life was to conduct this little pension. I
remember so well one long dining table and some of these
young men and girls--women--girls, I guess they were,
were going to operas. And so the first time in my life
I had ever been to an opera I guess. I went to these
operas and we always stood up in the gallery, because
they didn't have any money and I didn't have any money.
We always stood up in the back at these operas. These
young men were all preparing for the army, all not
knowing how many more years they had in life. They
had to be in the army. Well, I spent that summer
there. And then went over to Woodbrook in the autumn,
and I've told you the Woodbrook experience.

Fry: So that would be 1907, autumn, and--

Paul: Then I went to Woodbrook. And I finished in the spring
of 1908. And then I went first over to Paris to have
some more knowledge of something in Europe, and in 1908
went up to this Miss Lucy Gardner's charity organization
work. That's when I began really to take part in the
Suffrage movement.

        Maybe that winter I started at the School of
Economics. I guess I did.

Fry: I have here 1908 and '09 you were in the School of
Economics; that comes out right.

Paul: You see I went from this charity organization. Say that
we stopped our work in May at the Woodbrook and I went
over--maybe as little as two weeks, I don't know how long--
in France; and then came up and spent I suppose all the
first half of that year with this Miss Gardner. Then I
must have left and gone up to London to this student
hostel, to begin work at the School of Economics.

First Suffrage Tasks and the Clerkenwell Settlement

Paul: While I was at the School of Economics, I met one girl
especially, her name was Rachel Barrett, I
remember, who was a very ardent worker in the Women's

Paul: Social and Political Union, as they called it, of Mrs. Pankhurst's. I remember the first thing that I ever really did [for suffrage] while I was still at the School of Economics. This particular person, I think it was this Rachel Barrett, asked me if I would go out and help her in selling their paper, Votes for Women, in the street. So I did. I remember how very bold and good she was and how very timid and [laughing] unsuccessful I was, standing beside her trying to ask people to buy Votes for Women. So contrary to my nature really. I didn't seem to be very brave by nature. I remember very well doing this day after day after day, going down to the School of Economics, where she was a student and I was a student and other people were st students, and we would just stand out in the street wherever we were supposed to stand, on some corner, with these Votes for Women. It is what they did all over London. A great many of the girls in all parts of London were doing it.

Fry: Did you get some hostile responses?

Paul: Well, I don't remember anything about that. [Laughter] I don't know whether I did or not. I didn't think I was much of a success, but anyway I tried.

Then they began to ask me to speak outdoors at the street corners. Naturally they asked anybody, as I have always tried to do in our movement--to ask anybody to do anything that I could get them to do. So all we had to do was to tell what the movement was doing that week, what they were trying to do. I did speak, I guess, in a great many parts of London at little outdoor meetings, and indoor meetings when there was an election going on and they would meet in a schoolhouse perhaps and try to get all the people in that neighborhood to come in. The way you started, of course--they always started [new workers] by [having you] just introduce someone, someone who was an experienced speaker and would give you a little confidence so that you'd know you didn't have to go on; you could stop in a minute and now introduce the speaker. So that's the way I started, by introducing people. Then after a little while they would promote you to speaking yourself and having somebody introduce you--another new beginner.

We would go to the railroad stations in London and what they call the "tubes" (the subway) and in little parks. I don't know what we had for things to stand on, but they always had something we could stand on to

Paul: be a little above the crowd.

So then in a little while I decided I wouldn't
stay any longer in this Friends' pension, but I would
like to try to see a little more of the life of London.
So I went down to this Clerkenwell headquarters of the
Quakers and rented a little tiny apartment, or room, I
guess it was an apartment in Clerkenwell, in the very
poorest section of London you can imagine. And I became
one of their assistants in their Clerkenwell settlement.
It was very easy, you know, having been in settlement;
they would take you in and were glad to have you. They
would give you classes of people you were to instruct.

Do you want to go and get some lunch?

Fry: I'm out of ink in my pen.

Paul: Don't you think you'd better get some orange juice or
something?

Fry: Why don't we do that. We are just now getting into
your suffrage work and this might be a good place to
stop for a minute.

Paul: All right. I'll come out [to the kitchen]. We'll just
get a glass of orange juice.

Fry: Well, let me bring it in here to you.

Paul: I really don't want to stop. If you're going to do it,
I must make sure that you get everything that you want
[before you have to leave].

[break; tape recorder off]

Now if I am going too much into detail, you will
stop me, will you?

Fry: You're not. It's the detail that I need, because we
have the outlines and the general stuff.

Okay. So you are at Clerkenwell.

Personal Risk: Arrest in the Pankhurst Movement

Paul: Clerkenwell. This is where the Quakers had this little

Paul: sort of settlement house, headquarters anyway. So
then they asked me to come in and be one of their
assistants there. So I did. I had this little apartment
right by, so I fixed the little tiny apartment up and
made it the first little home I ever fixed up. I fixed
it up, I thought, and made it quite nice. I don't know
whether it was one room, one floor, or what, but it was
just the type that people were living in there. You
had to go down to the pump in the--it was built around
some kind of a little center place--and there was a
pump you had to get all your water from, walk down and
fill up your bucket of water or whatever you had.

Fry: Was there a long handle that you had to pump?

Paul: No, there wasn't any handle, but you had to go <u>down</u>,
with a bucket, to fill it for whatever you wanted to
take up to your room. It was the only water we had.
I can't remember about the toilet, what we had. This
was just--you felt that you were living the life and
that you could <u>see</u> what the life of the ordinary person
and all the handicaps and troubles and so on that they
had.

I stayed there. I still kept on going up to the
School of Economics and doing this work with the Quakers
in this little settlement and going to all the meetings
that I could of the WSPU. That was sort of my life.

I guess all that winter that was what I did because
it was in the spring [of 1909] when I was still at the
School of Economics I remember that I got a letter from
the Women's Social and Political Union asking me if I
would go on a deputation to, I suppose, the prime
minister [Asquith] (whoever was the head of the--a person
that they were going on deputations to in Parliament).
It was to be on a certain day, to be led by Mrs. Pankhurst
and it would probably mean that you would be under some
danger of being arrested and imprisoned, so you must
not accept this invitation unless you were willing to
do this. I remember hesitating the longest time and
writing the letter and not being able to get enough
courage to post it [laughter] and going up and walking
around the post office, wondering whether I dare put
this in.

Fry: Saying yes?

Paul: To say yes. (That's all you <u>could</u> say. If you didn't
want to go, you didn't write; if you would go, why then

Paul: they wanted you to write.) I thought maybe I could go under an assumed name, as some of the people were doing, because while I didn't object to going at all, I thought all my family and everybody I knew would object, so to save them from terrible disgrace [laughing] and a blot on our family escutcheon and so on, I thought, "Well, I will go under an assumed name." And finally I decided I wouldn't do that. So at last I got up enough courage to post my letter, saying I would go.

And I did go to the meeting in Caxton Hall in London, which you will probably come across in Sylvia [Pankhurst]'s book because all the meetings were held in Caxton Hall, very close to Parliament. I must read her book again to see what she says of all these affairs.* I remember Mrs. Pethick-Lawrence and Christabel conducted the meeting. They told us just what to do, where to meet, what to wear, how to act, everything. And then, we'll say the next day, we met. Mrs. Pankhurst led the procession. I imagine there were about a hundred people, but I am not sure how many. We marched--not really marched but we just walked--through the streets of London from Caxton Hall, very close, up to Parliament. There we were stopped and we were all arrested, and taken to the--I think it was Canon Row Street Station--I'd have to look it up [Canon Row]. But anyway to a police station that the suffragists were always taken to when they went to Parliament. That's where I met Lucy Burns. I had never heard of her--you know who she was, don't you?

Fry: Yes. [Later a close associate of Paul's in the suffrage movement in the United States.]

Paul: She was a student in Baden University in Germany and I guess she had gone over on her vacation to England. I imagine it was. Anyway, she heard of this deputation and she was always much more valiant than I. About a thousand times more valiant than I, by nature, I think. So she wanted to go right away on this deputation. She had a little United States flag of some type on her suit, and so I went up to her to introduce myself--we were the only two Americans there. So we became very good friends and continued to be all our lives until she sort of melted away in the last part of our [Equal Rights

---

*Pankhurst, Sylvia, The Suffragette, The History of the Women's Militant Suffrage Movement, 1905-1910, New York,

Paul: Amendment] campaign. But from that time on in England
we saw a great, great deal of each other.

Well, bail was given to everybody on [the deputation]
by Mr. Pethick Lawrence, who was a very wealthy man. So
he put up the bail for everybody. Now I remember he was
talking to me here in the police station, and he said
now would we be sure to be there when the time was
appointed for us to come to be sentenced. We were just
released on bail.

I remember so well. (Funny how you remember some
things and others you don't, though I have never thought
of it from that day to this. I guess I've never thought
of it since.) He sat down beside each person and said,
"Now I am leaving this money, and you be there at such-
and-such a date."

And I said, "You know I have a return ticket for
America on the boat going such a date, which is before
the time that I have to be there."

He said, "The only thing you can do I guess is to
cancel your return ticket because by order of the court
you have to appear at this time." So I did. I cancelled
my return ticket to America. Then somehow or other
this group never was called for sentence. Of course they
[the court officials] were very arbitrary. They did
what they wanted. Maybe it was such a large group
that they didn't want to put all these people in prison.
Whatever the reason was, they finally announced that the
case was dismissed.

I was at the School of Economics when this letter
arrived but it was just about the end of the term, and
that's the reason that I had gotten my ticket to go
home.

Since I had sent in my name for this deputation,
they supposed, of course, that I might be willing to
help in any of their militant efforts. Immediately,
it never failed, [laughter] everything that they got up
from that time after that was of a militant nature they
always sent me a note, saying would I take part.

First Imprisonment

Paul: Almost immediately they were going to have a meeting in
Bermondsey to protest against one of the members,
[Chancellor of the Exchequer] Lloyd George it was, Lloyd
George's speech which he was making as a member of the
cabinet; he was participating in the general opposition
to the suffrage measure. They all were. The cabinet
was united against us; as far as you could tell, they
were united.

So I went down, being asked to go, to speak.
Imagine I, knowing hardly anything about speaking at
all! And a group of people were asked to speak. That's
all we did: go outside the meeting and have a protest
meeting. But I learned then that you didn't have to be
an eloquent speaker as I thought you might have to be
and I knew I would never be. So anyway I agreed to go,
to make one more.

And the person who got up to speak first was instantly
arrested. And then the next one that she would introduce
was instantly arrested. So when it came my time to get
up and make a speech, my heart was calm [laughing]
because I knew I wouldn't have to make the terrible
speech [laughter] which was the thing that worried me
more than anything else. So I _was_ immediately arrested.
And that's the first time I was in prison.

Fry: What was the name of the town?

Paul: It was part of London--Bermondsey, one of the industrial,
poor sections of London. I may have some of these things
wrong, you see; I would have to refresh my memory, but
I think it was in Bermondsey.

So then we all were taken to the police station and
were not let out on bail at all and were convicted and
sentenced to prison, we'll say, for two weeks or something, maybe a month. It wasn't any very long period.
[pause]

So from that time on, I really did participate I
guess, almost entirely--I guess about everything I did
was from that time on in the suffrage movement.

To Scotland with Mrs. Pankhurst

Paul: I remember that Mrs. Pankhurst was going up to Scotland
to get up what they hoped would be a very large procession
through the streets of Edinburgh on October 9, 1909 to
start the movement there. And she invited Lucy Burns
and myself, two Americans, the only two Americans
perhaps that ever had taken part in the movement, to
drive up with her, which we were both of us very happy
that she asked us to do it.

Fry: Was it because she wanted Americans or was it just
because you and Lucy had been doing so well?

Paul: I don't know. I suppose she was going on this tour
and wanted to take some people along; maybe we had just
come to her attention in some way or other. I don't
know why she asked us to go, but we both were overjoyed
to be asked.

I remember she had a woman chauffeur, and this was
something absolutely unheard of. Nobody had ever seen
a woman chauffeur. It was unusual for a woman to drive
a car but to have a woman chauffeur--! So she was quite
a picture on her expedition. Only Mrs. Pankhurst, Lucy
Burns and myself, and this woman chauffeur. Then we
would stop at meetings along the way; great meetings
had been arranged for Mrs. Pankhurst, and she would make
one of her great speeches to enormous crowds; and then
we would go on to the next stopping place where she
would make another speech.

What they wanted to do was to organize this procession,
and I think that Mrs. Pankhurst thought that maybe we
could help her organize it. We both were going back to
America and we had no particular ties in England, and so
when we got up to Edinburgh--have you ever been to
Edinburgh?

Fry: No.

Paul: One of the most beautiful streets that you can think
of--Princes Street--goes from I think what they call
the castle, an old, old, old castle, down to an
equally historic place. It is between two very historic
places. They opened headquarters there under Mrs.
Pankhurst. And she had an assistant called Flora
Drummond (they always called her General Drummond)
.   .   .   .   '   .   .   ⁻   ,   (ʌ,   ⁴ ⊃ keep

Paul: up all your connections with these people that you
think were so wonderful.

So she asked me, and I think maybe Lucy Burns but
anyway she asked me, to go down to a meeting at Berwick-
on-Tweed (and by the way, that's another thing that Mr.
Gallagher asked me all about, so [that story] must be
in one of these books).

Interrupting Sir Edward Grey, Winston Churchill, and Lord Crewe

Paul: A meeting by [Minister of Foreign Affairs] Sir Edward
Grey; he was a member of the cabinet. We were not
supposed to go outside and make a meeting, but to go
inside and ask a question of him as to why the government
was obstructing the enfranchisement of women, or something
like that.

I remember the person that I was [assigned to]. I
was always sent along you know as a little girl assistant
to somebody important. This person that was put in
charge of this, I hope I can think of her name; her
husband was one of the foremost journalists in Great
Britain. (Previously at a meeting in London, where
various women had gotten up and asked questions and had
been thrown out of the meeting, there was a man named
Henry Nevinson. Did you ever hear of him? He has
written a book not exactly on this topic but on a related
one; he was one of the foremost newspapermen in England.
He got up in great indignation when all these women were
being thrown out and made a public protest. Then there
was another newspaperman who followed him and got up
and did the same. Probably I will think of his name.*
His wife up in Edinburgh helping Mrs. Pankhurst.) She
was sent down with me to Berwick-on-Tweed. She was to
make the speeches and I was to help her by introducing
her and so on.

So for one week we stayed there, and every night
we went out and spoke on the street corners of Berwick-
on-Tweed, in the marketplace or someplace where people
assembled. This was to acquaint the people of the town
with why we were protesting against Sir Edward Grey.

When the meeting came I think she went back to
London and I stayed on. Whether Lucy Burns was there

— — ·· —

*H. N. Brailsford

Paul: or not, I can't remember; it seems to me she was. But at all events I know that when the meeting was in full sway and Sir Edward Grey was talking about their great principles I just was told what I was to do so I did it, or tried to. I was supposed to get up and say, "Well, these are very wonderful ideals and so on but couldn't you extend them to women" or something like that. And when I did this (with great timidity, I am sure; anyway I got it out enough so that [laughing] I was heard), the police immediately took me by the arms and right out of the meeting. I remember I was most indignant.

They conducted me all up through the streets of Berwick-on-Tweed to the police station holding my hands behind me. I don't know whether with handcuffs or with what, so I was, I remember, so <u>blazingly</u> angry and--

Fry: They made you walk through the streets?

Paul: Yes, to take me to be arrested to the police station, or be booked, or whatever you did. So then I <u>was</u> arrested and I was charged with whatever I was supposed to be charged with and the meeting was over, and I guess Sir Edward Grey must have told them not to go forward with any prosecution of anybody or something like that. Because I was released.

So having done this little chore, Mrs. Drummond asked Lucy Burns and me to go together up to East Fife to arouse East Fife on this subject. Let's see, what was the name of that town--Dundee. We were sent to Dundee. We went out from Dundee into all the neighboring little towns. It was <u>so</u> interesting, the experiences; and we usually spoke on the street corners. They hardly ever had indoor meetings; it was in the summer.

Then there was to be a meeting by Winston Churchill, a great meeting, I think it was in a great hall in Dundee. And so we were asked to get up a meeting outside, a protest, which we undertook to do. And we did. We got up the meeting and we were both arrested and we were both imprisoned. I don't know for how long, but both of us were put in Dundee prison.*

---

*See Irwin, Inez Haynes, <u>Up Hill with Banners Flying</u>, Traversity Press, Penobscot, Maine, 1964, p. 10, for fuller account. This is the 1964 edition of Irwin's

Paul: Then when we came out, a very lovely woman by the name
of Miss MacGregor who lived in one of these beautiful
Scotch estates outside of Dundee, and who was a great
supporter of this movement, invited us to come out and
to be her guests and recuperate. So we went, both of
us.

I remember when we got there, we were far out in
the country, and Lucy Burns and I thought we would go
out for a walk, and Miss MacGregor was very much
embarrassed. She said, "You know, no lady goes out
without having a hat and a coat and gloves and so on.
I wouldn't want anybody to go out from my house without
being properly gowned." So we gradually learned all
the right customs [laughing] and conformed to them, I
guess all right. And this was at Invorkeelor.

Fry: How would you spell that?

Paul: I'll have to look these things up. I may find them
in Sylvia's book. I think it was [spelling] Invorkeelor
or something like that. That was the name of her town.
And the name of her house was [spelling] Abbeythune.
Maybe that was the little village she lived in. But
anyway we spent maybe two or three weeks there as her
guests.

Then we went back to Edinburgh, where the procession
was being gotten up. And that's the time they sent us
over to Glasgow, which you read to me.

Fry: And that's where you were arrested again? On the rooftop episode in the rain.

Paul: Yes, we were arrested there, but they didn't prosecute
the case. I remember they didn't. The only time I
went to prison in Scotland was in Dundee.

Fry: One question: When you were going into the Sir Edward
Grey meeting, how did you get inside the hall for that?

Paul: Berwick-on-Tweed? Well, they were public meetings;
people could always go in.

Then the procession came off. Both Lucy Burns and
I spent our time helping in every way we could in getting
it up. Doing all the things you had to do to get up a
big procession. It was a great success. The procession
was very beautiful.

Paul: Then when it was over we went back to London.

Fry: Any arrests on the procession?

Paul: No, no, no. There were no arrests at all. It was just
          a beautiful procession through the streets. There was
          no opposition; I suppose they had a permit. The only
          time we were ever arrested was when it was some protest
          against some members of the cabinet.

London, the Annual Meeting of the Lord Mayor, November 9, 1909: Alice as a Charwoman

Paul: Then when we went back to London in the autumn, (as I
          recall it, though I might find more in Sylvia's book)
          the first thing we were asked to do--Lucy Burns and I--
          was, as I can recall, to go to the meeting of the Lord
          Mayor of London [Nov. 9, 1909] which was held every year
          for some celebrity and to ask (probably the prime minister,
          but whoever was speaking) again about why they were
          holding up the suffrage movement.* And I will have to
          read more about it because as far as I can remember,
          Lucy Burns was asked to dress up and go as a guest--they
          got a ticket for her in some way--and to get up and
          interrupt the meeting. I don't remember whether she did
          or not, but she was always very courageous, so I suppose
          she did. I don't remember though.

          I was asked to go in as a charwoman in the morning
          when all these charwomen were going in, and go up where
          the gallery was and call down to make sure that if Lucy
          down on the floor didn't get her words heard, at least
          they would hear this from above.

          I was with another woman.

          [End of Tape 2, Side 1]

          [Tape 2, Side 2]

Paul: Maybe her name was Brown, I mean Nurse Brown, I always

---

*Pankhurst, Sylvia, p. 459-60. See appendix for text.

Paul: called her. Maybe it was Amelia. But the two of us
        were sent together to do this upstairs business. She
        was a nurse and I was a student. So we went there and
        spent the whole day.

Fry: As charwomen?

Paul: No, we just concealed ourselves. We got in as charwomen,
        and then we had to conceal ourselves upstairs somewhere
        in the loft. The police searched the whole building.
        I remember they came in and searched just where we were
        crouching down, and they even touched my hair, but they
        didn't--I guess they thought it was something else, so
        they didn't discover us. So we stayed there all through
        this day.

Fry: Were you in a closet or something?

Paul: No, we were just--we'll say some loft, over the--

Fry: Up over a ceiling.

Paul: Over the building. And it was not adjoining the place
        where the Lord Mayor's meeting was, but it was right
        next to it. So we were supposed to break a window and
        call down [into the meeting] because the place that was
        right above--it was too thoroughly guarded, I guess,
        probably, they thought.

        So we stayed there all day. And then I suppose
        Nurse Brown called down too--I don't remember a single
        thing except of myself. So I called down what I was
        supposed to call down and the police came rushing up and
        arrested us. She probably did the same. And whether
        Lucy Burns ever made her speech and so on on the floor
        I don't know. I suppose she did, but I don't remember
        because I don't think she was in prison with me.

Forced Feeding in Prison

Paul: Anyway, Nurse Brown and I were in prison, I think for
        about a month. And that is the time I think they
        started forcible feeding, I'm not quite sure. But
        anyway, we served out our sentence.

Fry: Pankhurst says in here that you had to undergo forced
        feeding.

Paul: It was started at a certain time, and I think it was
then. I don't think it ever was in a previous one
that I can recall.

So then when I came out I was invited by a very nice
Jewish family who belonged to this movement to come to
their house and recuperate. I was supposed to be very
ill [laughter] apparently, because I was a very frail
and fragile person anyway. I suppose I looked more ill
than I was. So I went to this home. It was lovely, oh
very cordial and warm and generous people. And I
stayed there maybe two weeks. I remember Mrs. Pankhurst
came to see me there and various people connected with
the movement came to see me. And then I got finally
my passage home and returned.

I don't know whether I told you all the episodes
or whether there were some others that I have forgotten.

Fry: Well, the one that you just told me, according to Sylvia
Pankhurst, took place in November of 1909.

Paul: And I came home in January, 1910.

Fry: What was your treatment like in the jails and prisons
that you were in?

Paul: Oh, they just paid no attention to us. You were just
locked up and you were in solitary confinement. You
never saw anybody. You were not given anything to read.
You were just left alone. Nobody paid any attention to
you whatsoever.

Fry: Did you get plenty to eat?

Paul: Well, we were forcibly fed you see. We didn't eat
anything.

Fry: What about in the other English jails you had been in?
You had this other sentence that you had to serve, and
you said you were sentenced for a short while after your
protest against Lloyd George.

Paul: About two weeks, I think. Maybe a month, but not very
long.

Fry: I just wondered if there was any--

Paul: I don't remember a thing. You know I still today don't
know much about food, or think much about it or care

Paul:　much about it.　So I don't remember a thing about the
food.　I guess it was all right.

Fry:　Apparently the hunger strike was one of the coordinated
strategies of the Women's Social and Political Union.

Paul:　Well, the hunger strike was the reason we were forcibly
fed.　Wouldn't have been otherwise.　And I don't recall
whether we went on a hunger strike before.　I know we
did the last time, but whether we ever did before or not,
I don't know.　Whenever they adopted finally as a policy,
which they did, of asking all the prisoners--the Women's
Social and Political Union would say, "Now if you want
to go, we want you to hunger strike or not go."　And so
you went in with that understanding.　When they adopted
that policy--and I think the policy was probably after
we were imprisoned in Dundee because I don't recall that
we hunger struck in Dundee.　We might have, but I could
look it up and see.　Whenever it was, we did.*

So that's the end of England.　I think I have told
you most of the things that happened.

Fry:　I think you have.

There's a note I picked up somewhere that in the
summer before, (1908) you were a resident worker for
Christian Social Union Settlement of Hoxton, London.
Did we cover that?

Paul:　Well, when I was staying with this Miss Lucy Gardner
in the Charity Organization work I told you the first
month [of the summer] I didn't stay with her because
I went up to have this training, we'll say a month.
I don't know whether I got there about July or June or
when.　Then after staying with her a little while and
I learned all about the Dalston region because I went
over always with my bicycle.

I must tell you one other thing.　While I was going
all over the place with my bicycle, going everywhere,
full of confidence and everything, which I still retain--
I don't seem to learn much through ages going by--I
came out from visiting one family, and here my bicycle

_____

*Pankhurst relates the first hunger strike taking place
in Holloway gaol, London, July 5, 1909.　Ibid., p. 391.

Paul: was gone. I had to walk home, and I never had a bicycle
from then on. I had no fear because I had read so many
tales about Scotland Yard. So I thought, well, Scotland
Yard will find it for me. But Scotland Yard never did.
I don't think they took any interest in finding it.

Fry: Did you walk <u>everywhere</u> after that, or how did you get
around?

Paul: I walked every place. Maybe they had some little buses,
I don't remember. Of course it was only one little
section you know, not an enormous section you covered.

When I was about to come home, Christabel Pankhurst
asked me if I would stay on as an organizer and be paid
a little salary,(they paid very tiny salaries, but they
paid a little salary) and give all my time to being one
of their organizers. And she made the same offer to
Lucy Burns. Same time. And Lucy Burns decided she
would and she did. And I decided I would still go home
and try to finish up my academic work and take a degree.
I thought it was perhaps the best thing to do. So I
came home. By myself.

SECTION II: THE USA SUFFRAGE CAMPAIGN

RETURN TO THE USA

From Suffragette to Suffragist

Paul: When I got home the suffragists in this country asked
me of course--naturally they would--to go to their
meetings. So I joined the one in [Philadelphia]. I
went right back to the University of Pennsylvania and
took a room in Philadelphia so I could go to classes
all the time; they still didn't have any place for the
graduate students and there were no other women there.
  They put me on the board of their Philadelphia
committee.

Fry: This happened right away?

Paul: Yes. After I came back, I remember when I made a speech,
they asked me to come in and speak to them and tell them
about the English campaign. I remember the head of it,
Miss Jane Campbell, who was the president, said, "You
know, when we asked you, we didn't know who you were
or what sort of person you were or whether you were
wild and fanatical or what you might be, but we thought
we'd ask you just because you are a figure now in the
minds of people. Now we see what sort of a person you
are and we'd like you to go on our committee." So they
were very welcoming from the very beginning. Even
though I think they may have thought we had done rather
[laughing] extraordinary things.

  Then they formed a committee for the first time
on having street meetings in Philadelphia and trying
to make this movement better known. So I was made
chairman of the street meeting committee.

Fry: That sounds logically like it might have been your
idea--bringing over the street meeting technique from
England.

Paul: No, they were beginning to start them in Boston and other places in this country, before we got back. Just the natural thing that comes in all political campaigns when you desperately want to get before the people; it is about all you can do.

So I took the chairmanship of this, and in Miss Katzenstein's book,* I think she tells about the first street meeting that she organized and took me to. I spoke. I'm sure it's in her book because it was the first time I met her when we started out on this meeting when I went in to see the people at the Philadelphia office. Then she got some kind of a conveyance for me and she went with me, and from that time on we worked together. Then that summer, all summer, we had these street meetings.

I was, let me see, I think I didn't start into the University of Pennsylvania until the fall, but all this time I sort of got into the woman's movement. And I was invited down to the national convention of the National American Women's Suffrage Association in Washington. I guess it must have been in the spring of 1912.

Fry: That was fall of 1910 when you started back at the University, according to my notes. Is that right?

Paul: I think so. I got back here in January I think. And I didn't enroll in the University right away but went to these different meetings, and, among others to one that was held in Washington (the first time I had ever gone to Washington in my life) at one of the hotels, their convention. Could it have been 1912?

Fry: Let's see. You got your Ph.D. in 1912.

Paul: No, this must have been earlier then. It was probably the spring of 1910, the year I came back. It would have been 1910 because Taft was the president of the United States and I presume he was president in 1910. We can look that up. Taft was a speaker at this convention, and Dr. Anna Howard Shaw, I think, was the presiding officer, and they invited me just because I had taken part in the English movement and I guess they invited

_____

*Katzenstein, Carolyn, Lifting the Curtain, the State and National Women's Suffrage Campaign in Pennsylvania

Paul: me to talk about that, I imagine. Whatever they invited me to do, I tried to do.

Then when it came time for Taft to speak (before or after--I don't know where I came in the program) Taft made clear that he didn't think much of this voting for women. All over the room people began to hiss, and he was unperturbed, but they did. [pause]

Nothing happened through the meeting excepting I got to know some of the different leaders of the movement and continued to know them always because of that first meeting. That was just one little--perhaps one week it took me down in Washington.

Fry: Any certain leaders that you want to mention?

Paul: I remember the women, but I won't say at this meeting because maybe I didn't meet them at this meeting. But I can tell you later who the women were I can remember.

A Ph.D. at the University of Pennsylvania

Paul: Then we went on--beginning I guess in the summer--to hold these street meetings and, let's see, this would have been 1910. I went back to the University evidently in the autumn of 1910 and stayed through 1911 and 1912. In 1912 I think I took my degree in June, my doctor's degree. Previously to that I had taken a master's degree. Whether it was the first year that I was back or whether it was the last year before I went, I am not quite sure. Anyway, I know what my thesis was for my doctor's degree. It was called "Toward Equality" and the same title I think I had for my master's. It was toward equality in the United States for women. And the previous one, I think my master's, was toward equality for women in Pennsylvania.

So on the basis of the Pennsylvania one, I just enlarged it to take in the country.

Fry: In this thesis--

Paul: One of the biggest things we did in our street meeting affair [?] --we had no opposition, but we didn't get much--I don't know, I wouldn't say very much assistance. There were just a few of us who did all the meetings.

Paul: We wound up by meeting in Independence Square, the
       biggest meeting. (I guess it was the end of the summer
       of the first year, 1910. It might have been a subsequent
       year.) And we had little stands for speakers all over
       Independence Square because of the great traditions of
       Independence Square, and I know Inez Mulholland came
       down and spoke to this meeting. We had the most
       illustrious people we could get. It was utterly, I
       thought, a thrilling meeting. The whole square was
       filled with people. We had a great deal of publicity.
       I could look up when that occurred. It is probably
       somewhere I could find. About September it was, of one
       year, I don't remember which year.

Fry: It will be probably in Katzenstein's book.

Paul: It might have been September of that year I came down
       to Washington. Perhaps it was because that year [1912]
       they had the National [American Woman] Suffragist
       Convention in Philadelphia and the person in charge of
       getting that up was Mrs. Lawrence Lewis.

Appointment as Congressional Chairman, National American Woman Suffragist Convention

Paul: She asked me to help her, which I did, perhaps because
       of this big meeting that we'd gotten up in Independence
       Square--but anyway she asked me to help her. So at
       that meeting I went--I suppose as a delegate; I don't
       know about that - but anyway I went to the meeting - and
       as a sort of assistant to Mrs. Lewis, helping her any
       way I could. That's when I was appointed to be the
       Congressional Chairman for the coming year, November,
       1912. The national Congressional Chairman had to go
       to Washington, you know. Lucy Burns and I were appointed
       and the resolution was offered by Miss Jane Addams at
       the national board meeting, that we be appointed and
       that we be given free reign and free hand in anything
       we wanted to do, excepting we were not to be allowed to
       send in a bill for anything that we spent and not to
       charge anything to the national treasury and not to
       spend even one dollar that we didn't ourselves raise
       or give. That's the only condition they made. That
       was the treasurer I suppose who made all those
       conditions.

Fry: N . . . . I . . . . vi . . . . L . y Burns at

Fry: her Long Island home in the summer after your Ph.D. was
        awarded, which would be somewhat earlier in 1912.

Paul: Well, I don't know whether it was that summer, I thought
        it was later, but maybe it was that summer--she came down
        and visited me at my little home in Moorestown. It
        must have been in the summer of 1912 I guess, because
        we were considering what to do about whether we would
        undertake this work in Washington. She came down and
        stayed with me a little while, and we discussed it and
        felt that we would _offer_ to come down and do this in
        Washington; maybe they wouldn't accept it, but we would
        make an offer. Then I went up to visit her to talk
        about it further. I don't know which came first, whether
        she came to me first, or I went there first, but anyway
        we had conferences, at least those two.

        Then at the time of the convention--I don't know
        whether she went to the convention or not--but I know I
        did. And we went--_I_ went at least, maybe she went too--
        to Miss Jane Addams to say we would like to offer to
        help in any way we could in the federal amendment
        campaign in Washington. And she said Mrs. William Kent,
        who was then acting as congressional chairman, didn't
        want to continue or couldn't continue for some reason,
        and they wanted someone to be on the congressional
        committee, and that she would offer our names, propose
        a resolution, which she did, and it was adopted with
        that one restriction.

Fry: I want to be sure I have this right. Did you and Lucy
        prefer to work on the congressional committee?

Paul: [Inaudible] a committee. This was [inaudible] open
        door [?], there was only one committee for the open
        door [?] meeting, only one committee for the congres-
        sional work. We didn't, I suppose, even know anything
        about it when we offered to go down and try to see if
        we could push it. Then we learned that there was Mrs.
        William Kent, wife of the congressman from California,
        who had been and who didn't feel able to continue, and
        wanted someone to take her place. I guess we were told
        that by Miss Addams; I can't be sure.

        Then anyway she said that she thought it would be
        a splendid thing for us to do, and she would be delighted
        to back it and would offer the resolution, which she did.

Fry: That's what I have in my notes--that Jane Addams brought
        it before the board and it was approved. The names I

Fry: have, that the committee would consist of, are, Alice
         Paul, Lucy Burns, Crystal Eastman (Max Eastman's
         sister); and then I have later Mrs. Lawrence Lewis.

Paul: Well, as far as I know only--that may be if there is
         some record that Crystal Eastman was on--I don't
         remember that. Crystal Eastman was a personal friend
         of Lucy Burns and I didn't know her. They had been at
         Vassar together, and it was my impression that after we
         got down there and began to see all the work that was
         needed and felt that we had to have more people, that
         she asked--we asked her together--Crystal Eastman to
         come down and join us, which she did. Or maybe she was
         already appointed, I didn't remember.

Fry: Well, my notes may be wrong because I think I got a lot
         of these notes from the History of the Woman's Party by
         Inez Irwin, so you see this might be wrong [in a secondary
         source].

Paul: Well, it might be true. Anyway she from the very begin-
         ning worked with us. I didn't think she did in the
         very beginning. I thought she came later.

Getting Set Up in Washington, D.C.

Paul: I went down alone on December 7, 1912, after I was
         appointed. I spent that Christmas in Washington getting
         ready for the opening of our little headquarters. Mrs.
         William Kent asked me to have Christmas dinner with them,
         I remember so well. She was the most stalwart and won-
         derful aide anybody could ever want, my predecessor.
         Extra, extra, extra, extra wonderful.

         Lucy Burns came down, I imagine about the middle
         of January, but anyway she didn't come down for quite a
         little while. I went into a little friendly boarding
         house on I Street in Washington right next to the Quaker
         meeting house and everybody there, I guess, was a Quaker
         or in some way connected with them. And I remember I
         had one little third floor room. And no headquarters
         of course, no office, nothing. And I told you that's
         when we got the Susan B. Anthony desk--I think I told
         you about that.

Fry: Oh, you told me, yes--but now you have to tell it
         again [to record it on tape].

Fry: How did you get the headquarters?

Paul: Well, they gave me a list of women's names in New York
         before I went--the New York people did in their head-
         quarters before I went down. These were all Washington
         members and officers and supporters. And so I started
         out.

         First thing I went to this little Friends boarding
         house which I think was the place that I went when I
         first went down to this convention that I had gone to
         when Taft was speaker. I learned about it anyway. It
         was in the _Friend's Intelligence_ here (that's the Quaker
         paper), always advertised, so I knew about it and I went
         there. So then I started from there, with no headquarters,
         to go through the whole long list that they had given me
         of maybe forty or fifty names to ask each person if she
         would join in with this effort we were going to make to
         take up again Susan B. Anthony's work in a rigorous
         form to really get the Amendment through Congress.
         Because Mrs. Kent, and I don't know who was there before,
         but ever since the death of Miss Anthony the national
         board had put all its efforts in state referendum
         campaigns and had regarded the Washington work as some-
         thing that had to be continued to the extent of having
         a speech made in Congress or something like that and
         having the _Congressional Record_ containing the speech
         sent all over the country; but it was all secondary to
         the state campaign.

         So when I went to these women I didn't go to Mrs.
         Kent right away, but I began on the list, maybe alpha-
         betically as they gave it to me, I don't remember. But
         I found one person after another after another had died,
         and then I found one after another after another after
         another had moved away and nobody knew their present
         address. So it narrowed down to not having so many
         left to see.

Fry: My goodness, it must have been an old list.

Paul: It showed how feeble was the movement there, anyway.

         And then I, among others, went to Miss Emma Gillette,
         who was the dean and one of the founders of the Washington
         College of Law which had been started as a college to
         enable women to study law, because at that time there
         was almost no place in the country you could be admitted
         as a student. Miss Gillette came from Pennsylvania
         and when she wanted to study law she came to Washington

Paul: thinking there was a law school here and it was the
Negro school, Howard University. And that was the only
place in the country she could find that would take her
in, so she went to Howard University and graduated
there.

Then when she graduated she joined forces with Ellen
Spencer Mussey, who was the wife of a Washington lawyer
and who had studied law herself in her husband's law
office and passed the bar examination to become a lawyer.
So there were two women lawyers in Washington, as far as
I know. One was Miss Gillette and one was Mrs. Mussey.
And they had set up this little Washington College of
Law, in order that the women would have a chance.

[Neighbor, Mrs. Scotty Reynolds, enters.]

Fry: Oh! Hi!

S.R.:   Am I too early?

Paul: Oh, no.

S.R.:   I'll put your groceries away, in here.

Paul: Lovely. [To Fry] Do you want to go and help her a
minute? I'll remember where we left off.

[Recorder off.]

Paul: --Forty or fifty people and almost everybody on the list
had died or moved away.

Fry: And you were telling about Ellen Spencer Mussey--

Paul: Miss Gillette, who was the first person I met who was
friendly and interested and still living. She was, my
goodness, such a wonderful woman. So she had been with
Mrs. Ellen Mussey. She had founded this Washington
College of Law where I took my first law degree, founded
in order that women might have a place to study law.

Fry: Did you say where you had taken your "first law degree"?

Paul: Yes, I took it there, after I got to know her long years
after. I didn't dream of taking a law degree then, in
1912.

I met Miss Gillette and she had a little law office
and real estate office in the basement of an office

Paul: building between what is now the Willard Hotel and the Washington Hotel on F Street in Washington. Do you know Washington well enough to know where that is?

Fry: Yes.

Paul: So I went to see her in this little basement office, and she was enthusiastic about helping, so I told her we probably would get up a procession in Washington, that we would try to, the day before [president-elect] Wilson came, that this was our big plan, and that if we did, would she be our treasurer? And she said she would be very happy to do so.

She then said, "Now why don't you go next door and there's an office in the basement just like mine, one long room, very simple, unpretentious, and I know it's for rent; the people have moved out."

And I said, "Oh, no, we couldn't think of it, I know we could never afford a great big place like this."

She said, "Well just go in and try, and I think they will be glad to have you and will put [on] a price you can pay."

So I did go in and they said they would rent it to us for $60 a month. So I said, "Well then we will see if we can raise $60 a month, and if we can, we will take it."

So we got our office next door to her. And this Mrs. William Kent, whom at that time I hadn't met but I went to see later, she gave the first $5 and said, "I will give $5 every month." So then we thought, "Well, with $5 guaranteed, maybe we could raise the $55" because it had been so impressed upon us by the national headquarters that we couldn't let any unpaid bill ever go to them. So we didn't take [the office space] then, but we thought we probably would.

Then I went to see Mrs. Helen Gardner, who was on their list, and she was _very_ cooperative. I think she was a writer of some type. I think she was very displeased that a young whippersnapper such as myself should be the chairman, because she talked about "Well they don't have much sense about who they put in charge" [laughter] and "all these undertakings which need great experience" and so on. I think she probably thought _she_ should have been made the chairman, but nobody had

Paul: known I suppose that she would even think of it.

So we sat in this room and finally I said, "If we do start up this procession, since you are in the field of journalism, would you be willing to be our press chairman?"

And she said yes, she certainly would.

THE COMMITTEE'S INAUGURATION PARADE, MARCH 3, 1913

Paul: So we gradually got, this way, some people. Then I
went to see the president of the little group in
Washington, which was very tiny. Her name was Florence
Etheridge. She was employed at the Indian Bureau in
Washington, and I had met her at the national convention
in Philadelphia because she had come down to represent
her little D.C. group at that convention. She had known
that up there we had talked about the possibility of
having a procession the day before Wilson came in, and
she wanted very much to do it.

But she said, "It is just impossible. We couldn't
vote to do it at the convention because we had nobody
to get it up and no money with which to get it up." So
she said, "Well, I think it would be a good idea. I
don't know whether it is possible."

So then she took me to see Mrs. William Kent, my
predecessor. I had put her off because I wanted to get
a little foothold before I went to her because she would
be the most important. And there I found such a
wonderful welcome and such a marvelous woman. Roger
Kent's mother, you know. Beyond words, a wonderful
person.

So she invited me immediately to come and have
Christmas dinner with them and, knowing our possibility
of getting a little headquarters, she said she would
give $5 every month, and she was from that time on a
steadfast supporter until she died. She was still a
member of our board when she died, not so long ago.

Fry: That $5 a month started a tradition with her, didn't
it, because I noticed--

Paul: She kept on and on, giving and giving.

Fry: Later she would have a "committee of a hundred" and a
      "committee of two hundred," always to pay your rent,
      as your houses got bigger and bigger and bigger

Paul: Oh, it was wonderful what she did.

      Then we decided to have a meeting and launch it,
      the whole program. So we held a meeting on the second
      of January [1913], which is the first meeting we ever
      held in Washington. I suppose it was held in this new
      little headquarters, though I am not quite sure.

      [Telephone rings.]

      [Tape off.]

Paul: All right. Now at this first meeting I presided and
      introduced the whole idea of a procession and so on, and
      I remember everybody there supported the idea and said
      they would turn in and help. And I remember among the
      people who were there was Miss Belva Lockwood, did you
      ever hear of her? I think she is the first woman in
      the country who ever ran seriously for the presidency.
      She was the woman who single-handed opened the Supreme
      Court to women. [Spelling] Belva Lockwood. She was
      one of the pioneers and she died of course a good many
      years ago. She was very nice. She came and she sort
      of gave us her blessing. And of course Mrs. William
      Kent came and Helen Gardner and all these few people we
      had gotten in touch with.

      Among other people that I haven't told you about
      that I went to see, one after another, the one that I
      suppose was the most important that I went to see, but
      I didn't know then, was Elsie Hill. She was the
      daughter, as I told you, of Congressman Hill. She was
      on my list.

Fry: And he was Congressman Hill from what state?

Paul: From Connecticut and from the district we are sitting
      in now. Our district. He was nineteen years in Congress
      and on very important committees.

      His daughter, who had graduated Vassar, had gone
      over and spent some time in France and knew evidently
      a little about French. So she wanted to stay on in
      Washington after she finished college to be with her
      family. She got a position to teach French in a high
      school in Washington, and when I got to her she was

NAWSA CONGRESSIONAL COMMITTEE'S
INAUGURATION PARADE, WASHINGTON, D. C.
March 3, 1913

Paul: teaching French, going off every morning and coming
back about four or five in the afternoon, I guess. I
remember so vividly going around--she had taken an
apartment of her own and [pause] my goodness, I remember
that interview so well She was so lovely and so
enthusiastic and said that she would bring her whole
college suffrage league into our march. And very--I
just--there was never a day from that time until she
died that we didn't work together over something.
Whatever we were working on, we worked together.

   As I said, then she came in and stayed with me after
my sister died up here. And all that china that you
were asking about in the kitchen that's in the left hand
side (we call it our [laughing] "common" cupboard),* she
bought almost all that china. I paid for the things, but
she went and bought them and stocked me with everything
I needed to have.

   And she got that little radio. A man stopped at
the door, and I said, "I just think I can't afford
another radio, I have this enormous one that's in here.
Now it's not much good, sort of worn out."

   She said, "I want one in my room that I can hear
the news every morning when I waken up."

   So I said, "All right, we'll buy that." And I
remember so vividly--it was only I think $17, but we've
had it every day, every day since she bought it. We've
had it there in our little kitchen.

   This was this first meeting. Then we had to get a
permit and I told you this before [off tape]. We
applied for a permit to have a procession, and the
national headquarters had been kept informed up in New
York about everything and they were very anxious for us
to have it. They thought it was a very good thing to
have this procession; it would have a good effect on
the suffrage movement all over the country. But they
were always harping on the fact that they couldn't
afford to pay anything toward it.

   So then we were told by the chief of police, as I

---

*Alice is referring to the cupboard of dishware for
everyday use, as opposed to more elegant china.

Paul: told you, that they would give us a permit for 16th
        Street, which is perhaps a principal residence street
        and where all the embassies are, nearly, in Washington.
        And that that would be a suitable background for our
        procession. We had asked for Pennsylvania Avenue,
        having been told by almost everybody we asked that that
        was the critical avenue where you always had your
        processions, from the Capitol to the White House, and
        that no one would pay much attention if we went down
        16th Street.

        So we said, "We just _must_ have Pennsylvania Avenue,"
        and they said,

        "Well that's fine, but we certainly won't let you
        have it. It's totally unsuitable for women to be
        marching down Pennsylvania Avenue."

        And so then Elsie Hill asked her mother--since her
        father was in Congress and the Congress supports and
        gives the money for the District [of Columbia] police
        and everything else--she felt her mother maybe could do
        something. So her mother said she would go down and
        talk to this--what is the name of that man, was it
        Sylvester?

Fry: His name was not given in any of the references I read,
        but you mean whoever the contemporary police chief was
        at that time.

Paul: Whoever he was; I don't remember. But I remember so
        well Major Sylvester _it is_ my impression that he was the
        one at that time. Anyway Mrs. Hill took Elsie Hill with
        her, and they came out of the interview with the permit
        for the Avenue.

        So then we had something to work on, and we got up
        a committee which divided up into all the different
        groups. One was to get the nurses, one the doctors,
        one the lawyers, one the college graduates, and so on.
        I found here my photograph just from going through
        these things; I will show it to you. And I was in
        that procession.

Fry: Oh, you did? Good!

Paul: Just by chance I found it.

        Is that somebody downstairs?

Fry: Yes, your tenants came in

Paul: You will excuse me one minute. I'll ask her if she's
       the one that's so chilly.

       [Interruption.]

       [Tape off.]

Paul: Well, I was saying that we had these committees for
       every department, and we succeeded apparently, [to judge]
       from the results, in getting very good leaders for each
       one, because you see between the second of January and
       the third of March wasn't very long to get up a procession
       in a city where you weren't known and where you had no
       workers and where you had about every obstacle that you
       could have.

Fry: And you had just moved into your headquarters, I guess?

Paul: Well we hadn't, I guess, moved in. Well maybe we had
       just moved in. But anyway we had nothing, and we had to
       raise all the money and we had to get all the women to
       march and so we put somebody in charge of the costumes.
       This was Hazel McKaye; I don't know whether you ever
       heard of her.

Fry: Oh, yes, Benton McKaye's--

Paul: Benton McKaye is her brother but the other famous one
       was Percy McKaye, the poet. She was considered the
       foremost woman pageant producer, pageant worker in
       America. I remember that one day somebody who was
       working with us said "There is coming to Washington
       tomorrow the best woman in the field of pageantry in
       the country, and it would be a good thing to get her,
       if we can, to help."

       So we went to her right away when she came. And
       then we became lifelong friends. Until her death she
       was always one of our supporters. And so she took over
       all the pageantry. She put on something on the treasury
       steps so that when the procession would go by, they
       would all see this beautiful pageant on the treasury
       steps being repeated and repeated. Elsie Hill was one
       of the dancers, I remember, in this pageant on the
       treasury steps. It seems to have been very beautiful.

       And the whole procession was so colorful. We had
       one section followed by another section in another color

Paul: and another and another. I walked in the college
section which Elsie Hill led. Each chairman got all
her own people and she wanted me to walk in her section,
so I did. So we each wore a cap and gown; ours was a
dark, very dignified little section. The one who had
the foreign section had very colorful costumes for women
of different lands. They each one brought their own
costume. So it was, I think, a very successful procession.

Fry: Who led the parade?

Paul: The national board of the National American [Woman's]
Suffrage Association because it was under their auspices,
you see. We were their committee. It started out that
way.

Dr. [Anna Howard] Shaw I guess was the leading person
on their board who walked at the head. I think that
Mrs. Mary Ware Dennett and a few of the other people on
the board--I don't remember who--were there. I remember
the national treasurer was there, the one who [laughing]
was always afraid of our sending the bills in. Her name
was Mrs. Stanley McCormick. All these people walked
at the head.

Well, we went out bright and early--I guess I told
you this too before, how we made an arrangement with the
people who were selling the tickets. I told you that,
didn't I? Do you want me to tell you over again or not?

Fry: Yes, please tell me about that. We didn't have the
recorder on before.

Paul: Some group had gotten a contract to put up the grand-
stands and sell all the tickets for [seats in] the
grandstand. I don't know what their contract was like.

Fry: For Wilson's inaugural--

Paul: For the inaugural procession. And so then they came to
us and asked, since they thought we were going to have
a pretty interesting procession the preceding day, if
they could make their ticket selling cover our day too,
and they would give us a percentage of all the tickets
they sold.

So we gave them a little tiny space in our little
tiny office, and there they had somebody selling tickets
all day long and all evening long until the day of the
procession. And they took in a great deal of money, and

Paul: it was one of the big helps in enabling us to pay all
the big bills we had from getting this up.

There had never been a procession of women for any
corner of the world or in Washington, probably; at least
nobody had ever seen it. [Faint noise and music in
background begins.] Nobody ever dreamt that women--you
were always seeing these Elks and people going around
in processions- but they never thought of women doing
such a thing. And so there really was a great interest
in it. A great many tickets were being sold, to our
astonishment. So we had a pretty good idea that there
would be a great many people there, apart from the people
who had written to us that they would come and be in
the march. And we had floats, a great series of floats.
Different towns and different sections of the suffrage
movement over the country that we would write to would
say that they would come and they would bring a float or
pay for their own float. The floats were a very
decorative part mixed in with this very great pageantry
that Hazel McKay had produced.

So when the day came, almost time for the procession,
we found that apparently the police were taking the
matter very casually. They said, "Well maybe a handful
of police could tend to it on the day before the inaugural.
And that then they would concentrate all their force on
taking care of the people at the inaugural.

We tried with not much success to get them to think
we might have a big procession and that they had better
be prepared. So then the night before, as I told you,
Mrs. Stimson's sister, Mrs. John Rogers (Mrs. Rogers
was the sister of Mrs. Stimson)--Mrs. Rogers said she
would take me down--she was on our committee--and talk to
her brother-in-law [Secretary of War Henry Lewis Stimson]
and see if he couldn't be aroused into the fact that we
really were in some doubt as to whether the police could
handle the crowds. So we went to see him.

At the same time they were having a big mass meeting
in I think Constitution Hall (you know, that's a D.A.R.
[hall])--I'm not sure--but in one of the big theaters,
big place in Washington. And Mrs. Catt, Carrie Chapman
Catt [was there]. [Tape runs out.]

[Tape 3, Side 1]

Paul: Well, I [inaudible] my first [inaudible] I remember
going to see Mrs. Catt in New York when I came back,

Paul: and sometime in the period between when I came back
        [from England] and when I started this movement in
        Washington, I had one talk with Mrs. Catt. I remember
        she said to me, "I feel that I have enlisted for life.
        This is something that cannot be done, [we] cannot get
        this federal amendment, and I did this deliberately
        knowing that I was enlisting for life." And I am sure
        she did; she was a very devoted member of the whole
        movement.

        So we asked her to come down and to speak at this
        mass meeting. It was the first time that we had any
        real contact with her. And she came and made a very
        powerful speech, people told me. I didn't go because
        I was out seeing Mr. Stimson at the moment.

Fry: [checks movement of tape.]

Paul: Do you want me to go on or is it stopping?

Fry: Yes, the recorder's doing fine.

Paul: So then Mr. Stimson said, "Why of course, if the police
        can't handle it, you can just count on me. I will send
        over our artillery" (from this place right outside of
        Washington where he was in charge of all the --) cavalry,
        I mean. He said, "I'll send over the cavalry. They will
        handle everything you need. Just call me up if you
        do have any difficulty." So that relieved our minds
        very much.

        The next morning we went out early, very early, to
        try to begin to line the people up in all the different
        sections. We had a grand marshall who rode on horseback
        with several assistant marshalls on horseback, but they
        were more for publicity. The grand marshall was a Mrs.
        Burleson; you know at that time there was a Burleson
        in, I think, the cabinet of Mr. Wilson [Albert S.
        Burleson, Postmaster General]. Anyway she was a very
        prominent Texan family, Democratic family. I'm not
        absolutely sure what her relationship was to [Secretary]
        Burleson; her husband was an officer at Fort Meyer. So
        she came in and practiced and rehearsed and everything
        else and was an extremely decorative person on her horse.

        But you couldn't do much because when we started out
        to form our people up, we had no place to form because
        the whole street was just--from one side to the other--
        was just filled with people. They were tourists, I

Paul: would say, who had all come to see the inaugural and gotten there the day before. They were there, mothers and fathers and children, just a great mass of people who had no interest except in trying to see a woman's march. They couldn't any longer buy tickets [for the grandstands] because they were almost all exhausted I guess.

So when we started out we had this mass of people and we didn't know how to get through; we tried to get through and we just saw it couldn't be done. We could never have this procession of maybe one thousand women or five thousand or ten thousand (whatever we had); we'd never get them through.

So we went to the phone to call Mr. [Secretary of War] Stimson, and he said--I don't know who went, probably I went but I don't remember--he said all right, he would do just as he had agreed the night before, and he'd have the cavalry there as fast as they could get there.

So they came all on their horses, prancing around, and of course they could easily open the way, which they did, so we could go a block maybe; and then the way was all closed again and they'd have to open the next block. So that, as I told you the other night, the march which was supposed to end at Constitution Hall at a certain hour, it was hours later before we even came in sight of Constitution Hall.

We had the meeting there all right, but on the way, for instance, there was this pageant of Hazel McKay's, which we had spent a great deal of effort on and it was apparently going to be extremely beautiful. So these poor people [waiting to see] the pageant--they had a separate grandstand built [for that], the sellers of this whole thing. Normally processions would go around in front of the White House, but this time they went in back of it so as to be opposite the Treasury and enable all the people who paid extra to have extra good seats [laughing] to see the pageant [laughter], so all these people thought they were paying extra to be in this place of advantage to see the pageant on the Treasury steps.

We had gotten very good publicity all the time we were getting up this procession because this Mrs. Helen Gardner I had gone to see turned out to be a super-whiz at this. She would arrive in the early morning and stay a'' i, .'. .' ' ' ' ' ' s 100%

Paul: wonderful, I thought. Didn't see how anybody could have been better. Well then--

Fry: Both Washington papers were faced, I guess, with prospects of filling their space between the time of the election and the inauguration--

Paul: Maybe.

Fry: --So you had some good--

Paul: Luck [laughing].

Fry: Also you were _given_ newspaper space.

Paul: You see, Mr. McLane [?], the owner of the _Washington Post_, gave us one million dollars and-- **

Fry: Then?

Paul: I don't know whether he did it for that procession or just after the procession, but he gave it to us, so we had the good will of the _Post_. [Pause.] That's the first big gift, I think, we got.

        Well anyway we had the cavalry working as hard as they could and very faithfully. People have written it up and I would like to read again that [Congressional] hearing [that took place later] because Mr. Gallagher tells me it is written up there that we were mobbed and people were very antagonistic and so on. But I didn't get that impression myself. My impression is of the police doing the best they could, having their leaders not providing enough policemen, and that they could not possibly, in any possible way, manage it.

Fry: Well, I have the reference on that Congressional hearing which followed.

Paul: Have you a copy of it?

Fry: I don't have a copy but Mabel Vernon has a copy.*

Paul: Has she? Well, I hope she will let me have it because

_____

*Mabel Vernon's copy could not be located for the final printing of this transcript, nor could the exact reference of the Congressional hearing. See _Sun_ article.

**The gift from the editor of the Washington _Post_ was $1,000. (Note by author [?])

Paul: I had two copies and I left these in the library and as
        far as I know they have both disappeared.

Fry: Well Doris Stevens' account intimates some sort of--

Paul: Well, she wasn't here though.

Fry: --harassment and so does the Irwin account.

Paul: I know they do, but Mrs. Irwin wasn't even a member
        of ours at that time, nor was Doris Stevens. I don't
        think--

Fry: And of course the <u>Suffragist</u> wasn't being printed at
        that time, so we don't have that for a record.

Paul: The only place where I could see [a record is] what we
        testified, because I testified [in the Congressional
        hearing] and I'd like to see what we said in the
        testimony. Because as I look back on it <u>now</u>, my
        impression is that the police were valiant in their
        effort to try to keep order and just about as completely
        at a loss for what to do as we were. And nothing saved
        that procession but Secretary Stimson sending the
        cavalry. I'm sure of that.

            I remember there were some protests from people
        thinking that the crowd had made remarks and so on they
        didn't like, but I don't know that there was anything
        worse than that. I remember Mr. Kent was one of those
        who wanted this investigation because his daughter,
        Elizabeth, a beautiful, lovely girl was on the float,
        (his and Mrs. Kent's daughter) and it seems that somebody
        had pulled her foot or done something like that from
        the crowd, something he thought was very insulting. So
        there were some people who seemed to think that the crowd
        had not behaved as they ought to behave, but I wasn't
        really conscious of it myself. I suppose I was so
        terribly busy trying to keep the people in line [laugh-
        ing] and get them not to go home disheartened, and keep
        our own little army together. But anyway we finally
        emerged at Constitution Hall at the end and had this
        meeting.

            Then immediately these Congressmen that somehow
        or other had been brought in touch with it--the one I
        remember the most was Mr. Kent--got this investigation
        started. And the chairman of it was the senator from
        Washington state. I guess his women had asked him to
        do it, because Washington had already become enfranchised,

Paul: you know. And I remember going down to see him in the morning and asking him about it and what we should do and everything.

Fry: (I think dinner is burning in the oven; let me go look.)

[Pause.]

Paul: And he was really enthusiastic, I imagine, because of the women back home. So I went to see whom we should ask to be speakers and testify as witnesses and so on and what they should do and everything--the procedure. And then I remember saying, "Well, I'll have to come in and see you probably a good many times about this, and what time would you like me to come?"

I remember him saying, "Oh, I'm always beginning my work at seven in the morning; that's the time to come." [Laughing] I got a very wonderful impression of Senators. I thought, "Here they are, all at work at seven in the morning. I have a hard time to get my eyes open at seven in the morning!" [Laughter.]*

---

*For conclusions on the March 3rd 1913 procession, see page 79.

INITIAL ORGANIZING

The Press Department and Florence Brewer Boeckel

Paul: Well, we had this hearing. Then Mrs. Gardner, who had
done such good press work, said to me that she wanted
to withdraw from our campaign. She said, "You know, I
did this press work on the impression that this was just
to make good propaganda for the campaigns in the <u>states</u>.
I don't believe in getting this federal amendment that
Miss Anthony was working for and never <u>have</u> believed in
it and don't want to have any connection with it. I
see from the way you are acting--you have these banners
saying 'We demand an amendment to the United States
Constitution'--that you are actually talking about
putting this amendment through. If I had known this I
certainly wouldn't have had anything to do with it. So
I want now to withdraw from all connection with it."

   So we said, well if that's the way she believes, we'd
have to accept it. So we did. So we never heard anything
more about her until the day of the ratification of the
amendment, when it was given--what do you do?--<u>proclaimed</u>
by the Secretary of State, I think it is.

Fry: Yes, a proclamation.

Paul: President Wilson gave the time of the proclamation.
(I suppose it was issued in the White House, but I don't
know where they give the proclamations from). Anyway,
President Wilson invited a group of women to be there
for this ceremony of the proclamation, and among others
was this Mrs. Helen Gardner, whom we hadn't seen all
these intervening years.

   And then he promptly appointed her to the first
position I guess he gave to any women, to be head (I
don't know whether it was head, but a member) of the

Paul: civil service commission, which had never had a woman
        on it. So she was then Civil Service Commissioner and
        had a good salary and a fine position and so on
        [laughter]. And of all the people who were invited to
        this final ceremony, not one of us was invited, not one
        of the people who <u>we</u> thought had borne the burden of
        the campaign--anyway had strived to do something--not
        one of us was invited or recognized in any possible
        [way], but all these opponents, every person who was
        there [had been] an opponent! I suppose Wilson was
        still so strong on his states' rights idea that--I
        don't know why he did this. Maybe they were more
        important people politically, or something or other.
        But it was so amusing. This one lady's resignation
        really hurt us, because if she had kept on with the
        publicity, we would have been much better off.

        So then we started to build up a little press
        department and--you may know all this. For about a
        year Elsie Hill and I, I guess, did all the publicity.
        I would write a little bulletin and Elsie Hill would
        come home from her school, and she would come in and
        take it around to the newspapers. She was full of
        enthusiasm and could get people all stirred up. So we
        continued to get, we thought, pretty good publicity,
        but it took a lot of our time and we wanted to get some
        one person to do it.

        So then Elsie told me of somebody who had graduated
        from Vassar that she knew, and she said she had been on
        a paper for a little bit of work up in Poughkeepsie when
        she was in college, and then she had now come down to
        Baltimore to be on <u>Vogue</u>, the paper, <u>Vogue</u>. So then she
        said, "I think maybe we could persuade her to come over."

        So we both went over to see her in Baltimore, and
        from the first moment we were so congenial; we all were.
        She was so--just <u>delighted</u> to be invited to come and do
        our press work, and she had a little money so she said
        she could pay all her expenses--and she came. And her
        name was Florence [Brewer] Boeckel. (She died, last
        year I think; I went to the memorial service for her.)
        So for maybe a year or two years she did this just as a
        gift. She came down to our headquarters in the morning
        and worked all day, as though she had been a regularly
        paid person. Then she married this Mr. Boeckel--do you
        know who he was?

Fry: No.

Paul: He had for years--and I think it still continues probably under his name, but I don't believe he does the work any more--I think it was something like the editorial research service, or something like that. But they didn't send out news articles like newspapers and news bureaus; they sent out only editorials, and he would write editorials. He was apparently very gifted in that field. He would write editorials giving the situation of different bills before Congress that the whole country might be interested in, and this service was bought all over the country. So it was the way that Mr. and Mrs. Boeckel lived, supported themselves.

So then she had a little son born, so she said that she thought she couldn't any longer do it as a free gift, so we paid her from then on a small salary, and she built up a <u>splendid</u> press department. We gave her one room in the headquarters. (By this time we had a building and not just one room.) She got two assistants, whom we paid, whom she chose. One was good at writing and one was good at interviewing. Then she got several stenographers and typists and mimeograph workers and people who clipped everything for her and kept clipping books-- she never had undertaken to do a news service; she just built it up without any experience. I would have thought she built up probably the best press service that I've ever known anybody to have for a volunteer organization in Washington. And she continued to our victory.

Fry: I've seen her name on the masthead of the <u>Suffragist</u>.

Paul: Yes, I'm sure you have. A great part of the time she didn't do the <u>Suffragist</u>, but toward the end she took over the <u>Suffragist</u> too.

Well, that's just telling about the beginning. I don't know whether there is anything else to tell.

Fry: That's just the beginning.

The macaroni and cheese is done. Do you want a break and eat now?

Paul: Oh, yes.

[Recorder off.]

[Background music ceases in subsequent taping.]

Field Organization and Mabel Vernon

Paul: [I've talked about] Lucy Burns, who came in our movement in England, really, and Mrs. Boeckel, so wonderful in the press,

Fry: Yes, we just finished Boeckel.

Paul: And Miss Gillette, this woman lawyer. So I thought I might tell sometime about how Mabel Vernon came in because I would like especially to put in the [two other] Swarthmore people, Mabel Vernon and Mrs. Walker.

Fry: Mabel Vernon came in in June of the year that we are now in, I believe, so maybe you could go into that.

Paul: The second year, 1914?

Fry: She came in 1913 didn't she?

Paul: No, I think 1914.

Fry: Well, we are now in 1913, according to my notes.

Paul: Did Mabel tell you she came in in 1913?

Fry: She told me you wrote to her, where she was teaching at Radnor, in the spring of 1913, asking her to join your efforts when the school year was out, in June.

Paul: Well, supposing I tell you right now about her, is that all right?

Fry: All right.

Paul: You see, when we began to think we would have to go out over the country and that we couldn't do this after we were severed from the National American and had no members and no branches of our own, we saw that we would have to form them to ever have any hope of influencing the congressmen. So we asked Mabel to become our first, what we called, organizer to go over the country. She was the first person we had outside of the few of us who were starting in Washington.

I went up to her school where she was teaching--she was teaching German I think, maybe she has told you this--in Pennsylvania and told her what our whole purpose was, to put this amendment into the Constitution.

Paul: And to do it we needed people who were good speakers
and who could go over the country and help arouse the
women, especially the women who were already voting, to
use their power with their own congressmen.

So she said she believed thoroughly in every bit of
it and that she _would_ like to come down and help and
would like to become a national organizer for that
purpose. So she was our first national organizer.
She accepted right away and she stayed of course till
the campaign was over. And then when it was over she
became the director of the whole campaign for the new
[equal rights] amendment. Then, after a time, she
stopped and formed her own People's Mandate, which was
for peace.

And of course you know how absolutely invaluable,
without words--we could never express what we owed to
her. Every place she went in the states she made
friends, and she could get up meetings with the greatest
ease. She had this great, great gift of speaking so
she could go in an unknown place and hold a meeting and
just put the place on the map, as far as our campaign
was concerned.

Financial Support for Workers

Fry: When she came, was she willing to live at her own
expense at first?

Paul: No, she couldn't because she was earning her living
as a school teacher, and we started by paying, I think,
when we began to pay anybody we started with one salary
for everybody that we paid, and that was $200 a month.
And at that time people could live on $200 a month.

Fry: Oh, yes. What about yourself, did you--

Paul: And then after we got a headquarters, she--I don't know
whether she stayed in the headquarters or not but she
probably did because almost everybody who was campaigning
stayed there--and then we never charged any of the people
[for board and room] who were doing this campaigning.

And about myself: When I started in the beginning,
the national [NAWSA] board, when they appointed Miss
Burns and myself, said they would of course pay no

Paul: salary to anybody. And we said, "Well, we don't want to
have a salary, but we would like to be reimbursed, not
by you, but if there is enough strength in the movement,
we would like to be reimbursed for any expenses we incur
if we go on trips or whatever we may do that would have
expenses." So they said, "All right, just provided
you raise the money."

So that's the way we did. Both Miss Burns and I
were the only two people in the beginning, you see, and
we both had our families back of us. You see, we were
still almost in the college age where your parents would
be looking after you. I remember Miss Burns' father had
been sending her the money to stay over at the University
of Bonn in Germany, and then he just continued it. Every
month he sent her a check down to continue the work here,
because he was backing her up.

And then my mother just did the same with me. She
gave us the money with which we started. If I went on
trips and so on I turned in an expense account and was
reimbursed; but otherwise in the beginning we practically
paid all our own expenses, our families did, I mean.
But don't put this in your story.

Fry: But this is something that's good to know, that you did
go down on your own expense. I think it shows a dedication not only of just you, but of your parents, too.

Paul: Then later on, when Mrs. [O. H. P.] Belmont came into
the movement and was so very wealthy, she announced to
me that she was going to give me a salary of $1,000 a
month. [This was during the Equal Rights campaign in
the twenties, probably.] I told her that I didn't want
to be in that position at all. I certainly didn't. So
anyway she did, she gave the check. So then I turned
the check over to the Woman's Party. I gave them for
the one year $12,000 that she gave to me.

Fry: That was a lot of money because she came into the
movement, when? About 1916?

Paul: She came in 1914. Our first year when we were put out
by the old National American she joined--she left them
and joined us.

Fry: So wasn't that a pretty big monthly salary in those
days?

Paul: It was, but I mean she had enough money, and I was only

Paul: explaining that I did have a salary, but I didn't keep the salary. I turned it over in full.

Fry: Well, that's important to know. Sometime somebody will be going through the party business records in the Library of Congress and they will come across an item of your big salary [laughter] and it's good to have an explanation.

Paul: At the same time they will come across my $12,000 donation in Equal Rights magazine. (I think it was after we started on the new Equal Rights campaign that she did this, because we made her president.) She said, "Now I am president. I can't do the work, and you are doing the work and I think you should be vice-president and I should pay you what I would be spending on it." That's when she gave me this money which I just said I didn't in any way want to be in this position. So then I turned it in. It was reported in our weekly magazine, donation from me, $12,000.

Fry: I'm glad we got that explained.

Paul: You see, I feel I owe a great deal really to my family. I must say that. They did always stand back of me. My mother did, my father did, and it was the money that my father made and that my grandfather made, which I inherited, partly, which enabled me to do it. It is a great asset, you know, to have a little money of your own you can fall back on.

Fry: Or even like this when you want to get something started, you don't have to worry about how you are going to eat for those first months before you get the organization set up.

Paul: Yes, and you don't know [whether] an unpopular measure-- and this was a very unpopular measure at the time--whether it will ever get much support. So it gave me--I feel I never could have done this, and Lucy Burns of course never could either, if we hadn't both had families that were willing to back us.

Fry: The question about that March 3 procession was whether the chief of police was removed or not, as is written up in these other books.

Paul: Well, I have told you all I know about that.

Fry: You told me that you doubted that he was removed. Then

Fry: I found another reference that said that at a later date he quietly retired to private life; so whether this was connected with the investigation or not remains a question, and we ought to point that out.

Paul: We ought to get that report that was made--you say Mabel Vernon has a copy of it. See what their recommendation was after all this testimony was in. But that's my impression, **strong** impression. I know that I never opposed this man in any way because I knew better; I knew perfectly well that he was in a hopeless thing for him to try with his inadequate force. That would be perhaps lack of foresight on his part or maybe it would have been impossible for him to get the extra money [for additional men], and therefore we would have never gone in to get him removed.

Anyway, we never did go in to get anybody removed. For anything.

Presidential Delegations Begin

Fry: That procession was March 3. Now on March 17 my notes say that you and three others went in to talk to President Wilson. He had called a special session of the sixty-third Congress for April 7. Do you remember anything about talking to him?

Paul: Yes, I led the delegation and I remember everything about it, I think. And one woman who went with us--does it give their names? Where did you get this from?

Fry: I think these notes came from Up the Hill, the second edition of Irwin's book.

Paul: I think if you look in this folder that you are in now for the 1914--I will tell you what I can remember and then you can look later--

Fry: It's right here. I think I've got it marked in the volume. [Names of other women are not given in Irwin's account.]*

*Irwin, Inez Haynes. Uphill with Banners Flying, Traversity Press, Penobscot, Maine, 1964. This is a second edition

Paul: One woman who went with us was Mrs. Ida Husted Harper,
          who was the historian, you know, of the suffrage movement,
          if I remember rightly. And one was the wife of a congress-
          man from Illinois, I don't remember who. She wasn't
          there long; her husband wasn't re-elected. And myself.
          I don't know who the fourth one was.

Fry: You see, this was before the Suffragist began coming
          out.

Paul: Oh, no, no. The Suffragist began November 15, 1913.

Fry: Yes, and you went in to see President Wilson on March 17,
          1913.

          [Discussion of date of first Suffragist.]

Paul: Yes, I remember it now because I know it was the end of
          our first year [that we began the Suffragist], and our
          first year was 1913. So maybe it wouldn't have given
          there the names of those people.

Fry: There's a report of the NAWSA congressional committee--
          which was "Congressional Union" by the time the first
          issue came out--that summarizes what it had done through
          the year. But it does not mention who went on that
          delegation; it just mentions that that delegation occurred,
          and that's all. So we don't know who went with you.

Paul: I know two of the people who went. One was, as I say,
          Mrs. Harper, who was this link with the old National
          American Woman Suffrage Association, and one was this
          wife of a congressman from Illinois, whose name I could
          look up of course, but he wasn't re-elected and I don't
          remember who he was. And there was a fourth one I
          think.

          Anyway, I introduced them and made the main presenta-
          tion, and Wilson was as he always was, you know: he gave
          the impression of being very scholarly, very tolerant
          and very respectful and completely in accord with the
          idea that women should vote. He explained how, as
          governor of New Jersey, he had supported it, how they
          had had a referendum and he had voted for it in New
          Jersey himself. And as a states' righter from Virginia,
          believing in all the states' rights traditions, he felt
          that that was the way to proceed, and he did not feel
          inclined to press for action by Congress. So we gave
          our point of view to him and we didn't, I think, change
          him at all; but he couldn't have been more courteous

Paul: and more considerate and more deliberate in giving us
        all the time in the world to say what we wanted to say.

Fry: As a resident of his own state, could you talk to him
        at this point as someone who had supported him in his
        recent campaign?

Paul: No, I didn't support him. I didn't support anybody in
        that campaign. I didn't have anything to do with that
        campaign. Women were not voting. I [resided] then in
        New Jersey and women were not voting in New Jersey. I
        mean when I did get to vote, I voted in New Jersey, but
        at the time of this campaign, I couldn't vote. So I
        didn't support him, I didn't have anything to do with
        the campaign.

        I just talked to him about the rightness of the cause,
        I suppose. I can only imagine that's what I would have
        talked about, and the importance of not wasting the lives
        of generations of women on these referendums--to the
        male voters of a state. It seemed so unfair and unjust
        to have to go forth and convert a majority of the male
        voters of a state to something, for the women who had
        the necessity of converting the majority of the men of
        a state.

        Well, he said there are two ways to get this, one
        by a federal amendment and one by the states' amendment.

        You know, I knew his daughter and I have a photo-
        graph of his daughter right here in this house, his
        daughter Jessie.

Fry: How did you come to know her?

Paul: I met her in one of the settlement houses in Pennsylvania,
        the Lighthouse Settlement. I used to go there a great
        deal because the head of it, Mrs. Bradford, was one of
        our members and she was the sister of Mrs. Lawrence, who
        was our national treasurer. So they gave a great deal
        of help. And Jessie Wilson was living for a time at
        that college settlement. I remember she was living there
        and I talked to her there when the New Jersey referendum
        was on, and she told me about the support from her father.
        She herself helped us when he became President down in
        Washington.

Fry: What did she do?

Paul: W-ll, f-- i-t---, w- h-d a re--r+i-- -r- r'rh+, just

Paul: across, at our headquarters, which was across the street,
you know, from where President Wilson was. She and her
sister came over and received for us. She was completely
and absolutely, I think, sympathetic to us. She perhaps
didn't differentiate between getting a state campaign
through and a national [amendment]; I don't know.
Anyway we telephoned over and asked her if she would
receive and she came.

I thought this first interview with Wilson was more
or less the same as we had every time afterwards. One
thing he was always saying, "You'll have to convert
public opinion, get enough public opinion in the country
back of this. At the present time there would be no
use of trying to get Congress to do this," and so on.
I had a great respect for Wilson, great respect for him.
And he was a nice type of man to have as your adversary
because you could be pretty certain of what he would do
in a certain situation

Fry: At least he was consistent and forthright, is that what
you mean?

Paul: Well, I mean he had the kind of a mind that you could--
you know some people you deal with you can't imagine
why they do the things they do. But [with Wilson], I
would feel [laughing] that we always knew beforehand.
If we planned a campaign, we would be pretty sure to
know what the reaction of Wilson would be to that kind
of campaign. I think he was a very great man, a very,
very great man. I was always so moved at the League of
Nations when I would walk down the street and see this
tiny little, maybe this long [measuring with her hands],
inscription to Woodrow Wilson--in French it was--"To
Woodrow Wilson, founder of the League of Nations." I
thought he did a marvelous thing in that.

Fry: Well, the next thing in my notes was that there was
another deputation to see him, that I think was led by
Elsie Hill, just a couple of weeks later.

Paul: There was a long series of them. It went on and on and
on through that whole year. Let's see; that was 1913.
They went on through 1913, [pause] and 1914 and 1915,
and 1916 I guess we kept up these delegations I'm not
sure when we stopped. Finally the President--it is my
recollection, vague recollection--he was getting mixed
up with the international situation, and the war seemed
to be in the offing, and he said he could not take the
time to see [the women] anymore, that they all said the

Paul: same thing and he said the same thing. And so then we said, "We will have a perpetual delegation right in front of the White House." That's when we began our picketing.

Fry: Yes, that was right after he was re-elected. Well, we will get to that.

Paul: Let me see when that was. That was 1917. January 10, I think we started them.

Fry: [Laughing] That's just the date that I have, January 10, 1917, and then the war broke out in April.

Paul: And we picketed with no interference from anybody January, February, March and April. [The picketing] was led by Mrs. Harriot Stanton Blatch, who had been on our own national board because after the victory of the New York campaign and referendum, her New York Women's Political Union (I think it was called, whatever it was in New York) voted to amalgamate with the Woman's Party. And when they voted to amalgamate with the Woman's Party, we asked Mrs. Blatch to go on our national board. She was one of the people, when we started on this picketing campaign, who was most ardent for us to do it.

Then to our great astonishment, we got a round-robin led by and initiated apparently and mainly due to Mrs. Blatch, urging in the name of all American women and so on, that we stop our picketing because of the war. She had married a British man, Englishman, and she was very pro-English. They got an enormous round-robin that they sent to us, and a great many people felt the same way and fell away from us, you know.

The old National American--you probably know all this--officers, the leading ones, took positions in the defense department of the government and moved down to Washington, not to work on the suffrage amendment, but to work in the defense movement, under whoever was Secretary of War. Dr. Shaw took such a position and I think practically everyone did.

Fry: Well, wasn't Harriot Stanton Blatch one of the leading officers of the National American Woman Suffrage Association?

Paul: No, she wasn't in it at all.

Fry: She had never been in that?

Paul: Never. She was the daughter of Elizabeth Cady Stanton, who had been one of the founders of it, but [Harriot] founded one of her own and it was modeled very much after the British one. I think she called it the Women's Political Union.

And all their membership was handed over to us. They just formally amalgamated. It was a help to us, of course. The reason they did it I think was that so many of their board members [advocated it]. This Mrs. Rogers, who, I told you, took me to see Secretary Stimson, was on her board, and Mrs. Rogers had always stayed with us, although she was always on the board of Mrs. Blatch's, too. And there were a lot of their women the same way, their leading women, who were also supporters of us. So when they won the referendum, they said, "There's nothing more we can do up in New York; we'd better turn in and help the National."

THE CHANGING RELATIONS WITH THE NATIONAL AMERICAN WOMAN
SUFFRAGE ASSOCIATION

The Congressional Union Evolves

Fry: During this period, in 1913, were you aware that the
         National American officers, like Dr. Shaw and so forth,
         did not want all this effort put out for a national
         amendment, that they wanted more state-by-state campaigns?

Paul: Well, I don't think that they did. I think that they
         were in back of us.

Fry: Well, they were back of you up to a point, and I was
         just trying to fix in time where that point was.

Paul: For instance, we had first of all, in [March, in] our
         first big procession, they headed it. Then our sub-
         sequent processions they--I don't know whether they
         came down physically or not--but I think that as far as
         I know we had their backing. Then that first year we
         had a meeting, I remember, in a theater in Washington,
         and Dr. Shaw came down and was the principal speaker at
         that meeting; it was in the summer.

Fry: Oh, in the summer? There was a--

Paul: The Columbia Theater, I think we had--

Fry: National Council of Women Voters on August 13 in the
         District of Columbia.

Paul: No, that was not it, that was totally different. That's
         something we formed on our own.

Fry: Well, they had a meeting in the Columbia Theater in
         December.

Paul: No, but that's their convention.

       We got up that convention and we paid $1,000--I
       never shall forget--ourselves; we had to raise the money
       for the hall in which it was held. I [had been] invited
       out to Dr. Shaw's home in Pennsylvania when they were
       planning the convention, and I said that I thought it
       would be helpful to have the national convention in
       Washington because we wanted to direct as much attention
       as we could to the federal amendment. The convention
       could go to see the President and it would be helpful
       to us, I thought. And--they were always this way--they
       said if we would get up the convention and would pay all
       the bills for the convention, they would come to
       Washington. So Dr. Shaw was heartily in favor of what
       we were doing up to that point.

Fry: Why wouldn't they share some of the responsibility for
       financing it with you?

Paul: Well, it's common in most women's organizations that
       the local place that has the convention--I suppose all
       groups, the American Legion, everybody else, do it that
       way--that the local people entertain and they bear the
       expense. Since their local [in Washington] was such a
       tiny little group that couldn't do anything, I suppose
       that it was natural [that] they wanted us to do [it],
       which we did.

       The first whisper of protest that I ever heard--
       there may have been whispers going on that I didn't
       hear about; I do think we made one mistake, which was
       that we didn't keep in constant--say almost every other
       day--connection, correspondence, by telephone or by
       letter or by going up personally--to make reports to
       the national leaders who were up there in the New York
       headquarters. I think if we had done so, we would have
       perhaps never had to have the two groups, because--[But]
       we were working so hard and had so little money and so
       little thought of anything but what to do the next
       morning, how we were to get through with the things we
       [laughing] had undertaken, that we just proceeded as
       though we were doing it--which we were--and that we
       would have the backing of everybody. But by the time
       of the convention, the national treasurer--her name was
       Mrs. Stanley McCormick--and Mrs. [Carrie Chapman] Catt
       made a protest at the convention against what we were
       doing, which is the first time that I realized it.
       Perhaps it was dumb not to realize it before, but I didn't.

Fry: That was the convention in Washington in December, 1913.

Paul: The one that we had gotten up. I remember our desire
to save money, so we asked Mrs. Kent if she would
entertain all the National board. She had a big house
and was the wife of a congressman and was very, very,
very, very wealthy. So she said she would.

Fry: Well, she had been a member for a long time, hadn't
she, of NAWSA? She was on their congressional committee
before you were.

Paul: Well, there was no division then. Anyway this convention
was coming, and I asked her, since we had the responsibility
of financing it, including the entertaining of all members
of the National board, would she entertain them at her
home? So that we wouldn't have to pay an immense hotel
bill. She said she would, gladly. And then I remember
they sent us word that they couldn't go to a private
home, that they had to meet constantly, every moment
almost, [and they could not be in any situation where
their time might be required for social niceties].

[End of Tape 3, Side 1.]

[Tape 3, Side 2.]

Paul: Are you taking this down?

Fry: Yes.

Paul: I figured it worked out all right, but we had to pay
[even] another bill, you see. So I had been thinking we
were on very good terms with the National; I didn't
realize that any rifts had occurred.

But at the convention Mrs. Catt (who had made one
big speech for us, as I told you, in the theater the
night before our first procession in Washington), she
got up on the floor, and of course she was a very
influential person, a hundred times more influential
than any of us were, and she--

I think I'd had to make the report [to the convention]
for the congressional committee, and so I made the report
saying we had this big procession and we had had so many
smaller processions, and we'd had so many deputations to
the President, and we raised so much money, which I
think was $27,000 if I remember rightly, not very much
but still a lot for us, and we had started a weekly

Paul: paper, which we had started just before the convention so people would see what could be done in the congressional field. We'd started it with no dire, sinister purpose but just to have a paper we could show at the convention of how needful it was to have some paper giving the congressional reports.

So Mrs. Catt said, "I want to inquire what has happened to the National American Woman Suffrage Association. It seems to me that there is something called the Congressional Union which is running the whole campaign on Congress," [tape volume decreases but words remain clear] and that we were--what did they say-- that they were the dogs and we were the little tail that was being wagged, or something like that. [Slight laughter] I remember it very vividly.

Fry: The tail is wagging the dog?

Paul: Yes, the tail is wagging the dog. We were the tail and we were wagging the dog. Is that the way it goes? Well, anyway, that was the simile she used. [Laughter.]

And she said, "Here they are even getting out a paper! Imagine such a thing!" And we thought oh we would get so much more support from our paper. We were very much astonished at this speech.

And then Mrs. Stanley McCormick, this very, very, very wealthy woman, I was told she was, from Boston, the treasurer, got up and said that not one penny of all this money, the $27,000 or whatever it was we raised, had come into her national treasury, and she thought that this was a situation that could not be tolerated that a committee--just a committee--should raise the money and keep the money.

So we saw something was not right. But I didn't suspect it before. And I don't think anybody else in our group suspected it.

Then Miss Jane Addams got up and she said, "I want to say that I do not agree with Mrs. Stanley McCormick" (you know these are not exactly their words of course, but this was their idea) "I don't agree with Mrs. Stanley McCormick at all. I made the resolution asking Miss Paul and Miss Burns to go down to Washington and start this work, and we made this condition, that they should raise all the money [standard volume returns on tape] in any way connected with the campaign and pay

Paul: all the expenses. I think they have carried out this
arrangement with the greatest possible honor and
conscientiousness. They have never turned in a bill
for even a 25¢ expenditure, and they have paid all the
bills and they have no debts to come back to the National
American. Every bill is paid that they have ever
incurred. Since this is what we asked them to do, I
don't see why we now turn around and criticize it."
That was her point. And of course she was a very
influential member of the National board.

And then Miss Gillette [got up], this lawyer whom we
had gotten to help us in the very beginning, who became
the treasurer of our first committee. It may be we
raised $27,000 for that procession and more later. I
remember $27,000 was raised for something.

Fry: There was a $27,000 total figure of funds raised up
through November of that year that I saw in a treasurer's
report. I think you had given that figure because you
had eleven months of the year totalled for the published
report in the Suffragist.

Paul: Whatever it was, it was the $27,000 that the treasurer
was having all this dispute about. So whatever the
sum was.

So then Miss Gillette got up and she said, "I was
treasurer for the movement here in Washington from the
beginning, from the first penny that was raised until
this procession was finished, then another treasurer
succeeded me. And I want to say from my experience
that phenomenal frugality was displayed, it seemed to
me, by the people who were running this campaign." She
spoke in general approval, and she was an important
woman, a very important woman because [she was] the dean
of the only woman's law school in the country. So she
spoke for us.

And then we saw there was a ripple of--some people
weren't our friends, we could see that. So then when
the convention was over they asked me, this board, if I
would continue for another year, but sever my relations
with the Congressional Union, which they thought was the
one that was wagging the dog or wagging the tail or
whatever the thing is. [Laughter.] The group that was
wagging them anyway had gotten out the paper, the
Congressional Union's paper, and by this time we were
using the name Congressional Union for Woman Suffrage.

Paul: The way that happened that we got a Congressional Union
was, that when we began to see how much it was going to
cost us to get up a procession--we had never gotten up
one, we didn't know what the thing would cost--we did
proceed I think with great frugality, but still we did
have certainly a tremendous number of bills.

I remember Miss Gillette coming to me and saying,
really in terror, "I just can't stand for these bills
that you are bringing in to me every single day. We
never, never, never can pay them." And then in a little
while she came and said,

"Well, I see. I don't understand how it is done,
but you are getting in a sufficient amount of money
always to cover your bills. And so I withdraw my
objection. You evidently know what you are about."
And so she supported us very loyally at the convention.

Well, when we discovered that if we wrote to somebody
in a state, the state treasurer [for National American]
would write back and say, "You have taken away one of
my chief financial supporters and I have to do my best
to win the referendum and I need every penny I can get,"
when we got protests from any place [where] we tried to
get any money, we thought, "Well, we will form a little
group who won't be involved in a state referendum
campaign and who can do everything they can to help us
by supplying members for our lobbying work, and for our
deputations and for our fund raising and so on.

Well now the National American had a series of
branches you could belong to. I remember that one of
them [requirements] required you to have three hundred
members before you could be a branch, in that category.
and you [the branch] had to pay so much--whatever the
sum was, I don't remember the sum--to the National
every year. So we applied to be affiliated with them
[National American] in this class, and we were accepted
[as a branch]. This was when we first began, probably
April or May of the first year, 1913.

Then it became a question of what we would--we
thought maybe we would get three hundred people and ask
them each one to give a part of whatever the sum was
we had to give, we'll say $10 each or something like
that. We called people on the phone and we got enough
to satisfy this requirement and the money requirement
and then applied to be an affiliated branch. At the
very begin , as.

Paul: So then we didn't know what to call ourselves,
and I remember that Mrs. Dennett, who was national
secretary, proposed this name--Congressional Union for
Woman Suffrage. I didn't think and I still don't think
it was very much of a name, but still, since she had
proposed it and was the national secretary, we thought
it would be a good thing to take it, so we did. We
called ourselves Congressional Union for Woman Suffrage.

And I remember we discussed it so much. We said,
"We don't know whether we have the right to say congressional
union; we are not connected in any way with Congress." And
I remember Mrs. Kent saying, "Oh, that will be all right,
we have a congressional boot"--what do you say, the
person who shines your boots?

Fry: Bootblack.

Paul: Bootblack is it? [Laughter.] "We have a congressional
bootblack and we have a congressional this, that and the
other. Why can't we have a congressional union for
woman suffrage?"

So we said, "All right. If you think the congressmen
won't object, we will call it that." So we did.

Well then it had raised--at least through the
efforts of this group--we had raised the money we had
gotten in; and we had gotten the people through the
efforts of this group who had gone on all our delegations
and all our processions and they were sort of our backbone. They were almost all D.C. [District of Columbia]
people who had almost no connection with the old
National American, never had had, so there was no
defection from them. And they had no state referendum
campaigns to be diverting them, so it seemed to be
working all right. We didn't expand it or try to make
it any bigger. We just tried to get the number we were
required by their regulations to have, which was only,
I think, about three hundred.

So then [when the convention was over, the board]
said, "Now if you continue as chairman you have to have
undivided loyalty and it must be to the National
association and their national committee and not divide
it with the Congressional Union."

We said, "Well, the Congressional Union's only
purpose is to raise money and get members to finance
th · · · ·⁻ ⁻⁻ⁱ⁻⁺⁺⁻ ⁻ ⁺⁻ʸ⁻ ⁻⁻ⁿ ⁻ w⁻ i.dn't

Paul: see any conflict at all. But I said I didn't think I
could function without <u>some</u> kind of a group to help us.
And so I [told them I] don't want to take it; I don't
want to disown the group that I have created and has given
us such enormous support. So I said then I just wouldn't
be [committee] chairman if that was the requirement.
First of all I had gone down [to Washington] to be
chairman only for a year and it had been a pretty big
personal expense to my family and to me, [pause] as well
as taking every moment of your time and your strength
and everything else, so I just said I had better not do
it then.

And they said, "All right, then we'd like you to go
on the committee all the same, but we don't want you to
be chairman."

So I said, "That's all right. I will certainly be
glad to continue on the committee."

Then they said, "Now we will ask Lucy Burns [to be
chairman]." Lucy Burns said about the same thing I
said. I don't know whether they put her on the committee, but anyway they asked her to be chairman. She
said no, she wouldn't be chairman.

So then we had a period with no chairman.

Then they announced one day that they had decided
on Mrs. Medill McCormick, and she had agreed to be the
chairman. We were very delighted because when we [had]
started our first little effort, I remember, getting up
the procession. She was one of the first people from
over the country who without any solicitation sent us
$100 to help with our first procession. And she had
always helped, <u>always</u>. And at the time of this national
convention in Washington--the delegation which we had
organized and planned way back when I had gone up to see
Dr. Shaw at her home in Pennsylvania--a delegation that
had requested an interview with the President [in
December of 1913]. Dr. Shaw of course led it as the
president, and I stood right beside her, I presume at
her request (I certainly wouldn't have done so otherwise)
and listened to this wonderful speech she made to the
President [Wilson]. Mrs. Medill McCormick was one of
those who helped me to get up this delegation to the
President. And we had gone to see various people--
newspaper people, all kinds of people, when we were
trying to get the appointment, which we hadn't gotten
too easily.

[Discussion of which presidential delegation this was.]

Congress Faces Two Amendments: March 2, 1914

Paul: So we thought this was a very wise appointment, and we
         were very happy over it. Mrs. Medill McCormick
         immediately asked me to be a member of her committee--
         well, I had already been appointed by the National
         board--and I asked her to be a member of our Congressional
         Union committee and she accepted right away. So we
         said, now we will have complete harmony because I will
         be on their board and she will be on our board and there
         won't be any possibility of conflict. So it seemed to
         me very good.

             By this time I decided I would take a little rest,
         [laughing] now that we had gotten the whole Congressional
         committee fixed up and the Congressional Union going
         forward, and although I had agreed and expected to go
         home at the end of the first year, I still didn't see
         exactly how I could go. So anyway I decided to go home,
         to my own home in Moorestown, New Jersey, and just rest
         for a time.

         [Discussion of time frame of previous story.]

             So then I went home and Lucy Burns took over the
         responsibility of the Washington work. And almost the
         first thing that happened was that I got a letter from
         her saying that the most unbelievable thing had occurred.
         That Mrs. Medill McCormick, without consultation with
         anybody as far as we knew, had introduced a new amendment
         to the Constitution. Senator Shafroth from Colorado was
         putting it in the Senate and Mitchell Palmer of Penn-
         sylvania putting it in the House, both of whom were our
         very good supporters, exceptionally good supporters.
         And that this amendment was one that would divide the
         whole of Congress into two groups, those who supported
         the one and those that supported the other, because one
         was to give women the vote and the other was to give
         women the right to a referendum on the subject, to the
         male voters of the state on the collection of a sufficient
         number of signatures, which seemed to us almost unthinkable.
         Well, Mrs. Medill McCormick took the position when we
         got back and we [looked] into these things--you know
         she was the daughter of Mark Hanna. You know who he was?

Fry: Oh, he was the big power, in Cleveland, Ohio?

Paul: Yes. I don't know if it was Cleveland, but in Ohio.
        He was one of the political bosses of the Republican
        party, national. And it was a great political power.
        And she was surrounded--she had married Medill McCormick
        up in Chicago--she was really surrounded by her father's,
        among other people, co-workers and they had convinced
        her that, as you looked over the world there was almost
        no place where women could vote; there were a few
        western states in our union at that time, but there
        weren't very many you know: Wyoming, Idaho, Utah,
        Colorado, a small group. And in Russia, Finland was a
        province of Russia and they could vote there, and--I'm
        not quite clear, I don't exactly remember at this moment
        what the situation was in New Zealand and Australia but
        I think it was in some provinces. But if you looked
        over the whole world, these were the only places women
        were voting, and they convinced her it was an impossible
        thing to take a great nation like the United States and
        go out of step with the rest of the world. She was
        thoroughly convinced of it. If by getting the referendum
        on [the ballot] in each state, maybe that state could be
        built up and it could be done, but the main thing to do
        was to get the possibility of these state referendums.

        Well, we told her we didn't agree with that at all.

Fry: When had you come back to Washington?

Paul: I came back right away when I got the message of this
        terrible thing. [Laughter.]

        By this time we had our paper [the _Suffragist_], and
        I think you will find in it, these volumes that you have,
        the editorials that we began to put out, week after
        week. Our editorials on this Shafroth-Palmer [bill].
        That was a big division.

        Then the little woman's Congressional Union met
        together, the leaders anyway, to decide what to do. A
        great many of them said, "Well, we think we had better
        disband. You can't fight this great National American."
        (Well it wasn't a very big one, still it was so big
        compared to us.) And they said, "Just the few of us,
        we can't go forth and try to put the [suffrage] amendment
        through, if they [in National American] all want this,
        they voted this--

        So we said, "Well, we will go up and talk to the

Paul: National board about this and see if we can't change
their point of view."

Fry: Was Lucy Burns one who said it was too much to fight?

Paul: Oh, no, no. She was always a very belligerent person.
She was always quite ready for a fight.

So we went up to the National board, made an
appointment to meet with them and I think all of our
leading people on our committee [went up]. I know Mrs.
William Kent went up; Mrs. Lawrence Lewis went. I went.

Fry: Was Maud Wood Park--

Paul: No, she wasn't in the picture then; I had never heard
of her at that time.

Then their national board met--Miss Jane Addams
came from Chicago, and Dr. Shaw and Mrs. Dennett and
their national treasurer. And I remember the national
treasurer sat there, this Mrs. Stanley McCormick, at
the meeting, and she took her chair and placed it so
her back was to the group and she sat there throughout,
us seeing only her back, to show her complete severing
of herself from everything that was going on. She
wouldn't have even had a conversation with us, I guess.

Of course Miss Addams was always very pacific, and
we were very pacific, and it seemed to us--I didn't see
how anybody could, it seemed to me just betray this
movement that had begun so many, many, many years before
[with Susan B. Anthony].

The Amendment before Congress at this time that we
were working for, you know that came up when we first
began [work on] our first procession: what amendment
we would work for. The whole National American didn't
even have any idea what they wanted to work for. So I
appointed a committee and asked them to draw up the
right amendment for us to work for when we were having
our first procession. We demanded "an amendment to the
United States Constitution enfranchising women," but we
didn't know what amendment or how to draw it up or
anything about it.

Mary Beard took the chairmanship and she came in a
few days--do you know who she was, Mary Beard?

Fry: [Laughing.] Oh yes, the historian.

Paul: Yes, and Charlie Beard's wife. And she was on our first
board when we formed our Congressional Union. So Mrs.
Beard came back and she said (she got people to be on
the [amendment committee] board who were competent to
judge this) what we should--You see we didn't have any
idea that there could be any dispute; we just took for
granted that what Miss Anthony had put in was the thing
that they had always worked for and Mrs. Kent had worked
for and we would just keep on. But when this question
arose, what would we work for, we then appointed this
committee to see what we'd better work for. So Mrs.
Beard made the report from her committee that we ought
to stick to this Susan B. Anthony original amendment.

So here we were. We were the only group sticking
to the one that had been introduced year after year and
we didn't see how we could make it better and we didn't
want to start and work for just the right to have a
referendum to the men of a state. No woman would be
enfranchised by that.

So we came back defeated from the National board.
They didn't seem to have any good reason, but they said
they'd appointed this committee and their committee
[chairman] Mrs. Medill McCormick had vast political
experience and great political wisdom at her command
through her father's affiliations, and it seemed the
wise thing to do and they stuck to it--although they
hadn't been consulted by Mrs. McCormick and hadn't known
she was going to do it. It was a strange attitude for
them to take. And maybe, again, if we had kept in more
daily contact with them we could have averted it. But,
that's the way it was.

The Separation from NAWSA

Paul: So we very seriously considered whether we hadn't
better just give it up and disband and go home, and let
them go ahead and do the best they could. But we
finally, all of us, agreed that--everyone of us came to
the same conclusion--that we had better turn in and try
to make another organization, because then we were only
an affiliate ourselves you know of the old National
American. And it would be pretty hard for the National
American to be trying to put one measure through Congress
and have one of their affiliates trying to put another
th .

Paul: So we said the only thing to do is to make ourselves
        a completely separate organization. And I think they
        came to the same conclusion, because we got a letter
        from them asking that--or suggesting--that since we
        were paying a rather high amount of money to them we
        could change into a category where we would pay less.
        You probably know all this.

Fry: No.

Paul: So they said, "You just send in your resignation as a
        whatever affiliate [chapter] you are, and then send at
        the same time an application to be in another [type of]
        group, and we will just transfer you." So we sent in
        the resignation and the request for membership in
        another classification where the expense wouldn't be
        so great, and they accepted our resignation but they
        didn't accept our application for the new one. So we
        were out, you see. We were just put out by this device.

Fry: Had you already decided that you wanted to be completely
        separate?

Paul: No, we had really expected to continue. We wanted to
        have unity in the movement, but we had expected to go
        our way and continue to work for our old Amendment.
        We decided to do it, but it was rather a hard decision
        to make because we didn't have any money, and our
        individual people didn't have any money, and we were
        all exhausted [laughing] by one vigorous campaign. It
        had gone at a terrific pace.

        So anyway we voted [to be separate]. All of our old
        congressional committee stood with us. Mrs. Kent went
        with us, and everybody who had been on the old committee,
        every single person, stayed with us. And so we then
        were the Congressional Union for Woman Suffrage as a
        new independent organization, not affiliated with
        anybody. That was I think in the late spring of '14.

        Then we had this constant conflict because we would
        use the "we demand an amendment to the United States
        Constitution enfranchising women," and they would say,
        "We demand the passage of the Shafroth-Palmer giving
        women the right to referendum " and so on, on this
        subject. It was the acme of the complicated for the
        congressmen and for the women of the country.

        So then they held what they called the Mississippi
        Conference, which was I guess an annual conference that

Paul: they had at that time. It was a conference of all the states around the Mississippi [Valley]. It was held in Iowa.

Fry: And this was NAWSA?

Paul: Yes. Well, this Mississippi Conference was under the auspices of the states in the Mississippi region belonging to the old National, because nobody belonged to anything else. There wasn't any other thing to belong to.

I went out to the conference to try to get this conference to endorse the old Susan B. Anthony Amendment. And I remember on the way out, I went with Mrs. Glendower Evan who was a very, very, very prominent woman in Boston belonging to the old National American, and she was passionate for continuing the old Amendment campaign. So she wanted very much to go to Iowa, and I went with her or she went with me, however it may be.

Fry: What was her name, Alice?

Paul: Her name? G-l-e-n-d-o-w-e-r Evans. She lived in Boston. She was a prominent member of the old National American.

Well, we stopped in Hull House [in Chicago] on the way out because Mrs. Evans was a great personal friend of Miss Jane Addams. And she was passionate about demanding the old Susan B. Anthony Amendment. So we explained it to Miss Addams that night--which is what you have to do all the time, explaining to the people who are important; that's what takes so much time, but we did do it with Miss Addams to keep her informed. We were her guests that night, and she devoted all her time to looking into it. And I don't think she took any active part; she was on the National board and so she was sort of bound to what they were doing. But we had a feeling that she was very sympathetic with what we were doing. So then we went on to the Mississippi Conference.

We met in the rooms of the different people during the conference where all the delegations from one state would meet. And I would go up and talk to a delegation, and somebody would go up and talk on the other side about the two amendments. I was trying to influence people as much as we could to stick by the old Amendment.

Paul: Well, then when it came to the floor of the
         conference, somebody got up and said, "We would like
         Miss Paul to explain to us what this"--because I wasn't
         on the program--"what this whole mix-up's about," and
         so on. And up got one of the officers of the Mississippi
         Conference and said, "Well, Miss Paul has been very ill
         and we don't want to tax her by making her make a
         report," or something. So I sat and listened in great
         astonishment at this, but I didn't say anything.

Fry: Had you been ill at all?

Paul: This time that I went up to--I think when I went up to
         [New Jersey] to take a rest, I think I went to the
         hospital, and there was some kind of an intestinal
         trouble I had gotten by eating some kind of apples or
         something. So my mother arranged for me to go into
         the hospital and try to get this thing cleared up,
         which they did, whatever it was. I wasn't very seriously
         sick. And I believe I did that during the time I was
         going to take this rest. I had sort of forgotten
         anything [about it] when I heard I was very ill.
         [Laughter.] I didn't say anything and they went on
         with all their reasons for the Shafroth-Palmer. And
         they got up a woman from Minnesota named Mrs. Alden
         Potter. I had gone out to Minnesota and spoken before
         their branch. (We had started in to go over the
         country and speak before every branch in the country if
         we could, and I had spoken there before the Minnesota
         one.) Mrs. Potter invited me to be her guest at her
         home--she was a Christian Scientist, very devout one,
         and gave me a Christian Science--what's the thing
         called, Mrs. Eddy's book whatever it is--Science and
         Health. We became very good friends by staying there,
         and so she said she would leave the old National
         American, that she would never work for this new thing.
         And a large section of their Minnesota people joined us
         in our campaign for the old Amendment; I guess almost
         everybody did.

         And Mrs. Potter got up and said, "Well, Miss Paul
         is sitting here and she doesn't seem to me too ill to
         explain things to us," or something [laughter]. I
         wasn't a member you see; I wasn't from the Mississippi
         region and I don't know that I was [invited]. I rather
         think that I just went. I can't remember that I had an
         invitation to go; I don't believe I would have had.

         So I did try to explain it, and I think then Mrs.
         Potter said, "Well, the Minnesota people, their board

Paul: and practically the whole group were all for continuing with the old Amendment." So there was not any <u>unanimous</u> support, I think, from Mississippi. There certainly wasn't any for our point of view and I don't think there was for any point of view. They heard it all and they disbanded.

But anyway I was regarded as a sort of pariah, an outcast in every possible way, at this convention. So everybody went back to Chicago, in order to get back to their respective places, and everybody stayed at the same hotel there--I mean most of the people I think-- just for convenience. Whatever the hotel was, it was recommended to us. I remember going down in the morning for breakfast, and here were all these people from all the different states in the union, and I remember not one human being spoke to me. I just felt <u>such</u> an outcast, and for a long time we were regarded in that way. [Pause.]

Howsoever, people like this Minnesota group and like Mrs. Donald Hooker--Katherine Hepburn you know, is her niece - Mrs. Hooker was the sister of Mrs. Hepburn up here in Connecticut and was a leader of the suffrage movement up here, and Mrs. Hooker was a leader of the suffrage movement in Maryland. They all belonged to the old National American. So Mrs. Hooker's group [formally withdrew], and of course that was because of this personal contact we had; we were so close in Washington that we went over to see Mrs. Hooker many times and she invited us often to spend the weekend or spend Sunday or something over there. So finally her whole branch formally withdrew from the old National American over the question of what we would fight for, and joined us. And then this New York one, as I told you, joined us, amalgamated with us when they gave up their own, just dissolved and recommended every member to transfer membership to us.

An Organization Emerges

Paul: So we gradually got support, sometimes whole states and sometimes parts of states. But from that year we spent--I spoke in a great many places over the country just to the local boards--we'd ask them if they would let me come and explain this. I remember going to Ohio, and that very foremost woman lawyer (Do you

: remember who she is out in Ohio? one of the first women
ever to hold high judgeship position?) Judge Florence
Allen was her name. You probably know who she was out
in Ohio. She was on this board and I think she was on the
court of appeals of Ohio, a federal judgeship. She had, I guess,
the highest position in the legal field that any woman
had ever held in the country. I remember she was at
this meeting. And I tried my best to explain it to
them, and I remember at the end someone said (I guess
it was the president, whoever it was) she said, "I
think it has been very interesting to hear all this,
and I think that we all feel that we had better stick
to our knitting." [Laughing.] I remember her words so
well, which meant to stick to what they were doing.
And even Judge Allen didn't speak up for us.

She meant stick to the Shafroth-Palmer Amendment.

: Yes. So as we went over the country, we got to know
the women. In every place we got some friends I
think. So gradually, to our amazement, while we hadn't
expected to get another [organization]. We thought we'd
be another group that would independently work for this
Amendment. We hadn't started out to build an organization, because that is a hard thing to do. And when you
get it, a hard thing to manage, and we really didn't
want one. We wanted to get the existing National
American to stop supporting the Shafroth-Palmer.

But oddly the only result was that our own
organization suddenly began to be an organization. So
that was, say, up to 1915. Then in 1915 Doris Stevens
went across the country speaking in place after place,
and Mabel Vernon had been going and I had been going,
and we had gotten branches in one state. We had been
down to Texas and got this Rena Maverick Green and got
this Clara Snell Wolfe, who became one of the greatest
supporters we ever, have ever had. She was the wife
of a professor of economics in the [University] at
Austin, Texas. And it is beyond words what she did.
It is just impossible to estimate the value of her work.
She was a very intellectual type. So then her husband
(this is just a diversion) was transferred up to the
University of Ohio, as professor of economics, head of
the economics department. So she went up to the University
of Ohio. In the meantime, she decided that she would
teach herself. She had no children and she was extremely
intellectual type of a person, so she had studied I have
forgotten what, something, and took her doctor's degree
in it and then got a position to teach in a college in

Paul: Ohio but not the same college as her husband. (But
        they seem to have all been in the same organization.)
        So then came the Depression and she was dropped on the
        ground that they couldn't afford in the Depression to
        employ two people in the same family, and she was married
        and she was married to this professor and so she was
        dropped. Happened all over the country, you know, at that
        moment, I don't know how many places that happened. So
        she then just turned in and devoted herself to the Woman's
        Party and did up to her death. She died about two years
        ago, I guess. One of the greatest blows we ever had when
        she died.

        But these groups brought in, you see, people so
        that gradually when the local wouldn't support the equal
        suffrage amendment, then we got a group of our own, until
        we formed branches in almost all the states.

Fry: Some of your organization started in 1913 because it is
        mentioned here [the Suffragist] that you had had
        mailings to suffragists all over the United States
        about the suffrage amendment that you were going to
        submit, and they responded. By the time Congress
        opened, which was in April of 1913, you had one woman
        from every congressional district in the United States
        on hand to give a petition to her congressman.

Paul: Yes we did, I know.

Fry: Goodness, how did you do all that?

Paul: That's what I said, we were so exhausted [laughter].

        Well, now you had better ask me some questions.

Fry: Let me go over this covering the years that you have
        just talked about and see if I have any mopping up
        questions.

Paul: Is this light good enough for you?

Fry: Yes, it's fine.

        Now, your amendment was introduced the opening day
        of Congress, April, 1913, by Representative Mondell,
        who was a Republican of Wyoming in the House, and
        Senator George E. Chamberlain of Oregon in the Senate.
        I think he was a Democrat.

Paul: Well, that was one year.

Fry: That was that year, 1913. So that the fight between the two amendments became known as the fight between the Shafroth-Palmer Amendment and the Mondell amendment.

Paul: We always called it the Bristow-Mondell amendment. I don't remember Chamberlain.

Fry: Yes, I wonder. Of Oregon.

Paul: Bristow was from Kansas, I think.

Fry: Well, his must have been the name finally assigned it, as the prominent one.

Paul: Maybe it was afterwards. It was usually known through the years, you will find it in almost everything, as the Bristow-Mondell amendment.

You see, the confusion was so immense, confusion among the women and the confusion in Congress as to why these two [suffrage] groups coming up with two bills. (Of course it didn't last very long because, as I said, as soon as the war came on these other people [NAWSA] all deserted and went into the war effort and we had the field all to ourselves. That was '17 and '18 and maybe part of '19 that they weren't there--till the war came to an end--they weren't there.) But when this confusion was so terrific, we decided we'd have to change the name of the Bristow-Mondell and call it something that would have some propaganda value, and that's when we decided to call it the Susan B. Anthony Amendment, because she had been one of the most prominent women in having it drafted and introduced.

And then to do that, we got up a pageant in Washington which Hazel McKaye came down and did for us. I remember going up to see her in Shirley, Massachusetts, the coldest little place that you ever saw, where she was living with her mother. I asked her if she would come down and put on a pageant to make people know who Susan B. Anthony was so we could call this the Susan B. Anthony Amendment and people would know something about it.

So she did come down and we had in a very big hall in Washington a very beautiful pageant that she put on honoring Susan B. Anthony. And from that time on we did it again and again, and again, and again. And we got a Susan B. Anthony stamp, you know, and we did everything to make people know who Susan B. Anthony was.

Fry: Oh, I didn't know you got a Susan B. Anthony stamp.

Paul: So then we called it the Susan B. Anthony Amendment, as against the Shafroth-Palmer. And it was just a device to simplify this campaign and make it easier for congressmen and easier for the women to know what they were backing.

Other 1913 Activities

Fry: You had problems getting it out of the House committee, in that Congress.

Paul: Well, we always had--we never in the beginning had any strength in Congress.

Fry: But you did get it reported out in the Senate. That was the first favorable report in twenty-one years, I think. It came out in June, and in June and July, CU-- the Congressional Union--had petitions circulated in every state. Then on July 31, when they arrived at the Capitol, you had another great big demonstration, with a motorcade--

Paul: What year are you talking about now?

Fry: 1913 still. There was a big motorcade to the Capitol that started at Hyattsville and came down to the Capitol with all of these petitions for the Amendment.

Paul: That's our first year, you mean?

Fry: Yes, this is 1913, your first full year. With a big demonstration of delegates. And you met with the members of the Senate committee, who made some speeches.

Paul: Where was this?

Fry: In Hyattsville, on the "village green."

Paul: Well, that wasn't anything very much.

Fry: But they had a big motorcade down to the Capitol.

Paul: Yes. That was gotten up; we created something, at least tried to--

Fry: It looks very big in the <u>Suffragist</u>.

Paul: Anyway, the thing wasn't one of ours, you know. In an effort to try to get women from the suffrage states, which we were then beginning, there was a Dr. Cora Smith King who had been a prominent member in winning the suffrage in the state of Washington. She had transferred her practice to Washington, D.C. from Washington state, and she was an officer of the Washington state branch of, I suppose, the National American. Anyway, whatever group [it was].

        [End of Tape 3, Side 2.]

        [Tape 4, Side A.]

Paul: She organized as well as she could, getting some women from every suffrage state to come or send a representative for a delegation they were going to take down to the Congress. Well, that was this one that she organized. She lived in Hyattsville and she organized it out there and she brought it in. It was very effective because these congressmen that they were going to see were their own congressmen and they were, themselves, voters.

Fry: I was amazed that you could get everything organized all over the United State. How did you locate all these women?

Paul: Well, we turned it over to Dr. King; she said she would do it. She got in touch with women in their own state and they authorized her to represent them, and she got in touch with women in other states where women had the vote.

Fry: One thing that interested me was that Mary Ware Dennett accepted the key to the town of Hyattsville from the mayor, so she must have been in on this. Isn't she on the board of the National American?

Paul.   Yes. In the beginning we worked, you see, much more closely together than we did later on. This was the first year before the separation had become quite so definite. You see there were only a few people, like Mrs. Catt, who seemed to have her heart very much in any animosity.

Fry: Then the next month, August 13 (that was just two weeks later) was this National Council of Women Voters, which was made up of women voters from the suffrage states.

Paul: That's what I am telling you about.

Fry: That's what you organized?

Paul: No, I wouldn't say we. We arranged through Mrs. King
        to get it organized--Dr. King.

Fry: Well, it seemed to have a president--Emma Smith Devoe.

Paul: That's right.

Fry: Jane Addams became the national vice-president?

Paul: Because they just got the presidential vote out in
        Illinois.

Fry: They had a mass meeting in the Belasco Theater. It was
        "hot and crowded." [Laughing]

Paul: Well, we really got up all these things and did all this
        organization work. But we were helped by the fact that
        we would send out the letters in Dr. King's name and
        Mrs. Devoe's--Mrs. Devoe Smith I think her name was.

Fry: Then I have another note here that in November, on
        November 17, a delegation of seventy-three New Jersey
        women came in to see the President.

Paul: Yes, that was Mrs. [Pikehurt? (inaudible)]. That's one
        of the things that Mr. Gallagher asked me about. I
        wonder where they get all that ?

Fry: I think it's written up in one of the early books,*
        and it's kind of amusing because you couldn't get an
        appointment with the President but you went on over
        anyway.

Paul: I didn't go but they did. But they came down--we had
        asked them to come down [to Washington] because they
        were from the President's state. You know we kept these
        deputations [to President Wilson] with anybody we could
        think of that might be a new group. We thought well, his
        own state women might be good, so we asked Mrs. [Pikehurt?].
        She was a member of the old National American; this was
        the first year when everybody was a member of the old

---

*Irwin, op.cit., pp. 41-42.

Paul: National American, the whole branch was. Anyway I
asked her--I remember it all very vividly--asked her to
come down and she came. Then when they were there [in
the headquarters], I called up the White House for them
to announce that they had arrived and would like to see
the President, and I was told that it was impossible
because he was occupied and so on. And then we said,
"Well, they would go over anyway and wait until he
could see them." So then when they went he did receive
them. It was just one of repeated deputations.

By the time we got through all these deputations he
certainly knew that there was a widespread interest in
the country. What he had asked us to do--to concert
public opinion--we were trying to do. That was our
point.

Fry: Another question I have is, Would you want to tell
anything about the problems of getting a suffrage
committee in the House? The Senate had formed a suffrage
committee; but the House continued to operate without
one, and they made you work through the sub-committee
of the Judiciary Committee.

Paul: There isn't much to say. I think that we thought it
might be a good thing to have a special committee,
but it of course didn't make much difference, just so
we got it done. As far as I remember, we never did get
a suffrage committee in the House, did we?

Fry: Well, you may have, along about 1917 or so.

Paul: I don't remember whether we ever did or not.

Fry: Seems like I remember that from my reading.*

Paul: You do a lot of things just in order to keep the subject
going, and of course I never thought it made much
difference which particular committee through all the
years. But if you could make an agitation about a
committee, you sometimes get to know friends and get
new friends and so on. While we might not have been
so anxious to get a report and have suffrage put in
the Constitution, they might think, well, why shouldn't
they have a committee? So we had all these little

---

*The House created a Suffrage Committee September 24, 1917.

Paul: devices, not that they were so important, but it was a sort of device to keep the thing alive

The Suffrage School

Fry: Another thing that you did later on is that you had a suffrage school; I thought that looked pretty impressive.

Paul: Yes, I remember all about it.

Fry: It's on page forty-two of December 20, 1913 _Suffragist_ and there's a class in parliamentary law, by Mrs. Nanette Paul, L.L.D.

Paul: Yes, I remember it all very well.

Fry: Elsie Hill.

Paul: These were all devices to keep the subject before the women of the country and to get them more informed, you know.

Fry: This went on for several days.

Paul: I know it did.

Fry: It looks like an awfully good training curriculum for anybody working in political organization work. You even have parliamentary law and a class in vocal culture and public speaking and one in press work.

Paul: We didn't devote--I don't know that we ever had another session of it; we may have had. But we only did this, again, in the way of keeping this before the women because I know perfectly well you can't stop and devote yourself to the physical culture of your speakers, studying parliamentary law and so on. You just have to spend most of your time in the actual work before you. Of course each one of these schools cost us a lot of time to make it a real success. It _was_ a good success. It was very, very successful.

Fry: Well, you must have gotten new workers out of it.

Paul: Maybe one or two. Not much.

Fry: Did you have very many of the schools?

Paul: I don't remember how big a school--it wasn't supposed
      to be a big school. At that minute they were having
      these suffrage schools all over the country. We
      weren't, but people were.

1914 - THE FORMATIVE YEAR

Nationwide Demonstration May 2

Fry: Now in 1914 the Suffragist in the April 11 issue talks
        about the nationwide demonstration to demand passage
        by Congress of the Bristow-Mondell suffrage bill. So if
        you can remember anything about the planning on that
        and how it was pulled off, it would be interesting.

Paul: Which one was that?

Fry: This was in April of 1914, and you wanted a demonstration
        in every state on May 2. Did you get one?

Paul: Oh, we certainly did. Crystal Eastman, who had come
        on our national board, went all over the United States
        (not all, but a considerable section) getting people to
        hold processions and meetings, whatever they could, for
        the original Susan B. Anthony Amendment, and then to
        send people to Washington on May 2 to have a big demonstra-
        tion there, which they did. The second one was very
        big and you will surely come across it here.

Fry: [Checking Suffragist.] Yes, there are quite a few
        pictures in the May 9, 1914 issue.

Paul: May 2 have you gotten to?

Fry: Yes, here's May 2. "From Ocean to Ocean Suffragists
        Celebrate Great Day. Women from every congressional
        district to carry resolution to Washington on May 9.
        Plans for procession to the Capitol."

Paul: Yes, that's right. That's when we had one woman, I
        think, from every district. That's when the police--I
        told you the other night--when the police had more
        ? .   .   ., .   .   ,   ers,

Paul: [laughter] because we had it limited to one person to
        every district, and they had a tremendous number trying
        to make a good reputation for the police department.

Fry: It says here you sold your <u>Suffragist</u> in cities all over
        the country; sales were most gratifying. Here's a song,
        "March of the Women," that someone wrote--Ethel Smith.

Paul: You know what that is, don't you?

Fry: I've heard it.

Paul: Do you know what it is?

Fry: No.

Paul: Well, when the women were imprisoned in England, Dame
        Ethel Smith, who was given her title of Dame because of
        her reputation in the field of music, wrote this "March
        of the Women," wrote the music for the "March of the
        Women" and wrote the words for the "March of the Women."
        And from that time on it was sung in every--it was sung,
        I think, when I was back in England, in the suffrage
        days over there. It was sung always in prison by all
        of the suffragists and everywhere at every meeting and
        so on.

        So then I knew about it, having been over there, so
        we brought it over here and had it sung at our meetings.
        And we still do. And the words are wonderful, you know.
        "Life, strife, these two are one." The words are superb
        in that. <u>I</u> think. And the music is stirring.

Fry: Yes, it is. I think Consuelo Reyes [companion of Mabel
        Vernon] has recorded that.

Paul: Yes, she's used it.

Fry: Here's a picture on the front of your May 16 issue of
        the front of the Congressional Union procession to the
        Capitol on May 9. So May was certainly your month.
        Here's this enormous, enormous crowd in front of the
        Capitol.

Paul: You see why we were so exhausted. You see why I have
        a "block" on my heart, the doctor says. [Laughter.]

Policy of Holding Party in Power Responsible

Fry: I can see why your heart is tired.

But 1914 seems to me to be an important year because that was when you really started working holding the party in power responsible and you began to influence the elections.

Paul: Well, it is the first election campaign that occurred after we [the Congressional Union] were created. We couldn't do it before.

Fry: Did you have any opposition to that idea?

Paul: Yes, tremendous. We had opposition to everything we did. Everything.

Fry: I meant within your own councils, when you were planning it.

Paul: No, our own people, we were the same type of people; we got on all right. We didn't ever have any opposition or anything. We adopted this program at this meeting up at Mrs. Belmont's, you know.

Fry: Oh, yes, at Marble House in Newport?

Paul: Yes. We called this meeting--it was a meeting of our, I think, of our executive board and our national advisory council, I think. And we laid before the women--I presided at the meeting--and gave the outline of what we wanted to do, and Lucy Burns, who had been doing most of the congressional work, made the splendid speech showing how the Democrats had caucused against us as a whole body, and we couldn't start and support individual Democratic candidates even though they were for us, when they belonged to a caucus that had taken the action against us, and so on. So this vote went unanimously through.

We had a great many people there who were from the old National American. For instance, Mrs. Hepburn,*

_____

*The actress Katherine Hepburn's mother and aunt were both active in the suffrage movement.

Paul: although their branch didn't do what her sister's branch did--withdraw from the National American. She went to this conference and voted for this, and I remember she wrote me afterwards and said, "The way you and Lucy Burns with your program swept us all completely into this movement is something I was very much impressed by" or something like that. So she was wholeheartedly--and she was a great power up in the state. So they had this dissension of course all the time in the old National American, with so many women trying to get the National American to stand with us, which they didn't succeed in doing.

Fry: National American had promised cooperation in this nationwide demonstration in May, 1914. Did they cooperate?

Paul: Well, I remember when we had this they had some kind of a float (maybe it shows in one of the pictures, I don't know) showing their support of the Shafroth-Palmer.

Fry: Oh. [Laughing.]

Paul: Putting it in our demonstration.

Fry: That wasn't quite what you had in mind, was it?

Paul: Well, most of the people that looked on had no idea what was the "Shafroth-Palmer." [Laughter.] It didn't make much difference. We didn't worry about it. It got us some more people.

Fry: At this Newport meeting at Mrs. Belmont's Marble House, my notes mention also that there was $7,000 raised.

Paul: Mrs. Belmont gave $5,000. After we had announced our program and so on, she got up and offered $5,000, which she paid.

Fry: May I ask you one more question that isn't quite clear to me?

Paul: Have you gone all through these records in the Suffragist for the things you are asking me about, have you gone through?

Fry: I have read the Suffragist.

Paul: The questions you are asking me, is that the period you have covered for your research, so far?

Fry: Yes. And there's one other thing that I want to ask
         you. The _Suffragist_ said that on this May 9 mass
         meeting and so forth in Washington, 531 delegates from
         various states presented resolutions to the committee
         of senators and congressmen, "which then were introduced
         on the floor of each house." This was the first time
         that suffrage had been up for debate on the floor of the
         House, although "Congressman Henry would not let the
         Rules Committee meet on it at first." Is that the
         right impression, that the petitions were presented to
         the senators and congressmen and then immediately
         introduced as bills into each House? Or was it?

Paul: Well, I think the petitions were presented in support.
         Usually you get your resolution introduced at the
         beginning of each Congress, and I imagine we did.

Fry: The purpose of this May march--

Paul: --was to back it up.

Fry: Was to back it up and make a demonstration in support
         of the bill?

Paul: That's right. All of our demonstrations were for that
         purpose. The only thing we changed in that was that
         finally we gave up Bristow-Mondell's name and put in
         Susan B. Anthony. In our demonstrations.

Fry: I wanted to ask you about the formation of an advisory
         council.

Paul: What year was that?

Fry: This was 1914. Harriot Stanton Blatch joined it in
         September; you had a lot of famous women on it from
         all over the nation. So I wonder if this was an effort
         on your part to get a wider base of support.

Paul: Yes. Of course. Mrs. Blatch may have founded it, but
         the principal person--

Fry: No, I didn't say that she _founded_ it. I just know that
         she joined it in September.

Paul: Oh, she _joined_ it. Well, the person who was the
         chairman, [pause] and I thought she was always the
         chairman, (maybe she wasn't in the beginning) was a
         Mrs. Elizabeth Rogers, the one I told you went with me
         to Secretary Stimson. She worked always as the chairman

Paul: of our advisory council. Everything we did, we would
have the advisory council there.

Fry: In getting an advisory council like that together it
takes a great amount of contacting women, and I noticed
they were from all different walks of life. Could you
give us any idea of how on earth you would go about
something like that?

Fry: Well, we got a chairman, the one that we wanted to be
a chairman (and I think it was Mrs. Rogers; I don't
remember any other chairman). Then she of course would
write to people she knew. She was very well known; her
family, Secretary of War Stimson, was very well known.
She had many connections. She got it together herself.
And if anybody heard of somebody she thought would be
nice to get as a member but would not be likely to do
much work--say some writer, some woman physician, or
something, somebody who was well known but she didn't
believe she would do very much work, then we would ask
her to go on the advisory council.

Fry: So how did you use this council then, just as names
for--

Paul: No. I just recall--I am almost sure they were at this
meeting at Newport, and I think they were at every
meeting we ever had.

Fry: So that they really did participate and gave ideas.

Paul: Yes. And they were willing to do that, you see, to
come to a meeting where a decision was to be made. It
was a very useful organization.

Fry: Well, the other thing that I would just like to hear
you talk about is how you handled the Democratic women
in trying to get them to campaign against their Democratic
candidates, in holding the party in power responsible.

Paul: You mean in the suffrage states?

Fry: Yes.

Paul: Well, we just used the same argument that we did with
all women: that women who had the vote now had the
obligation we thought--anyway they had the opportunity--
more than anybody else, to enfranchise the rest of the
women in the country. And we would appeal to them to
use their votes in a way that would help, and we'd point

Paul: out that the administration was formally against the
         enfranchisement of women, and if they voted for that
         administration they were voting against the freedom of
         women. That's all there was to it.

         You see, in each one of these election campaigns,
         we got women to go into every state, who believed this
         and who could get up and say it, and that way, I guess,
         we turned a great many votes. We didn't have to turn
         enough [votes] to defeat a man; if he just felt there
         was an unrest among his women on the subject, then it
         would be probable that when he came back he would use
         his influence in his party to stop this opposition,
         which was the case--that did happen.

Fry: Did you run into the stickly problem of having to
         campaign against Democrats who had worked hard for the
         Amendment?

Paul: Well, I don't know anybody who ever worked hard.

Fry: Or who had supported you in Congress?

Paul: But of course we did in the suffrage states because
         everybody was supporting us in Congress from the
         suffrage states.

Fry: Did you lose any friends in Congress?

Paul: I don't think we did. It made people [candidates] very
         angry, but I think they--of course they were angry when
         we diminished their support in their own states. But
         still they would probably always keep on being for the
         Amendment because the women were voting and very few men
         wanted to go against the votes for women in a state
         where women were voting. Of course in the Senate,
         Senator Borah [of Idaho] did vote against us. I think
         he was the only senator from a suffrage state that did.

Fry: Why did he? Do you know?

Paul: I don't know why he did. What he said publicly was
         that he was for it, and he thought people should get
         it the same way Idaho did, by their state referendum.

Fry: Oh, the same states' rights thing.

Paul: What he said was a defense. As to why he really was
         against it, I don't know. We had an organizer, Margaret
         Widemore [?] who went up to the state of Idaho, and I

Paul: remember she went down to the capitol where you could
look at--in that state--the signatures of the men who
were running and see what they had put themselves down
as supporting. In Idaho they did this. He'd put
himself down as supporting the national suffrage
amendment.

He came to see me personally in our headquarters in
Washington and said the same thing, that he was supporting
us, and he wanted us to know and to not continue any
opposition, which we were having in the beginning, against
him. He came into our office [in 1918] and sat down, in
a long talk, telling me this. And he told the senators
this.

And when this measure came up for a vote in the
Senate, when we were almost at the point we thought of
winning (and that must have been 1918 I guess; I think
it was in the winter), Maud Younger and I sat up--she
was our congressional chairman you know and a wonderful
chairman--we sat up together in the gallery. We thought
the vote was going to be taken in the Senate. We
thought we had the votes exactly, but not one over.
And she knew every man so intimately, she made that her
business, just to know them thoroughly and personally
and socially and their wives and everything. And so,
on the strength of her report and our own general
information, we thought we could risk the vote. And
from all over the country women came, packed and jammed
with people from great distances who came for this first
vote in the Senate on the equal suffrage amendment.
Maybe there had been earlier ones where it wasn't really
going to be passed, but this was the first one when it
looked as though it would go through.

So finally when all these speeches went on and on
and on and on and on, and no vote was being taken, Maud
Younger went down to see what the cause of it was. And
we went up to Senator Curtis, who was the Republican
Whip from Kansas, (later the Vice-President under
Hoover) and Senator Gallinger from New Hampshire who
was a Republican leader of the Senate (this was when
the Republicans were in control). We went up to them
and there they were, each one standing side-by-side with
a tally sheet in their hands, and we said, "Why in the
world don't you vote? All these women are assembled
to hear the vote and it's going on and on."

And they said, "Well, Borah has left us."

Paul: We said, "We think we have the votes."

And they said, "We think you have the votes too. We
thought you had the votes and we knew you had the votes.
And we were planning to take the vote. But when Borah
told us that he had decided to vote against it, we knew
we couldn't carry it because we would be one vote short.
And so," he said, "we have instructed all our leaders
on the floor of the Senate to just keep on talking, get
as much enthusiasm for it as they can, and then the time
will be up and they will move to adjourn, because we
don't want to be voted down, which would be very harmful
to you and to the Republican party. We don't want that
to happen." So we agreed with them that was the best
thing to do and the only thing to do.

So nobody really knows what happened to Borah
because we had had his pledge when he came to this
office personally--he took the trouble to come to an
unimportant group and sit down and tell their chairman
that he was going to vote for this measure, and please
not to make any more trouble in his state. And he went
down and signed it, and this Miss Widemore, I am sure,
was correct when she said she read it and saw his name
signed to things he would support. And then he told his
own Republican Whip and his own Republican leader,
Gallinger, because they said he told them he would vote
for it. And he didn't. So that postponed our Senate
victory for maybe half a year.

I guess you haven't come to that yet in the Suffragist.

Fry: Not yet.

After you had campaigned against the Democrats in
1914, the Amendment, which had been bottled up in
Congressman Henry's Rules Committee all that year, was
suddenly voted out, without recommendation, to the House;
he let it come to a vote in the committee.

Paul: Well, of course the purpose was to start to speed it
up.

Fry: Do you see that as a direct result of your work?

Paul: Well, we knew it was, of course. Because if you get on
the Rules Committee, there were a good many men--
Republicans and Democrats--and if they see signs of their
women wanting something and expressing it in their votes,
you see some of the senators and congressmen did have

Paul: their votes diminished--I don't know whether any of them were defeated because of this, but anyway their strength-- and they knew it, they always said so, they blamed it on us--Mr. Gallagher read me something I hadn't known and I don't know where he got it from, in one of these books probably. A statement by Mr. Taggart of Kansas, and you will come across it.

Fry: In the hearing?

Paul: On the result of the election, Mr. Taggart made these furious statements against us and oh, violent statements against us, that we had gone in and poisoned the minds of the women in his state and so on and so on. (He was from Kansas.) But then as far as I know--

Fry: He raked you over the coals pretty hard in a hearing; I don't know whether you remember it or not. And the transcript of the hearing was reprinted in the Suffragist. It was after the 1914 elections.*

Paul: Yes, because we felt--

Fry: He was really upset about it.

Paul: --it was good evidence (we put it in to encourage the women) it was good evidence to show that when they defected on this subject, it was making a congresssan give real serious attention to the subject.

[Discussion of date of hearing.]

Paul: We kept up the policy till the end, you see. And I am sure it was a very effective policy because it was an appeal to the solidarity of women, through all the highest motives they could have in voting, and it lifted the whole thing up to where they were standing for a great principle; we thought anyway, and they thought so too, evidently, so that they would put this principle above their party and everything else.

---

*Partial transcript is also in Irwin, pp. 119-124. The hearing was in December, 1915.

OPPOSITION

Paul: It was inevitable that it would have an effect on the
       congressmen. We didn't care very much whether we
       defeated them or didn't defeat them. We knew anyway,
       whichever we did, they would still probably vote as the
       women of the state wanted, which would be for it. I
       don't remember any man from the suffrage states who
       voted against it excepting Borah. And he made it clear
       that he wasn't voting against us, he was only voting
       for state referendum [slight laughter], to get it the
       same way Idaho had gotten it. But I think he must have
       had some other motive.

Fry: There must be a story there that we don't know.

       I thought that I detected, as I read through The
       Suffragist, every time a southern chapter was formed
       or something good would happen in the southern states,
       a little note of "Look, the South is coming around," if
       I read between the lines correctly. I wanted to check
       with you on this. Was the South a bit more difficult
       than other areas to get woman suffrage established,
       because of the race question?

Paul: Well, I don't think the race question would have come
       into it. Maybe the general conservatism of the South.

Fry: Well, there was an editorial in The Suffragist about
       how national suffrage would not affect white supremacy
       in the political world in the South, and I thought maybe
       that editorial wouldn't have been necessary if this
       hadn't been a problem.

Paul: Maybe, but it wasn't anything that was very serious.
       We just knew we had to go everywhere, and if we went
       to one state there would be some difficulties, and in
       another state another difficulty.

Paul: Now, I went down myself and formed a branch in
         Florida. We got one of the best members we ever had in
         the whole Woman's Party history, and that was Helen
         West, who later became the editor of our Equal Rights
         magazine. (We got an Equal Rights magazine after the
         Suffragist.) And at that same meeting we got somebody
         [from Florida] to come up [to Washington]; she was the
         oldest picket, and she was arrested and imprisoned.

Fry: Oh, yes.

Paul: And I remember when I went myself to Texas and formed
         that branch, and we got one of the strongest branches
         in the country through this Mrs. Clara Snell Wolfe,
         and she brought all these Maverick people in, Lola
         Maverick Lloyd and all these people whose children are
         still helping us. And South Carolina, we--by correspondence,
         not even going there--we got Anita Pollitzer, who just
         became the backbone almost of our movement. She came,
         you know, from Charleston.

Fry: Well, it seemed that there might be too--

Paul: And from Tennessee, for instance, (excuse me one word,
         one minute) we got Sue White. One of our members went,
         I think Maud Younger went down there and had a meeting
         and got Sue White to come up and stay at the headquarters
         and give up all her work. She had been a court stenographer
         and she came up and she just devoted herself to the campaign.
         She was one of those who burned the President's words in
         front of the White House, which was one of the hardest
         things anybody could have done. And she was from Tennessee,
         another southern state, you see. So I could go through
         all those southern states and tell of the very strong
         supporters we had.

Fry: Well, I thought that there might have been two other
         issues that kept impinging on the suffrage issue. One of
         them was the southern issues of states' rights and race
         relations, and the other one was the prohibition issue--
         liquor.

Paul: Well, the liquor interests were always considered, and
         many people still believe it is the main source of
         opposition. I don't know very much about the liquor
         interests, but they always had a formal representative,
         publicly representing them, speaking against the Amendment
         in every hearing as far as I can recall. And of course
         many people thought it was a very powerful opposition.
         I d...' .. w.   . w   . . . .   '. .r' * w. : an

From New York _Times_, 5 July 1975

ANITA POLLITZER, SUFFRAGIST, DIES

Founder and Ex-Head of the National Woman's Party

Anita Pollitzer, a pioneer fighter for equal rights for women, died Thursday at the home of her nurse in Queens. She was 80 years old and lived in Charleston, S. C.

Miss Pollitzer, the widow of Elie Charlier Edson, who died in 1971, was an organizer of the National Woman's party in 1913 and had served in various offices, including national chairman. She retired in 1949, becoming honorary vice chairman.

Over the years she had spoken in nearly every state and in Britain to plead for equal treatment for women.

One of the cases of injustice she cited was that of an American boy who had lived almost all his life in Iowa. Because he had been born in Mexico, the Immigration and Naturalization Service demanded he be expelled as an alien. If his one American parent had been his father he would have had United States citizenship.

She fought ceaselessly to permit female nationals as well as males to pass their nationality on to children born abroad.

Miss Pollitzer campaigned for suffrage in 39 states before the 19th Amendment, which became part of the Constitution in 1920, gave women the right to vote.

Another measure she backed was the Celler-Dickstein Bill which removed sex discrimination in the case of women who marry foreign nationals. One case she cited was that of a Vassar College graduate living in Paris and president of an American club there

Harris & Ewing

Anita Pollitzer as she appeared years ago.

who lost her citizenship after her marriage to a Frenchman.

Another was that of a woman whose family had been in this country since the early seventeen-hundreds. She went from Nevada to Europe, where she was married to a physician. When he was called to Army duty she decided to bring their three children to the United States but found that they were aliens and inadmissible.

The Equal Rights Amendment for which she fought so long is near passage. It was proposed in 1972 and since then 34 states have completed ratification, with 4 more needed for final adoption.

Miss Pollitzer, who was born in Charleston on Oct. 31, 1894, received a B.A. in 1916 from Columbia University and a master's degree in international law there.

She leaves a sister, Mabel Pollitzer.

A graveside funeral service will be conducted Monday at 1 P.M. in Chester, Pa.

Paul: would be the temperate half of the world, you know, and
        they didn't want to give them more power.

        And then this other one, about states' rights, there
        was no question that the states' rights movement--of course
        it was embodied in the old National American woman
        suffrage position. The women themselves were divided.
        I told you about how Mrs. Helen Gardner withdrew
        publicly from us and personally from us on the grounds
        that she discovered that we were really in earnest
        about putting the Amendment in the Constitution. And
        didn't appear again until the vote was won, when she
        appeared at the meeting giving them the pens I believe,
        for the proclamation. I told you all that.

        There is no question about that opposition; it
        was the voice of the President himself.

Fry: What do you mean, "giving them the pens"?

Paul: I told you how President Wilson assembled a group of
        people the night before the proclamation was issued
        and you know, they always sign it and then they give
        the pens, one pen to one person, one to another, then
        everybody goes away with a pen signed to some important
        document. So the people he assembled there were states'
        rights women who had opposed us. I don't know whether
        all of them were states' rights people, but probably
        they all were. Those I knew about were.

        And the other thing you said about the racial
        [issue]--. I want to tell you there was formed, and
        you probably know this, sometime while we were having
        the suffrage campaign I guess, a--let's see--National
        Association of Colored Women was its name (I guess you
        know all this) by Mary Church Terrell, who was the first
        Negro woman ever to graduate from a college, and she
        graduated from Oberlin. She married a judge in Washington,
        appointed by one of the presidents, a Negro judge. She
        got together a group of women that is still the largest
        and most important group of colored woman in the country,
        called the National Association of Colored Women. Well,
        they supported us always.

        In our first procession we had a group from Howard
        University which Elsie Hill organized. She went over
        there and spoke to them and got these colored women to
        come. At that first--I guess I've told you this--it
        was the only thing that brought dissension in our first
        procession. Have I told you about it?

Fry: No.

Paul: Well, she went there and organized these women and got
       them to come and--not this National Association of
       Colored Women, but just the women in Howard. She was
       having this [parade] section herself of college women,
       so she did that in connection with this, invited the
       college women in Howard to come, all of whom were
       Negroes.

            So they accepted and became one of the groups
       getting this up, and when this became public I began
       to receive letters from many, many, many, many splendid
       supporters we had, saying, "This is unheard of. We are
       certainly not going to come up and march in a procession
       where you have colored women marching." It reached the
       newspapers and they played it up to the utmost, to get
       dissension sowed in our ranks. It was quite a problem.
       It was extremely difficult because we had so many women
       saying, "There will be nobody from our town, there will
       be nobody from our state to do this," then lots coming
       forth in the newspapers inflaming everybody about the
       subject. [Laughs.] It was a very difficult situation.

            And so I remember how we finally solved it. We had--
       as I recall rightly, and I would have to check this--I
       think we had a men's section in this first procession,
       and I think these men were gathered together by a
       Quaker man whom I knew, whom I think was a distant
       relative of mine, named Mr.--I won't put his name,
       because I might be mistaken. This man said, "Well now,
       our group could be placed right next to the colored
       women because we have no objection whatsoever. We don't
       think anything at all about this fuss over this colored
       women's delegation."

            So it is my dim recollection--if only Elsie Hill
       were living I could ask her all these thing that I don't
       remember. I think in her college section--which is my
       section as I told you, walking--that we had this colored
       group, and it is possible that they had a whole separate
       section of colored women. But I think they were in the
       college section. I'm not sure about that, but there
       was a colored section anyway, a section of colored
       women. And so we put this men's group next to them,
       and the men's group were perfectly polite. Finally
       everybody calmed down and accepted it, so it was this
       men's group that really saved the day for us.

            And I want to tell you, this National Association

Paul: of Colored Women that Mrs. Mary Church Terrell formed
came in during the course of our suffrage fight, came
in later than this first procession, but from the time
they came in as supporters they have always stood by
us, up to the present time.

Fry: I saw your problem not as being one of lack of support
by the blacks but as one of--

Paul: Oh, it wasn't that. It was lack of support by the
<u>white</u> women.

Fry: Yes, because they didn't want any more blacks voting
in the South.

Paul: No, it wasn't ever that. I never heard of that before.
First time I have ever heard anybody say <u>that</u>. There
were not so many black people voting anyway because they
had this grandfather's clause and various things, you
know. They didn't worry about that at all. What they
were worried about was being personally associated in
any way with these colored women. On that ground they
left us--they never finally left but they threatened to
leave.

Fry: You mean in the organization?

Paul: Well, it came up about our first procession--they
weren't parts of our organization.

Fry: But after that--

Paul: The white women were parts of our organization but the
colored women who were coming in were not a part.

Fry: Judging from the <u>Suffragist</u>, apparently your workers
in the South were finding that the opposition there was
saying that if the woman suffrage amendment passed, it
might increase the number of Negro voters in the South.
The editorial that I read in the <u>Suffragist</u>, which is
in the November 14, 1914 issue, page three, pointed out
that the white women voters in Dixie will outnumber
Negro women two-to-one; and besides that, the property
and literacy tests rule out Negro voters anyway, usually;
and in states where there are more Negroes than whites,
"white supremacy could be continued to be maintained by
the same means as now prevails in these states."
Therefore the Amendment would not alter the proportions
of the black-white vote.

Paul: I think I probably wrote that editorial because I wrote almost all the editorials in the first few years of our magazine.

Fry: And it has a little chart to illustrate these points.

Paul: But I don't think I ever personally thought that this was a serious matter. Somebody was always thinking up some dread thing you had to answer.

Fry: I have some notes here on the opposition and I thought maybe you could fill out the picture. There was an opposition paper called the Woman Patriot, which was financed by a rich man named Wadsworth, and somewhere I picked up a note that this was a part of the Alice Longworth crowd.

Paul: [James Wolcott] Wadsworth [Jr.], you know, was the state senator [assemblyman] from New York, and then later defeated the congressman from New York [and became U.S. Senator], one of the most powerful men in Congress. And his wife, Mrs. James Wadsworth was the president of the association against votes for women. They appeared at every hearing, they were powerful women, wealthy women, and a powerful organization, and all over the country they had these branches. You know it was a very big force we were up against. And this was the leading, the crystallization, of the opposition by the leaders of this group all over the country.

Fry: Did this hit its peak in 1914, '15 and '16?

Paul: I should say it had its peak when the vote was taken in the House of Representatives [in 1919].

[End of Tape 4, Side A]

[Tape 4, Side B]

Paul: It was always apparently well-financed and extremely active and led by very prominent women who sincerely believed it was for the benefit of the country not to have the vote for women. Now what happened was they withdrew from the campaign, and I hope you read this when you get to the--it will be in the 1919 issues--have you read that yet?

Fry: I did, but it has been years ago, Alice.

Paul: You haven't read it right now, since you have been here.

Fry: I have read a few pages in it; but go ahead, what were you going to say?

Paul: Well, when the vote was taken in the House of Representatives the first time, it was taken twice. The first time was I think in the spring of 1919, but you can find it there in the Suffragist.* In order to defeat the Amendment, a man from Ohio who was considered an opponent, named--I think his name was [Hamilton] Gard, G-a-r-d [Democrat], but I would have to verify these things; I think it was that. Congressman Gard got up and offered an amendment to the Susan B. Anthony Amendment, which was before them for a vote, you see. (Maybe you saw this.) His amendment was to require ratification within seven years. And the reason for this was that the prohibition amendment had gone through with that addition. But there had never been one before; that was put in by the saloon keepers and so on to try to get the prohibition amendment defeated. So the anti-suffrage movement then adopted the same tactics and tried to put this seven-year amendment through.

And all over the hall cries came up of "Shame." They knew what he was doing, trying to defeat us by this. And so this amendment of Mr. Gard's was voted on and turned down, defeated. So then they had the original amendment, "The right to vote shall not be denied or abridged by the United States or any state on account of sex," with no limitation on it in any way.

And then (I think I told you all this before) then Mrs. Wadsworth--and you will find this in the Suffragist because I looked it up in our recent fight to keep the seven years out [of the Equal Rights Amendment].** I looked it up to check on what had happened--and Mrs. Wadsworth issued a statement right after the defeat of this measure to put the seven years on, saying that, "We realize that it is useless to go on any longer in opposing the equal suffrage amendment, now that the seven-year clause has been omitted, because without the seven-year clause, the women, if they don't win this year, they could go on next year, and next year and next

---

*The Amendment first passed in the House January 10, 1918, by a vote of 274 to 136--one vote to spare.
**The ERA was up for ratification at the time of the interview. A seven-year clause was added to it before passage by Congress.

Paul: year until they do win. There is no question it <u>will</u>
go into the Constitution. So we have decided to withdraw
from the campaign against it."

And so it was very wonderful for us because throughout this whole ratification campaign we never had a
whisper from any of these powerful women and the well-
financed organization of the league against votes for
women, because of Mrs. Wadsworth's withdrawal of the
whole organization from any further opposition. She
said, "It's useless, essentially useless. They have won
by defeating that seven-year [clause]."

I couldn't seem to get that over to any of our
women [last year]--that by putting the seven-year
[clause on the Equal Rights Amendment], they were
doing exactly what our opponents were trying to do in
vain back in the suffrage campaign, and the leader of
the campaign against votes for women was much more
powerful than any leader we have now, but she withdrew
and said, "We will give up the battle now. We won't go
into any campaign." And we went through all these
states and we never had anybody opposing. Other people
opposed as individuals, but we never had a group of
women opposing, which was our most formidable opposition.

Fry: And that seven-year clause now just gives hope to the
opponents of the ERA?

Paul: Well, it would give hope to anybody that has to try to
put something over that is difficult to put over. If
you limit the time in which you can oppose you limit
yourself, you see.

Fry: Did you ever have any indications that some of the
money for these antis [anti-suffragists] came from
liquor interests? Maybe some of the money in the
Wadsworth crowd, do you think?

Paul: We don't know where they got it from. They were all
wealthy women, that type of women.   ·

Fry: They had money anyway?

Paul: I don't know. We had no idea. But the liquor interests
were totally different. They had a personal motive:
they thought that women would be so given to temperance
that their own business interests would be destroyed.

Fry: There is one more opposition factor. That's some of the

Fry: newspapers. The <u>New York Times</u>: did you have trouble
with the <u>New York Times</u> and Adolph Backs? [Ochs]

Paul: Who was he supposed to be?

Fry: Apparently he was a writer or an editor on the <u>New York
Times</u> and was bitterly opposed to suffrage.

Paul: Yes, I think the <u>New York Times</u> was opposed. I don't
recall it was ever for us.

Fry: And there was a newspaper in Louisville that was
opposed.

Paul: I think a great many papers--I don't think we had very
much support from the press.

Fry: Oh, you didn't?

Paul: No.

Fry: Well, what I have been reading in the <u>Suffragist</u> are
the quotes from newspapers that <u>did</u> support you, so I
think that might give a kind of a skewed impression of
the support you got from the press.

Paul: When you say the <u>Post</u>, do you mean the <u>New York Evening
Post</u>? Did you say the <u>Post</u>?

Fry: No, I said the Louisville paper, and I don't know which
one.

Paul: Oh, Louisville paper.

Fry: It's referred to as "Waterson's paper," and I don't know
which one Waterson had. We'd have to look that up. But
I wondered if you remembered.

Paul: Well, as a whole, we had this wonderful person who did
all the press work for us and kept all the press work
for us, kept all the clippings and so on. We have the
clippings down there, a great many of them, in Washington;
you could go through and see. But my impression was that
we weren't getting much support from the press. I know
that we got support from a few, and we always recognized
it and knew who they were. One of them was a paper up
in Boston which was edited by Mr. Greuning; you know,
Senator Greuning. You know who he is.

Fry: Yes.

Paul: Did he die, by any chance? Do you know whether he
       died?

Fry: It seems to me he did.

Paul: Because in the middle of this election campaign, you
       know, he was the chief speaker for McGovern [in the
       campaign this year], his number one speaker. And his
       wife is a member of our national board, Dorothy Greuning.
       He went all over the United States speaking for McGovern,
       and then I heard over the television one day during the
       midst of the campaign that he was very, very, very ill
       and [it was]not known whether he would recover, and I
       never heard a thing about his death, so I didn't know
       whether he survived or not.

       Anyway [I was at his house and he] told me the other
       day himself that in looking through the papers for his
       memoirs which he was writing then, that he had found a
       letter from me, as national chairman of the Woman's
       Party, to him thanking him for the great help he had
       given in winning the vote for women, and he said he had
       kept it all these years and was putting it in his
       memoirs. Well, there were individual cases where people
       did go all out and help us. When we were picketing up
       in Boston, when the women were arrested on Boston Common
       all these times, he came to our aid.

DISCUSSION: SOURCES FOR HISTORY OF THE NATIONAL WOMAN'S
PARTY

Fry: Do you have the newspaper clippings in scrapbooks?

Paul: We have _volumes_ of them.

Fry: Where?

Paul: In the National Woman's Party headquarters.

Fry: Oh. But not in the Library of Congress?

Paul: No, I hope they are not. Mrs. Belmont, before she
        became interested in our [campaign] and joined us,
        when she first became interested in suffrage in general
        and was financial contributor to the old National
        American Suffrage Association, she bought a house on
        the corner of
        in New York City. I don't know which exact corner but
        just right there, that neighborhood, a whole building.
        She established a society called--I think she called
        it--the Political Equality Association, and she made
        herself the president, and she started in to try to
        work any way she could.

        Then when the National American practically threw
        us out, you know when they told us to resign and try
        for a membership in another form, she was their principal
        financial backer then. So she withdrew from them
        completely in indignation and joined us.

Fry: Oh, so that's why she entered the scene right then. I
        wondered what prompted her to do that.

Paul: We had gone to see her and gotten her interested a
        little bit, and she approved of everything we were
        doing. Then she was outraged when the National American
        acted this way toward us. It was in the spring of 1914,

Paul: I am pretty much worried, I am very worried, because
          we have a new chairman, and I think she is well-meaning
          but I don't think she knows very much about the campaign,
          or is at all the type of the women who built the organiza
          tion up. She was in the Bureau of Internal Revenue for
          years, she had some subordinate position there;* now
          she's resigned from the Bureau of Internal Revenue and
          has come down and taken our biggest room in the head-
          quarters, that no chairman has ever taken before, and
          filled it with her own possessions and just taken over
          the whole headquarters and all the money and everything
          else. And to my great alarm, just before I came up [her
          to live, this year], she came to me and she said, "I
          have made the most wonderful arrangement. I have gotten
          $10,000 for the Woman's Party. And you know what I have
          done? I am giving [the Library of Congress] all the
          records of the Woman's Party and they have agreed to
          put the whole staff of girls on sorting all our records
          and our filing cases and so on, and putting them all in
          the congressional library, as a gift to the Library."

          And I said, "But you haven't any right to do that.
          A great part of those letters are my personal letters
          that I have written over the country hither and yon,
          and Mrs. Emma Guffey Miller has written a great many of
          these letters, and"--you know who she was, don't you?

Fry: Yes.

Paul: "Mrs. Florence Bayard Hilles has written a great many
          of them; there are volumes and volumes and volumes of
          letters in these filing cases, and without the consent
          of these women, you haven't any right to do this." And
          I said, "All kinds of personal letters are mixed in
          there, and it would be a great violation of the under-
          standing on which these people came and wrote their
          letters here for us."

          But I don't know that I stopped her; I am not sure
          And I am so terribly afraid that I am going to learn
          that [she has done it]; she makes everything seem very
          plausible--so.

          _____

          *She had been with Bache & Company in New York--before
          the Internal Revenue. - Donald Paul.

Paul: when we were at our lowest ebb, when she joined us. She
had already bought this house and she had on the ground
floor a little office. Later on she gave this office
to us, and it was the New York City office of the
National Woman's Party. And she went, you know, on our
board, after about a year.

So in her office she employed a girl, a Jewish girl,
to search all the newspapers in the country that she
could search, and find any article about votes for women
and paste in her scrapbooks. They were about <u>this</u>
thick, and I don't know how many volumes of them,
several shelves of them. So I imagine that all these
people writing books come down there; they always go
through these press clippings.

Fry: Are those at Belmont House in Washington?

Paul: Yes, they are there. And I hope when you go down you
will go and see all these things.

Paul: Mrs. Butler Franklin, do you know her?

Fry: No.

Paul: Well, she is our first vice-chairman, and she is an
extremely fine woman, very fine woman. She is a second
cousin of Mrs. Belmont, lives out in Virginia close to
Washington and comes in quite often. Well, she called
me up and she said, "We are going to have a board meeting
and the subject is what to do with all the Woman's Party
documents."

I said to her just what I am saying to you. "These
must not be given away, and I think it would be absolutely
dishonest to do such a thing, and when the whole campaign
is over, we ought to do as we did when the whole suffrage
campaign was over: put some very responsible person in
charge of sorting the papers and discarding what should
be discarded and classifying them and cataloguing them
and then giving what we want to give to the congressional
library. But not just turn over to these dozen young
colored girls (what they have now, almost nothing else
in the congressional library) to come in harum-scarum.
No telling what we'd find left in the papers in the
congressional library. It would be a terrible, terrible
thing."

So I was going to say, if you get a chance to
impress upon this Mrs. Chittick--in case any papers are
left--the sacred duty that we have to preserve them and
not give them out to the world to people who know
nothing about their value, or what should be said or
not said.

Fry: Well, something like that needs to be gone over by
someone familiar with the Party first, I guess.

Paul: Yes, but if they get over to the congressional library
and these colored girls start--they will send everything
down and it's going to be in the manuscript department.
I remember when a man--maybe I told you this--came in
to see me who was writing the life of Jeannette Rankin,
did I tell you about that? And he came across a letter
from Mrs. Catt.

Fry: Oh, yes.

Paul: Well, we don't want that sort of thing to happen. If
Mrs. Miller has written a letter to somebody saying,
"Well, I think Miss Vernon is a not a very competent

Paul: person" (or something. She never would write such a
letter, but supposing something like that) such
injurious letters might happen to be left there by
chance. I think it is a dreadful thing.

Fry: Well, my experience at Belmont House last week was that
nothing is available to anybody, at least right now. I
couldn't even look at a copy of Irwin's book.

Paul: Well, maybe she didn't have one to show you.

Fry: Yes, she said she had several.

Paul: Well, why wouldn't she let you look at it?

Fry: She said she had no facilities to handle people like me
who come in wanting to see a copy of the Suffragist or
a book. I explained to her that I couldn't carry all
these things from Berkeley with me out here.

Paul: Did you tell her that you were coming up here?

Fry: No, I was trying to tape record Mabel Vernon in
Washington, which is what I told her I was about to do
at that time.

Paul: Well, that is absolutely outrageous!

Fry: There was just no way that I could come in and use
anything. So I don't think any materials are available,
right now at least.

Paul: Well, I am so afraid it is all going to go to the
congressional library; I am so terribly afraid of it.

Fry: Does she want to move that entire library over to the
Library of Congress?

Paul: No, she wants to take all these filing cases [of
papers], like my filing cases up here. I brought a
few up [to Connecticut] with me, which are my own
letters. If I had known what sort of person she was, I
would have brought them all up, while I had a chance.
I had a mover bring them up. It was very expensive,
but when I got this idea that she was going to put them
over in the congressional library and have them start
to sort and analyze and see what they'd keep and what
not, I was horrified. All my expressions of anxiety
didn't seem to have the slightest effect on her.

Paul: And then I thought it had; for a while I didn't
think she would do it. Then I got this telephone call
up here from Mrs. Butler Franklin, first vice-chairman,
and she said the subject was coming up and will you tell
me what you think we ought to do about it, and I told
her.

And so then she called me after the meeting and she
said, "Well, we voted to have a committee, and the
chairman of the committee is somebody who has never
been in our movement."

Fry: Oh, Chittick said to me that there was some professor,
a woman, who was going to take over the handling of
writing the history and get a grant to catalogue everything in the library. Maybe that's this person who's
head of the committee, do you think?

Paul: I don't know, but this was a woman, and Mrs. Franklin
said Mrs. Chittick seemed to have everything in hand
and know just what ought to be done. And she said this
was a wonderful arrangement she had made with the
congressional library, and "I am sure you will think so
too." Well, [laughing] I couldn't have thought so less,
but I didn't know what I could do way up here. The
meeting was over and they had voted it. They put it in
the hands of this unknown woman, totally unknown, I
don't know anything about her. She is chairman of the
committee to dispose of all our records, all our
tremendous effort through all these years is to be--

Fry: Well, I hope she doesn't dispose of anything that is
valuable.

Paul: Well, she will dispose of all the records. Records
are very valuable. Everything, she says, is now in
the hands of this woman. I hesitate to go down there.
I don't want to have a blow-up over it.

Fry: What had you given to to the Library of Congress before?
I remember going through quite a few boxes there.

Paul: I told you what we had given. At the end of the
suffrage campaign I told you this Miss Mary Fillbrook [sp?],
a lawyer and a member of the Daughters of the American
Revolution and very used to doing research, and one of
our own members. She was the one who opened the bar to
women in New Jersey. She was a young girl about nineteen
when she studied law in her father's office and then
wa ted t p   i e nd li vere t   r woman could

Paul: practice in New Jersey. So she went down, this young
        girl, and single-handed got the bill through to open the
        bar to women in New Jersey. She has always been a very
        good, wonderful feminist. (And she died recently too.)
        So at the end of the last world war or whenever it was
        that the Depression came, before the war or after the
        war--I have forgotten when it came [laughing].

Fry: Before World War II while you were in Europe.

Paul: Whenever it was, she told me that she couldn't really
        continue to practice in New Jersey because the Italians
        had taken over all northern New Jersey, and they had
        Italian judges, Italian court officials, and she said
        that first of all there is a prejudice against a woman,
        and then there is a prejudice against an American, and
        she said, "I can't get any case because the people trust
        me, but they know that when I go into court, I will have
        the court against me, against them." So she said, "I
        just can't get any cases." And so she said she was going
        to apply, if we approved, for a grant from this WPA,
        I think the thing was called, to catalogue all the
        records of the suffrage campaign.

        Well, we were very happy because I knew she would
        be the absolutely perfect person. Reliable and con-
        scientious, thorough and knowing everything about it,
        as much as I knew about the campaign; she would know
        everything. She would know what to be preserved and
        what to be discarded and how to classify it and so on.

        So she got the grant herself. She went forth and
        did it. The grant was for two years, if I remember
        rightly--this might not be correct, but it is my
        impression--and she was to employ as big a staff as
        she could on this amount of money they gave her. And
        I think--again I may be mistaken in the number but I
        think she employed twelve women, and she took the whole
        responsibility. We took one room in our headquarters
        and Mrs. Fillbrook had it wired all over with chicken
        wire so that nobody could possibly get in there to run
        off with any papers or anything. And there for about
        two years she worked. She had this staff, she directed
        the whole thing, and she saw exactly what they did, and
        then when it was finished we had an exhibit over in that
        great big lobby, you know in the front of the congressional
        library when you go up the steps, in that great big one.
        We had an exhibit of photographs from the beginning to
        the end of the suffrage campaign and of everything that
        made a good showing in the exhibit. Everything was

Paul: labeled by one of our members who was a librarian, a
very impressive exhibit I thought. So then the
congressional library asked if we would give all our
archives that Mrs. Fillbrook had gathered together of
the suffrage campaign to the congressional library.
And we said that we would <u>loan</u> them and we would be
grateful if they would protect them, because we didn't
have any paid librarian and we didn't have any fire-
proof building and we didn't feel we were as well
equipped as they were.

So they said all right, they would take it as a
loan. And every year they sent us a letter saying would
we like to convert it into a gift, and we would always
say no, we think we ought to keep title to these
possessions. (And we do.) And that we hope someday
that we could have a headquarters in which they could
be taken care of with a professional staff and so on.
We have had very good relationships with the Library.

Well now, building on that good relationship, she
is apparently trying to dispose of all the rest that
we have, just turn it over to them, not turn it over to
somebody who would do it for us.

And I wish very much, but I can't do anything with
her, that Mabel Vernon could be gotten to take a little
responsibility. We put her on this national board, and
while I am up here she could do everything that I could
do [there in Washington, things] I know she knows and
could do so well. But is she too old to do anything?

Fry: Well, it is hard for Mabel to get around.

Paul: I know, but when she does get around, can't she--I can't
see how she can let Mrs. Chittick do these terrible
things.

Fry: Mabel could do a lot by telephone, I think.

Paul: Or she could go up in a taxi. Consuelo always takes
her everywhere and helps her downstairs into a taxi,
helps her get over to our headquarters. And when I
came up here for the summer, that's the way it was
always, she came up quite often. But she couldn't have
come without Consuelo.

But I never could get Mabel to--I don't know why,
whether she has gotten too fatigued, or too bored by it,
or--I say, "Won't you do this, this is such a crisis,"

Paul: and so on. Just as if I had been in Washington, I
certainly would have done something about seeing that
you got that material. I can't see why Mabel wouldn't
do those things. She is on the board and can cast a
vote.

Fry: Well, she sees it as a very big problem. That's all I
know. Maybe if you called her--

Paul: She sees what as a problem?

Fry: Well, Miss Chittick.

Paul: I thought she was supporting Mrs. Chittick in every
way. She certainly was when I was down there. Of
course she doesn't like to--nobody else does either--
to get in any fight with anybody, but she is in a
position really to save our records.

Fry: Maybe if you call Mabel, it would help.

Paul: I had planned, you know, to go down to Philadelphia
and then I planned to go on to Washington. And then
when I discovered that I would have to pay $20 a day
to go into a hotel (I was afraid Mrs. Chittick wouldn't
allow me to [stay at] the headquarters), I thought
well, I will spend a lot of money and in that short
time I can't help Consuelo [with her audio-visual
history], which was my main purpose in going--I would
need more time, I was afraid. But I think maybe this
[recording we are doing] will do what she wants.

Fry: I hope so, yes, I think so.

Paul: I don't know what to make of Mrs. Chittick, really I
don't know what to make of her.

[Tape off.]

1915 - A YEAR OF FIELD WORK

Fry: In 1915, you were organizing a lot in the individual
         states, right?

Paul: Yes. And then we were making it all point up to the
         meeting in California, where we were going to concentrate
         on organizing as much support as we could from the women
         voters.

Fry: My notes here say, "On March 31 at an advisory council
         meeting Alice Paul announced plans to hold a convention
         in each state, and to elect a state chairman," and to
         make an organization in each state, and then send a
         delegate to San Francisco during the Panama-Pacific
         Exposition.

Paul: And that's what we did. You mean each suffrage state,
         it was.

Fry: Maybe so. Is that what it was, only each suffrage
         state?

Paul: Yes, I think so. Because we were concentrating on
         trying to get the women <u>voters</u> together, you see. Was
         this 1915? Yes, I am sure that is what it was.

Fry: Yes. Then in September you had the women voters'
         convention, in San Francisco. That must have been
         the suffrage states only.

Paul: Yes, that's what we were doing.

Fry: In the meantime you had had a couple more suffrage
         states come in in 1914, Nevada and Montana was it?

Paul: Yes, they both came in. They came in by state referendum.
         I don't really remember which year it was.

149

Fry: It was 1914.

Paul: In San Francisco--you know all about it from Sara Bard
          Field of course--we had this booth and so on, got up
          the big petition.

Fry: With Sara and--

Paul: She and Miss Joliffe were to carry it across the country
          [to Washington]. And Sara carried it [by car] with these
          two Swedish women; then Miss Joliffe came by train, I
          think. I think you ought to do this part extremely
          well because of the fact that you have done so much
          recording with Sara. She was such a big part of it.

Fry: I think it will be helpful to have Sara's manuscript
          deposited there with yours, so that both of them can be
          used together.

               I guess the only thing I wanted to ask you about
          1915, to complement what Sara has told, is how the idea
          ever came up of having women make a coast-to-coast
          automobile campaign in 1915?

Paul: Well, when we got this enormous petition, we wanted to
          get it to Washington and--I don't know much about an
          "idea"; it seems to me it would be a normal thing to
          think of.

Fry: You had had petitions brought to Washington before
          with--

Paul: This was the biggest one we'd ever had, and we wanted
          to get all the drama out of it we could.

Fry: And Mabel Vernon went ahead of them by train and--

Paul: She went ahead and arranged everything.

Fry: Each city.

Paul: Yes. Mabel has given you so much. Are we duplicating
          what she gave you?

Fry: No, not at all.

               There's one little note here. When Sara arrived
          in Washington there was a hearing before the House
          Judiciary Committee, with Congressman Taggert chastising
          you for your Democratic party opposition. Sara was

Fry: there and spoke; this was in late December, after Sara
        arrived. (That's the date on that Taggert tirade.)
        This was a hearing to get the bill reported out, and it
        was reported out and it was voted on in January and it
        lost in the House. That would be January of 1916. But
        it got a lot of debate on the floor of the house. Then--

Paul: I think you are doing this very thoroughly and very
        well, and I can't tell you how I rejoice over it.

Fry: Well, I am glad you are able to tie it all together
        like this. You can see how distorted it can be when we
        just take little bits and try to put them together. We
        still don't know what the full story is.

Paul: And how anybody at our national headquarters could
        refuse to cooperate with you is incredible!

Fry: Maybe I wasn't very good at explaining to her what I
        wanted, who I was, and what I was doing.

        I want to ask you some California questions. You
        had some problems along here with William Jennings
        Bryan.

Paul: When was that?

Fry: Well, in July, 1915 in California, William Jennings
        Bryan was there, and Sara had a conversation with him.
        He was just furious over the opposition from the Woman's
        Party.

Paul: Is that so?

Fry: Yes. And this is a marvelous conversation that is
        reported on page five of the July 17, 1915 Suffragist.

        Then there was another one. Sara was a leader of
        a four-hundred-woman deputation to Senator Phelan in
        California.

Paul: Senator who?

Fry: Senator James D. Phelan, a Democrat. I am kind of
        interested in whatever you can tell me of his attitude
        in this particular deputation. The Suffragist reports
        that he said that you shouldn't have campaigned against
        him just because he was on the Democratic side, and
        that you shouldn't go into other states to try to

Fry: influence elections. I think Charlotte Anita Whitney
        was head of that deputation to him. Sara was one of
        the other leaders. At any rate, can you tell me
        anything about Phelan's attitude?

Paul: No, I don't remember anything. Of course he wasn't
        ever any conspicuous person in our campaign.

Fry: I noticed that Joe Knowland, who is another Californian,
        made a marvelous speech on your behalf a couple of
        years before this, when he was in Congress.

Paul: That was later on, of course.

Fry: No, that was _before_, when he was in Congress, I think.

Paul: Yes. Senator Knowland I don't think was there in the
        suffrage days, was he?

Fry: This wasn't Senator Bill Knowland; I meant Congressman
        Knowland, Joe, the father. He was in one of his last
        terms in the House when he made this statement. He was
        a Republican, incidentally.

Paul: I think this will be so valuable too for things like
        this that you bring in. All the people who were
        associated in any way with these individual congressmen
        will be so interested in this.

Fry: We are always interested in California's congressmen
        and any new information we can get on them to round out
        their papers. [Pause.] Well, we will go breezing on
        into 1916 then. In April--

Paul: Of course, that was one of the very big things that we
        did, this women voters [convention] and having that
        booth and getting that petition presented with such
        an enormous number of people.

Fry: How do you rate what that accomplished?

Paul: Well, I think it accomplished everything we wanted.
        It was one of the big outstanding things I think that
        we did. The first convention ever held by women
        voters, you see. And getting them as far as we could
        get them lined up _for_ this policy opposing the party
        in power as long as it continued to oppose us. And then
        getting it dramatized by going across the country so
        the whole world--the whole country would know about it.
        I think it was very effective and very useful.

1916: THE NATIONAL WOMAN'S PARTY IS FORMED

Working for the Endorsement from the Democrats, Republicans, and Progressives

Fry: Well, you followed that up in April of 1916 with that big meeting--

Paul: That's the one in Chicago.

Fry: Not yet, I don't believe. [Reading.] This was the conference on April 8 and 9 in Washington that included members of an advisory committee representing thirty-six unenfranchised states. And the Congressional Union was "ready to undertake its most pretentious election campaign" and Alice Paul called for "an independent political party." There was a big procession connected with all of this gathering of women too. (I'm sure you never missed a chance to have a procession.)

Paul: That's when we decided to have what we called a National Woman's Party. Is that it?

Fry: Yes, I think so. And then you held your big gathering of the women--just before the other parties' conventions.

Paul: In Chicago [June 5-6-7, 1916]. But you see, it was made up only of women who could vote, and we elected Mrs. Anne Martin president in Chicago.

Fry: And you had a train that went from the East to the West to invite everybody, around the end of April. It went all around the suffrage states.

Paul: Well, we had three special trains. One was the Suffrage Special, we called it, and it went all around the country. Then we followed it later by one called the Prison Special, where all the people who went were

Paul: ex-prisoners.

Fry: That was not in this campaign though; that was later.

Paul: Later yes, that's right.

But you see at that meeting at Chicago we voted to carry this campaign in the coming election into all the states where women were voting. Just concentrate on that.

Fry: As you had done in 1914?

Paul: Only we did it on a much bigger scale.

Fry: Bigger because you had more <u>states</u>, or because you used more women?

Paul: No, bigger because we had just grown stronger. We had more women we could send out to campaigns, we had--we started off with this big convention in Chicago. Mrs. Belmont, I remember, got up and pledged, I think it was $50,000--the <u>Suffragist</u> will tell what it was--to defeat every Democrat. She didn't actually give the money later on. I don't know what happened to her. But she often--We got to know her through the years. She was very often full of enthusiasm and said, "I'll pay for this"--you know there are lots of people like that--and then when the time comes, they think, well, they guess they'd rather not. [Laughter.] So she didn't give us anything like $50,000 but I think anyway she got up and announced it at this great big meeting, do you have a Blackstone Theater, or something like that in Chicago?

Fry: Yes. That's right.

Paul: In Chicago. And that's where we had all these men come from the different parties and say what they would do.

Fry: Oh, yes. Now tell about that.

Paul: It's all there in the <u>Suffragist</u>. You can look through it.

Fry: You had the candidates coming to <u>you</u>. All the <u>Suffragist</u> says is that representatives from each party did come and did try to woo you to their cause and their party.

Paul: And I remember particularly well Dudley Field Malone,

Paul: who came for the Democrats. First time we had ever met
him. And he was of course an eloquent speaker. And he
became absolutely furious, [laughing] furious that we
would dream of opposing the Democrats. And he wasn't
able to give any real satisfactory pledge that they
would help us.

I think we had everybody come, every party.

Theodore Roosevelt

Paul: And at that time I think the Roosevelt party, which had
dwindled to a very little one, gave us an endorsement,
and the Prohibition party, and the Socialist party.

Fry: Yes, I have here that even before this happened, I
think about in May, Teddy Roosevelt announced in favor
of the suffrage movement.

Paul: Yes, but then at this time, his party did.

Fry: I thought maybe you would know what brought Roosevelt
around or who brought him around.

Paul: What date are you on now?

Fry: Well, this was in May just before you met in Chicago
in June for your first national convention.

Paul: There was a suffrage meeting held in New York--not by
us, I don't know who, but probably by Mrs. Blatch's
society, but some suffrage meeting--and I went up to it
just to be present, and Mr. Roosevelt was supposed to
be the principal speaker. I remember going with Mrs.
Lawrence Lewis, our national treasurer, after the
meeting was over, around up to the platform to thank
Mr. Roosevelt for the wonderful speech he'd made for
suffrage. Now perhaps that's the time that you have
that he came out.

Fry: Oh, may be.

Paul: But he did. Then I remember that we always regarded
him as an ally, always. And I think that this meeting
out in Chicago when his party--no, he had two conventions, the first one in 1912 when they formed this
Bull Moose Party, and I think that was the one when he

Paul: ran against Wilson and Wilson got in because there were so many candidates; the Republicans were divided between Roosevelt and whoever the other candidate was.

Fry: Taft.

Paul: I guess so. So then, he wasn't deeply interested but we regarded him as a friend. And when Hughes was finally nominated for the Republicans at that convention you know in Chicago [in 1916], we tried of course to get every candidate to come out--just as we tried this year to get McGovern--we're [laughing] still doing the same old thing.

Well, we couldn't get Hughes. Miss Alice Carpenter was one of the leading Republican women in New York and a personal friend of Roosevelt, and whom I had asked to try to get Roosevelt to use his influence with Hughes. We were getting everybody to go to Hughes to say, "Don't be such a fool. Do come out for this measure," and so on. So Miss Carpenter said, "I think that we had better go out and see Mr. Roosevelt," and she said, "I know him and I know he will make an appointment to see me, and if you will come along with me, because you perhaps know more about what's going on." So I said I would.

So we went out together to Oyster Bay and made an appointment to see him. I remember this so vividly. So when we went in he was all alone waiting for us, in a sort of library, I guess it was.

He said, "Well now, the great trouble is, in politics, that people don't seem ever to quite master this thought, that you not only have to be right, but you have to be right in time." And he said, "Hughes is undoubtedly some day going to come out for this measure. I don't think I can get him to come out now; he has to consider so much and take so long. He just hasn't mastered the idea if he should be president--he thinks this is right, apparently--that he must be right in time and let the world know." So he said, "I don't know whether I can do one single thing with him, but of course I think you are on the right track," and so on.

So then Mr. Hughes started on his campaign across the country. We had sent quite a good many delegations to Hughes himself and he was always saying this would require quite a lot of thought, and the idea of the state referendums and everything had to be carefully weighed and so on. So nobody had ever been able to get

Paul: him to say anything. So he started on his campaign,
and he first spoke in Wyoming, the first suffrage state.
He wouldn't commit himself in any way on the subject
of the Amendment.

And then he went on through the suffrage states,
down through California and so on, never committing
himself at all on the suffrage amendment in spite of
constant requests sent to him.

When he got back to New York, where they did not
have the vote, then, in a great speech that he made, his
final speech, he came out for the suffrage amendment.
It was just a perfect example of doing what Roosevelt
had said he would do. If he had timed himself to be
for it in all those suffrage states, he would have won
so much more support, and if he had kept silent, if he
had to keep silent, in New York--it was not a popular
measure there at that time--he would have been much
wiser.

So he finally did come out.

Fry: The Woman's Party had a hearing also before the resolutions
committee of each national party, to try to get the
Amendment in the party platforms.

Paul: Yes, we did.

Fry: For the first time, suffrage was put in party platforms,
although not the constitutional amendment. Can you tell
anything about what went on in those hearings?

Paul: Yes, I have already, I think, told you about that.

This was 1916, and when you were telling me that
the National American had rescinded its support of the
[rival] Shafroth-Palmer [bill], and I said it is hard
for me to believe that they did that in 1915 because I
can remember the tremendous opposition to us when we
asked for the federal suffrage amendment at this hearing
in Chicago.

I told you all that before.

Fry: Would you mind repeating it now?

Paul: Do you remember anything about what I told you?

Fry: Mmm--

Paul: Don't you _remember_ what I told you?

Fry: [Laughing.] I remember. But I want you to tell it to me as though I don't so I can get it all down on tape.

Paul: All right. As I said, I would have to look this up and see about that rescinding of the support of the Shafroth-Palmer bill, because when we went in 1916 to Chicago there seemed to be the greatest schism in there between the people who were working for the Shafroth-Palmer and the people who were working for the Susan B. Anthony Amendment.

Then to show you how it was, I said that we wanted to get first of all a headquarters to work from, and I appointed a Miss Sarah Chapman--

[End of Tape 4, Side B]

[Tape 5, Side A]

Paul: I had asked Miss Chapman to go out and find a head-quarters for us. At that time the different stores were giving their show windows to different groups of women, I suppose helping them in advertising, they thought. So Miss Chapman secured a shop in a very good location, with big show windows, and we were to have that for our headquarters throughout this campaign with the Republican and Democratic and all the other candidates.

Fry: [Labelling tape.]

Paul: Are you listening to me?

Fry: Yes! I am.

Paul: So then in a short time we received word from the owners of this business house that had the show windows that they had learned that we were not a group in good standing and so on, and that they were withdrawing their offer of the headquarters. So then we had to go forth and get another, which we did.

The chairman of the whole group out there that were getting up a parade through the streets of Chicago asked us to come in and join with them. They said they would like very much to have us do so because we had been getting up a lot of things with lots of people, and they thought we could help them. So we said we would be delighted to, and I went over to see her and

Paul: told her that what we always carried in our processions was "We demand an Amendment to the United States Constitution Enfranchising Women"--remember? I told you all this.

She said, "Oh well then, we won't <u>allow</u> you to come in our procession because we couldn't possibly, <u>possibly</u> put such a banner as that up. We are just saying that we believe in suffrage and we are asking the party to come out for suffrage for women."

So then we didn't go, and they went alone. A day of terrible storms.

Then they went in and we went in, separately, to the platform committee: two different groups with two different amendments. I am not sure exactly what they did get. They may have gotten an expression of approval of suffrage, I guess--maybe they did by that time. They did not get anything about, and we did not get anything for the suffrage amendment. So we were two groups. They were refusing to let us walk with them if we mentioned this enfranchisement of women by a federal suffrage amendment.

So it seems to me it is very hard to understand how they could nationally be taking this stand against any mention of this subject [the federal amendment]. And they didn't mention it at all in their presentation to the committees. But we did. I think we got only the Socialist, Prohibition, and the third party, Roosevelt's party--

Fry: Progressive.

Paul: But I remember later on in Congress, before Mrs. St. George became our leader for the Equal Rights Amendment, the congressman who had been leading the fight for [our Equal Rights Amendment] died or was defeated--was no longer there. So we had to get a new leader. I remember going to see Congressman [John Marshall] Robsion of Kentucky, a Republican, and asking him if he would become our chief sponsor. I remember his saying to me, "Well, you perhaps don't remember me but I remember you very well. I was on that platform committee in Chicago in 1916, and I remember you all coming in bedraggled, wanting to have the suffrage amendment before Congress approved by our platform committee. And we didn't approve it." But he said, "It made a very deep impression on me, and I am personally supporting it and I will

Paul: be glad to be your chief sponsor."

So I remember these very, very well--that hearing that we had there. Again it was the two groups of women, [and one] still asking for the Shafroth-Palmer as far as I could see, and [one] asking for the full amendment.

Fry: Well, at least suffrage did become a part of the platform in each of the major parties.

Paul: Just general suffrage, but not the federal suffrage amendment.

Fry: I think that was the first time that any kind of suffrage had been mentioned, but I wondered if it was more the National American's idea. I copied down what the Resolutions Committee of the Democrats said. Let's see, the Democrats recommended "the extension of the franchise to the women of the country by the states upon the same terms as men."

Paul: Yes, that's the state referendum.

Fry: And the Republicans said "Each state is to settle this question for itself."

Paul: You see, that was the position that the National American was taking.

So after all those years of Miss Anthony going to these conventions and so on, and working all by herself-- you see, it made me feel very sad to think that the women themselves would consent to work against themselves, but they did.

Now, what's the next question?

Fry: Well, I have that Wilson is still standing on states' rights and--

Paul: Yes, he was.

Fry: --he spoke to the Atlantic City convention of NAWSA. I think that was some time in the summer, when he spoke to them. And I wondered if this made hearts sink in the National Woman's Party?

Paul: Well, that was his position. There was not anything unusual about that. It wasn't very much of an event.

Paul: That's what he always said.

Fry: Then on August 10, 11, and 12--

Paul: You see, the thing that was bad about it all was that a suffrage organization that had had the tradition of working for many many years, before we were even born, for this federal suffrage amendment, that they would have at their national convention an address by a person who said he was against it! It gave support to our not getting it.

Fry: And just further divided everyone, I guess.

The Campaign, 1916

Fry: It looks like you had a planning conference at Colorado Springs. This was August 10, 11, 12, and again--

Paul: What year was that?

Fry: That's in the same campaign, 1916. You had representatives of the Republican and Democratic parties come to plead with you there. That's where you planned your big campaign and the organizers' work and so forth.

Paul: No, no, no. It wasn't. We planned all that up in Chicago.

Fry: Oh. Well, it says that there you were going to plan the protest campaign against the Democrats.

Paul: Well, maybe the protest campaign for Colorado. We had planned the protest campaign against the Democrats up in Chicago, when we elected Anne Martin to be the president of the National Woman's Party, made up only of women from the suffrage states.

Fry: Except that was before you definitely had word that the Democrats were not going to include it in their platform that year. You didn't know that until after you had your convention.

Paul: Well, I wouldn't say that. We knew when we went out there. The person who came to speak for the Democrats-- I told you how Dudley Field Malone who afterwards married Doris Stevens, stood there and argued on that

Paul: platform, I remember, until finally I guess the people who owned the hotel or the hall came and put down the curtain to send him home. He was in such a towering rage. When Mrs. Belmont got up and pledged $50,000 to defeat the Democrats, there was never any doubt in our minds up to that moment they were opposing us. The person they sent couldn't say anything that they were going to change their policy. That was the reason he was so angry. I don't see what we would do out in--I remember very well that meeting out in Colorado, but it was totally different from what you say.

Fry: Maybe it was just for Colorado then.

Paul: That was the meeting. I was there at that meeting. What date was it again?

Fry: August 10 to 12.

Paul: I remember that Hazel Hunkins--and I have told you about her over in Europe, I think, and how I went up with her to see Jeannette Rankin--this girl from Montana--to try to get Jeannette Rankin to vote against war, just unofficially, from ourselves. We had never seen her, but she came down from Montana. In fact you can probably find all this out in the Katzenstein book because Miss Katzenstein had gone out as our organizer to Montana in that campaign, and she had gotten this Hazel Hunkins interested. When we had our meeting down in Colorado Springs, Hazel came down. First time we ever met her.

She wanted to throw in her life work with us, which she did. She went on with us down to Washington and remained one of our workers until suffrage was won, and went to prison with us. We have some pictures of her heading the suffrage procession; she was going out to the White House to picket. She was a very lovely girl.

I don't remember it as being anything but just one of the organizing meetings that we had there. It certainly wasn't going to plan our policy because our policy had been planned and we had elected a committee headed by Miss Martin to carry it out.

Fry: So, in the big 1916 campaign, everybody went out and pitched in in the suffrage states, but we need a picture of how this was organized and how you--

Paul: Yes, it was all organized from Chicago,* and I was there
and stayed through the whole campaign organizing it. I
didn't go into any of the states, except I did go down
to Colorado for that meeting. For instance, in Chicago,
we had a big banner across the street: "Vote Against
the Democratic Party," and so on (I don't know exactly
what it said, but that was its idea) because they were
against the enfranchisement of women was the idea. And
we did it in all the states, had these big banners,
because we had so little time and money, and one great
banner gave your message pretty well to each big city.
We had somebody in every one of these suffrage states.
We usually sent two or three together.

We did just the ordinary things you always do. For
instance in Chicago I remember that the person named
Matilda Hall Gardner, who came from Chicago, came out
to help us. Her husband was the NEA representative in--
you know what the NEA is? National Enterprise--a great
newspaper [association].

Fry: Oh, yes. The newspaper association.

Paul: Well, her husband was the head of the NEA bureau in
Washington. She came to Chicago to help because she had
grown up in Chicago and knew a great many people there.
She took over, I remember, the question of getting up
parlor meetings, and she had little parlor meetings
every day practically to which we would send somebody
to speak trying to turn votes in that little district.
We just did the way anybody conducts a campaign. The
way the Republicans did and the Democrats did--only they
did it on a bigger and vaster scale than we were able
to do.

Then we took deputations.

Fry: To candidates?

Paul: [Pause.] I don't know whether any candidates came or
not, but if they did we would take deputations to them.
We had a great many street meetings in Chicago. We just
tried to put the question on the map and turn as many
women as we could. I remember one woman--you perhaps
know who she is and know her. She died two or three
years ago. Mrs. Avery Coonley. Did you ever know her?

Fry: No.

Paul: She and her sister were very wealthy women who had

*See Appendix Table of Contents.

Paul: inherited quite a fortune from their father, who came from Michigan. They were very public spirited. For instance, they gave the alumni house at Vassar, gave the whole building. They did a great many things. Her husband was in charge of the information service for the Christian Science Church. She was a very devout Christian Scientist, and somehow or other Elsie Hill had gotten to know her, I don't remember how. Elsie Hill was out there in Chicago with me, just speaking all the time. Of course she was a very good speaker, just never ended speaking. We were trying to change votes, as many votes as we could. We had a very prominent woman as our state chairman out there in Chicago and Mrs. Julius Rosenwald--did you ever hear of them?

Fry: Yes.

Paul: She went on our board out there. And I remember that simplified everything for us because anything that we would want, almost, by using Mrs. Rosenwald's name, it made it much easier for us to get. For instance, we didn't have to establish a big bank account or anything, because they knew Mrs. Rosenwald was on our board. It helped us a great deal. So we got very influential women out there in Chicago, I think, to help.

But, among others, Elsie Hill got to know Mrs. Avery Coonley, who was interested in progressive education and had started a kind of a school out there which she financed. Elsie, I guess, was interested in that and got to know her that way. Probably she got to know her through Vassar because they were both Vassar graduates.

She took me one day out to see Mrs. Coonley. We thought she would have a big circle, and if we would get these prominent women, each one would have a big circle, and it might be an easier way to get votes for what we wanted. I remember asking her if she wouldn't just not vote for Wilson, and not vote for any Democrats. She said she would have to think about this and so on. Anyway from that interview she became a warm friend and continued until her death.

I went out after the campaign was over (and Wilson had been reelected, of course; that's when we had all this campaign to get Hughes and didn't succeed) I went to see her to ask her for money then. I remember she gave about $750 or something. She said, "Now I want you to go to my sister, Mrs. Hooker, because we try to

Paul: make our gifts together, and if she knows I have given to the Woman's Party she will give to the Woman's Party. Probably the same amount."

So I said, "How did you vote?" She said, "I voted just as you asked me to vote. I voted for the prohibition ticket, all the way down the line." So we knew we were turning a great many votes. I don't--I suppose you were too young to know anything about the campaign when it came to California.

Fry: I have read about it.

Paul: Well, I think that's all I know about it.

Fry: Something kind of intrigued me, and I don't know whether you can throw any light on this or not, but according to the *Suffragist*, you had a very good kind of reporting system set up so that you were able to warn certain Republicans when you felt they were going to lose in certain districts in the West. The *Suffragist* intimates that you kind of established a reputation for knowing what the political winds were in each district around the West.

Paul: Well of course we did. We had to.

Fry: --That you had a better system operating than either major political party did.

Paul: Well, I don't know about that, but we always had in every state a group of women who kept us informed of what the situation was. You see, most of these men in the suffrage states all--in fact it was unanimous among them to support the federal suffrage amendment. So we were not out [to elect Republicans]. We were out to defeat all Democrats because they had caucused and were in power and could do it and wouldn't do it. But we were not out of course to elect Republicans. We didn't go out to do that, go out to do any party. We didn't care whether they voted like Mrs. Coonley, whether they voted Prohibition, Socialist, or Republican, whatever they wanted, [as long as it wasn't Democratic].

I have always thought it was one of the most powerful instruments that we could find and that we did use to change the Democratic party and change President Wilson, because of course, you know, it wasn't so long after that that he did change.

Fry: Yes, and Vance McCormick was the man who was chairman
of the Democratic party for that campaign. I believe
that after the campaign was over, he made a public
statement that by the next election, in 1918, the weak
places in the Democratic party must be patched up. One
of the weak places, he said, was suffrage, and the
Democrats should be doing something about suffrage
before then. Do you remember that?

Paul: No, but I am glad to know it. [Laughter.]

Fry: In your own evaluation, do you feel you were more
successful in your 1916 efforts than you had been in
your 1914 efforts?

Paul: Well, of course; we did it on a much bigger scale. We
had ourselves become much larger, stronger. We had
more women to go out to the different states. We tried
to send somebody, and I guess we did send somebody, from
Washington to every state. Those people who went in
with nothing to do but defeat the Democrats, could
accomplish more than getting some local committee [made
up of local people] that were doing like myself [now]--
having storm windows put on [laughing] and being diverted
by everything else.

Fry: Oh, I see. It really worked better if you sent someone
out into the state.

Paul: That's the reason we always did.

Fry: I should think that you also stood the chance of a local
person getting diverted into another campaign that was
going on there.

Paul: By sending somebody out, she had the one task of--if
there wasn't a good local committee--building it up
and guiding them. The whole thing, I think, worked
very well.

1917: THE FINAL PHASE BEGINS

Suffrage Banner Sneaked into Congress

Fry: Then the President took office. Did you have any doubt
         that he was going to omit the Amendment again from his
         address to Congress--as he did?

Paul: That would be 1916. We took it for granted he would.
         He had never changed his position that we knew of, at
         that time.

Fry: That was when Mabel unfurled her banner from the congres-
         sional gallery. In the middle of his address.

Paul: No. She unfurled that banner, as I remember, on a
         speech that he was making for the, I think it was the
         Puerto Ricans or some group.

Fry: You are right in that it <u>was</u> his message to Congress on
         what he wanted to do with legislation for that year, in
         January of 1917. Wilson had gone on eloquently about
         the suffrage that had been granted and the freedom given
         to the Philippines--meaning Filipino men.

Paul: Seemed to me--was this Filipinos? I thought it was
         Puerto Ricans or somebody.

Fry: Filipinos. And that was the moment that Mabel chose
         to unfurl her large banner from the balcony, which she
         has told me about in her interview.

Paul: Yes. There were others there, you know. It wasn't
         just Mabel.

Fry: Yes, there were five.

Paul: The way we got it done was through Mrs. Elizabeth Rogers,

Paul: the one I have told you so much about. Mrs. Rogers'
husband was the greatest authority probably in the
United States on goiters; I guess you know that.
People went from all over the country to him. We have
her painting now on the wall in the headquarters.

Fry: How did she help with this?

Paul: When she was a young and very beautiful girl apparently,
the daughter, I think, of a judge, anyway an eminent,
distinguished lawyer up in New Haven, and Dr. Rogers was
a medical student there, they became engaged to be
married. Suddenly she developed a goiter, and so he
said that he was going to devote all his time [to this]
because she would no longer marry him. She said, "A
goiter is incurable and I am not going to be your wife
and have this disfigurement," and also it had other
effects I guess on your body. So she said she wouldn't
marry him. And he said, "Well then, I am going to drop
everything else and find out how to cure goiters."

So he concentrated as a young medical student, and
he did discover a cure for goiters, which was the first
time it ever happened. So he cured Mrs. Rogers, and
she became his bride after that and married him. He
therefore, having for his own interest in curing Mrs.
Rogers, become an authority in this field of not only
goiters but everything connected with the thyroid and
so on, and so people came from all over the country.

I nearly always stayed with Mrs. Rogers when I went
up to New York instead of going to a hotel. She always
invited me to come, and to save expense I always went.
And also because I wanted to always be with her as much
as possible. And I remember when I would go in the front
door--it was one of the houses in New York where you have
on the ground floor your dining room, then a steep
stairway and then upstairs, sort of living quarters.
Well, I would walk up the stairs and it was almost
impossible to walk up because every single step was
covered by women seated there or men seated there
waiting to see Dr. Rogers because of their thyroid or
glands or something.

And finally, it got to be so that he would never
make an appointment. He took anybody who came and he
charged them all the same--I think $2 a visit. It was
almost a miracle the way they were cured. I remember
so vividly when I would go up. Mrs. Rogers, I would
find had [finally] been driven up to the top floor of

Paul: this big house--the only place she could sit or receive her friends anywhere, because the whole second floor, where he had his office was just filled with some more of these people.

Then he would never send a bill. But he had a secretary. Mrs. Rogers and the secretary together would contrive to send out the $2 bills to people. He was just a marvelous man in being unselfish--completely unselfish type, I thought.

So one day I happened to be there when this occurred: He came in and he told us--at the dining room table, all of us--that one of his Yale classmates had brought his wife to see him that day, and this Yale classmate had a wife who had shingles. Do you know what shingles are?

Fry: It's a rash, isn't it?

Paul: Something that goes all around your waist, I think. And [his classmate] was a member of Congress, and he was a very wealthy man, so he had taken his wife to Austria and all places in the world where they were supposed to be great experts on health measures to try to have the shingles cured. (It goes all the way around and I don't know what consequences it has.) He never could get any relief for his wife. [The congressman] said that people had been saying to him, "Why don't you take your wife to Dr. Rogers, why do you go all over the world?" And he said, "Dr. Rogers? I never would go to him; I was on the crew with him in Yale. He doesn't know one single thing about it. This man, all he could do was to be a good person in our Yale races," and so on. Finally, when he grew so desperate (and his wife was always getting worse and he was definitely very devoted to her) he said all right, he would swallow his prejudice against his fellow crewmate and go and see him. So Dr. Rogers told me that this day he has come with this wife.

And he said, "I saw in a minute what was the matter with her. It was very simple. I knew exactly what to do. I gave her some pills to take," and he said, "The whole thing disappeared; she is completely cured. There was no reason at all for all these years of hesitation. Very simple to anybody who is familiar now with all these glands."

So then this man talked to Mrs. Rogers and said, "You know, Dr. Rogers won't allow me to pay him anything.

Paul: and I <u>can</u>, because the only thing I have is quite a
good deal of money. I would like to pay him. He won't
allow me to give him a single ten-cent piece, and I
feel so indebted. This has transformed our lives, what
he has done for us." And he said, "If you ever need
anything in Congress, come to me. No matter what it is,
I will get it done for you because it will be a little
way I might repay Dr. Rogers."

So [later], when we decided we would have a banner
put out, when we knew this--you say Filippinos, whoever
it was--was going to come up, we could point out that
he was so solicitous for equality for other people and
not for people at home--just the same way we did when
we were burning his words, you know, later on. So Mrs.
Rogers said, "Now I think I have never asked Mr. So-and-
so for anything," this congressman, and she said it
was an impossible time to get a ticket to the gallery;
it always was these times the President spoke. There
were only a few tickets and they were given out to the
wives and so on and the diplomats. You couldn't. I've
never gotten a ticket; I've never <u>asked</u> for one because
I didn't like to be under obligation to anybody; but I
have never gotten a ticket to anything since I first
went up to Congress; to this day I have never gotten a
ticket. And we knew it was almost impossible. Mrs.
Rogers knew it was almost impossible.

So when we planned this idea of dropping the banner
on this subject, she said, "Now I will see if I <u>can</u> get
the tickets." So she wrote to this [congressman] and
asked him, since he told her always to ask for anything
that she wanted. She said, "One thing I would like to
do would be to have a ticket for myself and some of my
friends to go in for this opening speech of the President,"
on--you say Philippines--whatever it was [laughing]. So
she got the tickets and she came down to Washington with
the tickets, and so she gave one ticket to Miss Vernon,
apparently. I didn't remember whom she did give them
to. But she kept one ticket for herself. A little
group of four or five I think went in with their banners
concealed somewhere about their person. And then when
this moment came, I think they all put out their banners.
Or one long banner.

Fry: It was one big banner which Mabel laid down at their
feet once they got in, Mabel said.

Paul: Yes, I think they all put down the same banner.

Fry: And they all had a string then that they held it by.

Paul: So anyway Mrs. Rogers--it's not that I don't think Mabel did everything, because she undoubtedly did--but I just remember Mrs. Rogers then because that was the end that I was familiar with, of getting them in. And so they did. And then they were all asked to leave, as you know.

But it was very effective, very effective, written up in the papers, and I thought it was a very effective thing to do. But it was all due to this curing [laughing]. It couldn't have been done if we couldn't have gotten the banner in, and couldn't have gotten in--I don't know that we could have gotten in if it hadn't have been for this man's feeling of obligation to Dr. Rogers.

Fry: And that was just a little while before your picketing began.

The Death and Memorial of Inez Milholland

Fry: Now in the meantime you had the Inez Milholland memorial service.

Paul: Yes, and you know all about that I am sure.

Fry: You brought Sara Bard Field out from the West Coast to give a speech there.

Paul: No, we brought Sara for the presentation of the statues at the end of the campaign. I told you about the statues, do you remember, this morning.

Fry: Yes, she came out for that too. Okay, maybe she didn't come out for the Inez Milholland memorial service.*

Paul: No, she didn't, because the principal speech was made by Maud Younger. I remember this Mr. Gallagher (who interviewed me last week) said, "Well, I read that you told somebody that the way to speak was to read Lincoln's Gettysburg Address and then make the same kind of a

---

*Field's speech was the presentation of the memorial resolution to President Wilson following the service for I· · ꞓ ·. ·· ı.

Paul: speech." And I remembered it too. It was what I told Maud Younger when she said, "I don't know how I can speak in this tribute to Inez Milholland, or what to say." And so I remember she was the person who made the speech there.

Fry: We haven't mentioned Inez Milholland and her work on that 1916 campaign, or any of her other work.

Paul: Yes, do you want me to? I think I told you about it the other night. [Tape recorder not turned on then.]

Fry: Yes, you did. Of course there is quite a lot written about her as a result of her death. So you don't have to say very much now.

Paul: I will tell it if you want me to.

She had graduated, you know, from Vassar, and she'd become well-known because she was the person who organized this meeting in the [adjoining] graveyard at Vassar when the [college] president forbade--called her before him and told her that the board of trustees were not willing to have the college have this suffrage meeting. So then she got the same group she had gathered for the meeting (and who had arranged to have three speakers come) and took them out to the wall outside the college which separated the college from the graveyard. They all hopped over this wall, you may remember, and I don't know how she got her speakers in, but she got her speakers there too, somehow or other. So they held this meeting. It was such good publicity that people sort of remembered Inez Milholland as a result.

She then--I suppose she was about twenty-eight or something like that and she was already married and she had already studied law. She tried to study law at Yale and various good places, but they wouldn't take her because she was a woman. So she went to New York University, which then didn't have much of a reputation, and got a law degree there. Then she offered to come into our campaign, and she rode at the head of some of our processions, one at least. We have this photograph on many of our letterheads, you know, of her in that procession.

Fry: On the horse?

Paul: Yes.

Paul: She offered to go over the country and try to arouse women to vote against the Democrats, and her father, Don Milholland, didn't want her to go alone, so he said, "Well, I will pay all the expenses of my other daughter, Vida, and have her accompany Inez." Vida had a very beautiful voice, so it was arranged that she would sing suffrage songs or things related to it at every meeting and then Inez would appeal to people not to vote for the Democrats.

    I remember that she said to me, "I want to make one condition: at every meeting, I am the only speaker. The reason is that I am very timid and have no self-confidence and I think maybe I could appeal to women and get them to change their votes. But if there were another speaker there, I know myself that I won't be able to open my mouth. I will think she is so much better a speaker so I will say to her, "You go ahead and speak." I know that I can't do it unless I am left alone and I will _have_ to do it."

    So she started out and, I think, was very effective. The meetings, it seemed to me, were _very_ effective as far as we could hear. She was an _extra_ beautiful girl and _extra_, sort of, well [pause] she just was so _beaming_ with her belief in what she was doing. So extremely sincere. And she was doing it against quite a great deal of personal diffidence, as she said. So as the meetings went on, one by one by one, they seemed to me to be bringing in very good results. And then when she got to this meeting in Los Angeles and was speaking, she just fell to the floor and collapsed and she never regained consciousness. You know all that.

Fry: I didn't know that she never regained consciousness.

Paul: Nobody ever spoke to her or heard anything from her since.

Fry: Was it a stroke?

Paul: Well, I don't know whether you can have a stroke when you are twenty-eight, can you?

Fry: I don't know.

Paul: What the doctors out there said was that she had pernicious anemia and that she had not known she had it, and she had worked so extremely hard and just worn herself out and--it wasn't a stroke; it might have been

Paul: a heart attack--they said it was caused by pernicious
       anemia, whatever it was. So they sent her body back in
       a coffin to New York, because she was buried up at her
       family home up at Westport, New York.

       And then immediately, in a very short time, in about
       a week--we got up this memorial meeting in the capitol
       and sent a message from the memorial meeting to Presi-
       dent Wilson urging that no more sacrifices like this be
       made necessary in the effort to get the enfranchisement
       of women. And Mrs. William Kent offered the resolution,
       which was good because she was a congressman's wife.
       We had the ceremony up in the Statuary Hall, and then
       she took it down with a delegation to the President.*
       [Inez Milholland] was one of the very wonderful women
       we had. Very tragic to lose her so young and so soon.
       On her first speaking trip.

       Well, now what's the next one you have to ask?

Fry: It seems that Wilson's response was another one of "I
       can't as the leader of my party do anything that my
       party doesn't want me to do or take any stand that my
       party doesn't want me to take." The accounts I read
       emphasize the extreme disappointment of the women after
       this meeting as they filed back across the street to
       suffrage headquarters. They were gloomy and rather
       silent. Do you remember?

Paul: The only thing that I remember was that somewhere along
       there, I don't know which day, but somewhere along in
       this time--he said that he had received so many delegations
       and they said the same thing and he said the same thing
       and he now had the great world responsibilities because
       of the threat of war and he couldn't see any more delega-
       tions. That's my recollection. And so we then said,
       "All right, we will send this perpetual delegation. And
       you won't have to see it; we will just hold up banners
       reminding you."

_____

*Sara Bard Field's address to the President is on p. 192,
Irwin.

The Decision to Picket the White House

Fry: At the meeting that was scheduled to be held at your headquarters right after their deputation to Wilson, was it a new decision then to start the picketing, the direct result of Wilson's response to your delegation? [January 9, 1917.]

Paul: No, I think it was the general situation of not being able to go with any more delegations to him. That he had announced. I don't know when he announced it but somewhere around that period. I always supposed it was because he was getting so involved. There was a very great threat of war, you know, and we might get in it, and it seemed very natural.

        We had quite a long discussion--I guess many days and weeks, maybe--before we decided to start any pickets. When you start you have to be prepared to come through for a long time or it is ineffective. So we finally decided to do it. Then we started it, whatever day we did start it, in January--[January 10, 1917.]

Fry: Do you remember anything about the pros and cons of picketing that were discussed at the time?

Paul: No, I don't. I think that just as if you and I should decide whether we should go out and picket somebody today, it would be about the same thing. Would it be useful? Would it be possible to carry it out? Could we get enough people to carry it out--because you can't possibly do anything effectively unless you have it over a long stretch; we knew that. I don't know. Women volunteered to go right away. You see it is like everything when you mull over what will you do. I think it is always the same. There are lots of pros and cons on any step that you take.

Jeannette Rankin Votes Against War

Fry: Then in April, war was declared.

Paul: Yes, April 7.

Fry: Could you relate to me again--for the tape recorder-- the incident of Jeannette Rankin?

Paul: Oh yes. I can.

We had known Jeannette Rankin, not intimately, but known her because the first year we went down in 1913, when we were a committee of the old National American, the National American had sent Jeannette Rankin down to be what they called an organizer to work with us. So we had gotten to know her. She was mainly on the legislative work, going up and seeing congressmen, but we didn't get to know her too well. Then she disappeared, and I don't know exactly what she was doing all that time.

Then she suddenly appeared [as a congresswoman] in this victorious campaign in Montana, the time that Hazel Hunkins came down; she had worked for her, you see, up in Montana. We got up a meeting in conjunction with the National American to welcome the first woman member to Congress and held it in one of the hotels in Washington. Jeannette Rankin spoke and I spoke and I don't know who spoke for the other group.

So then we didn't see her again until this vote on war was to come pretty soon. Hazel Hunkins by that time, as I said, had come down, and was working in our Washington headquarters, and was our only real Montana connection with Jeannette Rankin, so she and I went up together that night when she was to vote. We said, "The Woman's Party welcomes all women who work for equality for women, whatever they think about war. And we have in our picket line women who are strong supporters of the war and people who are strong opponents of the war. We don't take any stand on this as an organization.

But both of us take a stand as individual women, and we wanted to tell you how we feel, just so we could feel that we had said this to you, whether it meant anything to you or not." And so we told her we thought it would be a tragedy for the first woman ever in Congress to vote for war, that the one thing that seemed to us so clear was that the women were the peace-loving half of the world and that by giving power to women we would diminish the possibilities of war--

[End of Tape 5, Side A]

[Tape 5, Side B]

[Sounds begin from a radio in background, dimly.]

Paul: --the only place we would go I presume that night.
She came upstairs to see us and talk to us up in the
gallery.

Then she went down, you know, and the first time
around that her name was called, she didn't answer.
And the second time when they went around to all the
people who didn't answer, you remember, she said--I
think these were her words, I remember it very, very
clearly--she said,

"I want to stand by my country but I cannot vote
for war."

And now this man from this University of Georgia
is writing her life. I told you he has been up [to
Washington] quite a number of times and stayed at our
headquarters. (I don't know, if Miss Chittick won't
let people in the library, what anybody will do [now],
because he has come in there and gotten so much material
for her life.) And had so many talks with me about
her [Jeannette Rankin], telling him all these things
that he doesn't know. He always comes and stays with
us, and pays for his room upstairs so he can work there.

So I was talking about him to Jeannette, the last time
she was there at our headquarters (she almost always
stays with us when she goes to Washington) I told her
that I had told him about this time we went up to see
her, and I said, "I don't know whether you remember it
but I remember it very well." And she said,

"Oh, I do remember it very well, because it was
about the only support I received from women in my
vote." And she said, "The most enormous pressure that
you possibly can conceive was brought to bear upon me
by the suffrage leaders on the ground that I would put
back the suffrage cause if I voted opposing the war."
So she said, "I was invited up to the home of Mrs. James
Lee Laidlaw"--you probably don't know her but she was a
very well-known woman then in the suffrage movement in
New York, and a lovely woman, a wealthy woman and very,
very lovely woman. And she said, "I wouldn't have
believed Mrs. Laidlaw would have done this thing, but,"
she said, "Well, Mrs. Laidlaw invited me up, she had
people come to see me, she entertained me, there was no
kind of pressure that she didn't bring to bear, as did
the other suffrage leaders, to get me to vote for the
war."

177

Paul: And then you know I told you that this man who is
writing her biography came in and told me that he found
this letter from Mrs. [Carrie Chapman] Catt, written
to a personal friend. (And probably Mrs. Catt doesn't
know it is in the congressional library--and that's the
harm of getting these letters put in without people
classifying them and going through them.) Mrs. Catt
just let herself loose against Jeannette Rankin in this
letter, and said, "It is impossible to say how much I
detest"--and so on--"Miss Jeannette Rankin"--I am not
saying the words, of course I don't know the words because
I didn't see the letter--"how terrible had been the action
of Miss Rankin, in casting that vote against war. It has
put the suffrage amendment maybe back years and years and
years and years, what she has done." So this man who was
writing her biography [laughing] came across it and then
told me about what it said.

I knew that's what was happening, that that was
their attitude. So I was very proud of her [Jeannette].
I think she was superb.

So when Congress came along to our measure, of course
she was extremely helpful. She spoke for it, helped in
every way because she was on the inside and could do
what we couldn't do. And in all the speeches, she tells
me, she always said, "I am the only woman in the country
who ever voted or who ever will vote or who ever can
vote for the enfranchisement of American women," because
the day that she voted it went through, of course it
was no longer to be voted on. They got it.

DETAILS AND DESCRIPTIONS OF THE WOMAN'S PARTY AND ITS
OPERATIONS

Working on the Suffragist

Fry: The only other questions, before we get into the new
      section on the suffrage campaign picketing, have to do
      with the administration of the National Woman's Party,
      just little things, I might just run through them to
      see if you can tell anything.

Paul: Do, please.

Fry: Did you write a lot of the articles in the Suffragist?

Paul: I wrote a lot of the editorials. I didn't write any-
       thing else excepting whenever we didn't have an editor.
       For instance during the period that we were having our
       1916 election campaign, we had nobody at that moment
       who was editing the paper. I remember that I did it
       from Chicago, and I had to not only write the editorials
       but I had to assemble and so on all the material. I
       remember I just didn't see how I could do it. I decided
       that I would stay up all night every other night; one
       night I would go to sleep, and the next night--because
       all through the day you were having telephone [calls],
       you were having people, and you couldn't do anything--
       so at night when everybody had gone and the charwomen
       came in to clean the building and so on [I would work
       on the Suffragist]. We had this big room down on the
       street, as I told you, with big show windows, and it
       was very safe because you were exposed through every
       window. Nothing really could happen I think in the
       light. You just would seem to be one of the late workers
       in the office. So every other night I took up the
       Suffragist problem, and we got it out all through the
       election campaign. That's the only time that I took
       the whole responsibility of the paper.

Fry: How long did that keep up? I don't see how your health held up, missing your sleep every other night.

Paul: Well, as I tell you, that's what this doctor says, I have a heart block. [Laughing.] I don't know whether I have or not.

Fry: You are still one of the most active and brightest people I know your age.

Classes of Woman's Party Members

Fry: I thought you might like to give a few statements on the types of women that were in this campaign. For instance, it wasn't a lower class working women's campaign, was it? It was primarily handled by women who had independent means or who had time to do this and who were in a position of influence and power. These were the women who really seemed to do the work. Is this impression right?

Paul: Well, see, when we went to prison, the woman who was in the same room with me in the psychopathic ward was Rose Winslow and she was, as far as I know, I think she was a Polish immigrant. Completely what you would call the working class.

Fry: I know that you did have some labor women.

Paul: Then we had Nina Saboroden who was the one who gave us our suffrage song because in prison she would always sing this haunting melody which we adopted as the Woman's Party song. "The Walls That Hold Us," you remember [hearing Consuelo's recording of] that song in our words. But she of course sang it in Russian; she was a Russian immigrant. Her father, we will say, was a tailor or something like that. We had, it seemed to me, every kind of--from the beginning to the end--every kind of woman.

Fry: Yes, you did, Alice. But I mean in your general profile. You know, there are different kinds of campaigns. Some campaigns just start with organizing masses and masses of people, which you did not have the time or funds to do, you told me a while ago. So it seemed to me that what you had done was choose women who were in strategically imp

Paul: I think more that we chose anybody who would come. We sort of put up a banner when we began to work for this Amendment all alone, about fifteen of us you see, the start of the little group, after the National American cast us out and put in another amendment. That's the reason we didn't know whether we could survive or whether we ought to do it or try to do it even; and so all we did was to put up this banner of what we stood for. The women would come. Wherever you went, women would come. And whoever came, we welcomed. Whoever she might be.

Fry: In your positions of leadership, did you have a preponderance of college-educated women?

Paul: No, we never thought about it.

Fry: It appeared to me that you did.

Paul: Well, we didn't. It is very likely that--I remember that in this campaign--not this campaign but the Equal Rights Amendment campaign, that the AAUW, American Association of University Women, of which I was a member then (almost all college women joined it) and it had its headquarters in Washington--they sent a letter to every member of Congress signed by their executive director of their national headquarters, opposing the Equal Rights Amendment for women. I went over there to see Miss M. Carey Thomas of Bryn Mawr [president, 1894-1922], who had been a strong supporter always of ours, and asked if she would come down to their coming convention in Washington of this association [AAUW] and try to stop this opposition. She said she would.

Mrs. Lawrence Lewis and I--Mrs. Lewis was always our strongest woman in Philadelphia--we went out together to see her [Miss Thomas], and she said she would and she did. She came [to the AAUW convention]. Immediately she tried to use her great influence as the foremost woman college president in the United States, the foremost woman educator, perhaps (and I think the greatest woman in the field of education we ever had in America). She had a great deal of prestige we thought. She proposed that [AAUW] take up this whole subject and study it and immediately rescind this action that they had taken, and she carried it.

As a result of that meeting in Washington this

Paul: executive director was probably dismissed, or anyway she disappeared, the one who had sent out this letter-- her name was Mina Kerr from the University of Wisconsin who had been employed as their executive director. She didn't get a wholesale endorsement of the Equal Rights Amendment, but she got the endorsement of having nothing to do with this letter that was going to every member of Congress, disowning it.

Then they sent out a letter to every member of the AAUW giving the pros and cons on this amendment, and Miss Thomas wrote the pros and sent it around the country and so for a time we heard nothing more in the way of opposition from the AAUW.

Then came their meeting out in Oregon, and by some trick, it seemed to us--because people didn't know it was coming up--they brought this subject up and voted to oppose the Equal Rights Amendment. They had withdrawn their opposition some years before. So I went up to see Miss Thomas again. By this time she had retired as being president, but I met her at some relatives' home in Maryland, in Baltimore, and told her this whole tale.

She said, "Well, I have decided never to go to another convention of the AAUW or have anything further to do with them. I have done the best I could; I created the organization." She said, "College women today are so different from the college women in the early pioneer days when every woman was a personality. Now they all do what the popular thing is." And that has been my experience with these college women too. They haven't been much of a help to us.

Fry: In the days of the suffrage movement were they more individualistic? Is that what she meant?

Paul: No, she meant back in the early days when they were beginning to--early days of college education for women. Her early days when she became president of Bryn Mawr and started something unheard of, which was a girls' college with equal academic standing to the men's colleges. You know Woodrow Wilson was one of her professors. And she went forth and she had a doctor's degree from Zurich herself and was a highly educated woman. She was a Quaker, by the way. And she got up a group of people, of professors, that were equal to those in the men's colleges. She lifted up college e͏   fore.

Paul: And I had the same feeling about these college
women. You see, in our own college, Swarthmore, which
Lucretia (Coffin) Mott helped to form, only Mabel
Vernon and Amelia Walker and Martha Moore ever
stood with us. I don't think we had much support from
college women as college women. Our members might
have gone to college or they might not.

Fry: Well, the reason that I brought that up was that I
have run into this as a complaint I've received in my
own work for the Equal Rights Amendment: that it's an
elitist movement. I wondered if this had been true of
the women's suffrage movement. And if you had that as
an issue. Probably wasn't an issue then.

Paul: Well, I don't think it is an issue now either. I never
heard anybody raise that idea before, that we gave
preference to college women.

Fry: Oh really? It isn't that you give preference to them;
it is that they are the ones who are interested in it
and the implication is that--

Paul: Yes, but do you know that of all the women's organizations
in the United States, the AAUW was the next to the last
to support the Equal Rights Amendment. When we tried to
get the Equal Rights Amendment endorsed at the first
hearing in Congress, you know everybody spoke against
it but ourselves at that first hearing; no one else
said a word for the amendment. Then we started out on
this campaign to go to all women's conventions to try
to change the thought of American women--not to change
Congress, because there was no use changing Congress if
you couldn't change the thought of American women,
because the women would dictate what Congress would do,
now that they had the vote. So we stopped much work
with Congress and went off to try to change women's
attitude on this subject. And of all these organizations
which have come, one by one by one by one till now we
have practically every one in America, the last one to
come in was the University Women last summer in Houston
[Dallas?]--next to the last one. The last one was the
League of Women Voters. They came in this very year
in the autumn.

Fry: Was that your old NAWSA grudge that has kept the League
out for so long?

Paul: Well, it might have been in the beginning, but I think
at present very few of them ever heard of it.

Fry: Yes, I should think most of them wouldn't care about it.

Paul: Didn't know anything about it.

          I don't know why. They were just all out for
          protective labor laws, that was all there was to it.
          So I feel very proud of our organization, I mean of our
          women in our group as a type of woman, because you know
          women of every experience and every walk of life you find
          have this same feeling for building up respect for their
          own sex, power for their own sex, and lifting it up out
          of a place where there is contempt for women in general.

          I always feel, <u>always</u> I think, when I go into a
          little group, I don't know whether a single woman will
          respond, but very often <u>one</u> woman at least responds.
          You don't know <u>who</u> it's going to be.

Fry: There was no prototype that you could always be sure of,
          a type of person who would always be a pro-suffrage
          person?

Paul: No. No.

Fry: Okay.

          The other question that I have on administration is
          on the inner workings of the Party. It was prompted by
          a note in the <u>Suffragist</u> in June, 1914, that Mary Marsh
          Lockwood had to resign as treasurer, and that from May,
          1913, to June, 1914, the treasurer's task had grown from
          one desk to seven large departments, each one equipped
          with officers and stenographers. That was the first
          time I got a glimpse of how rapid your growth had been,
          and how enormous--

Paul: What is that? I don't understand what you are talking
          about.

Fry: There was a very nice thank-you article written for her
          in the <u>Suffragist</u>, and it mentioned that when she first
          started there was one space in the office at 1420 F
          Street designated for the treasurer's desk. It told how
          she went ahead and worked at her job there even though
          all the distractions were around.

Paul: That's right.

Fry: Then by June of 1914 it had grown to seven departments,
          ea

Paul: Well, that must have been when we moved over--I don't remember when we did move over from our little basement room to the Cameron House, the Dolly Madison House. Then we had a whole building, of course.

Fry: Yes, this was after you moved.

Paul: I don't remember when we moved, but we must have moved before June, then. When we rented this building known as the Dolly Madison House and out in the back of it--I think this was this building--No, I don't believe it was though. It must have been later when we were put out of the Dolly Madison House and had to go across to the house that had been William Randolph Hearst's. I think that's the one that had this great big building, sort of an annex. And we had a carpenter cut it up into a lot of little offices, so that the Suffragist could have one office and the treasurer, one office, and so on and so on and so on. But if it was 1914 we hadn't done that yet.

I suppose that's just taking all the space that we had in the building.

Fry: Well at any rate it sounded like you had a pretty complicated organization and that just keeping things going from the standpoint of the treasurer and getting the Suffragist out and these routine things that had to be done all the time was quite a challenge.

Paul: Well, it certainly was.

Fry: I don't know how you did it. You must not have slept much then either.

Paul: Now my dear, I think you are getting sleepy. And I think I'm getting sleepy. Shall we go to bed and get up in the morning?

Fry: [Laughing.] Yes, that's a good idea.

[Tape off.]

Fry: What about representation on your board?

Paul: When any group in our organization didn't seem to have very many members, much representation, then we tried to put one woman from that group on our board, so that everybody would, in the direction of the movement, would have, people would feel they had a part in it.

Fry: Was this from any interest group or from any social class?

Paul: For instance, we didn't have very many Negroes in our group, although the National Association of Colored Women, as always, worked very closely with us. So we put one Negro woman, who is one of our ablest and best members, on our national board and she is there now, you see. I remember we had one woman of the Farmer Labor Party--out in Minnesota. She certainly was not a person who had any college education, didn't have any of these things you are talking about, any wealth or any social position or anything. But we put her on our national board. That was back in the suffrage days. And then she finally became our state chairman because she was so extra good. So we have had all types for state chairmen in different states. We only judged them by whether they wanted to help and were eager to help and were really helping.

Fry: Well, last night we--

Paul: And secondly, did you have enough breakfast?

Fry: Oh, absolutely.

[Conversation about the milk.]

Paul: Are you finding much or not finding much?

Fry: Oh I found so much in this 1917 Suffragist, Alice, I hardly know where to start.

Paul: Now this [taping] will be very helpful, I think for Consuelo [Reyes].

Fry: To review, we ended last night with the memorial service on Inez Milholland, and then you talked about Jeannette Rankin and her vote against war--

Paul: She came into our campaign you know, so completely--we should point out that we had this welcome meeting for her--you probably found it in there. And then we had her vote so she was a big feature, I think. She ought to have a photograph and such in Consuelo's [audio-visual] list, don't you think so?

Fry: Yes, I do think so.

Paul:]   :.   , "   · , ·s she

Paul: always says, who ever voted or who ever will vote for the enfranchisement of women in Congress.

Fry: She was one of the sponsors, too, of the [suffrage] bill in that war session that followed. That was one of the things I wanted to ask you--

Paul: The session that it went through was 1918 wasn't it, is that what you are talking about?

Fry: Well, right now I am talking about the 1917 session in which it did not go through.

Paul: No, but the 1917 was on war when she cast her vote--

Fry: Yes, but right now I am talking--

Paul: She cast her vote on the enfranchisement of women in 1918. Is that right?

Fry: That's right. What I am talking about is the 1917 war session when she couldn't vote on it because it never got to the floor.

Paul: I mean it wasn't there for a vote.

Fry: No, it was not there for a vote, but do you know what she did specifically to try to get it to the floor, because it was, as usual, in the House Judiciary Committee.

Paul: Are you asking me?

Fry: I am asking you, because it says that she was the "sponsor" of it, but I guess it had a lot of sponsors.

Paul: Well she was of course committed to it. When they say a "sponsor," probably--at that time we didn't have an official list of sponsors--she was committed to vote for it and support it and of course she did. We kept in pretty close contact with her, and whatever she could do which wasn't much because everything was turning around the war then. Even all the women's suffrage groups, as I say, were turning, working for the war. So it wasn't before Congress and it wasn't coming before Congress; and then as I recall, in 1918, they had first one vote. Then in 1919 they had a second vote. Or else they had them both in 1919--there were two votes, I know, in the House.

Fry: Yes, I don't have that chronology right here before me.

Paul: You haven't gotten to it yet, I guess.

That's the time that she cast her vote for us anyway. It must have been in 1919 vote in the House. And it was the previous one, then, when they voted down the seven years. That's the reason we paid so much attention to that one because it resulted in our not having to bother with the people working against us.

I think when you go through all this, it is--from Consuelo's point of view--it will be very helpful because it gives a pretty vivid idea of what drudgery was in it. Doing it over and over and over again. Just as when you showed me the [story about our banner to the] Russians' [delegation to President Wilson], you know. I said, well we had this problem: how can we make it interesting and exciting and dramatic, on and on and on and on, the same plea, the same women (an organization of the same women although different women), and the same plan standing at the White House gate. Naturally it would get completely dull unless we could think up a new one.

So when these Russian people came (I had forgotten all about it) we immediately seized it as something different.

Fry: That was when you had the banner--

Paul: Not only that, but over and over again you notice how we changed what we were doing. We would have women from some one state come, or women from some one profession come.

It was another thing--this is just apart, not to be put in your record at all--when you asked me if we didn't--are you taking this down?

Fry: Yes.

Paul: Could we stop it right now? I just want to tell you something about what we brought up last night.

Fry: Okay. Well, go ahead and we will just make a note here to the typist to not transcribe it.

Paul: All right. I don't object to it being transcribed, but it's not pertinent to what we are talking about now.

Last night you said to me that there was a general idea that college women were the women who were conducting this campaign, and I said it was such a new idea to me. I thought about it after I went to bed and I was thinking, well maybe in our present campaign. Of course in our first campaign not every woman went to college. Today almost every woman--it is hard to find one of the most obscure and the most impoverished that doesn't go to college. It doesn't mean much.

But in our present campaign, most women have gone to college as far as I know. Mrs. Chittick, our national chairman, I have never heard of her having gone to college; she has never mentioned it. No one has ever heard of it. She may have gone but she has not revealed it to anyone that I know of. Normally you talk about, "when I was at Vassar, when I was at whatever." Which was your college? You told me but I have forgotten.

Fry: Well, I have three.

Paul: Well, all right. [Laughter.] Anyway, if Mrs. Chittick had ever been to college, she would certainly meet somebody who was from a college and somehow or other we would have heard of her college, but we never have in connection with her. Our first vice-chairman and one of the most powerful people now on our board, Mrs. Butler Franklin, the cousin of Mrs. Belmont, I am absolutely positive has never been to college. So there is our first vice-chairman and our national chairman, and I could start and go down the list and think of a lot of people, I am sure, that even in our today's group have never gone to college.

I think if you are in any kind of a campaign for anything, anything under the sun, whether reform or not, you naturally tend I guess to attract to yourself (if you are trying to do something, you want people's help) people who are somewhat akin to you in beliefs and experiences and so on. I don't think I have ever attracted more college women than any other because I don't have much interest in college. I know it takes a large slice out of your life that, in my opinion, you could use better if you hadn't gone to college. So I never even inquire whether a person has gone to college if they want to come into our group. I don't care. I

Paul: think that it would probably be better if they hadn't been, because they will have a little more originality, perhaps, and independence.

[Background radio sound stops.]

So I thought you might try to somehow or other get that idea across--that this was a <u>classless</u> <u>movement</u>. I always felt you go into a crowd and you get up and you make an appeal and somebody comes to you, like Helen Hunt West came up to me, and from that time she never faltered. She just dedicated her life to this campaign. Well, it just struck a kindred note in her. And I found out afterwards that she had Quaker forebears; [laughing] maybe that had something to do with it. Some little time before. But she just was a <u>born</u> <u>feminist</u>. When somebody presented a way to expedite this, she gave up everything else and threw herself into it. Then you don't ever think, have you been to college or not. You just think well, here is a kindred soul; she feels just the same way.

Fry: Yes, I think it is clear, too, from the examples that you have given of getting specific women to come to work, that your concern was not whether or not they had been to college, but what particular talents they possessed that the party needed at the time. In most cases your--

Paul: Well, I never cared much what talents they possessed. We tried to get--and I suppose Mabel Vernon did and all the other people who were trying to get people--we tried to get people who were enthusiastic, because there is nothing in the world that is more important than that, enthusiastic and eager and consecrated in their feeling about the movement. <u>Anybody</u> could be of service, you see. There was always something she could do.

Ages of Members

Fry: Well, this brings up another characteristic. Let me try this idea out on you. It seems that this was a young women's movement; although you had a few old women in it, it was the youth and vitality of it that distinguished it.

Paul: No, I don't think that's true at all, and I very much

Paul: oppose people saying that because it was so <u>totally</u>
untrue. I think that the people today make a great
mistake in putting so much emphasis on youth, because
we didn't do that <u>at all</u>. I can remember when Lucy
Burns and I went down to Washington, and we were certainly,
we would say, <u>young</u> women, and we were always being more
or less criticized as taking--pretending to take--a
position of leadership when we were so young and inex-
perienced and everything else. It was only the fact
I guess that we had been in prison and had <u>some</u> experience that people overlooked [laughing] our being so
young.

But most of the women who came in were not of our
age at all. For instance--I told you Mrs. Lawrence
Lewis, who was one of the very <u>greatest</u> workers we ever
had. She was a mother and had three grown-up sons, one
grown-up daughter; her son was a physician and the other
son was a lawyer and the third daughter was living at
this Lighthouse Settlement I told you, where I met Jessie
Wilson, President Wilson's daughter. Then one of our
greatest helpers was Miss Lavinia Dock, did you ever
know who she was?

Fry: No, how old was she?

Paul: She was an older woman. She was one of the first people
who was ever arrested and, I don't know, she might have
been sixty-five or something. I got to know her when I
went to the School of Social Work as they call it now,
the School of Philanthropy we called it. She was one
of the distinguished lecturers who came there. She was
a great world authority, more or less--she was a nurse
and her field was everything to do with these things what
they call venereal disease and things like that. And
she lived at the nurses' settlement in New York which
was just around the corner from us. So I just got to
know her as a humble little pupil of hers in this School
of Social Work.

So when we began to try to gather a group together
in Washington, all these people I had ever met or knew
I would telephone to or go to see and ask if they would
help us. So she came right down. She was the founder
of the International Nurses' Association. (When this
visiting nurse of mine came here [this year], I said,
"Did you ever know of Lavinia Dock?" She said, "Of
course, we all studied her textbooks. She is one of
the greatest, greatest women ever in the field of
nursing.") And when we started to have the picketing

Paul: and being arrested, she was one of the first group, I
am almost certain. If she wasn't the first, almost the
first. And no one could possibly say she was young. And
here she was, a professor; all these younger people
were still going to school to people of the age of Miss
Lavinia Dock.

And then there was another one who founded the nursing
school at Yale, and I will look up her name. She was
about the same age, of course, as Miss Dock. And she
was very cultured and what one would call an upper class
person. She went into nursing and she was very shocked
to find--I won't say shocked, but she was distressed to
find--that the women in the nursing field were, she
thought, not very suitable to be nurses. She thought
maybe they had had nursing training, but they hadn't
had anything else. So she went to Yale and persuaded
them to open a school of nursing and make it a regular
school like medicine or law or anything else, of the
university, on the same scale, the same standing. And
it was set up. Women students then did start to go in
and become nurses, who never would have had a chance to
have that training before. Do you want me to go on?

Fry: [Looking out the window.] Yes, go ahead.

Paul: I thought you were looking at something.

Fry: I was watching your--your tenant is leaving, and I thought
you might want to know.

Paul: Yes, because [laughter] now we can turn the thermostat
[more laughter]--as soon as she gets out of the way
safely.

Well then she was one of our pillars. She got this
great National Association of Nurses to endorse and
support us and work with us. She was certainly not a
young woman at all.

And then, of course, Mrs. Belmont was not a young
woman. One time in Washington Mrs. Belmont conceived
the idea that she might give a dinner at the Willard
Hotel where she always went, where she had been a patron
for years, to sort of try to move into the social world,
to try to attract some people who might not come otherwise. She gave this dinner and she told us to invite
whom we wanted, all our national board, all our state
chairmen, everybody that had been important in our
m   bout

Paul: six hundred or something like that. Maybe one thousand. Enormous, enormous dinner. And I remember this person from Yale (whose name I can easily find I'm sure in the Suffragist) she was one of the--well, we say one of the leaders that we naturally invited.

Then there was this other, Izetta Jewel Miller. Do you know anything about her?

Fry: Yes, I know that she is a Californian.

Paul: She is a Californian now; she never was before.

Fry: She was from Virginia?

Paul: West Virginia. Well, when I went to Washington, she was in what they called the stock company of Washington, and she was a most admired and beloved, and most beautiful, and most successful young woman actress that there was. She then married Congressman Brown, and she was the first woman in the country that ever presided at a national Democratic convention, after we got the vote. It never had happened before. And she brought her little daughter June up [in the Woman's Party]. I would say June would have been a young worker, but the one who was really the person who was always working and doing everything was the mother. We have paintings of both of them in the headquarters, down in the living room. You may remember.

Fry: I do.

Paul: Now this was Izetta Jewel. You couldn't think of the Woman's Party without thinking of Izetta Jewel. You see, none of these women were young. At this time, after she married Congressman Brown, she took over the state chairmanship of West Virginia, which her mother had had, and was all through this period coming up to our meetings in Washington as a state chairman of West Virginia.

Fry: Was that through the suffrage period?

Paul: Yes, through the suffrage period. I remember her saying to me one time, when I was perhaps impatient I guess, or something, about people asking so many questions, she said "But you know, I have taken this long trip up from West Virginia just to ask you these questions [laughing] so I'll know what to do." I remember so vividly.

Paul: So when you think of the people who put through
          that campaign--Mrs. Florence Bayard Hilles you can
          never call a young woman; she was one of the most
          active people and of course she was grown up with a
          grown-up daughter at the time we first met her and a
          sister of a United States senator; she was about the
          age of the senators and so on.

          Well, I can just go on and on and on. Mary Beard,
          who became the chairman of our committee to decide on
          what amendment we should work for: well, she was
          certainly not a young woman. Her husband was already,
          and she was already [herself] established. I knew all
          about them when she told me her name was Mary Beard.
          I said, "Well, are you related to Charles Beard?" And
          she said, "Yes, I am his wife." Well, everybody knew
          about them. She had had time to make fame for herself
          and her husband in these books she was writing. So
          you did not have much feeling that we tried to get
          young women, or old women; we took any women that we
          could get, of course. I would not say that our movement
          was a young women's movement at all.

Fry: Well, I think I have read this statement made by
          people who were contrasting the advent of the Congres-
          sional Union with the leadership in the National American
          Woman Suffrage Association. That here was Alice Paul
          who was under thirty, I guess, weren't you in 1914?

Paul: I am almost sure that the year I went down I was twenty-
          seven, because I had just taken my doctor's degree and
          I think I was twenty-seven.

Fry: And Lucy Burns--

Paul: --was about two years older, I guess.

Fry: Who were the young and vital leaders, and that that
          gave the campaign a character. Now I know--

Paul: But that wasn't true, you see. Now for instance, Mrs.
          Richard Wainwright (here was her husband who was the
          admiral, you know). She was our house chairman and
          she got us this new headquarters when we moved from
          this little basement place. All these people--Mrs.
          William Kent; there was never anybody who was more
          active every single day than Mrs. Kent. So we didn't
          really have any such feeling at all, at all, that we
          were immature and all the things that they were trying
          to say we were. They were really trying to say I was,

Paul: you see. And that Lucy Burns was perhaps. But anyway
they certainly had it out for me. [Laughing.] They
thought that I was immature and I didn't know what I
was doing, I was unreliable and I didn't know what were
good things to do and what were bad things to do in the
campaign and all.

Fry: Well, now when people look back on this, I think they
tend to see your youth as an advantage instead of a
disadvantage, to the movement.

Paul: But that's what I want to avoid, their thinking so,
because it wasn't true. It was a very stable group of
women from the very beginning. You can tell from all
these people I am telling you about--these are a few
that just cross my mind. Now Mrs. Robert Baker--if
you look in this magazine, and Maud Younger. They
were not young--Mrs. Baker was our political chairman
all through the suffrage campaign. She had one desk
and one room all to herself. She was the one who went
to see all these senators and governors and everybody.
She was the wife of a physician and she had three sons;
I think one son was still in Harvard and the other two
sons were out in the world; I think one of them was in
the army. Anyway, you couldn't possibly say she was a
very young person. And then this Mrs. [Forest?], who
got up most of our pageants and all that sort of thing,
she was not young at all. So the people that we got
in who were young, when we started to do it--I think--for
instance, I remember Anne Martin--you couldn't possibly
call her young. She wasn't old either. She was--you
wouldn't have thought her a particularly young woman.
She's the one who ran you know for Senate [in Nevada.
And do you know Betty Gram Swing?]

[End of Tape 5, Side B]

[Tape 6, Side A]

Fry: Yes, I do. Is this the same Betty Gram who right now
puts out the Congressional Digest?

Paul: Yes, but now, of course, she is retired more or less.
Her son does it. Anne Martin went, among many other
people, over the country to try to explain the picketing
and make people sympathetic to it and so on, and she
stopped in the University of Oregon. There two young
girls were thrilled at the idea of being invited town
to Washington to participate, and they came.

Paul: I remember so vividly when they came. People went
        to me and said, "You must quickly see these two girls
        and see that they don't go back to Oregon because they
        will be of such tremendous help to us." One was Betty,
        who became Betty Gram Swing, you know. She married
        Raymond Swing, remember. She was young; she was still
        in college. The sister Alice was in college with her.

        So we enlisted them right away and they turned in
        and we gave them small little salaries to pay their
        expenses so they could stay on. And they did stay on;
        they stayed to the very end, I think.

Fry: But that was the exception rather than the rule in age?

Paul: No, I wouldn't say it was the exception. I just--till
        you told me of it, I never heard or had given much
        thought to this view. I know that you go out now to
        the [1972] Democratic convention we are told, this is
        all youth, wanting what they want. You know they even
        call and say we are standing for this minority and that
        minority--women and youth. And you can't fail to
        realize it over the television sets, what they are
        emphasizing, the great beauty of the youth. (You must
        know that.)

Fry: But that's even younger, and that's in a different
        context from what I am talking about in 1914 and '15.

Paul: Oh, it is the same thing.

Fry: These people are even younger I think than the young
        ones in your movement.

Paul: Well, those I met haven't been any younger. In this
        liberation movement.

Fry: Eighteen to twenty-two year olds. And I am talking
        about those who were in their late twenties, for the
        most part, who came to your movement.

        At any rate, you have convinced me that it was a
        multi-aged movement.

Paul: When you say, about this "women's liberation"--I haven't
        met very many, but those I have met--for instance, when
        I was in this hospital in the spring, somebody came in
        to see me, and she said she was a nurse down the hall
        for some man who was very, very ill and had a terminal
        disease. I think she came from Austria. (I have

Paul: forgotten where she came from, but it was some foreign country.) She was all ablaze with this woman's libera-tion, and she brought me in a paper to read, all about homosexuality and so on. I didn't think much of this person. I certainly didn't.

But you wouldn't have said she was so _young_. She was old enough to have come from another country and gotten an education and spoke English and everything in this country. Now she was a professional nurse earning an enormous salary by going and being a nurse for these people with great wealth in the hospital in addition to their hospital nurse.

I have met just a few of them. Now there is one of them called Gloria Steinem. I have never met her but this magazine that the girl brought in was this Gloria Steinem's magazine.

Fry: Is that the one called _Ms._?

Paul: I don't know what it was called, I don't remember. I gave it back to the girl, she wanted it back; I just glanced at it and I didn't read it.

But this Gloria Steinem I saw over the television at the Democratic National Convention. We had been trying, as you know, to get our Equal Rights plank in, and we had an extremely difficult time, _extremely_ difficult, because all the women's liberation were wanting to put in all these other things. So here I saw this Gloria Steinem get up and make a speech for all the things that _they_ wanted. Other girls--other women--I'd say _women_--they didn't give the appearance of being teenagers at all--

Fry: No, they are not.

Paul: I think that these teenagers you talk about are people-- they are not, I don't think, the leaders who are guiding these movements.

Fry: No, they are the new voters who were just enfranchised.

Paul: Yes, I think that's what they are.

Anyway, I wanted to say this.

Comparisons with Women's Liberation

Fry: Is there any way, Alice, that you <u>could</u> characterize
the women in this movement? Is there any trait or
characteristic that any of them had in common?

Paul: Yes, I always thought there was one thing that they all
had in common, which I presume you have. (I don't <u>know</u>
[laughing]; I think you have.) It was a feeling of
loyalty to our own sex and an <u>enthusiasm</u> to have every
degradation that was put upon our sex removed. That's
what <u>I</u> had anyway. It was just a principle that I--if
I belonged to <u>any</u> group and that group was regarded
with contempt, given no power, and handicapped in every
possible way it seemed to me, I'd have an impulse to--
for instance, if I had been in India when they were
fighting for the freedom of India, if I had been in
Ireland when they were fighting for the freedom of
Ireland, I can't imagine not [helping out]. Just as
when I went as a student to England, I just couldn't
<u>dream</u> of sitting down and seeing these women having
such a hard fight--which was also, I thought, the
universal fight of women--and not wanting to share in
it.

As I say, when Alice Morgan Wright got up and left
her sculpture work in Paris--she was very successful--
and came over, we just became sisters right away. We
just felt the same way, although I didn't meet her
over there--not till after she came back to this
country.

It seems to me that's been the only thing that
united us. So many women think, "What's the difference"
and, as you know, through the suffrage campaign, we
didn't have very much support from the women of the
country; we had this big and powerful organization
<u>against</u> suffrage for women, and almost no group <u>as a
group</u> came in to help us. You just had to go forth and
get individual women to do it.

I think it is the same feeling that Margaret [Webb?
inaudible] must have had, I've always felt, and Abigail
Adams and so on down, and Lucretia Mott, and I know, I
just feel I <u>know</u> that they had that feeling. They
never talked about [personal] advantages. These people
talk now about equality for women, liberation of women,
they are always talking about <u>advantages</u> to women--how
you will get promoted, and how you will get more pay,

Paul: and so on, and so on, and so--which is such a different
       feeling from the dignity of your sex that you are
       trying to get, and the freedom. So I think if we get
       freedom for women, then they probably are going to do a
       lot of things that I would wish they wouldn't do; but it
       seems to me that isn't our business to say what they
       should do with it. It is our business to see that they
       are free. Just as each country, when it gets freedom,
       then you don't [tell it what to do]. George Washington,
       after he got it, didn't start in and try to tell the
       Americans how they must live and what they must do and
       so on. I feel our duty the same way. Now. [Laughs.]

Born Feminists

Paul: Well, do you agree with that, or not?

Fry: I do agree with it. Sure I do.

Paul: Because I thought, I suspected--I haven't asked you
       anything, but I took for granted that you were of this
       point of view.

Fry: Yes, well, I am, and when we have lunch or dinner, why
       I can tell you more about it. I just don't want to
       take up our time right now to fill this with my
       experiences.

Paul: But I mean if you tell me you agree with it, that's all,
       I would be sorry if you didn't. [Laughter.] I meet so
       many people, and it's rather rare to meet somebody who
       does feel this way.

Fry: Is it rare?

Paul: Yes, very rare. You can see from what people do with
       their lives. Here was a great national campaign [last
       year] where this ERA measure was one of the measures in
       their platform. Well, even the women in [George]
       McGovern's own staff, even the women in our group, like
       Mrs. Colby, who could say, "Oh, well, we telephoned down
       to Mr. [Frank] Mankiewicz" [head of the McGovern campaign].
       It is not anything that they think is a burning need for
       the country.

       There are just a few people over the country and
       now I try to keep in touch with them by telephone, like

Paul: this [Ohio chairman] Mary Kennedy. Well, they are born
        feminists and they cannot help themselves; that's the
        way they were born, that's all there is to it. And this
        Georgia Lloyd, who just called me up from Illinois.
        [Vacuum cleaner noise begins.] One here and one there
        in the different states saying, "Now this ratification
        campaign is on, what shall I do?" But about one, you
        see, out of the _millions_ of women there must be in
        Illinois, is all on fire over this. And usually they
        are so much on fire that they transform their states.

Fry: And you work through these that are really on fire in
        the various states, from your telephone here?

Paul: That's the only way. I remember once asking Helen Hunt
        West [down in Florida?] to do something. She said, "You
        know, till the _end_ of my life you may _know_ that this is
        the only thing I am going to do, so don't worry about
        me. I am always going to be here to do the next thing
        that has to be done."

Fry: Real commitment. Let me test this tape recorder and
        see if it's coming across with the vacuum cleaner on.

Paul: How is my voice? Am I speaking too loud or too low?

Fry: It sounds perfect to me. Just fine.

Paul: Because it is only for you to get the notes from.

Fry: Comes across loud and clear, fortunately.

Paul: Well, now let's go back to your [outline].

CONTINUING RELATIONS WITH NAWSA

Loss of "Woman's Journal"

Fry: Well, 1917 was a year of all the arrests--

Paul: And 1918 was. It began, I remember, when we entered
        the war in 1917.

Fry: Just before we went to war.

Paul: Do you remember who the chief of police was there?

Fry: Yes, I took his name down [searching for notes]--

Paul: Is it Sylvester?

Fry: Yes, he was the first, and then there was a Major
        something-or-other [Pullman] later on that year.
        Sylvester was the first one.

Paul: You know, I was telling you before that when I thought
        back to who was chief of police, I could only think of
        Major Sylvester. I wondered if he had been on as early
        as our first procession [in 1913]. I didn't know
        whether he was the same one or not.

Fry: I don't know about 1913, but in 1917 he is named as
        the chief in charge.

        There were a few things going on in the background.
        Can we cover them before we get to the picketing and
        the arrests?

Paul: All right.

Fry: These are factors that might or might not have influenced
        the movement. I wondered if you were able at all to

Fry: profit from the one million dollars that was willed for
suffrage propaganda to Carrie Chapman Catt by Mrs.
Frank Leslie.

[Vacuum cleaner noise stops.]

Paul: No.

Fry: Was any of that helpful?

Paul: No, we never had one single dollar, of course, of it.

Fry: I knew you didn't have any money from it, but I thought
maybe _their_ propaganda campaign might have helped yours.

[Vacuum cleaner noise starts again.]

Paul: No, no, no, no. Their propaganda campaign was _against_
what we were for. You see, Mrs. Catt used it to
establish a magazine and that magazine replaced the
old Woman's Journal, which had been supporting us. And
this new one didn't support us, at all.

Fry: I noticed that a magazine was established.

Paul: That's the main thing that they put their money into
as far as I know. Let me see. Frank Stevens--I don't
know whether you know who he is; he is the president of
our Men's League for the Equal Rights Amendment--and he
was not the president, but he was a member of the Men's
League for Woman Suffrage in the suffrage days. When
he was a young boy, just graduated from Dartmouth, he
went up--he told me this and I know him quite well--he
went up to Boston to find some work, after he graduated
from college. By chance, he got a position in the
circulation department, the business end, of the Woman's
Journal. (You know what the Woman's Journal was through
all these years.) And so he told me so much about how
they sympathized with us and helped us, and I knew they
had. I had gone up to see Alice Stone Blackwell who was
the editor, the daughter of Lucy Stone. So then he told
me how they finally gave up their paper when Mrs. Catt
got this enormous bequest which enabled her to start
one on a far bigger scale than theirs. The Woman's
Journal was given up and was replaced by this one of Mrs.
Catt's. Of course, I told you how hostile Mrs. Catt
was to us.

Effort to Re-unite

Paul: I don't know whether I did tell you--that--now what's
        that person's name out in Wisconsin--that woman writer--

Fry: Oh, in Wisconsin?

Paul: Yes, she was a very well-known woman writer.* [Pause.]
        Well, I thought you just might know her as a writer.
        But I will go on and tell you about her and I will think
        about her name.

        At all events, this young woman out there--I guess
        she was young, about thirty or forty--anyway she was a
        very prominent woman in the United States in the field
        of authorship, and so she was a member of our organiza-
        tion in Wisconsin, also a member of the old National
        American, as nearly everybody was of that type. She
        conceived the idea that she would unite us--have I told
        you this?

Fry: No.

Paul: And so she called me up and said, "I am going to arrange
        a meeting at the Willard and will you come and bring
        anybody you want to bring to it to meet with Mrs. Catt,
        whom I am going to ask and insist that she come because
        I am a member of her organization, to stop this constant
        friction between these two groups, which is so bad for
        the women's movement and so bad for our ever getting the
        vote."

        I said, "Yes of course, we will." Lucy Burns, I
        know, went, and we took one secretary to take down
        everything. That's all we took. Mrs. Catt came.

Fry: May I ask you a question? Was this the meeting with
        Maud Wood Park?

Paul: Oh, mercy no.

Fry: Okay.

Paul: You will know this woman, I am sure. [Pause.] I just
        can't remember what it [the name] is.

Fry: It will pop into your mind.

Paul: I haven't thought of her since all these years and

*Probably Zona Gale

Paul: years.

Well, at all events, Mrs. Catt arrived with some people on her side and I think Mrs. Whoevershewas said now she had brought us together thinking that we could solve whatever difficulties we had and so on. She told what she thought we ought to do and I said, "We certainly, for our group I knew, would do every one of these things, be glad to." We didn't want to have this continuing friction.

Then she turned to Mrs. Catt and Mrs. Catt said, "I want to say that I will fight you to the last bit." That's the last word she ever said that I ever heard from her in my life, and she got up and walked out with her little group. So her paper was used that same way.

Fry: That was after the Woman's Journal changed to a thing called the Suffrage News?

Paul: Was it?

Fry: That was the name of this new magazine that was put out with the one million dollars.

[Vacuum noise stops.]

Paul: I don't know what it was called. But it was a loss to us when we lost the Woman's Journal. When you just asked me that question, did we profit by this bequest, well we certainly didn't. And then Mrs. Catt used this money always--and I suppose she was very conscientious and thought she was doing the right thing.

The Retracted Invitation to the International Suffrage Alliance

Paul: But then when suffrage was won, I went over [to Europe], just sort of to--rest and so on, I guess. I was invited by Mrs. Belmont, anyway, to come over and stay with her a little while. I went over and stayed in England and met the president of the--what was it called--International Suffrage Alliance. That's the International to which the National American was affiliated. And her name was Mrs. Corbett Ashby. I telephoned to her and made an appointment, and went out to see her and she invited me out to lunch at her home.

Paul: I remember she said to me, "Now we would like very much to have the Woman's Party join us. [Vacuum noise starts again.] Of course we have the National American Woman Suffrage Association and we would also like to have the Woman's Party affiliate with the International." She was the International president. I said, yes, of course, we would like to. Naturally we would like to affiliate; now that we are through with our own campaign for getting the vote, we would like to affiliate with the women who are doing the international work, which really had been started largely by Susan B. Anthony, this international movement which Mrs. Corbett [Ashby] actually then inherited.

She said, "I am going to write you a formal invitation to affiliate with us."

I said, "All right, and we will accept it I know, because I know without asking that all our people would be in favor of doing this." Mrs. Belmont by that time had become very fervent in her work for this and she had moved over to live permanently in France to be with her daughter, Madame Belzan, as you know--Belzan had been the Duchess of Marlborough. So they were both living in France. So we accepted.

When Mrs. Belmont knew we were coming, she said she wanted to make quite a large gift to the International. Of course, she was primarily interested in the International. She said she would entertain the International and do all the things that she could do and would also make a financial gift to them. So we chose a group of people to go over, most of whom paid their own expenses, and we put in a few people who couldn't pay their own expenses. It was a very great, very big and I thought, very good delegation. Maybe twenty people or thirty people perhaps. For instance Elsie Hill went and she spoke French and had been teaching French. And Mabel Vernon went and Doris Stevens went, all of them. So it was a good group.

Before, I think before they left, they received word from Mrs. Ashby that they wished to withdraw their invitation to us, because Mrs. Catt who had been the International president before Mrs. Ashby, had felt that we were not a desirable group to have in the International and had said that she would give no more money to the International from her Leslie fund if they allowed us to become members.

Paul: So I wrote back to Mrs. Ashby. I think you will find
all this in the _Suffragist_, probably. It ought to be
in the _Suffragist_ right at the end of the suffrage
campaign. I said well we have had the invitation, we
have made the plans, the people were all ready and
prepared to go and probably whatever differences there
might be could be ironed out at the convention. If
there is anything in our program that is not in harmony
with their program, we could settle it maybe at the
convention itself. All the people who went on the
delegation were in accord with that. They all felt--
Mrs. Belmont was in accord--they all thought we don't
want to be suddenly told by Mrs. Catt whether we can
go or we can't go to an International convention when
we have been asked by the International president and
when we had certainly won the vote in our country. We
shouldn't be put in this position. So they went.

   Lady Rhondda went over, whom we had gotten to know
very well, from England; you have heard of her I think.
She was the head of what we called the Six Point Group,
a group which belonged to the International and was very
up-and-coming and forward-looking. So when they got
there, Lady Rhondda was so incensed at what was going on
that she rose and withdrew all her delegates and would
have nothing further to do with the convention. I don't
know at what state of the proceedings she did this, but
she did withdraw, I guess her whole organization, as far
as I know. [Vacuum cleaner noise diminishes.]

   We had asked Mabel Vernon to make the main speech
for us, because of all the people who were there, we
thought she was our best speaker; she _was_ in my opinion,
without any question, obviously. People have often said
it is a pity Mabel Vernon didn't die after that speech
because it was the most wonderful speech that could ever
have been made by a human being. [Laughter.] Everybody,
everybody said this to me, who ever made any report about
the convention. They said this was the high point of her
life, it was such an _amazing_ speech. The point had come
up of whether [our American delegation] should be seated
or not seated, that was what it was. She made the speech.

   I think it was after that speech, maybe, that Lady
Rhondda said, "Now if you don't seat them, I withdraw."
Of course she was a powerful person too. But the whole
thing, the only thing that came up was well, they
couldn't afford to lose the Leslie money. I mean that
wasn't put in the _speeches_, but that's what the whole
thing was more or less about. Mrs. Catt was insisting

Paul: upon this. I don't think Mrs. Catt was there. I am
sure she wasn't.

Mrs. Belmont was like Lady Rhondda. She [Belmont]
was aroused to such a point--oh my goodness. So she
said that she cancelled all her promises to give the
International all this money, which would have been a
great deal if she had continued, and she was going to
give it to the local suffrage organizations in France,
which she did, which more or less put them on their
feet. But they were not connected, I guess, in any
way with the International. So we were voted down.

I think that the point on which we were voted down
was--of course they didn't [mention] the money part,
but I knew from my letter from Mrs. Ashby what the
point was. What they said was, if I remember rightly--
Mabel will remember better than I, I am sure, this
whole meeting because she led the fight there. But
what they said was, if I remember rightly, that they
couldn't have two organizations from the same country
that had different policies. We had the policy of
complete equality and they had the policy of protection
of women. I remember somebody later from Holland who
came over to our country and she said, "You know, I
think that the death, really of the International took
place at that meeting, because after all, most of us
do stand for complete equality." And I found they did
when I went over [later] and I became a member of the
International Committee on Law, I think they called it,
of the International Council of Women. I discovered it
was true. Those women over there were all pioneer women,
you see, that were in the women's movement in Europe.
They were not like the great mass of, as you say, [laugh-
ing] college women, that are flooding the marketplaces
now and don't have any particular pioneer spirit. They
were still in that pioneer stage over there when I went
over later, and I don't know that I ever met a person
that wanted protection. So this was not a--well, it
was something that could have been solved at that convention. They certainly were not obliged to put people
out because they stood for complete equality. These
were the people who said, "Oh no, all these poor working
girls and working women who work at night," and all that,
you know?

Fry: What was the name of Catt's organization at this time?
Was it still the NAWSA?

Paul: W ', ' /1 + .+r r.   izatior. She belonged to it

Paul: and was a leader in it. They never changed their name until suffrage was won, you know.

Fry: I thought this was after our suffrage was won.

Paul: Yes, but it was almost immediately. I wouldn't know about that point. I don't know what day they changed their name.

Fry: The other thing I was wondering, Alice: Do you happen to know where the papers are, or the proceedings of this meeting? [Vacuum cleaner noise stops.] It would be nice to have a copy of Mabel Vernon's speech.

Paul: It certainly would. I doubt if they kept such good records as that.

Fry: You don't know if there are any proceedings. If they are, they might be where, in England?

Paul: I haven't the faintest idea who is the International president now. You see, we never became members of it. When they refused to take us, we were invited by the International Council of Women, which was the one which was founded in 1888 in Washington by Susan B. Anthony and all our women, you know--Frances Willard, all those people, you know about that I am sure. Well, they invited us to become members and we accepted, so we have always belonged to that group. But the others have an organization, I am sure, and a headquarters somewhere in the world--the International Suffrage Alliance. Now let's get back to your questions.

Fry: Back to the United States. That was a marvelous answer to that question about the one million dollars from Mrs. Frank Leslie.

Paul: I wouldn't put it, ever, in your records, you know. I don't like to have attacks on anybody going down in history.

Fry: Well, you will get this back, and if you would like for the typist to leave that out--

Paul: Well, you can just judge yourself. I don't want this to be something that is going to be a source of friction and so on down through the ages.

Fry: I wouldn't either. [Laughing.] Its time should have run out by now, as far as the friction is concerned.

Fry: There were also food riots. Five thousand women in New York were demanding government action to bring down the cost of food. Did this displeasure on the part of women and their frustration at not being a part of the political establishment for such actions as this, was this useful to you, do you remember?

Paul: Do you remember in reading whether that's the one that Mrs. Belmont participated in?

Fry: Let me see. [Reads.] No. It's just a little item here on page 4 of the March 3 Suffragist, 1917. The mass meeting was the culmination of rioting in many sections of the city.

Paul: What was the mass meeting?

Fry: It was this five thousand women who "met in and outside of Forward Hall in New York City last week." They passed a resolution to the President demanding government action to bring down the high cost of food. It refers to "vigorous action of women in New York and Philadelphia and other eastern cities."

Paul: I know there was a period there where people were opening all kinds of soup kitchens and so on. Mrs. Belmont was one of the people who did it. All the people of a philanthropic nature who were sort of expected to do these things, were doing them. But it didn't cross our path, one way or the other. I wouldn't have known it excepting for having known Mrs. Belmont was doing it all the time.

Fry: This may be something different because in this President Wilson backed an appropriation of $400,000 to inquire into the food situation.

Paul: Yes, I just remember that this was going on. Women were--not only women--everybody was having [to struggle]. It was one of those economic crises, but they came and they went, you know, all the time.

THE TURNING POINT: MILITANCY

Unifying the Party

Fry: On March of that year [1917], you held simultaneous
        conventions of the Congressional Union and the Woman's
        Party, and they voted to unite into one organization.

Paul: What? [Fry repeats the question.]

        Yes. Well, it wasn't exactly a convention. That
        was just a group, I think, of the leaders. You see, we
        had formed the Woman's Party of the members of the
        Congressional Union in the suffrage states and called it
        the Woman's Party for political reasons. Then we were
        confronted with two. We had all the women in the non-
        suffrage states who were Congressional Union, and the
        women in the suffrage states calling themselves the
        Woman's Party.

        I remember the person who did most of this business
        was Mrs. Belmont because she liked the name, National
        Woman's Party, and she was of course very influential
        in our board because she was giving us so much financial
        help and was also so much help in every possible way.
        So I don't know whether people thought the Woman's Party
        name was so wonderful, but we knew we had to have the
        same name. Our members in Nevada, for instance, who
        were members of this national headquarters in Washington,
        even though they called themselves Woman's Party members,
        were on the same relationship to the national board as
        the women, we will say, in Kentucky, who were in the
        non-suffrage states.

        I remember our meeting together and I think Anne
        Martin and a few people who had been elected out of
        that meeting nationally, and probably our national board,
        I don't know that it was a real convention, but does it

Paul: say it was a big convention? It was just an agreement
to change our name, and make the name National Woman's
Party for all the women, all Congressional Union members
wherever they were.

Fry: It is called the "union convention," in the write-up
here.

Paul: Say anything about it particularly?

Fry: Oh, it has a long article on it, the essence of which
is that this will unite the two organizations and it
will culminate in picketing of the White House, and
it also culminated in women trying to get in to see
the President, who, on March 4, had just taken his
oath of office for his second term. And he refused to
see them.

Paul: And who led that delegation, does it say?

Fry: Let's see. There were nearly a thousand women. (That
will be in the next issue here, March 10.) It says
here, "Even the women's personal cards with the resolutions to be presented were refused transmission to
the President."

Paul: Didn't say who? In the photographs, does it say who?

Fry: [Reads.] "The leaders of the delegation were Miss Anne
Martin of Nevada, Mrs. William Kent of California, Mrs.
Darrell Wieble of North Dakota--

Paul: I don't remember her.

Fry: --"Miss Mary Patterson of Ohio, Elinor Barker of
Indiana, Mrs. J. A. H. Hopkins of New Jersey."

Paul: Oh, yes. She is one of our very important women.

Fry: And Mrs. Florence Bayard Hilles of Delaware.

Paul: I see what we did. Mrs. Hilles was in the non-suffrage
states just as an example and Mrs. Hopkins was in a non-
suffrage state, and Mrs. Kent was in a suffrage state,
and Miss Anne Martin was. As I recall--I remember very,
very, _very_, _very_ vividly--I remember we met and we agreed
and said we could go forth now as one group--

Fry: It was a drenching rain.

Paul: Was there? [Laughter.] I remember the only point that
       I think maybe there was some [question of who should be
       the leaders]. This is March 7, 1917, was it? Just
       before we entered the war?

Fry: March 4, just before we went into the war.

Paul: We went to war April 17. All right. But this is the
       only thing, that there was a difficulty was who would
       be the board and who would be the leaders of this
       [united] group. I think Miss Martin, perhaps--Mabel
       woudd know much more about this than I--I think that
       Miss Martin and some of the people felt she had been
       elected at the convention in Chicago [in 1916] and she
       should be the new chairman. Anyway I remember talking
       to her about it. It either had to be Miss Martin as the
       chairman or I as the chairman because I was of one group
       and she was the other, you see. And so I told Miss
       Martin that I wished she would become the chairman and
       take it over. I had done it, I thought, maybe long
       enough. And that I would become a vice-chairman and
       work for them. She said no, she would rather have me
       continue and that she would be vice-president. I don't
       know whether that's how we settled it or not, but I
       think we did.

Fry: [Searching Suffragist] I am trying to see. Oh,
       "Officers were elected unanimously at the morning
       session. Chairman Alice Paul, vice-chairman Anne
       Martin, secretary Mabel Vernon."

Paul: Yes, that is what I have been thinking.

Fry: And then Lucy Burns and Mrs. Belmont and Mrs. Brannan
       were all on the executive board. Mrs. Gilson Gardner,
       Mrs. Robert Baker, Mrs. William Kent, Miss Maud Younger--

Paul: You see, none of those were such young women--

Fry: --and Doris Stevens, Florence Bayard Hilles, Mrs.
       Donald Hooker, Mrs. J. A. H. Hopkins, and Mrs. Lawrence
       Lewis. All those now were on the new executive board.

Paul: Well, that was a magnificent group of women. I want to
       point out that, with the exception of Doris Stevens,
       none of them could possibly be called young.

Fry: [Laughter.] All right.

Paul: B   ʼ ̄   ᵗʰᵉ   ʳᵉˢᵗ ᵒᶠ ᵗʰᵉᵐ   ᵉˣᶜᵉᵖᵗ Anne

Paul: Martin. But we didn't have any real friction. I don't--
I always felt that she really didn't think it was quite
right that she was replaced, but it was done without
any **apparent** friction.

Fry: And yet she did not want--she wanted you to be the head,
you said.

Paul: I really think she _didn't_, is what I mean. But anyway,
when I asked her to take it, she said, and I said I would
be just as happy to be vice-chairman, maybe happier.
Anyway she wouldn't. Whether she thought the financial
responsibility was too great, or having to come to
Washington and having to spend every minute of her time.
But she didn't.

So from that time we were the National Woman's
Party, you see. We had been incorporated--let's see,
we were incorporated in 1918, the next year. We had
never been incorporated.

Fry: Well, this was an enormous demonstration with women
from nearly every state and each one carried her state
banner and so forth.

Paul: Well, that delegation to the President--does it say who
took the delegation? Miss Martin, I guess.

Fry: Yes, I think so.

Paul: Oh, well, that's one of the biggest we ever got up. I
know _that_ was a day that it was drenching, drenching
rain.

Fry: Yes, and around and around and around. It was Inauguration Day. All during this time there was no problem of
violence or outward crowd hostility, apparently.

Paul: You see, we were never arrested until the war had been
declared and we kept on [picketing]. That's when I
told you we got this round robin headed by Mrs. Harriot
Stanton Blatch, urging us--our _own_ _women_ you see, began
to revolt against us because we wanted to go on with the
picketing and they wanted us to stop the picketing. The
whole National American was _solidly_ against us because
they wanted to go right into the war, and wanted to
push Jeannette Rankin and everybody else into the war.

Fry: And then we did get into the war.

Paul: And we got into the war on April 7.

Fry: And on April 14--you may have forgotten this, I thought
it was worthy of note--the first war losses were mostly
women. It was a munitions factory explosion in Chester,
Pennsylvania. One hundred eighteen were reported killed
with more expected to die.

Moment of Decision

Paul: I remember at the time that I was called up by this
Major Sylvester [on the Washington police force],* and
he said that they had decided that they could not permit
this picketing any longer in view of the war and so on.
And that he wanted to warn us that if anybody did go out
again on the picket line, it would be their duty to
arrest us. And we said, "Well, we think it is our duty
to continue to go out," so we did.

From that time on, while they were arresting the
women, of course, that sort of [laughing] inspired the
crowd I think to great excitement.

Fry: Yes, when you carried that famous "Russian banner," your
first arrests came.

Paul: Yes, it was later on.

Fry: That was in June of 1917.

Paul: We began to be arrested pretty soon, I think. You can
find an account of the first arrests that were made, I
think you will find there this Lavinia Dock I have been
telling you about. I think in this first group that
were ever arrested was Katherine Morey, one of our very
wonderful Massachusetts women.

[Break for lunch.] [Tape off.]

Paul: --when we'd be arrested. That was really a big high-
light [in Woman's Party history].

---

*Doris Stevens says it was Major Pullman, in Stevens'
Jailed for Freedom, Boni and Liveright, New York, 1920,
p.

Fry: Didn't you get that message from the police _after_ they had already arrested you a few times?

Paul: No. He sent a formal [message]. I received it and I remember it very well. And then we didn't know exactly what to do, and various women, among them Katherine Morey I can remember, said, "All right, then we will have to have people _willing_ to be arrested, and I will come down and I will be one." So she came down from Boston and she was one. And Lavinia Dock, it is my recollection, was the second one.

I am sure you will find them there [in the _Suffragist_].

Fry: Their names should be right here because here is the story.

Paul: That is after it got going. This wasn't the first arrest at all, [in that issue you have] now. We didn't have any of that excitement or violence or anything.

Fry: No.

Paul: I might have been in the first group, but I don't think I was.

Fry: [Reading.] Katherine Morey?

Paul: Morey, that's one. She was.

Fry: And Lavinia Dock?

Paul: Lavinia Dock, yes she was. Have you any other--Is that table clean enough?

[Tape off momentarily.]

Fry: Which was the turning point?

Paul: When people were willing to continue with that picketing when [they knew they would be arrested]. There was a big division in the women's movement, you see, when they sent this round robin from so many influential women headed by Mrs. Blatch to demand that we stop the picketing, and the White House had the chief of police call us up. So it was really a big turning point. That's when our militancy really began. This going out and standing there with our beautiful banners wasn't anything very militant. But this really was, I would say, tne beginning of the militancy. Have you any other names? I was sure

Paul: I was right in Morey and Lavinia Dock. They must
record that people went out that first time and were
arrested.

Fry: Well, there is a good chronology of all the arrests in
the July 21 issue.

Paul: No, but I--oh, no, no, but right here when we were first
arrested we had to put it in [the Suffragist]. Because--
my goodness! I want to tell you one thing, may I? We
were--a meeting was being held over in Pennsylvania
somewhere and one of our well-known women, Mrs. Frederick
Howe, was chief speaker there, and in the midst of the
meeting, the press called up and said so-many women
had been arrested in Washington, and people were dumb-
founded at this meeting, that we were all being arrested
and well, it was just, the whole country was just all--

[End of Tape 6, Side A]

[Tape 6, Side B]

Fry: "...Lucy Burns, and I"--and "I" is Katherine Morey
because she is writing this article--

Paul: Were they imprisoned this time? I presume they were
but I don't remember.

Fry: [Reading.] Here is an account of the chief of police
telephoning you. It was after the pickets had greeted
the Russian mission at the gates of the White House with
your famous Russian banner, and--

Paul: Oh, but that wasn't the Kaiser Wilhelm banner.

Fry: No, this was the one that said,

"PRESIDENT WILSON AND ENVOY ROOT ARE DECEIVING
RUSSIA. THEY SAY WE ARE A DEMOCRACY. HELP US
WIN A WORLD WAR SO THAT DEMOCRACIES MAY SURVIVE..."

Paul: That's right.

Fry: --And so forth. Then, in this story by Katherine Morey,
she tells that when she arrived in Washington on receipt
of a telegram from you she found a tense situation. That
two women had the day before greeted the Russian mission
at the gates of the White House with that Russian banner
and a mob had torn it down. That mob action had sent

Fry: the story of the banner with its inscription all over the country and into the capitals of Europe as well.

Then Tuesday morning, Lucy Burns and she carried a similar banner over the lower White House gate but a few boys had destroyed it with the police "looking placidly on." One of the banners said "Democracy should begin at home." And a great crowd began to surge up and down the street and they "stood motionless." And then when she was in having lunch at the headquarters, another mob charged upon other pickets and tore their banners to shreds. The police warded off that mob and protected the pickets, and then that evening the chief of police telephoned that the Woman's Party could not again hold banners of any kind before the White House.

Paul: Is that all they said?

Fry: Well, she says that you were "amazed."

Paul: But he did say, in phoning, he said, "We have to say to you, if you do persist in going, and we hope you won't, that we have no alternative except to arrest you. These are our instructions." Something like that.

And I said, "Well I think that we feel that we ought to continue and I feel that we will continue."

The First Arrests

Paul: Then I probably notified people and said--because people were coming all the time and offering to stand [and picket] before the White House--and I said, "If you come now, you will have to be prepared for arrest. You will have to." I remember Katherine Morey saying, "Well, I am willing to be," and I remember Miss Dock, and the reason I remember both of them so well is that they did say they were willing.

But I would like to know who the others were who went out that day, and were arrested. And also I would like to know whether they were imprisoned. Because this event is one of the things Consuelo [Reyes] ought to concentrate on [in her audio-visual history].

Fry: There's a good editorial in the next issue of the _Suffragist_ which I guess you wrote, and that's the July 7 issue--

Paul: That's a long time--July--I think the arrests began long before that.

Fry: --It says here six suffragists are tried, and the ones who were tried were Katherine Morey, Leah Neil--

Paul: Who?

Fry: L-e-a-h N-e-i-l.

Puul: I don't remember her.

Fry: And Mabel Vernon, Lavinia Dock, Maud Jamison, and Virginia Arnold. That was from the June 27 incident when "six American women for the first time in the history of this country defended their right peacefully to promote suffrage." They were arrested and charged with obstructing traffic.

Paul: How long were they sentenced for? You know, you should get Mabel Vernon to tell you this. She was in this group.

Fry: I think she did, in our interview.*

Paul: She probably remembers the names of the people who were arrested with her. I would like to get in touch with those women who were first arrested if any of them are living.

Fry: Well, those are the ones, apparently.

Paul: The one you call Neil, I don't know who she was. I know who Virginia Arnold was; I know she was from North Carolina; and I know who Maud Jamison was.

Fry: [Reading.] Well, the judge found them guilty as charged, of obstructing the highway in violation of the police regulations and the act of Congress, and he imposed a fine of $25 in each case, or, in default of that, three

*Vernon, Mabel, The Suffrage Campaign, Peace and International Relations, Regional Oral History Office, 1976.

Fry: days' imprisonment. So they were each sentenced to three days in the district jail because they refused to pay the fine.

Paul: And did they go to the district jail?

Fry: Yes, they stayed in three days.

Paul: And that was the first time, in July--

Fry: No, it was written up in July and the trial was in July, but they were arrested in June 27.*

Paul: June 27 [22]? Well, that's the big day I'd mark in your book as the beginning of the real militancy.

I remember this meeting now, out in Pennsylvania. It was Mrs. Frederick Howe. Did you ever hear of Frederick Howe?

Fry: No.

Paul: He was a government official, [Commissioner of Immigration; Port of New York] and Mrs. Frederick Howe--what was her name--I remember she was a speaker at this meeting, and she was one of our most distinguished women-- when they got this news that electrified them all. Horrified them all. And it led to many resignations from our ranks, you see. They didn't want to have anything like this happening. So we sort of emerged from all this with, maybe, the sturdier feminists, people who wanted to continue anyway.

Fry: Yes, it would certainly be a purge of the faint-hearted.

Paul: Not so much the faint-hearted, but the people who didn't think it was important enough to upset the country about.

Fry: It is kind of interesting that on July 19, then, Wilson unconditionally pardoned sixteen women who had been sentenced to serve sixty days in the workhouse at Occoquan.

Paul: Well, that was natural in the beginning.

---

*The very first arrests were on Friday, June 22, of only two women, according to Irwin.

Fry: No one <u>asked</u> him to pardon them.

Paul: Who were they?

Fry: [Looks through <u>Suffragists</u>.]

Paul: I think this is the one led by Mrs. Hopkins of New Jersey.

You see how valuable it is to have a record like this. It's one of the things that upsets me so terribly: we are having just as many things happening today, but we have no record being made. We have no paper [published now].

Fry: I know; and that's also why we need to tape record more people.

Paul: We need a paper so desperately.

Fry: We might note that there is a record of the arrests from June 20 on, a good chronology here on page 7 of the July 21 issue. [Pause.] It helps to straighten out that date of the first arrests and the first convictions.

Paul: You know, we always marched out with a little group. It is my impression that a little group in which Miss Lavinia Dock was one, and so on, (I didn't remember Mrs. Lewis was in the first group) but at all events, I know Miss Morey and Miss Dock were, and they marched out just as we did each morning, without any particular banner. That was the time they were arrested, because they had gone out in defiance and absolute noncompliance with this order from this Major Pullman. But we don't seem to find anything in there about it.

Fry: There is a story on that day's arrest. You are talking about June 25 Monday--

Paul: Yes, but that was of two people who were going out with a particular banner which was inflammatory, but I don't think that that was exactly--well, it is not what I have remembered. I just remember having a long consultation, "well, what shall we do?" when we had gotten this order. You know, I couldn't arbitrarily change the whole policy of the Woman's Party. Everybody there talked it over and communicated with people like Miss Morey, who was one of our leading women in another state, and so on,
w   ı to

Paul: stop us picketing, we could always call on her. And
then I think we got in consultation with these people,
and then we had lots of serious discussion naturally,
because if we embarked on something we knew we embarked
on, we had to stick by it, which was going to be pretty
difficult. We didn't know whether we would get anybody
but ourselves that would be willing to be arrested,
which might have crushed the whole thing. So when we
thought we had consulted enough people, then we just
deliberately took about six women--about that number--
that were willing to be arrested and who wouldn't cave
in if they were arrested. And they started out. But
there is no indication in the Suffragist of anything
like this having occurred. All we started in with was
this inflammatory banner, [according to the Suffragist]?

Fry: No, that was five days before, when the inflammatory
banner was carried.

Paul: Oh, it was. I thought you read that they had gone out
with that inflammatory banner on this particular day
and that these two people had been arrested.

Fry: A quotation from the President and one from Susan B.
Anthony was carried on this particular day (June 25,
Monday) with fifteen suffrage flags and they were
displayed on the picket line--

Paul: Oh, then we had fifteen people. That was splendid.

Fry: Or maybe seventeen. Five of them were arrested,
surrendering their banners, twelve were arrested and
ordered to appear for trial when summoned. That episode
was on Monday, June 25. Then two days later, they were
sentenced.

Paul: That was after the Major Pullman had sent his ultimatum,
was it?

Fry: Yes, it was.

I think the very first arrests were on Friday, June
22, which was three days before.

Paul: Would it be too much for you to look up in Miss Katzenstein's book* and see what she says, because she, I

---

*Katzenstein, Carolyn, Lifting the Curtain, The State
[illegible] In [illegible] [illegible] [illegible] sylvania

Paul: think, went into all of this with the greatest thorough-
ness when she wrote this book.

Fry: She has some dates. [Reading.] It looks like it was
Sunday, June 24, when the police major called you and
warned you.

Paul: It was Sunday, anyway. You got the day, it was Sunday?

Fry: Yes, it was June 24. And on Monday, June 25, quite a
few women went out and were arrested, Miss Burns and
Miss Morey. Their case had not been called.

Paul: It never was.

Fry: I don't know--I am only reading this--as of July 21 it
had not been called. But those who were arrested--

Paul: And you gave me last night the names of about six people
who were arrested and I know you had somebody named Neil
whom I never heard of. And then we had Maud Jamison and
Virginia Arnold and Mabel Vernon and Miss Lavinia Dock,
and Miss Morey.

Fry: But you think the real red-letter day, Alice, is the day
of the very first arrest? Or the day the first women
went to prison?

Paul: No, I think the first arrest, because if you decided to
be willing to be arrested, you change our policy, you
see.

Fry: Well, that was June 22, and then June 27 was the day of
the first sentencing.

Paul: So I think the day of the first arrest would be the
turning point. (Excuse me a minute, I am going in to
get my check for Mrs. Dolley [housekeeper].)

    Well, now I think that's very important that we got
through that period.

Fry: Yes, the first--

Paul: And then she gives those little summaries that you could
use, that there were all together what number arrested
and what number imprisoned.

    I told you in the very beginning of that book, she
tells about how we held our first open air meeting in

Paul: Philadelphia, in the opening part of the book.

Fry: Yes. On page 206 Katzenstein sums up, [telephone ring interferes] "More than five hundred were arrested during the agitation over the whole campaign, and out of these 168 served prison terms, some of them several terms." That's a big number of women, five hundred.

Paul: It's really quite amazing. Because you see it wasn't at all--today it's sort of commonplace to be arrested, but it was certainly extremely [laughing] unusual at that time.

Fry: Especially for women who were very cultured and, as you were pointing out, who absolutely would never think of even picketing in any other circumstance.

        [Tape off.]

Paul: The first women who did it gave it such a good start because the women were of such prestige. For instance this Miss Morey was of a very distinguished family up in Massachusetts. There is a statue to one of her ancestors as you go out to Brookline. I used to go up and stay with her mother up in Brookline. Her mother was our state chairman. Every day we would drive home from our little headquarters on--what is that great park you always speak in in Boston--Boston Common, wasn't it--right there on the Boston Common we would drive home to the Morey house. There we always passed a statue of her great grandfather. It was a very well-known family.

        So these people kind of gave it a standing; it wasn't quite so hard to get the others to follow, I think.

Fry: Well, [reading] I notice here in this court case, the names listed are the United States vs. Mrs. Julia Hurlburt of New Jersey, Mrs. J. A. H. Hopkins of New Jersey, Mrs. Minnie D. Abbot of New Jersey, Mrs. B. R. Kincaid of California, Mrs. Paul Reyneau of Michigan, Miss Anne Martin of Nevada, Mrs. Amelia Himes Walker of Maryland, Mrs. Florence Bayard Hilles of Delaware, Miss Janet Fotheringham of New York, Mrs. Gilson Gardner of Washington D.C., Miss Doris Stevens of Nebraska, Mrs. John Winters Brannan of New York, Miss Mary H. Ingham of Pennsylvania--

Paul: She was a very distinguished woman. Every one of these people was very well known.

Fry: Mrs. John Rogers, Jr. of New York.

Paul: That's the one I was telling you was such a chum from
         the very beginning. She was [Secretary] Stimson's
         sister-in-law.

Fry: Mrs. Rogers?

Paul: Yes. Secretary of War Stimson.

Fry: And Miss Eleanor Calnan of Massachusetts and Mrs. Louise
         P. Mayo of Massachusetts.

Paul: Is that the end?

Fry: That's the end of those listed in that litigation.

Paul: Yes, so there was a very--my recollection is that Dudley
         Field Malone, who was a _very_ close friend and associate
         of Mr. [Woodrow] Wilson, and campaigned with him and had
         been given by him the position of Collector of the Port
         of New York. He was then married to one of the big
         Democratic political families in New York--I have
         forgotten what her name was. He showed every sign of
         being quite infatuated by Doris Stevens. I guess he
         was. You said twenty-six--[Tape off momentarily.] I
         am sure he got those women out, that's all I am trying
         to say.

The Presidential Pardon

Fry: Out of jail and pardoned? Wasn't that later on?

Paul: He knew Wilson so well.

         [Interruption, housekeeper.]

Fry: This was July 19 when the President unconditionally
         pardoned sixteen women who had been sentenced on a
         technical charge to serve sixty days in a government
         work house at Occoquan. Everyone seemed to feel that
         the pardon was what we would today call a "cop-out"
         by President Wilson. (There is a good write-up here
         on the trial on page 7 of the _Suffragist_.)

Paul: Anyway Mrs. Hopkins, I think, took a very good position.
                                                      t have

Paul: done, and they didn't want to be pardoned by the
        government for something that they considered was right
        and proper that they had done. So all by herself, she
        wouldn't accept the pardon.

Fry: And the very next day she went out and picketed and--I
        suppose was arrested?

Paul: No, she wasn't arrested.

Fry: Oh, there was a time right after that pardon when they
        didn't arrest anyone.

Paul: The only one who wasn't arrested that I know of was
        Mrs. Hopkins when she went out. Nothing would induce
        them to arrest her [laughter], because it brought up
        the whole question of whether Wilson did have the right
        to pardon them, you see.

Fry: Which was a legal question they didn't want to get into.

Paul: They certainly didn't want to. Her position was quite
        right. You can't pardon a person for something that--
        you are not in position to be giving a pardon. I
        thought it was very gallant what she did. Then we went
        on with our regular picketing, and we were regularly
        arrested, as far as I can recall.

Fry: Things got livelier and livelier, it seems, as the
        summer wears on. The Suffragist carries comments of
        the police encouraging the attacks of hoodlums, and in
        one of them in August there is a note that you were
        knocked down three times and a sailor dragged you clear
        across the sidewalk trying to tear off your suffrage
        sash for a souvenir. And there were no police around.

Paul: Does it say that in there? That's another question [Mr.
        Gallagher asked]. I don't know where this man got all
        these things.

Fry: That's August 15.

Paul: And I said, "I don't think I have ever heard of it or
        remember a single thing about it--ever being thrown
        down--and I don't see how I could be thrown down and
        not remember."

Fry: Don't you remember even being kind of frightened by
        all these crowds around you?

Paul: No. I don't remember. Maybe I <u>was</u>. I was more sensitive
       I think, not to any of these crowds and that sort of
       thing, but to the general feeling over the whole country
       that you were the scum of the earth and all that.

       Charlie--[tape off while Miss Paul talks to carpenter.]

Fry: The thing we haven't brought out here is that <u>most</u> of your
       banners were not inflammatory, that you were quoting
       President Wilson's own words, back to him. [Laughing.]
       I think we kind of missed that point here.

Other Consequences

Paul: Of course, really you know, we weren't addressing
       President Wilson, we just were addressing the people
       of the country.

Fry: Yes.

Paul: To try to get those words over to the country.

Fry: Well, you had another big one on Bastille Day and then
       on through August, and in the meantime, in September,
       there was a so-called investigation of Occoquan Workhouse.

Paul: By some member of Congress?

Fry: No. This was the one written up in the <u>Suffragist</u> as
       just a whitewash. Dudley Field Malone was ready to be
       your counsel for it because in the meantime he had
       resigned [from Port of New York] in protest.

Paul: Yes, but who was conducting it?

Fry: The investigation was called by the District of Columbia
       commissioners? There was a hearing which was secret.

Paul: Was Dudley Field Malone conducting the investigation
       for us? Representing us?

Fry: He was representing the women who had been in Occoquan
       and some of the men too. He was prepared, but when he
       got up there, the <u>Suffragists</u> say that this hearing was
       secret and Malone refused to take part in a secret
       hearing; he wanted a public hearing.

Paul: Oh, yes. And he couldn't get it.

Fry: He couldn't get it. And what happened was that the board of charities gave a whitewashed report and Superintendent Whittaker was reinstated. By that time it was October 2. A lot of other women were in. There was a period there where they began to not send suffragists to the workhouse but kept them in the jail.

Paul: Yes, I thought in the beginning, they went to jail and only afterwards to Occoquan.

Fry: It seems to go back and forth. During this investigation they didn't send--

Paul: It seems to me that I was in prison toward the beginning, I know I was in with Mary Winsor and Lucy Branham I remember, and we were in the district jail.

Fry: This says on October 20 you were arrested.

Paul: October? No, but I think I was arrested before that. When was the time when I went in the psychopathic ward? I think that was the first time.

Fry: Well, I missed it if it was earlier than October 20.

Paul: Because this man [who interviewed me last week], Mr. Gallagher, told me all about that. And all about how this newspaperman who was close to the President came out to interview me and how they put me in the psychopathic ward and the head of St. Elizabeth's came to interview me. He must have gotten that all from the Suffragists. You haven't come across any of that?

Fry: That's in Jailed for Freedom* and yes, I have come across it.

Paul: You haven't come across it here in the Suffragist?

Fry: Not yet. But you had been sentenced to seven months in jail.

Paul: No, but that wasn't the first time. That was the second time.

---

*Doris Stevens, op. cit.

[Discussion of succession of jail terms.]

Paul: The first time, as I say, I remember, was in the [summer in the] very beginning of our going to prison, and Mrs. Lewis had gone up to see Mrs. Dora Hazard in Syracuse, who was the wife of that great man up there in Syracuse who had the Eastman Kodak Company and all those things, I think; she was on our advisory board, or something, or the New York City board, or something. Mrs. Lewis went up to see if she would advance the money [because] this was the time that we were put out of our old headquarters. You know, I told you about how the man came and said they couldn't have people going to prison--

Fry: Did he really put you out?

Paul: Yes, I told you all that.

Fry: You said, off the tape, that your landlords were unhappy. I didn't realize that they really put you out of your headquarters.

Paul: Well, maybe we could have resisted, but we didn't. He came in, I remember so vividly, and I was in bed. I guess I was just lying down for a rest or something. And he came in and sat down, very courteous, a lawyer, I presume he was, and said that the estate he was representing would like to request us to leave as soon as we possibly could. It was embarrassing to them to have people going to prison from this building and connected with this whole affair.

So I said, all right, how much time would they give us and so on and we would go and immediately try to find another place and go as soon as we could. So we were, really, just put out.

Then we had the problem of finding a place and we couldn't find a place right away, so Mr. Dash--Herman Dash--you have probably come across him many times; he was a real estate man who was also a very good personal friend. He found a place just across the street on Lafayette Square, but just a little tiny--apartment more or less. So we transferred ourselves across there and put things in storage I guess somewhere--I don't know what else we did with our possessions. Maybe we left them in the Cameron House until we could really find a place.

Then we did find that the owners of this building

Paul: that I think is now occupied by the Brookings Institute,
just right across from Cameron House, said that it was
for rent. Whoever had been there had left; it was
empty, I believe. I think this Mr. Dash, this real
estate man, found it for us. They said they would rent
it to us if we could pay $1,000 a month and one year in
advance or something like that. And just almost that
very day we got that ultimatum I was sentenced to
prison and the only two I can remember being in with
me were Mary Winsor because she made a daily prayer
for _all_ the prisoners [laughter] and Lucy Branham
because she was in the cell next to me and she was
always telling me how to eat, saying, "Now, shut your
eyes tight, and just take a bite, and then you will
have it down." [Laughter.] This was because the food
was so bad we really couldn't look at it. And I never
shall forget her. She was such a courageous girl. She
instructed me so much on how in the world we could ever
swallow the slice of bread that was given us [laughing].
But I don't remember anyone else.

But I remember Mr. Dash coming and saying, "Well,
Mrs. Lewis has returned." She was our treasurer. I
would love, in these things, to get some honor paid to
all these wonderful women. So Mrs. Lewis [had] said
she would go up and try to do the terrible thing of
raising this sum of money. And she went up to see this
Mrs. Hazard. Mr. Dash came down and asked if he could
see me as a client of his--I don't know whether you say
"client"; we were a real estate, not a law client or
whatever you are.

So he came in and came up to my little row of cells
and was assigned to a seat, and I think I went out and
sat down beside him, and he said, "Well, Mrs. Lewis has
come back with the $8,000 we had to raise." I think it
was $8,000 she raised, in addition to what we already
had. So he said, "Now I can make out the check and we
will take over the building." And that is when we moved
into--not our present but our last headquarters.

Fry: That was where?

Paul: Just about where the Brookings is. Do you know where
the Brookings is? Right down on Lafayette Square, about
two doors down from the White House.

Fry: Oh, I see; well, Brookings has now moved to Massachusetts
Avenue.

Paul: Did they. I didn't know that. It used to be the William
       Randolph Hearst residence. It was owned by his estate,
       I guess, or by somebody who had inherited it from him.
       And they asked this enormous rent and we raised it, and
       paid it. By the time we came out, we could go into our
       own headquarters where we stayed until the campaign was
       over. But that was very early in this campaign.

Attack on Headquarters

Fry: And it was after a crowd had tried to attack your previous
       house, too. Could you tell us anything about that? The
       night that a mob surged across Lafayette Square and--

Paul: Yes, but did you find that in here?

Fry: It is mentioned.

Paul: Well, what does it say there?

Fry: It will take me so long to find it; I don't know the
       exact date.*

Paul: Oh, it will?

Fry: Yes, but it mentioned that there was a pistol shot or
       some kind of a shot that went into the window--

Paul: That was very early in the period you have been going
       over. It was <u>very</u> early.

Fry: It sounded like it was fairly scary.

Paul: Well, I can remember that there was an actual invasion
       of our headquarters. The only time it ever happened.
       They did fire shots; some shots went, I think, through
       the windows there. I don't know that there was anything
       more than that.

Fry: It was shortly after the police chief had issued his
       ultimatum to you. It was within a little while after

---

*August 14, 1917.

WHEREAS, in the city of Washington, D C, about 350 feet from the White House premises is a building known as the Cameron House, in which is located headquarters and main ...s of a woman's organization at which is continually con-...ated women of character, courage and intelligence, who from various sections of the United States, and

WHEREAS, on three successive days, to wit. the 14th, . and 16th days of August, 1917, on said days immedi-following the closing of the day's work by the clerks and ...yees of the Executive Departments, hundreds of these ...s and employees, acting with sailors, then and now in the ...ce of the United States Navy and in uniform at the time, ...oldiers, then and now in the service of the United States

..., also in their uniforms at the time,—and these clerks, em-...es, sailors and soldiers, and others, formed themselves ...nobs and deliberately, unlawfully and violently damaged ...aid headquarters and offices of the said woman's organi-...on by pelting rotten eggs through the doors and windows, ...ing a bullet from a revolver through a window, and other-...damaging said Cameron House, and also violently and ...fully did strike, choke, drag and generally mistreat and ...?e and abuse the said women when they came defenseless ..., the streets adjoining as well as when they were in the ...aid building; and

WHEREAS, the organized police of the City of Washing-...n, District of Columbia, made no attempt to properly safe-...rl the property and persons of the said defenseless women, ...h..n the contrary, said police even seemed to encourage the ...s acts of the mob, and

WHEREAS, such lawlessness is in the Capital of the United States and within a few hundred feet of the Executive Mansion and offices of the President of the United States, and

WHEREAS, these attacks upon defenseless women are not only an outrage and crime in themselves, that prove the

perpetrators and those lending aid to the same to be cowards, but in addition, create throughout the world contempt for the United States and set a vicious example to the people through-out the United States and the world at large, of lawlessness and violence, and encourage designing cowards and manipula-tors everywhere to form mobs to molest the innocent and de-fenseless under any pretext whatever, and

WHEREAS, there seems to be no activity or attempt on the part of any one in authority in the City of Washington, District of Columbia, nor by the government officials to ap-prehend, arrest or punish those perpetrating the violence, on account of which the same may occur indefinitely unless Con-gress acts in the premises; and

WHEREAS, the legal status upon the premises stated would excuse the occupants of the Cameron House if they were so disposed in firing upon the mobs aforesaid, and thus create a state of greater violence and unlawry, to further injure the prestige and good name of the United States for maintain-ing law and order and institutions of democracy; therefore be it

Resolved, that the Speaker appoint a Committee of seven members to investigate into all the facts relating to the violence and unlawful acts aforesaid, and make the earliest pos-sible report upon the conditions, with the purpose in view of purging the army and navy of the United States and other offi-cial departments, of all lawless men who bring disgrace upon the American flag by participating in mob violence, and also to inquire regarding the conduct of all government employees and the police of the city of Washington, District of Columbia, with a view to maintaining law and order

*House Resolution 171 by Representative Jeannette Rankin, October 5, 1917, as reprinted in Doris Stevens's Jailed for Freedom, Boni and Liveright, New York, 1920, p. 352-3.

Fry: that.

Paul: Yes, I thought it was a little way after that. I
        remember when--very well--one of our members, who had
        been chairman of one of our committees--and these people
        were all assembling around there [outside] and there was
        lots of noise and so on. Without a word, I saw her get
        up and go out the door, and she never came back. [Laughter.]
        It was a very alarming thing, and people didn't want to
        be in any way associated, so it was, "Well, now, this is
        the limit. I am not going to be here any longer."

        But I don't think any great violence was done to the
        building. People were very terrified, that was all.

Alice in Prison

Fry: The other thing I wanted to ask you about was your
        hunger strike. By November 24, you had gone thirty
        days without food. There's a note about that. And
        there's a lot in the Suffragist about the leader being
        imprisoned. You managed to smuggle out notes some way.

Paul: I guess this time I was in the psychopathic ward, wasn't
        I?

Fry: It doesn't say that yet, but you were smuggling out
        notes.

Paul: Well, I don't remember anything about smuggling out
        notes.

Fry: You don't? Well, they printed one from you in the
        Suffragist, and a lot of times your notes were things
        like telling people what to do to get ready for the
        December convention; in other words, business of the
        party.

        And then suddenly, everybody was released. This
        time they were released on a writ of habeas corpus in
        a U.S. District Court in Virginia. This was by action
        of Dudley Field Malone, because he alleged that when you
        had been transferred to Occoquan, it was illegal.

Paul: I wasn't to Occoquan, I was to the psychopathic ward.

Fry: But a lot of the prisoners had been taken to Occoquan.

Fry: Do you remember the immigrant Polish girl, Rose Winslow? She was in jail with you.

Paul: Yes, she was also in the psychopathic ward with me. The only person who was transferred to the psychopathic ward, but this was toward the end of the whole campaign. I think if I look in Mrs. Irwin's book, I can probably find this, easily.

Fry: We should mention in the record about this long quotation from you that Doris Stevens put in her book.* It starts on page 215 and it is on your experience in prison and in the psychopathic ward. It ends on page 228. It includes the visit from the journalist, David Lawrence.

Paul: Read that to me, please.

[Tape off. Fry reads the passage.]

Paul: I certainly owed a lot to that Dr. White because it would have been so very easy for him to have given an adverse decision and I might still at this moment be in the St. Elizabeth [psychopathic ward].

Fry: That's right! That's a chilling thought.

Paul: And all that, I owe to Dr. [William A.] White.

Fry: We might point out that he is the one who first interviewed you, the "alienist."

Paul: Yes, but he was the head of St. Elizabeth's [Insane Asylum], you see, and I know that he gave an absolute, absolute statement [for my release] because he came up to see us later in the headquarters when I was there, and we got to know him fairly well. And he just completely, he said, would have nothing to do with it. He wouldn't in any way consent to have me transferred to St. Elizabeth. And he had the final say as the head of St. Elizabeth. So I have always felt the greatest sense of indebtedness to him. And so I am afraid [I might have stayed there forever--like many, many, many, many, many women over the country.]

Women in Mental Hospitals

Paul: All the time you were reading this I was thinking of a

*"The ... ireed r", r tevr , New York, 1920.

Paul: woman who called me up I guess the day before Thanks-
       giving it was. From Washington. She said just about
       everything I said. She was the wife of a judge in the
       court of appeals in Illinois, and he had gotten a
       divorce from her and married somebody else and the home
       that they had she felt she had built up equally with him
       which they had lived in for maybe fifteen or twenty
       years, and suddenly she was put out and this other woman
       was put in. She tried through all the ordinary ways of
       protesting, getting a lawyer, and no lawyer would take
       her case because he wouldn't take a case against a judge
       of the court of appeals. It would be a difficult thing
       for him ever to survive as a lawyer, perhaps, in Illinois.

            She had come down to Washington about two years ago
       while I was there in Washington and I was called up--
       (Do you want to hear this or not? Maybe I am diverting
       you too much--I will say it very fast.) Well, she came
       to me (not that I think you can do anything about it
       but it is so typical of what is happening to thousands
       of women is what I mean). I was called up by the
       Annapolis Hotel and they said, "Somebody has arrived
       from Chicago and she wants very much to see you." And
       I said, "All right, please send her up." And it was
       quite early morning, and I said, "I will have breakfast
       for her and invite her as my guest." So she came up
       and then she told me this tale and that she had come to
       Washington because she could get no justice out in
       Illinois. Her husband when he divorced her had given
       her a very tiny little alimony on which she couldn't
       survive, and she was so harassed by being constantly
       threatened that they would put her in an insane asylum
       if she made any trouble for this judge. So she thought
       she would come to ask for help.

            So I said, all right, first of all I would give her
       a little money; she said she had none at all, just
       enough to pay her bus fare down to Washington. So I
       did, a tiny little sum. Then I said we would entertain
       her for a while at the headquarters and not charge her
       anything and she could have her room and her meals there
       while she was looking around to see what she could do in
       Washington.

            She wanted to go to her congressman and her senator.
       So I called up the congressman, Senator Percy's office,
       and made arrangements for her to go see both of those
       offices and be received; otherwise, I guess, she never
       could have gotten in. She did get in very easily in
       the congressman's office, and I think Senator Percy's

Paul: office she didn't because they said she had already
been there and there was nothing they could do for
her or something like that.

    This all happened this previous time; we did every-
thing. Absolutely everything that I could think of to
do for a person to--but we didn't have much--you couldn't
hold her down. She was fluttering here and fluttering
there, and going hither and yon. She went over to the
Supreme Court and wanted to speak to the chief justice
and things like that. She went down to the attorney
general's office and wanted to speak to the attorney
general and she was each time being turned away as
perhaps out of her mind.

    So finally, one day, after about a week or ten days,
something like that, she just announced she was going
back to Illinois because her case was coming up. And
I said, "I don't advise you to go back, because if you
get into this court, they may put you in an institution."
But she went anyway. And right away you forget these
people, so I had forgotten even her name when she called
me up just now.

    She said, "Now I am back in Washington and I went
up to the headquarters and the person who is there, who
is named Miss Chittick, wouldn't have anything to do
with me and just swept me out of the house. So I found
a little colored maid there and she told me your telephone
number and so I telephoned you on the long distance. I
have rented a little tiny room out in the suburbs, from--"
some name, sounded like a Polish name, long--long involved,
lot of consonants thrown together--and she said, "They
just want to get a little money so they let me come in
for a week, but I have to pay this rent or I can't be
even here. So now I want to come right up to see you."

    And I said, "Well, I don't know that there is a
single thing I can do from here, but if you will give
me your number and so on I am going to see what I can
do and I will try to." But you just come up against
this helplessness of people, men as well as women, I am
sure, who are being sentenced to these institutions.
You know even our Mrs. Hilles, our wonderful Mrs. Hilles,
died in some kind of an institution, and her daughter,
probably it was money, I don't know what else. One only
child was a daughter. Her husband had died, her daughter
married a Catholic man.

[End of Tape 6, Side B]

[Tape 7, Side A]

Fry: Your position as leader of the National Woman's Party
meant that if you had gone into St. Elizabeth Insane
Asylum that you would have stayed there? It seems to
me that surely they could have gotten you out.

Paul: Well, people are so apt to say, "Well, this lady
unfortunately was very good in her way, but she was
mentally unbalanced." People are apt to believe it, I
am afraid. I know that there was absolutely nothing
the matter with Mrs. Hilles, and I think the cruelty
of her daughter's doing a thing like this, probably
under the influence of her husband, and maybe under
the influence of the church at this time, to get possession of her fortune--we don't know what motive
animated them. You wouldn't think that it was possible
when you know the record and type of Mrs. Hilles, that
she could die in this institution. So I could have
died in this institution, and be there this moment. So
I think it was Heaven protecting me, I guess.

The Campaigning Goes On

Fry: Should we go on to some of the things that were going
on outside of the prisons at that time?

Paul: Whatever you want.

Fry: You did have speakers going around all over the country.
Wasn't there a train for suffrage?

Paul: Yes, we had two trains. The first was the Suffrage
Special and then there was the Prison Special. The
Suffrage Special was a group of women, I think we took
one car on a train, and we sent [women] like Mabel
Vernon the same way she [had] organized for Sara [Bard
Field in 1915], we had people in every state where the
Suffrage Special would stop get up a big meeting. And
you will find all that, of course, in the Suffragist.
It was just to spread--another way of doing something
different so as to perhaps get a little publicity on it.

Fry: And you had a very dramatic story to tell at this time.

Paul: And then came the next one, which was the Prison Special,
in which we took the women who had been in prison. They

Paul: went in their prison costumes and they got out and they spoke at these great, great meetings in their prison costumes. It was all, you know, general propaganda to hold the Democrats up to a bad light and so on.

Fry: When you look at the chronology you can jump to the conclusion that your picketing was very effective because just right after your picketing got started Mr. J. A. H. Hopkins tells about talking with President Wilson [about July 18, 1917], and Wilson asked him what he thinks he should do about the suffragists and finally asks him if he thinks--

Paul: It was his wife, you know, who wouldn't accept a pardon. My, what a wonderful woman.

Fry: Wilson was considering making suffrage a war measure at that time. And he asked Hopkins if he could find out about what would happen if he decided to put in suffrage as a war measure and would he please find out how it would be received by both the Senate and the House. And then right during this time the House Judiciary Committee voted that only war emergency measures should be considered.

Let me run down the chronology for this period. The Senate, which had voted out the suffrage bill on May 15, finally reported it out again with a favorable report on September 15. But before that, on July 19, Wilson unconditionally pardoned the sixteen women. In the meantime the state of Maine lost its suffrage referendum something like two to one.

Back on the Hill on September 22 the House finally created a Suffrage Committee. That happened on September 22 from Chairman Pou. How did you pronounce that?

Paul: [Phonetically] Pew.

Fry: And this was interesting because President Wilson had finally asked Chairman Pou to consider his request to establish a suffrage committee just a few weeks earlier, after your picketing began. Then on October 6 the war session adjourned. (And that was also when you were first arrested.) It adjourned without suffrage being considered.

On October 25, Ohio loses a suffrage referendum. Women continue to be arrested. On November 12 there were forty-one arrested. (At least it is talked about in the November 12 issue; that may not be the exact date.)

Fry: And then right after November 24, I am not sure of the exact day here, all suffrage prisoners were released on the writ of habeas corpus. It looks as if when Congress closed the suffrage newsletters sound optimistic.

Paul: That was the end of '17.

Fry: That was the end of '17. Then in December, I guess, you had your big meeting of the National Woman's Party.

Paul: Wilson made the announcement that he would support the Amendment. He went up to the Senate, you know, and made this--

Fry: That was the next December, you know. That was in 1918.

Paul: 1919 was it?

[Tape off to straighten out chronology.]

Paul: --and constant insistence through the picketing were the two methods that we used.

Fry: And one was constantly opposing the Democrats, you were saying?

Paul: Well, the policy of opposing all the Democratic candidates, in all the suffrage states, I mean, using the votes of women to win it for us. We couldn't have made it political issue by opposing it in any of these other states which weren't even for it. I think that was the more important thing that we used, and because we had a constant supply of support from behind at home in the Sen te and the House. Because as I said, I don't think anyone but [Senator] Borah ever opposed us, or ever voted against us. I don't remember anyone else from the suffrage state.

Fry: When Maine lost the suffrage referendum in September--

Paul: So many of these lost. Pennsylvania lost and New Jersey lost it. You had so many of these go against us.

Catt Backs the Federal Amendment, September, 1917

Fry: In the suffrage magazine of September 15, Carrie Chapman Catt says, in response to the Maine loss, that all

Fry: suffrage forces of the nation will unite in the near future and concentrate in Washington for a drive on the federal amendment.

Paul: That's wonderful. Now when did she say that?

Fry: That was in September of 1917, after Maine lost but before the New York referendum.

Paul: That's simply amazing that, she finally did come out for it.

Fry: And I think England, at that point, had finally won equal suffrage; Russia had it and Canada was about to have it.

Paul: I know, but Mrs. Catt had opposed us for so long that I don't remember that [laughing] she ever did come out. That was 1917? Really? In the midst of war.

Fry: Well, I wonder if she ever really did?

Paul: Well, you say she said so.

Fry: [Reading.] She says that "in the near future" that they would do this. Maybe they never did?

Paul: I think at that time they were all working in the defense [effort] and maybe they thought that they could make some kind of a bargain about that.

My goodness, as you recall all this, I realize what a very great resistance Mr. Wilson put up to something that he said he believed in.

Fry: [Laughter.]

Paul: Almost impossible to believe.

Fry: I wonder what he did with things that he opposed?

Paul: Yes. Exactly. [Laughter.]

Fry: Well, later on Jeannette Rankin performed another service. She got the House to pass a resolution appointing a committee of seven to investigate Occoquan just at the end of the session, so I guess that that investigation came up--

Paul: And then, you know, the only member of Congress that

Paul: came out--actually came, ever, to visit any prison to see what was happening, was the father of Lindberg, did you know that?

Fry: Oh, I thought--well, Jeannette Rankin visited it a couple of times, according to the Suffragist.

Paul: I don't think so, because I asked her about it the other day and she said, "No, I never went out there."

Fry: Oh, really? Well, there is a profile of her given in the Suffragist sometime in the fall of 1917, one of those issues, and it mentions in there that she had visited the women, either in jail or in Occoquan.

Paul: Well, then, of course, if it is in the Suffragist I am sure it is true, but she had evidently forgotten it the way [laughing] I have forgotten being thrown down. Because she told me that. She said she was sorry she never went but she never did. But I do remember Lindberg (we didn't know the famous son then) because he was a member of Congress, and he was the only one that I ever recall that went out to really see what was going on in the prison when all this fuss was being made.

President Wilson Comes Around

Fry: [Reading.] Well, I do have a date to announce: that on October 25 Wilson publicly endorsed suffrage as a war measure.

Paul: When did he do that, in a speech to Congress or what?

Fry: I don't know how he did it, but it could not have been in a speech to Congress if Congress had adjourned its war session; I don't think there was anything going on.

Paul: I would consider that you would maybe mark that as one of the high points for Consuelo.

Fry: Do you remember that great day?

Paul: No, I don't remember it at all. We knew that he was coming along but I don't recall any one day when something happened.

Fry: Well, I guess there were a lot of indications by that

Fry: time, that he was on the verge of coming out.

Paul: Yes. But which particular day--the time that he made
it public to the world was when he went up to the Senate
and made this appeal. Of course that was almost the
end of the campaign.

       That was a great speech. We have had it mimeo-
graphed and all through our present [Equal Rights
Amendment] campaign we have been circulating it, to
show what one President did for equality for women, to
try to encourage the others.

Fry: [Searching.] Here it is on page 6 of the Suffragist,
Saturday, November 3.

Paul: He made the speech before the Senate?

Fry: No, he did not. You were in prison, incommunicado.
On October 25, 1917. That's why you weren't in on it.

Paul: I wasn't in prison when he made that speech though.

Fry: President Wilson was speaking to a delegation of New
York women who asked him to encourage the voters of New
York state. (Oh, this isn't the Amendment.) He endorsed
suffrage "for the women of this nation as a war measure."
He stated clearly that "the war burdening the country
cannot excuse the leaders of any party in neglecting
the question women are pressing upon them." And he
says, "The world has witnessed the slow political
reconstruction and men have generally been obliged to
be satisfied with the slowness of the process, but I
believe that this war is going to so quicken the convictions and the consciousness of mankind with regard to
political questions that the speed of reconstruction
will be greatly increased, and I believe that just
because we are quickened by the questions of this war
we ought to be quickened to give this question of woman's
suffrage our immediate consideration."

       Now he knew that legislation (the article goes on to
point out) in New York state lies outside of his power.
He knew too that "millions of women and men who demand
that he pass a federal amendment in the next session
were listening to him." So he "set out the case for
national suffrage like a political leader who sees the
side he must take on a national issue while at the same
time he bade godspeed to the New York election, required
by the occasion. His statement assures suffragists of

Fry: action from the administration that has kept women dis-
         enfranchised. Already there have been clear indices that
         he planned at last to act. The reporting out of a long-
         buried amendment in the Senate at the end of the war
         session and the creation of the Suffrage Committee in
         the House prove that the pressure of women's agitation
         had forced the Democratic leader to turn from his
         obstinate stand against national suffrage." It ends
         by saying, "It is no longer safe to oppose federal
         suffrage. The President comes all the way to endorse
         it. President Wilson has learned his lesson. The
         National Woman's Party will hold him now to action in
         the December session of Congress."

Paul: Well, then in the December session, he probably made
         this appeal, the speech I remember.

         [Tape off.]

Fry: This particular volume of the Suffragist has a lot of
         the first-hand notes from women in prison and we can
         encourage people who use your manuscript to look it up
         here. I noticed here some prison notes of Rose Winslow,
         and here are some by Mrs. Mary A. Knowland describing
         that "night of terror," which was November 14.

Paul: Oh, she would be a very good person. I told you--remember--
         that when I went to Florida, when I was talking about age--
         that the oldest picket was the one who came up and
         volunteered. That's that Mrs. Knowland.

              We used to have so many pictures. We [released] the
         photograph of the oldest and the youngest picket.

Fry: Did somebody in National Woman's Party know Mr. Joseph--
         how do you pronounce his name--Tumulty?--

Paul: Tumulty.

Fry: --who was private secretary to Woodrow Wilson?

Paul: Yes, what about him?

Fry: Well, apparently he told members of the National Woman's
         Party in December, "Of course I am with you" and promised
         to speak to the President about the federal amendment.

Paul: No, but--I know he was Wilson's secretary--Tumulty was
         [also] the personal lawyer for our Mrs. Emma Guffey
         Miller and her family, you know. Senator Guffey of

Paul: Pennsylvania, of course, a very prominent Democrat.
        Tumulty the senior, when he left when Wilson went out,
        he started a law office, and then we inherited the son,
        so we have Tumulty the son now as our attorney.

Fry: Well, apparently somebody was able to arrange a deputation
        to Tumulty, senior.

Paul: December 26.

Fry: What year?

Paul: Let's see. [Reading from Irwin, op. cit.] What year?
        [Laughter.] Too bad that they don't put the date of
        the year on the top of each page or something. Well,
        let me see if I can find the year [tape off] the Senate
        passed the suffrage amendment. But what[ever] year it
        is, I have the date, and it was, if you look, September
        26 it was.

Fry: Well, the Amendment passed the House January 10, 1918.
        So maybe that was in September of 1918.

Paul: But in the Suffragist, could you see the year you are
        on?

Fry: The President's speech there just before the Senate
        almost passed it, is on page 7 of the October 12, 1918,
        issue.

Paul: Well, I think you ought to mark that for Consuelo.
        Another highlight.

        It lost by two votes.

Fry: After five days of debate?

Paul: Yes, is that it?

Fry: And this eleventh hour appeal by the President.

Paul: That was an eloquent and marvelous speech. As I say,
        we had it so many times mimeographed and sent over the
        country as far as we could. That was really the
        culmination of the battle.

THE FINALE

The Battle in the Senate

Paul: I notice in this book it says that hereafter, having
gotten the President, we turned our picketing to the
Senate because that was our next obstacle.

   We were two votes short. The President first went
up and made the speech, and then over in Versailles he
cabled back here for the last vote, Senator Harris of
Georgia.

Fry: Yes, for the final vote. All this time you were
continuing your--

Paul: We continued to picket now the Senate because the
President was no longer--we had no longer any enemy
there.

Fry: Did you move the locale of your picketing over to
the Capitol or to the Senate Office Building?

Paul: No, we just picketed on the steps of the Senate Office
Building.

Fry: Right up to the time that the President made his speech,
you were burning his words in the park. Did you personally
participate in any of that?

Paul: No, but I--we had a very beautiful picket line and I
showed you the photograph of it. We went out from our
headquarters to hold one of these speeches and on
Lafayette Statue we began, "Lafayette we are here!"
[Laughter.] And each time that a person got out
"Lafayette we are here," she was promptly arrested. I
was, I suppose, managing it, seeing they got there and
everything, but I wasn't up making a speech. It was

Paul: very beautiful, these girls that made these speeches. So suddenly I was just arrested, because some policeman came along and just arrested me because I was obviously engineering this outrageous affair. There they were, you see, [showing a picture] each one holding up the President's words.

Fry: Oh, that's beautiful. [Laughter.]

Paul: Putting a little flame and "Lafayette we are here!" [Laughing.] Then she was pulled down.

Fry: Yes, I see. She is holding it up very much like pictures of boys burning their draft cards today--hold it up high and put a match to it. But these are all dressed in white flowing gowns. It is the beautiful pageantry of it that is different from our protests today.

Paul: That really is lovely, don't you think? I mean it sounds sort of violent, "burning the President's words," but you see [laughing] it is not particularly so.

Fry: And there is not a big mob, they are all evenly spaced, much as they might be in a pageant.

Paul: But I remember I was way far out and suddenly was arrested.

I think maybe that's the time we were taken to the old abandoned workhouse [Occoquan].

Fry: Oh, were you arrested more than twice? I mean more than two or three times?

Paul: I think I was arrested three times, and the one you read about to me I think was the last. And I remember this one, which I hadn't gone out to be arrested, but I was. And I was imprisoned, I think. Of course, I remember being in the old abandoned workhouse. Elsie Hill was in that prison with me and also Hazel Hunkins. And then I think the first time [I was arrested] was when I was in with Mary Winsor, as I said, who made the prayer. I thought it was Lucy Branham, but you read she was in with me the last time.

Well, now we have gotten that date fixed and Wilson's speech. Now the only remaining thing is the two votes.

Paul: I know when the [successful] vote was, in the
Senate--I know exactly where to look--the vote in the
Senate was in June*--because that sent it on to the
states for ratification--so we all know that. That was
June, 1919.

Fry: To get this chronology straight, the Amendment first
passed the House, January 10, 1918, by a vote of 274 to
136, a two-thirds majority with one vote so spare.
Exactly forty years to a day from the time the suffrage
amendment was first introduced into Congress. That was
the session that the Senate failed to pass it by two
votes.

Paul: That was January, yes. Well, then the House met again
and passed it in the spring of 1919, I think.

Fry: Yes, the House passed it again May 21, 1919, 304 to 89.
And on June 4 it passed the Senate and was up for
ratification.

Paul: I think the House voted on it twice that spring.

Supporters Willaim Boise Thompson and William Randolph Hearst

Fry: You had a mass meeting in Palm Beach, Florida. Do you
remember Colonel William Boise Thompson who was chairman
of the Ways and Means of the Republican National Committee?

Paul: I certainly do. He gave us $10,000.

Fry: Yes, and he said that "the story of the brutal imprisonment in Washington of women advocating suffrage is
shocking and almost incredible. I became accustomed in
Russia"--let's see, he had been a member of the United
States Red Cross Mission in Russia--"to the stories of
men and women who served terms of imprisonment under
the czar" and so forth. And he says, "I wish now to
contribute $10,000 to the campaign for the passage of
the suffrage amendment through the Senate. One hundred

---

*June 4, 1919.

Fry: dollars for each of the pickets."

Paul: Yes, indeed, I will never forget it. And they telephoned up and said, "How many pickets had there been?" Because he was giving a hundred dollars for every picket who was imprisoned.

Fry: They telephoned to you?

Paul: I don't know whether it was to me, but anyway to the headquarters.

Fry: Did you know right off the top of your head, how many there had been?

Paul: No, we had to scurry around and find out how much it was. [Laughing.] This was Mrs. Lawrence Lewis, who was our national treasurer, you know. She organized the meeting down in Palm Beach, and didn't know Mr. William Boise Thompson at all, but he walked into the meeting. And then she telephoned up--I suppose it was she because she got up the meeting--and asked us to find out quickly. (We didn't know, I believe,) how many people had ever been in prison. So we quickly got the number and phoned down to her. And then she went to Mr. Thompson and said this is the number so then it came to $10,000.

Fry: I see you had the support of William Randolph Hearst in editorials calling for suffrage.

Paul: Oh, always from William Randolph Hearst, always. Always, never failed. You know his mother, Phoebe Hearst, was one of the greatest women of the country and was a great leader in the suffrage campaign. When we formed our little branch out in California she was a friend of Mrs. William Kent and helped with forming our Woman's Party branch.

Fry: Yes, that makes sense.

Paul: And you know that set of furniture we have down there was given by Mr. Hearst, you know that don't you?

Fry: Where, Belmont House?

Paul: Yes. It was made by slaves down on a plantation in Louisiana. Mrs. Hilles had always been in political life because her father had been such a great secretary of state, Senator Bayard, you know. Secretary of State B------. ~ ~ · · · · · · · · · we

Paul: have ever had because of building up a friendship with Latin America. And so she grew up in that political atmosphere, and so did William Randolph Hearst. And so she had known him since childhood. So when she became a national chairman of the Woman's Party, he gave her a check one day, I think it was $1500. Anyway quite a large check. He said, "Now I wish you would put something in your new headquarters that you are getting"--(this one up on Capitol Hill--that was our original one; we bought it. The old brick capitol)-- "in memory of my mother, Phoebe Hearst." So Mrs. Hilles went down to Louisiana and she bought the set of furniture that is [now] there in the living room-- two sofas and big chairs and little chairs and so on. And she got a set of furniture that had been made by the slaves on one of the plantations down there.

We have had it re-covered twice. When we were re-covering it the last time, Mrs. Longwell--and I think you must know all this--wrote to Mr. Hearst and went personally to his office in New York to say that since this is a set that your father (the present William Randolph Hearst) gave in memory of your grand-mother and it is getting pretty dilapidated, and we would like, if we could get a modest estimate for putting it back in shape, if you would be willing to pay for it.

And she thinks that--she was under the impression that the answer was yes, find out what it would cost and so on. I don't think she ever saw him personally, but I think this was the reply she got from his office. So then she got an estimate and sent it up and the reply came back very cold, everything connected with donations from the Hearst family is in the hands of a Hearst Foundation or something. And no interest was manifested at all. So finally Mrs. Longwell and her friends, Wanona McGuire and some others, Wanona McGuire's sister, mainly, I think, paid for it themselves.

But he was always--the Hearst paper always helped us. And Mrs. Hearst was always a member--that is Mrs. William Randolph Hearst.

The Last Votes

Fry: To go back a moment, I think I have found that first

Fry: attempt to force a vote in the Senate that you spoke of. It occurred on May 19, 1918, and this was when friends interceded when it was shown that not enough votes were pledged to secure passage. So they postponed it.

Paul: That's the time I told you about when Maud Younger and I went and talked to these two men, Curtis and Gallinger, that's right.

Fry: Yes, it says the Republicans, led by Senator Gallinger, provided skirmishes from time to time. And the administration was accused on the floor of blocking action. Alice, did you think there were two votes lacking when it was up for the next vote October 1 of 1918, after the President's address to the Senate?

Paul: Well, of course, I guess everybody knew there wasn't.

Fry: Why couldn't you have postponed the vote that time too? [It lost, 62 to 34--two votes short.]

Paul: Well, we didn't postpone it the first time. The Republicans thought it was better and they postponed it.

Fry: Then on February 10, 1919, it was introduced in the Senate and it lost by one vote. So it was reintroduced, and in the meantime Woodrow Wilson came back from Europe.

What I wanted to get down, Alice, was the way that apparently they changed the wording a little bit to get the vote of Senator Gay of Louisiana, in February of 1919 I think.

Paul: I know. They did, you see. It was on states' rights, you see, again.

Fry: And the National Woman's Party--

Paul: --would have nothing to do with it.

Fry: So it never came to a vote, because Senator Weeks of Massachusetts, who was a Republican anti-suffragist, objected. And then Senator Sherman of Illinois, a Republican suffragist, objected. And then the session was closed so it did not pass the Senate.

Form 1201 2

WESTERN UNION
TELEGRAM

CLASS OF SERVICE	SYMBOL
Telegram	
Day Letter	Blue
Night Message	Nite
Night Letter	N L

If none of these three symbols appears after the check (number of words) this is a telegram. Otherwise its character is indicated by the symbol appearing after the check.

NEWCOMB CARLTON, PRESIDENT   GEORGE W. E. ATKINS, FIRST VICE-PRESIDENT

CLASS OF SERVICE	SYMBOL
Telegram	
Day Letter	Blue
Night Message	Nite
Night Letter	N L

If none of these three symbols appears after the check (number of words) this is a telegram. Otherwise its character is indicated by the symbol appearing after the check.

RECEIVED AT 127 N. CENTER ST., RENO, NEV. ALWAYS OPEN
1306 SF 72 BLUE

1919 MAR 1 PM 8 52

MC WASHINGTON DC NF 1

MISS ANNE MARTIN   176

153 NORTH VIRGINIA ST RENO NEV

VOTE LACKING TO PASS SUFFRAGE OBTAINED TODAY WHEN SENATOR
GAY LOUISIANA ANNOUNCED WOULD VOTE FAVORABLY NECESSARY TWO
THIRDS NOW PLEDGED SENATE AND HOUSE AMENDMENT CAN PASS BEFORE
CONGRESS CLOSES IF WE CAN SECURE ROLL CALL DANGER NOW IS FROM
FILIBUSTER PRESIDENT CONFERRED WITH JONES NEWMEXICO ABOUT AMEND-
MENT JONES ENDEAVORING HAVE VOTE TAKEN TODAY SENATE PLANNING

RECEIVED AT 127 N. CENTER ST., RENO, NEV. ALWAYS OPEN
ALL NIGHT SESSION PLEASE HAVE TELEGRAMS SENT PRESIDENT AND
YOUR SENATORS URGING THEM NOT TO LOSE THIS LAST OPPORTUNITY
ALICE PAUL.

1919 MAR   M 3 57

The Battle in the House

Paul: I want the Suffragist.

Fry: The 1919 Suffragist? I am going to read from your editorial that says on January 10, 1918, the vote on the suffrage amendment in the House of Representatives was 274 to 136, only one vote more than required. And on May 21, 1919, it was 304 to 89, 42 more than the required two-thirds. Again the greatest support for the Amendment is from the West.

Paul: Well, in that article, then, they must give an account of it.

Fry: Do you want me to go ahead and read it?

Paul: Not the editorial.

Fry: Here is a mention of the introduction of the Amendment. It was introduced by six members in the House--

Paul: No, I don't mean that. Is that when it passed?

Fry: Yes. It tells about it being referred to the Woman Suffrage Committee. You are particularly interested in the House?

Paul: I'm very interested in the House because that is when they struck out the seven years, you see.* Is Mr. Gard [mentioned] there? Because I know it was at the bottom of the first column.

Fry: [Searching.] See, this article says that in the House there were no hearings. On Tuesday morning, May 10, the first meeting of the committee was held and it was decided to report it favorably. [Pause.] It doesn't mention [a seven-year clause].

Paul: You haven't the article I am talking about.

[Tape off.]

Fry: Why don't you just go ahead and tell what happened.

---

*A seven-year deadline for ratification. This limitation had been added also to the Equal Rights Amendment when ᵀ ᵢ ᵢ ᵢ ᵢ ᵥᵢᵉʷ ver strong ᴬ

Fry: Don't you want to go into that seven-year clause that
was attempted?

Paul: I was just going to show it to you, try to show it to
you [laughing], but it doesn't seem to be in this issue.

Fry: So I think you ought to tell it to me and let me get it
down on tape because it is something that needs to be
hunted up later. We need to have a record of it here.

Paul: Well, I will tell you all I can remember. That when it
did come up--whatever date, and I don't know when the
date was. I rather thought it came up twice in the
House--

Fry: In May*--

Paul: It was the first time that it came up after a new session
began you know, with the Republicans, and the prohibition amendment having just had the seven years put in.
Mr. Gard of Ohio arose and just moved the addition of
the words "provided that it is ratified within seven
years." And the whole chamber resounded with cries of
"Shame!" And it was voted down.

        And then on the next page was a little statement
that we had in--I don't see why I can't find it here--
by Mrs. Wadsworth--it was the top of the next page.
(And I had it copied so many times, is the reason I
remember, in Washington to use it with people I couldn't
seem to move very well.) At the top of the next page
was a statement by Mrs. Wadsworth [head of the anti-
suffragists] withdrawing all sort of efforts to defeat
the Amendment, having lost the seven years. Because,
as she said, "With no time limit, the women would keep
on and on and on until they will undoubtedly ratify
this. There is nothing further we can do. We have lost
our campaign." Later I used her statement trying to
try to show these women how they were misjudging the
importance of the seven years they were trying to put on.

Fry: Later on in the ERA.

Paul: How these present women were trying to put it on [the
ERA] and how they were making a mistake. Perhaps they

----

*January 10, 1918, and May 21, 1919.

Paul: would realize, if they saw how the leader of the
        opposition withdrew all opposition, so we didn't have
        to meet any opponents at all from this organization
        against the votes for women, when we tried to ratify.
        That's all there was to that.

Fry: Okay. And now--

Paul: Now ratification--we went along fairly quickly, I think.
        We began immediately, the very next day, and appointed
        a committee headed by Mrs. Lawrence Lewis to head the
        ratification campaign. The states that we had to go to
        we went to, from the national headquarters.

        [We didn't go to] the states where the campaign was
        very easy, such as, I remember, Iowa, where Senator
        Cummins of Iowa said he would give me one postage stamp,
        and "That's all the campaign would cost you, because I
        will"--he was a very powerful man in the state of Iowa
        apparently and powerful politically, and so he said, "I
        will have this brought immediately before the legislature
        and you won't have anything to do." So we didn't go into
        Iowa. Iowa ratified right away. If I remember, Wisconsin
        was the first state to ratify, I think it was. The
        father of the president of the suffrage organization
        came down--his name was James--came down to Washington
        with the ratification to get it in number one.

        And so it went along pretty happily. We lost, for
        instance, in some states, and finally when--we lost in
        Connecticut, we lost in Virginia, we lost in Maryland,
        we lost in Delaware.

Fry: That Delaware battle was quite a long heart-breaking one
        because there for about three or four weeks, it looked
        like Delaware was going to be the state that would have
        the distinction of being the final state to ratify and
        put it into effect. And then it fell through.

Paul: Well, when we were getting down to the very end, of
        course, it dragged along, because we finally got it as
        you know through President Wilson conferring with the
        governor of Tennessee and asking him--as a fellow Demo-
        crat--to call the legislature. And then that was a long
        and very dramatic campaign--I think maybe Mrs. Irwin
        gave an account of it in this book*--in Tennessee where,

_____

*op. cit.

Paul: if I remember rightly, they did not pass it in the
       beginning, and then reassembled and did pass it.
       August 28.

       Well, that's about the essence of the ratification
       campaign. It was August 28, 1920, and it was submitted
       to the states in June, 1919. So it took us from June
       1919 to August, very little over a year.

Fry: And that was just in time for the women to vote in
       the presidential election of 1920.

Paul: It was between Harding and Cox, of course. Harding
       was the Republican candidate. So we went out and had
       deputations to him, deputations to Cox and all those
       things.

Fry: Well, let's see. How many states was it? Thirty-six?

Paul: Thirty-eight.

Fry: Thirty-eight that was required, and you--

Paul: It took thirty-six then, thirty-eight it takes now.

Fry: You got thirty-five fairly rapidly. Why did it take so
       long to get that last state? Was there more resistance?

Paul: I wouldn't say that it went so rapidly. It went along,
       but we tried in a good many states to finally consummate
       it when we got up to thirty-five. Of course, that was
       the place--that's exactly what the seven years can do
       to us, you see--they could hold you off and get enough
       counter states to defeat you.

Fry: In the ERA, exactly.

Paul: I do want to have that preserved about that vote, and
       when we are through all this, I will take it and try to
       see, if my eyes are a little less fatigued. Maybe I
       could find it.

Fry: Well, there's a chance that it might be in that first
       vote in the House, which was--

Paul: No, it wasn't.

Fry: The first time it passed the House?

Paul: ꟼ, , , , . ꓔ⸗   ⸗⸗ ⸗⸗⸗⸗ ⸗⸗⸗⸗ ⸗⸗⸗ ⸗⸗'⸗en in

Paul: 1919.

Fry: It wasn't the 1918 vote?

Paul: No, the 1919 vote because it was then that they withdrew.
This was the last vote before we went to the states for
ratification, and the organization against votes for
women withdrew from the campaign then, at the beginning
of the ratification campaign, because they said, "We are
now defeated. We can never, never defeat this unless
we have that seven years' limitation." It was clearly
true that if we were defeated in seven years, we would
have tried eight years, nine years, and ten years. And
they said that is something that the [suffragist] women
will accomplish.

Ratification

Fry: What sort of campaign organization did you have for
ratification? Did you just continue with your same
organization?

Paul: Yes.

Fry: Did people tend to zero in on states like Delaware and
Tennessee that were the hoped-for final states?

Paul: Well, Delaware wasn't exactly the hoped-for final state
in my opinion. It was--any state. We were hoping to
get Connecticut. I remember the same time we worked in
Delaware because it was a little state and it was Mrs.
Hilles' own state, you see, and her brother was a senator
and her father had been secretary of state from there and
it was a powerful political party. We had all the women's
organizations there back of us. I went up there and
stayed through most of the campaign in Delaware and the
DuPont family were backing us. Nearly every DuPont
woman was on our board up there. And there was a
Senator Al Lee.

[End of Tape 7, Side A]

[Tape 7, Side B]

Fry: Mabel Vernon doesn't remember the Delaware campaign for
ratification, but the Suffragist shows that she did work

Fry: in it.

Paul: She _didn't_? Yes, she was the _key_ to it.

Fry: _You_ will have to tell about that, [laughing] because she
didn't remember it.

Paul: How extraordinary. I don't see what she _could_ remember
if she couldn't remember Delaware.

Fry: She remembered the suffrage campaign but not ratification.

Paul: You see, Mrs. Hilles was state chairman and she conducted
the campaign in Delaware. And I know that Mabel went up
to help her and went over the state, and Betty Gram Swing
went up and went all over the state. I went up, and Mrs.
Lawrence Lewis went up, a great many of us because it
was a small state and we thought it wouldn't be difficult.
And the National American Woman Suffrage Association
there worked in complete--completely with us. There was
no conflict at all. We knew the president very well and
she worked just as harmoniously as anybody else. But
we lost it anyway. They didn't vote us down, they just
didn't act.

They just had so many problems about their orchards
and their pruning of their [laughing] trees and their
peach trees and so on. We went almost all over the state
into every little village and it seemed to me we talked
to almost every woman in the state, but they were
absorbed in their own agricultural problems and such
things.

Fry: The _Suffragist_ mentions that there was an argument
going on in Delaware between the head of the Republican
party there and the Republican governor. There were
two factions in the party. The governor was very strong
for suffrage, and the chairman of the state Republican
committee was determined to fight the governor on every
issue, and so he fought ratification.

Paul: Does it say that in the _Suffragist_?

Fry: Yes, I think it was one of your editorials in the
Suffragist. I wondered if you might remember that.

Paul: I don't see how that could be--

Fry: Dan Layton, state chairman of the Republican party in
Delaware, was opposing the suffrage amendment because

Fry: he was having a factional fight with the governor.
This was just briefly explained in the Suffragist.

Paul: Yes, I didn't realize that there was a--I hardly see
how that could have been; and I don't think I wrote an
editorial to that effect. Somebody else must have
written it. Because I think the DuPont family were all
Republicans and that was a very powerful family; and
this Al Lee family were all Democrats and that was the
other great political family. And I remember talking
to the governor myself. I think he was a Republican.

Fry: Yes, and he was all for it.

Paul: I know he was.

Fry: And even the national Republican committee held a meeting
and passed a resolution for the Delaware state committee
to get behind suffrage, and they still wouldn't do it.
But the governor continued in his support.

Paul: As I say, as I recall, they didn't vote. They just let
time slip by with their agitation over other subjects.

Fry: Yes. Then on June 23 President Wilson appealed to
Tennessee in a telegram to Governor Roberts.

Paul: That's right.

Fry: I wanted to ask you, were you very worried about all the
matters that were going through the courts at this time?
There was a question that came up of whether women could
be allowed to vote in the election because the states
hadn't had time to pass their election qualification
laws to cover women, like the poll tax and the literacy
test.

Paul: Well, you see, it was put in the Amendment itself,
"Congress shall have the power to enforce this by
appropriate legislation" or something like that. We
went to see Senator Walsh of Montana, who was supposed
to be the greatest constitutional lawyer, and we asked
him what should we do to provide for what you are talking
about. And he said, "Oh, you do nothing. There is no
question about this at all, this will go. We don't have
to consider this. Congress is not going to take any
action directing the states what to do, they will do
what they want--each state do what it wants." So we
never had any trouble about that.

Fry: The Supreme Court did rule in your favor in one state--
I think it might have been Ohio, if I remember. And it
ruled in your favor before the election.

Paul: There was some technical point, and in that case Mrs.
Lawrence Lewis got her son, who was this young lawyer
as I told you, if not in the firm, he knew very well
William Draper Lewis, who was the dean of the University
of Pennsylvania Law School and a great constitutional
lawyer. So Mr. William Draper Lewis and his son,
Shippen   Lewis, and I think they got a third lawyer,
they just handled that Ohio case for us so we didn't
bother with it.

Fry: The thing I noticed was that you had said, in the
Suffragist that you'd better get two more states, just
in case the ratification in these states [are invali-
dated by the courts].

Paul: Well, we did. We got one more and that was Connecticut.

Fry: After Tennessee, right.

Paul: Well now it seems to me that as far as your thing, that
you really have covered the whole field pretty well from
the beginning to the end.

WHAT NEXT?

Alternatives

Fry: Well, I notice that right after it was ratified there
        was a series of articles and meetings called "What
        Next?" in the Suffragist, talking about what to do.

Paul: Then, you see, what we had to consider was, should we
        dissolve because we had been formed just for this
        [suffrage], or should we continue. And we really--I
        think I would have dissolved it because you just reach
        a point of such extreme fatigue you can hardly go any
        [laughing] longer, you know. Anyway I didn't want to
        go ahead and take the responsibility of raising any
        more money, and I had the responsibility, I thought, of
        paying up all our bills at the end of the suffrage
        campaign because we had about $10,000 of bills we had
        to pay.

        So Maud Younger and I took a tiny apartment together
        and we started out. She didn't try to raise the money,
        but she started to help so we could have a little place
        to live and try to get the new organization started.
        Elsie Hill was made the new chairman, you know. I
        didn't even go on their new board because I wanted to
        be so free. So that took about half a year, of just
        raising the money to get the bills paid. Maybe a year,
        I don't remember exactly how long it took us to pay it
        all off. But we did.

        And during that period we tried to find a permanent
        headquarters where we didn't have to be subject to our
        landlords putting us out and also having to pay such an
        immense amount for rent as we had been paying--$1,000
        a month you know, for some period. At the beginning of
        this period, when we were raising this money and so on,
        we started in on putting the suffrage statue in the

Paul: Capitol and having our final convention to wind up
everything, which we held in February 15, 1921: Susan
B. Anthony's birthday, our final convention.

At that convention, many people came. For instance
I remember Miss Jane Addams came, and she said, "We hope
you will just merge in with the Women's International
League for Peace and Freedom and devote all your time
now to peace." And a great many of our members wanted
us to go into the peace movement.

A great many members, for instance Lucy Burns, she
just said, "I don't want to do anything more, I don't
want to be on any board or any committee or have anything
more to do, because I think we have done all this for
women and we have sacrificed everything we possessed
for them and now let them--They say they want all these
things, better salaries and better positions, and married women the right to work and married women the
right to have their own earnings and married women the
right to be employed by the government even if their
husbands are employed,"--she said, "let them fight for
it now. I am not going to fight for these married women
any more." And she didn't. She never--I don't know if
she even came to our final convention. From that time
on she never gave any help, and she was a very devout
Catholic, and I think she devoted herself entirely to
her family and her church, until about a year ago, she
died.

So at this last meeting perhaps the person who did
the most to get us to continue was Mrs. Donald Hooker,
our state chairman in Maryland. She was _very_ eager to
go on. She said the Woman's Party was a peculiar type
of women that, if they should all disband, we'd lost
that type of women who is so devoted to building up a
respect and so on and a belief in the power of women.
We can't afford to lose it. So Elsie Hill was made the
first chairman, and Mrs. Hooker pretty soon was made the
national chairman.

Fry: Let's see, was Mabel Vernon the secretary at that point?
No, Mabel went to Europe at this point and then she
didn't come back until about 1924 or '25 and at that
point she became secretary of the Party.

Paul: Did she?

Fry: [The masthead of _Equal Rights_ shows her as secretary]

Fry: for about four years, 1924-1929, something like that.

      In the meantime, Alice, was there ever any thought
      given to joining with NAWSA, now that the vote was won,
      in the League of Women Voters that they were forming?

Paul: Oh, no. You see, almost immediately we went to this
      meeting in Paris that I told you about,* the meeting
      of the International [Suffrage Alliance]. I went over
      as I told you, to visit with Mrs. Belmont and consult
      with her about how much she would do if we went on in
      this new organization, what we should do. And I told
      you I went over and saw Mrs. Corbett Ashby and then had
      this invitation. And I remember Mabel going over for
      that meeting. I didn't know she stayed four years.

Fry: She didn't stay that long, but she did go for a little
      while.

Paul: The only time I knew of her going was for this meeting
      in Paris where she made this remarkably wonderful and
      moving speech.

      Well, we could hardly think of merging with this
      group that was keeping us out of the international
      world, and if we hadn't been asked by the International
      Council of Women we wouldn't have been in the interna-
      tional movement at all, unless we'd formed our own
      group. And here we were being kept out of this organiza-
      tion on the grounds that we were standing for complete
      equality while they stood for protective labor legislation
      and protection of women in all fields. Well, we could
      never merge with them. So I never heard of anybody
      proposing that.

      But I should say that the biggest movement was to
      have us disband--the people who said they were too tired
      to go on themselves and they didn't know anybody else who
      would take up such a big burden (that was Lucy Burns' idea
      as I said)--and the people who were determined to have
      us go into the peace movement which was a very, very big
      movement. I mean not the peace movement was such a big
      movement, the desire to substitute peace for equality
      was a big movement in our group.

-----

*See p. 203.

Fry: Yes, I think that's where Sara Bard Field left your group.

Paul: Well, she never formally left it.

Fry: Not _formally_.

Paul: You see she had never been in the--every time we asked her to do anything [special] she would do it, but I don't think that she ever was one who took any responsibility, other than that. I never was conscious of her leaving because she was always, we supposed, still--just as when we went to her at the time of the founding of the United Nations and took for granted that she would of course be with us, and she was. She agreed right away to do everything; she _always_ agreed to do _whatever_ we asked her to do. But we never had her go forth, we'll say, like Maud Younger on her own initiative into taking any leadership.

Fry: She was kind of your special speaker and person who--

Paul: She was somebody who believed in us and supported us and every time we needed her help and asked for it she gave it. And her greatest gift in our movement was her speaking ability.

So we had all these little meetings of the branches and then we had the convention. At the convention I remember Miss Jane Addams getting up and from the floor saying, "I hope you will all decide to join in with the Women's International League for Peace and Freedom, make that your future." And Crystal Eastman went with a very involved feminist program. I don't know whether she went to the convention, but she drew it up beforehand, to be presented to the convention, which she felt was an extremely good one. But it was--well, we didn't give a second thought to it. It was more embracing everything that Russia was doing and taking in all kinds of things that we didn't expect to take in at all. [Pause.]

Debts and Transition

Paul: I think Mrs. Belmont wanted us to continue. When we finally decided and voted that we would continue (she wasn't at the convention) and that we would get a headquarters, then we signed all these notes for the

Paul: headquarters, over years and years in which we would
be given time to pay.

I told you that we had this meeting in New York
beginning to raise money again--this awful raising of
money, such an awful task. I was staying with [Mrs.
Belmont] on Long Island that day, and we drove in together
to the meeting in the home of Mrs. Havemeyer, who was a
very wealthy woman, very wealthy, and one of our members,
had gone to prison with us. So then Mrs. Belmont got
up and said, "I will pay off all the notes." You know
that; I have told you that before.

Fry: Is that the $10,000 that you were talking about that
you owed?

Paul: Oh, no, no. This was the $155,000 that we signed for
to pay for the new headquarters.

Fry: Where?

Paul: The headquarters that was the old brick capitol. You
see, prior to that we had rented the headquarters down
on Lafayette Square. And the moment that we were through,
the February 15 meeting, had had our convention, we
moved out. I remember that I spent the last night in
the headquarters with Katherine Morey. There was nobody
left but Katherine Morey and myself as far as I can
remember. And we were packing and moving everything
that we could.

We first had a sale at the headquarters and Mabel
Vernon I think was the auctioneer. Of course she was
always our best speaker at everything I think. So we
auctioned off everything that we owned because we didn't
know whether we could get another headquarters or afford
it or anything because then we were faced with paying
off all our debts. I was faced with it anyway. So I
remember our kitchen, which was well-equipped--are you
taking all this down or not?

Fry: Yes.

Paul: --because we had had a regular lunchroom and dining
room where we'd served lunch and dinners, I think. And
breakfast too, I imagine. And it was very successful
from the point of view of having very many people come
to it. And this Lucy Branham's mother started it. I
know she said, "Well, there is not one single thing I

Paul: active and so eager. The only thing I know how to do
is to keep house." And she was a <u>very</u> distinguished
Baltimore family, Mrs. Lucy Branham and her mother. So
she said, "I would like to come over and open a dining
room for you and see if I can't make some money for you
because I have no money to give--make some money by
having a nice dining room."

So she opened one and it was a <u>tremendous</u> success
because it was right on Lafayette Square, right by the
White House. All the newspaper people, with the Bureau
of Information for the government were in the neighboring
building. So they <u>all</u> came in and had their lunch there.
Practically all the newspaper people in the United
States, it seemed to me, who were in Washington for the
war, came in to our lunchroom.

So when we got to auction it off, I remember we got
$1,000 for their dining room equipment, and its good
will. So that is one of the ways we paid off our debts
in the beginning.

Then still perhaps with $10,000 left to pay after we
had paid off all these things, we just started in this
tedious work of dollar by dollar, ten dollars by ten
dollars, a hundred by a hundred, getting enough in to
pay it all, which we did. And that went up until almost
the time for--[pause] yes, that was <u>after</u> our convention
because we had our convention at that headquarters, I
remember. It was right <u>after</u> the convention we did that.

There was a unanimous vote at the convention when
we finally took the vote, because people had talked it
over so long and it was clear that so <u>many</u> people wanted
to continue. So we felt, well, so many people <u>want</u> to
continue. There was only one thing if we were <u>going</u> to
continue: it was perfectly clear we never would, <u>never
would</u> have it continue for anything excepting complete
equality, to try to follow up the whole emancipation
program of 1848 [Seneca Falls resolutions] and bring it
to a conclusion. So <u>that</u> we were all agreed on at that
convention.

Then there was the question of whether anybody would
undertake it. And finally Elsie Hill said she would
undertake it. And she took the chairmanship, and I
stayed on and helped her until we paid off all the money
and until we raised the money for the new headquarters.
Then, since I wasn't on the board, I then stopped, more
or less.

Fry: Could you tell again how you discovered the new head-
       quarters and how you finally bought it, because that
       wasn't taken down [on tape] when you told me before.

Paul: The new headquarters? [Pause.] Before I leave the other
       point about selling the things: you see, a few things
       like the Susan B. Anthony desk that had been given to
       me in the beginning, and just a few of these things plus
       our records, was all that we moved out of the old head-
       quarters. Everything else in the old headquarters--if
       it had been loaned, we returned it to the person; if it
       had been bought, we sold it. So we started almost <u>over</u>
       again without anything. The new little committee under
       Elsie Hill rented, I think, one or two very tiny offices--
       maybe one room or two rooms, I'm not sure--and just went
       on with the work in a formal way, not anything excepting
       answering the mail and doing the things you had to do,
       while I was raising the money to pay off all the old
       debt.

       And all this period we felt if we were going to
       continue at all, we had to have a headquarters again.
       And we didn't want to continue with a thousand-dollar-a-
       month place we were in that was costing so much. So,
       we thought this new equality campaign would be pretty
       much centered on Congress rather than one specific thing
       that would be centered on the President. So we looked
       up around Capitol Hill and we found this building, which
       was quite a dilapidated building, which <u>had</u> been the
       home of Congress, as I told you, in the time of President
       Monroe who was inaugurated there, right after our
       capitol was burned down by the British.

       Then it had been used as a prison for the officers
       and important prisoners in the time of the Civil War.
       Mrs. Serat [?] had been a prisoner there and it was well-
       known as the prison where important prisoners were
       placed. Then it was used as a home by different people,
       the last one being Justice Field of the Supreme Court.
       His niece was Mrs. Charlotte Anita Whitney; it belonged
       to his estate. So she helped and cooperated with us in
       making the arrangements for buying it. And this same
       Herman Dash, who had come to see me that time in prison--
       I told you how Mrs. Lewis got $8,000 to complete the
       amount due on taking the place when we were put out of
       Dolly Madison House; I told you how we had to, and the
       only place we could find was this William Randolph Hearst
       place which some estate was renting for $1,000 a month;
       and I told you how Mr. Dash, when I was in prison (that
       must have been one of these earlier imprisonments) came

Paul: to see me and said, "Well, Mrs. Lewis has gotten the money and now you can move out everything you have into this new headquarters," which was our final headquarters.

Well, getting this up on Capitol Hill, the same Mr. Dash again arranged everything for us. At that time the Capitol Hill building was owned by three different owners, I think. It was owned anyway by more than one because we first bought one of the three--it was three buildings joined together you see--we first rented one of them and then we bought all three and had it all joined and it was one big building. Through Mrs. Belmont's help, you see, we paid off all the notes, she paid off all the notes, and we had it without any mortgage or encumbrance at all. We got it in 1922, I think, and we sold it in 1929 to the government.

Fry: And that's where the present Supreme Court is, did you tell me?

Paul: Yes.

Fry: It was built in the 1930s--

Paul: It was destroyed to make way for the Supreme Court, this old building, which was a very sad thing to happen. You never can restore a building with that history.

I remember one night some people came to stay at the headquarters and we put them upstairs in one of the rooms that we didn't use very often, and they came down in the middle of the night it seems, and slept out in the garden or something like that, and they said, [laughing] "What is the matter with that room that you put us in? All night we seemed to have some kind of ghosts or spirits talking about the Civil War and so on."

We had at that moment staying in our headquarters a person who was always herself--Edith Ames, she was then our national treasurer--seeing people and having them speak to her--what they called extra-sensory, isn't it? She was a perfectly normal person as far as anybody could see, but she would say, "Somebody did come and stand by my bed last night and they said this and this and this." There was--well, these people said, "There was not any question, that somebody came here and talked to us for hours about the Civil War."

We said, "Well, it was a prison in the Civil War and the prisoners from the South were imprisoned in

Paul: that room where you were."

They said, "Well, they are certainly still imprisoned in that room, and we are not going back in that room again." [Laughter.] It was an extraordinarily interesting headquarters with all this--it was so <u>full</u> of the traditions of the time of the British coming and burning down our capitol and the congressmen being suddenly pushed out in the cold and having to go over there and Monroe had to be inaugurated in front of this old whatever-it-had-been--an old tavern, I suppose, in the beginning.

Fry: That's really fascinating in view of the renewed interest now in the extra-sensory world. Did this other couple know it was supposed to be haunted by ghosts?

Paul: Oh, no. They didn't know anything about it. I don't know--it was a couple--who they were, but I just remember some people. We might have had several rooms upstairs in that place, but they all had the same experience whoever the people were. [Laughing.] So it was an extremely interesting building anyway, when we sold it.

But I wouldn't put any of this, I think, in your present one [manuscript] because it seems to me [enough] if we end up with the ratification having gone through and the aid that the President did hold true to his statement that he would help us and see it through. He certainly did. I think made that ratification possible, and it was a hard fight, the ratification. It was a very, very, very, very, very hard fight.

And then [you can] state what we agreed to do, which was to adopt the old program of 1848. We had taken up one plank only, which was suffrage. Can you imagine how these women felt when we had these resolutions? You know, there are two pages of [Seneca Falls] resolutions of things they would work for in 1848. Well, the people [in our suffrage campaign] had pretty nearly killed themselves, had no money left and no strength left and no health left or anything, [laughing] like Lucy Burns more or less, to think up all these other things of 1848. It was, "Let those other women take up something, I am not going to take up any more." [Laughter.]

Equal Rights Amendment at Seneca Falls in 1923

Fry: Was this at your Seneca Falls meeting? You had another meeting at Seneca Falls like the original one [in July of 1923].

Paul: No, that Seneca Falls meeting was just to commemorate Seneca Falls. It was the seventy-fifth anniversary.

Fry: But you did submit an equal rights amendment wording.

Paul: Yes, by that time I think I had gotten all my awful bills [laughing] out of the way and paid. It is just amazing that you can have a--I always sympathize at the end of these Republican campaigns, Democrat campaigns, because I know that somebody is being left with these awful bills. Because you really would have thought, with wealthy women like Mrs. Belmont and so on that, while certainly one couldn't be too grateful for all she did, after all they all sailed away on their own lives. Suffrage was won and now the thing is over. We certainly had a hard time then.

But I would end up, it seems to me, by saying that when the ratification was over, we celebrated by putting in the Capitol the statues of the great pioneers who in large measure had started the modern campaign at Seneca Falls [in 1848]. It was one of the really big things we did, because it was starting women to have a feeling of respect for women and by putting statues of women in the Capitol when it had always been a Capitol of men. Until Jeannette Rankin no woman was venturing into the--like you say venturing into the Cosmos Club. And that then when we had a convention on and presented the statue to the Capitol, the last thing that we did in the suffrage campaign was that we voted to go on. Elsie Hill was very gallant and courageous and took the leadership.

Well then by the end of two years had gone by, we sort of I guess [laughing] gathered up some more strength. And this was a really very wonderful meeting up at Seneca Falls. There we proposed not only would we work for equality but we would work for an equal rights amendment to the Constitution. And we started on that campaign. That's enough to finish up with.

Fry: And you did submit a wording of the amendment, which is in that issue of the _Suffragist_ (or I guess, maybe it

Fry: was called the <u>Equal Rights</u> by that time).

Paul: The amendment read—I made the speech, you know, presenting this [amendment]. Of course, by this time I had recovered enough strength [laughing] I think to feel convinced that we ought to go ahead with the campaign and we ought to do it in the form of another amendment to have <u>complete</u> emancipation as our goal. So the amendment that I proposed—and I said, "This is just a tentative proposal because we have asked a good many lawyers to work on the form and so on, and the wording doesn't make much difference if we agree on what we want." So I presented this:

> "Men and women shall have equal rights throughout the United States and every place subject to its jurisdiction."

That said it all, and I said, "That's what we want, let's say what we want, and if they can find—"

That's when I started in to study law because I thought, "I can't do anything without knowing as much as the people who will be our opponents. I don't know anything whatsoever about law."

So I then went up and lived at the headquarters and early morning about six I went to the American University and enrolled in the law department, and I got my bachelor's degree in law,

And then I thought, "I really don't know much, I must say, still about law, as far as being able to cope with the people who say you can't have any such amendment as that." So you see we went around from person to person who was supposed to be a great authority   I went up myself to see Dean Pound at Harvard, who was supposed to be the greatest authority on constitutional law in the country, and Mrs. Lewis had her son work on it, and Elsie Hill met her husband when she and I went down to see him in the George Washington University law school to ask him to work on some kind of an amendment to the Constitution.

Fry: You mean, a man she later married?

Paul: Yes, her later husband. That's where she met him.

Everybody drew up things, and we knew they wouldn't do. But I thought I wasn't very well-equipped to be

Paul: making judgments on this subject, so then I went on and took a master's degree in law at the American University. And then I thought, "Still I really don't know very much about this--it is such a vast subject"-- we had to study Roman law and all kinds of laws of all--things like that, quite a lot to do. So I then took the doctor of law. By that time I felt really I could talk to people on this subject, because I knew that they didn't know very much either. My feeling of complete ignorance they seemed pretty much to share.

So then the Judiciary Committee of the Senate paid no attention to us at all. We went to all the national conventions of the Republican party and the Democratic party that intervened, and the first hearing we had in 19--this is just for your _information_ you know, not for this article--but 1923 was the first hearing on the subject of the new amendment, and the amendment was "Men and women shall have equal rights throughout the United States and every place subject to its juris-diction."

Well, at that hearing--and this seems almost impos-sible to believe--all the women's organizations that came now with the votes in their hands so they counted for something (while before nobody paid much attention to us or to anybody else when we went to hearings because we were all voteless) now became a great power, even more power in the minds of the congressmen and the senators than they really had, because they didn't have back of themselves any united, strong group that would always stand together on this subject. But they got up and spoke and the congressmen certainly felt they had power then. All of them spoke I think _against_ the Equal Rights Amendment. And if they didn't speak against us they remained silent. They didn't speak _for_ us. So we were the only group that spoke for the Equal Rights Amendment when it was first put in.

The Biggest Obstacles

Paul: Then we saw just what Lucy Burns and all these people thought we would find. Our problem would not be the Senate and Congress and the President, because now we were voters and had this power; but it would be changing the thought of American women because more than half the country were now new voters, and if the new voters through

Paul: their own organizations went up and said, "Please don't
have a thing to do with this, we don't want women
working at night, we don't want women standing up to
work and we don't want women to lose their alimony and
we don't want married women working when their husbands
are working," and all these things that they said. (You
know what they say.) Well, we said, "Now we have a
wholly different task, which is to change the thought
of American women, really.

So we started then to one convention after another
after another and kept it up until this year. We are
still keeping it up, the last one being the League of
Women Voters and the one before that the AAUW [American
Association of University Women]. I have told you all
this, I think, before.

Fry: Well, yes, and I remember myself taking long lists of
women's organizations to use with congressmen for you.
By 1971 huge numbers had gotten behind the Amendment.

Paul: I know, but you see our task through these years was
this monotonous one of getting these women to change
their minds to make them see what this principle meant
and so on. So that's what has taken, more or less,
all these years to do.

Well now, we went to convention after convention
of the political parties. It was in 1940--this is just
in case you are interested, all for your own information.

Fry: This is marvelous, Alice, to give me a good overview of
this.

Paul: Well, in 1940 for the first time we got in the Republican
platform. Then in 1944 we got it in the Democratic one.
That was a very hard-fought fight. Then we had it in
both. Well, by that time Congress began to--

Fry: When did Republicans--?

Paul: 1940. 1944--Democrats. And that's when we finally
began to work with Mrs. Emma Guffey Miller because she
was so prominent in the Democratic party. She came in
and joined us then and laid our fight before the Democratic National Convention to put it in the platform,
and we got it in.

Wording the Amendment

Paul: Well, then Congress began to pay more attention to us. It was in the political party platforms, and the Judiciary Committee of the Senate began seriously to consider the wording.

I remember going myself to--while I was not national chairman I went down whenever I could to try to help--I went in to see Senator Burton, I remember, from Ohio, who was on the Supreme Court later. At that time he was on the Senate Judiciary Committee. I went to talk about how it could be worded. I remember him saying, "Well, Senator Austin of Vermont, who is perhaps the most concerned man on the Judiciary Committee, and I have worked and worked and worked and worked and we still cannot find the wording that we think will express what you want."

So this went on. We had asked Dean Pound, and the versions that everybody had given us we knew enough at least about law to know we didn't want it. A great deal of this responsibility fell on me because I was now beginning to know a little bit about law, you see. So I think it was in 1943 that finally we took a draft to-- Mrs. Broy went with me; she didn't know very much about it but she was our political chairman so she went with me--to see Senator Austin. We handed him a draft, "Equality of rights under the law shall not be denied or abridged"*--what we now have, you see, the one that is now through Congress. So he studied it for a time and then he said, "Well, I really think perhaps this is just exactly.right. I don't see anything the matter with it. And I think it will probably give you just what we all have in mind. But I wouldn't want to do it without Senator [Joseph Christopher] O'Mahoney of Wyoming who, on the Democratic side, is the chief person working for this measure."

So Mrs. Broy and I then went up to Senator O'Mahoney's office. He was just departing for Wyoming where he lived,

---

*The Amendment read, "Equality of rights under the law shall not be denied or abridged by the United States or by any state on account of sex.
Congress and the several states shall have the power, within their respective jurisdictions, to enforce this ar   take
ef

Paul: but he studied it and he said, "Well, you can go back and tell the senator that you just left that I will be, anyway, the second senator and I will support it, so you will have probably the man who is most concerned on the Republican side and the man who is the most concerned on the Democratic side." So we did.

Then we were asked to make sure that the women of the country who had already (in a few cases, not many, but a few organizations had) endorsed the old amendment, "Men and women shall have equal rights," these two men said, "We don't want to put this in and then find that the women won't stand back of us. So will you get the signature of the responsible person in every woman's organization that has endorsed the old amendment ('Men and women shall have equal rights') saying that they approve of the new amendment." So that's what we started and did.

We drew up a paper with the new proposed amendment addressed to the Senate Judiciary and called up each women's organization or had them come to see us, or in some form or other had them consider it, and we got a page of signatures of all these different women's groups. None of them knew enough to have any objection! Especially when we said we thought we could get the Senate Judiciary to support this. You see, the difference was, the old one said, "Men and women shall have equal rights throughout the United States and every place subject to its jurisdiction." They took the position that while they personally were for equal rights throughout the United States, they didn't think Congress had the right to interfere so much in the lives of <u>individual</u> people; they thought it ought to deal with the <u>government</u>; the <u>government</u> should not deny equal rights. So when we changed it to saying, "Equality of rights under the law shall not be denied or abridged <u>by</u> <u>the</u> <u>United</u> <u>States</u> <u>or</u> <u>any</u> <u>state</u> on account of sex,"

[End of Tape 7, Side B]

[Tape 8, Side A]

Paul: then they all signed, they all signed their approval of the new one.

Fry: That fixed that.

Paul: And so we went down to the Judiciary meeting the next time it was held and--I remember this so very vividly--I

Paul: remember one of our members said, "It is so useless to
do this. You know that Judiciary Committee; they will
never do this. They won't listen to us. They won't
even read it, they won't care, they don't care anything,
they are just against us."

This was one of our officers from Virginia, a very
fine member. And you know you are so pulled down by
this defeatist attitude and discouragement. (Of course
you have been through all that; you know what it is.)
Anyway we did. And quite a group of maybe forty or
fifty women assembled in the hall outside the Judiciary
Committee, and I had the paper there, full of joy
myself, with all these people saying, "You are just
wasting your time. That committee will never care
twopence about it, will never look at it; we can be
sure of that."

So anyway I sent the guard in to tell the senator
that I was out there, as he had asked, with the paper.
He came out and took it in and presented it to the
Committee. Senator O'Mahoney was there and gave his
report as he had promised to give and the whole Committee voted--I think the whole Committee voted unanimously, but I am not absolutely positive about that--anyway
the majority voted to report out this new version.*

So from that time on we had this one that we now
have before Congress, which is more limited because
when it says, "shall not be denied or abridged by the
United States or by any state" it is only a prohibition
on the government of the country. An individual family,
such as you and your husband, can have inequality with
you the head of the family or he the head of the family
or anything you want to do. It is not interfering with
any private business or anything excepting where the
government has some regulation on the subject, which
I think is the right thing myself. So, from then on
there was never any deviation, until this new thing
that has now been sent on to all the states for ratification.**

---

*The Senate Judiciary Committee voted it out 9 to 3 on
May 11, 1942. The House Judiciary Committee voted it
out 9 to 7 on July 22, 1942.
**Paul is referring to two changes in the Amendment:
(1) putting a seven-year deadline on ratification, and
(2) in the enforcement provision, leaving in "Congress"
bu
st   th were

Paul: Now this campaign in a very different one from the
other campaign because the other one concentrated on the
President. Suffrage was something that we thought was
sufficiently in existence because we already had a
number of states where it was in existence, and there
was not any conceivable reason why it should not become
universal for our country. But this one, you couldn't
possibly start out to put something in the Constitution
that all--practically all--women of the country who were
supposed to benefit from it were opposed to. And that
is what we were confronted by, which was a very hard
thing to be confronted by.

When you think of the long hold-out by the AAUW--
imagine taking all these years, and this very great
educator I told you about, M. Carey Thomas, coming
down and succeeding in having AAUW's name at least
deleted from the letter sent to every member of Congress
saying we are opposed to the Equal Rights Amendment.
(They wouldn't support us; they just agreed not to fight
us.) See what we were up against was about unbelievable.

Fry: You were starting from scratch like Susan B. Anthony, I
guess, did in the very early days of suffrage, or would
it be even worse than that?

Paul: I think as far as law and government, the Amendment
won't do away with all the innumerable phases of the
subjection of women; but as far as government, it seems
to me, it completes the emancipation of women as far as
I can see.

Now the thing that I think is before us next is to
work with the women of other countries where we have
almost all gotten the vote now and try to make the power
of women so clear and recognized that we can really make
the world according to the ideals of women as well as
the ideals of men.

I don't think we can do it all alone in our country.
We've got to do it with the women of all countries
because so much is being done through the United Nations
now and it increasingly will be. While I am not very
keen on our meddling in other countries, still we seem
to be involved to do it, so when we meddle, it will be,
I think, essential to have the power of women guiding
that meddling--if we can't keep them from meddling.

I really think, if we can concentrate now on the
thing that you are preparing for your library, that we

Paul: really have covered the suffrage field.

Fry: Yes, you have.

Later Leadership in the National Woman's Party

Fry: There is one thing I need to know later on if I go into some research preparations for this ERA section. Can you tell me <u>when</u> you were in Europe and who ran the ERA campaign while you were working in Europe?

Paul: Well, you see, I have never run the ERA campaign since I went out as the national chairman. I have never been national chairman excepting about two years which was in the last World War, when I came back and was living up in Vermont in this little cottage I had up there, on the lake there at East Charleston. It seemed that nobody would go on with the campaign. They hadn't at that time agreeed even on the amendment, because they were having all the opposition in the Judiciary Committee and it was before this new amendment was put before them.

   Mrs. Harvey W. Wiley was the national chairman and she didn't want to run again although she was honored and beloved by everybody. But she just felt she couldn't do it any more. (She got out this <u>Equal Rights</u> magazine for part of that time.) So then I was elected at this Philadelphia convention in 1942.

   I came down and took over the campaign all through '43 and '44 and '45 I think, and during that period we sent women out and got the equal rights clause in the United Nations Charter you know, in San Francisco. That was '45. That was perhaps the biggest thing we accomplished in that period. But anyway that is the only time I have had the financial responsibility and the real responsibility for the campaign. And then Anita Pollitzer was elected in the next convention, which I guess was in the autumn of I don't exactly know when.

Fry: Is Anita Pollitzer still alive?

Paul: Oh, yes. She is the one, I think I told you, I talked to her the other day over the telephone--and she says that she has very much upon her heart, if she can recover her strength. She has been very ill, because

Paul: her husband died, as you know, and they had been such a devoted couple. She had for him one of these nurses from Jamaica, one of these colored women, and I think had a night nurse and a day nurse. And then he died. She was so exhausted at the end with perhaps the terrific campaign of taking care of him, she had an operation. They took out almost all the interior of her body and didn't know exactly what was the matter with her although she has had the--you know her uncle, I think I have told you that before--was one of the great surgeons and doctors of America. Ginsberg, I think his name was. But anyway, whatever his name was, he was one of the great Jewish doctors of the country and her brother and her nephew are all doctors and are all devoted to Anita. She has had a great, great, great deal of medical help but she has not gotten anywhere. I drove into New York to see her not very long ago, and she said that she can't walk, even in the little apartment she has, she can't even walk to the door. Somebody has to walk with her or she will fall. And her voice seems almost to have gone. Did you know her at all?

Fry: No, I never did, Alice.

Paul: Well, she was one of our most, most wonderful workers, so I hope everything you write will pay real tribute to her. She was the most remarkable person. She had the most beautiful speaking voice and she could have been a great actress, I think. She is Jewish, you know, and had all the things that the Jewish have with all the great talents, and she just had a flair for knowing what to do always. And in the suffrage days she had been down in South Carolina and teaching up in the University of Virginia.

She lived in South Carolina, in Charleston. And she was teaching at the University of Virginia in the art department. And so when somehow or other at some meeting we had enlisted her interest, she started every weekend to save all the money she was earning to come up to Washington to help us. And then she would go back and do her teaching every week and then come back again. That's the way we got to know her.

From that day on she has just been a pillar. So for a time she was our national chairman and now at this very moment she is down in South Carolina with her family and she is thinking--at least I proposed it to her and I think she is thinking about it--if she can get

Paul: her strength back, she is going to write the history
of the Woman's Party herself. And she would do it
marvelously. She writes so well and with so much--she
just has a great gift for writing and for everything
like that.

And she has a sister, Mabel Pollitzer, who is our
state chairman in South Carolina and whom I have talked
to over the phone many times about this ratification.
(And you know South Carolina has just turned us down.)
So I think if her sister would help her, because her
sister is perfectly well and strong apparently, that
maybe Anita could do this. Because she has all the
records through the years up in her little apartment.
She told me she was going down, she would have to take
the colored maid on the train because she couldn't go
alone.

Fry: To South Carolina?

Paul: Yes. And she would stay there two weeks and then come
back. Because all her papers and all her husband's
papers--a tremendous volume of them are all in their
apartment. It's worse than mine as far as papers and
books go, I am afraid.

The people who now engage in writing or think about
writing about the history of the Woman's Party in book
form really, seriously devoting themselves--when I asked
Anita if she wouldn't do it, I know she would do it well,
if her sister could help her enough through all the
mechanical parts, save her strength. Another one is
this Mr. Fox who I think I told you is coming to see me
in the Christmas vacation from Kansas University. He
is writing his book, not on the Woman's Party but on the
women's movement, and he seems to want to put quite a
great deal of emphasis on the Woman's Party part of it.
Another one is Dr. Dorothy Rogers you know, up in Oswego,
I think I told you about her. I just got the letter
from her saying would I cooperate with helping her if
she would come down here. So her mind was set on doing
this. She has brought out several books which are
travel books and then she has brought out quite a number
of books on psychology, and they are, she says, bringing
her in a very big income. She is herself professor of
psychology up in Oswego University or College, whatever
it is, and this is a textbook which has received enough
support from college professors over the country so all
the poor students are supposed to buy one of Dr. Rogers'
books. So she says it has turned out to be extremely

Paul: profitable, textbooks. She wrote me and I will show you her letter. She said would I cooperate with her and help her put out this history. I don't think she knows much about it.

Another one is Ernestine Breisch Powell. I don't know whether you know her. She is our leading member in Ohio, a woman lawyer, I told you, who had been the tax lawyer with her husband. She has been through the campaign, and if she does it, she would bring out a solid book like that Susan B. Anthony book, a big thick book which would be absolutely carefully done and accurate. The trouble is that her husband just died of a heart attack, suddenly, and she is left with this enormous law firm responsibility and is trying to get her young son trained in so that he can maybe handle it.

Then there is a woman out in Los Angeles who wants to write a doctor's thesis--her name is Baker--on the Woman's Party, who has written to me for help. So I can see it is becoming enough in people's minds now so that it would be a right time to have this written. Of course they could write all of it--not bring it out till the ratification had occurred, so that could be included, too.

Fry: When you said that you had only been head of the equal rights movement for two years--

Paul: Chairman of the National Council, we call it. You see, according to our constitution--and I had better give you a constitution so you will have it, just as a supporting document--according to our constitution, every chairman, on ceasing to be a chairman becomes an honorary chairman. We are supposed to have an election at least in every four years--the same time as for the president. The chairman can go out if she wants to before, just as Mrs. Longwell did, but she cannot stay in more than four years. Of course in the suffrage campaign I stayed in from the beginning to the end. Then we made this constitution that the time for any chairman would not exceed four years, and every outgoing chairman, if the convention lets her, becomes an honorary chairman. And we have always elected all the outgoing chairmen as honorary chairmen excepting one, and there wasn't enough support for her so she wasn't elected. So I am an honorary chairman, and in that capacity I have gone down and tried to help each chairman when she wanted some help.

Fry: Well, Alice, I have the idea, this impression, though, that

Fry: you were the <u>continuous</u> leader and spirit and energy
        behind this campaign.

Paul: Well, I wasn't <u>supposed</u> to be, but you can't always--
        even if you don't have officially the responsibility,
        if you care very much about something you do your very
        best, to help. Each chairman who has come along almost
        has been less able to give her time and less able to
        take responsibility almost, even though she is chairman,
        than I have been. For instance, our previous chairman
        (I don't know the new chairman at all, Mrs. Chittick, I
        don't know anything much about her, and what she is
        like or anything) but the previous chairman was Mrs.
        Longwell. Mrs. Longwell was out in California a great
        part of the time, and you know these things are happen-
        ing in the capital and it's hard to do it. So I stayed
        on a good part of the time while she was chairman, trying
        to help. Just as when you came down, you know, I think
        she was out in California. The time that I sent you to
        help with [Congressman] Don Edwards.

Fry: Well, you sent me to help with Don Edwards both times--
        she was there once.

Paul: No, but what I really sent for you for was when Edwards
        was chairman of the House subcommittee and everything
        was depending upon him, and we weren't having very good
        access to him. That's when I really sent for you and
        you came.

Fry: No, she wasn't there then.

Paul: That's what I thought. She wasn't. Well, it was
        situations like that: I would try to help because she
        wasn't there.

        Well, then the chairman before that was Mrs. Brook-
        head: she came over just as regularly as anything, as
        though she lived in Washington, and often she would come
        over and stay for weeks and weeks and sometimes for
        months. But her husband suddenly had a stroke of paralysis
        and she just couldn't leave him. She had to give him
        medicine every hour and that sort of thing, and she didn't
        have enough money to pay for a good nurse. So then
        although I was only honorary chairman (I got on very
        well with her, we were very sympathetic with each other)
        I stayed on and helped a great part of her regime. And
        of course Elsie Hill and I were always so close together
        that when she was struggling along I always tried to
        h   .   .   very

Paul: movement of course to go out and get new leaders, and
that is what we keep trying to do.

Fry: But this one was so discouraging at first, it required
somebody who had a commitment for a long-term effort.

Paul: Which was so discouraging?

Fry: ERA. When all the other women in the country were so
against it. My thesis is that if there hadn't been
someone like you, who had an idea of a long-term effort
over a long period of time and a real commitment to it,
that it could have just fallen by the wayside.

Paul: Well, of course it could. But that's all any campaign
needs, isn't it?

Fry: No, but you were really starting from scratch.

Paul: I mean a campaign that's involved as much in the changing of the thought of the country as this did. I guess
they are always about like this. Probably Frances
Willard and her temperance, and all these people have
all faced the same thing I guess.

Fry: What I am groping for is the sense of what to research
to trace the history of ERA, and I wanted to be sure
that I had an accurate impression that even though other
women had been chairman, you were in there and fighting
for ERA all the time, except when you were busy in
Europe with equal rights.

Paul: You see, if you are an honorary chairman, the way we
put it in our constitution is that all honorary chairmen
are supposed, if they possibly can, to continue to help
the movement in any way they can. That's the way we
created it so that we wouldn't be left always with the
new chairman and she might be good or she might not be
good. She might start us off on some strange course,
but it wouldn't make any difference--all the past chairmen can assemble and try to keep it on the right track.
I just don't really know whether--we now have a new
chairman--how she is going to turn out, whether it will
be helpful or not helpful to try to help her; I don't
know.

Fry: I can't tell. Let me turn this off.

THOUGHTS ABOUT QUAKER FOREBEARS

Paul: Of course, you have all kinds of ancestors. Probably
       there are some that are very much--to be proud of these
       people, I have the same reverence for religious freedom
       and for every kind of freedom that they had. So I am
       proud that they took the stand. But now this Grateful
       Penn--

Fry: on your mother's side--

Paul: --was the sister of Admiral Penn, who was the father of
       William Penn so when the King of England was in great
       debt and wanted money very much, you know he borrowed
       money--at least I believe in all history books they say
       this--from Admiral Penn, who was an admiral in the
       British navy. He repaid his debt by giving this land
       over in America to William Penn. Well then Ann married
       and I will have to look it up in my chart to see what
       was the name of the person she married, but her son, or
       grandson, one or the other--I guess it would be her son--
       was the first cousin of William Penn. He made this
       ancestor of mine, and I think his name was Crispin, the
       first chief justice of Pennsylvania and a member of the
       governor's council (whatever that was called) that set
       up the government of Pennsylvania. (I think this is it,
       but I have this in my chart, so I can verify these
       points.)

       So then when this chief justice started over to
       America he took his daughter with him, who had married
       a John--if I can remember this rightly, I think his name
       was Blackpan--but anyway the man that she married was in
       prison as a Quaker leader and I believe died in prison,
       I think so. So then the father took the young widow with
       him over to America.

       The father was to be the chief justice and one of the
       three commissioners to set up the colony. By the way, I

Paul: just met somebody down in Washington whom I had gone to
Swarthmore with, and she was telling me that her great,
great and-so-on grandfather was one of the three com-
missioners appointed by William Penn, I guess, to set
up the colony; and I said, "Oh, so was one of mine,"
and so we found that we were cousins. And this person
I think was somebody who comes down to see Mabel Vernon
all the time, let me see, quite often.

But on the way over, anyway, this chief justice
died, so this young widow--

Fry: Before he ever got to Pennsylvania?

Paul: Yes. So the young widow--and of course the only reason
he was ever appointed, I think, was because he was the
first cousin of William Penn. The young widow arrived,
and so William Penn asked her to come and stay with
him. And so she did. She lived and brought up her young
son in his home, which is one of the historic places
they always show you in Philadelphia, a little bit out
in the country. I have been there and visited it.

Then for one or two generations, and I have forgotten
just how they go, but I do have it in my chart I think,
emerged this lady whose portrait is hanging here up on
the mantelpiece, who was my great-grandmother. Her name
was Letitia Penn Smith. She was a direct descendant of
the widow that was living in the home of William Penn.
And she married my great-grandfather, a Parry.

In the meantime I was invited to join the--what are
these things called?--Magna Carta Dames. That's the
people who they think can prove are descendants of the
people who drew up the Magna Carta. It seems that I
qualify through this sister of Admiral Penn, and I will
find out what her name is from my chart; he was the
descendant of one of the groups that drew up the Magna
Carta. So there is a Magna Carta Dames up here in
Connecticut, and so they invited me to become a member
so they have traced the whole thing, so I am perfectly
sure it is correct.

Well, I think it makes no difference to anybody,
because you can be a disgrace to your ancestors. It is
also, I think, in our movement a strength to show you
have deep roots in the country and your ancestors helped
to build it up and so on, and I feel sure your Roberts
is one of the early Quakers.

Fry: I hope so. I feel inspired to go back and look up my
genealogy charts to see if I really had one.

Paul: Well, I am going to look up your Roberts here in mine.

Fry: To tie this up, when Letitia married your great-grandfather, who was your grandfather?

Paul: My grandmother was Alice Stokes. So Letitia had to be
my great-grandmother. Oh, then this so [gesturing to
picture on the wall] must have been the son of Letitia.
I am sure now, what it was.

Fry: And what was his name?

Paul: His name was William Parry.

Fry: That is where the Parry's enter.

Paul: Yes.

Fry: So did Letitia marry a Parry?

Paul: Yes, but I will have to get out my chart and show you
because I really can't remember But I thought while I
was up here I would get some genealogist to take my
chart and finish it out.

Fry: [Reading book.] On your father's side, this starts
with the Winthrops of Massachusetts, the governor's
sister, Jane, who married Thomas Gostlin. Her daughter
was Anne who married Thomas Fones, and Anne lived from
1586 to 1619 and they had a child named Elizabeth who
was born in 1610. And there is a book on her--

Paul: Did you ever hear of Ernest Thompson Seton?

Fry: Yes.

Paul: This book was written by his daughter.

Fry: Anya Seton. And the name of this is The Winthrop Woman,
in case anybody whould want to refer to it. Now the
heroine Elizabeth's brother from a second marriage is
Robert Feake.

Paul: Yes, I want to tell you that she first married her first
cousin, who was the son of the governor, and came with
him and the governor when he set out for America to start
the little colony that he became the head of.

Fry: Oh, that was--she married Henry Winthrop.

Paul: So she set out with her father-in-law who was Governor Winthrop, you see, and her husband, John Winthrop--

Fry: Henry.

Paul: Was it Henry? And arrived here anyway in Massachusetts. The day that they landed, or the week anyway that they landed (and I think it tells it all in this book here), there was a terrible storm, and he was swimming, a great swimmer apparently, and in the Massachusetts Bay somewhere up there where they were landing he was drowned. So she suddenly lost her young husband. Then she married this Robert Feake. He was the lieutenant governor under Governor Winthrop and he was a very prominent member of the colony. He was the one who got the grant of land down here in Connecticut. One thing I wanted to look up and see was if by any chance she owned all around Greenwich--the whole of that territory, which is right close to here, to see if my little cottage by any chance is on that original land, because it would be very nice.

Fry: Wouldn't that be something.

Paul: I would feel so much more at home.

I don't know how you got me started looking up this because I've really never done it.

Fry: That's a very decorative coat of arms, Alice. You should have some jewelry made up with the rabbit on top and the lion underneath.

Well, at any rate, to carry that down from Feake, Elizabeth and Feake were married--

Paul: I read you the dates. That's on the back page of the book, inside. It's halfway down the page, I think. "Were duly married and became famous and persecuted Quakers." Did you find it?

Fry: "Elizabeth's daughters," let's see, "Hannah Feake and John Baum," that's the one.

Paul: She is the one that became the Quaker minister. First time that we had any Quaker in that family. They were all Puritans.

Fry: Now, what's the relation of Hannah to Elizabeth?

Paul: That was her daughter. The reason that I took an interest in this book when Elsie Hill told me about it was because this told me my great-grandmother, beyond the Feake period.

Fry: And Hannah Feake married John Baum in 1656 and their biographies are readily available because he is the one who kept holding the illegal Quaker meetings and was finally banished to Holland where he got the--the King?--

Paul: He got the Estates General to direct Governor Stuyvesant to stop this interference with religious freedom.

Fry: And that is known as the Flushing Remonstrance of 1657?

Paul: Well, now that remonstrance, I don't remember from the dates whether it was before or after he went over to Holland, but it was a very famous document which was sent, I suppose, to Governor Stuyvesant--maybe it was sent to the Estates General; I don't know where it was sent.

Fry: From John Baum?

Paul: No, from all the people that he gathered together. There were a good many people who signed this remonstrance.

Fry: Like a petition.

Paul: And that's what the stamp was about, to celebrate the birth--one of the births--of religious freedom in this country, the issuing of this remonstrance.

It tells you if you want to read it right in the front: [Interruption: books dropped on tape recorder.] Elizabeth, the heroine in this book, stood by Anne Hutchison; you know she was expelled for her religious views. I am almost sure it says [Elizabeth] took this stand in the colony where her former stepfather was the governor. She was rather prominent in the colony and she took this stand against the way they were expelling Anne Hutchison, I think.

Fry: And also against a determined army captain bent on the massacre of her friends the Savinoy [?] Indians.

Paul: So she was a rebellious type.

Fry: S·   ,   ·   -   ··   o refer

Fry: to as his "unregenerate" niece. That's a good family
       tree [laughter].

Paul: I think your genealogy's real experience is very exciting.
       Everybody's is.

Fry: We don't all have such distinguished people on our family
       trees, Alice.

EQUAL RIGHTS IN THE UNITED NATIONS CHARTER

Fry: Tell what you know about getting the equal rights clause
put into the United Nations Charter.

Paul: Just what I have already told you, I guess.

Fry: Yes, that was our first evening together when we were
talking about what we were going to talk about. I didn't
really get it down at that time; I didn't take any notes
on it or tape it.

Paul: Well, I told you, you know, that after the suffrage
campaign I was only one-time national chairman after I
was not reelected after the suffrage campaign, I just
stopped everything. And then I was asked to come down
and actually elected and asked to come down when the
World War [II] broke out, and I came back for that
reason from Geneva, where I had been, you know. I came
back in 1941. Are you talking about this period?

Fry: Yes.

Paul: Well, I came back in 1941 in the spring and felt that
there was no possiblity of going on with the work in
Geneva, when from all indications we would very soon be
engaged in the war ourselves. So when I came back I
found that there was nobody here who wanted to go on
with our own campaign, which was very exacting in the
way of requiring raising money and spending all your
time in Washington. Everybody was engaged either for
the war or against the war or some kind of war activities.
So I was asked to come down and take over the chairmanship. Which I did. I came down in 1941. Is that the
year we went in the war? In the late autumn, about
December, I guess.

     I was elected as chairman at the national convention
held in Philadelphia in the preceding November, and

CHARTER OF THE UNITED NATIONS

Adopted at San Francisco June 26, 1945
Ratified by the United States August 8, 1945

Provisions on Equality for Women

PREAMBLE

"WE THE PEOPLES OF THE UNITED NATIONS
DETERMINED . . .
to reaffirm faith in fundamental human rights, in the dignity and worth of the human person, in the *equal rights of men and women* and of nations large and small .
have agreed to the present Charter of the United Nations and do hereby establish an international organization to be known as the United Nations."

CHAPTER I
ART. 1.

Purposes and Principles.

"The Purposes of the United Nations are:

. . .
3. To achieve international cooperation . . . in promoting and encouraging respect for human rights and for fundamental freedoms for all without distinction as to race, *sex*, language or religion . ."

CHAPTER III:
ART 8

Organs.

"The United Nations shall place no restrictions on the eligibility of men and women to participate in any capacity and under conditions of equality in its principal and subsidiary organs."

CHAPTER IV:
ART 13.
SEC I

The General Assembly.

"The General Assembly shall initiate studies and make recommendations for the purpose of ·

. . . .
b. promoting international cooperation in the economic, social, cultural, educational and health fields, and assisting in the realization of human rights and fundamental freedoms for all without distinction as to race, *sex*, language or religion . . ."

CHAPTER IX ·
ART. 55

International Economic and Social Cooperation.

"With a view to the creation of conditions of stability and well-being the United Nations shall promote:

. . . .
c. universal respect for, and observance of, human rights and fundamental freedoms for all without distinction as to race, *sex*, language or religion."

ART 56.

"All Members pledge themselves to take joint and separate action in cooperation with the Organization for the achievement of the purposes set forth in Article 55."

CHAPTER XII
ART. 76.

International Trusteeship System.

"The basic objectives of the trusteeship system   . . shall be:

. . . .
c. to encourage respect for human rights and for fundamental freedoms for all without distinction as to race, *sex*, language or religion . . ."

(Note The italics above are not in the official text of the Charter.)

NATIONAL WOMAN'S PARTY
144 B St., N. E.
Washington, D. C.

Paul: during the period that I was chairman, one of the most
important things that we ever did was to help in getting
equality for women written into the United Nations
Charter. That we did by sending out a delegation of
women for that one and only purpose to San Francisco
to try to have it put in the charter, in as many places
in the charter as possible, covering every aspect it
was possible to cover. So there was pending before the
United Nations the resolution introduced by [Field
Marshall Jan Christian] Smuts of South Africa conveying
the same idea that we were trying to express: complete
equality in every field of endeavor that the United
Nations would take up. Finally it was placed in the
charter in the opening sentence reading something like
this (and before you go I will try to look up the exact
words): "Reaffirming faith in the worth and dignity of
the human person, the equal rights of men and women and
nations great and small," then it goes on, "we hereby
establish the United Nations."* So it was saying exactly
what we were trying to put in our own national constitution and in the very words that we would want, so we
gave it all possible backing.

The United States delegation however, was very
powerful of course, in this first opening meeting to
found the United Nations, and there was one woman only
in our delegation--Dr. Gildersleeve--dean of women at
Barnard College. She objected very much to this statement submitted by Smuts and largely on its English; we
couldn't comprehend [her objection] at all. So one of
our members who was out there representing the National
Woman's Party, Anita Pollitzer, had been in touch with
Sara Bard Field at Los Gatos, California, because Sara
Bard Field was one of our honored and beloved members
in California and she had been seeing her just personally.
Anita informed us in Washington that Sara Bard Field was
entertaining Archibald MacLeish, a member of the United
States delegation, the next day in her home for dinner.
She thought that if Sara would take up with MacLeish
the importance of having this in the charter, maybe she
could get him to use his influence to bring this to pass.
So Anita Pollitzer then went back to --

---

*"...to reaffirm faith in the fundamental human rights,
in the dignity and worth of the human person, in the equal
rights of men and women and of nations great and small...
do here establish an international organization to be known
as the United Nations." From the preamble to the Charter
of

[End of Tape 8, Side A]

[Begin Tape 8, Side B]

Paul: ask Sara if she would do this, take this matter up with Mr. MacLeish when he came to visit her for dinner and see if he could possibly save the Smuts declaration by removing the opposition of the American delegation, and she said she would do her best.

Then Mrs. Pollitzer telephoned to us that this interview with MacLeish had occurred at Sara's home at the time of this dinner she had arranged and that Mac-Leish had said he would certainly make a supreme effort to bring this to pass and that he now reported that the American delegation had agreed to support it.

It was put in, and not only put in the preamble in the opening of the whole charter, just as we had wanted and Smuts had wanted, but it was amplified in a good many sections making it specific with regard to other specific points.

Is that all right?

Fry: That's fine.

Paul: One of the very biggest achievements that it [the Woman's Party] helped to bring to pass.

AFTER-DINNER CONVERSATIONS

Susan B. Anthony's Desks

Paul: The other thing you asked me to tell you about when we got the tape, I think, was about the Susan B. Anthony desk.

Fry: Oh, yes. Do you have time to tell me about that tonight?

Paul: I have time to tell you about anything because this is my last chance, you see.

Fry: Well, all right, but you could tell me in the morning.

Paul: No, I'd rather tell you now.

Fry: You look so bright-eyed right now, you might as well go ahead.

Paul: I think in the morning, if you are going on a plane, you have a lot to do.

When the National American Woman Suffrage board, acting upon the request and suggestion of Miss Jane Addams, appointed Lucy Burns and myself as members of their congressional committee to go down to Washington and do what we could for the passage of the federal suffrage amendment, which Miss Anthony worked for so long, we had no office to begin with and no place from which to work. The first thing we did was to put a little notice in the newspapers saying that we were coming down to take up the work that Miss Anthony had laid down when she had to give up going to Washington, and we were going to open an office and start a procession, if we were able, through the streets of Washington, to occur the day before the inauguration of the new President Wilson.

Paul: When this notice was read by Miss Anthony's former secretary, named Rachael Brill Ezekiel, Mrs. Ezekiel telephoned to me that when Miss Anthony left Washington she expected to come back again but she did not because of her death. Mrs. Ezekiel was in possession of her desk that she had left behind. She said that, having read in the paper about our trying to go on with the work of Miss Anthony, she felt that she ought to turn the desk over to those who were going on with Miss Anthony's work. And so she had called me to say she had the desk, what should she do with it, would I like to have it?

I said, of course, we would like to have it; we had not yet even gotten an office, much less a desk. We were getting an office in this little basement on 1420 F Street, so she said she would have the desk brought down to us. And she did.

The desk arrived, and we opened our office with only one piece of furniture, the Susan B. Anthony desk. We continued to use this desk all through the suffrage campaign and all through the following campaign for complete equality for women, and it is still at the headquarters of the National Woman's Party in Washington.

Fry: Now what about this desk, back here on your sun porch?

Paul: Well, after the suffrage victory, one of Miss Anthony's admirers (and perhaps a co-worker, I don't know whether that's true or not) named Miss Cary Harrison, who was a very active worker in the National Woman's Party for the votes for women, presented this desk which she owned, having somehow or other acquired it from Miss Anthony, and presented it to me in gratitude perhaps that I had gone on with the work of Susan B. Anthony. I rather think something was printed on there but I'm not quite-- I'll have to go and look and see. I can't remember just what it was.

Fry: And that's the rosewood desk. The desk that's now in Belmont House--Do you know what kind of wood it is? It's very dark.

Paul: I don't know.

Fry: On this one the wood grain shows through better and it looks like rosewood.

Paul: I'd like very much to have the other one too.

Fry: It ought to be saved for posterity.

[Tape off.]

Responses to Civil Disobedience

Fry: I would think, Alice, that you would have had quite a feeling of support for any action of civil disobedience, as a result of your Quaker background.

Paul: We didn't do civil disobedience, of course, in our movement.

Fry: Oh. When you went to jail?

Paul: I suppose you would call it civil disobedience, but we didn't think of it that way.

       Anyway I was just saying, I just meant the reason I haven't kept up with my college as much as I should have was the feeling that they were anything but pleased with me, for having--

Fry: For heaven's sake. Do you think that's true now?

Paul: No, because last year they wrote me a note saying they wanted to confer a doctor's degree upon me. So I'm sure they didn't think so now. Somebody, some person--

Fry: It's fashionable now to have gone to prison for a cause. But that surprises me that a Quaker college--

Paul: But I think through all those years when we were not succeeding, not having won, it was just a general feeling with everybody, the women's movement, everybody.

Fry: That you could not be respected if you went--

Paul: Well, I mean the more and more things we did. There was certainly a feeling of regret among everybody, it seemed to me.

       That's the reason I was very much tempted to go to prison under an assumed name when I was in England. I thought I would bring so much disgrace upon my family and everybody I knew, and so on.

Fry: Wasn't it Emerson and Thoreau who had that conversation in prison with one inside and the other outside. Have you ever heard of that exchange?

Paul: No.

Fry: I think Thoreau was inside prison and Emerson came to visit him--

Paul: I didn't know Thoreau was ever in prison.

Fry: Well, maybe it was Emerson who was in prison.

Paul: I didn't know Emerson was in prison.

Fry: Well, one of them was. To be arbitrary, we'll say that Emerson said to Thoreau, "Good heavens, what are you doing in there?" and Thoreau said to him, "And what, may I ask, are you doing out there?"

Paul: [Laughter.] That's very, very good.

Well, now I suggest you go to bed and I will get out my Roberts lineage [chart] and see if I can trace your ancestors.

[Tape off.]

LOBBYING: METHODS, WOMANPOWER, AND MAUD YOUNGER

[At breakfast table.]

Fry: The story on Maud Younger, the lobby chairman, is in
the March 22, 1919, issue of the Suffragist, as a re-
print from the New York Times of March 2, 1919. This
says "Many rumors have been afloat in Washington about
the methods used by the suffrage lobby in bringing
pressure to bear on members of Congress."

Paul: Are you sure you had enough breakfast?

Fry: Positive. And then it tells about how, at the headquarters of the National Woman's Party in Washington,
there is a card index so extensive and detailed, political and personal, that twenty-two different cards are
required for each senator and representative. And then
later on it gives a list of the cards. Card number one
contains his name and biography from the congressional
directory. Number two, the key card that talks about
ancestry, nativity, education, offices held and general
information. The next card is a subcard, more on birth
date, place, number of children and so forth; it just
goes on, where he went to school, where he went to
college, his religion, his military service, his occupation. Number fourteen is what newspapers the member
reads, and those that have the most influence on him
and so forth.

It all sounds fairly innocuous but valuable information to you. His suffrage record is on one card. So
maybe you could just repeat what you said before off
the tape, about how this file was built up and how
Maud Younger and everybody operated.

Paul: All right, just let me swallow my tea and orange juice.
I think maybe I better--

Fry: This isn't a very good article. [Machine off.] Let's
        see, Alice. You told me that although you had this
        elaborate card index system that it had kind of grown
        naturally and that actually you and Maud Younger had
        most of the information in your heads by this time
        anyway.

Paul: Well, no. I said that as long as you had a congressional
        chairman like Maud Younger who endeavored to know person-
        ally every member of the Senate and House, and really,
        we thought, succeeded, you were not dependent on our
        card catalogue. But it was part of her organization in
        her department.

Fry: The article says that when a lobbyist starts out for the
        Capitol she receives a lobby slip which has a list of
        entries to bring out fully all the information that she
        obtains and then on that slip, under the heading "Exact
        Statement and Remarks," are remarks made by the congress-
        man to the lobbyist. An example was given: on one card,
        the congressman had told the lobbyist, "Put me down on
        the mourner's bench, I am thinking about it." So that
        apparently this file builds up a running account of how
        the congressman is feeling about suffrage. All of these
        are filed in the Library of Congress now, we should note.

Paul: Well, we loaned it to them, the whole catalogue. It was
        in our loan; I suppose it is still there.

        But as I said, Maud Younger always said, "What I do
        is to take the temperature of the members of Congress
        and then inform the people at home of how at this parti-
        cular moment he is feeling on the measure."

        Now, do you want to ask questions, or are you doing
        it now?

Fry: I am doing it now. The tape recorder is on. I am
        trying to get kind of a picture of the whole lobbying
        activity that went on. Maud Younger was in this for
        about four years, right? Had been the head of it, I
        gather. This article says she was in it for three years,
        and this is March of 1919.

Paul: I met Maud Younger when we went out to the Convention
        of Women Voters at the San Francisco fair in 1915. I
        remember vividly how I met her. We were--I was in a
        car with somebody or other out there, with various
        people. We were going somewhere to a meeting on
        equality for women in the political field. We passed

Paul: her and she stopped in her car--we had never met at all--
and talked about everything and I said, "Now you come
down as soon as you get through with what you are doing
and help us in Washington."

And she said, "I certainly will," and responded with
great joy at the whole thing. And that was 1915.

Not long after she came to Washington and took a
little apartment and began to come in to try to help.
Soon she saw she couldn't operate from her apartment;
she had to be right in the headquarters. So she moved
into the headquarters and stayed in her particular room
until the campaign was won. Then she took one little
office as her congressional office. From that time on
she took complete charge of all congressional work. I
would think that no organization could have ever had a
more, greater leadership really, in that particular
field that she took under her charge. So she got a very
good secretary, a young woman from Kentucky, whose husband
was employed in the government as a lawyer, and this
secretary was always there. Whenever the lobbyists went
out she would get all the instructions from the secretary,
and when she came back the report would be filed. It
was the most ship-shape, business-like little office.
It was perhaps not so helpful to Maud Younger because
she knew the congressmen so well anyway, but helpful to
everybody else, especially to the congressional chairman,
who at that time was Anne Martin of Nevada. She would
take all these reports and write letters back home to
people and report what the temperature was at that particular moment of this particular congressman.

Then at the very end, people in Congress began to get
rather interested in seeing that they had a very good
record here. Then when we placed it in the very end [of
the suffrage campaign] in the congressional library, at
the request of the congressional library, the loan, they
were particularly interested in the card catalogue from
their point of view, for the use in their districts, when
we began on the same plan [for the ERA campaign] for which
Maud Younger still was the head. She started the whole
congressional campaign on the Equal Rights Amendment,
you see.

She built it up until she finally, in the Equal
Rights Amendment campaign, she did even more on the
congressional work than she did in the suffrage campaign,
perhaps, because she bought a house right next to our
headquarters so she could always entertain congressmen

Paul: or entertain their constituents, especially at breakfast.

I remember morning after morning going over and eating breakfast with her with Senator Curtis, who was the Republican whip. He became a great friend of Maud Younger's. Then this card catalogue became, in the minds of the congressmen, almost a privilege, to be on the card catalogue list.

Fry: They began to ask you to be on it, or what?

Paul: I don't know whether they asked, but they were more enthusiastic about seeing us and having it reported just as it should be, you see.

Fry: A progress report, their accomplishments on equal rights?

Paul: No, I mean the man would take it, it would be something he could use in his district, to show what the women said about him in this report.

Fry: Right.

I wish that somehow we could get the feeling of the effort and so forth in the lobbying. One thing I was wondering about was how could you tell who to ask to go lobby and who not to go.

Paul: Well, we never felt there was anybody who shouldn't go. We always thought everybody who wanted to go--especially of course we wanted them to be people from the man's district or the man's state; no congressman could have his time taken up with constant visiting from somebody who is not in his district and he doesn't have any responsibility for--but anybody who came from the state and wanted to help, we sent her over to see her congressman or see her senator or see both. Then Maud Younger, of course, undertook with her own little lobby committee, to see everybody. Then we would know whether it was safe to bring a measure up for a hearing, safe to bring it up for a vote, safe to bring it up in a committee, and we would know where we were weak and where we ought to be getting more meetings started in the districts and [with] the people, and so on. I guess it is just exactly like all these professional lobbyists, because you know lobbying is a very big profession now in Washington. They would probably think our little efforts were very amateur.

Fry: I wish I knew how to compare such a, as you say, ship-

Fry: shape, well-run lobbying office with the other kinds of
        lobbying that were going on in 1919. This article from
        the New York Times is a very long article and either it
        is because they were so anti-suffrage that they wanted
        to make this sound ominous or it is because lobbying done
        this way was usually not quite as thorough and as
        businesslike and organized as this was.

Paul: I think that's really an effort to show that we were
        trying to get votes by threatening congessmen with things
        we had found out about them, which, as Maud Younger said,
        is totally and absolutely as far away from our thoughts
        as anything could be. I never heard of any information
        that we ever even received that was derogatory to a
        congressman. We didn't go after that. We went after
        things that were related to what his position was on
        this particular subject, and what were the groups in his
        own district who were the people he was trying to please.

Fry: And what his habits were. They bring this out in this
        article. The reporter asked Maud Younger, "Why do you
        want to know the habits of the congressmen?" She says,
        "For several reasons. If they get to their offices
        early, the one that comes at 7:30, this is often the
        best time during the day to see them. And if a member
        is a drinking man we want to know that. One of our
        lobbyists may go to him and not know what's the matter
        with him, or how to evaluate his answers." She says,
        "In 1913 the money we allotted for lobbying was $10.
        Since then we have raised more than $425,000. Our
        expenses in Washington this year will be $100,000."
        Was that just lobbying expenses?

Paul: No, I think that's everything about the headquarters.
        We didn't break it up. For lobbying we had only one
        expense really, and that was the secretary in Maud
        Younger's office. She was a volunteer worker and all
        the lobbyists who came were volunteers. We didn't have
        any paid lobbyists. We never, never from the first day,
        ever did we have a paid lobbyist.

Fry: They would simply live there and probably get their food
        and their meals?

Paul: I don't know about their meals, because we always had
        this little restaurant. Well, they would come to Wash-
        ington and stay with maybe the--I remember one from
        California who always stayed with her congressman who
        always lived just outside of Washington and they would
        always stay with Mrs. Kent [wife of Congressman William

Paul: Kent of California] because she had this big, beautiful home. Lobbyists from many parts [would stay there]. I remember one young girl came down from Utah and her father was a friend of the Kents and so they invited her to stay there the whole time she was there. She stayed there and she just turned in, just worked extremely hard day after day after day. Then she went back to her home in Utah.

And another one was invited by one of our members, Mrs. John J. Waite, who had a large and beautiful home She was our Connecticut state chairman so she was always taking in two or three people who came to help and they would stay weeks and months or days, as it might be So almost all the members would--of course there were too many people to put them all up in our headquarters.

Fry: In the last couple of years of the campaign, could you give some idea of the volume of lobbying? How many people, would you say, was the average number of--

Paul: Let's put it on, don't you think we'd better keep this on the suffrage? I'd like to keep that one campaign--

Fry: This _is_ suffrage I am talking about.

Paul: You mean how many people were working on lobbying?

Fry: Yes. Because what we always read about for those two years are the picketing and the prison experiences, and we need more information on what was going on in the halls of Congress by the Woman's Party. I thought if you could just remember the numbers--

Paul: of people who came--

Fry: --to lobby. To give us some indication.

Paul: Well, nearby places where we had a big membership like Philadelphia, it seems to me, there were always a great many coming and going, like Maryland and so on, New Jersey. Then the far away places, they would do as Maud Younger did, come and try to make a stay and see everybody they possibly could and then go home.

It was just something that went on all the time. For instance I told you how Anita Pollitzer was teaching at the University of Virginia and came up every weekend. The first thing we sent her over to do was to go and see her congressman, and she was so enthusiastic and so good,

Paul: just almost all the time she came she was just doing
        that, doing the congressional work. Some people just
        naturally fell into that. Some fell more naturally
        into, say, helping in the library or whatever it might
        be that they were attracted to.

Fry: Were you doing any lobbying yourself during these years?

Paul: Oh, yes, sure. In the beginning, it seemed to me that
        I had to do it all because before Maud Younger came,
        before we had any chairman, we just started in, not
        knowing anything at all about how the people stood in
        Congress. Lucy Burns and I did, together. And then
        sometimes we would get somebody, I told you the National
        American Woman Suffrage Association sent down Jeannette
        Rankin to help. She was their paid organizer, so when
        we got started we had her. She spent all her time going
        up (that's before we won the vote in Montana, you see).
        Practically everybody who came, turned in, went to see
        the people they thought they could.

            We were not received with any great enthusiasm. It
        was just a necessary evil the men had to put up with
        [laughter] especially in the suffrage states, where
        they felt they had to receive the people. Then we
        worked particularly on trying to get women from those
        states, I mean to be in a lobbying group.

Fry: Then as the years progress in the suffrage campaign,
        did you continue to lobby, all the way through?

Paul: Yes, but not very much. Unless it was some person it
        was necessary to see. Remember I told you, I think,
        after we had this first procession and they decided to
        have a Senate investigation, I went up myself to make
        all the arrangements necessary. That's what I usually
        did for a hearing or anything like that. I told you,
        when I said to Senator Jones, "Well now, when shall I
        come to confer with you about this--it looks as though
        it might be going on for some time," and he said, "7:30
        in the morning I'm at work." [Laughter.]

Fry: So primarily, yours was more and more limited to testify-
        ing at hearings, is that right, before the committees,
        in the latter stages?

Paul: Well, no, it was more going up and seeing about [arrange-
        ments]. Well, something like this with Senator Jones
        that somebody had to make all the arrangements for.
        It wasn't testifying. I suppose I did but that wasn't

Paul: the point. It was to go up and arrange it. Or when we
were going to have a question of bringing up a measure
or not bringing it up, say with a senator like Senator
Curtis, Maud and I would usually go together and see them
and make all these plans with the committee chairman as
to whom they would like us to have and, in case they had
a hearing, when would be a proper time for it from our
point of view to risk a vote, and whether it was worthwhile to stress this thing or that thing or the other.
Just--you know, you couldn't hardly conduct a campaign
and not try to know just what ought to be done from the
people who would know the most on the inside. See, we
always had some good friends--

Fry: --who would keep you informed?

Paul: Well, with whom we could confer and know we were getting
the right kind of information. I wouldn't call that
lobbying exactly, but it was working with the members of
Congress. I'm sure that's what all these professional
lobbyists do, that that's the way they proceed.

Fry: Did you have the congressmen's administrative assistants
then to deal with that we have now?

Paul: No.

Fry: You could talk more directly to the legislator himself?

Paul: Oh, yes. A hundred times simpler then, a thousand times,
I guess. This business of not being able to see your
congressman and so on, I don't remember an experience
like that.

Fry: In the committee work of the Judiciary Committee or
the suffrage committees, did you work any with the--what
do they call it--the executive secretary of the committees,
the person who is paid to do the work of the committee?

Paul: You had to do it somewhat but I don't remember. We might
have a preliminary talk, perhaps, I suppose. I don't
remember any slowing up of things because of any, as it
is slowed up now, because of all the stages you have to
go through before you can get to anybody. I mean just
as when I asked you to come out and see if you couldn't
take on Don Edwards; well, we didn't have to go to all
that effort then in the suffrage campaign. We could go
to see the congressman himself, usually.

Fry: Judging from my experience, we were able to get a lot

Fry: of information on which members or for instance on
          whether the bill was going to be reported out in four
          weeks, if it was an adverse report, how much time we
          would have left to work in getting that bill re-
          considered--all that sort of thing we could find out
          from the executive secretary of the committee. I
          wondered if you had a person like that then?

Paul: Maybe they had them but I don't think they had the power
          they have now. I don't remember even knowing whether
          they had any particular secretary. Of course every
          senator and congressman probably had some secretarial
          help.

Fry: But I am talking about the Judiciary Committee secretary.

Paul: They undoubtedly had some. See, there wasn't this
          great, enormous staff like there is now.

Fry: You just didn't have to deal with that bureaucracy
          then.

Paul: No.

Fry: Is there anything else that you can think of that would
          help us get an accurate picture of the lobbying activities?
          I have run out of questions on it, but I still feel like
          the picture is fairly fuzzy.

Paul: In what way is it fuzzy?

Fry: Well, if I were writing a book, trying to describe the
          pressure and the combined dedication and enthusiasm and
          the snap and the crackle around the House on the lobbying
          that was going on for suffrage, I wouldn't have any
          sharp picture.

Paul: I think if you would look through all the photographs
          it would be very good, because we have people standing
          outside the door of a committee and you find them there.

              I remember the first one we ever had, I think I was
          coming down the steps of the Capitol--the first year it
          must have been, back in 1914--from one of the committees,
          and I suppose there must have been other people coming
          down too. Where we would have a feeling of almost
          hopelessness: how would we get it out of this committee
          with all the difficulties we were experiencing. So many
          of those lobbyists, and then all those great thousands
          of people--when you showed me one [picture] the other

Paul: night, or I showed it to you--assembling there with petitions and so on. It was all lobbying. Any time any big enormous group like that came, then they [congressmen] saw people.

I think there is something in that part of it that Consuelo could very well portray by taking picture after picture of these great groups of people--almost every time anybody looks at this magazine [the Suffragist] here they seem to be so surprised and say, "Well, we never had any idea that the lobbying consisted of this great number of people coming." I suppose it was the first time that this did occur, because all these [instances of big demonstrations and delegations of] people now are more about anti-war and so on. We never heard of such then. As far as I know we were the only people who ever lobbied.

Fry: Oh, really, so that part was fairly unique then.

Paul: Yes, I don't think there was any other group that was sending delegations. You see in that photograph that we always use as a postcard with Susan B. Anthony going up all alone, that's what the lobbying had been as far as the women's movement was concerned.

Fry: I was going to ask you if you knew what the lobbying had been the year before you took it over.

Paul: I have told you many times how Mrs. Kent said how she gave back change from her $10 [annual expense allotment].

Fry: I knew that.

Paul: Beause all she had done really was to write a few letters and get a few speeches made perhaps and have them mailed over the country. There wasn't anything like this personal, starting in to visit every man and to visit every committee and to visit the key committee that we had to have.

I don't know whether there were all these professional lobbyists. I never heard of them, they may have been there; but now, of course, it is a regular profession.

People [lobbyists] have an office and an enormous staff. They entertain, usually, a great deal and try to conduct their lobbying in a social way. Then they usually, well, as still now, if it is a man lobbying for,

Paul: oh, we'll say the laundry industry, whatever it may be, this one man with a secretary, maybe two secretaries, maybe ten secretaries, really do press work. And it would affect that congressman. And they concentrate on the few people that may be necessary to the laundry industry at home that they are sent down by, and report back.

I remember one time recently when we were having a great deal of trouble with the United Automobile workers and they were spreading out into Indiana, where the factories were going and therefore the United Automobile Workers were going. And they were becoming a force, as far as we could see, but we didn't <u>know</u>, against us, from Indiana. And so, one day when I was talking to our first vice-chairman (<u>now</u>; I don't know what she was then, but she was on our board) Mrs. Butler Franklin, and I said, "If we could have a little better idea of what is going on in this United Automobile Workers and whether they are putting a great deal of energy into opposing us or not, it would help us."

And she said, "Well, my brother"--you are not putting this down, are you?

Fry: Well, it's on.

Paul: Because I couldn't put this down. She said, "My brother is vice-president," (I think) "of a very big industry." I believe it was gas, or something like that, where it was a question of pipelines. It is vague in my mind.

And she said, "He is here visiting me now and I will ask him about Indiana because he has lived in Indiana."

So she came back and said now she knew everything about it. "Just call up Mr. So-and-so," whose name I don't know. "He is our chief lobbyist; he is paid a large sum to get better legislation on"--pipelines, we'll say, I'm not sure of this. "And he will know everything that is to be known about what the United Automobile Workers are doing, whether they are a force that has to be reckoned with now, or whether they are such a minimum force in Indiana, whether they are not important, and what attitude they are taking on this subject, whether you can count really upon the support of the senators and congressmen from that state," so she told me.

Paul: Then she got him on the phone, the lobbyist, and then
she asked me to take the phone. She said, "He is talking
away but I can't make out very much what the situation
is, so will you talk to him?"

So I talked to this man. He said, "Now if Mr. So-
and-so," (whatever her brother's name was) "wants me to
get this information, of course I will get it for you.
It would take me maybe two hours or three hours. That's
what I am here to do. I am paid by that firm," by the
gas company, we will say it was, "and he [Mrs. Franklin's
brother] is the vice-president, one of the most important
officers. If he requests it, it is my business now to
find out, and I will call you back." And he did.

And he said, now--let me see if I remember what he
said--"Now you say you want information that bears on
the Equal Rights Amendment. If Mr. Walter Reuther and
the UAW are for the Equal Rights Amendment or against
the Equal Rights Amendment, I don't know anything. You
must know about that, I don't know a single thing about
that. But if they are against you, there is not much
chance you are going to get any of the congressmen and
senators from Indiana. They may give you all reasons
and so on, or may be hesitating, but you probably won't
get them.

"But if by chance Mr. Reuther and the UAW are _for_
what you are working for, then you needn't worry at all
and you will have all their support." He said, "We
know [these men now] have recently become one of the
great political forces in the state of Indiana through
the transfer of so many of their industries, of their
automobile factories, and so on up there."

Well, that's the way they were working, you see.
And we would always try to just know as much as we could;
naturally that's what anybody would do. These regular
professional lobbyists they are more unknown figures;
of course the company who employs them, sends them down,
knows if they are skillful in sending in accurate
information and helping with the things they are supposed to be helping with. It is done quietly, nobody
knows about it. Ours was just done in a more--in a way
to try to make public opinion _for_ what we were after.

Fry: Are you talking about both the ERA and the suffrage?

Paul: Now, I am talking about the suffrage. That's the reason

Paul: we were doing that, just <u>publicly</u>. Like the time when we sent down two women from each congressional district. It was no secret lobbying. It was just very publicly staged, while the paid lobbyist, the professional lobby-ist, it's more secret, you know. More hidden and concealed, people denying that they <u>are</u> lobbyists and all that sort of thing.

Fry: A lobbyist from one of the industries once told me that most of his work, in fact nearly all of his work, was to <u>stop</u> bills that might be hurtful to the industry. Yours was to get a bill put <u>in</u>, which he said was much more difficult to do. It is easy to stop a bill, there are a million steps along the way of legislation where it can be killed. But to put a bill in and <u>avoid</u> it being killed--

Paul: But I think the lobbying is always the same problem--it is to achieve a particular purpose. Ours was unpaid people and the professional lobbyists are paid. You know when they put through the bill requiring registra-tion of all lobbyists--

Fry: That was about '47 or '48?

Paul: That was after suffrage victory. I remember very well what happened. We had a chairman. I don't remember for the minute particularly which one it was. She was one of those people who is always very meticulously careful about carrying out the letter of the law, and so she insisted--we said, well that lobbying law was not made to apply to us, we know that. We are not in that class at all, what they call lobbyists. They wouldn't call us lobbyists.

But nevertheless she registered us. Then you were subject to every kind of report and restriction, report-ing,I think maybe every month, just what you had paid for your lobbying and whom you had paid it to and how much had been for railroad fare and all these things. It was a dreadful situation.

I think this was the first--probably the one who did all this was Mrs. Murrow who was a lawyer from Florida, and she got the organization into such a tangle in every possible way because she was down in Florida and couldn't very well keep track of things, I think. So one Jewish man who was a professional lobbyist, persuaded her to put him in charge of all the lobbying and every activity

Paul: practically of the Woman's Party. And when I told you all of our chairmen have been made honorary chairmen but one, well, this one got us into such an awful mess [laughter] that nobody would elect her to be an honorary chairman. But at all events, a new chairman came in and this new chairman was Dean Agnes Wells, dean of women, of the University of Indiana. And also she was national president of all deans, the association of deans.

[End of Tape 8, Side B]

[Tape 9, Side A]

Paul: (If ever I say a single word critical of anybody, leave it out, will you, because I am only saying it for you.)

Fry: At any rate, she was very prominent.

Paul: Well, she made, oh, a splendid chairman. She retired as dean. This was during the World War [II] and they said well, we can't let you go because we are going to increase your responsibilities because we can't get a professor of the stature that we need excepting if we let you take over the mathematics department and the astronomy department. So instead of being a dean--her specialty was mathematics and astronomy--she was in charge of all these great responsibilities.

Well anyway, she said, "I think I will just go up to see my Senator Ferguson of Michigan." (She came from Michigan.) And afterwards she asked him if we must again register under the lobby act. And Ferguson (who later became a judge and he was a distinguished lawyer) he said, "Oh no, the lobby act is not for people like you at all." So we then had the supporr of at least the statement of one senator as to what the lobby act was. So we all said, "Well then, we don't think we ever should have registered and we are not going to register," so we never did from that time on.

Every once in a while some poor lady comes down and she is intimidated by someone saying, are you properly registered under the lobby act. "Oh!" and they come back trembling all over. [Laughter.]

Fry: Well, I'm going to have to stop. I've got to get on that airline bus in twenty-eight minutes.

Paul: Then I think that I will proceed to stop too, and I

Paul: think I will mail you Elizabeth Roberts' genealogy.

[End of Tape 9, Side A]

End of Interviews in November, 1972.

SECTION III: THE SUFFRAGE CAMPAIGN REVIEWED

1914: EVOLUTION OF CONGRESSIONAL UNION'S ORGANIZATION

Alice Paul Leaves Suffrage Campaign

[Tape 10, Side A. May 10, 1973. All Side A has a buzz and static.]

Fry: First, I'll just run down some questions that have emerged from research I've been doing since we last talked. Maybe this will help you warm up--it's about the early years of the Congressional Union: we didn't talk very much last time about how you evolved your organization, setting up council and so forth.

There was a lot of pressure about a year after you first organized the Congressional Union to hold a general election and have an elected national council to run it--all of this sort of thing. These things are going to be found by the scholars who will be delving into your papers, because Ivy Kellerman-Reed wrote a lot of letters about it. She was a woman early in Congressional Union out in one of the states; I don't know which one.

Paul: I never heard the name.

Fry: Her correspondence is in the collection at the National Woman's Party. At any rate, she is only representative.

Paul: It would be so much better if I could think who she was.

Fry: I think Mrs. Donald Hooker also was a part of this; this was the group that was campaigning for a constitution and so forth. They were opposed by the ones who wanted to have a very efficient, lean organization that could make decisions rapidly. How did you handle this? Because this was a threat to your authority.

Paul: I can hardly see that. We were appointed by the National

Paul: American Woman Suffrage Association as a committee, you
        know. We came down as a committee of this organization,
        almost the only organization for suffrage (I think there
        was the College Suffrage League also) in the country.

Fry: But this happened afterwards.

Paul: No--I know, but when we arrived that's what we were and
        what we continued to be for the whole first year.

Fry: That's right. And then--

Paul: So we didn't form anything but to get enough members in
        the District of Columbia and round about where we knew
        people who would turn in and help in the work of this
        committee. But you know all that [from our previous
        interview].

Fry: I know all that. And you told me about the break--

Paul: They made only one requirement, that we shouldn't send
        a single bill for a single dollar to the national board,
        and must raise all the money, and must do all the work,
        because they wanted to spend all their money and their
        work on their state referendum. And that was the purpose
        for which they appointed us, to have somebody who would
        continue what Miss Anthony had been doing. She didn't
        even have a committee. She just had herself when she
        went down [to Washington] with the National American,
        but by that time they were lucky enough to have Mrs.
        William Kent as their chairman.

        And then Mrs. Kent just couldn't continue, she said,
        possibly. They had given her $10 and she had handed back
        the change to show how little they were doing and how
        necessary it was to have some people who would concentrate
        on it. So then when we came we added to the committee;
        the committee that they had appointed was only Lucy Burns
        and myself, with power to appoint anyone else we wanted.
        So Mrs. Kent went on our board.

        We got an extremely good, powerful board with all of
        the members, of course, of the National American like
        Mrs. Kent. Of course our little tiny board of, say,
        fourteen people--Mary Beard was on our board, and Miss
        Emma Gillette, who was the dean and founder of the
        Western College of Law. It was an extremely good board
        we had. Crystal Eastman went on the board from upper
        New York. And that was printed; it's in all the early
        i̇

Paul: And then, in order to have a group that would start
         in and help with the interviewing of Congress and the
         raising of money and the putting on of functions as a
         money-raising body, we formed this little "Congressional
         Union for Woman Suffrage" we called it. The national
         secretary of the old National American, Mrs. Mary Ware
         Dennett, was the person who suggested the name of Congres-
         sional Union for Woman Suffrage. I don't know that it
         was a very good name but anyway that's what we started
         with.

         In order to be a part of the National American,
         every group had to have a certain number, I think three
         hundred members. So we established some dues, say a
         dollar--I'm not sure what it was--and got the three
         hundred members that qualified us to be an affiliated
         group with the old National American. And throughout
         that first year that's all there was to it. They were
         to help the congressional committee.

         At the end of the year, they first asked me if I
         would continue but not continue with the Congressional
         Union, because they said it was--

Fry: They didn't want you to be head of both?

Paul: It wasn't that. They said they didn't want the money
         to be--We had raised so much money, you see, that their
         national treasurer got up at the national convention (her
         name was Mrs. Stanley McCormick. There were two of
         them. There was Mrs. Stanley who was the national
         treasurer of the National American)--She got up and said,
         "Now I think we've raised," it seems to me, "$27,000
         for this first procession," the National American's
         procession. That's all in that book that I gave you
         here, that hearing by the Senate on that first parade.
         I think it was about $27,000. She said, "Think of all
         that money going into this national procession in Wash-
         ington when we need so much for the state referendum
         campaigns." She wanted all the money raised to go--
         according to her plan--into the national treasury,
         because it was the national committee, to be spent by
         the national board as they wanted.

         At the convention then Jane Addams got up, as you
         may remember, and she said, "I had offered the resolution,
         you remember, to appoint this committee, and I think they
         have been extremely honorable and have carefully paid
         every single bill. They have left no debts and no

Paul: obligations and have put through a very remarkable campaign at no expense to us whatsoever, so in every possible way it seems to me they are to be thanked and commended." And _especially_ (she didn't say this) but this was especially true because we at that very moment when Mrs. Stanley McCormick was making her protest, the hall, and it was a very enormous hall, one of the biggest in Washington--we were paying a thousand dollars for the rent of the one week that we had it for their convention. We were paying all the expenses for the convention.

Fry: You mean the Congressional Union was?

Paul: Yes. Because we considered that was part of our duties. They said they were coming to Washington for their convention, and it seemed our duty to provide the hall and so on. So we paid it. And also we arranged for the entertainment in the homes of different people, especially Mrs. William Kent, the congressman's wife. All the board came, so it saved them from having any financial expense. So I thought that what we had done was quite right and proper.

So then when they said would I take it on and be only the Congressional [Committee] chairman so there wouldn't be this question of the money we were raising being in the treasury of the Congressional Union, there it was, you see. We didn't _have_ any money in our little Congressional _committee_ at all. So I said no, I didn't want to do that. I knew that you couldn't put through any campaign without some kind of [financial] assistance. And because the states would say, "Look here, we need it for our referendum."

Then they offered it to Lucy Burns, and she said the same thing. She didn't want it. She wouldn't do it under those terms. Then they had a time to find somebody and they finally found Mrs. Medill McCormick, who, we thought, had been a very good choice. She was the daughter of Mark Hanna, the great Republican leader in Ohio. She said she would want me to go on her national committee if she was going to be the congressional chairman, which I did; and I asked her to go on our Congressional Union board, which she did, so we would always work together and know just what was going on. So it started out very well, _until_--and we thought probably all of us would go home. We had taken it for a year, and all of the people who had just come in for that one year, we didn't want it to go on any longer.

Fry: You mean in the Congressional Union?

Paul: We didn't want to go on into any campaign. When the
new board was appointed, when the new congressional
committee was appointed and put under the chairmanship
of Mrs. McCormick, we felt we could then give it up,
you see, and not continue any longer. We never formed
it, at first, with the thought of its being a perpetual
organization, or an organization at all.

Fry: Oh, really? I thought you had formed it to work on
suffrage until suffrage passed.

Paul: No, it never once entered our _heads_ to do that. We
formed it to make possible the first year we had undertaken. When we had undertaken to do it and we weren't
allowed to have any money from the national treasury,
we had to get it from _somewhere_. So we formed this group
[Congressional Union] to do the work, as volunteers, to
raise the money which we had to pay. Which they did.
We raised, as I said, so much that the national board
wanted to have it. Probably she [Mrs. Stanley McCormick]
didn't know of this condition under which we agreed to
take it in the beginning. So suddenly, after she [Mrs.
Medill McCormick] was appointed, there didn't seem to be
any particular reason for our going on. But that's
probably what we _would_ have done.

Fry: But you would have retained your chairmanship of the
committee?

Paul: No.

Fry: Not that either.

Paul: No, no, no. Because I said that if _I_ went on, I knew that
there must be some kind of a group to do this work for
us, to raise this money for us. And they didn't want
this to be.

Fry: Were you going to leave suffrage, the whole organization?

Paul: Well, we didn't have much of an organization. We had
only about fourteen people on our national committee.
We formed this little group [the Congressional Union] to
help us; that's all there was to it.

When this all happened I went home. Mrs. McCormick
finally agreed to come on our board and we had this little

Paul: group which she could continue with or not continue
        with if she wanted to.

NAWSA Introduces Rival Amendment

Paul: So I went back to my home in New Jersey and sort of
        decided I would take a rest since it had been a very
        strenuous year. I had hardly gotten home when I got
        this note from Lucy Burns saying, "A most dreadful thing
        has happened. Mrs. McCormick, without telling us a
        thing about it, although she is on our own little Congres-
        sional Union board, and without apparently telling
        anybody, has introduced in Congress the Shafroth-Palmer
        amendment." You remember reading all about that.*

Fry: That would be the resolution for the amendment, only it
        was different from your amendment.

Paul: Let me tell you what it was. It was this. And you
        certainly can't write this thing up without making it
        very clear what it was.

Fry: I'm sure we have this.

Paul: It was this: Any state legislature was required, by an
        amendment to the Constitution--"upon receiving a petition
        of (some sufficient number) must have a state referendum"--
        to the men of the state on the question of suffrage for
        women, that is, suffrage for that state. If it had gone
        through Congress by two-thirds vote of both houses and
        been ratified by three-fourths of the state legislatures,
        made up of men at that time, all that women would have
        gotten by amending the Constitution after doing all this
        work and spending all this money, would be the right to
        have a referendum. So no woman in the whole country
        would have gotten the vote. It wouldn't have given the
        vote to women. Mrs. McCormick had been persuaded by
        those--which has happened again and again in our experi-
        ence--by these men politicians, who were all friends of
        their fathers, that it was impossible, impossible to get

_____

*The Shafroth-Palmer was introduced in the U.S. Senate
March 2, 1914.

Paul: the vote for all the women by a federal amendment. It
could not be done, the one that Susan B. Anthony had
labored on all these years. They said, "She never got
it, and if you look across the world at that time [blank
tape] excepting for Wyoming and the few states like Idaho
and Montana and some provinces in other countries, there
was no place in the whole world where a woman could vote."
There was no place in Latin America where a woman could
vote. There was no place in Africa where a woman could
vote. There was no place in Asia where a woman could
vote. And in Europe the only place was Finland, which
was a dependency of Russia; it was a province, I presume,
but I don't know exactly what it was, but it was not
an independent country. And there were some territories
down in Australia and New Zealand--not the whole countries,
but some place where women of Australia or the women of
New Zealand could vote--I think there were some provinces
in both; I'm not quite sure. But if you looked over the
world, it was an unheard-of, unthought-of thing. A few
people out in Wyoming and Idaho, and so on, a tiny
minority in our country; and in Finland, a tiny minority
in all of Europe, not even an independent country; and
in Australia and New Zealand, not even countries either,
just in sections.

So they persuaded her that what we were trying to do
and what we had been trying to do the whole year and
having a big procession for and all the lobbying and
everything else, was doomed to defeat. It couldn't be
done. The only thing to do was to gradually--they said
gradually the state referendums, some of them, were won,
and by making it obligatory to have a referendum to all
the states, some more would be won.

That, I thought was the most terrible proposal that
could ever be made. So I went back to Washington, and
we asked for an interview with the national board of
the National American and practically our whole board--I
remember Mrs. Lawrence Lewis was one of the most prominent
people on our board, and Mrs. Burns, and several others--
went up and met with the national board. They summoned
all their people from all over the country to this
national board meeting.

We tried to explain why we thought that this amendment, which had been announced in 1878, introduced in
Congress by one of the California men, one which Susan
B. Anthony had worked for so heard year after year--we
said everything we could think of as to why we should

Paul: continue it. I'm sure all the people on the board were
        very conscientious people, trying to do the best they
        could for women. But they said, "Well, we know so
        little and Mrs. McCormick has all these positions and
        friends in Congress who know so much about it all and
        think it the best thing to do, and have already
        introduced it."

        Miss Addams sat there for two days, and I think she
        was--we always thought she was completely with us, more
        than anybody else, because she had been the person to
        propose the resolution that we go down there [to Wash-
        ington] in the beginning. So it was a very sorrowful
        few days that we spent there. We just got nowhere. We
        certainly did fail. Whether we could have done it better
        I don't know. But I think. We had very sincere and
        honest people like Mrs. William Kent, very powerful
        people, and so our little board was completely united.
        There wasn't a dissenting person on our little Congres-
        sional Union board which we had still. And we just
        couldn't convince them.

        So they said, "We think we'd better go ahead and
        continue our effort all over the country for the state
        referendums and it will be a help. It will make it
        easier to have a referendum because sometimes a legis-
        lature refuses." That was their philosophy.

        So then this idea that we had all had of packing up
        and getting back to our respective homes as soon as we
        could really vanished, because we thought, "We can't
        go away and leave the whole woman movement without
        anybody working in Congress if women are ever going to
        get the vote."

The Congressional Union Reconfirmed

Paul: So then we started in. There was nothing but the
        little Congressional Union then, you see.

Fry: Which Mrs. McCormick was it who was chosen to lead the
        congressional committee?

Paul: Mrs. Medill McCormick, Ruth Hanna McCormick, daughter
        of Mark Hanna.

Fry: Around January I think.

Paul: Well, we continued along with our same little basement
        office, and the first thing that happened was that women
        over the whole country who just naturally, without any
        argument from us or anybody else, thought this was a
        very fatal mistake [this step] that the National American
        had taken. And the first group, as a group to act, was
        out in Minnesota. They sent word and asked me if I
        would come out and explain this whole thing to the
        women there because they were very much opposed to
        dropping the Amendment they had all been working for and
        that they were all committed to.

        So I did go out and spoke at a meeting that they
        had, and spent about a week I guess. Quite a great
        many of their own board--the meeting that they got up
        was presided over by their state president, Mrs. Euland.
        She was a Scandinavian woman, very fine woman. They
        had a splendid group of women out in Minnesota. Anyway,
        a good many of them wanted to become members and asso-
        ciate themselves with us, but we didn't have any--we did
        have a little [individual] membership; I suppose they
        paid a dollar or something but I don't remember much
        about that.

        But then the state of Maryland, led by Mrs. Donald
        Hooker, a remarkable woman, a wonderful, marvelous, mar-
        velous person, who had a great command over her own
        branch--they would do anything she told them to do--the
        whole branch voted to sever all relations with the old
        National American, withdraw from it completely, broke
        with them completely and wanted to join with us. So
        then we suddenly, not wanting in the least to become a
        national organization, had a branch. And we suddenly
        had some individual women out in Minnesota.

        That spread all over the country, and I took a trip.
        I went to a great many--I don't know how many--states.
        I spoke to the state boards trying to get them, not to
        join us because we didn't want to be an organization,
        but to try to get them to refuse to go along with this
        new Shafroth-Palmer bill.

Fry: Also, about this same time there was discussion by your
        group of the strategy of holding the party in power
        responsible, in the 1914 election campaigns.

Paul: That was formally adoped later. This split was over

Paul: this thing. When the split began we had already
started our paper the Suffragist [November, 1913].
Everything I'm saying is down there because we took it
up week by week. We got the Suffragist out every week.
The main thing we labored on and talked about all the
time was the importance of sticking to the original
amendment. There you will find page after page
after page after page. It was about all we talked
about. We sent the paper, of course, all over the
country wherever we could get anybody to take it.

And then Crystal Eastman (she was on our national
board) went out on one of these very successful trips
across the states trying to--we had only one thing--
trying to get people to come back to the original
amendment.

Fry: Who did you see when you went to these states? The
chapters of the National American?

Paul: We went to the state committees of the National American,
with whom we had been working the whole previous year.
So we knew them. They had come to Washington; we had
corresponded with them. We also gradually, without
wanting it or thinking about it, we suddenly found that
we were getting little branches in different states who
would not go along with the other amendment. That's
the only thing that caused the Woman's Party to come
into being.

Fry: Was this when your amendment was the Mondell?*

Paul: We didn't have any name for it then. Shafroth-Palmer
was because Shafroth was a senator and Palmer was a
House man, and they introduced it.

[Interruption for adjustment of furnace thermostat.]

We still didn't have any idea of having a national
organization, of being anything very permanent, although
it looked as though we might have to be permanent to get
the old National American to come back to the fold on
the subject of which amendment we were working for.

---

*According to Irwin (ibid.), the Amendment at this time
was referred to in the name of its main sponsors in
Congress--the "Bristow-Mondell Amendment," and later
became the "Susan B. Anthony Amendment."

Paul: You see what an extraordinary situation it was.

Fry: At this point, did you still prefer to work with the
          National American, if they had let you?

Paul: We never thought of being <u>anything</u> but the National
          American. There had been for a long time two groups,
          one the National and one the American. This was before
          I ever came along. By the time we arrived everybody
          was in just one.

          Supposing you belonged to a church and the church
          suddenly went off on something quite contrary to what it
          was formed to do. You wouldn't be thinking about
          whether you wanted to work <u>with</u> them or not. You would
          be thinking about bringing them back to what they <u>should</u>
          be working for, what <u>we</u> thought they should be working
          for.

          We discovered that there was immense support for
          our view. For instance, the most powerful woman in the
          women's movement in California, in your state, was your
          own Mrs. Kent on our board. I think everybody out
          there--I never heard of anybody who didn't support the
          position we took. Charlotte Anita Whitney was in the
          College Woman's League. And Mrs. Phoebe Hearst. All
          these people were great followers there. Maud Younger--
          she was one of the most powerful people in that state.

          You see, it was such an unheard-of thing when women
          who had worked for a long time, for generation after
          generation and had seen steady progress made, suddenly
          [saw] it completely abandoned, because you see, they
          [National American] were completely abandoning the
          vote-for-women campaign federally.

Fry: I understand that Carrie Chapman Catt and Dr. Shaw,
          who were leaders in the National American, said that
          the Shafroth-Palmer bill was just to be a <u>supplement</u> to
          the other one. Did you understand this, and could you
          explain that to me? How could it be a supplement?

Paul: Well, I suppose it could be, being an attempt to <u>oblige</u>
          legislatures to have a referendum. <u>Some</u> of them might
          be successful, and then that would give more support in
          Congress as it would then be a suffragist state and
          would be more apt to support it. I suppose that way it
          could be.

Paul: But of course when you face it, when you go down
to see a man and your measure is introduced and you speak
before a committee and the hearings and so on, and you
speak for the one that's going to give the vote for
women if it ever goes through, and other people speak
for the other measure before Congress, which is to make
a referendum (for the men of the state, not the women
of the state) obligatory; if a sufficient number of
people sign a petition, to an ordinary congressman or
to an ordinary woman it's a very complicated situation.
And so these women [we talked to] absolutely couldn't
comprehend why, when Miss Anthony had been going down
there [to Washington D.C.] year after year and they'd
all been supporting what she was going for, why they
suddenly dropped it. And I don't see, I can't imagine,
I really never could comprehend any reason whatsoever
for it. [Laughter.] But it went on. They continued
their campaign. I'm not sure what year they gave it up.
There was a convention, I think, in Louisville, where
they voted it down.

Fry: It wasn't terribly long after that.

Paul: You see, we got into the war in 1917. And since the
whole National American devoted itself to the war effort
and practically ceased everything, it more or less left
the field to us. So after a time we didn't realize that
there was any counter-force at all. Everybody seemed
to be working for the original amendment.

        But our whole coming into being as a separate organi-
zation and continuing was due--If they hadn't introduced
that Shafroth-Palmer we never would have thought of
having a separate organization. I'm sure we would have
closed up our headquarters and gone back to our respective
lives, whatever we were trying to do before we went
down there.

Fry: What would you have gone back to?

Paul: I? I don't know because [laughter] I haven't stopped
to think about what I would have done if I didn't do
this.

Fry: I can't imagine you not being in the suffrage movement.

Paul: Oh no, I don't know. I certainly [would have been] in
the suffrage movement. I don't know if I would have--I
was in the suffrage movement when I was a student in

Paul: England, and when I was a student in the University of Pennsylvania. You can do all those little things and still it's not your life.

Fry: I read somewhere, I think it was in somebody's thesis--they mentioned that you one time thought that you would be a college professor.

Paul: I suppose everybody in those pioneer days, when there weren't very many women going to college anyway and almost no women taking their doctor's degree, it would have been a natural thing to do. The few women who were graduate students the same time I was, I guess they all became college professors.

I had what was called the Moore fellowship at the University of Pennsylvania. I was so surprised when I met Dr. Crawford (out in California) and she was, of course, such a very distinguished dean of students at the University of Southern California. When she began to be active in our campaign, I met her once when she came to Washington. She told me that she had studied at the University of Pennsylvania and had had the Moore fellowship. I said, "Well of all things! I had the Moore fellowship I don't know whether before or after you"--I guess she must have been after me, I'm not sure. I remember that it was after I had come back from England where I had been imprisoned as you know. Everybody I knew I supposed looked rather askance, rather embarrassed to know a person who had been in prison. Certainly everybody in my family, everybody from Swarthmore, it seemed to me everybody thought it was rather a disgraceful episode in my life. I went to the University of Pennsylvania when I came back. I had gotten a master's degree before I went to Europe and had studied at the University of Birmingham and the University of London (the School of Economics); so when I went back I thought that now I would finish it up.

I remember Christabel Pankhurst coming to me when I was in London and saying, "Wouldn't you stay on as an organizer for the Women's Social and Political Union?" They paid a very tiny sum, but up to that time I had been paying all my own expenses. I said, "No, I've started to get this doctor's degree; I think I'd like to go back and finish it."

So I went back to the University of Pennsylvania, where I had taken my master's degree. The professor of

Paul: economics, whose name was Dr. Simon Patton--he was a
        very great professor in my opinion--came to me and
        asked, "Wouldn't you like to have a fellowship at the
        University of Pennsylvania?"

        I said, "Well, I thought I had burned all my bridges
        that time when I went to prison. I didn't think I
        could ever aspire to any honor like this."

        He said, "Oh, we don't think that way at all. If
        you'd like to have the Moore Fellowship, it's now open,
        and we want to offer it to you." So--I felt just--oh
        so grateful to this man.

        [Tape off. Interruption for dinner preparation.]

Fry: How did Mrs. Belmont come over to you?

Paul: You know Miss Crystal Eastman, don't you, who she was.

Fry: Was she Max Eastman's wife?

Paul: Sister. Crystal Eastman was one of those on our little
        Congressional Union committee, our original committee.
        She was very helpful. You know her mother was one of
        the first women, perhaps the first woman minister in
        America, very, very well known in the women's movement.

Fry: Did she work in suffrage or equal rights?

Paul: I don't know whether she worked or not, but she was the
        mother of Crystal who worked. Crystal went to Vassar.

Fry: Well, you would know if her mother was a part of it.

Paul: Well, I think her mother died before I ever knew Crystal.
        She was just a tradition of being one of the first woman
        ministers in the country. Crystal was a member from the
        time she went on our committee until she died. She knew
        so many people, and she was always trying to get them
        to come in and help in the campaign. She took one trip
        over the country which was _very_ successful and where she
        got a _great_ great deal of help.

Fry: Was this the same time that you took yours around for
        the opposition to the Shafroth-Palmer amendment?

Paul: No, she did it first.

Paul: So--she was always insisting that we do something
to get Mrs. Belmont to take part in this movement because
she was somebody everybody knew about because of her
great wealth, and so on. I remember when we were getting
up this first procession I don't know how many people
were always insisting that we give a very prominent
place to Mrs. Belmont, that she was the sort of person
who liked to be known to everybody and to be conspicuous,
and so on.

So they said, "What you must do is put her on one
of the three floats." I thought, "What a funny lady
she must be, to want to be on a float." I never had
heard of anybody who wanted to do that. You had to
labor and toil to get people to sit up above all the
crowd and be on a float. But I thought that since they
all said I must write to Mrs. Belmont I wrote her a
letter asking her if she would preside over one of
the floats in this first big procession. I don't
think she even answered me. I guess she thought I
was another lunatic come into the movement to ask her
to go on a float.

But then when Crystal was always pursuing this and
I said, "Well, I did do what you asked me--I asked her
to be on a float." Suddenly one day I had a telephone
message from Mrs. Belmont asking me if I would come in
and have dinner with her and then spend the night so we
could discuss the whole break that we had had over the
new amendment. She was always working, of course, for
the old National American, and I think perhaps paying
for their headquarters, it was very much [?].

So I went up and had dinner with her. Then I spent
the night there. She was one of these people who doesn't
like to go to bed until very, very, very late. So she
wanted to talk, on and on and on. We talked the whole
evening until two in the morning or something like that.
I guess that night she said that she had decided that
we were the ones who would be able to put the amendment
through, and it was insanity to be starting on just
getting a referendum to the men of the states. So most
of the people of course didn't sever their relations
with the old National. They just belonged to both.
But she definitely cut off all her connections--

[End of Tape 10, Side A. No words were lost here in
the tape copying.]

[Tape 10, Side B]

Paul: --some form of an organization.

Fry: I think the issue was over--

Paul: It was very simple maybe. Maybe they were a more elaborate one.

Fry: This was before a constitution was drawn up. Do you remember any discussions over whether to have a general election for officers by the general membership?

Paul: I think we always did. You see, we were such a tiny little group. Whatever we drew up--we had lawyers on our little board like Mrs. Gillette, as I told you, the dean and founder of the Western College of Law--I think we probably just asked one of them to do all that sort of thing for us. I don't remember a thing about it.

Fry: It was probably just part of your ordinary evolution, so you wouldn't especially mark it in your own memory.

Paul: Whoever this Mrs. Reed was--you say she was writing us letters--

Fry: Ivy Kellerman Reed. Also Mrs. Donald R. Hooker was involved trying to help get a constitution written, and so forth.

Paul: Yes, she was the one who joined almost immediately, before Mrs. Belmont even. At the time she joined she was one of our most powerful and prominent people. So anything she asked we would certainly have done. Maybe she was the one who did get us a constitution. (I can't remember one thing about getting the constitution.)

Fry: Well, okay.

Paul: She was one of the most involved and devoted and _ardent_ and enthusiastic workers we ever had.

Carrie Chapman Catt's Opposition

Fry: Was Carrie Chapman Catt ever sympathetic to your cause after the Shafroth-Palmer amendment was put in?

Paul: See, she was International president. I guess we mostly heard of her as International president.

Fry: Then?

Paul: Then.

Fry: I thought she would be in on the National American board meetings.

Paul: No, no.

Fry: Wasn't she there?

Paul: I never heard of her.

Fry: Carrie Chapman Catt?

Paul: I never heard of her being present at anything. She was International president. She was supposed to be looking after things in Europe. This was something Susan B. Anthony really started, the whole international. She went over to Germany and started it.

I don't know what she was before, but when we came along she was International president.* The first time I ever saw her, we had a big mass meeting in one of the theaters in Washington the night before our great parade-- our first procession, we called it, not a parade [March 3, 1913]. We asked Mrs. Catt to be the great speaker on this occasion as the International president of this whole movement. She did. I didn't go to the meeting because I think the meeting was the night that Mrs. Rogers and I were going over to see Secretary of War Stimson about sending police. I remember the meeting was going on and I didn't even get to the meeting.

Fry: Yes, you told me about that.

Paul: That was the meeting where Mrs. Catt made a very splendid speech, the night before our procession. We asked her to do it. I don't know whether she spent her time in Europe. I don't remember ever hearing about her one way

*Carrie Chapman Catt was elected president of the National American Woman Suffrage Association in December, 1915. She remained the United States leader of the International until 1923. The outgoing NAWSA board in December, 1915 v⌐ ⌐ ⌐ ⌐ ⌐ be r⌐ eventually.

Paul: or the other until the end of our first year in Washington at the national convention where we paid, as I told you, an enormous rent for this hall and expenses entertaining the board and such things. At that convention I had to make the report for the Congressional Committee, which I did. I remember when I finished Mrs. Catt arose. I don't know that I had ever seen her or spoken with her before. She was there, of course a very important person in that national convention. I remember her getting up and saying after I finished the report, "It seems to me that the tail is really wagging the dog." Isn't that something they say?

Fry: Something like that.

Paul: That idea. She said, "Here is somebody telling about an official organ that they have, and it's only a <u>committee</u>. What business has a committee having an official organ, getting out a weekly paper?" I remember this very well [laughing] because it was such agony to us to get it out, and we expected a little praise! She said that this was all wrong. "We have to do something about this, this relationship. This committee is getting to be more prominent than the mother, the organization itself."

So she made this protest, and then the treasurer, as I said [laughing], got up and made this protest: What in the wide world did we mean by not turning all the $27,000 they raised into her treasury? That's when Miss [Jane] Addams got up and said this was according to the agreement. She made a very fine speech.

But nobody that I had heard of said anything to support Mrs. Catt. Usually, you know, in a convention people don't say very much. They all sit and listen.

Then the next time, I think, I ever heard of Mrs. Catt--but I don't want all this recorded down [and attributed] to me.

Fry: It sounds like something so far that we could find anyway in the proceedings of the convention. It's already in print.

Paul: I know, but you don't like to be seeming to be hostile to any of your fellow-workers.

Then we had the division over the Shafroth-Palmer. As far as I know Mrs. Catt didn't ever appear in that one

PAUL: way or the other or have anything to do with that except of course that she was officially connected with the side that was working for the Shafroth-Palmer.

Then--I'm sure I told you this--Zona Gale was a famous writer at that time, greatly respected and greatly admired. She had belonged to us, as so many people did, formally joined us and also kept on with the old National American. She conceived the plan of having a meeting at the Willard Hotel, which she arranged, at which the two groups would meet together and iron out their differences and we would have one society again and not have two. This was--I don't know which year, but I imagine around 1918.

Fry: That late?

Paul: I'm not sure about that date. It might have been, because, you see, the war came, and then Dr. Shaw and I guess almost all her officers took different positions in the defense movement in Washington, official positions, I suppose they were paid, I don't know about that. But they gave _all_ their time and _all_ activity that we were aware of ceased. So it was much better for us. We didn't have any friction because there was nobody to have any friction with; they were all over in this other camp.

I think it was at this time, somewhere along there, that they had their Louisville convention and withdrew the Shafroth-Palmer.

Fry: In late 1917, according to my chronology, they voted to back the federal amendment. The Shafroth-Palmer may have been withdrawn even before then, but they still wanted to put their emphasis on state-by-state referenda. Is that right? And then finally in late--

Paul: No, this convention was over the Shafroth-Palmer. That was what this fight was about, whatever year it was.

Fry: And it was in Louisville.

Paul: It's my recollection. And I'm almost certain that Mabel Vernon attended it. I think she told me about being there. I think she was out in Nevada helping Miss Martin somewhere in that campaign; I guess that campaign was 1914. Then there was a later campaign out there [when Anne Martin ran for Senate]. Anyway she was somewhere in the West and she went down to this convention.

Paul: I guess that was it.

Anyway they did vote to do it [drop the Shafroth-Palmer].

Now what time of year and what year was it that Zona Gale conceived the idea of uniting the two groups? It seems to me it must have been toward the end of the war because I don't think there was much friction when they were busy in war work and we were--they had no use for us, of course. And Jeannette Rankin was one of those Mrs. Catt was very angry with because she cast this vote against the war. That was 1917. So Mrs. Catt must have been there then. Because I remember about her terrific appeal against Miss Rankin.

At this meeting, as I recall it, Zona Gale told of the importance of working together and not having a moment in which women couldn't get along together, and so on. That was her general theme.

I think I spoke then and said that we were in harmony with everything she said, of course, but we were certainly not going to abandon the amendment we were working for. And I remember Mrs. Catt spoke up for _her_ point of view, and she said, "All I wish to say is, I will fight you to the last ditch."

I'll never forget her speech, because it was so cryptic. And up she got and walked out. That was the end of the whole attempt. I guess that's the last time I ever saw her.

Fry: There's a letter she wrote to the _New York Times_ in 1914 in which she disclaims the activists, strategy of Congressional Union. She wanted the world to know she had nothing to do with it.

Paul: I'm sure of that, I'm sure that was her attitude.

Fry: Do you remember her letter?

Paul: No, I never heard of it. I don't think I ever knew there was a letter. But she was completely remote from our experience. We never saw or heard of her very much as far as I can remember. I remember one time that I did actually talk to _her_. (I can't really remember when it was. It might have been perhaps at that first procession in Washington when she made this big speech for us.) But

Paul: I remember she said, "I have always felt that I <u>enlisted</u>
        <u>for life</u> when I went into this movement." She was
        opposing the idea that we had that we might be able to
        <u>get</u> the vote. She said, "When you have more experience
        you'll know that it's a much longer fight than you have
        any idea of."

Impact of Congressional Union's 5% of the Suffragists

Fry: Another thing that National American kept saying, after
        you really got started, was that the Congressional Union
        (or the Woman's Party, depending on what year they were
        saying this) only had about 5% of the suffragists and
        they had the other 95%.

Paul: I'm sure that was true.

Fry: I wondered if true, how important it was.

Paul: [Laughing.] Well, of course it would have been easier
        for us if we'd had all the ninety-five. But it certainly
        was true. There was no question at <u>all</u> about it. That's
        of course what made our work much much more difficult.

Fry: Was the rank and file out in the states really divided?
        Did a number of them belong to both, for instance, after
        you got all set up?

Paul: I told you how we never would have had enough to have a
        society, never would have had a society forced upon us,
        if there hadn't been <u>some</u> support for the old amendment.
        That was just a question, I think, of there being so
        few women in <u>any</u> organization. The old National American
        was a small organization, a tiny little organization.

        I know when I went down to Washington I was driven
        by their headquarters in New York when we were the
        Congressional Committee. I was given a list of their
        leading members so I could get started on our congression-
        al work. I started out to call on every one of these
        members or telephone or in some way to get in touch with
        them. I worked for quite a good many days before I
        found a single one, because they had either moved away
        or they had died; somehow or other there was no trace
        of them.

        I went on and on and finally--of course I knew Mrs.

Paul: Kent was there, my predecessor--and I went around to call
        on her. She was of course the best person in the world
        one could have to work with. And then I knew about Miss
        Gillette, the founder of the Western College of Law, and
        I went to see her and she became our treasurer. And
        Mrs. Kent agreed to go on our little committee and so
        did Miss Gillette. And the third person I found who
        was actually living in Washington was Mrs. Helen Gardner
        who later became the first Civil Service Commissioner in
        the United State, appointed by Wilson when we got the
        vote, the first thing he did after we got the vote. So
        she agreed to be our press chairman. So we started with
        three people: the treasurer, a press chairman, and Mrs.
        Kent, a former chairman who was just one of our--she
        gave our first donation to us for our headquarters,
        which was $5 a month. It wasn't until we got $5 a
        month promised that we dared even to have a little head-
        quarters. Before that we had to just work from our own
        bedrooms; Lucy Burns' bedroom, my bedroom was all we
        had before that.

        You can't imagine how unimportant, poor, without
        any reputation, any friends or anything--[laughing] we
        wondered what we'd taken upon ourselves. And then when
        we were suddenly thrown out of the old National American
        by their taking up this other amendment and then they
        didn't even want us to be a member of their society, to
        be an affiliated member or anything. So they practically
        put us out. And we practically put ourselves out,
        because we weren't going to be part of anything that
        was working for the Shafroth-Palmer. Well, you felt all
        womanhood almost was against you. So every word they say
        about our being 5%--I'd say we might have been 1%, [laughter
        not as much as five.

Fry: But later on, by about 1916, you had grown. By 1917 I
        believe you had organized and had some kind of a chapter
        in almost every state.

Paul: We did, of course, we had to. We couldn't do anything
        else.

        We were talking about people who joined up and left
        the old National American. Another one was Anne Martin.
        She was the head of her [NAWSA] state branch in Nevada.
        She left them completely too and she became our congres-
        sional chairman and she continued in that up until the
        time she ran for the senate herself.

Fry: What I'm trying to get up is a picture from you on the

Fry: impact of the National Woman's Party versus the impact of the National American.

Paul: Impact on whom?

Fry: On Congress and on the President, in getting suffrage.

Paul: We felt that we were the one that made all of the impact, because they weren't even trying to. First they went off working only for state referendums, officially, and then working only for war, officially, so--

[Interruption.]

You see, the first impression we probably made on Congress, was not whether it was the National American or ourselves. It was that big procession; it was an impression of course of enthusiasm, interest, excitement on the part of women which they probably never imagined, because it really was I think extremely successful and powerful, and had a great deal of publicity because it was new and there never had been a procession in Washington with women before.

Then we kept them up. We had another one on May 9. So that's one way in which--it wasn't _their_ group or _our_ group or any group. It was _women_ for the first time being conspicuous enough to be recognized by Congress as demanding something they wanted.

And then you see when you talk about growing, the coming in of Mrs. Belmont brought her whole Political Equality Association into our camp. So we had these accretions that came without any thought or planning on our part, but just because of the fact that really we were, and history certainly shows we were, on the right track in keeping to this original amendment demanding in simple English the vote, which all women could comprehend. And they couldn't very well comprehend this complicated business of petitions and so on being obligatory by action of Congress through the medium of putting it in the national Constitution. It was a very long and complicated process to try to get the vote.

Assessing Results of Holding Party in Power Responsible

Paul: T ·· · · · · · · w· ·· · w ·· · · political

Paul: field. All congressmen could comprehend our going
around and campaigning only among women who had the vote,
to arouse them to use that vote for all the unenfranchised
women. That certainly was an enormous turning point
in the attitude of Congress toward us. Because even if
you didn't defeat a congressman, after all, these women
voters were making to them something appealing to all
their altruism and selfishness to come in and stand by
other women who were not as lucky as they were. And
there was nothing a congressman could say to his own
women voters in defense of not doing it.

We did it on such a tiny little scale. We tried
to get two women to go to each state. We paid their
expenses, not any salary but expenses, for which we
raised the money with great difficulty but did pay it
all. Mrs. Belmont and a few people like that helped us
to make it possible. They had this meeting up in her
own home at her invitation, August 1914, when we adopted
that policy.

Fry: That was the now famous meeting at Marble House.

Paul: It wasn't so famous.

Fry: Well, when you research awhile, everything keeps referring to it.

Paul: Anyway, she invited us to come and have a conference,
which we were going to have anyway to draw up an election
policy, to have it there. Doris Stevens, who was one
of the best organizers that we ever had or could have,
extremely good, went up in advance and stayed there,
took a little room somewhere, and worked with all the
prestige of Mrs. Belmont behind her. She got all the
people that Mrs. Belmont thought were of any importance
in Newport to come to the public meeting we had after
we had the meeting in her home and adopted this policy.

The meeting was very successful. I remember Mrs.
Thomas Hepburn, sister of Mrs. Donald Hooker, was the
unquestioned leader of the suffragists here in Connecticut, just as Mrs. Hooker was the unquestioned leader down
in Maryland. Mrs. Hepburn came to that meeting at Mrs.
Belmont's. She was the state president of the old National American. When you say, did many of the leading
women leave, well, she didn't leave. She continued as
state president but she also continued as one of our
members and came and spoke and voted at that meeting up
there in Mrs. Belmont's. So unanimously we--

Paul: I made the main proposal at the meeting what we
should do, and then Lucy Burns, who was a very eloquent
speaker made a long speech, I remember, showing the record
of the Democratic party, how very bad they had been on
this subject. And of course the attitude of President
Wilson was completely hostile, and so when we took the
vote it was unanimous.

Then I remember Mrs. Belmont standing in the back of
the room, intensely interested, because she always was
a great fighter. She was just a born born fighter.
Whenever there was a fight on she took the leadership.
So she arose and said she wanted to do what she could to
further this and she would now give us $5,000, which was
the biggest gift we had ever had. It seemed to us
enormous. And it was, for us.

Then we did go to every state where women were voting,
sent in two people who were the best we could find who
were willing to go. Everyone of them did very, very good
work. At the end of the campaign there wasn't any question
now in the minds of the senators from those states that
they were going to support this measure.

I remember Senator Wesley Jones from Washington
state. Washington was one of the recent ones that had
gotten the vote. I remember that we were trying to
have somebody get up and begin to speak about this on
the floor of Congress. (You can't have a movement to
introduce a bill with nobody ever speaking for it in
public.) I remember going to see Senator Jones and asking him what time I could see him in the morning. He
said, "I'm always in my office at seven o'clock." [Laugh-
ing.] That impressed me so much because I felt I had to
get down there at seven. I don't think he meant that,
but anyway I made a great effort and got there at seven,
when he began his work.

He had conducted this hearing and I gave you a copy
of it [to read] which Consuelo sent me, of the Senate
investigation of the procession, of all the attacks--
they weren't really attacks, just unfriendliness--that
happened that day.

Fry: On the parade in March of 1913.

Paul: Yes. So I did go down to see him and got the hearing
arranged.

Fry: This was the hearing for the investigation, or the
hearing on the [Bristow-]Mondell bill?

Paul: You mustn't say Mondell because it was Mondell one year
and somebody else the next year.

Fry: Well, 1914--

Paul: We called it the Susan B. Anthony Amendment. That's
the reason we did it, deliberately, to try to educate
the women of the country that that was the Amendment,
the Susan B. Anthony Amendment, we were working for,
that they had all been working together.

Fry: So it could be called the same name each year.

Paul: Not so it would be called the same each year, but so
that it would be called by a name that the women would
know which one they wanted to support, we hoped.

Anyway, I went to see Mr. Jones to ask him if he
would make a speech and he said, "Yes." At that time
whatever we asked those few men from those states
(Mondell, whom you always talk about was, I think, from
Wyoming--or I have a feeling he was from Washington.*
Bristow was from Kansas. "Bristow-Mondell"--)

When Senator Jones got up I went to sit in the
gallery, very proud of the fact we were going to have a
speech, [laughing] thinking that all women would rally
because we were notifying everybody, and all senators
would be enthused. I believe that nobody was on the
floor excepting Senator Jones making his speech, and I
think almost nobody was in the gallery except for myself.
[Laughing.] It shows what worlds we had to do before we
we could get this measure through.

But that was just the beginning of making the congressmen want to do what we wanted them to do, even to make a
speech to an empty house and gallery. He was willing
to do it because we had fought out in that state and had
sent a very wonderful girl out there to do it, Margaret
Whittemore, with somebody else with her. We usually had
one very good person and the other person was more or
less an assistant so they wouldn't be all alone.

---

*Mondell was congressman from Wyoming.

Paul: When you said, "impact on Congress," I think that
by organizing the women voters in every state where the
women had the vote, when a new one came in like Kansas
we went there, you see. And Washington was a new state.
Gradually a few came, but then immediately we got those
congressmen by including them in whatever election
campaign we were having. So after the first election
campaign, which was in 1914, we went next in 1916 and
and we kept it up every year there was an election
until by the end I feel it was one of the main things
that put the Amendment through Congress.

Fry: Did you run statistics all the time? Or how did you
assess what influence this policy was having on elections
and so forth?

Paul: We knew pretty well from the attitude of the men. I
remember, for instance, a man from Kansas when we decided to go into Kansas which had just been enfranchised
more recently. One of the congressmen from Kansas
telephoned and asked me to come down to his office in
the House of Representatives and talk with him about
this announcement that we were sending two women out
to Kansas to warn the Kansas women to oppose him on the
grounds that he had supported the Democratic caucus of
opposition to the suffrage amendment. He just besought
me not to have anything to do with it. He just went to
me because my name was publicly in the papers as having
had something to do with it.

          Naturally no congressman wants you to go into his
district against him even when he can't tell and you
can't tell what the outcome will be. But it probably
will have some little effect. In some places it
probably had a great deal, in some places very little.
But certainly we had enough so it was recognized
everywhere in Congress, that this was a group which was
attacking anybody in the one place it could attack--
where we had women voters.

          So we had this meeting in California at the time of
the world's fair [Panama Pacific Exposition, in 1915]
where we had a booth from the beginning to the end of
this campaign; you know all about that. Part of that
whole effort there was another step in organizing the
voting women. It was something that we worked on all
the time. We would go from one state to another after
these voting women.

Paul: There was an organization formed, I don't remember
        what it was called. One of the leading women in it was
        Dr. Cora Smith King from the state of Washington, who
        had led in the campaign to get suffrage out there. They
        held a convention in Washington, which we persuaded them
        to have, so that the congressmen there who had never
        visualized before could see right in their own capital
        these voting women coming. Then of course we had them
        all vote to oppose anybody who would oppose the Amendment
        or who did not support the Amendment. Every device we
        could think of was used to build up this idea of the
        women voters standing together <u>against</u> the party which
        was against <u>them</u>.

Fry: One thing I ran across, Alice, in all my reading, was a
        letter from your "Uncle Mickle Paul." He says, "Stop,
        think and decide: Is it an advance or a retreat to
        destroy instead of building up a force to aid in the
        battle for justice to women." He is talking about hold-
        ing the party in power responsible.

Paul: He was the president of the Democratic Club of Pennsyl-
        vania. He came from a Republican family. Nobody else
        in my family had ever been anything but Republican. He
        started out as a drummer boy in the Civil War.

        My father was too young to be in the war. But he
        was a little older. And so he always explained to us
        this extraordinary thing that he was a Democrat. He said,
        "You see, my experience in the war of getting to know
        all the common rank of soldiers so well and what their
        terrible problems were and their great heroism, and so
        on, has made me so different, perhaps from my brother,"
        (who was my father and who was more conservative).

        At all events he was always a champion of the under-
        dog and was made the president for a time of the Democratic
        Club, I think, of Philadelphia (it may have been the
        state). And he was elected to the state legislature as
        a Democrat. But he always upheld me, you know, always.

Fry: He just hated to see you fight the Democrats.

Paul: I don't know about that; I don't remember this letter.
        At all events, when I was in prison in England, and my
        father wasn't living, and my mother was horrified and
        wrote to the British ambassador protesting against this
        terrible treatment of an American girl student in England,
        and so on. I never knew this until recently but my

Paul: uncle's daughter, my first cousin, is still living in Philadelphia, and every time I go over there I go and see her. She told me that my mother came in to see her (my cousin's) father wanting to know what on earth to do because she didn't have any husband to consult about this tragedy that had come to the family. My uncle said to her, "Oh, don't worry about that. She is doing something very splendid. I'm very proud of her." He always stood up for me. Look at his photograph out here.

Fry: In 1916, when you also were fighting against the Democrats, I ran across some letters that were written to "Dear Organizer" from you. Apparently you sent it out to all your state organizers. It sounds like you were having trouble getting the women out in the states to really make it clear that they were supposed to be asking people to vote against Mr. Wilson and the senatorial and congressional candidates of the Democratic party.

Let me quote from it here. You say, "I find in looking through our press clippings that they frequently state that we are holding meetings and trying to arouse interest in the national suffrage amendment but that nothing whatever is said about voting against President Wilson and the Democratic national candidates." Then you say, "I think we cannot be too explicit in telling the people just what we are asking them to do at election time."

Paul: Of course, that was the whole point.

Fry: And you say, "We will, of course, arouse more antagonism by this course than we would by vague generalizations, and the result undoubtedly will be that people will resign."

Paul: I'm sure when I wrote that, that was exactly what the situation was and always is. This very week, for instance, when I was talking to our state chairman down in Alabama, she said, "Now the tactful thing is, not at all what you are saying." (But what I was saying I know is the right thing.) She said, "It's so important to have no apparent difficulties with Governor Wallace, that [we] mustn't say anything about the Equal Rights Amendment."

Fry: To Governor Wallace?

Paul: No, to the state, to anybody. It's the same thing exactly.

Fry: You go on to say in this letter--

Paul: The whole power that we had was in the effort, whether we took away one vote or a thousand votes, to diminish the success in the campaign of the party we were opposing. And now [1973] our great need is to get this ratification of the [Equal Rights] Amendment through, not to have all the people in Alabama rising up and saying how wonderful is equality for women, but not to touch the Amendment. That's no good at all. She said, "I think it would be so much better..."

Then Mrs. Longworth called me and said, "I don't know about this. I think we had better soft-pedal anything about the Amendment."

[End of Tape 10, Side B]

[Tape 11, Side A]

Fry: Another thing on this was your mentioning that some people would undoubtedly resign. Did you lose many people over this policy? When you think about your organizers, as you look back on it, do you remember that you had any further difficulties in getting them to come around and emphasize this business of fighting all Democrats, including those supporting suffrage?

Paul: Oh no, that's what they went out to do. That's what they purposely went for. But you know when you go with a set purpose and you find that people look askance at you and the newspapers are critical of you, certainly you begin to think, "Well, maybe I'd better not mention that too much."

That is just the way they say now, "Well, look here, don't mention the fact that Governor Wallace came out for the complete Equal Rights Amendment." But these people are so determined, all these NOW* people and the left people are so determined to defeat Governor Wallace if they can that they say, "Think of the trouble you will have with so-and-so if you bring up all these points, if you bring up the draft, if you bring up the thing that they object to. So just don't mention the

---

*National Organization of Women

Paul: Amendment at all."

How in the world are we ever going to get this thing
ratified if we don't even mention it because it's unpopular with some people!

Fry: It seemed that a lot of this strategy, too, was to
create a controversy so you _could_ get in the newspapers
and you _could_ make a mainstream issue. That's what your
letter sounds like.

Paul: It wasn't that we were trying to get into the newspapers.
We were trying to make a congressman feel that all these
meetings of all these earnest housewives all over this
state were maybe going to be a danger to him, and then
maybe he would come back and do something, whether we
were in the papers or not.

Fry: You had some other problems with your organizers. It
looked like in the correspondence I was reading (in the
Anne Martin collection) and in the telegrams that went
back and forth between your office in Washington and
these outlying states, every organizer had her strong
points and her limitations.

Paul: Did she?

Fry: Yes, let me give you an example here. Apparently you
tried to get Harriot Stanton Blatch out to speak, and
she wouldn't speak to anyone any more until after the
election except at engagements already made and except
to _large_ audiences. She would not speak to small
audiences.

Paul: Well, that was all right.

Fry: But your problem was, she was in Nevada and Utah at that
time and [laughing] there weren't very many large
audiences available in those states.

Paul: About Mrs. Blatch--she was the president of the Woman's
Political Union, I think it was called, in New York
state. It was a very big and successful organization.
Then New York won, and the organization voted to disband
and to ask all their members to join the Woman's Party
and throw in their strength with us. Mrs. Elizabeth
Seldon Rogers--I've told you about her--she was one of
their most powerful women. Mrs. John Winters Brannan
was perhaps the second most powerful woman. They had
always been on the national board of the National Woman's

Paul: Party, for years, and were backbone of our organization, so they wanted immediately to have the Woman's Political Union throw all its forces into helping us. Mrs. Blatch wasn't so ardent about it, but she concurred. We voted to put her on the national board. So at least there were those three women from New York on the national board; there may have been others.

She was very ardent about starting the picketing. At the meeting where we had to decide whether or not we would begin to picket the White House she was probably the most vigorous person in speaking for it and wanting us to start. And we did start in January 1917.

Then, in April 1917 we went into the war, and so we didn't discuss changing our policy; we had started to picket and so we expected to go ahead and picket. And we did. We didn't have any vote about it or anything. We just continued.

She then resigned from our national board [laughter] that she had just been put on, on the grounds that this was unpatriotic. She then proceeded to get up what you call a round robin. It was late when it arrived to us. It was a long, long document with many signatures, I guess headed by Mrs. Blatch, anyway instigated by Mrs. Blatch, simply demanding that the Woman's Party stop its picketing. This was an unpatriotic disloyal step. She had married an Englishman and a great part of the time in the suffrage campaign while we were campaigning she was over in England looking after the financial interests of her children, because her husband died in England. I remember that Mrs. Brannan finally sent her a cablegram which said, "We demand that you come home and tend to your organization."

So she did come home because of this demand from her people at home. They thought that here in this very critical time that she ought to be there if she was going to continue as president.

So when you tell me about Mrs. Blatch, the period that she was with us was quite short.

Fry: This was October 1916, and, specifically you were hunting for someone to speak at Ely and McGill, two little towns in Nevada. You suggested that Gail Laughlin speak there instead of Harriot Stanton Blatch.

Paul: She was in California so she could go over easily.

Fry: Yes, and you thought that she might be better than Blatch under those conditions.

Then there was somebody who didn't want to go more than so many miles from home. And there was another one--

Paul: An organizer? Who was she?

Fry: I don't have her name down here. And--who was the one who died in the middle of a speech?

Paul: Inez Milholland, my goodness.

Fry: Inez Milholland didn't like to be on a platform with another speaker, because she was afraid--

Paul: I told you that, didn't I?

Fry: Did you tell me that?

Paul: Yes.

Fry: It was also in the telegrams and so forth.

Paul: I want to tell you about Inez Milholland, one of the greatest women we ever had in our movement. You know, we have that painting of her on horseback, on a white horse. We've used it ever since. My goodness, she was a wonderful girl! A wonderful girl! But she was a very modest sort of person. I told you this before--she said she wanted to make only one request, that she be the only speaker. She said, "You know, with a second speaker, I always know in my own bones that I'm not a good speaker and that she would be so much better, so the result is that I simply remain silent. I'm unable to overcome this feeling that poor speaker as I am I still ought to do it. So, if I'm the only person I _know_ I have to do it."

As a result, she was just a _superb_ speaker in the way of moving her audience. She was _extremely_ beautiful and so radiant and lovely. And then she had this lovely sister--that was Vida Milholland--who always sang these wonderful songs that their father paid all expenses to have Vida go with Inez so she wouldn't be alone on the trip. So they were a marvelous combination.

There are so many people in every place where you get up a meeting that can't rest until they have gotten

Paul: themselves on the platform making a speech. We always
had so many people <u>determined</u> to speak. It has been one
of the hardest things in ever getting up a meeting, the
number of people who are offended if you don't make
them a speaker. So that's what she wanted to avoid.

So we got her successfully from the first meeting,
which was in Wyoming, to the last meeting when she fell
unconscious on the platform in Los Angeles, with no one
else ever permitted on that platform, hard as it was,
excepting Vida with her lovely songs, and whoever introduced her. So no matter how <u>determined</u> some of these
queer people were to get up and have a chance to speak
before an immense audience, we kept them off the platform.

Fry: My question is, with communications the way they were
those days I just don't quite see how you were able to
keep all of this coordinated.

Paul: Why not? I don't see how you could do it any other way.

Fry: It must have taken <u>most</u> of your time to do that. Did it?

Paul: It did of mine. I always thought I spent all my time,
ninety-nine per cent of it, raising money (which I guess
I did). Then far too much on just <u>doing</u> this work of
seeing that every little detail went all right way out
in Wyoming or wherever it was. But I never thought we
ever had anything but the utmost and the most wonderful
cooperation from all the organizers. I never thought
there was a single organizer who hadn't been good.

Fry: I'm just referring to the way you had to route different
ones. How on earth did you keep track of all of them?
There were so many going so many places all at the same
time. You had more than just your organizers, didn't
you? You had speakers going out like Sara Bard Field
who wasn't necessarily an organizer.

Paul: The organizers were supposed to be able to speak, but
that wasn't their purpose of course. It was to go and
arouse the people and have lots and lots of people, the
local people speaking, in the suffrage states. Nobody
cared very much, say in Kansas, if somebody from--Like
what this lady said to Mrs. Chittick [the other day],
"Nobody cares very much when you come down from New York
and the campaign is right here in Louisiana to have <u>you</u>
speak. You would do more good if you would come and get
some of these Louisiana people to speak."

Paul: So that was the organizers' point of view; that was
what they had to do.

Operating with Congressional Rules and Committees

Fry: There was something I wanted to ask you awhile ago when
you were talking about the Susan B. Anthony bill in the
1914 session. It was actually brought to the floor in
the Senate in that session and then voted down and
killed. What gave you the idea of having that bill re-
submitted in the Senate during the same session, because
that had never been done before to a bill in the Senate.
Do you remember that?

Paul: No. I don't remember whether it had ever been done
before, if that's what you mean.

Fry: You said, in a letter at that time, that it had never
been done before but that you thought you could get the
senators behind this and get the rules suspended.

Paul: Did we do it or not?

Fry: You did; it _was_ re-submitted.

I just thought maybe you knew something about that,
because it seemed like a pretty big thing to attempt,
to get the Senate rules suspended for that. You were
establishing a precedent.

Paul: That's what we have been trying to see if we could do
up in Maine now, see if we could get it [the ERA] re-
submitted, re-introduced I mean, [for ratification].

Fry: In your letter you said that you thought a lot of the
senators would back you on this, because they wanted to
get this precedent established so that if _they_ had a
bill killed they could re-submit it.

Paul: Yes, that would be so.

Fry: Remember your efforts to establish a suffrage committee
in _both_ houses? After you mentioned it to me, I wished
I had asked you to spell out the advantages of having a
special suffrage committee instead of a subcommittee in
the Judiciary Committee.

Paul: Well, I don't know that there's much to spell out. On any subject, if it has great interest, you have to have a special committee. For instance, they have a special banking committee, banking and currency now.

Fry: That's an on-going committee, isn't it?

Paul: Yes. So would the suffrage one be until suffrage was won.

Fry: I thought maybe there was some reason that you did not feel it was to your advantage to continue to use the Judiciary Committee, which normally would handle it.

Paul: The Judiciary Committee has such a tremendous number of points--everything connected with that whole judicial system comes before the Judiciary Committee.

Fry: It was really easier to get a new committee formed and get those men to meet, than it was to deal with men who were already meeting?

Paul: Everybody was meeting on some committee.

Fry: Well, okay, I thought maybe I had missed a point there and I wanted to give you a chance to explain it if it needed to be explained.

Paul: No, I think it's just an ordinary custom to get your subject to have enough interest in it to have one committee deal with it. People are apt to go on the committee that they are interested in. I think they are always establishing new committees on subjects where there is considerable amount of public interest.

Fry: Was this done a lot then?

Paul: This was done before we were even born, back in the time of Susan B. Anthony, somewhere they started this Suffrage Committee. When we arrived there was a committee in one house and not in the other. We accepted it. We couldn't do anything else. We just took the Suffrage Committee and did the best we could with those men, and we took the other committee and did the best we could with them.

Fry: You did get a suffrage committee in both houses eventually.

Paul: I don't recall that, but maybe we did. I know we started

Paul: with one in one house. Whether we got another one created--

Fry: Yes, you did. You got one in the Senate.

Paul: I suppose we were probably having better luck with our Suffrage Committee, so we wanted to get one in [the other house, too].

Fry: There was a Representative Burns from South Carolina. In 1916 in the spring he called for an investigation of your lobbying finances.

Paul: Did he?

Fry: Yes, but the investigation never came off. This hit the newspapers at the time. Do you remember anything about that and do you know why Burns did this? Can you tell us anything about Burns and his part?

Paul: I don't remember. I could look it up, but I don't remember now.

Fry: Well, I thought I detected the fine hand of Alice Paul, because after all these threats and so forth he never did have the investigation. [Laughing.] Maybe you had a story behind that.

Paul: No, I don't think so. People were all the _time_--what year was this?

Fry: The spring of 1916, before the election in 1916.

Paul: After 1917 they were always charging that we were being financed by the Germans, because the war was on, and all these women in the National American and all these people who were for the war said we were interfering with American defense and therefore it was perfectly clear that the Germans were financing it. Always. I remember the many times that many people wanted to investigate this.

But you know we published in the [_Suffragist_ and] _Equal Rights_ magazine, a separate magazine, every single two-penny contribution that we ever got. You've noticed them probably there. That was a great protection. I'm glad we did. But I don't seem to remember about Burns.

Fry: Did you have a congressional investigation over this charge of being financed by the Germans?

344

Paul: No, no. No one ever made an investigation. First of
        all, we had so little money that there wasn't much to
        investigate.

Fry: In our other interview you mentioned in passing the
        "Hazel Hunkins issue." Do you know what that was?

Paul: What do you mean, "issue."

Fry: I don't know. Maybe some controversy. I probably under-
        stood what you meant at the time. Maybe you can clear
        it up. It was referring to the first two or three years
        of the existence of the Congressional Union.

Paul: Hazel Hunkins joined us in 1916, I think, because I
        remember very vividly when she joined. She came down
        to a meeting we were having and I was there at that
        meeting in Colorado Springs. She came down from Montana
        right after the election. Then she just joined and went
        down with us to Washington. She took over the business
        management of the Suffragist and lived at our headquarters
        and was one of our very best workers. So I don't know
        any issue about it.

Fry: We may have just gotten the wrong word transcribed there.

Paul: Then she went over, you know, to England. The only
        conceivable thing (that I never would have said was an
        issue because nobody was concerned with it) was that she
        had strong principles against getting married, for some
        reason. I remember once when I went over to England
        (when I was in Geneva) and I had dinner with her. She
        said, "You know, I've tried to be faithful to my principle
        that you should never have a marriage ceremony." (I
        don't see any point in that myself, but that's what she
        thought.) She said, "Now I'm beginning to have some
        doubts about it because I feel very passionately on the
        subject of vaccination. I'm determined that my children
        who are going to a British school where they require
        vaccinations should not be vaccinated. So I have sent
        a protest and said I won't permit it. And they have
        said that they don't care whether I permit it or not.
        Only the father's consent is necessary against vaccina-
        tion, to prevent it. If your husband doesn't want it,
        then, of course we wouldn't have any vaccination." So,
        she said, "Now, they seem to think that I have no real
        say in this matter because I'm not married to Mr.
        Hallinan."

        So I can remember that. But that was not exactly

Paul: an issue, telling me of the difficulties she had encountered. And gradually, through one thing after
another, she began to call herself Mrs. Hallinan, and
then I guess she was married by common law. I guess
she never did have this marriage ceremony. But she had
a very happy marriage.

Fry: That may have been it. We may have been referring to
that particular belief as something held by a minority
of women at that time, that would reflect on the suffrage
campaign or something like that.

Paul: She didn't _talk_ about it.

I remember very well once somebody from the government coming to see me about Hazel Hunkins. I think
perhaps it was years afterwards when she came back and
for a time stayed in this country and tried to earn
some more money for some reason or other. Her husband
was a very distinguished, I think United Press correspondent, a war correspondent, and so on. Maybe she
was having financial difficulties, I don't know what it
was. But she came back for a time and did work maybe
two years and she got a position with the government.
I was extremely busy at the time. I really didn't know
very much about her.

Anyway, this man came up to say that before employing
her in something that had to do with the security of the
country, some kind of thing that was very important,
they wanted to know more about her and could I tell more
about this Hazel Hunkins.

So I started in and told the man everything, how
she had been an organizer for us and gone to prison with
us, had been our business manager for our magazine,
everything I could think of. Then I said, "Then she
married Mr. Hallinan and went over to live in England,
and she's been living in England and I haven't heard
much about her since. Something like that." Then I
believe I said, "I really believe she _didn't_ marry,"
[laughing] that she had some principles on this subject.
He said, "Oh yes, we know all about that. No, she
wasn't married."

So he hadn't contradicted me. I just thought I
would say all these things and he would see how little
I knew.

She had never engaged in any public propaganda on

Paul: that subject.

Fry: She didn't make a campaign of this?

Paul: Oh, she never mentioned it one way or the other.

Congressional Union Becomes the Woman's Party

Fry: More on this organization--the Congressional Union
remained separate from the Woman's Party until, March
of 1917, as I understand. Is that not right?

Paul: No.

Fry: Because at that time they consolidated. Anne Martin
was head of--Woman's Party? You were head of Congressional Union? Is that wrong?

Paul: No, we changed our name from Congressional Union for
Woman Suffrage to National Woman's Party at the earnest
request of Mrs. Belmont, who had become a member of our
national board. [Different] people were always much
concerned about this thing, or this thing or this thing:
she was very concerned about our name. I was not a bit
concerned about our name. I didn't think it made any
difference what our name was. But when she wanted it
so much we all said all right and we couldn't see any
reason why we shouldn't take the name she thought was
so important. She said, "It has so much more strength
and more dignity and for future times it will be a
stronger, bigger name that will help put the woman
movement into a better position." She was very genuine
and sincere in what she thought.

So I suppose at one of our national conventions we
must have voted to change the name.

I remember this about Anne Martin.

I think we first changed it just for the women in
the suffrage states that we were trying to mobilize.
We called it the Woman's Party. I don't think we had
"national." Everybody whom we enlisted out there--by
that time it was growing to be a very big group out there,
with all this campaigning--And we called that the Woman's
Party. But that was because of this effort of Mrs.
Belmont to have something called the Woman's Party.

Paul: Then we thought, "The name seems to be generally
        accepted. People like it. Congressional Union for
        Woman for Woman Suffrage is much more limited and less
        understood." Finally we said, "We'll make it universal,
        for the whole." At the time it was one of the many
        things we did to try to develop this woman voter idea.
        We had a convention in Chicago and we called it the
        Woman's Party Convention. That's what Mrs. Belmont was
        trying to get us to do.

        Then we voted--it was 1916--to go into the election
        campaigns in all the states, appeal to all the women
        voters to stand by the Woman's Party, which was to be
        the woman's political organization for those states.

        I remember Mrs. Belmont was so pleased that we did
        it [laughing] and so full of interest that she got up
        and pledged on the platform some tremendous sum of
        money. I forget how much it was, but I think we can
        find it in the Suffragist, $50,000 or $100,000, I don't
        know what. It was some enormous sum. The meeting was
        extremely successful. Dudley Field Malone was a very
        eloquent speaker. He came to say what the Democrats
        would do. All because we had a "woman's party."
        [Laughter.] It was really marvelous. Then Mrs. Belmont
        just astounded everybody with this enormous gift she
        was going to make to make this possible, to put it
        through.

        Then we elected Anne Martin to be the president of
        the Woman's Party, for this election campaign. Then we
        went into the campaign which was against Wilson, you
        know, in all the states. I think this was in 1916.

Fry: Yes, according to my notes'.

Paul: And then--I don't know what we called ourselves. But we
        then decided, at the request of Mr. Kent, to incorporate;
        we had never incorporated. [Searching her memory] I
        know there was some little trifling thing--somebody--I
        just vaguely remember--somebody was threatening to sue
        us over some very little thing--I don't know what. But
        anyway Mr. Kent--I think there was not anything to it,
        I don't know exactly what it was, some bill somebody
        had incurred. So Mr. Kent, who was very, very wealthy,
        as you know, said, "Now look here, these people--you
        are getting to be a big organization and to have a big
        headquarters and everything else," and he said, "As long
        as you are not incorporated people are going to bring a
        suit against Mrs. Kent," although she had nothing to do

Paul: with it, whatever this little episode was. She didn't
       even _know_ about it. He said, "They know that _I_ have a
       great deal of money, and all these shysters are out to
       try to bring these nuisance suits, and then you pay off
       to get rid of these people. I have a very _very_ skillful
       lawyer, and I want you to give him all the facts and let
       him incorporate you for my own sake and my wife's sake.
       I'm so afraid we'll be the victims of some other person--"
       whatever that man was now threatening just to get some
       money from us.

       So we did. Mr. Kent incorporated us, paid for the
       whole thing. If you don't have the articles of incor-
       poration I'll give them to you. We still have them.
       When we won the vote it was very fortunate for us we had
       such a skillful lawyer, because we didn't have to re-
       incorporate. He put it in a way that would cover any
       possible future.

       So, it was around this time that we took the name of
       National Woman's Party. The Woman's Party was in the
       West. _We_ were probably still the Congressional Union.
       When he incorporated us as the National Woman's Party.
       We incorporated in 1918, in the spring.

Fry: Was control of this shared between you and Anne Martin,
       or how was this worked out?

Paul: No, she was in charge of everything that was the Woman's
       Party, just the women in the western states. She was
       complete president and everything of that. Those women
       in the western states were all members of our national
       organization. We wanted her to take it over, you see,
       being a western woman, or in that section. So she
       agreed to do it.

       But we all, eastern women, worked with her. I
       stayed in Chicago through that whole election campaign.
       She went down to Nevada with Mabel Vernon to work there
       and had other people with her there I guess.

       All this business of keeping the organizers going
       in all those states, Mrs. Belmont, who was an _eastern_
       woman, was paying for a large section of it because she
       had promised to do it, paid for more than anybody else
       did. And we raised all the rest of the money for it.

       Then, after the election campaign, that was 1916, I
       think that Anne Martin took a trip around through the
       West, because I remember she got Alice Gram and Betty

Paul: Gram (Betty Gram Swing) when she went to Oregon and
        spoke there. They were students. She got them to come
        down to Washington. So, she went visiting various places
        out in the West.

        Then she came back and stayed at the headquarters
        in Washington, just as before. Then when it came to
        starting the <u>National</u> Woman's Party (which we decided
        to call the National Woman's Party probably before we
        were incorporated. Sometime along there--it must have
        been at one of our conventions.) I know the question
        would have been then whether Anne Martin should be the
        president of the whole one or whether I would continue.

        So, I asked her to do it. One is always glad in
        the middle of a campaign to have someone to step in and
        take up the burden. But she didn't want to do it. At
        least she <u>said</u> she didn't want to do it. So I suppose
        she didn't want to do it. So I continued, because there
        was nobody else to continue. And I continued until it
        was over.

Fry: The voting western states continued to be sort of an
        entity, it seemed like, because I notice when the de-
        cision was made to picket, that at first someone recom-
        mended and the council approved this, that western women
        would not picket because they already had the vote.
        Picketing would be done just by the eastern women. Then
        later this was changed. Do you remember that?

Paul: I don't remember it.

Fry: Later on more and more western women came to picket and
        [laughing] no one turned them away I guess. Is that
        right? You don't remember that being a big issue?

Paul: I don't remember that at all, because Betty Gram Swing
        came in in the very early days, and she was from the
        West. Her sister, Alice Gram, was from the West.

Fry: Had you ever thought of this as just something being
        done by the non-voting states' residents?

Paul: No. To get people to picket wasn't very easy, and we
        weren't in any position to lay down anything that would
        keep anybody from doing it if she wanted to do it.

Fry: There are about a hundred letters of resignation on file
        over that picketing. I don't know whether that was a

Paul: Well, of course every person is a loss. I'm surprised
there weren't more than that.

[Interruption.]

Fry: I wanted to ask you awhile ago about Ida Husted Harper.
Could you tell me where she was in all of this evolution
of splitting off, and so forth. She was pretty old then,
wasn't she, Alice? I'm not sure of the ages of these
people we were talking about.

Paul: She was the age of Dr. Shaw and Mrs. Catt and all the
rest. When we came along she was what they called one
of the elder statesmen, that idea. We were all brought
up to have great reverence and respect for her when I
went into the movement. When we had our first delegation
to President Wilson we asked her to go. I think the
delegation had four people on it. One was the wife of
a congressman, and I think that Mrs. Harper was one of
the four. We thought that she would give prestige,
connection with the past, and so on.

I don't recall ever having any contact with her, or
meeting or ever seeing her until after the suffrage
victory in 1920. She didn't cross our path; she lived
up in New York. She never opposed us--if she did we
never knew it. She didn't help us--if she did we didn't
know it. She was in some kind of a different world up
in the old National American Woman Suffrage headquarters.
We just never saw her.

HISTORY OF THE SCULPTURE OF SUFFRAGE PIONEERS, ADELAIDE
JOHNSON, SCULPTOR

Paul: When the suffrage amendment had been won, I guess we all
thought, everybody thought that we ought to have some
tribute to these pioneer women. We knew that the bust
of Susan B. Anthony was on the steps on the lefthand
side of the Metropolitan Art Museum. We knew that there
were these busts, because Mrs. Belmont had always had
them in her home from the first time we met her. We
were still, of course, down on Lafayette Square.

[End of Tape 11, Side A]

[Tape 11, Side B]

Paul: We knew vaguely about these statues, that there were
these three busts. So I went up to New York. I think
I went first to see Mrs. Adelaide Johnson, I'm not quite
sure. But anyway I began an investigation, as we all
did I guess, to find out where these busts that we had
heard of were, to see if we couldn't get them to the
Capitol and present them to Congress. I remember going
to see Mrs. Johnson (wherever she was at that time. I
guess she was living up at the Dolly Madison House. Is
there something called the Dolly Madison House in New
York?)

She told me all about this. She said in the time
when Susan B. Anthony and Elizabeth Cady Stanton were
living she had gone somewhere, to their homes probably,
and from life had made the busts of both Elizabeth Cady
Stanton and Susan B. Anthony. She said she made the
one of Lucretia Mott from a photograph. She said that
these three were all made at the request of a committee
in the old National American Woman Suffrage Association.
They had arranged for her to make the busts, as a young
promising woman sculptress.

Paul: When they were made, among people who contributed
was John Greenleaf Whittier and people of that type,
who wanted these women honored. They had paid her
whatever they were supposed to pay her for making them.
She had gone over to Italy and had made the busts there
in Italy, because she could get better marble and better
labor.

She said that when she made them, they were put in
storage. There was a committee in charge of it and the
only living member of it was Ida Husted Harper. All
the others who had contributed had died. She said, "I
don't think Mrs. Catt ever liked my statues. She didn't
think they were good. I don't think, because of Mrs.
Catt's influence with the National American, that they
will ever take those busts out of storage and will ever
put them in the Capitol. I think if it is to be done
that we will have to do it, the Woman's Party. I don't
own them, because I was paid to make them, and I have
been paid and that's finished for me. But I think the
best thing to do is to go and see Ida Husted Harper and
find out the legal situation and what she would like done
about this and so on."

So I did go and see Mrs. Harper. It was perhaps the
second time in my life that I ever talked with her. She
said, "Well, Mrs. Catt is very opposed to those statues
ever being put in the Capitol. She says they're not
worthy from the point of view of their artistic value,
and she doesn't want the National American to have anything to do with it. I don't think she can be changed
on this. I am the only living member of that original
committee that raised money and paid Mrs. Johnson and
put them in storage. I think that I would have the
right to transfer all my legal rights to you, to the
Woman's Party, if you will put them in the Capitol.
Because that's what they were made for.

"In the interval some of them have been copied, like
the one that somebody had made and put in the Metropolitan. They thought it was a good enough statue to
put on the stairway so everybody who ever entered the
building could see it."

So we then decided to form a committee to put the
busts in the Capitol, the purpose for which they had
been made. We told Mrs. Johnson that we were going to
do it, and that Mrs. Harper had transfered all the rights
to us. Mrs. Johnson said, "Well, in that case, if they
are to be in the Capitol, I made them when I was a very

Paul: young sculptress, a very young woman, and I could do much, much, much better work now. I have been making busts all these years. I would like to go over to Italy, where I got the Carrara marble before, and make a new set, not use the old ones."

This was shortly after the suffrage victory, which was in August, so we thought that we would have our wind-up convention on Susan B. Anthony's birthday-- that's what we finally voted to do--the following year because we had to pay all the debts off of the suffrage campaign and we thought it would take us from August up until the next February. We thought that would give time to Mrs. Johnson to make the new busts, and of course we would arrange to get them into the Capitol.

Do you want me to tell you all this?

Fry: I think you told me the story of how you got those statues into the Capitol and how you raised the money.* But I am glad to have the Ida Husted Harper connection. I thought too that maybe she had been one of the ones who would have considered going with Congressional Union during that split, but apparently she wasn't--

[Interruption.]

Fry: The only organization that didn't come when you presented the statues at the Capitol--

Paul: They were received by Speaker Gillette of the House on behalf of Congress. The chairman of the meeting which presented them was Jane Addams, who we thought would unite all women pretty well. The speaker was Sara Bard Field, as you know, who made the speech presenting them. We invited every woman's organization that had anything to do with the suffrage movement to come and place flowers. I remember several days afterwards when we were cleaning up over there in the corridor we found a little bouquet from the National American Suffrage Association. They hadn't sent anybody, and whoever had delivered it, (evidently some expressman or somebody) apparently some guard just took it and put it in the corridor. So they didn't send anybody from that organization. Practically everybody else had somebody there--

---

*This story was related late one night during the
Ṁ⸱̄ ⸱̄ ⸱ ⸱̄⸱⸱ ⸱ Ṅ⸱ ⸱ ⸱ ⸱ ⸱ ⸱̄ ⸱.--Fry

Paul: every conceivable kind of woman's organization.

Fry: [Laughing.] That's kind of poetic: their flowers got
        put in the corridor.

Paul: So absurd, after all these years, to think of these
        little petty divisions that were so unworthy.

Fry: Did the National Association and you work together
        toward the end, except for the picketing?

        [Interruption.]

Fry: Who helped you organize the parade in 1914?

Paul: Lucy Burns was the only person on it besides myself,
        a committee consisting of Lucy Burns and myself; you
        know that. Then, in the course of the getting up the
        procession we got to know Mrs. Beard. She went on our
        committee. Mrs. Lawrence Lewis of Philadelphia came on
        our committee; she was a tower of strength. We had a
        very effective group. And Elsie Hill went on our com-
        mittee; she took the college section. Each person took
        a section that they organized.

Fry: And you only had two paid typists at first to help you
        organize this?

Paul: Those two typists didn't do any organizing. They just
        transcribed letters for us.

        [Interruption.]

NEWSPAPERS AS SOURCES FOR THE SUFFRAGE AND EQUAL RIGHTS
STORIES

Paul: We had these big volumes of clippings in Washington.
        Mrs. Belmont had her secretary paste them together.
        Have you seen that clipping book?

Fry: No, I haven't seen it yet; I want to look at that this
        morning.

Paul: Some volunteer put those together. Mrs. Belmont employed
        a person, a young Jewish girl, who now wrote a very
        kindly letter to the <u>Washington Post</u> about Mrs. Belmont
        the other day. She pasted them together. We have
        <u>volumes</u>, which show the enormous amount of publicity
        we were getting then.

        Then, when suffrage was over, practically our whole
        national board that had carried that campaign wanted
        to stop because they were so completely fatigued and
        worn out. We elected a whole new board, and of course
        there wasn't anybody working very hard on the raising
        of money. So one thing that they stopped altogether
        was any press department. We never had a press depart-
        ment from the time suffrage was won. And we don't have
        any now, never had it at all.

        But we didn't care whether we had it or not. We
        thought in the suffrage campaign we <u>needed</u> it very much
        because we were trying to have a short campaign to get
        it into the Constitution. This other looked as if it
        would be a long, long campaign of changing the thought
        of all American women on the subject. So that's one of the
        reasons we economized. And that's the reason we had so
        little in.

Fry: That's why the role of the Woman's Party isn't known
        as well in the Equal Rights campaign probably.

Paul: Yes, that's true. With all the government communiques going out from Washington, unless you steadily are thinking up something that will make it news and employing somebody to do it, you just don't get it done, especially now that in the country as a whole journalism assumes such a big part, which it didn't in the early days.

Fry: We have more in the media now.

Paul: Of course when we went to Washington there was no woman up in the press gallery. There were no women signing their names to the articles going out. One of the places that the suffrage movement helped to open to women--we always had a little tearoom always at our headquarters where most newspaper people used to come. The people that were doing the press for us were headed by Mrs. Florence Boeckel. They formed this Women's Press Club, which now exists. It was formed there in our little tea house by Mrs. Boeckel and two of her people who worked with her, a little group of three women: Eleanor Taylor Marsh, Florence Boeckel was the head, and Alice Gram Robinson. You ought to interview Alice Gram Robinson because she is still living and she, you know, gets out that Congressional Digest. Do you know that paper?

Fry: Yes. I met her briefly. Do you mean those three women started the press club?

Paul: Yes, and they are always considered by the press club-- there is no dispute about it--I think they always have at the head of their magazine or whatever they get out, "founded by Florence Boeckel, Eleanor Taylor Marsh, and Alice Gram Robinson."

Fry: More women in the press is a spin-off that I didn't realize came from the suffrage campaign.

Paul: By their giving out these press releases and doing it so professionally and so well--Florence Boeckel could never have been exceeded. We never could, never have had a better person than she was.

Fry: And they gave out the press releases and they--

Paul: Well, they wrote them and did whatever they--we gave them one room in the headquarters. Florence Boeckel had graduated from Vassar and had married a man, Richard

Paul: Boeckel, who was a professional newspaperman in I think
Poughkeepsie--wherever Vassar was. She had gotten to
know him there, then she came down to Washington. She
first came down to Baltimore; I think she was on <u>Vogue</u>.
And Elsie Hill, who was one of our chief people, of
course, in the beginning of the suffrage campaign, knew
her and went over to see Florence Boeckel whom she had
known from Vassar. I went with her. We said wouldn't
she like to come over (since she apparently had enough
money so she didn't have to keep the <u>Vogue</u> position) as
a volunteer and take over our press department which we
didn't have. Would she create it. So she came and
stayed until suffrage was won.

[Some background static develops for a while on tape
during discussion below.]

Paul: Then by always being available to the press, and we
were right there in Lafayette Square where all the newspapermen would come in; we had this one office which we
gave them. First Florence Boeckel had no assistants,
then she got Eleanor Taylor Marsh, [interruption] then
Alice Gram Robinson who had come down from Oregon when
Anne Martin went out to speak there and she had interested these two college girls still in the University of
Oregon. They both came down to help (and later they
both went to prison). So she stayed on, and we paid a
tiny little salary to them. They had somebody who did
all the mimeographing and someone who took all the
dictation and all of that. So they got quite a little
staff, a very, very, for us, expensive staff compared to
the rest of the work where we didn't have any profes-
sionals. Actually I think it was extremely well done
for that period. Anybody who goes through our press
clippings can see how well done it was.

Fry: Tell me about the beginnings of the Women's Press Club.
Do you mean it grew out of this little group of women?

Paul: Well, they just got the newspaperwomen together, the
few that there were, and formed a club while they were
there, toward the end of the seven years that we worked
there. And that club of course developed and grew to
be quite a big power, I think, in our nation. The first
woman (you might add to this story) apart from us--she
was our first member, in fact, in Washington was--I can't
think of her name. She was the first woman ever to be
allowed to sign her name to reports going out from the
big bureaus--Her name was Winifred Mallon. She lived
 ̄ ̄   ̄   ̄   ̄ ̄   ̄ ̄   ̄ ̄   ̄   ̄ ad in

Paul: Washington was Winifred Mallon.

Fry: And she was the first woman to have a by-line in the press in the wire services?

Paul: One of the first. When we got to know her she was on the _Chicago Tribune_ and this was before we met Florence Boeckel and started to have our own little press department. We had nothing but a little basement room, 1420 F Street, one room, nothing else. You had to go down the steps to go in.

Just across the street was the _Chicago Tribune_ office. And somehow or other we got to know Winifred Mallon, who was there. She lived up on Capitol Hill with her mother and other members of her family. She would work all day I guess and all evening getting the material off to the _Chicago Tribune_, which was her livelihood. Then she would start in and write the little press bulletins for us before we ever had any press department. She would write up whatever happened and give it to us so we could give it out the next day. We did have a typist, that much. And we had a volunteer person who was taking care of the press by interviewing the people who came in. So it was a _wonderful_ thing she did for us. And also putting it in her _own_ things that she sent out [to the _Tribune_].

Later on, I think she was one of the presidents of the Women's Press Club after it got started. She remained until her death one of our strongest members. She had very little money, so what she did was whenever anybody came to Washington to help and we couldn't pay for their going to hotels, and so on (and they often couldn't pay for themselves), she would take them one by one by one, as they came up, to her home. I don't know _how_ many people who came down to help in those early days stayed as guests at the home of Winifred Mallon where her mother and the other people who lived there were very hospitable and took care of them.

Anyway, later she became the president of the Women's Press Club.

So that was really the way we started our campaign, was through this Winifred Mallon, our press work. So, in any story, I'd like to have her built up. Then she left the _Chicago Tribune_. (And I'm not sure whether she ever signed her name to the _Chicago Tribune_ articles.)

Paul: She grew in stature in the press world so that she became in a much higher capacity on the staff of the New
York Tribune. She was there up until the time of her
death. And of course, Mrs. Ogden Reid was one of our
great supporters, as you know, one of the owners of the
New York Tribune.

After she went over to the New York Tribune, we had
a very direct line into the Tribune. We could get a
great, great, great deal of publicity there. First of
all Mrs. Reid herself for us, very strongly. (I
think she was on our national advisory board, but I'd
have to look that up. I'm not perfectly sure.) And the
publicity that Winifred Mallon was able to get--she had
a free hand and could write up an enormous amount for
us in the New York Tribune.

So we had all this going when Florence Boeckel came
along and then got it all put in a very systematic and
orderly way down in one big room that we gave for the
press. [Laughing.] Now that's the end of that one.

Fry: [Laughing.] Very good! This report that was done in
1926 on the National Woman's Party:* Why did Mrs.
Boeckel get this out?

Paul: Because she got out everything--

Fry: I mean, do you know what the purpose of this was?

Paul: That was the year there was held in Paris a world convention of the International Alliance for Suffrage for
Women. We had been invited to send a delegation because
we had just gotten the vote. She made this so our delegates who went over would have something in their hands.
You probably know all about this.

[Pointing to photograph on page 11.] That's Anita
Pollitzer and myself putting flowers on the grave of
Susan B. Anthony. I have on the wall the original
[photographs] over there. These people who are just
getting out this thing in Ms.,** the photographer took
this one on the wall, she took it all apart and photo-
graphed it so as to put it in Ms., coming out in June.

_____

*"The National Woman's Party 1913-1926," pamphlet, 16 pp.
**Gurovitz, Judy, and Hofner, Evelyn, "Suffragists Still
Going Strong," Ms., July, 1973, pp. 47-49.

Paul: When we got over there, Doris Stevens and Mabel
Vernon--Mabel Vernon was sort of in charge--Mrs. Catt
sent word to them. She had been the old International
president; she no longer was. She sent word to the new
president who invited us to come, named Mrs. Corbett
Ashby. [You remember I told you] she invited me personally, when I was over in England after we had won the
vote, to her house for lunch and asked me to have the
Woman's Party affiliate. She said, "We need more branches,
to have money. Mostly the countries in Europe have only
a few pennies they can give. We want some branches in
America. Would your branch that has just won the vote
become a branch?" So we said we would. So we had this
big delegation that went over, about twenty or thirty
women.

     When they got there the letter was read from Mrs.
Catt, I think it was read at the convention. If not it
was read to people of importance, saying, "If you admit
the Woman's Party to your International Alliance, I will
cut off all help from the Leslie million." Mrs. Catt
had received a legacy of a million from Mrs. Leslie.
And that was to keep the International going. So in
view of that, they voted down--after all our delegates
were there--they voted that they wouldn't keep them.

Fry: I think Mabel Vernon told me about that too. She made
a very eloquent speech at that time.

Paul: This is when we dedicated our headquarters in Washington
[photograph, pp. 7-8].

Fry: That's a big crowd.

Paul: This was our old headquarters, you know. This is where
the Supreme Court is now. That's the old building.

     This is of one of our delegations going up to the
Capitol [photograph, p.5]. Here is a delegation to the
President [photograph, p.4].

Fry: This is the one to President Coolidge for the Equal
Rights Amendment.

Paul: That's the little pin that we gave to everybody who
picketed the White House [inset on p.3].

     That's a meeting at Lafayette Square [p.3]. I was
arrested there. Everybody got up on Lafayette's statue,

Paul: you know. We had about one minute, "Lafayette I am now come here." And they arrested us.

Fry: Lafayette's words, "Lafayette, we are come"--too inflammatory.

Paul: I think our declaration of principles is here. That's the new one that we adopted [pp.1 and 2].

Fry: New compared to the old Seneca Falls declaration of principles?

Paul: Based on that. We took Seneca Falls and brought it up-to-date. When we started the Equal Rights campaign that we were going to work for. At that time when we began ours only one of the things that they were going to work for had been achieved, which was the vote. So we put in our new one. We had a meeting and adopted this as our program.

Fry: I'd like to have a Xerox, or some kind of a copy, of your declaration of principles for our appendix. Maybe I can get this copied downtown.*

Paul: You see the great trouble is that when a whole new board comes in that hasn't lived through any of these things they don't know which to save or which to throw away.

[Interruption.]

This is the last thing I'm going to show you. The day that we dedicated our headquarters, we started a system of getting what we called "founders" of this new movement. And everybody who was a "founder" had to give $100. We drew up new membership cards, a whole system, starting a new permanent group as against the old group. This [a framed citation] is what we gave to the founders.

Fry: What was the year of this?

Paul: 1923, I guess, the day we dedicated the headquarters. You'll find the date on all these things. 1922 was it?

[Interruption.]

---

*See appendix.

Fry: For the record, this is the inscription of the founders'
       award. It's illuminated in gold and purple with vines
       and flowers and it says:

>   "Greetings to our honored founders.
>   "We taste the spices of Arabia, yet never
>   feel the scorching sun which brings them forth.
>   "To those women of the National Woman's Party
>   who have borne the heat and burden of the day
>   we now pay reverent tribute; especially to
>   those who, for a time, gave their liberty
>   that we might gain a fuller freedom.
>   "This scroll of honor is committed to the
>   future, an imperishable parchment, illuminated
>   by the vision of a small band of faithful
>   women, who, inspired and led by
>
>   Alice Paul [name of each founder]
>
>   nobly have striven and nobly achieved in making
>   that vision come true.
>
>   "'As one lamp lights another nor grows less,
>   So nobleness enkindleth nobleness.'"

[Interruption.]

PASSAGE THROUGH CONGRESS

Amendments to the Amendment in the Senate, March 1919

Fry: I'm talking about the 1919 introduction of the Amendment into the Senate, when Senator Jones of New Mexico first refused then introduced a variation of it. I'm looking it up here to see what the variation was, to see what happened, because that's the only note I have.

Paul: I don't remember that point; I certainly can't--

Fry: Yes, it kind of surprised me.

Paul: I'm glad you are such a scholarly type; it's a protection to us.

Fry: Here it is. I don't think it means very much and it probably disappeared the next week. But it does tell about it here. It says, "Introducing suffrage resolutions has become quite the rage up at the Senate."

Paul: Who wrote this article?

Fry: This is in the Suffragist of March 8, 1919. It's not signed.

> "Senator Jones of Washington, Senator Gay of Louisiana, Senator McKellar of Tennessee all have their own private little resolutions which they offered to the committee on woman's suffrage. Senator Jones of Washington, a Republican, was first, and got to re-introduce the original Susan B. Anthony Amendment following its defeat, because no motion to reconsider was in order and because Chairman Jones of the committee, [the senator from New Mexico], had refused to do the re-introducing himself.

Fry: The others followed with new versions of the
proposed amendment of their own. And last
week Chairman Jones of New Mexico offered
one himself."

That's what was confusing me. Because he up to
this point, as the chairman, had been handling only the
Susan B. Anthony Amendment.

"He couldn't withstand it any longer. He
too must introduce a resolution. So after
a conference with the President"--

Paul: Yes, I can see how that works.

Fry: --"he read before the Senate a still newer version of
the Susan B. Anthony Amendment"--

Paul: This is exactly what we are facing now in the legislatures that have turned it down, that they can't reconsider.

Fry: Yes, on the Equal Rights Amendment. Now, let me
see--

"which also was referred to the committee on
woman's suffrage. The new resolution differs
very little and not at all materially from
the original and yet it was hoped that in
its wording it might serve to conciliate some
previously hostile senators. This hope has
not been entirely in vain, for Senator Gay
of Louisiana, who had made the statement that
his own resolution, providing that the states
should have the exclusive right to enforce the
provisions of the measure, was the only one for
which he would vote, and has since stated that
he would vote for Senator Jones' new resolution."

Now Senator Jones' new resolution provides that--
let me see--two-thirds of each house of Congress con-
curring therein,

"the following article shall be proposed to the
legislatures of the several states as an amendment (and so forth)...and when ratified by
three-fourths of the said legislatures shall
be valid...the right of citizens of the United
States to vote shall not be denied or abridged
by the United States or by any state on account

Fry: of sex."

          That's Section One. Section Two--

Paul: That's the original amendment that we were working for.

Fry: So that's not what he changed. Maybe he changed
          Section Two.

Paul: Yes, maybe in the enforcement part.

Fry: "The several states shall have the authority
          to enforce this article by necessary legis-
          lation, but if any state shall enforce or
          or enact any law in conflict therewith,
          then Congress shall not be excluded from
          enacting appropriate legislation to enforce
          it."

Paul: Yes. Well, that's just the enforcement clause and that's
          not part of the Amendment.

Fry: Was it new? Was that the different part?

Paul: I think when it went through it said, "Congress shall
          have the power to enforce this article by appropriate
          legislation." That's my memory. Somewhere up here
          where we always gave the text--the version we always
          proposed, I think on the editorial page we always had
          it, down at the bottom somewhere.

Fry: Here it is. Okay. The original Susan B. Anthony
          Amendment.

Paul: Could you read it right through? I'd like to hear it.

Fry: Section Two says, "Congress shall have power by appropri-
          ate legislation to enforce the provisions of this
          article." He had made additions to that. That was the
          only thing.

Paul: Of course that didn't affect the Amendment itself. It
          was only an enforcement thing. Now they have taken out
          the "several states" altogether in our new one [the Equal
          Rights Amendment]. As long as they don't touch the
          Amendment, I think it's all right. But of course by
          changing the enforcement clause you imperil ratification.

Fry: In this, the Suffragist goes on to say that "Senator
          Jones' substitute resolution is practically as acceptable

366

Fry: as the original." So I gather this was not a problem then for the Woman's Party.

Paul: No, but probably they didn't go along with it. You see, you are reading 1919--

Fry: March 8, yes. "This resolution has already been reported favorably out of committee and Senator Jones hopes to present it to the Senate on Monday."

Paul: It was the following June if you will turn to that, that they voted on it.

Fry: Yes, I have that.

Paul: Let's see what the text of that one was.

Fry: They voted on June 4.

Paul: Here's the place you will undoubtedly find the text that they voted on. I think this was merely a device, because Senator Jones of Washington was a great friend of ours. He was the one that got up the whole hearing.

Fry: Oh, is that the same Senator Jones?

Paul: I suppose so, I don't know that there were two.

Fry: Well, there was one from Washington [Senator Wesley L. Jones], and I keep getting them mixed up.

Paul: This isn't the Washington one?

Fry: This is the New Mexico one that introduced the bill, Senator Andreus Aristides Jones, the committee chairman.

Paul: The first you read to me was introduced by Jones of Washington, and then you said, "Senator Jones of New Mexico."

Fry: They both introduced an amendment change.

Paul: Anyway, they were trying all of them to change the enforcement clause to make it not the same amendment, so they [wouldn't lose the right] to reconsider. It's almost always a parliamentary ruling that you can't reconsider [the same measure]. You have to reconsider within three or five hours or something; then that's finished. Then you can't later on reconsider in the

Paul: same session of the legislature.

       That's what we're up against now in a state like Maine. However much you may want to you can't do it.

Fry: The Amendment in its final version has the original Susan B. Anthony enforcement section too in it, the version that was passed June 4, 1919.

[End of Tape 11, Side B]

[Tape 12, Side A. May 11, 1973.]

Party Endorsements

Fry: Let me look at our chronology here. You began picketing in January 1917. Congress adjourned on October 6 of that year, the same day that you were arrested. You were carrying a banner which read, according to the Suffragist, "The time has come when we must conquer or submit. For us there can be but one choice. We have made it." You were arrested then and sentenced to seven months in October 1917.

Paul: I think that must have been at Lafayette Square. We had a long procession led by a beautiful girl from Michigan.

Fry: A week before the next session reconvened, December 3, 1917, all women were released from prison. Then on December 10 a date was set for a vote in the House; they decided to take up the suffrage issue on January 10 of 1918. This was Chairman Pou's Suffrage Committee in the House. You may also remember that in September or 1917, a month before you were arrested, the House had voted and it had lacked seventy-three votes for passage. So they took it up again on January 10 and the House passed it with only one more vote than was needed.

       The Senate then became your big problem, I guess. You had to have eleven more votes than you had pledged.

       But in February, and I thought you might remember how you did this, or what you did to bring this about, "the first favorable expression of the national Republican party was when the Republican National Committee commended House Republicans for their votes for suffrage." [According to Inez Haynes Irwin, opus cit., p.341.]

368

Paul: You say that's the first time? The National Republican
        Committee? I think we got it in the platform in 1916
        in the one headed by Theodore Roosevelt, the Bull Moose
        one, but we didn't get it in the Republican National,
        I'm sure about that, in 1916. So this I suppose would
        be the first. I don't remember.

Fry: The same day in 1918 the National Democratic Executive
        Committee held a telegraphic referendum of their national
        committee and it showed two-to-one in favor of the
        suffrage amendment.

Paul: In 1916 they hadn't put it in when we went to them in
        Missouri, I remember, at their convention. At the Repub-
        lican Convention and the Democratic conventions we made
        a tremendous effort.

Fry: What I read about that was that in 1916, when the parties
        put it in their platforms, they came out for suffrage,"
        but they did not come out for a national amendment; the
        Democrats specifically recommended state-by-state suffrage,
        but it was in their platforms for the first time.

Paul: I remember Chicago just vaguely (because I haven't thought
        about it from that day to this--I have to go back and
        think about it), because it seems to me--

Fry: Would you like me to get those platforms, the quotations
        for you? [See quotations from platforms, pp. 371-372
        below.]

        [Tape off.]

Paul: They did exclude the federal amendment. Borah, that was
        his point.

        Let me just tell you about my greatest memory. (It
        may not be right.) 1916 was two years after the Shafroth-
        Palmer had been introduced. It showed by their actions
        that they were still--something that you or somebody
        said to me indicated that they [NAWSA] thought they really
        did not stand against the federal suffrage amendment,
        but I think you said they regarded this as a supplement
        [to our amendment].

Fry: That the National Association--

Paul: Now that this is all past, this is what they do say, that
        this was supplementary and they were always working for

Paul: the national amendment. I told you at the time that was so completely untrue because here it was two years later and the National Association, under a very fine woman out in Chicago, decided to try to get up at the time of the conventions a procession through the streets in support of suffrage. We had just gone out and opened a little headquarters to work for a platform resolution on the suffrage amendment. This leading woman out there invited us to join in with their procession and to come around and discuss with her how we would participate and help in getting up their procession.

So I did go and talk to this person, a perfectly lovely woman, and she said, "Of course we can't allow you to have this banner that you are always carrying at the head of your processions, which demands an amendment to the United States Constitution, because we are trying to get the state constitutions changed through the Shafroth-Palmer amendment." (Not an amendment to give the votes to women but only to give the right to a referendum.) Then I said that we wouldn't go in any procession that didn't have the complete demand for complete equality to obtain votes for women in the Constitution itself. Therefore, we said, "We won't participate."

So they went ahead with their procession. And we said we would just go to the resolution committee with our fight. So that day we did go. It was a terribly stormy day. Everybody came in dripping, with umbrellas and everything. They presented the demand just for suffrage. That's all they did, and I think that was incorporated, if I remember rightly. And we presented the demand for the equal suffrage amendment to the Constitution, not just to say we believed in suffrage. So we didn't get ours.

Then we went down to Missouri to the Democratic one and with about the same result. They [NAWSA] were absolutely opposing our amendment in both hearings.

Fry: There's a very bitter editorial in the Suffragist on that.

Paul: At that same time in 1916 I'm almost certain that the Socialist convention put in a plank for the equal suffrage amendment. At least their leaders did. And at what they called the Bull Moose convention, which was also

Paul: put one in.

Fry: You managed to get Charles Evans Hughes, the Republican presidential candidate, to come out for the Amendment.

Paul: We didn't get him at the convention. We didn't get him until the end of the election campaign in November. I told you how I went out to see President Roosevelt at that time. It wasn't until he came to this final meeting in New York that he came out for us, after going through all those suffrage states where it would have helped him and not being able to make up his mind yes or no. Because his party didn't have it in its platform. President Roosevelt had it in his party [platform]--that's my faint recollection.

Fry: Here is Wilson's interpretation of the Democratic suffrage plank. This is in the July 1, 1916 Suffragist. It says, "On June 19 President Wilson sent to Mrs. Carrie Chapman Catt, president of National American Woman Suffrage Association, the following letter. This is a reply to a telegram from her asking what the suffrage plank in the Democratic platform meant. His letter is, 'My dear Mrs. Catt'--

Paul: I don't think she was president. She was of International American, of course.

Fry: This calls her "president"--

Paul: Probably people didn't even know whether she was president or not. She was president of the International anyway.

Fry: Wilson says that he wishes to "join his fellow Democrats in recommending to the several states that 'they extend the suffrage to women upon the same terms as to men.'"

Fry: So then in 1918 you did have this expression from both national committees. I have a note here that the Democratic telegraphic referendum was somehow inspired by the women who worked so hard in 1916, with the Democrats down in St. Louis.

Paul: Oh no no.

Fry: They had something to do with inspiring this telegraphic referendum in 1918? You don't think this is true? Do you know how that happened, who got them to make that

Fry: referendum?

Paul: I don't remember a referendum at all.

Fry: The Democratic central committee sent out a lot of telegrams to Democrats all over the states.

Paul: I think any action they took was because of the campaign by the women voters in the states where we were having them oppose the Democrats. That probably brought the matter before them so that they began to look into it. Now I'm sorry, but I've got to get this check written [for the carpenter].

Fry: During this interruption, let me quote the following for the manuscript from the Suffragist of June 17, 1916, page 4:

"SUFFRAGE IN THE REPUBLICAN PLATFORM"

"Already members of the Republican committee on resolutions which drafted the suffrage plank in the Republican platform have made haste to say that it in no way declares against the federal suffrage amendment. Senator Sutherland states on June 8 that the plank, while recognizing the right of the state to settle the question of suffrage for itself did not declare against the right of the nation to settle it also."

From the Suffragist, July 1, 1916, page 6:

"Democrats and Republicans are now busy defending the suffrage planks in their respective platforms with the plea that one is no worse than the other. This is strictly true.
"Both planks declare for the principle of woman suffrage, advocate state action upon the question, and say nothing whatever about federal action.
"The Republican plank reads: 'The Republican party...favors the extension of the suffrage to women...but recognizes the right of each state to settle the question for itself.'
"The Democratic plank reads: 'We
r   _   .v . . r   . . :r . i..

Fry: to the women of the country by the states
upon the same terms as to men.'"

From the Suffragist, July 8, 1916, page 6:

"Suffragists are keenly aware that the
suffrage plank in the Progressive platform
reads, 'We believe the women of the country,
who share with men the burdens of government
in time of peace and make equal sacrifices
in time of war, should be given the full
political right of suffrage both by state
and federal action.'"

From the Suffragist, July 22, 1916:

"The draft of the Socialist platform
in its political demands declares for
'1. unrestricted and equal suffrage for
men and women;
'2. the immediate adoption of the
so-called Susan B. Anthony Amendment
to the Constitution of the United
States granting the suffrage to women
on equal terms with men.'"

From the Suffragist, July 29, 1916, page 5:

"The Prohibition party, meeting at St.
Paul July 19 and 20 adopted in its platform
the ringing demand for national women's
suffrage. The plank embodies the text of
the Susan B. Anthony Amendment." (It was
already on record, prior to this, of being
in favor of woman's suffrage.)

[Tape off.]

A Senate Vote Not Called

Fry: --What you see is two things together that pushed this
into Congress--and into the Republican and Democratic
national committees' endorsements: the Woman's Party
campaign against the party that didn't support the
Amendment, and the picketing.

Paul: Well, I mean the particular thing that came up [as a

Paul: result] then was action in the House. That was the first time, wasn't it, that it was voted on in the House, passed in the House?

Fry: I'm not sure that this was the first time.* But it <u>was</u> passed 274 to 136 on January 10, 1918.

Paul: I think that was the first time it went through. What month was that--January?

Fry: Yes and this was apparently before the newly elected Congress took its seats.

Paul: Then I think on March 4 the new Congress came in if I remember rightly. Then we had to begin again and get it through the House again, because it always had to go through both houses. The first time we failed in the Senate by--I'm not sure whether we were voted down or whether we didn't have the roll call.

Fry: Do you remember those times when it was scheduled for a vote in the Senate and Senator Andreus Aristides Jones who was the chairman of the Senate Suffrage Committee--

Paul: Oh, from New Mexico. What was that name?

Fry: [Laughing.] He is usually called A. A. Jones. He didn't call up the Amendment, because there were three votes absent. That was in May, 1918. So they set a new date.

Paul: I think it was prior to that, sometime in the winter.

Fry: You may be thinking of 1919.

Paul: No, it went through in June 1919 the Senate. But the previous winter, I think, it came up and we had a marvelous attendance of everybody in the woman's movement almost, because we thought it was going to be voted on in the Senate. Have you come across that? It must have been after it went through the House. I know exactly what happened and I'm sure the <u>Suffragist</u> must have recorded it. I've probably told you this before. Maud

*On January 12, 1915, the House had defeated it--over a year before the issue came up in the party platforms. (Stevens, Doris, Jailed for Freedom, p.348.)

Paul: Younger and I were sitting together up in the gallery. We had the votes--we knew we had the votes and everybody else knew we had the votes. That's the reason we had such an enormous number of people coming. I remember people coming down all the way from Buffalo and Syracuse and many places. As we all sat there time went on and they debated and debated, made speeches, and speeches and speeches and speeches. Suddenly Maud Younger and I said, "We'd better go down and see what's happening. Pretty soon they're going to begin to go home. They can't sit here talking forever. What on earth can have happened?"

So we went down together. She had this marvelous relationship, which I hope you'll make clear in all your accounts, with the senators [congressmen] in the House [Congress] because she had rented a house up on Capitol Hill; there never was a congressional chairman like that. She paid all expenses and she gave party after party after party, very nice intimate social little ones until she got to know these people personally, their wives and their children and everybody. So she knew them so well that she could go up and talk to most any man on a personal, friendly basis. I couldn't do any of those things. I practically never went up to Capitol Hill, so I didn't know them personally. But I went with her.

There at the entrance to the Senate chambers was Senator Gallinger who was the Republican leader from New Hampshire, a very great friend of ours, and Senator Curtis (who later became vice-president under Hoover; then he was in the Senate). One of them was the Senate leader--they both had high political positions whatever they were. They were standing each one with a poll in his hand.

We said, "Why in the world don't you start the vote?"

They said, "Well, we'll tell you--Borah has changed his mind. We had him. He promised us to vote for us. We put him on the poll. We assembled all these people to vote and gave word to you and all the women to come to hear the vote. And now we dare not, because we're one vote short. We've been spending all this time with Borah trying to get him to stand firm and he won't. And we can't do it. So now we've sent word to the men just to talk and talk and talk, make good records for themselves in their states, get good publicity for themselves so they won't be too down on us for having gotten them

Paul: into this poll. Then we want to just adjourn, the time
having expired that we had allowed."

That's what they did. I never, never will erase
the memory of that occasion from my mind. It's so
vivid still.

Then we started to rebuild strength so we would be
able to proceed without Borah. I don't know just when
that was but it was probably in the winter.

Fry: It sounds like it was perhaps the first of October,
1918, vote. They had a long debate of four or five
days in the Senate.

Paul: No, it was only one day. It was called for the vote.
It wasn't a debate at all.

Fry: They had been debating for three or four days when they
called for the vote in October 1918.

Paul: No no no, not this time.

Fry: This day it failed to pass by two votes.

Paul: No no; no vote was taken this day.

Fry: Then that must have been a previous Congress.

Paul: It didn't come up at all to a vote. They were determined to pass it, you see. We had passed all the
debating period and it was up to the point where they
thought--of course the Republicans were in control of
the situation; it had to be after that November election
or they wouldn't have been in control [of Congress]; and
they were in control, or it wouldn't have been Gallinger
and Curtis there that we saw.

Fry: I'll find the date on that and put it in.*

Paul: That was the time when the sentiment had changed and
you had the feeling that the Amendment fight had been
won. Because here we had enough votes--excepting for
whatever the reason on Borah's part was. All through

---

*Votes were scheduled and speeches made on the Amendment
in the Senate on both May 10 and June 27, 1918. Both
r ' . .   J '   1 * *.. 1 .' .. ' * lack of
  .(. ,   ~.   . . '. . . . .   r'. Irwin, op.cit.
  pp.))))-(. j

Paul: that period of the ending of 1918 and the beginning
        of 1919, somewhere along there.

Filling in Chronology: the Senate and the President

Paul: You were trying to tell me about 1919, weren't you?

Fry: Well, in 1918 the Senate did have a debate for quite
        a long time, from September 26 to October 1. Wilson
        addressed the Senate for suffrage finally, and the
        next day--

Paul: What day did he make that address?

Fry: It was about September 30; the exact date is not given
        in the Suffragist.

Paul: We had many thousands of mimeographed sheets, so that
        date should be easy to get. Even this past campaign
        we've been using it all the time with the Democrats.

             That was September, you see.

Fry: The point is that they did take the vote and it failed
        to pass by two votes.

Paul: When?

Fry: September 30 or October 1.

Paul: The vote wasn't taken at the time he made the speech.*

Fry: Well--do you want me to read it to you in Irwin?
        "Wilson's appeal had started only two weeks before.
        He had written to Senator Shields of Tennessee in the
        summer and Senator Baird of New Jersey asking them to
        back it..."

Paul: He got that last vote when he was over at the Peace
        Conference in Versailles. He cabled back that he had
        the last vote.

----

*Paul is likely referring to Wilson's first public
declaration in favor of the federal amendment eight
months before, on January 9, 1918.

Fry: This happened before then.

Paul: I know it did. It had to happen before then. The speech happened before.

Fry: This was just a month or two after the Woman's Party began carrying banners at the Lafayette statue across from the White House.

Paul: That was a <u>continuation</u> of our picketing, only we just moved across the street.

Fry: Then when this failed to pass the Senate by two votes, Inez Haynes Irwin says that then you began picketing the Senate on the steps of the Capitol. Do you remember that?

Paul: Yes, that's right.

Fry: That's the period I'm talking about now. There was a lot of picketing and a lot of arrests, a lot of "detentions."

Paul: Anyway, the whole picketing was one. The whole year of 1917 was picketing. I was saying the result of it at the end of the year, plus the election campaign in 1916, brought us high up to the point of general expectancy that the victory was around the corner.

Fry: There was a winter vote scheduled in 1918, but the Senate recessed on November 21 without any further consideration of suffrage.

Paul: That was an election year, was it not? Not for the presidency but for congressmen.

Fry: The election was just over; this was November 21, 1918.

Paul: They must have had that recess for the purposes of the election.

Fry: That would have been after the election, wouldn't it? That was November 21 that they recessed.

Paul: Anyway, what was the next thing after they recessed and came back?

Fry: When they came back, Wilson on December 2, 1918, included suffrage in his formal message to Congress, and then he sailed for France.

Paul: He didn't include it in his message. He made up a
special appeal. It was an appeal that he made to the
Senate, a personal appeal because the feeling had got to
such a point that he did this and made a wonderful
speech, which we've used from then on.

Fry: Yes, it's quoted in both the _Suffragist_ and in Irwin.

Paul: Now what time was this that he went over to France?

Fry: That was December 1918.

Paul: When was the Armistice?

Fry: November 11, 1918.

You were arrested a lot during all this time. At
any rate, the burning cauldrons and all of this sort of
thing were going on.

Paul: They were when he was at Versailles.

Fry: That's this time--the winter of 1918-1919, December and
January of that winter. And on January 1, New Year's
Day, Irwin says, you "started the watchfires of freedom."

Paul: Then, he must have been over in Paris by that time,
because we didn't start--

Fry: That's right. He had left in December.

Paul: In the winter of 1918.

There wasn't any _message_. There was just an appeal
that he made because the feeling in the country had grown
so great, and he had changed his mind personally.

Fry: He was asking the Senate to get behind it.

Paul: I know he didn't get any vote at the moment.

Fry: The vote was set for February 10, 1919. Two days before
that the President was burned in effigy in the urn; it
was a cartoon of him that you burned.

Paul: I know. All that period we were having those watchfires.

Fry: And it was defeated by one vote on February 10, although
the new senator, who was Senator Pollock of South

Fry: Carolina, voted for it.

Paul: The new senator that carried it, when we finally got the total number, was Harris of Georgia. That was in June, when we got it.

Fry: How did you get him on your side?

Paul: The President got him, President Wilson. Senator Harris was over in Italy doing something or other. President Wilson got in touch with him over there and cabled back, telephoned back, communicated back in some way, with our Democratic leaders. The main person was Matthew Hale, the main person who was working on the Democratic side to get this done. He got word (some said directly to him, some said through somebody else) that they could now count on Harris, that he had given his pledge to the President to be back and vote on it when it came up. I guess you'll find all that.

Fry: My note says that Tumulty sent a cable to President Wilson to confer with Harris, who traveled from Italy to France to meet with Wilson.

Paul: I know that they met; I don't remember where they met but evidently they met at Versailles there. Probably Mr. Hale was the one that we dealt with altogether. I don't know what his title was but he was a very prominent Democratic leader, a very wonderful man.

Fry: Was he former chairman of the Progressive national committee? Inez Irwin says he was, on page 427.*

Paul: I don't know what he was, I don't remember. We dealt with him because he was the person outside of Congress who would do the most for us. All our relationship with Senator Harris was through Mr. Hale with whom we dealt. Mr. Hale may have asked Senator Tumulty to send a telegram, very likely he did. Because he was very close to the President.

Fry: Do you remember Senator Keyes?

Paul: Of West Virginia? Yes, but he never took any particular part.

---

*. p'   / ' t.,   ^^^   s t t   .

Fry: He was still one of the unknowns who leaped on the
        bandwagon right at the last minute. At any rate, on
        May 21 the House passed it again.

Paul: Let me get these dates in my mind. The first time it
        came up in any place and it was passed was when?
        January or February of 1918?

Fry: In January of 1918 the House passed it.

Paul: I guess that was the first time it was ever passed.
        Then what happened? What's the next vote?

Fry: There were some votes set but not taken in the Senate
        because you didn't have the votes to pass it.

        The Senate brought it up on October 1, 1918, and it
        failed to pass by two votes.

        The Senate recessed, and so forth.

        Then there was Wilson's appeal to Congress.

        The next vote was in February 10, 1919; the Senate
        voted again and it failed by one vote. Then in--

Paul: Wait a minute. Let me see if I have this in my head.
        In the beginning of 1918 it went through the House. Is
        that right? Then at that time that's the only victory
        we'd had--the House in 1918 at the beginning. Congress
        came to an end with no favorable action excepting that
        one vote. Then we started in 1919, March 4 I suppose--
        because Congress used to begin then--so then we had to
        do it a _second_ time in the House, and they _did_ vote it
        a second time in the House.

Fry: Yes, the House passed it again on May 21, 1919, 304 to
        89; then on June 4 it passed in the Senate--

Paul: --Then it went over to the Senate and passed in the
        Senate. So it never passed in the Senate but once, and
        it passed in the House twice. It told in the _Suffragist_,
        I remember, that in that _second_ vote in the House, in
        the debate Mr. Gard, representative from Ohio, proposed
        the seven-year limitation because it got to such a point
        that they thought the only way they could defeat it now
        was not by an outright vote against but by making dif-
        ficulties in ratification. So they--this was brought up
        by Mr. Gard.

Paul: I looked this up recently when the seven-year
[limitation] was put on [the Equal Rights Amendment]
by Mr. [Senator] Bayh and we saw the same thing was
happening. This time when it was brought up in May,
when Mr. Gard proposed this, all over [the chamber
you could hear cries opposing it].

[End of Tape 12, Side A]

INDIVIDUAL EFFORTS FOR THE EQUAL RIGHTS AMENDMENT

George Gordon Battle

[Tape 12, Side B]

Fry: May I read the title of this onto the tape so we'll
        have exactly what we are talking about?

        This is "Excerpts from the Brief in Support of the
        Equal Rights for Women Amendment," by the late George
        Gordon Battle, distinguished jurist of Virginia and New
        York. It was submitted to the Judiciary Committee of
        the Seventy-seventh Congress and printed as a Senate
        committee print by the U.S. Government Printing Office,
        Washington D.C.

        Excerpts were presented to the platform committees
        of the 1944 and 1948 Democratic National Conventions.

Paul: It was presented by Mr. Battle, personally, before his
        death. The Battle family was an old and distinguished
        Virginia family. Mr. George Gordon Battle went up to
        New York after he became a lawyer and established a law
        firm. I think he was head of the firm. Does it give
        the name of the firm?

Fry: No, it just says he was a "distinguished jurist."

Paul: Anyway, when Mrs. Belmont inherited a large fortune from
        the Vanderbilt family, after her divorce from Mr.
        Vanderbilt and his death, she needed, she felt, a lawyer
        of the highest possible rank to look after her affairs.
        She made a search to find the person who would be the
        best person to help her, because she knew nothing what-
        soever about managing her investments and so on, and
        she finally asked Mr. Battle to become her lawyer. She
        told me that the retaining fee that she paid him was
        $1000 a month. And in addition, any time that he took

Paul: a case she paid him also for that individual case.

So when Mrs. Belmont began to help the Woman's
Party and finally became our national president, we
began to have some dealings with Mr. Battle, especially
about money that she was giving to the national headquarters to enable us to complete the purchase by her
actually paying off all the notes that the Woman's Party
had signed when we originally contracted to buy the
headquarters, the old brick capitol.

Then Mr. Battle, getting to know about our work,
said to us one day, "I don't understand why you don't
get a lawyer of great knowledge of legal position of
women in the country that you are trying to change, and
of knowledge of our political make-up in Washington, to
just take this thing over and present it to the Judiciary
Committee. I feel sure that Congress will be more
willing to pass it if you do do this."

We said, "Yes, we know, but we don't know how to
get enough money to pay a lawyer of the type you describe." He said, "Oh, I'll be glad to do it for you
and I wouldn't charge anything."

So that's the way we came to have the aid of Mr.
Battle from that time on. The first thing he did was
to prepare a brief to be presented to the Judiciary
Committee of Congress.

He said, "It's very simple for me to do this. I
have a large staff who will look up all the details
for me and everything and I will merely prepare the
brief. I will go down to present it personally."

So he did. The next hearing we had he went down
and personally presented this brief. That was the time
we got our first favorable report from the House
Judiciary Committee.

Then, shortly after--this was in 1944--he went
out to the National Democratic Convention as a delegate--
I presume a delegate, as a member of the convention in
some capacity. And we went out to present our appeal
before the judiciary platform committee asking for a
plank in the Democratic platform being drawn up in
1944 at the Democratic National Convention. (Four
years before we had gotten a plank in the Republican
platform.) The Democratic National Convention met that

Paul: year in Chicago. I went out personally to it.

The person who took charge of our presentation
was Mrs. Emma Guffey Miller, who was then on our
national board.

Mr. Battle went before the platform committee
personally and gave these excerpts from the brief that
he had prepared for presentation to the committee in
Washington. At the meeting at which the platform
committee recommended to the national convention that
they adopt the plank, Mr. Battle was heard, and he I
think was one of those who helped immensely in our
victory, because it was put in for the first time in
the national Democratic platform and used in their
campaign and from that time continued up until it was
finally passed by Congress.

I'd just like to add this so that our gratitude to
Mr. Battle can be made clear. Through the years after
this first help that he gave, Mr. Battle always was the
person to whom we went when we had any legal matter
coming before us. When we were acquiring the old brick
capitol as a headquarters, he drew up all the papers
concerning it and put in the deed from Mrs. Belmont to
the Woman's Party including the provisions that are in
the deed now that tried to safeguard the property forever,
as long as we wanted it safeguarded, from anything that
might take it away from us.

He put in, for instance, a clause that this property
"should be used only for the advancement of women and
for no other purpose." It would revert to the heirs of
Mrs. Belmont if it were used for some other purpose,
or if the management was turned over to men and taken
away from women, and if salaried positions and positions
of authority (positions paying considerable amounts to
any person) were taken away from women. We did all this
so what happened to the Red Cross wouldn't happen to us.

You know, the Red Cross was founded by a woman,
Clara Barton, and all the money was raised and the work
that was done at the beginning was done by women, Clara
Barton and her associates. And then as it became a great
and important and powerful and wealthy organization it
fell again into the hands of men. So the women have
very little to do now with the running of the Red Cross.

When we tried to have a bust of Clara Barton put down

Paul: in the Red Cross building (Adelaide Johnson was making
these busts of Susan B. Anthony, Lucretia Mott, and
Elizabeth Cady Stanton) some of our members wanted to
raise the money to have one made of Clara Barton. We
asked the Red Cross if they would accept this, and they
said they didn't want anything (the people with whom we
dealt; maybe another committee wouldn't do this) but
they didn't want anything related to Clara Barton in
the form of a portrait or bust or anything else.
Because their headquarters had gone completely over
to the control of men.

So we were trying to protect our headquarters. Then
at each successive step whenever any legal problem came
up, such as whether to change the wording of the Amendment and accept all these different variations that
people wanted, all the struggles that we had, to keep
it just on equality for women and nothing else so that
it couldn't be attributed in any way that we didn't want,
one of our greatest supporters was Mr. Battle. This was
always so, and without any charge at all he would always
give us his advice which was of such value to us. (Now
that's the end of that one.)

Pearl Mitchell Sayre and Emma Guffey Miller

Fry: Can you tell about Mrs. Pearl Mitchell Sayre from
Oklahoma and her role in the---

Paul: We got to know Mrs. Sayre first at the Republican
Convention in Philadelphia, I think it was about 1948.
Mrs. Sayre worked for many months in Philadelphia before
the convention opened in the general capacity of a member
of the committee in charge of the convention. She joined
the Woman's Party and became a very ardent supporter and
helped us in every way with our preparation to present
our case to the platform committee. From that time on
she was always on our national board as representing
Oklahoma, her home being in Ardmore, Oklahoma. Then,
when Eisenhower became President, she took a delegation
from the Woman's Party to the White House where one of
the chief aides of Eisenhower--he was an Oklahoma man
who had been introduced to Eisenhower by Mrs. Sayre--
endeavored to help her in pushing forward the Equal
Rights Amendment claims upon the attention of the
President and getting support for it.

Paul: Mrs. Sayre continued always up until her death to be one of the national officers of the Woman's Party. She was one of the vice-chairmen year after year. She was unfailing in trying to put the Equal Rights Amendment into the Constitution.

Fry: In this 1948 convention, did the platform committee adopt a resolution backing the Equal Rights Amendment?

Paul: It was first adopted in 1940, and so there was no difficulty at all [in 1948]. A few speakers led by Dr. Mary Sinclair Crawford, Dean of Students of the University of Southern California, who was another one of our national officers. The principal speaker was Anita Pollitzer, who was also on our national board. All the arrangements were made by Mrs. Sayre so that we might have this good presentation of our case. But there was no difficulty whatsoever. The platform committee accepted our draft exactly as it was presented and exactly as it had been presented at all conventions beginning in 1940, of the Republican party.

Fry: Did she come to Washington to help lobby the Oklahoma senators?

Paul: She didn't exactly lobby. She of course was a person who was so high up, (she was national committeewoman from the state of Oklahoma for the Republican party,) that she would--I wouldn't say lobby, but would invite senators important to us to have lunch with her, for instance, to discuss the matter, and almost invariably they would agree to what she was asking them to do.

          [Pause.]

          I'm trying to think of some more about Mrs. Sayre.

Fry: All right. [Pause.]

Paul: I think I'll have to go back and fill this in later.

Fry: All right, if you think of anything else, I'll take it down.

Paul: Let me tell you why I'm hesitating.

          [Tape off.]

Fry: --in Pennsylvania?

Paul: Yes. That's because of the great political work that Mrs. Miller did.

Fry: Did you say Emma Guffey Miller?

Paul: Yes. You know, when she went on our national board and began to help us, then she took, as her special place for working, Pennsylvania naturally. Then she got the Federation of Democratic Women Clubs, which she belonged to, to <u>unanimously</u>--they had a convention to which someone came from every precinct, it was so well organized--and all of these women were pledged to support, to get the endorsement of their congressmen if they could. And the Republican women were rather spurred, I think, by all this to do exactly the same. So we had a unanimous vote when it was taken in the House this last time, it went through both times, you know. It went through the first time the way we wanted it. The second time it was the way Mr. [Senator] Bayh wanted it; the wording was the same [as his]. Only <u>one</u> single person from Pennsylvania voted against it. Mrs. Sayre had about the same control over the voting from Oklahoma. Some of these states we didn't bother about. We had such a good person there.

Fry: She was that effective?

Paul: Her capacity was the same as Mrs. Miller. Mrs. Miller could do all this because she was on the National Democratic Committee. And Mrs. Sayre could do it because she was on the National Republican Committee.

I wanted to tell you another thing. On the National Republican Committee, for several years they had an executive committee. On the executive committee there were only two women, and one of these two women was Mrs. Sayre. She had a supremely important position.

President Richard Nixon

Paul: Now I want to tell you--this is just of no importance for your manuscript, so you might turn it off. But I want to tell you about Mrs. Sayre.

When Nixon was vice-president under Eisenhower, we were trying to get greater activity of course from him.

Paul: When he became a congressman he announced he would be a
sponsor in the House, and when he went over to the
Senate he announced immediately he would be a sponsor.
But we never had any push that we could see. So we were
trying to get greater support from him. There was some
particular thing that was up that was affecting women.
(I've forgotten--I probably could think of what it was.)
But at the moment, anyway, we were wanting to get somebody to talk to Nixon who would be powerful in his own
party and get more activity from him in supporting this
particular measure.

Fry: It was not the Equal Rights Amendment?

Paul: No, but it was something that was along the line of the
Equal Rights Amendment. I think that--it seems to me it
was something to do with all contractors dealing with
the federal government having no discrimination on the
grounds of sex. It was before Congress and we were trying to push it. It was in harmony of course with the
Equal Rights Amendment. If the Equal Rights Amendment
had gone through we wouldn't have needed it, but in the
meantime we did need it.

So I went over myself to Nixon's office and talked
to his assistant. I remember very well, it was this girl
Rose Mary Woods, and I asked her if I could make an
appointment for two very important Republican women who
were coming shortly to Washington, to come and see Mr.
Nixon. I told her that what we had proposed, and very
much had to heart, was this non-discriminatory measure
about government contracts. (I think this was what it
was about.) So she--the two women who were coming for one
of our own National Woman's Party national board meetings
were Mrs. Sayre and Dr. Mary Sinclair Crawford. Dr.
Crawford had campaigned for Nixon, and she told me herself
that she had canvassed her whole congressional district
personally as thoroughly as she could. She had even
gone, she said, into every saloon in the whole district,
and really labored for Nixon's election. I told all
this to Rose Mary Woods and she gave me some other
secretary and so they said all right, they would make
an appointment for this particular day when the women
would be here.

So when the day arrived that they were to come, I
told them we had this appointment which I thought was a
perfectly secure appointment. And they came a little
bit, I guess, early, but at any rate they managed to be
there at the time of the appointment. They went over.

Paul: I went with them to introduce them and see that
        everything went all right. And when they got there,
        Nixon wasn't there, and I think he left word that he had
        gone off to Pennsylvania to make a speech at some college
        or something like that, and left his secretary.

        They said, all right, could they speak to the
        secretary. Of course, here we had two of the highest
        women in the Republican party, Mrs. Sayre on the
        national committee and Dr. Crawford had been the chairman
        of the campaign committee for Congressman McDonough when
        he was running for Congress on the Republican ticket.
        They were both Nixon supporters, and great Republican
        supporters of course.

        So this secretary came out, and was anything but
        cordial. He didn't even ask them to sit down. Can you
        imagine two people of this rank! He kept them standing
        while they tried to talk about what it was about. They
        said, well, could they make another appointment for some
        other date when they could arrange to come, and they
        said if they couldn't come themselves they would arrange
        to have someone else come to represent them to deal with
        this whole subject with Nixon.

        The secretary was very casual. He said he would
        take it up with Nixon. He didn't know, since he was
        such a busy man, whether he could possibly see anybody
        on this subject or even see them if they came back, or
        see anybody in their place. It was finally left that he
        would notify them whenever Nixon could see them and they
        would endeavor to come back again. Dr. Crawford was
        then leaving for Europe. She was going to be back in
        some short space of time. Mrs. Sayre was leaving again
        for Oklahoma.

        I kept calling and calling and asking if Nixon had
        been able to arrive at a date when he would be able to
        receive these women on this subject. And finally we all
        gave it up. It was always being deferred. Nixon was
        always too busy; his secretary hadn't been able to see
        him and hadn't been able to bring it before him, and so
        forth. Of course it's one reason I suppose why Nixon
        hasn't been as effective a president as he might have
        been.

Fry: On equal rights wasn't it rather difficult to get Nixon
        as a president to come out for the Equal Rights Amendment?

Paul: I', ⸱ ⸱ ⸱ ⸱ ⸱ ⸱ ⸱ ⸱ ⸱ ⸱ ⸱ ⸱ when he

Paul: was first elected as a young congressman it was one of the subjects that he espoused as soon as he got into Congress. We always of course asked each man as he came to be a sponsor. He made himself a sponsor right away, the first year, and continued to be a sponsor as long as he was in the House. When he went over to the Senate he was immediately asked to be on the Senate sponsor list, and he became a sponsor immediately.

When he was vice-president, of course Eisenhower went much further and put it in 1957 in his message to Congress as part of the administration's program, the first time any president had done that. That was his second term. Naturally he spoke not only for himself but for his vice-president when he gave his administration's program.

When Nixon was running hemself for the presidency, he issued a statement (and I can give you this to put in your record here) stating his complete support for the Equal Rights Amendment. That was when he was defeated by Kennedy. Then when he became President--I remember we were getting statements from all the candidates for the presidency in 1968; that was the time we got Governor Wallace and all the others. We got statements from--everybody running for the Republican nomination, then from everybody running for the Democratic nomination. I think there was appreciably nobody running who didn't give us a statement of support for the Equal Rights Amendment.

After he was elected President--first of all before he was elected President, after he had been nominated, he appointed as manager of the women's division of his campaign Louise Gore, who was our own legislative chairman, as you know. Louise Gore was installed in the old Willard Hotel with an enormous staff of assistants to campaign among women, to organize the women of the country for the election of Nixon. This was the first time he ran. [1968.] There was no question at all about his supporting the Amendment. It was something Louise Gore was so strongly for herself, officially for. And the statement he had issued was [sent] widespread over the whole country.

Then, after he was elected, we hoped that he would really give a big push. Louise Gore undertook, as our legislative chairman, to keep the matter before the White House all the time. She went down to the White House to confer with the person whom the President had appointed

Paul: to be one of his liaison contacts with Congress. So she
worked with this particular man, to get him to understand
thoroughly the Amendment, the arguments to be used, like
any group going up to lobby. He was equipped with everything she could give him.

After a time when she went back to see how everything
was going and to push further, he had been changed and
assigned to another department. So she had to begin
all over again with another person who was given to her
to work with. She kept on but didn't have any very
great success because Nixon's mind was evidently on
getting something else through Congress, not particularly
on getting our amendment, although he had--[spoken] for
us.

It wasn't until this present year when the Amendment
had gone through Congress, and of course Nixon, through
Louise Gore who was able to have the lobbyist who went
up to the President on other matters, always encouraged
to be as strong as they could for this measure too. It
certainly helped in getting it through. I feel perfectly
sure. Getting it through the House, I mean, and getting
it through the Senate.

Fry: I don't remember Nixon coming out for it while it was
going through Congress.

Paul: Well, he had come out for it in his whole election
program.

Fry: Hadn't it already gone through Congress then? [1972]

Paul: No, it didn't go through until 1970. It went through
the House for the first time. In 1968 he was elected,
wasn't he?

Fry: And at _that_ time Nixon came out for the Equal Rights
Amendment?

Paul: No, I _told_ you he came out first when he was campaigning
as a young congressman.

Fry: When he was _President_, did he ever try to--

Paul: It was part of his _program_ in his election campaign
that he was campaigning for, the statement that he gave
out. We circulated it, and everybody else working for
the Republicans. We were not working for the Republicans,
t   , \--   - ̇   ..   · ́   ʍ .i support

Paul: this measure. So when Louise Gore took over the organizing of the women of the country for him it was one of
the planks in the Republican national platform that he
had unequivocally supported and in his election campaign
had issued this statement, which I have here, appealing
to the voters on this specific question. So there was
no question about it. Then, for the very first time--
not for the first time because Eisenhower was also
doing it--we had the staff of the President working
with Louise Gore. I know this because I talked it over
and over again with her before she went and when she
came back and what she said and what they did, urging
each man that the President might have some influence
with, as they were doing on <u>all</u> measures that they were
trying to get through.

But they weren't putting any great volume of pressure
on this. I <u>know</u> that they weren't. Because the person
to whom we owe the most thanks, Louise Gore--she wouldn't
have been appointed chairman, an unpaid position,
honorary, to organize the women of the country for Nixon
if she hadn't had his <u>ear</u> and his approval. One reason
I think he appointed her was--you probably know all
about her--her home is one of the showplaces of Maryland,
a great, very beautiful estate; there she has had many
fundraising meetings, among others, for Nixon; she did
raise a great deal of money for his campaign. So she
was given as cordial reception as possible when she went
up to try to push for the thing. The doors were open to
her and people were assigned to her to work too. So,
I think when we got it through it was with the cooperation
and support of the White House.

But it wasn't until this [present] election campaign
came on and had gotten quite a good way toward success
that suddenly Nixon issued a statement, which had wide
publicity. I have it here. I can show it to you if you
haven't seen it. He said, "We are officially joining
the ratification campaign and doing everything possible
to see this measure become part of the Constitution."
And of course it wouldn't have gotten in the platform
again without Nixon's support; but you do have the planks,
I guess.

Fry: No, I don't have a copy of the Republican planks, and I
don't have a copy of Nixon's statement anymore because
I gave them all away.

Paul: Suppose I get you right now the platform, because I have

Paul: it right here. I got it out to file it last night, thinking I must file it because I use it all the time.

Fry: All right.

Paul: It got in at the Miami convention, as you well know. It couldn't have gotten in if he hadn't wanted it, and what he did want got in. Nixon controlled this Miami convention.

It was very interesting to see that in the Republican platform at last--what we kept emphasizing and calling to their attention all the time--they emphasized that they were the first political party to come out for the Equal Rights Amendment. Not only to just say we'll do it now, but --. I think I'll mark the page and let you look at it and I'll go get the Democratic one for you.

Here is something I got out for you last night, which is a nice summary from a newspaper written by Carolyn Katzenstein before her death. Here is the governor signing it, the ratification of the Nineteenth Amendment. This is Mrs. Lawrence Lewis on our national board. It's a very good story.

Fry: This is 1955, August 21, the Sunday Bulletin of Philadelphia, Section 4, page 6. This is a good twenty-two year history of the Equal Rights Amendment.

Paul: I think these clipping ought to be kept with your compilations.

Fry: I can Xerox it.

[Discussion of Xerox quality.]

Fry: I want to ask you one more thing about Nixon.

Paul: Well wait a minute--did you find the one where he says that we were the first?

Fry: Yes, it says, "our party being the first national party to back this amendment" (that was referring to 1940).

Paul: This is the Democratic one which is equally good. Only they can't say they were the first.

Fry: This is on page (Roman numeral) 111-16, the 1972 Democratic National Convention. I wish I could take these

Fry: with me and copy them, but we'll just have to refer
         to them as being in the platform books that come from
         the two 1972 national conventions.

         The Republican platform book for 1972 has the equal
         rights platform on pages 60 and 61. The title is: "Re-
         publican Platform, a Better Future for All."

         The thing that is sticking in my mind, Alice, about
         Nixon is that few days or weeks of lobbying that I did
         for the Equal Rights Amendment--was it in '69 and '70?--
         I remember the judiciary subcommittee in the House was
         split along party lines with the Republicans voting
         against it and the Democrats voting for it (with the
         exception of one). At that time we were _trying_ to get
         President Nixon to come out and say something to those
         Republicans.

Paul: But let me tell you. We were trying to get him to push
         harder the whole time. We never stopped trying to get
         that final push, which he made only a few weeks ago.
         It came out first in the Michigan paper, the Detroit
         paper, then it was spread all over the United States.
         It was some statement given, I believe, to the AP
         [Associated Press] or something like that. It just put
         the party wholeheartedly back of it.

         It was really what enabled us to ratify up here in
         Connecticut. Because the legislature voted it down, and
         [then] the new election of last Novemeber, there was a
         Republican sweep up here which replaced Democratic control
         by Republican control. Just about that time--the governor
         was Republican--and the governor called a press conference.
         (As you probably know--I don't want to put this in the
         book at all.) At the press conference he announced that
         he had changed his position.

         [End of Tape 12, Side B]

         [Tape 13, Side A. May 11, 1973.]

Paul: We began our appeal to the National Republican Committee
         as a whole to come out for it so that the ratification,
         in accordance with the platform pledges, would perhaps
         insure a ratification. And it was through this support
         that we got from the National Republican [Committee]--
         but this is all an inside, intimate thing about the
         campaign which mustn't be put in your book.

Fry: Well, let's put it under seal then so nobody will use it until much later.

Paul: No, no. Don't put it down. I'm not going to tell you if you put it down because we never could get another state if I began on telling you all this.

Fry: Why don't you put it under seal for five years?

Paul: No, I don't want to do that.

Fry: Well, we've _got_ to get it down for history; but not for use immediately.

Paul: No, no, no.

[Tape off.]

Paul: Anyway, in a part of this general effort that's been made to get the Republicans to back the ratification in accordance with their own pledges in the platform--it was through that effort that we succeeded in getting this enormous vote up here in Connecticut.

Then, this was followed up by the President, probably in reply to questions from newspapermen, giving out this statement, "We're backing up to the hilt, in every possible way, the ratification." I must get one of the copies of this if I have it. I have it here and I'll show it to you. I gave it to Mrs. [A. Scott] Reynolds, the lady next door, to paste in the clipping book we're starting up here on the ratification. So, I can show you.

That brings him--oh!--completely and _wholeheartedly_ and absolutely _back_ of the ratification. Now, if we could only _keep_ him there [laughs] and _hold_ him to it now the tide is running the other way, now is when we really _need_ that Republican support. I'm hoping we will take it one state by another, and work through the Republican national headquarters to make this seem a politically wise move for the Republicans and Democrats in one legislature after another.

Because that's the way it was put through in Connecticut. When you had even the governor committed--a--a--even a press conference had been _called_. You see what a thing we had to overcome. And we went to the national headquarters of the Republican party and succeeded in getting such support that the governor turned

Paul: around and came back again. Then he was evidently
entrusted by the national leaders to put it through
because the governor always had enormous power of putting a measure through the legislature.

So, at the present time, we've got to begin again,
I think, to obtain greater support from President Nixon
than we're getting. Suddenly it's more or less stopped.

Fry: Maybe he can give more attention to it and a lot of other
things once Watergate is straightened out.

Paul: Of course, the National Committee has a new chairman,
Congressman Bush, who was, you know, up at the United
Nations. He came from Connecticut. His father was for
many years a United States senator here. That was the
reason we were able to, without the White House, get
this political support from the Republicans.

Fry: I see. Do you know Bush?

Paul: No, I've never seen him. We just got in touch with him
by telephoning and then he responded right away.

Now what's the next question you want to have
discussed? We've gotten away from your chronology
but now I guess we've gotten a chronology [of our own?].

ASSESSING THE TACTICS OF THE NATIONAL WOMAN'S PARTY
IN THE SUFFRAGE CAMPAIGN

Fry: Alice, we don't have any statements from you on that
         final whirlwind, from about the first of 1918 to the
         middle of 1919. If you feel like it now, I wish you'd--

Paul: What kind of a statement did you mean? I mean, we found
         the things that we did [laughter]--

Fry: We've outlined the things and pieced them together from
         the Suffragist now, but what I'd like to know is what
         your impressions are of what you personally were doing
         in that period. You were in and out of prison and it
         seemed like you had a lot of things to direct. When
         you were in prison, who kept the pressure up in Congress?
         Were you able to direct it from prison?

Paul: Yes. But I was never in prison for any very great length
         of time, you see.

Fry: Except that fall of 1918.

Paul: I think that was a month, if I remember rightly, that I
         really was in prison. But that wasn't a very long
         period.

Fry: Did the discontinuity of people going in and out of
         prison make a problem in the campaign to keep all of
         these things going in this very busy time?

Paul: You mean was it a problem, because so many women were
         in prison, to keep the campaign going?

Fry: Yes. And the jobs that they would be assigned to,
         because some of your leaders went to prison.

Paul: Nearly all of our leaders went to prison.

398

Fry: Yes, who had definite administrative jobs in the party.

Paul: That wasn't very difficult to arrange. Somebody else would always take on whatever it was.

Fry: How did you decide when you wanted to picket and when you personally wanted to go over?

Paul: Whom we wanted as pickets?

Fry: No, when you, as the coordinator of all of these activities, would picket and risk arrest and imprisonment. I'm asking, How did you decide between those two alternatives: staying at headquarters, where you were invaluable as the leader and the coordinator of the whole campaign, or showing your support in personal participation in the picketing and getting yourself arrested (as you did more than once) but having to face the fact that that would deprive the whole movement of its chief coordinator and executive at that time?

Paul: I never thought of myself as a coordinator. [Laughter.] The last thing in the world I ever thought of being was coordinator. But of course you can't lead people to do something that you won't do yourself. I never had any particular problem about that.

Fry: You say you didn't see yourself as "coordinating" all of this. What did you see your job as?

Paul: I just had--had the main responsibility of doing whatever had to be done.

Fry: [Laughing.] And there were a lot of women involved in it too.

Paul: We never had any problems that I saw along that line.

Fry: What about the health of the women who went to prison and things like that? Is this something that you can remember and tell me about?

Paul: I don't think it ever injured anybody's health. It was for a very short time; it wasn't any great hardship.

Fry: How do you see this last year and a half of the suffrage campaign along a continuum of importance in the whole suffrage campaign?

Paul: It was the culmination, of course, of all the efforts that had been made since 1648 [1848], when our first petition was presented. I think the part that the Woman's Party contributed in coming along, toward the end--because we took probably the leading part in the last seven years, but not any before this last seven years because we came into existence seven years before the final culmination--I think that the women in the Woman's Party succeeded in increasing the support and arousing the enthusiasm of women all over the United States to an extent that it had been never aroused before.

I think that by standing in front of the White House and calling the attention thereby of all political leaders in the country from the President down and, really, calling the attention of the whole country to the desire and demand of women for political equality, it gradually brought it to having a foremost place among the different reforms that were being advocated. It impressed upon Congress. It impressed upon the President.

When women were actually being imprisoned for it, it made it a still more insistent demand that the country had to give thought to it. Then, I think, by taking it into the field where women who were already voting were lined up with the women who weren't voting, and were using their votes and their political power to make it something that was politically useful to members of Congress to be supporting, was one of the biggest things that was done to finally put it across.

Fry: Did you feel at any time that your tactics of fighting the party responsible and your tactics of picketing and going to jail created more opposition to suffrage from people that felt this was improper?

Paul: No.

Fry: [Laughing.] Do you remember ever worrying that this might have been a disadvantage?

Paul: No, no. No. I had no doubts about that point, [laughter] any of those points.

Fry: Okay. [Laughter.] That seemed to be what the opposition would always dwell on.

Paul: Yes.

Fry: Speaking of that, I noticed that the Prohibition Party
        also came out for the Amendment. Did you consider that
        an advantage or a disadvantage?

Paul: Yes, of course.

Fry: You thought it was an advantage?

Paul: Yes.

Fry: Weren't you afraid you'd lose the vote of all good drinkin'
        people?

Paul: No. [Laughter.] I believe myself that women by nature
        are the great force for all these things that are con-
        structive and up-building to a nation.

THE NATURE AND ROLE OF WOMEN

Fry: Do you?

Paul: Yes. I think men contribute one thing and women another
thing, that we're made that way. Women are certainly
made as the peace-loving half of the world and the home-
making half of the world, the temperate half of the world.
The more power they have, the better world we are going
to have.

Fry. And that with the vote--

Paul: Don't you think so?

Fry: No, I haven't made up my mind yet about how much is
intrinsic in women and how much is a part of their
perceptions because of the role society has thrust upon
them as being the chief homemaker and the chief raiser
of children and so forth.

Paul: Yes, but being raisers of children just makes them all
these other things. [All these other things] come, don't
you think, from the role that women have in the world.
They are going to make the home for the children, for
their husbands, and so on. It's--they want to make it
the best possible home and the best possible community
and so on; you have a force that's not thinking all the
time about going out and fighting somebody in the
economic struggle or in any other struggle.

Fry: But what if women do go out and fight in the economic
struggle or in the political struggle? Then they're
not any more responsible for rearing their kids than
their husbands are.

Paul: No, but I think these qualities that they have, however
we've gotten them down through the ages and ages--but
wherever you go to a new country, as when they came over

Paul: and discovered this country and they found the same role, more or less, for women and the same role for men.

       When I spent two years in the School of Economics in London, I had a Professor Westermarck , who was a Danish professor. Every half year, if I remember rightly, he would go down to some more or less undiscovered part of the world where people were in the most primitive life that he could find and he studied the whole marriage system and family system and so on. Then he would come back and lecture on that field to all of his students. I had the great privilege, I think it was, of being one of his students.

       The thing that so impressed me was that every place he came back from all fresh with what he'd discovered, the system of marriage was the same. He wrote this book, The History of Human Marriage, which was a textbook at that time all over the world in universities. So, wherever he had been, the one thing that I can always remember that was about the same: the role of women, the role of men. Women were the peace-loving, constructive part and men were the aggressive, fighting part.

       So, I look forward to when we get real equality and everybody can be what he or she wants to be, so that we'll have a very much more perfect world in which to live. I haven't any doubt about it at all.

Fry: But what about the present movement, Alice, toward equalizing the roles of male and female in society so that there is not a distinct role any more? Do you think that when that happens--

Paul: Well, of course, our effort is to give an equal opportunity, as when we were trying to get through these measures about all government contracts. It's the simplest thing in the world: if we tax men and women equally, certainly we should give an equal opportunity to the contracts on which this tax money is spent.

       These long, long, long, long fights we had over each little detail, because all the time we were working for the Equal Rights Amendment we took one measure up after another, after another; that's just a sample of them. And you find somebody would come forth for the principle, but they wouldn't be for the application of the principle.

       Now it seems to me that when women have, not only in

Paul: government contracts but in every field, an equal chance,
they will naturally go into the things they can do the
best, and they want to do the best. Then we'll see.

Fry: Related to this is a question that I've been wanting to
ask you. After the vote was won, there was--

Paul: If all my answers, you know, aren't sensible, just skip
them when you have them transcribed.

Fry: I'm fascinated and I'm learning a lot, too.

SECTION IV: THE EQUAL RIGHTS AMENDMENT

THE CONTEST FOR THE NWP TO SUPPORT OTHER CAUSES, 1921

Fry: After the suffrage was won, there was a big proliferation
        of women's organizations, as you'll remember, to put
        forward these very things that you're talking about that
        women have a natural concern with.

Paul: You mean that they were trying to get the Woman's Party
        to take them up? Is that what you mean?

Fry: I don't know. That's what I want to ask you. I know
        that the Woman's Party <u>didn't</u> take them up, but that
        there were causes like voter education for women, and--

Paul: Suffrage was won in August, and we voted for the first
        time in November. We had the problem then: "Well,
        should we dissolve?" because we had been formed for the
        purpose of getting the vote, although we had been in-
        corporated in a way that left it open to anything for the
        advancement of women that was included in our program.
        But we actually undertook in our own minds to try to
        get the vote and that's all we tried to do. We didn't
        look forward beyond because that seemed to be a
        Herculean task that was enough to undertake. So, when
        we had the vote, we had this problem: "Well, shall we
        now dissolve, or shall we--?" We never had a permanent
        home, we just rented, of course, because we thought it
        was temporary. And we called this convention, as I told
        you, on the birthday of Susan B. Anthony, February 15,
        1921, which we thought would give us sufficient time to
        make up our minds what to do, and sufficient time to
        pay off all the bills we had left over from the suffrage
        campaign. So, at that convention, we did have all these
        different points that women were interested in presented,
        people being extremely anxious to get us to take up their
        particular problem. You know that, I think.

Fry: Just from my readings. There were things like maternity
        and child medical progress that was the concern of one

Fry: group, and peace, and child labor laws (which had been going on during suffrage too, I notice) and the education of women on issues for voting (which became the League of Women Voters) and protective labor legislation, as well as equal opportunity for jobs--all of those things. So I wonder if you could shed some light on who really did come forward with some of these ideas and what the discussion was about them in the National Woman's Party and how you finally decided.

Paul: At this convention, it was a large convention held in the big hall of the Washington Hotel. Representatives came and were given every chance to talk. [Small interruption.] Oh, is it dinner? Let me just tell you quickly then. Miss Jane Addams came and sat in the front row. I remember I presided at this convention and she was right down in front of me. She said that she hoped--and she was a very beloved person by the National Woman's Party because she stood by us always so strongly and faithfully when we were being--usually when we were being attacked by somebody, she certainly didn't vary in her support. So, she said, "Now, I hope you'll all join us in coming into the Women's International League for Peace and Freedom." That was a very strong feeling among most of the delegates, that peace was, after all, the next thing to work for.

       We had succeeded when they didn't think we could succeed in such a short time in getting the Equal Rights Amendment in the Constitution.

Fry: You mean the suffrage amendment.

Paul: I mean the suffrage amendment. So, for the moment, we were regarded with some respect and as powerful people that they'd like to have take up their reform. That was I would think the strongest effort that was made: to get us to become affiliated with or in some relationship with the Women's International League for Peace and Freedom, of which Miss Jane Addams was the international president.

       Crystal Eastman, who was much more to the left I would say than most of us, drew up a whole program of all kinds of social reforms that she wanted us--a very good program, she thought it was. Maybe it was, but it was sort of more like--well, we'll say the program that had been adopted by Russia in general. And these people were not only wanting it, but they wanted it with such intensity, the di--

Paul: [laughter] when we didn't at once leap into taking up
another one of these measures.

Some were very strong for anti-vivisection. [Pause.]

Fry: What about birth control?

Paul: [Simultaneously.] Some were all for throwing all our
effort into the Republican party. Some were for throwing all our effort into the Democratic party. Many
were for throwing all our effort into the Socialist party
and into the Labor party, whatever labor group there
was. Oh, that was an enormous, enormous campaign to get
us to go into the field that the Consumers League, with
Florence Kelley, was into. That was tremendous because
so many of our women had helped put through these special
labor laws for women.

Fry: Yes, right. And Florence Kelley--I've seen her name in
the suffrage books. She used to help with the suffrage
campaign.

Paul: Oh yes. She was one of our strong members in the suffrage
campaign. She was a leader in the campaign and had a
meeting in Washington to which she invited all women's
organizations to try to get them all to form a sort of
coalition to work together for what the Consumers League
was working for. She was one of the strongest people
in trying to get this put in in our program. Well, we
kept saying, "But we stand for equality and your special
labor laws are not in harmony with the principle that
we're standing for."

So we had these debates day after day, people coming
to our headquarters and asking us to meetings over in
the country where they were discussing what to do next,
just because it was a group of women who were being
credited with having won something that was important to
win and maybe we'd win something for them. [Dinner is
called again.] I remember these just bitter fights with
the special-labor-laws-for-women people.

Fry: Let's take up on this labor question when we come back
after dinner.

Paul: All right.

[Break for dinner. Tape on during dinner.]

Paul: Those who were on our national board had worked
together so long and had borne most of the burden of
raising the money and of doing the work, because it was
practically all a volunteer group. One thing that united
us was that we were so anxious that if it did continue,
if we could find any group that was willing to continue
(because we were too exhausted to start right in again
on another campaign) that we wanted to continue just
for equality for women. We wanted this first movement,
from the very, very beginning in the colonial days,
which was equality, nothing else. That one that I just
showed you, from Lucretia Mott and Thomas Wentworth
Higginson and all through the 1848 convention when for
the first time they made a more formal presentation to
the world of their demands. Down to our time, the thought
or mainstream of the women's movement had been for equality and that was all it was. The whole difference in
rights should be wiped out, and [so] we wanted to go on.
It was going on and all until this really had been
accomplished, till not only equality in political rights,
but equality in all rights had been won. We thought that
was something that ought to be done and we hoped somebody
else would rise up and do it. [Laughs.] That was our
general feeling.

          So, we elected a new board and we most of us tried
not even to go on the old [new] board so it would have
a whole clean field to work in. Elsie Hill took the
chairmanship and a good many of our people were finally
put on the new board. [Interruption.] So then, according to Mrs. [Sarah T.] Colvin, who wrote this up--I never
had known that she disagreed with this (because she had
been on our national board) until he [Robert S. Gallagher
of American Heritage] told me what she said and read it
to me. She probably wanted us to take up one of the
groups that were, say, more like Crystal Eastman's, to
go in for more radical reforms in labor. I think that
was probably, probably her idea.

          Anyway, what she wrote was, she said [something like],
"We all went down with such glory and happiness to this
convention, and we all wanted to present our programs
for what we ought to do next. But," she says, "we
really didn't get any chance. There was no general
discussion on the floor. We didn't have a real debate
of all the different things that people had before them,
which we ought to have had. But, instead, they voted
to continue because it had sort of been thrashed out
through all these months and the different people said

Paul: they would continue. They would go on the new board and would help and so on. And they all voted. Almost the whole convention voted for this idea of equality, to go on into that."

She said, "Well, the rest of us just went home feeling frustrated. We hadn't had a chance to present our programs, which we thought would have been much better, and we thought this was about the worst convention we'd ever been to as far as people not having a chance to talk about what they wanted to talk about."

So, I said to him [Mr. Gallagher], "Well, this may all be true. I didn't realize it. I thought the whole question in most people's minds was: 'Should we continue or not? If we do continue, can we find some group that will be willing to really devote their time to it and their money to it and not just vote to continue and then disappear?'

"When people got up and said they wanted to have us join the Women's International League for Peace and Freedom, or they wanted us to form a new peace society, just change our organization into a brand new peace organization, a great many of them wanted that." I said, "There really wasn't much discussion because in the minds of most of the people that were leaders in the convention, the only problem was: 'Should we continue or not? Can we find the people who will do it?' The idea of deviating from the equality thing we just didn't even register. [Laughing.] We knew a few people wanted it, but we didn't think there was any feeling in the convention for it. So, when people got up and presented it and nobody got up and said much in support, we weren't trying to suppress any discussion, but there didn't seem to be anybody that wanted to discuss that."

Fry: Was the equal rights concept then looked upon as a unifying concept of all these diverse interest groups?

Paul: No.

Fry: It wasn't seen as some symbol of women's equality like suffrage had been?

Paul: Well, you see, we never thought there was any great mass of people in the country that wanted equality. We knew we wanted equality.

Fry: Who's we?

Paul: We of the Woman's Party wanted equality. That's what
        we'd started out to do, to make a reality of what was
        drawn up, as you can see from our declaration of
        sentiments that we drew up, our Declaration of Principles.
        It's the same thing exactly. We didn't add to or sub-
        tract from 1848, which was the first convention, the
        great convention that started the women's movement in
        this country, as you know. We were just taking one
        point in their program and trying to bring it to pass.
        We always had perfect loyalty to the whole program and,
        if we could continue, we knew that the thing must extend
        to get the whole program a reality.

        So, all the things that Mrs. Colvin said were
        certainly astonishing to me because I didn't realize--I
        knew that one or two or three people were sort of leaders,
        we'll say, in wanting us to go into a woman's peace
        organization, and others were leading us and wanting
        us to go into forming a whole new society. I mean, take
        the same society, but have a whole new program of what-
        ever reform they had for trying to bring peace. So,
        with each group--we knew Mrs. Florence Kelley and two or
        three people thought the most important thing was special
        labor laws for women.

        Well, they said their say; there was not any uprising
        from people; there wasn't any discussion because the
        main group of the Woman's Party people all did want
        equality. They just wanted the whole equality program.
        That's what had brought us together in the beginning
        because we all thought equality was the most important
        of all the things that we wanted to work for.

Fry: Who were the specific women who were supporting you at
        this time in this stand?

Paul: There wasn't any supporting me or supporting anything at
        all in the way of any individual person.

Fry: Well, I guess it was a group from the National Woman's
        Party--

Paul: But, I mean, the Woman's Party group--we supposed, or I
        supposed in my innocence, that almost every Woman's Party
        person was--I never even dreamt that one person on our
        national board--Mrs. Colvin--thought there was something
        else more important, such as the labor movement (which
        I think she thought was more important--I gathered from
        Mr. Gallagher, the one who told me about the book, that

Paul: Maybe it was more important, but for us, who were
working on the equality program, our only question was:
"Should we continue?" not what we should continue for.
There was nobody supporting anybody else; we _all_ thought
that way.

Fry: What was Florence Kelley's reaction, then, when she
found out that you were going to go ahead with an equal
rights amendment?

Paul: Well, of course, at that time, we didn't have any equal
rights _amendment_.

Fry: It wasn't an amendment. It was just equal rights, yes.

Paul: No, it was just to get equality between the sexes.
Whether we'd have an amendment to the Constitution--we
hadn't even thought that far.

Fry: What was her reaction to that?

Paul: As soon as she saw that we were really going to try to
do it, I told you: she called this meeting at the Dodge
Hotel and invited all women's organizations to try to
get them all to [interruption] support her special labor
laws.

Fry: We'll start there after we finish dinner.

         [Break.]

PROTECTIVE LABOR LAWS VS. THE ERA

The Meeting Called by Florence Kelley

Fry: When you say "the meeting at the Dodge," is this Kansas?

Paul: The Dodge Hotel in Washington. The societies that she wrote to sent one or two people. Three went from ours-- Mrs. Lawrence Lewis, who'd been our national treasurer all through the suffrage campaign nearly, [sculptor] Adelaide Johnson, who more or less represented the old school of Susan B. Anthony, with the busts she made and so on, representing those people who'd worked over the years and years and years, and I. [Interruption.] We were the three from the Woman's Party and nobody agreed with us, not one person, from any of these societies.

Fry: Now, one of the labor groups was the Consumers League.

Paul: Yes, only it wasn't a labor group.

Fry: It wasn't a labor group and yet it was this labor question where you differed with them, is that right?

Paul: It wasn't a labor group at all. It was people who were consumers, I understood. I wasn't a member, but I understood they were a group of women consumers who had been organized by Florence Kelley to use the power of consumers to benefit women in industry. That was what it was, not a labor group at all.

Fry: I see. Could you tell me again, Alice, about the meeting in which Florence Kelley and her group apparently decided against supporting the Equal Rights Amendment?

Paul: Anyway, the Consumers League objected to the Equal

Paul: be wiped out. We said it <u>wouldn't</u> be wiped out because
equality in laws affecting industry could be made by
every state to apply equally, under the Equal Rights
Amendment on the ground that they'd worked very hard
to get special protection for women and this would be
wiped out. We said it <u>wouldn't</u> be wiped out because
equality in laws affecting industry could be made by
every state to apply equally, under the Equal Rights
Amendment, to men and women employees. Any benefit
that occurred would be beneficial to any person--we
thought. The benefit should be--

[End of Tape 13, Side A]

[Tape 13, Side B]

<u>The AAUW on the Fence re: ERA and Equal Nationality
Rights</u>

Fry: We'd run out of the tape and I didn't turn it in time,
but all we missed was what you said about the letter
that the AAUW was sending around to Congress at about
this same time--Mina Kerr's.

Paul: No, it wasn't the same time. It was a <u>result</u> of this
meeting. I don't know what action the others took; they
all appeared to be supporting, and stated that they were
supporting, special labor laws for women. But the AAUW
[American Association of University Women], of which I
was a member at the time, sent a letter, an official
letter signed by Mina Kerr--she was their executive
secretary at the time--to Congress. Whether to every
member or not, I don't know, but to everybody they
thought was important to communicate with, saying that
the AAUW was opposed to the Equal Rights Amendment and
hoped no action would be taken to further it.

When this happened, Mrs. Lawrence Lewis from Philadelphia, our national treasurer, and I went over to see
Miss M. Carey Thomas, president of Bryn Mawr, who had
been one of the founders of the AAUW when it was leading
women and she was, of course, perhaps the woman who'd
done more than any other woman to lift the--[Interrup-
tion.] In all events, I was telling you who Miss M.
Carey Thomas was, in case you don't know. (But you
really will know all that, I'm sure.)

So, because of her relationship to the AAUW, she'd

Paul: been the woman who had probably done more than any
other woman in the country to lift the educational
institutions in the country, to give opportunities to
women, and to Bryn Mawr, which she'd brought up to the
same standard in the academic world that the men's
colleges had. She made this very great gift to the
education of American women.

So, she said that she would come down to the convention that was about to be held, their national convention
to be held in Washington, and do her level best to have
the AAUW withdraw its letter, which she had not known
anything about and certainly hadn't been in any way
consulted about it. So, she did come and she wrote up--
offered a resolution repudiating this letter. The AAUW
voted, after she'd made this appeal to them, to make a
study of the subject of the Amendment and not to take
any position of opposition or support or anything until
they'd looked into it, which was a very good resolution,
we thought.

Then, Miss Thomas agreed to (and did, herself) send
out and write the case for the Amendment and to send it
to all the AAUW clubs over the country in the effort to
put the Amendment side before all the college women.
Someone else was delegated to send it on the other side.
So, they began, then, a study of the subject and also
informed Congress that they no longer stood against it
and were making a study of the measure.

Fry: They were neutralized, then, as I understand it, for
many, many years. Is that right?

Paul: They kept on their "study" program until a meeting in--
but you'd better verify all these things from the AAUW
because I'm not very--I resigned after a time from them,
over the nationality of women question. They would not
support the nationality of women, but their international
whatever they called it--

Fry: The international organization of university women?

Paul: No, no. They had a department in the AAUW, I guess
on international work, something like that. The chairman of it, the head of that department, a paid person
by the AAUW, (all of our memberships were going towards
paying her salary)--let me see. She was Esther Calkins
Banning, and you may remember her. No, Esther Calkins--
she married another person. You could easily find out
who this person was, this director of the international

Paul: work. I think Esther Calkins <u>Brewer</u>, perhaps. She
married a Jewish man. She came from California; maybe
the California women would remember her.

But she took a strong position when we were trying
to get the nationality of women in our country, a bill
to give American women equal nationality rights as a
part of our Equal Rights Amendment work, you see, in
our equal rights campaign.

After suffrage was won, one of the first things we
did was to try to give women the same nationality rights
that men had, instead of a woman's nationality following
her husband's on divorce or marriage or on naturalization.
And the nationality of the child, at that time, followed
the mother only if the child was illegitimate. A child
born abroad of a foreign father and American mother had
the nationality of the mother only if the child was illegitimate. If it was legitimate, our country just
didn't recognize it any longer. We didn't recognize
the mother as any longer an American (although she was
an American) because she had married a foreigner, and
we didn't recognize the child because the blood of the
mother was never recognized at all, excepting when it
was an illegitimate child. We were trying to get this
whole law changed, and we <u>did</u> get it changed in 1934.

In 1934 came forth then a great opposition from the
lower people in the State Department, not the top. The
top man was Secretary Hull, who was in sympathy with
us, but the lower ranks weren't. So, they had introduced
in Congress a bill to have a commission set up to study
the question of nationality of women. Three people
were to be on that commission and it was to be a paid
commission. So, we didn't oppose it or support it. We
did nothing with the bill, but we put all our effort
on getting our own bill through. We did get it through
in May, May 24, 1934.

At that time, this Esther Calkins (Brewer, we'll
say) had an article which appeared almost the day that
our bill went through, in which she spoke passionately
supporting the commission set up to study the matter.
I tried my level best then, as a member of the AAUW, to
do something about it. I didn't make a dent in this
Esther Calkins--Breunaur [?] I believe it was, Esther
Calkins Breunaur's position. And here came forth this
article. Instead of supporting an equality program for
nationality, they, by having this article in their
journal by their paid officail on the subject, gave their

Paul: support to the lower people in the State Department,
and I think they did it in order to promote--well, the
people in all the organization and all the staff were
trying to stand in well with the administration. Esther
Calkins [Breunaur?] [was]. So, that's the time I resigned
from the AAUW.

So, therefore, I don't know so very much more about
it [AAUW and the ERA] after that. But I do know that it
continued to be studied, perhaps in a perfunctory way,
by both sides being questioned, the propaganda for both
sides being put forth before their branches. Until one
of the national conventions, which met in Oregon. At
that time, they, I think, gave their--they apparently
withdrew from studying the Amendment to taking for
granted that the organization was for their previous
position of being against the Amendment altogether.
Then, after a time, it seems to have come back to being
just a question of study, because I know at the Washington convention, our national chairman, Dr. Agnes Wells
at that time--she had been the dean of women at the
University of Indiana--then she became our national
chairman, she went out while she was our national chairman to the AAUW convention in Washington state and made
a great effort to have them support the Amendment. But
she didn't succeed. They still took the stand that they
would look into it further or something like that.

Then, at the Minnesota convention, which was still
later, I know that they voted because they wrote to us
and said so. The vote was exactly the same: we'll say
200 for, 200 against; 200 for the Amendment, 200 against
endorsing the Amendment. The person that can give you
all of this if you just telephone down to her [in Southern California] and get it when you go home is Wanona
McGuire, because she went down two years ago--she was on
the national board, I think, of the AAUW. At Dallas,
Texas, I think, the convention was held. I know she
telephoned up to me at night and said, "Well, at last,
through all these years and years and years, we've
endorsed the Equal Rights Amendment."

Fry: Yes. It had always failed by a small margin, I guess,
for many years.

Paul: No, I don't know about that, whether it had a small
margin or not.

Fry: But it had never passed before that convention in Texas,
a   .   .'   .   .   .

Paul: I don't know that it came up very many times. I know that [once] when it was coming up, probably right after the Oregon convention, when they took the first steps that seemed to be more positively endorsing the opposition, I went over again to see Miss M. Carey Thomas. By that time she had resigned and was no longer living out at Bryn Mawr; but she was visiting, as it happened, in Baltimore. So, I went over to see her again and told her, "We need your help again."

She said, "Yes, but I think that the type of women that are in the"--Goodness! I mean, I shouldn't be saying this, I guess. But--"The type of women that are in the AAUW now are not the type that [they] were in the pioneer days when we were trying to open educational opportunities to women. I think that I won't make any further efforts. I think, as far as I'm concerned, I can't do anything more with them."

But her support was just the same, _her_ support, of course.

But at last--and more or less, of course, it was Wanona McGuire, who carried on the work, who was the one woman on the inside who went forward with it more steadfastly, I thought, than anybody else.

Fry: As a matter of fact, Alice, I happened to be there at Belmont House when she called with the good news that they'd finally passed it, and I was the one who took the telephone call and carried the news to you and the others who were having dinner in the garden. She said that they'd been working on it for years and years and years.

Paul: Of course, they had been. We all know that. But I think she'd give you the details. I don't know you _need_ it, but for your work.

Fry: It is probably available in collections on the AAUW.

Paul: But I've just sketchily given it from the outside, how it looked to us.

Fry: I never did know precisely what AAUW's objection was. Was it just this protective legislation issue?

Paul: Well, I don't know what it was.

Fry: Could you explain to me what issue was it that was so

Fry: difficult for you on this equal nationality rights for
       women? You see it's hard for me to understand, sitting
       here now in 1973, how anyone _could_ have opposed that and
       on what grounds they would have opposed it.

Paul: [Pause.] I don't know that you would say that they _op-
       posed_ equal nationality for women, that anybody did that.
       But in the practical point of view from what was before
       Congress, the measure before Congress was that a commis-
       sion should be set up to _study_ this question. When we
       went to Congress to ask that--I think about January we
       had the bill introduced--for complete equality in the
       field of nationality of women.

EQUAL NATIONALITY RIGHTS

The Montevideo Conference, 1933

Paul: In 1933, at the Montevideo Conference of American
Republics, we had gotten through the Inter-American
Commission of Women, which we had formed and through
which we could operate, have a voice in affairs at the
Conference of American Republics. We had gotten this
set up, you know, in 1928 at the Conference of American
Republics that met in Havana, Cuba.

One of the things that this commission began to work
on--you see, one of our own officers, Doris Stevens, was
made the international, I suppose you'd call it, chairman; anyway she was chairman of the Inter-American
Commission of Women. As we were trying right up to
getting the votes to get equality of nationality for
women, she succeeded in having them take this up at this
Montevideo, and the treaty was passed there, as you
know, adopted there, and submitted to all the American
republics for their signatures, their ratification for
complete equality for women in the nationality field.

After getting the vote, of course, it was one of the
most logical and reasonable things to go to see that you
not only had voting rights, but that you had equal rights
to your own nationality, to keep it on your marriage to
a person having another one. If you were naturalized,
to be able to be naturalized in our country, and to change
your nationality in any way you wanted (an American
woman), that they could have their own passport and that
they could transmit the nationality to their children--
even if married to a foreigner, that is--that our
country would recognize it. That was the essence of
what we were trying to do.

So, the State Department, which was the part of the

Paul: government the most concerned, of course, was the
author, through some of its lower-down people, of this
bill to have the subject studied. So, while the American Association of University Women probably would <u>not</u>
be opposed of course to equality of nationality, they
did refuse to support us on the ground that they
approved this policy of the State Department of having
a thorough study of the whole subject, of how it should
be set up and how the details should be worked out and
so on.

So, I wouldn't say they were exactly opposed, but
they would not support our effort to have the measure
passed right away because they said they approved this
other policy of having it all studied.

Now, you know, the husband of Elsie Hill was one of
the three men who was appointed by our government when
their bill finally did pass. But they didn't get their
bill through--it didn't make any difference to us
whether they did or they didn't. We said the State
Department could study it to their heart's content, we
were still going to put our measure through. And we
did get ours through, as I say, the 24th of May in
1934, I think. You can verify that, but I think it was
the date, because I remember it because we worked so
long and so hard.

I rather think this commission to study it got
through later. I'm not sure when it got through because we paid no attention to it. This was set up and,
as I say, Elsie Hill's husband, who was working then, I
think, in the Justice Department, was made one of the
three people on that commission to study. They had a
little staff to work through and all the facilities of
the government to make this study [laughing] and they
kept on studying. I think it was five years. Then they
made a report. We didn't pay any attention to the
report; we don't know what they reported. I think one
was from the Justice and, say, one from the State Department, and I don't know who the third one was. Three
men.

Anyway, when this went through both houses of
Congress--May 24, I think--in the morning, in the afternoon we put the measure through the Senate ratifying the
treaty at Montevideo, which had been for complete equality
for women. It was in 1933 that it went through at
Montevideo and it was presented by our United States
de   ⸱   ⸱ ₁   ⁻ ⁻ ⸱ ⸱   ⸱ W men.

Paul: It was presented by the Inter-American Commission of
Women, but it was really through the efforts of our
United States group, led by Doris Stevens, who was one
of our own officers who went down to Montevideo, of
course, the chairman of the Inter-American Commission
of Women.

At that time, we gave most of the money, for
instance, for the Inter-American Commission of Women
because, I think, through that whole period we raised
quite a lot of money and we did everything possible for
them until they became so official that the commission
itself was later on financed by the Pan American Union
itself.

So, when this went through at Montevideo, we of
course couldn't ratify, although we'd helped get it
through at Montevideo. We'd been the main force of
getting it through, with all our support of the Inter-
American Commission of Women and having the chairman
from our country and from our own organization.

It was, I think, the following January after the
Montevideo treaty was voted. I guess we had no dissent-
ing votes in Montevideo. We then, of course, wanted our
country to ratify, not only all the other countries,
but ours. We couldn't do it since we didn't have
equality at home. So, that was the reason that we
concentrated at _that_ moment on getting it through our
Congress. We had it introduced in the beginning of the
year and worked for it steadily until it was ratified.

Fry: Who helped you in this in Congress? Do you remember any
special congressmen who were good friends in all of this?

Paul: Well, the nationality question we took up for the first
time when they were starting to work on the World Code
for the World Court at the Hague. The conference was
called to consider drafting the Code; it would be the
code that the whole World Court would carry out. The
United States began to do that.

The Conference for Codification of International Law

Paul: The first conference, I believe, was in 1930. I have a
little draft. Maybe I could get the date of that for you.

Fry: I think I have it here. Let's see. [Looks through papers.]

Paul: If you don't have it, I think I have it and can get it. I'm almost certain it was 1930.

Fry: Yes. In 1930, there was a plenipotentiary person to the Conference for Codification of International Law to be held at the Hague in March of 1930.

Paul: That's what I thought the year was. Anyway, we sent over a delegation there and we persuaded the government to send one official person as a voting member of the college for our country. That was Emma Wold.

Fry: Oh yes. It was almost Doris, wasn't it, your chairman of the Inter-American Commission? I think that there was some move to get Emma Wold and--just a minute. [Looks through papers.]

Paul: Where did you get all this from?

Fry: I just picked it up in a letter in the Anne Martin collection in the Bancroft Library.

Paul: [Are you speaking of] Doris Stevens? She's the one who wrote Jailed for Freedom.

Fry: Yes. Did she go, or did only Emma Wold go?

Paul: Well, this was what happened. [Interruption: music from apartment below.] The sequence was this: When this conference was called, when we were just beginning to work on the nationality of women for our country. We learned that this Codification of International Law was going to be started about that time, just almost after the Inter-American Commission was formed, which was in Havana in 1928 at that Pan American Conference. It was set up. And we then started to work on this subject through the Inter-American Commission of Women.

Doris went over to the Hague as the chairman of the Inter-American Commission of Women. Then we thought we might probably--she undertook to go before the conference ever started and try to press from the outside, as we had always to do at international conferences. Then we thought maybe we could even aspire to get somebody on the conference itself as part of our United States delegation.

Paul: So, we went to President Hoover to ask that he
         appoint somebody.

Fry: Was it easy to see Hoover about that?

Paul: You could always get to see him. We never had any
         trouble getting to see him at all. He was always ac-
         cessible. So we sent quite a large delegation to him
         and asked him that the United States support at the
         Hague complete equality in every field that might come
         up in international law within the code.

         Then it developed that in the draft that they were
         going to work on, one of the first articles dealt with
         nationality, including the nationality of women. So,
         it became extremely important, we thought, and we sub-
         mitted the name of Emma Wold, who was one of our law-
         yers who'd been in this group that was working with
         Burnita Matthews. I've told you other times of how
         Burnita Matthews undertook one of the first things we
         did. She undertook for us to put through this study
         of all the laws in this country. I told you how we
         began this with Burnita and then we raised enough money
         for her to have an assistant, and then another assistant,
         and another assistant, until she had about twelve. (I
         remember telling you all this.) They were making this
         first survey that was ever made of the legal position of
         women in our country.

         So, among others who helped her and one of those
         who was perhaps the best in helping her, from the point
         of view of doing that all the time for a much longer
         period--some of these other lawyers came in for a short
         time and then went on to their private practices or
         something, but she [Emma Wold] stayed on working in
         this group. So, she was a very logical person to have
         go and a very good person. We were perfectly sure that
         she would be steadfast and stand up in every possible
         way for what we wanted. So, President Hoover appointed
         her. Then, while this was pending, before he appointed
         anybody, one of the people, perhaps in the White House,
         that we talked to, but I don't know who it was--

         Mrs. Harvey [Anna Kelton] Wiley was one of those who
         undertook to have an appointment made; she may have been
         our national chairman, I'm not sure. But I know she
         came back one day and she said, "When I went to see this
         particular man, he said,"--this was part of our general
         work of trying to get Emma Wold appointed--"he said,

Paul: 'Well, how is it you're asking for Emma Wold? The person that I've always been meeting in all this international work was Doris Stevens. Why not have her?'"

Mrs. Wiley said, "Well, of course, we would like very much to have Doris Stevens too. We're not saying it has to be Emma Wold, but we wanted a woman and she seemed to be perhaps the best qualified person who had indicated an interest in going." Then she said, "We could take them both in our arms," or something like that.

So, after all, we then gave our support also to Doris to show that we were not only supporting Emma, but supporting Doris. But I guess it had gone so far that it had probably already been decided to appoint Emma, so she was appointed and Doris continued, as she had planned in the beginning, to go for the Inter-American Commission of Women and work for it from the outside. So, we worked for both. We were for anybody who could be appointed and who would be willing to go and take the time to go and so on.

So, we did have Emma on the inside, which was a big step forward, because I think she was the first woman who had ever been appointed by any government of the United States to participate as a full-fledged member of the delegation from our country in an international conference. As far as we knew there never had been such a thing before. So, it was another big forward step, and she was a very good representative and did everything she possibly could.

Fry: Did you go too?

Paul: No, I didn't go. I never thought of going. [Laughter.] It never entered my head to go.

At that conference, we had a hearing at which Doris presented the case from the outside for the Inter-American Commission, just taking the one point of the nationality of women because that turned out to be one of the first subjects that they were to have under discussion. It looked as the whole old point of view with regard to nationality of women would be incorporated in the World Code, and not the equality view at all, because all the governments of whe world were having in their own laws the subordinate position of women with regard to nationality and everything else.

Paul: So, then we started to try to get President Hoover--do you want me to talk about this?

Fry: Yes, I do. This is very interesting. I wanted to start a whole session on all of this international work.

Paul: Well, we then started to try and get President Hoover to stand for complete equality in nationality. You see, we didn't have it in our own country in 1930. The man who helped us the most with this was Dr. James Brown Scott, and he's given me a photograph and I'm going to put it up here because he did so much for us. He was then president of about everything in the field of international law.

They had a headquarters just opposite the White House, on the opposite side, almost next door to where our headquarters had been on Lafayette Square, right across from the White House. And they were still there. I think it was then called the headquarters of the Carnegie Foundation for International Peace, or something like that.

But anyway, he was the president at that time of the World Organization of International Law. I remember that just about the time they were going to vote over in the Hague and we saw that it was going to go no along the equality--that the Code would not open on the equality basis as we wanted it to--he went over twice that very morning to see President Hoover for us and said, "I want, as president of this International Law Organization and so on, to tell you that what these women are asking for, from the point of view of international law and so on, is perfectly right and proper." Then he went back a second time because Hoover had been the first time a little bit--well, I mean, he had not known it was this important for him to intervene after he'd sent a delegation over there, to instruct them.

So then when Mr. Scott came back and told us what the President said, we suggested further things that he might emphasize to him, the great importance of a World Code not starting on the basis of inequality. So, he went back a second time to see the President. I remember very vividly that he came back and said, "Well, Mr. Hoover said, 'Well, now, just stop talking. Just get out and leave me alone so I'll have _time_ to get this message over. I will send the message right over saying th-- ... ...es not

Paul: recognize equality for women in this World Code.'"
So, I'll have to check this again, but what I think
happened was that we didn't vote. We abstained. We
did not give our support to this.

And the result was that since the United States
was such an important member after our participation
in the World War and we had a bigger say, a bigger
voice, I think, in international matters, so the vote
was to refer the whole subject to the League of Nations.

Fry: I see.

[End of Tape 13, Side B]

[Tape 14, Side A. May 12, 1973.]

Paul: And so the question of nationality of women--I'm not
sure what way it came before the League of Nations, but
it came before the next assembly. It was put on the
agenda of the next assembly of the League of Nations,
and that's the reason that we started to go over to the
League, because having gone this far and putting our
hand to the plow, we had to more or less follow through.

Now after we had got the Inter-American Commission
of Women committed to this (and certainly we did because
if we hadn't manifested all this interest, probably some
other subject would have been taken up by them first)
but they did take up the whole question of the treaty
on this subject in 1933, after we'd gone over to the
League and gotten the League working on it also. Then
when it went through in the Montevideo Conference, we
then undertook with great vigor to make our own country
to do what we were advocating now in the international
field. So that's the way we did; we had them put through
the nationality of women treaty in the afternoon, after
we'd made our own country absolutely equal, as far as
laws could do it, in the morning. This was May 24, 1934.

Then you said, who helped us? (when we first started
this whole thing with your question, when I began to tell
these other points, how we worked). When we first began
on the nationality of women, there was one woman in Congress who'd had trouble in getting in because she'd
married a foreigner. Under our law, normally, she would
be considered to have been no longer an American citizen.
But she'd run for Congress and been elected and was in
Con   .   .   w: the

Paul: daughter of William Jennings Bryan. She was elected from Florida.

So when we campaigned in our own country, we naturally went to the one woman in Congress at that time. Perhaps there may have been another woman in Congress, but she was the logical person because she was having a problem of establishing her own nationality rights so she could sit after she was elected. I went over, I remember, myself and saw her in the Methodist building where she was living and had a long talk with her. She said she wasn't in a very good position, she thought, to take the matter up because people were challenging her own right to be in Congress and on this very subject.

So then we went to Hamilton Fish and asked him, and he did it. He took it up with great enthusiasm and called a hearing on the subject. Then we did as we always did at hearings--got the speakers and so on. I presided, as far as our delegation was concerned, and introduced the people and spoke for complete nationality rights for women. Hamilton Fish told me that it couldn't _possibly_ have been better. We got very good publicity about it. We had daughters of Americans whose mothers had lost their nationality and so on.

One very lovely young American girl--we would have said young American girl--had Austrian nationality because the mother had married an Austrian officer who'd been killed in the First World War and she was over there when her little daughter was born. Then, the mother tried to come back to our country. You may probably know all about her. She was the sister of Maud Younger, our congressional chairman. But she couldn't go back and she couldn't get any money sent over to her because she was an enemy alien--this American girl and the American mother, Maud Younger's sister, who had married, as a Californian, an Austrian--or Hungarian; I don't know--it was Austria-Hungary.

Fry: It's probably written up in _Equal Rights_ somewhere.

Paul: I can't remember whether he was Austrian or Hungarian. Anyway, she married a foreigner--an officer in a foreign army. Of course, she married before the war broke out; but when the war broke out, naturally he was involved, and he was killed. So Maud Younger's sister was suddenly the widow of this very distinguished Austrian or Hungarian--whichever it was--family, and she sought to

Paul: come home with her little daughter.

She got as far as Switzerland and then she couldn't get a passport to come home; she was stuck in Switzerland. She was an enemy alien, you see, by our laws.

Fry: Both she and her daughter.

Paul: Yes, were enemy aliens. So Maud Younger, all through this time, was sending her family--of course, it was a very wealthy family and she'd probably married, as so many women do (the sister) into families that were not very wealthy over there but had titles and such. So Maud Younger was always sending money over to her sister and her niece. All the property that they owned in this country was taken over by the alien custodian; you know, that department took over all the property in America of--you remember that department probably called the Alien Custodian Office, I think it was--they took over the ownership and the administration of the property of the enemy aliens in this country. So they didn't have any of their property left or anything.

It wasn't until the end of the war that Maud Younger succeeded, and was helped a great deal by the fact that she was our congressional chairman and was seeing all the people in Congress who could help. Somehow or other they got it arranged so that she could come back to this country with her little daughter--who, by this time, after staying a long time in Switzerland before she could come back, because she was in this position of having lost her passport, lost her American nationality--when she did come back, we were having a hearing. And I remember this young daughter was one of the speakers; she was very moving.

Fry: Was this 1933? You said, "After the war," and I didn't know which war you meant.

Paul: The First World War. But sometime during this period, before our nationality bill went through in 1934, we had a hearing at which this young girl spoke. But all these things were organized by Hamilton Fish.

Then, then there was a great deal of publicity and everything seemed to be going our way, Mr. Fish called me and told me that Mrs. Ruth Bryan Owens had come to him and said, "Now I've gotten my nationality straightened out more so long; that I will w   r   a
l   .   .   A 'r T .' '   iK T .e women's

Paul: cause."

He said, "Well, at the time when nobody would take
it up and it was a very unpopular measure, you were
asked and you refused. I took it up and I've gotten
everything up to this point where we think the nationality bill will be in a position to go through; and I
think I'd better just stick to it and go on." Of the
people who helped us, he was one of the best--very, very,
very best--because he began when nobody <u>wanted</u> to be
associated with it.

Then, it was introduced in the final year--1934--I
think (but I'd have to verify it) by the chairman of
whatever committee was in charge of it. He was a
Jewish man from New York City, not a very powerful man;
Dick Stein I think his name was. You know, I haven't
looked this up since 1934 and I might be mistaken, but
I think it was Dick Stein. I suppose in <u>Equal Rights</u>
in 1934 we could find it.

He introduced it with the firm belief that it was a
ridiculous thing and wouldn't go through--couldn't
possibly--but he would introduce it for us. I think he
was chairman of the committee and that was the reason we
asked him to. But he didn't give much hope that he could
ever do anything with it.

But nevertheless it went through in the morning, and
in the afternoon we ratified, through the Montevideo
treaty. So that was the end of the thing on nationality.
You see, we always took some measure and had not only
the Amendment that we were working for, but whatever
particular thing that happened to be before the country
that was discriminatory.

Fry: This interested me because whereas with suffrage, there
was <u>no variance</u> by the Woman's Party in working for any
other issue, any other bill, even though it might relate
a little to suffrage. I wondered if you saw this as a
change in policy, when equal rights was the main goal?
You did have more diversity.

Paul: No, but of course our situation was so very different.
After we got the vote, all these congressmen were people
the women could ask to do various things. Before, when
we had the little handful of congressmen who were re-
sponsive to women--the women of Wyoming and two little
states--

Fry: The voter states, yes.

Paul: And all the rest, we were not in a position to ask them to do anything. But then, we concentrated on having the women who <u>were</u> voters ask their congressmen the one thing of getting us the key to the vote for all the women; I think it was a logical thing to do.

    <u>After</u> we got the vote, and women were beginning all over the country to ask congressmen to do this for them and that for them, we tried to do the one thing only of keeping, as far as our organization was concerned, what we asked for--something that was part and parcel of the Equal Rights Amendment. The Equal Rights Amendment, if it had gone through then, would have settled all the nationality problems and all the others. I think it was very reasonable. We didn't have to argue it, nobody ever disputed it, ever questioned it. We just felt natural to do that.

    A measure like nationality was coming up; our country was taking a stand on it because it happened to be one of the opening sections of the world code; our government was publicly participating in it. Well, that sort of thrust you into taking up nationality. Of all the things that you might have taken up, that was the current one that happened to be before Congress.

Fry: I have one more question to ask you on this. What other organizations were working for this equality of nationality act?

Paul: I don't think any other ones. Anyway, women had just gotten the vote and the organizations weren't taking much part in working on national measures at all, unless somebody gathered them up, as Mrs. Kelley did, to try to get them to oppose the Amendment. And we didn't go forth to <u>get</u> any others; we just undertook to do it and be glad we had the field to ourselves and nobody interfering very much excepting this--I don't know that any other organization opposed. Opposed the nationality measure, I mean. I don't know that any other did.

RELATIONS WITH ORGANIZED LABOR

Maud Younger

Fry: There was a National Women's Trade Union League. Did
          they give you much trouble on the Equal Rights Amendment?

Paul: No. They were part of--supporting--the AFL, CIO, the
          general labor movement. We didn't come into contact
          with them as individuals at all.

Fry: My guess is that they would have opposed the ERA.

Paul: It was such a small little organization; I don't re-
          member anything about them. Now, Maud Younger, for
          instance, who was our congressional chairman, in our
          group was the leading woman who was in the women's
          trade union movement. You probably know because you
          must know all about the Californians.

Fry: No, I don't; I don't know much about Maud Younger.
          [Laughter.]

Paul: You know who she was, don't you?

Fry: I know that she handled the lobbying and the congres-
          sional contacts.

Paul: She belonged to a quite wealthy San Francisco family.
          As a quite young woman--young girl almost--she undertook
          to help the waitresses from a waitresses' union. She's
          written a good many things in popular magazines about
          this.

              Then this waitresses' union, under her leadership--
          she did everything, I guess, that was done--succeeded
          in getting through an eight-hour law for women in
          California, which I suppose was one of the first that

Paul: was ever passed in the country. It was then challenged--
its validity and so on--and I suppose presumably by
people who were in some way involved in restaurants or
hotels that tried to have the law thrown out. It was
not only for waitresses, but the eight-hour [law]
covered a good field, I guess. (I haven't looked it
up.)

Then it was carried to the Supreme Court of the
United States by the people who had a personal interest
in not having the eight-hour law for women. She
carried it there herself and financed the whole campaign
and paid all the expenses, largely; maybe other people
helped, but she was always supposed to be the main
person back of this. The eight-hour law was sustained
by the Supreme Court, for women. So she was regarded
in all this protective labor law group as the mother of
the eight-hour law for women.

When we first met her, it was in 1915 when we went
out to [San Francisco] have this women voters' convention which we organized to be held out there at the
time of the [Panama-Pacific] fair, and in conjunction
with all the people who were going to the fair.

I remember that I was in one car going to some
meeting in the street and passing a car with Maud
Younger in it, whom I didn't know and had never perhaps
heard of, but at least I might have known her name.
For some reason--perhaps the drivers of the two cars
knew each other (I suppose there was just ordinary
people driving, not chauffeurs at all) anyway, we
stopped, and somebody introduced me to Maud Younger
over in the other car. That's the first time I ever
saw her.

She was then completely engaged in this protective
labor law for women movement. I just invited her,
saying, "We're going back to Washington; won't you come
help us in Washington," or something or other. Later on
she turned up in Washington, came and took a little
apartment, and said she had come to see if she could
help. Then she began to help; she was so wonderful,
we made her our congressional chairman. Finally, she
gave up the apartment, came over, and took a room in
our headquarters where she stayed, in our headquarters,
and by paying for a room and so on, up until suffrage
was won, as you well know.

Paul: Then, when we started in on our <u>new</u> campaign of
equality, of course equality ran <u>counter</u> to all these
special labor law ladies. Some came out against us and
were just flatly against the Amendment.

Maud Younger was so much on the inside; she'd been
the national treasurer of this women's trade union
league. She was very perturbed, naturally. We certainly didn't want to lose Maud Younger, whatever else
happened, because in the suffrage movement she'd built
up this great power in our organization, and we didn't
want her to stop because of this difference with the
trade union people.

She thought a long time about it and she finally
decided this was the right principle, and that all the
efforts she'd been making for women in industry had
been right, in her opinion, and they ought to be extended
for everybody, not make it for one sex.

Everything to do with labor, we always turned over
to her. She still had many strong friendships. I remember that--well, one of the principal people in the AF
of L--I don't remember what his name was--who was always
representing the AF of L in things in Washington, would
always leave it to her. They had any number of social
affairs always going on. She would go to all these
social affairs, from us. But she kept up this very
cordial relationship with the people she'd known for
so long, from Gompers down.

I remember when we were picketing, and Gompers was
making apparent some objection and passed by--I don't
know whether she ever picketed or not (that was in the
suffrage campaign) anyway, if she wasn't actually picketing herself, she was there with the pickets. Maybe she
was picketing herself; I don't know.

I remember that Gompers passed by, and he was rather
frowning or something, I guess. She said, "Now, don't
you forget, you <u>taught</u> me to picket; you were the one
who trained me to be a picket," and so on. [Laughing.]
But she had this very good relationship with them.

Your question was about the Women's Trade Union
League, and I guess that's all I know about it, that
she always was our liaison and on very good terms with
them.

Fry: Didn't you have an industrial council in the Woman's

Fry: Party that was headed by Josephine Casey?

Paul: For a little while. I remember the name Josephine Casey and I remember that, when I came back from Europe, she was the chairman. Did you know her?

Fry: No, I just picked this up from the *Suffragist*. Her name was there, and I thought that maybe she also was a good liaison between you and the labor groups.

Paul: No.

Fry: She was a former ILGWU [International Ladies' Garment Workers' Union] organizer, apparently; that's the only note I have on her.

Paul: Was she? I don't think I ever knew Josephine Casey at all, but I do remember the name. We did, of course, when we began the whole campaign for the Equal Rights Amendment, we had an excellent person--a splendid person-- named Isabel Kendig to take up our membership work.

We hadn't worked very much on membership while we were working for the vote. People joined and so forth, but we didn't seek to have an organization; we didn't care much about it. Then when we'd gotten the vote and we began to have an organization we hoped would be on a permanent basis for some years to come--until we got equality for women anyway--we started a membership department.

Isabel Kendig

Paul: Isabel Kendig was one of the very few people we started on a paid basis because she'd agreed to do it, to take this membership work. She'd been a volunteer and we didn't know too much about how well she could succeed or not, but she wanted to try it. We raised some money and gave her a little salary.

She's also known as, I think it was, Mrs. Howard Gill, if you've ever heard of her. She'd be a good one for you to interview.

Fry: Somehow I connect Isabel Kendig or her husband with Harvard.

Paul: I think she later went up and got a degree at Harvard,
herself, after she left us. But at this time, she was
the mother of two or three little children and the wife
of Howard Gill. She was one of the few women at that
time who was making a point of keeping her own name.
She called herself, when we first knew her, Sally Gill;
I think her name was Isabel but she was always called
Sally Gill. Then she developed, before she became our
own chairman of membership, a desire to be known as
Isabel Kendig. I remember her coming to me one day and
saying, "From now on, I'm going to be Isabel Kendig;
please call me always that."

She was an extraordinarily good organizer. She
started out and we gave her free policy and I think she
must have begun about 1922 or '23, somewhere along in
there, because I think we persuaded Mrs. Belmont to be
responsible for her salary so that we could really try--
when we got Mrs. Belmont to be the president--try to get
an organization formed for her. She took an interest in
that and so we were assured of _her_ salary and we gave her
an office. I think she probably typed herself, but we
may have given her a stenographer and so on.

But she was able, anyway, to build up our membership
to about sixty thousand in a very short time.

If you go into the secretary's office in Washington,
just across from the chairman, you'll see these rows
and rows and rows, up to the ceiling, of card catalogue
drawers.

Fry: In Belmont House?

Paul: Yes, just across from the chairman's office. They've
been kept in there ever since. After she stopped the
work--I think I was in Europe when she finally stopped--
because I think she was going with her husband when he
was transferred up to Massachusetts or somehwere. (She
did take this doctor's degree, I think, or maybe a
master's degree, took something at Harvard.) But anyway, for several years she kept on doing this.

The first thing she did was decide to organize by
councils, and take each profession and get a chairman
for that profession and let them build up the memberships. She had a lawyers' council, doctors' council,
nurses' council--we had every profession there was.

Fry: O'- ' ' ·· ·, · ··· · — · ·· ˈat

Fry: came about.

Paul: So when you're talking industrial councils, she started
         that. And she got them themselves to choose the head of
         their councils--the most distinguished doctor, the
         most distinguished lawyer, and so on. She would perhaps
         invite her, but she would say that the women themselves
         [in the field] must decide whom they would like to have.
         And then these council heads were supposed to have their
         meetings.

         As long as she directed it, I mean--such a good
         organizer--I was no longer even hardly taking any part
         in any of this except in trying to get Mrs. Belmont to
         do all these different things and get them started. I
         went over to Europe and stayed there off and on and
         didn't do too much or see too much of what was going on
         in Washington.

         I remember coming back and finding that the member-
         ship was no longer being looked after very much because
         Sally Kendig had gone. But she now lives right outside
         of Washington and she's still--she seems to be--a very
         good well-wisher for us, but to have sort of been drawn
         into her own family life.

         When you ask about the industrial council and
         Josephine Casey, you see I'm not telling you very much.
         But I can remember when I did come back--I think that
         was when I came back to be the chairman in 1941, in
         the war time--I believe it was then that Josephine Casey
         (I'm beginning to remember about her) and I found that
         we were paying her a salary and she was working over in
         Pennsylvania. I think that I discontinued it myself
         because I thought it was costing us a great deal and
         we were not getting anything very much from it.

         I think then we got an unpaid chairman--Ella Sherwin.
         Have you never come across her name in the Suffragists?
         She was very very active and wrote a great deal, so I
         think you'd--she was a very excellent chairman of that
         industrial council.

Fry: Did you keep these councils through the forties and
         fifties?

Paul: We had one chairman after another; if the chairmen don't
         keep working on these things, they're apt to dwindle,
         and most of them didn't do so very much work. They just
         f r   ·ry much
         inter + i   .

Bolshevik Charges

Fry: I ran across something that today is amusing; I wanted
       to ask if it was a problem for you then. Because you
       had this organization of different councils, the Woman's
       Party was criticized--just a minute; let me see if I
       can find the source here--for being set up like that be-
       cause the Communist party was also set up like that.

Paul: [Amused.] Oh, is that so?

Fry: Yes; I wondered if you had any problems with these al-
       legations of being Bolshevik (or something like that)
       in the twenties.

Paul: No. Maybe people accused us but I never heard of it.
       No; we were much more apt to be accused of being too
       conservative, you see. Because so many, almost all our
       members [laughing] seemed to be of the conservative
       school.

Fry: There was a periodical called The Woman Patriot that
       seemed to be ferreting out all kinds of organizations
       that were communistic or Bolshevik. I believe it may
       have been something put out by the DAR [Daughters of the
       American Revolution]. And it charged the Woman's Party--

Paul: No, not the DAR. I'm a DAR member and I've never heard
       of that. It certainly was not put out by the DAR. I
       have their paper here; it comes every month. It has
       no name; I think in the front it just says, "Daughters
       of the American Revolution."

Fry: At any rate, you don't remember any problem, then, of
       being accused of your work being dictated by Moscow or
       anything like that?

Paul: Oh, I don't doubt that people would say that; they would
       probably say it all now when we're trying to have this
       Amendment ratified. It's a favorite thing for people to
       say, you know--dictated by somebody.

Alice Paul and a Union

Fry: On this labor thing, I read a little note somewhere that
       you had once been in the milliners' union. What did that

Fry: refer to? Is that true? I thought maybe you have a
       labor background that we hadn't touched upon.

Paul: The first years I was out of college, I think I told
       you, I had this college settlement scholarship or some-
       thing that way. You know what a settlement house is and
       how they work?

Fry: Yes.

Paul: Ours was down in the Jewish-Italian section on the East
       Side of New York.

Fry: Did you have anything to do with a union?

Paul: Of course, all of our people would naturally be the
       poorest people almost in the city and presumably belong-
       ing to some kind of such organization. But I rather
       think that we did form a union--helped it. This is the
       sort of thing we were trying to do all the time, was
       trying to help these particular people, who were all
       foreigners, in getting--just like any settlement--it
       settles there to try to help its community.

       I wasn't a member of it, of course, but I vaguely
       remember that one of the things we did--maybe it was
       milliners--was helping some group of women who were try-
       ing to get into a union. They couldn't get into--because
       most of the other unions wouldn't take them in without
       being apprentices and all sorts of things you know, and
       they had a hard time with the unions, as you well know,
       I presume, if you know anything about the labor movement.
       What we were certainly trying to do was to help the
       women get their own unions so they wouldn't be debarred
       from all union benefits. So very likely, there was a
       milliners one that we were working on.

Fry: That's probably where it comes from.

       The other thing that was going on in the early
       twenties was the formation of the joint congressional
       committee--Women's Joint Congressional Committee--which
       was a committee [loud hammering on roof above begins] of
       all the people who were working with Congress to get
       legislation passed that women were interested in.

Paul: Yes, and I was the one who formed it.

Fry: Well, it came out in opposition to the Equal Rights
       A · - .

Paul: It came out _for_ the Equal Rights Amendment. It was
       formed and it is still existing and the present chair-
       man is Mrs. Nina Horton Avery.

       [Hammering stops.]

Fry: That's a different one; we'll talk about it.

Paul: It was called the Women's Joint Legislative Committee
       for Equal Rights.

Fry: That was the one that was formed in the forties, right?
       When you came back from Europe?

Paul: Yes, and I formed it when I was the chairman; this little
       period when I was the chairman, one of the first things
       I did was to ask the women to come together who were
       working for the Amendment and form a joint committee,
       which we did. To our first invitation, I think we got
       only two people who accepted. There was the Woman's
       Party itself; then the American Medical Women sent a
       group or a person to represent them, and the National
       Association of Colored Women, and ourselves--I think we
       were the ones who were at that first meeting. Is that
       what your records say?

Fry: Yes it is, but--

Paul: That's my memory, very vague memory.

Fry: I was asking you about one that was formed in the early
       twenties--the Women's Joint Legislative _Conference_, with
       Mary Dreier as chairman. They pushed five new laws for
       the protection of working women, and she was the moving
       spirit of New York's National Women's Trade Union League.

Paul: I knew Mary Dreier because I went to the School of
       Philanthropy--now they call it the American School of
       Social Work--the first year that I was out of college,
       when I was living at the college settlement. Every
       morning I went up and spent the whole morning there in
       that school. Edward T. Divine was the master, the dean,
       or the head of the school--whatever it's called--and
       Mary Dreier was one of the students. I was another
       student, so I knew her. She was the sister of Mrs.
       Raymond Robins, you know, who was then the president of
       the National Women's Trade Union League. Mary Dreier
       was her sister.

       I knew her quite well that first year. Then, after

Paul: I got my degree and started down to be in Washington,
        I'd lost all contact with her, although I greatly
        admired Mary Dreier. If I'd known she was the head of
        a committee against us, I certainly would have done
        something about it. But I never even heard of it until
        this moment.

Fry: Oh, you weren't aware that they were working against
        the Equal Rights Amendment?

Paul: Well, I never heard of this committee, as far as I
        know. They were perhaps working up in New York and I
        didn't know anything about it.

Fry: That may be.

Paul: Because I certainly never heard of Mary Dreier opposing
        us--never knew it.

Fry: Well, maybe she didn't; it's something we should check
        up on, and go back to some original sources.

Paul: I don't know; maybe she did. Maybe they had some con-
        gressional committee operating. I certainly didn't know
        there was one. When we formed ours, we thought it was
        something new and original, to get them all to work for
        us. Of course, a good many by that time had come out
        for the Amendment.

Fry: That was twenty years or more after this first one that
        I'm talking about. It's hard to tell how real committees
        are when they exist on paper.

Paul: Well, it's very likely that there was a big powerful
        one in New York, but we wouldn't have known about it
        perhaps.

Fry: It may have been strictly a New York thing.

RELATIONS WITH WOMEN'S ORGANIZATIONS

The General Federation of Women's Clubs

Fry: I wish now that you could tell me (again--for the tape
        this time) about the General Federation of Women's
        Clubs and put down their relationship to the Equal
        Rights Amendment--

Paul: I told you how when I did become national chairman for
        a moment--the only reason I remember particularly about
        that organization. I became national chairman in 19--

        [End of Tape 14, Side A]

        [Tape 14, Side B]

Paul: [It was] one year we had our convention in Philadelphia.
        I was elected there, and I was living up in Vermont when
        I was elected. They asked me if I would come down, by
        telephone, and take over and be the chairman. I think
        that I came in about November '42. But one could easily
        find that out by the Equal Rights who would have the
        chairman list. I came back in '41 and I went up to my
        little cottage and was staying there, and I think that
        convention was that autumn--1942, I think. I'm not sure,
        but somewhere around there.*

            Anyway, it was the next year--'43--that we got to
        the point of trying to get all the women's organizations

        _____

        *The bulletin, "Silver Anniversary of Suffrage Amendment:
        1920-1945" issued by the Woman's Party, lists the chrono-
        logy of "national chairmen" to 1945. See appendix. Alice
        Paul was elected chairman at the October 23-25, 1942
        Biennial Convention.

Paul: that were against us off of our backs if we could. I
thought the most important one was the General Federation because it was the biggest in the country, and we
had our Mrs. Wiley on our board, who was the national
legislative chairman at the General Federation.

She was the person really who accomplished it, because she went to their national board meetings and
herself tried to persuade them not to take this stand
against the Amendment. Then when she failed, we adopted
the plan of trying to see if they wouldn't--we not all
agreed on the plan, I won't say--I was trying to get
them to take a referendum with their membership. I told
you how Mrs. Wiley found that she couldn't seem to make
any impression on them about getting them to change
their policy of opposition because they had all this
staff advising them that this was the proper course.

Then she proposed to them, which we all wanted her
to do, "Why don't you make sure of this by consulting
your membership?" They said, "Fine idea; we'll be glad
to." Then they took a referendum, and by 1944 they'd
completed it. It showed the support in the organization
was for the Equal Rights Amendment, although in Washington they were speaking in hearings and so on against it.
Then they immediately said, "Of course, whatever our
membership votes, we carry out here in Washington."

So they disregarded and brushed aside all the advice
of their staff and followed the advice of their membership, as it had voted.

The next year, for the first time, they came and
spoke [to congressmen] with us. From that time on,
every single time we had a hearing, always, wherever
the hearing had been--before Congress, or the national
committees of different political parties--wherever it
may be, always the Federation has been our splendid
ally and supporter.

Fry: I was wondering about the character of your membership
and the character of the Woman's Party membership. Did
they overlap much at this point, do you think?

Paul: No, our membership was always very tiny. We didn't go
in for a big membership because we thought that there
were enough organizations by this time in the country,
of women, and all of them had to spend enormous amounts
of time and money on just organizing. We thought the
e   *   A   ı⁻ ʼ ʼ ˅   ı ˙ ˙ ˙ry

Paul: to get each one of the national organizations to come
        out for it with its membership, not try to build up a
        duplicate membership of our own. I think it was very
        wise to do it that way.

        Now, by following that policy of getting organizations,
        the membership, as the people give their memberships, is
        up in the millions. To take the time to build up an
        organization of millions, we wouldn't have been able to
        have gotten very far [laughing] with the whole campaign
        of teaching so many women if we tried to do it de novo,
        get new women and so on, with all these organizations,
        like the [American Association of] University Women.

        For instance, this last ratification, when Congress-
        man [John] Wold telephoned to me and said, "To get this
        ratification through in Wyoming, you'll have to get
        some of the more conservative women." Then, immediately,
        by having the University Women's whole organization
        ready to help you, you get a supply of women voters so
        quickly.

        The Task of Changing Women

Fry: When you were first made aware that you were not going
        to have in the twenties the support of the other women's
        organizations, at that time did you have a different
        idea towards--

Paul: I don't know that we were made aware that we wouldn't
        get any support, but we had expected universal support;
        we thought, "All these women have the vote now in their
        hands; naturally they'll want to get everything for women
        they can get." We were very much astonished to find we
        didn't. The thing that stands out most in my mind was
        people who thought we were going to imperil their ali-
        mony, and the people who thought we were going to imperil
        their support from their husbands, and the people who
        thought we were going to endanger the health of women
        by opening them to working tremendous hours--all night
        and so on. I don't know that we thought all women--that
        we were going to have no support; I don't think we thought
        that.

Fry: From bigger organizations. Well, I was wondering about
        the problem then, which you told me you faced at that
        time. You said you recognized then that what you had

Fry: to do was educate other women about it.

Paul: We really thought it was more than educate; we thought
         it was really <u>changing</u>. I thought we were going to have
         to simply change the thought of the women of the country,
         because they were being led--of course, most organiza-
         tions didn't take any stand on the subject at all--but
         those that were working vigorously, like the General
         Federation of Women's Clubs (and Consumers League was
         a small one)--you see, we did from the very beginning
         have the women physicians; there was some that we al-
         ways had. Of course, they never hesitated--and women
         nurses; some we just counted on from the beginning
         because there were so many of them in our own ranks.

         But we knew that the thought of the country, we
         could see, had not come around to supporting the idea
         of equality for women. In fact, it perhaps hasn't
         come around even today to get a ratification.

Fry: It seems like this was a wholly new problem for the
         Woman's Party, that of mass education and changing the
         opinions of great <u>masses</u> of women.

Paul: No, it was the same kind of a campaign for suffrage,
         certainly when we started in <u>our</u> little group. As I
         told you, when I came to Washington, I couldn't find
         but about three women who were willing to have anything
         to do with the suffrage amendment, of the long list that
         the National American had given to us.

Fry: That was for the federal amendment idea?

Paul: No, I couldn't find any on any suffrage list at all;
         there wasn't any kind of an organization at all.

Fry: For working with Congress, you mean?

Paul: No, for working for suffrage in any way. They told me
         Mrs. William Kent had been chairman of the committee
         appointed, and she couldn't produce any women; nobody
         could produce any women [laughing]--there just weren't
         any.

         And certainly the opposition of these powerful
         groups, such as the one led by Mrs. Wadsworth, were
         well financed and powerful in prestige by being con-
         nected with Congress. You can't <u>imagine</u> the feeling
         that you had as you look over the whole United States
         '   w r ((' ' ,   , and

Paul: most women apparently not thinking about it one way or the other.

So I think our campaigns, as far as I know, have always been the same.

Fry: That the main problem is making the issue visible to women, making them conscious of it?

Paul: Making women _want_ it. You can't suddenly get the vote for women if the women don't want the vote, never heard of it, thought of it, and don't care about it one way or the other.

Fry: One of the _Equal Rights_ magazines--

Paul: For instance, the first thing I did in this country myself, when I was at the University of Pennsylvania, since I'd been in prison in England, as I said, I was given all these invitations to come and tell about [laughing] this extraordinary career. I remember one place I was asked to go and I did go and made a speech, and I was the only speaker. When it was over, some man came up and spoke to me.

He said, "You know, I guess you made up this tale. I don't believe for one single moment anything you said tonight. I don't think you ever _were_ in prison." It was so _inconceivable_ to anybody in this country. He was a very nice man [laughter]; he was really quite sincere in thinking I was letting my imagination run away with me. [Laughter.]

Of course, at that time, nobody had ever been in prison in this country, and they couldn't imagine such a thing. They thought, "Well, in telling about her life abroad, she makes it very exciting by saying how other countries are so peculiar."

I think you have to do in life, if you're trying to help some measure, the thing that that day seems to present itself to you; you don't sit down and make a long plan of what you're going to do. And if you discover that what you're trying to push before Congress and get action on, that nobody else practically is asking for that, you know you've got to go forth and get some allies. Then you try to get the people who seem _most_ possible. And if they're in an organization, then you'll get a good many of them at the same time. I

Paul: guess everybody does exactly the same thing; they go
forth and try to get all the organizations in their
community, whatever they may be, to work for the same
purpose.

QUESTIONS RAISED BY EQUAL RIGHTS NEWSLETTER

Fry: There was an interesting legal work-up on the connection
       between your efforts in the international field to get
       equality for women, and what might be accomplished in
       the United States as a result of that. This was a
       brief article that appeared in the Equal Rights magazine
       saying that, according to past legal opinions, if the
       United States ratifies an international accord or treaty,
       this becomes a part of the highest law of the land here.

       At that point I wondered if this effort really was
       two-pronged. In other words, you not only would have
       gotten an international agreement, but you also would
       have gotten equality between the sexes by virtue of the
       United States government having signed a treaty. This
       was the United Nations--

Paul: No, but that wasn't the real point. Whenever the
       United States was about to take action in the inter-
       national field--when we knew they were about to take
       action, as we did when the World Code was being started
       and as we did at the Conferences of American Republics
       where we were always represented by our government--[it
       was our task] to try to see that whatever they did, not
       because we wanted in this rather--well--unusual way to
       try to amend our own laws--we never thought about that--
       we thought about seeing that they didn't do anything
       adverse to equality if our government was participating.

Fry: I think this was in reference to the United Nations--

Paul: Of course, we were not members of the United Nations
       when we were over there.

Fry: I mean this was later after World War II, after the
       United Nations had been formed in San Francisco. I
       think it was in reference to the equality-between-the-

Fry: sexes clause.

Paul: Yes. I gave you that little leaflet, didn't I?

Fry: Yes you did, and you told me a short story about getting it in the Preamble of the U.N. Charter in 1945.* Then later, there was a commission established under the Human Rights--

Paul: And we established that; nobody else did that at all but the Woman's Party.

Fry: Now that's what we don't have any information on at all, except what's in Equal Rights magazine. So I hope you can tell me a lot about how that commission functioned.

Paul: Yes. We've never done the whole equal rights [story] from beginning to end. We've never done that at all because we left off with the winning of suffrage, I think.

Fry: Yes. So we want to be sure to bring that in.

Paul: Yes, but that's a later development. It wasn't until 1938 that we formed the World Committee. We first formed the International Committee. The International Committee was just a committee of the Woman's Party. Then we voted in 1938 to form a world committee that would not be just a Woman's Party international committee, but would be one that would take in other countries who wanted to work with us.

But I think that had better come later. We did record our actual work for equal rights, but we weren't far enough along to venture, to try to work in [the story of] other countries.

Fry: All right. I guess I do have a few questions where things aren't quite clear from my reading of the Equal Rights magazines here last night.

Paul: And did you read the first two volumes?

---

*See page 285

Fry: Yes.

Paul: All right, then, let's begin there.

Submitting the ERA the First Time

Fry: All right. You and I have covered a part of that: your
early meetings and the decision and the Seneca Falls
conference and so forth. But I wondered if you could
tell about the first time you submitted the equal rights
measure to Congress.

Paul: Yes, but that will all be in that first issue, if you've
read that.

Fry: I know. I thought maybe you could tell us how you did it
and what efforts it took, and if the response was very
difficult--if it was hard to find a congressman that
would submit it.

Paul: Well, it wasn't a bit difficult because it was right
after the suffrage victory, and anything anybody asked
congressmen to do--anybody connected with the suffrage
victory--they were received with great respect which, as
I told you before, was so totally different from the way
we went up when we were still trying to _get_ suffrage.
The response not only of congressmen but of everybody.
Everybody. Suddenly we were regarded as having some power
in the world. I mean, people were coming to you wanting
you to get things for them. Women were coming wanting
you to have them promoted in the government because they
never could get the positions they thought they ought to
have, and wanting to be appointed as ambassadors and
everything they imagined, we could suddenly have so much
much power. All women began to flock down to Washington
to get for themselves something.

Congressmen began to suddenly have women secretaries:
when I first went there, there was no woman secretary in
all of Congress and they never heard of such a thing. You
walked into an office--all were men. And the press
gallery--you look up and all were men. Everywhere--all
the employees, the people earning their living by being
sent to [work for] Congress were [men], because the
congressmen were trying to build up votes among their

Paul: constituents, who were men. Therefore, if they had a secretarial position paying a good salary, they found some local man. And then they found a local assistant and another and another and another and a telephone operator. It was just a man's world that you walked into in the Capitol.

Fry: Something else on the context of this work in these early years that I wanted to ask you about was the attitude toward constitutional amendments, because at this time Prohibition was in effect through one constitutional amendment and a lot of people were having second thoughts about the ERA, some historians say, as an amendment.

Paul: It was the one just before us, the eighteenth.

Fry: Yes. And there was another constitutional amendment then being attempted for child labor laws. This never was ratified, but it would have been before the judiciary committees at the same time ERA was. (It was a miserable failure.) I wonder if you ran up against a problem of opposition from people who felt that constitutional amendments were getting out of hand.

Paul: No, I never heard of that. [Pause.] You see, when we had this introduced, we had our amendment introduced before we were aware of the lack of support that would come from the women; we didn't really discover that until we had the first hearing. And I told you how much Senator Curtis had helped in the suffrage campaign. He was a very powerful man; he wasn't then vice-president but he was extremely powerful. Maud Younger, who had known him so very well. I showed you the picture of that first dedication of our headquarters which was in about 1922, and I think there was some senator in that photograph that was addressing us, or some congressman.

We were at that moment, while we were putting the Amendment in--it was not really until we had our first hearing that we discovered how really little solidity there was back of this equality movement among women. Congressmen hadn't discovered it. When we asked Senator Curtis, he considered this was a really proper recognition of his great effort in getting the suffrage. And Mr. Anthony thought it was a proper recognition of the great part his family had played in it. And so, there was not any trouble at all about that.

I... y... r ar r w discovered

Paul: all these women arriving, saying--these women who
        nobody had paid the slightest attention to when they
        came to a hearing before because they didn't represent
        anybody, anybody who was a voting power. It was only
        when we could get groups from the few states where women
        did vote--that little group we formed of women voters
        that had the meeting out in California at the fair and
        so on. But normally, if a woman came there [to a
        committee hearing] and asked something, she was just
        put aside as--nobody had to pay any attention to her,
        whether she wanted it or not.

        But this time, at our first hearing after we got
        the vote, everybody came and said, "I represent two
        million women," or whatever she said she represented. Well,
        that was two million voters and was a totally different
        situation than when she came before. So of course, we
        had supposed that when they came with the vote in their
        hand, and they would have this immense effect on Congress
        and that they would all be for complete equality.

        We were [laughing] really thunderstruck when we
        heard them get up and talk about this ridiculous point
        that they wanted to preserve their alimony. It seemed
        to us ridiculous because, of course, they could have
        alimony given to the husband, and it has been given
        to the husbands over and over again since. We didn't
        see what in the world was the matter with these women.

        So that's when we saw that it was perfectly useless
        to go and say, "Will you stand with Senator Curtis?"
        because suddenly all the men were being made aware that
        this was not a very popular measure for the women. And
        the women suddenly caught it.

Fry: That was pretty ironic.

Paul: Most of the thing the women saw in it was to get some-
        thing for themselves, to come down to see if they could
        be secretaries, and they could be clerks of committees.
        Did I tell you about this Mrs. Gilbert, who was phoning
        me the other day from Kentucky? She came from a miner's
        family, from Hungary, who'd settled as mining immigrants
        in the woods up in Pittsburgh. Her family earned enough
        money to send her to a little school down in Washington;
        she went there and learned to be a secretary. She went
        over [laughing] and got a position as a clerk immediately
        and then was married by the chairman of the committee.
        He then ran for governor and died three days before the
        e   ,   d because

Paul: he got the Democratic nomination for governor. It was a state where they were electing only Democrats. So she would, in that short time, [laughing] have been the wife of the governor of one of the great states of the country.

That was what was happening. All these women were dashing down to get something for themselves, and were getting it because they were voters suddenly. That's the reason that you walk in Congress now and you go in the offices, they're largely women.

Whether to Become a Political Party

Fry: When you were trying to get support and so forth and round up any kind of political segments on your side, did you think about the Woman's Party as a regular political party? There's a speech from Mrs. Belmont in which it sounds like she is proposing--and this is very early, like 1921 or something, when she first became president--she was proposing that the National Woman's Party be made into a regular political party, as a third party (or fifth party, or whatever the number was then).

Paul: Well, she always wanted that--I don't mean wanted, but she always thought it would be wise to nominate women for--get the Woman's Party to nominate women for as many offices as we thought we could carry.

Fry: And run them as members of the Woman's Party?

Paul: Yes. And perhaps we could have pushed it further than we did. It was pretty difficult under the election laws to comply with all the things that you had to do in the way of signatures of people to allow you to get on a ballot. She didn't realize, of course, any of those difficulties, and when we--On one occasion, I remember, when she was _very_ anxious to have us do it, and she wanted to run them from the President down, you see. So we made a very careful study of what we had to do. At that particular time we couldn't do it because the time limit made it impossible. You had to, a considerable time before you put your candidate in the field, you know you had to comply with so many requirements in the way of bona fide signatures from citizens of that

Paul:　You couldn't just walk out and say, "I'm going to become President of the United States and I'm going to put my name up."

　　　　If it was going to be put up by some group calling itself anything under the sun--if any labor group now tries to get a party--they all find the same thing, as you well know, I'm sure.

Fry:　Did you ever consider throwing yourselves into one of the already established political parties, and in that way working--

Paul:　As I told you, at our first convention when we decided to go on, this is of course was what many people--if they were Democrats they wanted us to throw our strength in the Democratic party, Republicans into the Republican party. We wanted nothing but equality; we couldn't very well suddenly consolidate [ourselves] with the--the people who were most anxious to do it was the Progressive party; they had made themselves finally into a party and had given wholehearted support to us.

　　　　I think, Mr. J. A. H. Hopkins, if I remember rightly--you know, when you think something from forty years ago, [laughing] it's hard suddenly to remember it, when you see you haven't thought of it once since. But I believe it was Mr. J. A. H. Hopkins, who was the husband of Alison Hopkins, who was our New Jersey state chairman--this was a quite wealthy man and had a marvelous wife who went to prison with us. He therefore became very much interested. He had succeeded in getting his Progressive party actually recognized as a party, complying with everything about the number of members they had to have and so on. He was very determined to do everything he could to get the Woman's Party, when it came to having a new program after suffrage won, for having them vote to join his Progressive party, as a party. We would throw all our strength and money and any power we had into building up this Progressive party. I don't know how he was going to work it out but that's what he wanted.

　　　　That's just to answer your question, "Did they ever really contemplate it?" Well, we didn't contemplate it but he did.

Fry:　But it was never really seriously discussed or anything by the Woman's Party?

Paul: Oh yes, it was discussed by us, because they came to us and spoke before us, he did and other representatives, and showed all the merits of our being able to take a bigger part in political life more quickly and easily if we identified ourselves with a <u>successful</u> group that <u>had</u> been able to start in as a political party. But then it would have committed us to all of their programs, you see, and we wanted to stick to <u>one</u> program. We thought we could do it better--and I think it was the right decision--much better by just sticking to the issue and trying to get all parties to take it up, than to become a part of one party which has many issues.

Whether to Support Women Candidates

Fry: Yes. In 1924, you chose the course of trying to get women [to run and be] elected to Congress. Do you remember that?

Paul: I wouldn't say that.

Fry: It seemed to be a big push [according to the <u>Equal Rights</u> newsletter].

Paul: No, no; I wouldn't say that. We may have made more of an effort for somebody, but we <u>always</u> tried to get women elected to Congress. [Pause.] That was two years after we put the Amendment in; maybe that was the first time we ever went into a--

For instance, one of the people who worked hardest to get elected was Anne Martin; I don't know what year that was. We really put a great deal of power and effort into getting her into the Senate. Her papers will show what year it was. We sent out Mabel Vernon and other people to help her. We raised money for it, and we gave her a large farewell luncheon in Washington at which Julia Lathrop, I remember, opened with a speech. She was the head then of the Children's Bureau; you know who she was. And we had many people wanting us to go in. If we'd had more money and more women and more strength, of course we could have done <u>better</u> in that. We had a <u>constant</u> series of women coming and wanting us to go into their election campaigns and help.

Fry: In doing this, did--

Paul: But we just couldn't do all.

I remember one woman coming to us, and she wanted to come to Congress--but she was such an un--we didn't know her; we just knew she existed. But she came down to Washington-- and she was very insistent. And I remember saying to her, "But just why? You've never helped in our campaign; you've never done anything particularly to connect to [it]. Of all the women in the United States--so many other women--why would we suddenly start in and do all these things you're asking us to do for your election campaign up in New York?"

And she said, "Well, you see, if you should say you'd want to run for Congress in my district, you could never be elected. Maybe you could be elected somewhere, but you could certainly never be elected in my district, and I probably can be elected.

I said, "Well, just why do you think you could be elected so easily?"

She said, "You see, I live in a Hungarian district and my husband is a Hungarian, and I am (something else) I am a Jewess, (let's say). I can get all the Jewish vote; he can get all the Hungarian vote, and I think I can be elected if I can get the support of some well-known group of women."

So we had these all the time, but we didn't--I thought she was a purely selfish immigrant who'd arrived in this country and wanted to use us for her own personal advantage. She didn't even have any principle she was trying to further or anything, but thought it would be nice to be a congresswoman and have an enormous salary and not have anything to do but to go down and sit in Congress. So we had all types who wanted us to help.

Fry: I thought maybe there was a problem of getting women to run, because there weren't very many women candidates that year, just as there are not now. I understood there were Woman's Party organizers who went out to try to find women in the states to run.

Paul: No, we never did that. Our problem was finding enough money and workers to help effectively. We didn't want to go into a campaign and say we were going to help them and not be able to help them.

Paul: I remember Izetta Jewel Miller. I worked very hard myself, I must say, on trying to _get_ enough money and enough help for the women that we did try, but I don't think there was too much enthusiasm. I can remember one time--I was _sorry_ about this--Izetta Jewel Miller, one of the _very finest_ members we had ever had in all our lives or ever could have (her painting, you know, is up in the living room)--

Fry: Yes; beautiful woman.

Paul: And a wonderful woman, absolutely superb. You have regrets, as you look back at the things you didn't accomplish. One regret that I have is that we didn't get Izetta Jewel Miller into Congress. She wanted very much to be a congressman. Certainly if I had been down there in Washington at that time, I would certainly have, I think, devoted all the time I had and strength I had to getting the money and getting the women in doing this.

Fry: Where were you?

Paul: I guess I was probably over in Europe, but I wasn't anywhere in Washington. After I ceased to be national chairman, I just came and went when there seemed to be some crisis. But I remember coming back and finding that Izetta Jewel had asked wouldn't we come down to her state, send speakers, and you know this is a lot of work to do and a lot of money to raise. Because in order to get the speakers down you have at least to raise the money for their traveling expenses and such. I know what it cost when we helped Anne Martin; it was a very expensive campaign for us, sending out all the things that we had to send. So, that board at that particular moment just shrugged its shoulders and said that nobody could undertake all that had to be done; we just said we couldn't help her. She ran anyway, but she was defeated.

Fry: Oh. Earlier than that, wasn't she the lady from West Virginia who was the first one to speak before a national political convention?

Paul: First one to preside.

Fry: She presided at the--Republican convention? if my memory is correct on this. So she must have had a pretty powerful--

Paul: I don't remember which one she presided at, but she was a Democrat, so she must have presided at the Democratic National Convention.

Fry: She's the one who was so remarkable because she _was_ the first. Of course, they didn't let her preside for a very long period, but long enough anyway to preside-- she's the one that I told you that didn't even understand how to use a microphone. She talked to the person next to her and said, "I'm going to tell my little daughter; she'll be so proud. And wouldn't Susan B. Anthony be proud if she could see me standing here!" The whole little colloquy went out over the whole great audience with not the faintest idea on her part that we'd heard the whole colloquy that she'd entered in with her neighbor there. [Laughing.] It was so sweet and charming.

Fry: When you were thinking about these women running, and supporting women for Congress, were you going to support them whether they were for the Equal Rights Amendment or not?

Paul: No, we certainly wouldn't have ever dreamed of doing such a thing. Anyway, nobody would have ever _asked_ us unless she was assuring us that she would support it.

Fry: I thought at first you planned--

Paul: Nobody in this whole world ever had any idea that we would do such a terrible thing as betray the woman's movement by trying to put somebody in Congress who was not for equality for women. It was unthinkable!

Fry: Okay. One of the books says that at first the Woman's Party planned to support _all_ women candidates, regardless of their position on the Equal Rights Amendment.*

Paul: No.

Fry: And then after that you narrowed down to just those who'd already come out for it.

Paul: Well, they needn't have _already_ come out for it. You

O'Neill, William O., _Everyone Was Brave, The Rise and Fall of Feminism in America_, Quadrangle Books, Chicago, 1969; p. 283.

Paul: know the type of women that are in the women's movement; you can't conceive of it. Suppose you were working for temperance; you don't suddenly get somebody who's never showed the slightest interest in the temperance movement and try to put them in. WCTU [Women's Christian Temperance Union] wouldn't do such a preposterous thing.

Fry: I know, I agree it doesn't make sense. Was the idea that you would campaign to get women to vote exclusively for members of their own sex, regardless of the party?

Paul: What?

Fry: I was wondering if the idea behind this was to urge women to vote for members of their own sex, regardless of the party. Such as in the suffrage campaign.

Paul: You mean that after we tried to assist somebody--

Fry: For Congress.

Paul: When Anne Martin was running for the Senate, of course we tried to elect her; I suppose the people out there who conducted the campaign--she naturally directed her own campaign--would be to get--she told what her platform was, what she would stand for, and I don't exactly see [what you mean]. Would we ask women to vote for her regardless of her party? She was running on the Democratic ticket, I imagine; I don't know, but I presume it was. The people we sent out to help her were probably guided by her wishes of whom to ask, where to campaign. We didn't try to direct a campaign of anybody, you know. If they wanted our help and we wanted them to succeed, we tried to furnish them with whatever things they needed.

Fry: For instance, when Mabel was sent around the country in 1924 to help women who were running and to encourage others to run, did--

Paul: I don't know that we ever went in for that purpose particularly.

Fry: I was wondering at that point, Alice, if you could remember what you and--

[End of Tape 14, Side B]

[Tape 15, Side A. May 12, 1973]

Wording and Intended Meanings of the ERA

Paul: There's really not too much necessity, I guess, for us
going into those years because we were paying off
this--I was staying in a little rooming house with Maud
Younger; we got a little tiny apartment together. I
started to pay off all our debts and she started to
begin mainly on how to start the new campaign with
Congress. So there wasn't anything but sort of prepara-
tory work; there wasn't anything the Woman's Party was
doing but just sort of cooperating. And Elsie Hill
was then our national chairman, so I don't see there's
much to say about that.

   I mean, we were submitting possible amendments.
We weren't doing much ourselves but we were asking
possible advisers, like Dean Pound of Harvard and so
on, to tell us how to get equality because they voted
it, of course in 1923, on the one that we drew up ourselves because nobody had ever drafted anything for us.

   For all that period, Elsie Hill, as I told you,
met her husband and she married by going down to the
George Washington University and seeing the law
professor of domestic relations to ask how in the world
we should present something to Congress; we don't know
what to present.

   He undertook to draw up something. Then we
asked Mrs. Lawrence Lewis's son who belonged to a very
prominent law firm in Philadelphia (but don't put that
down; I don't want to get his name into it because we
didn't use his draft); that's just to tell you what we
were busy about.

Fry: This is Seneca Falls before 1923 when you were first
trying to draw it up?

Paul: Yes. This was between 1920--The first thing we did was
start to try to remove discrimination by going to the
state legislatures. We did get a great many of them
removed. If I can find them before you go, I must get
you this little history that nobody seems to have given
you; it's gotten out by the New York City committee--
chronological history giving the dates and the number
of bills we got through and all of that. It was gotten
out I guess about 1960 or something.

Fry: Maybe this is it by Dora Ogle?

Paul: No; it was done by the New York City committee. By Nina Broderick Price, the one I was telling you to go see. The New York City committee paid for it, published it, and drew it up.

Fry: That would be very helpful if we could have it.

Paul: I had it here; I showed it to somebody the other day. I'll try to go through some of these papers before you go and get them for you; they have all the dates.

Fry: In the meantime, I have this that will cover us up to 1949, which is a very thorough chronology.

Paul: I'm not so sure whether it's very accurate because Mrs. Ogle was very faithful and a very good worker, but she was--she wasn't any too good on accuracy. She had wonderful, wonderful spirit. She had very bad diabetes and would go into comas and just pass out completely.

[Interruption for lunch.]

Fry: I wanted to read into the record the resolution from Seneca Falls. It says:

> "Be it resolved that in order to bring the complete equal rights ideal to the victory that was won for suffrage, we undertake the following program: the securing of an amendment to the United States Constitution stating, 'Men and women shall have equal rights throughout the United States and every place subject to its jurisdiction.'"

So that was the version you were using then.

Paul: I made that speech, you know, and presented this resolution.

Fry: Yes, that was yours.

Paul: Yes. We did this because, at that time, we had--for two years of Maud Younger and Elsie Hill had been going around trying to get an authority to formulate

Paul: something for us. They hadn't formulated anything that we were willing to accept. And so it seemed as though, which usually happens you finally have to do it yourself. Then I just drew up one myself.

I stated in this whole speech that these were just the ideals we were to strive for, put into ordinary, simple English. I think it was about that time that I decided to go to law school myself so I would know a little bit how to do this. And I did, as you know; I got a bachelor's degree and a master's degree and a doctor's degree, thinking each time desperately, "Maybe I'll learn a little more."

But I didn't learn very much [laughing]. But at least it gave you a feeling that you could talk to these lawyers and that you would know what you were talking about.

When I presented that resolution, I don't think I'd started law school. I think I was just putting the idea before them of what we were going to try to put in. Then we always took the position that if we could change the wording to make it any better, it could be done; that the wording wasn't final but that the idea of what we were trying to put in the Constitution was. That showed its purpose perfectly.

I think it was about '43 when I came back from Europe and so on and I found we weren't making any progress really with the Judiciary Committee and I thought, "Now we can get down to the question of wording. They're taking it seriously because they've agreed to put it on their national platforms, both Republican and Democrat." And that's when we had the final version, which we drew up ourselves.

Again we couldn't get anybody on the committee. I remember going to see Senator Burton once, who later was on the Supreme Court. He was then a senator. This is one of the first things I did when I came back and became a chairman.

I said, "Just why is it you never get to the point of changing this amendment if you are not willing to pass it in the form that would be best, not only to get what we want but to have a possibility of being adopted by Congress?"

Paul: I remember he said, "Senator Austin and I have
worked and worked and worked and worked and worked and
worked on this wording, and we can't seem to arrive at
anything that would be what you want to accomplish and
still be a possibility of getting it through Congress."

So then, after we found that nobody showed any
signs of ever drafting anything on the committee itself,
as though we'd never get it through because they'd
say--

[Interruption--food brought in.]

Paul: And that's the way we finally got the present one; we
drew it up ourselves and we took it down to Senator
Austin--Mrs. Roy [?] and I took it--and he said that
as far as he was concerned, it was perfect. If Senator
O'Mahoney would support it, who was leading on the
Democratic side--Austin was Republican--with the new
wording, he would bring it before the committee. That's
the present wording--"equality of rights under the law"--

It appeared that the problem of the Judiciary
Committee and of the friends that we had--not people
opposed to equality but friends who were only working
on the points of--like Burton and Austin--of getting it
through--said the main difficulty was that in "men and
women shall have equal rights throughout the United
States and every place subject to its jurisdiction,"
there's a problem of how Congress can establish equal
rights, which means complete equality, in fields in
which Congress has no--nothing to do.

Fry: No jurisdiction?

Paul: Saying "equality shall not be denied by Congress or by
any state" government it meant. And then if equality
was denied by some church or by some individual in his
home--the main thing we would have gotten, which was
preventing government that did have jurisdiction from
ever doing anything that was contrary to the equality
program. And we did it, really, by basing it on the
suffrage amendment which was drawn up the same way.
"The rights of the citizens of the United States to vote
shall not be denied or abridged by the United States or
by any state on the grounds of sex."

So we said this has been sustained in every way, is
now accepted as far as the Constitution. If we use the

Paul: same wording and instead of the "right to vote." put "equality of rights under the law"--(We put in our draft "equality of rights before the law" and that was the only change that was made in the form we submitted.

Fry: What's the difference between "before the law" and "under the law"? Is that significant?

Paul: Well, Mr. Austin and Mr. O'Mahoney accepted "before the law." Then we took it over to Judge Sumner, chairman of the House Judiciary [Committee], whom we knew extremely well over the years, and he said that he thought we'd better say "under the law."

The Judiciary [Committee] of the Senate was willing to take "under the law," and since it was apparently going to get more support in the House by saying "under the law" [we used it]. I think "before the law" perhaps isn't quite as thorough-going and all-covering; it would mean people coming before the law with their problems and so on, rather than "under the law" being everything that is in the legal field at all.

So we accepted that. Then Senator Austin said, "Now I'm not going to propose this to the Committee unless I know that all the women's organizations are going to be in accord."

Fry: Before you get to that part, can I ask you one more question on this wording and the intent of it? I remember that one of the arguments against the Equal Rights Amendment is that it only pertains to equality of treatment in the federal government or in state government jobs and positions and things like that. How limited is its effect, if it gets ratified?

Paul: All legal matters; anything that's under the law.

Fry: Would it pertain to a private business practice?

Paul: Yes; everything.

Fry: It would?

Paul: It cannot be denied by the federal government or the state government on the grounds of sex. That is, you can have all the inequalities in a private business you wanted [pause] if that business is not an area in which the state government and the federal government have
s   .   come

Paul: under some general business codes and so on in the
        state, and not just the people [who] are employed by
        the government, but all businesses. I guess there's
        almost nothing that isn't licensed in some way or
        another, where the government's voice appears. [Pause.]

        If the state government, we'll say, on the ground
        of sex--this particular business you're talking about--
        would be considered as having denied or abridged equality
        on the ground of sex, if the code under which this
        particular thing were operating--say their right to give
        a license--the state would be denying it [equality of
        rights] by having a business operating under its own
        code that was denying it. Do I make it clear?

Fry: I see. That's quite clear.

Paul: Of course, that's the reason we're having all the opposi-
        tion.

Fry: Because it does pertain to private business, is that it?

Paul: Yes. For instance, the American Tel and Tel (isn't it
        called?) [American Telephone and Telegraph Company]--
        their vice-president came down and testified at a
        hearing where we testified--Louise Gore testified for
        us--very recently. This was a question of whether they
        could continue their present policy of having pensions
        that did discriminate on the ground of sex. The vice-
        president of the American Tel and Tel spoke for continu-
        ing the present policy of allowing lower pensions to
        women than to men. This is what the vice-president said
        in his speech, which he made quite briefly down in a
        meeting in the Labor Department:

        He said he'd suffered tremendous loss when they
        gave equal pay under the equal pay bill, which went
        through in Congress; the Amendment hadn't gone through,
        but the equal pay bill had. It doesn't cover everything
        but it happened to cover the American Tel and Tel. He
        said, "We have such an enormous number of women employees
        that when we had to put the salaries of all these women
        employees--telephone operators--over the whole United
        States up to the point that we were paying the men, it
        almost bankrupted us.

        We have now a new proposal that's being agitated
        and the Labor Department is now looking into it, in
        which they propose that all people who are no longer
        em[ ]   ]   , "all

Paul: have the same pensions. If they do this, with the
great pension burden now on the American Tel and Tel,
we don't know whether we can survive. It will certainly
be a great cost to our stockholders and a great cost to
the American public, who'll have to pay higher telephone
bills every month. And whether this equal pay bill,
which requires equality in payment in certain occupa-
tions including ours, but says nothing about pensions--
it says 'shall not be any lower pay for telephone
operators'; it doesn't say 'for [pensioners?]'"
[laughter]--the pension business.

Then Senator Dirksen made the report from the
commitee before [whom] the whole problem was pending
recommending that it should not include the pensions.
and that bill didn't go through because Congress
adjourned before it got to the bill. But it was
reported from the committee, advocating only the
existing people should not be paid less.

All these problems, of course, are making a new
group who are rather opposed to the Amendment because
they foresee, with the experience they've had with the
equal pay, which was rather small and limited--but still
it gives them enough damage for them not to want to
see it made into a federal amendment which would cover
everything. That's a little side thing that's not
very important, I guess, but--

Fry: Except it is a big problem because we must have many,
many industries that have been set up and run with
expenditures set for lower pay for women than for men,
and it's going to be very painful for them to switch
over and also include equal pensions and everything
else.

Paul: Yes. That's just a concrete illustration today of the
people who would normally be for the principle, but
there's certainly great difficulties. Well now, what's
your next question?

Fry: I notice there is a new name who introduced it in the
Seventieth Congress, which was 1928 and part of '29.
Then it was still introduced by Representative Frederick
W. McGrady of Pennsylvania, and I wondered if he was a
new friend, at that point.

Paul: I remember that, but I know I was in Europe when he
introduced it. We had somebody down there working from
Pennsylvania who asked him. I suppose Mr. Anthony hadn't

Paul: run or had been defeated--I don't know.

BEGINNINGS OF INTERNATIONAL WORK

Fry: I'd like to go into the story of how the whole inter-
       national aspect of the Woman's Party got started.

Paul: I think we'd better finish up equal rights--

Fry: You mean the national?

Paul: --because it was, oh, much later, in 1938, that we voted
       in our national convention held in Detroit, Michigan,
       [that] in addition to having an international committee
       as we had all during this period--a Woman's Party
       International Committee--to try to form something that
       would be like the other organizations. [Women's
       International League for] Peace and Freedom was inter-
       national; the International Suffrage Alliance was
       international. We thought we had formed so many
       contacts, had so many friends, were doing so much in
       the international field, that it would be a good thing
       to do. So we voted that.

Fry: Well, I'm talking about the international work that got
       started in the twenties, when--

Paul: Well, we did it first by just doing it where our own
       government took part in [an international] conference,
       having an international committee that would handle
       that subject.

Fry: You told me about the one in 1926 with the International
       Suffrage Alliance.

Paul: Oh, we didn't mean international in that sense. That
       was an international woman's organization that we had
       been invited to join, and we returned now when we got
       there. Then we did join another one, which was the
       International Council of Women; we're still members,

Paul: unless Mrs. Chittick has refused to pay the dues.   But
         until I left we were still members.

Fry: You joined it in the twenties?

Paul: I don't know what year we joined, but it was founded
         in Washington in 1888. That was the first international
         gathering of women I guess ever held in the world, and
         it was held in Washington in 1888 and formed the Inter-
         national Council of Women. That's before there was
         any Woman's Party, of course. The leaders in doing it
         were Susan B. Anthony and all the people associated
         with her, and Frances Willard and all the people associ-
         ated with her, and May Wright Sewall of Indiana and
         all the people associated with her.

             These women were the foremost women in the woman's
         movement, in different fields of course. Frances Willard
         was in the field of temperance and Susan B. Anthony in
         the field of the franchise. But they worked together
         on all these things. I mean they were equally working
         for the vote. So that's a very famous meeting--1888 in
         Washington--and that was the date of the beginning of the
         International Council of Women, the first in the world,
         long before the International Suffrage Alliance was
         formed.

Fry: Was the National Woman's Party officially involved in
         the meeting of the Pan American Republics in Cuba in
         1928?

Paul: Yes. I told you how we sent down a delegation because
         they were bringing up the subject of something to do
         with the status of women; it was on the agenda, and
         we certainly didn't want our government going down there
         entering into international relations with all these
         Latin American countries on something affecting the status
         of women without much knowing what they were doing.

             We went down and there's a photograph in the chair-
         man's office of the national headquarters of Mrs.
         Clarence Smith, who was our national chairman at the time
         and who led our delegation down there, directing the
         whole plenipotentiary conference, and we've noticed it.

Fry: And then they elected Doris Stevens as their first
         chairman?

Paul: No no no. We went down to present the equal rights

HEADQUARTERS, WORLD WOMAN'S PARTY
Geneva, Switzerland

Paul: treaty, which by this time we had formulated. Maybe
we formulated it _at_ that time. "The contracting
states undertake that men and women shall have equal
rights throughout their respective countries," all
the countries agreeing to this international treaty.
We proposed an equal rights treaty there, and I believe
that was the first time we proposed it. I think this
photograph shows Mrs. Clarence Smith presenting it to
this whole conference of plenipotentiaries, including
our delegation--United States delegation. That's the
reason we went, because our delegation was going to be
called upon to act on this subject, so we thought we'd
watch over them.

And then they defeated this proposal that Mrs.
Smith put before them--our whole delegation put before
them, our whole Woman's Party delegation. When they
defeated it, we then proposed that the Conference of
American Republics set up a commission--it had
commissions on highways and everything--a commission on
the status of women to study this problem, because we
couldn't get the treaty itself, but to study the
problem of a treaty on equal rights for men and women,
and that it should be called the Inter-American Commission on the Status of Women. I think that was the
title.

That went through. The person who perhaps did
most to get it through was James Brown Scott who was
one of the delegates and who became a deep, _warm_
supporter of our whole equality campaign when we asked
him to help us down there get this commission set up.
So they voted then to set it up.

Dr. Scott had great power, as I said before to you
when I talked to you, there because he was president
of the World whatever it's called--International Law
Association. So it was set up and it's continued.
And I wanted to tell you they had not so very long ago
an anniversary meeting and they asked to have a delegation come up to the Woman's Party headquarters and thank
us publicly for having founded the Inter-American
Commission of Women, because of course we _did_ do it.
In the beginning we paid all the bills that they had;
then we persuaded the Pan-American Union to give them
an office, and gradually they got sort of established
within the organization. So now they're all on their
own; we don't have to do anything more for them.

Paul: Have you any questions about all that? But I'd
         much rather, if we could, go ahead with equal rights;
         I'm so afraid that that'll get left out if we don't.

Fry: All right. I thought it was kind of significant that
         by the mid-twenties you did have a definite interest
         in the international thing. And then you left for
         Europe--

Paul: You know if your government is starting to make treaties
         that involve the United States' treatment of women, you
         have to watch over it; you haven't any choice. But
         incidentally, it's helped us, I think, to get to know
         the women of other countries and so on.

              All the time I was in Europe, I was put on the
         International Council of Women ever since we joined them.
         They had an International Council of Women Committee on
         Laws, I think they called it, and every country had a
         right to put one woman on. Mrs. Clarence Smith was the
         chairman at the time; so she wrote to them and said
         that our country was asking that I be put on because I
         was the only woman in our organization staying over
         there at the League in Europe and could go to their
         meetings.

              So they put me on this International Laws Committee,
         and all the time I was over there--I'd not only authority
         to represent our National Woman's Party at home (and we
         had no standing in any possible way because we were not
         a member of the League, you see; our country wasn't a
         member) but then by being on their International Laws
         Committee, I could also speak for the International
         Council of Women.

Fry: I see, and did you find that this really did help in
         your work?

Paul: Of course, it helps greatly to have a formal close
         connection with the oldest and biggest international
         woman's organization in the world, because it is the
         oldest and the biggest, far and away the largest. In
         most countries in Europe, the suffrage movement wasn't
         so developed, and so the International Suffrage Alliance
         was a very small group very often, but every country that
         I knew of had a big flourishing Council of Women.

              Therefore it is important for us to retain our
         membership in it. But we had an unceasing campaign at

Paul: Two hundred dollars a year to this International
       Council of Women and what's it doing for us?" So we
       have a little battle every year, and I'm not so sure
       when I'm going out but what they'll drop paying their
       two hundred dollars; then we'll be out. It's something
       I've got to look into.

       [End of Tape 15, Side A]

       [Tape 15, Side B not recorded on]

ENDORSEMENTS OF ERA

Minnesota Farm Labor Party

[Tape 16, Side A. May 12, 1973.]

Fry: We were talking about the Minnesota Farm Labor Party
        endorsement, Alice, which was your first.

Paul: It wasn't anything very important. I was out there at
        the time and I remember. Wherever we went, we tried to
        get endorsements. It was just part of the general
        endorsement campaign. And the Farm Labor Party was
        strongly supported by our national chairman, I mean our
        state chairman, Mrs. Sarah Colvin (who later became our
        national chairman) and I stayed with her and heard all
        about the importance—stayed in her home as her guest
        while I was there, and I heard all about the importance
        of the rising Farmer Labor Party that they thought
        might become a great force in the country.

        We had this one member in the legislature, I think
        she was in the legislature, Myrtle [Cain? or King?] and
        so she took the main part in actually getting the
        endorsement. Later she did so well in that that we put
        her on our national board and she became one of our
        national board members. And in this recent campaign that
        we had for [Senator Eugene] McCarthy when he became our
        chief sponsor and a candidate and supposedly was going
        to make a great effort to put the Equal Rights Amendment
        through (which he didn't turn out to do) but at all
        events, we tried to help in his primary.

Fry: When he was running for President?

Paul: When he was running for President. And Myrtle [Cain? or
        King?] at that time was in charge of his Minnesota
        office right just now when we were working with him. So

Paul: she has continued all these years, and now she's our state chairman, you know, in Minnesota.

Fry: A little bit before this, Wisconsin passed a state statute on equal rights, but I think it included an exception so that it didn't cover all women.

Paul: How do you mean, a state one?

Fry: I think in 1922 Wisconsin passed a state law on equal rights, although it had a--

Paul: They did, but they had exceptions. It was not completely-- you know this is the time that we drafted the laws for all the whole forty-eight states as fast as we could do it. And we got one ready for Wisconsin because we had a very extraordinarily active group up there in Wisconsin at that moment, and they undertook to get the whole state to do it, to make it the first in the country.

Fry: Was this the same group of women who enabled Wisconsin to be the first one to ratify the suffrage amendment?

Paul: Well, they all worked together. But the person who ran this campaign was a person named Mabel Putnam. (You'll find her in the [Equal Rights magazine]--and one who helped a great deal was this writer--I told you about her before, now what was her name. I will think of her in a minute. I have told you about her before because she did so much in that first Equal Rights Amendment campaign out there when it was put in in Wisconsin. Let's go on to something else.

Fry: It was kind of interesting in Seneca Falls; I think someone proposed a resolution to try to get this exception removed from the Wisconsin statute at that point.

Paul: The one that we drew up and that they offered [in Wisconsin] was complete equality and I think it was--I know it was in the field of labor, whether it was ex- cepting employees of the state legislature or what I don't remember, but it was something. It was added in the legislature itself, we didn't get it [our version] through. But this was the first equal rights law in the country, passed after we began our campaign.

National Association of Women Lawyers

Fry: The National Association of Women Lawyers endorsed you.

Paul: Yes, and that was because in Washington we had so many
       women lawyers, they had the convention out in California
       and Burnita Matthews was the national president and she
       submitted it. I was a member of it [NAWL] then and I
       went to the meeting in Washington where we drew up the
       plan of trying to get the first endorsement, I guess it
       was the first endorsement we had of any organization.
       Perhaps not the first because some of them just auto-
       matically went right over from the suffrage, which I
       told you was the National Association of Colored Women
       who worked in the suffrage campaign, and the women
       doctors.

Fry: I thought woman doctors came in in 1943, about ten
       years later. Maybe it was a different--was there
       another group in the early twenties?

Paul: I think I told you about having a meeting of this joint
       committee we formed, because they had always been with
       us. I don't think that they ever varied from starting
       with us in the suffrage campaign.

Fry: Oh, I see. That is why they show up in 1943, because
       they responded to this joint legislative committee--to
       be a member of it.

Paul: Yes, we sent this invitation to all the societies that
       were working for it and they were the ones who were
       willing to join this committee. The others who were
       working for it of course still didn't want to join the
       committee in the beginning.

Fry: At any rate Burnita Matthews I guess was the main worker
       for getting the women lawyers' endorsement?

Paul: We didn't have any trouble. All the women lawyers we
       knew were for the Amendment. There weren't too many
       women lawyers in the country, you know.

Fry: What about the American Bar Association? Did you have
       a lot of trouble with that one?

Paul: It is one of the last ones we've gotten. I don't feel
       we had trouble, but we were at it and got it in

Paul: their opinion I guess to think much about us. We had it introduced year after year, but it was rather ignored because they thought it would never materialize into being a reality. But recently they did endorse. It is one of the newcomers.

National Federation of Business and Professional Women's Clubs

Fry: As near as I could tell, the next endorsement after the National Association of Women Lawyers--which was early thirties--was 1937, the National Federation of Business and Professional Women's Clubs.

Paul: That is right.

Fry: Business and professional women are not "working" women in labor unions. I wonder what their objection was for so long. Were they objecting to the ERA threat to the protective legislation anyway?

Paul: They _supported_ it at all events--special labor laws. I'd like to tell you these things for yourself, but I don't like to put them down as source material for other people.

Fry: Okay, let's label this for my record only.

Paul: Well, you can put _that_, because that is known to everybody.

[Miss Frances] Perkins at that time was secretary of labor and in the cabinet, the first woman ever in the cabinet, and the whole administration was for special labor laws as a result. Mrs. Roosevelt was. Miss Perkins was in the Labor Department under Roose-- velt and was taking a very strong stand for special labor laws for women. And the Business and Professional--is it off now?

Fry: No, it is on.

Paul: Can you turn it off for a minute?

Fry: I was wondering if you couldn't explain, in a way that you felt was innocuous, about the very interesting thing that some of the women's organizations were more

Fry: interested in getting their officers into highly-paid
       government positions, and you felt then that this
       interfered with their support for the ERA movement.

Paul: [About the Business and Professional Women's Clubs'
       endorsement] Is all this being taken down now?

Fry: Do you want me to turn it off?

Paul: If you would like really to know what happened, I'd
       like to tell you.

Fry: Okay. But I won't _remember_ it, Alice. I would like
       to take it down, but just mark it.

Paul: I don't want you to remember it, but I would like you
       to _know_--have a real picture in your own mind of what
       this fight was.

Fry: Can't I tape it and we will just mark it not to tran-
       scribe?

Paul: No. No. It might get transcribed by mistake.

Fry: Okay.

       [Tape off.]

The Women's Bureau (Department of Labor) vs. the ERA

Fry: About the 1926 Women's Industrial Conference that left
       equal rights off its agenda, and Gail Laughlin and
       Mabel Vernon managed to get the floor so that there was
       debate on ERA from the _floor_: now do you remember that?

Paul: Yes, very well. That wasn't anything very important,
       though.

Fry: Well, I guess it was important in that it showed the
       attitude at the time of the difficulty of dealing with
       something like the Women's Industrial Conference on the
       ERA.

Paul: Oh, it wasn't anything important. It was just a tiny
       little conference in Washington. It was under the
       auspices of the Women's Bureau. They were always having

Paul: these conferences all the time, you know. They had all
         the financial backing of the United States government,
         they could send letters everywhere and get people to
         come down to conferences, and this was just one of
         many, many, many.

         And at this one we deliberately--deliberately
         thought we would just would go into the enemy camp
         because the Women's Bureau was the enemy camp, one of
         the great enemy camps of the Amendment. And at this
         conference, Gail Laughlin was going to be in Washington
         and she was a very outspoken person for--she was
         passionate, one of the leading people in the country, in
         opposing special labor laws for women. So we thought it
         would be--I imagine that that was the reason that we
         particularly thought of doing it while she was there.
         And she was the leading, only outside person that we
         had there. She came down from Maine and was a member,
         I think, of the Maine legislature. Anyway she was a
         very prominent Woman's Party member, and she was one
         who had converted probably most of the Woman's Party
         leaders in the beginning before anybody was thinking
         about it. She was out there campaigning against special
         labor laws for women, long before we ever knew there
         was such a problem.

Fry: That's good to know that she had also played that role.
         Well, this was written up in the book as quite a
         sensational thing.

Paul: What book is that?

Fry: I'll have to check the bibliography. It's one that
         came out quite recently on the women's movement.*

Paul: I wanted to tell you that when I was out in California
         the first, I guess, first time I met Gail Laughlin.
         She lived in California, you know, a long time. After
         she graduated from I think it was Wellesley, she went
         out with a very close friend she had who lived in San
         Francisco and they worked together out there in
         California for the vote. So when we came out for that
         1915 [Panama Pacific] Fair she was, of course, a leading
         California woman that we got in touch with.

         _____

         O'Neill, William L., Opus oit., pp. 283-85.
         See also Equal Rights, January 30, 1926.

Paul: I remember she began right away to talk about the
subject that was so dear to her heart, to get women away
from the special protective laws and to stand for
complete equality and so on. We were only thinking
about getting the <u>vote</u> then. And I remember so vividly
meeting her, and of course it was all a new idea to me.
I hadn't thought about special labor laws once at all,
hadn't thought about it at <u>all</u>. Of course I knew that
when I lived in the college settlement, people were
taking these special protective laws for women for
granted. We didn't hear any discussion of it.

    And I remember that I said, "Well, will you just
explain it all to me." And she said, "No, I don't
think I will explain it to you. All you have to do is
just think about it, that's all you do, do nothing but
think and then you will know."

    So I proceeded [laughing] to think about it, and I
just felt, "Well, how true this is. I can't think of a
reason in the world why we <u>should</u> have the special
labor laws for women." It became very clear to me. So
that was the way she--I guess she talked to everybody.
But she was the great leader in thought in that field.

    And so it was probably for that reason that we
asked her to go to this conference, I imagine. It was
a conference to which anybody could go, a government
conference, to discuss this subject. And she was a
great speaker, and of course a lawyer, and knew all
about parliamentary law and [laughing] how to hold the
floor--get the floor and hold the floor--so everybody
that we could think of that we could persuade to take
the time to go down to the conference, we sent so she
would have some supporters.

    As far as I can remember, she got up and made some
kind of a motion, something that gave her the floor to
speak on her favorite topic [laughing]. It was such a
relief to us to find somebody else who wanted to get
up and talk about this subject so we didn't have to do
it. So she did, she took the floor, and she had a plan
by which she turned it over to somebody else--

Fry: I think Mabel Vernon was there.

Paul: Was she? Well, I don't remember, but probably she was.
If you have her name, she probably was. She was in
Washington, so it would be very natural for her to go
t- - - ' ' , , , w ' .t', u ' -' 'p aker.

Paul: She had a voice that could be heard everywhere. So
whenever we had anything when speaking came in, we
always asked Mabel to be sure to be there. She was a
very eloquent speaker, I thought. But especially, she
had this wonderful voice.

So anyway, whether they could speak or not, seems
that Miss Laughlin had some plan which she devised which
[laughing] was proper from a parliamentary point of
view and, I suppose, having been probably in the legislature already (I'm not sure about that though) that
she knew how to manipulate these things. But somehow
or other she contrived to grant some time to somebody
else, as far as I can recall.

Having gotten the floor, I suppose, in a perfectly
normal way, then she granted some of her time to someone
else, so they kept on, just capturing the whole meeting
with a protest against the Women's Bureau. And so the
result was (and I suppose you know all that--probably
they put it in this article that you were talking about)
that--Hoover was President then and certainly was very
much of a supporter of the Equal Rights Amendment when
he stopped to think about it; every time that we had
anything where he came into it, he seemed to be always
with us.

And his secretary of labor was named Davis, from
Pennsylvania. So Secretary of Labor Davis (I don't
think we took any initiative in this) but he [Davis]
seems to have thought it was something you should look
into--that there was this storm of protest at this
conference about what the Women's Bureau was doing. And
so far as I know, without any suggestion from us, he
stated that he would like to form a consultative body
to assist with the Department of Labor, Women's Bureau,
and he would invite the Women's Bureau to choose three
people that they would like to be on this consultative
body and in harmony with the point of view with the
head of the Women's Bureau--who was the head then, do
you know?

Fry: I don't have her name down here, Alice.

Paul: She was the head, at that time, who was the one who was
so many, many, many years--she came from Norway--and for
years she was the head of the Women's Bureau, for years
and years and years.

Fry: I know, she was quite the symbol of it. But it will be

Fry: easy to fill in. [Mary Anderson]

Paul: But whoever that woman was, she was the head of it at that time, and then he sent a letter to the Woman's Party asking us if we would appoint three members to be on this consultative committee. The people who were appointed were Maud Younger, who was our congressional chairman, and Doris Stevens, who was then--I think she was our national organizer or something like that, and myself. And so we were half of the consultative body.

And so then the Women's Bureau set a date for a meeting of this consultative body, and they certainly did everything they could to defeat us. They certainly were--Mr. Davis didn't evidently make clear to the head of the Women's Bureau his displeasure over this or his anxiety over it, of having part of his department causing so much outcry against what they were doing. Because when we got there, the head of this--whoever this Women's [Bureau] head was [Mary Anderson]--she said, "Well, of course, our time is very limited. We are not employed to work beyond four-thirty or four" (or whatever it was) "and we must make this very brief."

And we said, "Well, look here. You are getting a salary for <u>sitting</u> here. We are getting <u>no</u> salary for sitting here. We come from some distance." I believe this was after Doris Stevens had married Mr. Malone and gone to live in [Quilton?]. I remember saying, "Well, Miss Stevens has had to take a trip down here and not only is she not paid for coming and sitting here, but she has had to pay her trip down and back to sit here. We are not even reimbursing her for that. And if we're willing to come and stay the whole evening and discuss this measure at our own expense, why shouldn't you be willing to at your expense?"

"Oh, no, no. Oh, not at all. We of the Women's Bureau always leave at half-past--anything we do, we do in the Women's Bureau time for which we are <u>paid</u>, we don't do one single thing after that"--She couldn't have been more--ooh!--<u>uninterested</u> in making this women's consultative committee amount to something.

She said, "Now the thing we must do. It is very important to get information, and I think the Woman's Party can look up <u>this</u> and can look up <u>this</u> and can look up <u>this</u> and can look up this."

And we said, "We are to look up all these statistics

Paul: and all these laws, and you have all this force here, all employed? Why would we go forth"--before we'd ever started to look up all the laws in the United States, you know, and they didn't know what the labor laws were, they didn't know what anything was, apparently from what they said.

"Now you just investigate in this state whether there's a law on this or there's not a law on this. So I will assign this to you, and this to you, and this to you." This was the type of a woman this woman was. Merciful, goodness me. I never, never, never, never believed there could be such a woman, seriously, [laughing] as this woman that we met. So we didn't really, I think, get anywhere.

I remember Maud Younger when we came out saying, "I certainly was proud of the Woman's Party, prouder than perhaps I've ever been of the Woman's Party, when I saw what types of women we had and what types of women they had." Because she was one who really had investigated before she decided to take this great step that she took, after being the mother of the eight-hour law in America. And none of these women had a special labor law to her credit, or had actually gotten one through the Supreme Court or done what Maud Younger had done. And here she was standing against them! It was perfectly true, our people seemed so superior to these people who were all sitting there with their nice big salaries and just breathing incompetence. I think it was probably out of that that we got started on--perhaps we were already started but we were perhaps encouraged to keep on with our surveys we were making of the laws all over the country. What year was this?

Fry: This was 1926 so you had, I guess, already begun some of your surveys.

Paul: This meeting was in 1926?

Fry: That is when the conference was that began all of this.

Paul: Well, immediately this meeting was right after the conference, you see.

Fry: Well, then, that would have been 1926.

Alice, something else, I think, came out--

Paul: The next thing that happened was--We got nothing, no

Paul: discussion of anything, only discussion "Would this one look up this law," and we said, "We won't." And we didn't get anywhere. And we went on having this meeting, I guess, once a week or once a month whatever time they had it. We were sure we were making no impression, having no effect whatsoever on the Women's Bureau.

And then we were one day having a meeting over in Baltimore, which Mrs. Hooper had organized, a very large luncheon. And I went over to be one of the speakers. And I remember the telephone--I was called to the telephone before I made my speech. And there was someone saying, "We've just received word from the Women's Bureau that they have decided to have no more meetings of the women's consultative group." So when I went in, I just announced this, that the whole thing has now been abolished by act of--I don't know she could do it, one woman, but she announced there would be no more meetings. So we did have no more meetings and that was the end of it.

Fry: Also--and I think you can record on this--the conference did ask that a study be undertaken and two years later a report was published--

Paul: What conference?

Fry: This Women's Industrial Conference. As a result of the debate on the floor, they voted to have a study under- taken of the Equal Rights Amendment and protective legislation.

Paul: The only thing that I know that they voted--I don't know whether they voted it, but the only thing I know that came out of it was this immediate action by the secretary of labor. And maybe he considered that this was a study that we were going to make, but we certainly didn't--

Fry: I don't know--

Paul: No other study was ever undertaken but that one was being undertaken by this consultative committee that I ever heard of.

Fry: By the Women's Bureau? Weren't they always publishing studies on the status of women and things like that?

Paul: I don't know what they were publishing at that time.

Paul: the Equal Rights Amendment. But this was a three people for, three people against--I wouldn't have said that it was to make a study. It was to advise the Women's Bureau so they wouldn't--the way it was put to us was we were to be a consultative committee to help the Women's Bureau from making the mistakes that then the secretary of labor thought they'd made. It was obvious that they'd made a mistake, because there was certainly not any. I think at that conference, not any feeling of success on the part of the Women's Bureau that they had come off with glory. Because all the meeting was, through Miss Laughlin's efforts, a meeting of condemnation of the Women's Bureau, and I guess this was all manufactured that it was to be that they were going to make any study, because certainly they made no study when we were there. A study could have been made by hearing the points of view that we were certainly able to present.

Fry: I think this was their departmental study, and sounds like--

Paul: But this was a department study; they said that we do this all on Women's Bureau time, in the Women's Bureau. It was certainly, I would have thought, you could call it a study; but the result of the study would have been a complete division, the Women's Bureau taking one point of view, Woman's Party the other point of view.*

---

*The Women's Bureau study which was published two years after the 1926 conference is footnoted by O'Neill (opus cit.) on page 285. The reader is referred to Henry
R   rey,
N   .   .   .   .

TIME SEGMENTS OF ALICE PAUL'S WORK IN EUROPE

Fry: Did you go to Europe then late, in the late twenties?
        I don't know what dates you were in Europe and when you
        were back here on the scene with the Woman's Party in
        Washington. There seems to be no chronology anywhere.

Paul: After suffrage was won, you mean?

Fry: Yes. After suffrage was won, I assume that you were on
        the scene in Washington for about eight years, is that
        correct? And then you went to Geneva--

Paul: I don't know being that much "on the scene"--

Fry: At what point do we leave the Washington scene and go
        to Geneva?

Paul: Well, before I went to Geneva, I went up and bought
        this little cottage up in Vermont.

Fry: Did you buy that in the twenties, before the world
        codification conference?

        [Interruption. Tape off.]

Paul: --been trying to help always.

Fry: So even when you were in Europe you were helping here?

Paul: No, no. I consider that "helping," in Geneva; but I
        mean I did that as a result of a vote, you know, that
        we took in 1938, when we voted to form a world committee.
        But I'd rather just go ahead [and complete the section
        on the Equal Rights Amendment].

Fry: Yes, that's what I want to do.

Paul: I can't remember exactly when I went up and--

Fry: Then there was no break for you then?

Paul: There was never any break.

Fry: You were consistently involved with the Woman's Party
effort for the Equal Rights Amendment here in the United
States, and we can go ahead and talk about it, just go
continuously down the line?

Paul: I have been all my life, [never] having varied on that.

Fry: I thought there might have been a time when you were
for several years in Europe.

Paul: The longest time I stayed in Europe was the time we
opened our world committee headquarters, which was in
I guess in 1939. Let me see. [Pause.] Maybe we
opened it in 1938.

Fry: Well, we are not to that yet.

Paul: I don't think so. I think it was in 1939. I can look
all these things up very easily. I think we opened them
about August. When did the World War start?

Fry: Hitler marched into Austria I believe in March of 1938.

Paul: But we started when they went into Poland; that is
when the World War started.

Fry: That was I guess 1938?

Paul: No, it wasn't that; I don't think so. Well, anyway it
was somewhere around there and I stayed--it must have
been 1939, September 2, 1939, I believe. Then I stayed
all through 1940 and then it was in 1941 that I knew we
were going into the war. And everybody in Europe knew
we were going into war. They all said, "It took us so
many years to get the Americans in the first time [World
War I], but this time, we'll do it in a year," they
were always saying. And we did, we went in in 1941 I
think. And so I came back, I think, in the spring of
1941. You see, I wasn't over there a very long time.
I was in Europe all of 1940, part of the spring of
1941, and maybe half of 1939.

Fry: What about ten years before that, how long were you
there?

Paul: I never was there any definite--any very long time

Paul: before. I just went over for some specific thing to
do.

USING PUBLICITY MEDIA IN THE TWENTIES

Fry: Then there is one more thing I want to ask you about,
before we leave the 1920s and the Equal Rights Amendment.
[Interruption.] In the twenties you started broadcasting on radio, I believe. The reason I think you
probably did was that in the 1923 Equal Rights magazine,
on the cover, it depicted a woman broadcasting over the
radio for equal rights. And then I noticed that later
in the twenties, you had regular weekly broadcasts over
the National Broadcasting Network or something. Do
you remember any of that? I thought that was a good way
to educate women.

Paul: When was this?

Fry: In the twenties. Nineteen twenty-three was one date,
and I think the other one was 1928 or 1929 when you had
your regular weekly broadcast. I wondered if this was
national.

Paul: We didn't have any. Some local place may have. It
was never done very well.

Fry: In the Equal Rights magazine they said it was over the
National Broadcasting--

Paul: Maybe Mrs. Hooker did it; she was very good. She had
a very good branch. Maybe they did it.

Fry: Now all of this time in the late twenties, you were
still introducing it into Congresses, and Senator Nye
emerged--

Paul: From North Dakota, yes.

Fry: --for the first time in 1929, yes.

Paul: As the chief sponsor?

Fry: As the chief sponsor, yes, for the Senate, and Frederick
        McGrady was still sponsoring it for the House.

Paul: Yes, McGrady, I remember that he did, but he didn't--and
        I remember that I was away in Europe when they did it--
        he was never, didn't keep it up very long. Maybe one
        Congress or two.

        You see, the reason we didn't do broadcasting and
        those things was because we'd spent so much money over
        in the suffrage campaign and then we had this debt that
        we had to pay in the end. It took a long time, it took
        about half a year, I guess, to raise the money. Then
        when we started in something that looked as though it
        might be a campaign of a good many years, the one thing
        that I think the new board particularly didn't want to
        do was to get themselves into having this nightmare
        of money raising because the new chairman, Elsie Hill,
        had never taken much part in money raising. She did do
        the very big thing of authorizing and signing herself
        the always tremendous number of notes for the head-
        quarters, and that was about as big a task as anybody
        could want to take upon her shoulders. So we just gave
        up making any attempt to do press work on the scale
        that we'd done it in the suffrage campaign. Because we
        thought, well, the other things were so pressing that we
        had to do, so I know that we didn't have any kind of a
        professional backing of anything like broadcasting. Maybe
        some of the local places did it in some of the states.

Fry: Well, I ran across a printed speech that had been made
        as one of the weekly broadcast series by the man who
        was head of United Press for Washington. And this was
        a very eloquent speech on behalf of the Equal Rights
        Amendment; I think he was the husband, I am not sure,
        of somebody in the Woman's Party.

Paul: I am sure these were done, but--as they are done today,
        we didn't do it on any very big scale.

PRESIDENTS HARDING TO EISENHOWER

Franklin Roosevelt Administration Opposed

Fry: There was one other question I wanted to ask you and that is about your presidential delegations. I wanted to ask you to evaluate for us the value of the presidential delegations. You saw Coolidge, and Harding, and Hoover each time you had the Equal Rights Amendment submitted--

Paul: Well, we always had it submitted, it was never _not_ submitted.

Fry: And that was when you saw the presidents, I guess.

Paul: No, no. No, no. Of course, you always tried to keep it before the presidents and we went to all the presidents excepting [Franklin] Roosevelt, who wouldn't receive us.

Fry: He wouldn't?

Paul: But up to that time, we never had any difficulty. Up until Roosevelt's time.

Fry: Did the presidents _after_ Roosevelt receive you?

Paul: Yes, Truman.

Fry: And Eisenhower?

Paul: Yes, we never had--he was the first one who put it in his presidential message, you see.

Fry: Well, how was it that President Roosevelt never met with a Woman's Party delegation?

[End of Tape 16, Side A]

Paul: [While tape is being turned: transcribed from
interviewer's notes:] When Eleanor Roosevelt was
first in Washington, she invited all the women's
organizations to the White House except the Woman's
Party.

We had an extremely good state chairman in New
York, Mrs. Clarence Smith, who worked--

[Tape 16, Side B. Audio note: volume rather low.]

Paul: --for the Equal Rights Amendment. But in New York
the special labor laws for women were working a good
deal of hardship to a great many women, and so they
were always coming to our New York office asking us to
go up and testify for the women because they couldn't
afford to go themselves and they didn't know enough to
say what to say. When women were being laid off in
great numbers by special labor laws, then the women
affected would want to go up and make a protest at
Albany. But they wouldn't go up themselves, because
they didn't know how to do it they thought, and would
come and ask us to do it.

So Mrs. Smith was constantly going up to hearings
in the name of the Woman's Party and having other people
go with her, making protest against these laws. And
Mrs. Roosevelt was always appearing with the labor
leaders **for** these laws and she began to have a tremendous
feeling of opposition to the Woman's Party while she
was governor's wife, because of all this. When she
came to Washington, it was transferred to us. She
just--we were just completely ignored, as though we
didn't count for anything, and it wasn't until after
she was out of the White House and was with the United
Nations, you know, that she finally came out with a
statement saying that she'd withdrawn her opposition to
the Equal Rights Amendment.

I was there when she did it, I heard it from the
gallery. We didn't know she was going to say this, but
she did. And we rushed down to the--I didn't, but I
think Anita Pollitzer was with me--and somebody else
rushed down to the American mission at the United
Nations, to say, "Have you the text of what Mrs.
Roosevelt just said? We just heard her say, 'I have
withdrawn my opposition to the Equal Rights Amendment.'"
So we got the original statement that was given out by
the American mission that day quoting what Mrs. Roosevelt

Paul: had just said. So it was years later before she ever
        withdrew her opposition.

Harding, Hoover and Coolidge

Paul: Now before Roosevelt was Hoover. Hoover actually went
        out of his way to support us and that was at the Repub-
        lican National Convention and I was there so I know about
        that myself. That in 1944, this was; he was no longer
        President.

Fry: What about in 1928?

Paul: But in 1944 he was no longer President, but that is
        when we were trying to get the Republican convention.
        We already had it in the platform four years before,
        and it was a great fight to see it didn't come in a
        second time. And so we had the actual support of
        Hoover there, I remember. That is when he wasn't
        President then.

        But when he was President he asked us for the
        different things that came up, for The Hague, for
        instance. But we hadn't gotten to the point where we
        had enough members in Congress where it was practical
        to try to print it through.

Fry: I have a quotation from what Coolidge said when you
        went to see him.

Paul: What did he say?

Fry: This is from a newspaper account in 1972 so it's not
        a--but it says that he said, "This is something of a
        novel experience for me. I have been engaged somewhat
        in legislation on the other side in attempting to
        protect women from possible impositions. But if the
        womanhood of the nation want a change, having demonstrated
        their ability even before they got the vote, I haven't
        the slightest doubt that Congress will respond favorably."
        (Meaning with the Equal Rights Amendment.)

Paul: Who wrote that, because I think that is about what he
        did say.

Fry: I don't know who wrote it. This was in the Sunday
        issue, December 3, 1972, in the San Francisco Chronicle.

Paul: It wasn't signed?

Fry: No. I suppose the editor of this dug it out. The writer goes on to say, "That was the promise President Calvin Coolidge gave two hundred fashionably gowned women of the National Woman's Party."

Paul: This delegation went out to see him in South Dakota--

Fry: That was 1923.

Paul: I think he was spending a vacation in South Dakota or something like that.

Fry: Yes, that is what I understand.

Paul; Seems to me that's where we went.

Fry: It was in South Dakota.

Paul: Anyway, [in the ERA campaign] we didn't emphasize the leadership of the President the way we had done with Wilson, because there was--well, we had so much to do to sort of get the Amendment idea off the ground, it seemed to us, with the women's organizations. We felt we had to do [that] first, get some little more substance to demand from the country, but Harding was--let's see, I know the first delegation we took to Harding [pause]--I believe he was always a supporter, but it's not very--and I led the delegation, I remember, and introduced people to him. But we had on our board then, a woman from Ohio whose husband was one of the chief backers of Harding. Do you remember what her name was? I'd have to look it up.

Fry: No.

Paul: And she had constant access to Harding. Could always arrange interviews and everything else. Seemed to me that, as I remember it, that he seemed to have the sort of answers of the same kind that more or less Coolidge gave. "Well, if the women want this, of course." And this lady, whoever she was, asked him to come up and make the main speech at that photograph I showed you in the little report--1926.* There was a man speaking.

---

*"The National Woman's Party, 1913-1926." Pamphlet. [illegible] NWP headquarters.

Paul: It wasn't Harding because Harding didn't show up.

Fry: Was he supposed to show up?

Paul: Yes, he was supposed to be our main speaker.

        I think there is [also] a photograph of Harding
        in that one.

Fry: [Checking pamphlet.] It has a picture of a delegation
        to President Coolidge at the White House. And yes,
        here is a picture also of a delegation to President
        Harding.

        It says that three deputations have been sent to
        Coolidge, including one composed of New England women
        from his own part of the country, and a delegation of
        wage-earning women to urge the Equal Rights Amendment.

Paul: And what's it say about the Harding one?

Fry: It doesn't. It's just a caption under a picture.

Paul: Doesn't say anything about it?

Fry: No, he doesn't make it in the text.

Paul: Well, isn't there a delegation to him?

Fry: Yes.

Paul: It doesn't say what we were asking him?

Fry: It just says "Members of the Woman's Party appealed
        to President Harding."

Paul: Then it was presumably about the Equal Rights Amendment.
        I didn't know whether it was over some other topic.

Fry: Would there have been another topic?

Taking Related Issues to the White House

Paul: Yes, we often went--I know we went to Hoover, for
        instance, about the world code, you know. [Pause.]
        And I know we organized a delegation to Roosevelt which
        he did receive, but it wasn't a Woman's Party delegation

Paul: particularly but we got it up, of repealing what they call 213. Do you know what 213 was?

Fry: Was that one of the NRA [National Recovery Act] codes?

Paul: No, 213 was the Economy Act put through under Hoover trying to stave off a depression by which only one of the two spouses could be employed by the federal government.

Fry: And if you were married, one of the spouses had to resign, and it was nearly always the wife.

Paul: Yes, that's it. It was Section 213. They called themselves the 213ers. And we helped very, very--we practically did the whole campaign for those women, so they always say. And we gave them an office in our headquarters without any charge and we raised the money and engaged an organizer for them and one of our officers, Mrs. Hooker, paid the salary, I believe, of this organizer.

And then we called up all the women's organizations and asked them, one by one, if they would join in this campaign to have 213 repealed. And then we finally--I think I was away at this time--finally got an audience with the President for all this combined group of women to President Roosevelt. So I meant, we did take up other things than just the Amendment, you see. Always we took up any crisis that was affecting women.

Fry: What about jury duty, Alice? We haven't talked about that and that may be something that you were involved in because I noticed Equal Rights magazine would sometimes include a map. The white states were the states in which women were still not allowed to sit on juries, and there was a big discussion--

Paul: Well, of course, these were all published because they were arguments for why we needed the Amendment.

Fry: This says that, "Hearings have been held also on minor points covered by the Amendment, such as equalizing citizenship rights of married men and women, giving jury service to women of the District of Columbia, giving equal contract rights to married women in the District of Columbia, and the equal application as to men and women of pension laws"--which you mentioned to me--"Through these hearings not only has the attention of Congress been concentrated upon the equal rights

Fry: question, but the attention of the whole country has been called to this unsettled problem still confronting Congress." Let me note that this is from this little pamphlet, "The National Woman's Party, 1913-1926."

Paul: Yes, was there anything you wanted to ask about that?

Fry: Yes. That since you must have been busy on a lot of these other issues, I wondered if there were any others who were given space in the NWP headquarters. For instance, the move to get women on juries or anything like that. Let's see, I believe you said you didn't go into the old Margaret Sanger group of birth control.

Paul: No, we didn't take it up, but we let her have meetings-- have at least one meeting, maybe many, in the head- quarters.

Fry: On into the thirties it seemed that from the Equal Rights Amendment--

Paul: Now in 1928, you see, was the first time--that's in the twenties, if you're doing the twenties--first time we went to an international conference. That was the one in Havana.

Fry: Yes, and I think you've talked about that.

Paul: I did, yes. Out of it we got the Inter-American Commission created.

Fry: Is this right? In 1933 there was the Montevideo Conference--

Paul: After it was created, you see. Every five years at that time, they had the Conference of American Republics. So the _next_ one, after it was created, was the one in Montevideo. And so we got it created in Cuba, and at the first time they met afterwards, we got to the Montevideo Treaty.

Fry: How much work was there going on in the Woman's Party between 1928 and 1933 on that treaty--especially on the equal rights terms of it?

Paul: Well, our main work was on an equal rights treaty on all subjects, an equal rights treaty which we were trying to get the women's organizations' international [sections] to endorse. I told you the Business and Professional Women had endorsed it. And then we presented it at

Paul: Montevideo and I think there were four countries that
       agreed to sign it at Montevideo, but that was not
       enough to make it very universal among the American
       republics.

Fry: Did Ernest Gruening have something to do with that?
       He was later governor of Alaska and senator.

Paul: Yes, and his wife was on our national board, Dorothy
       Greuning. No. No, he didn't. The only time we came
       in contact with Senator Greuning was--of course he
       supported the Equal Rights Amendment when he got to
       our Senate, but when he was a newspaper editor--I guess
       editor, or owner, something or other, up in Massachusetts,
       he aided us in our suffrage campaign.

Fry: Yes, I think I've got that. Well, I had a little note
       here; I thought he did something in Montevideo. Maybe
       he was covering the meeting or something.

Paul: I don't remember him at Montevideo. He's the one who
       told me what he did himself up in--I wouldn't have
       remembered, but he's writing his memoirs now and one day
       he told me that in writing his memoirs he was going to
       put in the letter that I had written to him thanking
       him for his great help on his paper in the time we were
       working for suffrage up in Massachusetts. Must have
       been the time, I guess, that we were burning the
       President's words on Boston Common; we were being
       arrested. So he said, "Oh, you know, I did so much
       to help and you wrote me this wonderful letter and I'm
       printing it in my memoirs." So he told me that not so
       long ago.

THE WOMEN'S BUREAU NEUTRALIZED VIA DOROTHY GREUNING

Fry: How did his wife get interested enough to be on your
       board? Do you know?

Paul: She was one of those few women who attended this very
       historic gathering at Vassar when they had their
       meeting in the cemetery.

Fry: Oh, and they wouldn't let the suffrage speaker on the
       campus? Was that a suffrage speaker?

Paul: Yes. They invited three distinguished women in the
       suffrage movement, and Inez Milholland was getting up
       the meeting. And the president sent for her and said
       the board of trustees was not willing to have this
       meeting at Vassar. And so the women who were interested
       in the meeting, including Dorothy Day--Dorothy Greuning--
       decided to hold it next door, which was in the graveyard.
       So they all went out and hopped over the wall--I guess
       you know this tale because it's so famous--and how they
       got the three speakers out there, I don't know, but the
       speakers came anyway. [Laughter.] And the whole
       meeting was held over there in the graveyard.   It was
       very convenient, it was right next door. Then they
       apparently, somehow or other, hopped back or walked
       around the wall or went in the entrance, I don't know
       how, but they had the meeting anyway.

       And she has been a very ardent suffragist all
       these years.

Fry: Was she active in your suffrage campaign?

Paul: She may have been, but I don't know her. I mean, I
       don't know--of course, I don'tknow when she married Mr.
       Greuning. If she was his wife by any chance when he
       was up in Boston, I suppose she was perhaps encouraging
       him. I never even knew any of this until Consuelo came

Paul: along and somehow I discovered that she had been in this Vassar meeting.

Fry: Consuelo Reyes? That's where I found out about it too, from Consuelo and her audio-visual story of the history of suffrage. In the thirties--

Paul: Just to continue that--so when I learned that she had been in that meeting, we got in touch with her from the headquarters right away and got to know her and found out what a champion she was and had been all her life. And I asked her to start in and help us now, and she agreed right away and went on our board.

Fry: What position was her husband in at that point?

Paul: I guess he was still senator. And she went on the board. She took it very seriously, and the thing that she took up immediately was to try to get the Women's Bureau from continuing to stab us in the back. The first thing she did was to call me and say, "I have, I think, gotten Mrs. Esther Peterson to the point where she will no longer continue the Women's Bureau policy of opposing the Equal Rights Amendment. And I want you to come up and have tea with her." And she said, "I'm having nobody but you because I don't want to get it complicated by lots of people talking and she's agreed to come on condition that there's nobody else."

And when I was calling a taxi to get ready to go, I remember--I can't think of who the people were, but certainly great alarmists--and they said, "It's absolutely unsafe for you to go up through Rock Creek Park all by yourself in a taxi. You may never come back." They said, "You don't understand the terrific opposition there is to you on the part of the Women's Bureau and all the people in that field." And so one person who was there said, "You simply can't allow it. You can't get in that taxi alone and go; it will just look like some ordinary accident, but you will never be seen again."

Fry: My goodness.

Paul: So one of the people who was there and the only one I remember who was there at the headquarters, finally said, "Well, then, if you're determined to go,"--I just said, "I have to go. There is no question at all that I certainly have to go to that meeting. Nobody here seems to have a car. The only way I can get there is

Paul: to go in a taxi and I can't tell what the taxi man may
        do, I'm sure, but I don't see any other way to get
        there."

        So then one person spoke up and said, "Well, if
        you're so determined to go, then I'm going to go in
        that taxi with you." And they were really most extra-
        ordinarily serious about this idea.

        And that was Margie Leonard, who was our Massa-
        chusetts chairman. How she happened to be there at
        that moment, I don't know. I think it was she. But
        anyway, I remember that when we got to Mrs. Greuning's--
        I knew Mrs. Greuning wouldn't be a party to anything
        like this. But I didn't know anything about the Women's
        Bureau, about this terrible Esther Peterson, that they
        all considered so terrible that she would do anything
        she could in opposition to our Amendment campaign. So
        anyway, when we got to Mrs. Greuning's, and went in
        safely--nothing happening to us [laughing]--and kept the
        taxi man to take us home again. (I think it was that
        way.) Mrs. Greuning was lovely beyond words, a beautiful
        hostess, had a beautiful tea, and--but she was very
        concerned about what to do with [laughing] poor Miss
        Leonard. And Miss Leonard was quite an important person
        and used to being treated with great respect, because
        you know she was about the only woman in the John
        Hancock Life Insurance Company, in the legal department,
        and had been there ever since she graduated from the
        law school. So she was used to being treated with
        great respect and so on.

        So Mrs. Greuning, having promised Mrs. Peterson
        nobody would be in the room but Mrs. Peterson, Mrs.
        Greuning and myself, she said, "Now, I think that you
        had better stay here."

Fry: Speaking to whom?

Paul: To Miss Leonard. "And because Mrs. Peterson wants this
        to be a very private interview where she is going to
        possibly state that she will no longer oppose the
        Amendment." So I couldn't see anything objectionable
        at all to what she said, but it seems that they had a
        kitchen, with somebody in the kitchen preparing the
        dinner at that moment, and they sort of placed her in a
        little kind of a hall outside of it. So she was prac-
        tically being consigned to the kitchen, because there
        wasn't very much but the kitchen and this little ante
        place.

Paul: At all events, it appeared that she was somehow or
other seated in the kitchen. And [laughing] up to this
day, whenever we talk about that interview, she says,
"Yes indeed, that person who put me in the kitchen"--
[laughter]. And evidently the person in the kitchen
wasn't very welcoming, and probably nobody is very
welcoming to somebody coming into their kitchen. But
she's always had a great grievance against Mrs.--a
personal one [laughing]--against poor Mrs. Greuning,
who had the best motives in the world.

       So then Mrs. Peterson did come, and she said, and
I know that she said this, that she would never again
participate in any [pause] active opposition to the
Amendment. I don't think that she said that she would
support it. But she said, "I have written against it
and spoken against it and debated against it, but I've
made up my mind not to do so in the future." So of
course, it was a big step, I guess.

Fry: So they were neutralized at that point?

Paul: And that was a very little while ago, you know, while
Mrs. Peterson was still down at the Women's Bureau.

Fry: Yes, that would have been fairly recently if it was
when Greuning was a senator.

Paul: But I mean Mrs. Peterson was by that time assistant
secretary of labor as well as being head of the Women's
Bureau, and she remained there, I think, until Nixon
came in. And it was Nixon, I think, who appointed
Mrs. Koontz, the Negro woman. Nixon came in in 1969,
didn't he? I think he won in 1968, and so by 1970
probably he'd gotten Mrs. Koontz in probably. So it
must have been around 1970, I suppose. That would be
about two years ago.

Fry: When this happened with Mrs. Peterson?

Paul: Yes.

Fry: It was right at the end of her tenure then.

Paul: Yes, it was very recent.

       And then Mrs. Koontz came in, and she continued
really the same opposition of Mrs. Peterson, the historic
opposition. And it wasn't until a new secretary of labor

Paul: was appointed--I think his name was Hodgson [James D., appointed June 10, 1970], but I'm not sure about that-- and Mr. Hodgson, almost the first thing he stated was his support of the Equal Rights Amendment--publicly stated it. And thereupon Mrs. Koontz came out for the Amendment. But prior to that she had been continuing the opposition.

Fry: Had you sent a delegation to see the new secretary of labor?

Paul: No. He did it right away. I think Hodgson is no longer there, if I remember it rightly. Is there a new one since?

Fry: Yes, but I'll have to fill that name in. [Peter J. Brennan] I'll check on the Hodgson name, too.

Paul: And there's a new woman appointed. So you know who she is? I don't know who she is, in place of Mrs. Koontz.

Fry: No, I don't. How is she toward the ERA?

Paul: Well, you see, all that has happened in the time since I've sort of been out of it for a year. I don't know. I don't even know who she is.

Fry: I'm about to change the subject. [Laughing.] If you have anything else to say on--

Paul: I was going to say that if you would excuse me a moment, I'll go and see Mrs. Dolly [housekeeper]. And maybe now you can take your orange.

[Tape off.]

THE WOMAN'S PARTY IN THE 1930S

Inequalities of the Depression

Fry: As I was going through the Equal Rights magazine in
the thirties, the thing that hit me as an impression
was that there was a general slowing down of the
movement. Now is this a true impression or is it
just one that one gets from reading the Equal Rights
magazine? There were so many difficulties involved in
fighting these minimum wage and maximum hour laws, all
these things that were against women, that it seemed
to sap a lot of the vitality of the movement.

Paul: I don't think it did. [Pause.] It doesn't seem to me
that it did. Of course, I wasn't in it so very much
myself, as I had been in the suffrage campaign, so I
wasn't--and each new chairman, I think made her particular contribution the sort of thing that she could do
the best. And I thought it was a very wholesome growth.
All of those of us who worked so hard in the suffrage
campaign, as I told you, deliberately tried to get
another generation to take on this one. And they
didn't take it on as much as we had believed they would.

    I thought the thing that we basically tried to do
was to get the women of the country [aware]. You see,
in the suffrage campaign there [had been] more lethargy
and indifference and so on in the part of women, but we
didn't have people actively going to legislatures and
getting measures through prohibiting women to vote and
so on. Here [in the equal rights campaign] we were
having the whole labor movement, almost, guiding the
woman movement. And of course, the Labor Department
was an expression of it. Here was a Labor Department
with a woman movement as only a subsidiary of the labor
movement. And instead of having an Equality for Women

Paul: Department, a women's department, we had it as just a
       little sub of the Labor Department. And so the problem
       we had was so completely different from the voting
       problem.

       And here we have, as you say, minimum wage laws
       for women, all kinds of things being enacted, through
       the power of the labor vote, and it all had to be
       [dealt with]--and it was different in different states.
       It was certainly a hard thing to do. And it seems to
       me, I don't think there's any question now but that the
       thought of the country is for equality for women in
       industry and in earning a livelihood and so on. All
       these fields that, a short time ago, the whole thought
       of the country was on the other side. So I think it's
       really been a very great achievement.

Fry: Certainly when one reads these articles from the
       thirties, you can see this big, big difference. That
       then women were losing their jobs because of the enact-
       ment of minimum wage laws that applied only to women.

Paul: Yes, of course.

Fry: And, as you say, this appeared to be true in many
       states and in the District of Columbia it was at least
       tried. (I haven't followed it through to see if they
       got one.)

Paul: Now each of our chairmen was so different, and each
       one, I think, played a big part in making this change,
       and the thing that united all the group--it was a very
       little group, but it was [laughing] all of one opinion
       on this subject anyway. That group didn't perhaps get
       any bigger numerically, but the people who came to that
       opinion increased and increased and increased, until now
       certainly the vast majority of women, I would think,
       are today of the same point of view that we had when we
       started this whole crusade in 1923.

       Christian Science Church Help

Fry: I noticed that one of the chairmen was Mrs. Steven Pell
       of New York for a while at least. Sarah Thompson Pell,
       from 1936 to 1939.

Paul: . - w   .   ..

Fry: This is in 1937, and Anita Pollitzer at that time was
        a vice-chairman with Gail Laughlin. The thing that--

Paul: One thing for instance--as I told you, when we came up
        before the Business and Professional [Women's Clubs],
        (and I say her name was Dorothy Schuler [?] but it
        might not have been, but you can easily find out what
        it was. It's my impression that's what it was.) But
        when she got up to speak and made this speech [for
        debating the Equal Rights Amendment]--against the whole
        board and against the whole administration in Washington
        that was headed by Miss Frances Perkins, a member of the
        cabinet and head of the Women's Bureau--we asked her
        afterwards how this all happened, how could she have done
        this thing. What made her do it? It was wonderful for
        us but we were so unaware of her support. And we dis-
        covered that she was a Christian Scientist and that they
        all have teachers--do you know anything about Christian
        Science?

Fry: Not much.

Paul: Well, their system is to have teachers who are accredited
        by the church, and there are only a few in the country.
        I think there are about thirty in the United States* and
        maybe about thirty more all over the world. My sister-
        in-law is one of them. That's the reason I know a little
        bit about it. So any person who is really an ardent
        Christian Scientist always enrolls in one of these
        classes and then they give them some kind of recognition
        as having been a student with an accredited teacher.
        Well, Mrs. Pell was an extremely devout Christian
        Scientist, a very, very, very, devout Christian Scientist.

        So she had a teacher--she enrolled in one of these
        classes--and his name was Mr. Heitman and she made him
        thoroughly aware of the Woman's Party and went to him
        when we asked her to be national chairman. (She told me
        all this herself.) And she said she wouldn't become
        national chairman unless he thought it was the right
        thing for her to do, and he looked into the whole
        matter and he strongly urged her to do it. And then
        when there was a question, should she run for a second
        term, he strongly advised her to do this. So we learned
        from Mrs. Pell that this mysterious Miss Schuler, who

_____

*There are over a hundred in the United States, and many
more than that all over the world.--Donald D. Paul.

Paul: got up and made this great defense, was one of her
fellow students under Mr. Heitman. So she had been
thoroughly indoctrinated by Mr. Heitman in the importance
of the equality-for-women movement. Naturally, Mrs.
Mary Baker Eddy was a woman, you see, who founded that
church.

And so then, when I went down in 1942, I guess it
was, to become the national chairman when the war was
over and (I told you when nobody would want to take it
and I was elected in Philadelphia) one of the first
things I did was to begin to see if I could get some
newspaper support because we never had an editorial
support for the Equal Rights Amendment since we introduced it--of any importance, maybe little papers, but
no big papers. And I went down to the office of the
Christian Science Monitor to see if they wouldn't take
the lead. (This was before Mrs. Pell came along, a long
time before Mrs. Pell. I think. I have forgotten just
when Mrs. Pell was chairman.* At all events, it doesn't
make much difference.)

When I talked to the man in the office, he said he
knew all about this, he said, "because I've talked so
much to Mrs. [Perle] Mesta"--Mrs. Mesta, you know, is a
great Christian Scientist--and he said, "Mrs. Mesta's
told me so much about this and about the Woman's Party.
And I am all for your Amendment, and I will see what I
can do about bringing it up with the editorial staff
of the Monitor, putting in an editorial for you."

[End of Tape 16, Side B]

[Tape 17, Side A]

Paul: And he said, "Well, I'll just write up to Mr. Canham
the editor." You know who Mr. Erwin Canham was, I
guess; the editor of the Christian Science Monitor--

Fry: Yes.

Paul: So he said, "I'll write to Mr. Canham." He called me up
and said, "You know, I find Mr. Canham is even more
enthusiastic about this than I am. And he says he'll

*Sarah Thompson Pell was chairman 1936-1939.

Paul: take it up with the national board, and they will decide
        whether or not the _Monitor_ should come out for this.
        And there is no use in your going up because Mr. Canham
        is going to present it to them himself." He said, "I
        think that's the best thing to do."

        So then he telephoned again and said, "Mr. Canham
        says that he presented it to the board. He [had]
        found on the board, one of the most influential members
        of the board, Mr. Heitman and that Mr. Heitman [had]
        said, 'Well, I will propose this and get the endorsement
        of the Christian Science board.'" And so then he called
        me again, and he said, "Mr. Heitman has presented it.
        He's gotten the national board of governors"--or whatever
        they call it in that church, board of trustees, maybe*--
        "and they have voted upon Mr. Heitman's recommendation
        unanimously to support the Equal Rights Amendment. And
        they directed Mr. Canham to have an editorial to that
        effect." So you see, when you think of what one person,
        Mrs. Pell, did, these are far-reaching things that have
        maybe affected, enormously affected, the final result.

Fry: And at the time they appear to be little things, but--

Paul: So I mean, each chairman has been doing the thing that
        maybe has had enormous results, but each one in a more
        or less different field.

---

*Board of directors.--Donald Paul.

THE ERA ENTERS CONGRESS

First Times Out of Committee

Fry: I'd like to talk about the legislation in the thirties for the Equal Rights Amendment, because there were some important milestones, it looks like.

Paul: All right.

Fry: On January 3, 1935, this chronology says that it was introduced in the House as Resolution number one by Representative Lewis Ludlow of Indiana and it was the first favorable action ever taken by the Judiciary Subcommittee of the House, or of either house, according to this.

Paul: Now there's one whole issue that I noticed in that pile [of Equal Rights magazines] that I gave to you. The heading was--this was the House now?

Fry: Yes.

Paul: And I think it was the year the Republicans came in and we didn't have Mr. [Imanuel] Celler's opposition--What are you doing over there?

Fry: I'm just writing on the tape, labelling it. Go ahead.

Paul: Well, I think this is an extremely important issue, and I would get it out if I were you. And I know I put it over there, so it must be in yours.

    Yes, that was a big day when we got it in the House.

Fry: [Searching.] Well, there's nothing between December of 1934 and March of 1935 in these.

Paul: I remember [1947] because Anita Pollitzer was elected [chairman of WP] and some people didn't want her; it appeared to be because she was Jewish, as far as I could make out. So we had a very terrible time--

Fry: Because the mail ballot that you'd had was not considered legal, was that it? Was that the grounds that they challenged you on?

Paul: No. I don't of course know what the reason was that they were so determined she shouldn't be chairman.

Fry: I read about that in the Equal Rights magazine. That was the contested Woman's Party election that finally had to go to court.

Paul: So anyway, I stayed on--well, I was no longer chairman because she'd already been elected, and I had voted for her and--when we get to that I can tell you more about it.

But at all events I think I was still in Washington, either as chairman or being there to help Anita in the troubles that had developed, when we got that report from the House, is what I'm talking about. So I didn't think it could have been 1936 [1935].

Fry: In 1945 it was reported out from the full House Judiciary on July 12, with a recommendation that it "do pass"--

Paul: 1945? That's what I thought.

Fry: But 1935 was the first time it had been reported out from the subcommittee of the House Judiciary Committee.

Paul: Well, that didn't make so much difference. It was getting [it out of the whole] Judiciary itself, getting it out before the House. And I think that was the year the Republicans were in control of the Committee--

Fry: In 1945?

Paul: Well, I don't know whether it was 1945, but I think that whenever they reported it out, it was because of Republican control.* They took it away from [Emanuel] Celler

---

*Republicans won control of both houses in the 1946
e⁻ ⁻ ⁻ ' ⁻ ' ' ⁻ ⁻ ⁻ ⁻ ⁻

Paul: [who consistently opposed the ERA]. See, he couldn't
be chairman because the Republicans took over. And I
think I was no longer chairman [of WP] in 1945. I don't
think I was still chairman, but I think I was there
helping Anita. I think. Because 1945 was the year we
got it in the Charter of the United Nations.

Fry: And you may have been there?

Paul: I know I was in Washington when we got it in the Charter.
Anita went out for the Woman's Party (I think as chair-
man, but I know she went in whatever capacity) to San
Francisco.

Now take another cup; it's nice and hot. I'm
taking this to keep me up as long as you need me.

Fry: I'm sure I'll fold long before you do.

Well, what about the Senate Judiciary Committee?
It was reported, without recommendation but it did
report it out, in March of 1938, with a nine-to-nine
vote.

Paul: Nineteen thirty-eight? I know when they reported it
out all right. And it was under [Frederick] Van Nuys;*
he was chairman. And the next year it was reported out
in its new form, whatever the next year [of getting to
the floor] was after the first year. And I thought it
was about 1943--

Fry: Nineteen forty-one the subcommittee reported it out and
then in May--

Paul: Which are you reading? [Dora] Ogle's [chronology]?

Fry: Yes.

Paul: Well, as I say, I'm never sure about her.

Fry: That does go right along with your memory, however.
Then the Senate Judiciary Committee reported it out on
May 11, of 1942, a favorable report.

---

*Senate term 1933-39.

Paul: And when was the next one?

Fry: After that?

Paul: Of the whole committee.

Fry: Nineteen forty-three.

Paul: Yes, I think that's the [Senator Warren R.] Austin one that I told you about [when we had its new wording in the bill]. You know, where I told you he said he would report it if we got the signature of every women's organization. I think then for some reason I stopped.

But I wanted to tell you we did get the report signed. We got a recommendation of one page on which every organization signed its name, to supporting this version. It went through [the Senate] in 1970; and it was reported favorably that year [1943] by Austin.

Fry: Yes, and that's exactly what she says here. The new wording of "equality of rights under the law"--

Paul: Yes, it was 1943, wasn't it?

Fry: Yes.

Paul: That's what I thought.

Fry: May 28. And the House Judiciary subcommittee, about three weeks later, reported it out unanimously.

Paul: What about the full [committee]?

Fry: Nope. I don't see anything else in 1943, Alice.

Paul: You mean the House didn't do it in 1943? When did the House do it next, after 1943?

Fry: In 1945, "the first favorable report ever made by the House Judiciary Committee" was made in 1945.

Paul: All right, then we'd better look up 1945. I'll look it up when I've finished my tea. Because I remember what it looked like on the front [cover].

Fry: It's in these that I brought over from Anita Pollitzer's. Shall I read it?

Paul: Yes, that's the reason I just saw over there; you must

Paul: have seen it too when you looked through those.

Fry: No, I didn't get up to 1945. This is an article in
Equal Rights, volume 31, number 4, July and August, 1945,
by Amelia Himes Walker, the lobby chairman of the
National Woman's Party.

Paul: You know, she was our national chairman once. She was
with us and went to prison with us in the suffrage
campaign.

Fry: The page next to this of the previous issue, they
announce that the executive committee postponed a convention due to the death of President Roosevelt.

Paul: Well, Truman took over, [pause] so I don't see where the
Republicans would have come in. [Pause.] Does it say
who was chairman of the Judiciary then?

Fry: Representative Fadjo Cravens, a Democrat of Arkansas--

Paul: Oh, yes.

Fry: --made the report on behalf of the House Judiciary.
(It doesn't say he was chairman.)

Paul: Yes, now I remember. But it must have been a later
one when the Republicans came in. Because of course,
he was a very prominent Democrat. I was there at that
time that report was made.

I remember perfectly. It was made in about three
minutes and Mrs. [Cecil Norton] Broy and I were, I think,
the only people who went over for it. We knew it was
going to come up, and we went there to be there and hear
all the discussion and everything else that we could.
There were very few people in the room, and we sat down
more or less outside where we were supposed to sit.

And suddenly we learned, I suppose from Mr. Cravens,
who was a very, very good friend of our cause, that it
was through. And we said, "But we've been here waiting
for it, we didn't know it had even come up."

And he said, "Oh, yes. We don't do things very
slowly. We did it right away." So it was about as
undramatic a meeting as you could go to. We never even
heard a word said or saw anybody get up, or saw anything.
How they ever did it in about one minute, I don't know.
B - . . . nd you

Paul: see, if it was after the death of Roosevelt (it says so--what you just read me) we would have had, our greatest opposition was removed.

Fry: I wondered if that had anything to do with it. The Committee made a long statement about it, I believe.

Paul: And who signed it, did Mr. Cravens sign it?

Fry: Yes, Amelia Walker says that Cravens was the person who made the report "on behalf of the Committee," and I guess the Committee then signed this report. But it's a very long statement.

Paul: It probably gives the history up to that time.

Fry: Not particularly--

Paul: What was the next time on that list?

Fry: --the Committee report mentions the 1944 platform support of the Equal Rights Amendment, and it quotes the party platforms.

Paul: Oh, yes. This was the next year.

Fry: No, this was the platforms of the year before.

Paul: That's what I say, and this was the next year.

Fry: That's right--

Paul: So evidently it was the platform that got it.

Well now look here, when was the next time? I think it came up a second time when the Republicans came in.

Fry: Yes, the next time was in the Eightieth Congress. The bill was introduced by Representative John Marshall Robison with 102 co-sponsors and had a hearing in the subcommittee of the House with a favorable report on May of 1948. That was when both houses were Republican.

Paul: That's it, then.

Fry: And also, a favorable report from full Senate Judiciary Committee. So both of those voted it out favorably, but there was no vote taken on the floor.

Paul: I know.

Fry: The first vote had been taken on the floor of the Senate in 1946, July 19.

Paul: Oh, yes. That's right. We got a majority.

Fry: It was thirty-eight to thirty-five. You got a majority--

Paul: We got a majority, but we didn't get a two-thirds. What year was that? Nineteen thirty-six? Or 1946?

Fry: Nineteen forty-six.

Paul: It had to be 1946 because it was after we put it in the Republican platform.

Fry: July of 1946.

Paul: Yes, I remember that vividly. [Long pause.]

The Turning Point--1940

Paul: I wish that perhaps now women could have a more respect-ful, if you had more repect for the campaign for the equality for women and for the women who took part in it. Because when I came along from England as just a young college student, I had never heard of the name of Elizabeth Cady Stanton, and only vaguely of the name of Susan B. Anthony. Just it was a name I knew I'd heard, but I didn't know anything about her.

        And I only knew about Lucretia Mott because her painting was up in the head place of honor in the collection hall where we met every morning. All the students met and every day I looked up at Lucretia Mott, and we had a fellowship that was called the Lucretia Mott Fellowship. And that was because she was a Quaker, and they had preserved her name. But in the woman movement, I didn't know she had anything to do with the woman movement.

Fry: It's hard to think of you not knowing that at one time, Alice. [Laughing.]

Paul: But I meant, nobody knew it. Nobody who had just an

Paul: ordinary college education had ever been told a thing
about these or ever heard of it. And the woman movement
wasn't enough developed so that people were talking
about the generation before them. They were just tiny
little groups of women meeting together, talking about
how could they get a few signatures to a little petition
and so on, when I went to these meetings.

So then I really think that by encouraging one of
our members to start a [postage] stamp--a Susan B.
Anthony stamp and things like that, and having pageants--
we had one great pageant in Washington put on by Hazel
McKaye on the life of Susan B. Anthony: this was the
time that we were trying to get people to follow the
old Amendment. We thought if we could identify it in
any way in their minds with some heroic woman who had
been outstanding, it would help.

Fry: Today they call that consciousness-raising--

Paul: Do they?

Fry: ---Of women about women.

Paul: Is that so? I didn't know it. At all events it certainly has been--and then we started having meetings
every birthday of Susan B. Anthony in the capital, and
birthdays of Lucretia Mott once in a while, Elizabeth
Cady Stanton once in a while. And then we started
having meetings, general meetings in the capital in
Statuary Hall, for instance, on the death of Inez
Milholland and we started out to make Inez Milholland
known and revered. So that's one--I think when you
think of this period, not only did it--as you can see
very easily--in a very short time, change the feeling
of people toward accepting an amendment to the Constitution.

I think the turning point was in 1940 when for the
first time we put it in the Republican convention platform. (And by the way, that was done by one of the
delegates from Oklahoma, so when you try to get Oklahoma
into the field [to ratify the Amendment], remember that.)
The person who did it was Mrs. Perle Mesta. I was in
Europe in 1940 at our headquarters in Geneva, but when
I came back and became national chairman, and started
to try to get it in the national Republican convention
platform in 1944, and I went to see the leading Republican
women who were going out there, one of them was Miss
Ja ⌐   · ' ⸣ · ⸍┐ ┌ ⸍ ┌ ' ┬ ┬ ┐ ┌ ⸍ , a

Paul: delegate from New York, and I think she was perhaps
the most influential leading delegate, woman delegate.

Accidental Inclusion in Republican Platform

Paul: She said, when I said, "You see, the Republicans put it
in their platform," they said,"'Yes, we did. And that
was all in error. It was all a mistake.'"

Fry: [Laughing.] Oh. Really?

Paul: It seems at that time Mrs. Mesta was one of the delegates
from Oklahoma and of course that was her--I guess--birth-
place, where she grew up anyway. And they had some kind
of a hotel in Oklahoma City, Scrivner Hotel, is there
such a thing as that?

Fry: Skirvin.

Paul: Skirvin Hotel. That was their hotel that the family
owned, and I think it was through oil that they acquired
this fortune because she came, she said, of a very
humble origin in--went to some little, very ordinary little
school. And anyway, when they got this great wealth in
the family and she married a Mr. Mesta then, after she
became wealthy, who was also an Italian. He was an
Italian who had come in, had some kind of a business
in Pittsburgh which prospered. So by that time she
was--she was always, it seemed, a Republican. Now she's
a Democrat, you know.

So she went up as a delegate from Oklahoma to
Chicago to the Republican National Convention. And it
seems that she tried to get our plank in the platform,
(so Mrs. Mesta told me) and it seems that they put in a
kind of a plank which the women had drawn up which was,
I guess, just rather vaguely for equal rights, not for
the Equal Rights Amendment, apparently.

But you mustn't put this in your thing--my goodness
me, [laughing] it's a very private secret.

So then she said that the delegate on the platform
committee from Oklahoma, of course, knowing Mrs. Mesta
(she was standing somewhere around waiting to see what
they were doing about this particular plank) he came

Paul: up to her and said to her, "Now we've done it, here it is."

She looked at it and said, "That's all wrong. This is not what we want at all." And it was what Miss Todd and the other Republican women had all handed in. Perfectly all right, but not for the Equal Rights Amendment at all.

So he said, "Oh, well, I thought this is what you wanted."

And she said, "No, this is the way it should be: just a frank endorsement of the Equal Rights Amendment, in a few words."

And so he said, "Well, my goodness me, I'll have to have this substituted right away in our report, because we certainly don't want to make this mistake."

So it was substituted and read to the convention. And all these women said, "Well, who played this trick on us?" and so on. So, [laughing] my goodness, the hostility of Miss Todd and all the other Republican women that I went to see to ask them to help us again! And they said--

Fry: That took place in 1940?

Paul: Yes. I was there in 1944, but I wasn't even in the country in 1940 when this happened, and I didn't know one thing about it, the greatest possible--thank heaven I didn't know! So I'm sure they were sure that I had nothing to do with this trick that had been played. And I said, "Well, anyway it's in, and we certainly have to continue with it." And very reluctantly they didn't stage any opposition.

And so I remember I sat in my bedroom and called up practically every woman delegate to the convention, and said, "Now be sure you get our plank back again in 1944." And we got it in. But that, I think, was the great turning point.

Then I went--and the Democrats were going to meet in about two weeks or three weeks. So after it was in the Republican one--there were other people with me, you know, I wasn't doing all this alone, but all the I ... w ... , w l, l w ... ... w en I

Paul: first met Mary Kennedy who's turned out to be such a
        wonderful person. She came up to help, I think with the
        Democratic one.

            Anyway, I stopped on my way down at Mrs. Miller's--
        Emma Guffey Miller's home out in the country near
        Pittsburgh, I think it is, out in the country though, on
        the farm. And told her all that happened at the Repub-
        lican. And I said, "Now we have it in, could you take
        the leadership and come up and put it through in the
        Democratic one?" Because we knew she was going to be a
        delegate, she knew she was, and she was just beginning
        to be interested in this campaign.

            So she came up and she really--Mrs. [Perle] Mesta
        by this time had become a Democrat, so this year she was
        at the Democratic convention and was on the platform
        committee. So Mrs. Mesta and Mrs. Miller together
        really got it into the Democratic one. Then we had it
        in both. Absolutely, unqualifiedly for the Equal Rights
        Amendment.

            I think that the years from 1923 to 1940 were all
        building up to this culmination when it went into two
        platforms. And from that time on it was only, really--
        1944--the one you just told me went through in 1945 in
        the Democratic [Congress]. Nineteen forty-five was the
        Democratic, yes, because of Cravens. It was carrying
        out, of course, what that platform had said. And then
        in 1946 was the vote. And I remember that because I was
        there then.

The 1946 Vote in the Senate

Paul: And that was another trick that was played on us,
        because Mrs.--whoever the [WP] chairman was, I'm not
        quite sure who the chairman had been--but the new chair-
        man who came in right then at that moment almost was
        Ernestine Breisch Powell from Ohio. And she didn't have
        time to organize her forces or strength or anything else,
        when someone telephoned, "Within fifteen minutes the
        Equal Rights Amendment's to be introduced." I was there
        with Ernestine Powell trying to help her get started.
        And [the caller] said, "It's going to be introduced in
        the floor for a vote." It had gone through the
        committee.

Paul: Well, you know, this was simply an impossible situation.

[Interruption.]

So let me see--it was in the Senate it was coming up. I think our chief sponsor at that time in the Senate was Senator [Homer] Ferguson of Michigan. So we asked Senator Ferguson if he could defer the vote. Does it say anything about Senator Ferguson?

Fry: No, I only have the names on the committee here.

Paul: No, I'm not talking about who was on the committee, who was the chief sponsor. I think he was the chief sponsor at the moment. Anyway, he was the man who helped us the most.

So he went around to all the leaders trying to have this deferred, saying, "Well, the women aren't ready. They just haven't had any notice of this. There is nobody here to see the different senators." And he couldn't hold it off. So our opponents arranged it so we had this vote taken just by surprise. But we did get, of course, a majority, and that was because we'd just gotten it in the platform.

And so I remember I was so depressed because--and I guess everybody else was--that we did get a majority but we didn't quite get the two-thirds. And so Mrs. Miller, who had gotten it in the Democratic platform with Mrs. Mesta's help, said she wanted to take me over and talk to her brother, the senator. Senator [Joseph F.] Guffey was a senator and a very powerful senator, Democratic senator. And I went over--I remember very well his room was just covered, every inch of it with portraits given to him with signatures and so on, of all the illustrious people in the country, I guess.

And he said, "Well, it's nothing to be discouraged about. If the first time you get a majority vote, it's doing very well. And the next time we'll probably be able to get the two-thirds." But all this feeling of success not being too far away we've really had since we got it into the two platforms.

Fry: It's sort of like the rabbit running after the carrot--

Paul: And we've gotten more, I suppose, a great deal more of...

ERA AND THE HAYDEN RIDER 1950-1971

The 1950 Narrow Escape

Paul: And that was 1946. And then four years later we got the
       two-thirds, you know, in the Senate, but that's when we
       got the [Carl] Hayden rider. So you always seem to have
       one [problem]. The major point I think you have to have
       in your equipment is patience [laughing] if you engage
       in a reform of this type that you have to get through a
       legislative body. And my goodness, the ways they can
       oppose you! And if you could only have--the people
       were not so impetuous, if they could only have a little
       more trust in the people, usually, in the people who
       are doing the work to know that they know what the next
       thing should be. Because when this Hayden rider came
       on, what do you think the University Women [Business
       and Professional Women?] did but to endorse it!

Fry: Why would they do that?

Paul: Yes, why would they?

Fry: Now was that the same Hayden rider that was put on
       last year when I was lobbying?

Paul: There's only one Hayden rider.

Fry: So it was the same thing that was in 1970, 1969, in the
       bill.

Paul: Well, every year, the Hayden rider was always, always
       a thorn in our flesh. And you know they nearly got it
       through in 1950, almost got it through. You probably
       know that.

Fry: I knew it was sometime in the fifties.

Paul: But it was in 1950 that it went through the Senate by a big majority right over to the House. Now when it went, nobody knew it was coming up. Senator Hayden didn't know it was coming up. Nobody. And he was a very, in my mind a very fine man, Mr. Hayden. Very, very, very, _very_ friendly to the cause of women. And he was known and famous almost for the things that he did for women secretaries and clerks and so on over in the Senate.

Fry: Oh.

Paul: He just couldn't possibly be more fatherly, more kindly, and more concerned. And he was powerful so he really could help. So when this happened we went over to see Senator Hayden to talk to him about it. It had gone already to the House, ready to be voted on.

I was up in New York working at the United Nations trying to work with Elsie Hill on what we were doing over there, our little World Committee. And I discovered, somehow or other, somebody informed us, that the Business and Professional [Women] were employing a lobbyist, paying her a salary, Marjory Temple was her name, to get the measure through the House, and it was almost ready to go through.

Well, now, if it _had_ gone through, it would have gone on to the states and probably been ratified, and here we would have had it in the Constitution, as a result of all these years of labor, _in_equality written in for women!

Fry: I'm trying to remember how the Hayden rider was worded--

Paul: [Pause.] It was almost something like this: "This article should not be construed to impair any rights, benefits, or"--something--I can't remember the third thing--"now or hereafter conferred by law upon persons of the female sex."

Fry: Yes, which was again that old bugaboo of special protections.

Paul: "This article should not be construed to impair any rights, benefits, or _exemptions_" --I believe that was it--"any rights, benefits, or exemptions, now or hereafter conferred by law upon persons of the female sex."

Paul: Well, immediately we called up all the women's
        organizations when this happened. (Yes, I know now, I
        was down there [in Washington] when this vote was taken
        and then I went back to New York. We thought nothing
        more would happen about it.) It was such a dreadful
        thing. Now I want to tell you while the Senate was--
        now all this you can record if you want to. But when
        Mr. Hayden introduced this, Mrs. [Representative
        Katherine] St. George told me herself--Mrs. St. George,
        you know, was our chief sponsor in the House. Do you
        want to hear this?

Fry: Yes, it's right here [in the 1950 Equal Rights] while
        you're telling me about it. Marvelous.

Paul: Well, she told me that--of course, she wasn't a senator,
        but she said she'd gone over to sit with Margaret Chase
        Smith, the only woman in the Senate. They didn't know
        anything about the Hayden rider, that it was coming.

        They thought it [the Amendment] was going to go
        through; we had the votes so we thought it was going to
        go through. We had enough votes to carry it that day
        in 1950, and I can remember now I came down from Vermont*
        just on purpose for the vote. I was up in my little
        cottage, and the people telephoned and asked me to come
        down because it was such a crucial vote. They said,
        "We want everybody to come down who can possibly help."

        So I went down to try to help, never knowing about
        this Hayden rider, and no one else knowing it was coming
        up as far as I knew, excepting whoever was engineering
        the Hayden rider, and I don't know yet who it was. So
        Mrs. St. George said that she went over, and all relaxed
        feeling that it was going through with nothing for her
        to do and she would just sit there and hear the roll call.

        And then when Hayden got up and proposed this rider,
        she said she and Margaret Chase Smith immediately--saw
        immediately what it would do, that it was impossible,
        she said. So they divided the hall. And she said as
        rapidly as they could walk they walked down the different
        aisles and stopped at every man that they thought they
        might affect and said, "This is not what women want."

---

*Where Alice lived when working in the United Nations.

Paul: And said, "We haven't time to explain it to you, but
we know this is not what they want. They want the
Equal Rights Amendment without this rider." And she
told me that when it was over, she said, "Of course in
a very few minutes by the time it was ready to be voted
on, we couldn't do much. But we do know that not a
single man that we said, 'Please trust us. We know
what women want. Don't do this'--and we selected the
people we went to of course," she said. And every single
man voted against the Hayden rider that they had time
to talk to. And she said, "Of course, if we'd had
time, had an hour, we could have defeated the rider.
But it was so quickly pushed through by somebody, we
don't know by whom."

So then I went over to see Mr. Hayden. I was, I
think, with Cecil Broy. She was always such a wonderful
person to lobby with. Just a very good person. She
was the widow of Congressman Sisson [?] of Mississippi,
and she had long experience. He was in Congress twelve
years and was chairman of the Ways and Means Committee,
for part of the time anyway. A very powerful congressman, and she could always get access to people, by
calling up and saying, "I'm Mr. Sisson's widow, may I
come and see you?" So we went together to see Hayden.

That's the first time I'd ever had a talk with
Hayden--

[End of Tape 17, Side A]

[Tape 17, Side B]

Paul: And this is what Hayden said. He said, "As I was
walking into the hall and going to vote for the Equal
Rights Amendment as I had told you always that I would
do," he said, "a young man came up to me whom I'd given
desk space in my office"--because he was always doing
that sort of thing--

Fry: Hayden was?

Paul: Yes. This young man came and said he was out of work
and he wanted to try to get some assistance from various
congressmen and senators in trying to find a position,
and he couldn't afford to stay at a hotel and he couldn't
afford to have any place from which he could work, and
could Senator Hayden help him, and so Senator Hayden said,
"C   ,   ,   .   desk.

Paul: Make yourself at home." And that was the type of man
he was. And so when he told me this, I'm sure that is
what he did do.

[Interruption. Tape off.]

No, I didn't meet Senator Hayden in the hall. I
told you, Mrs. Broy and I went in to call on him, after
we [had] been told by Mrs. St. George, you see, that all
the people that she and Mrs. Margaret Chase Smith spoke
to and had time to speak to, voted against the Hayden.
And we wanted to find out now all about it, how it
happened to be introduced and so on.

Then Hayden said that he was taken completely by
surprise when this young man walked up and said,

"This amendment which you're going to support and
which is a very good one, of course, is not acceptable
to everybody on the ground that it may perhaps deprive
some women of advantages that have been won for them,
and that people will think they are doing a good thing
for women, they really will be doing harm to some women
who will lose what advantage has been won for them."
And he said, "Now here's a draft I wish you'd look at
and see about putting on this as an addition. Why not
safeguard and make this a better thing for women?"

Senator Hayden said to the young man, "Well, I'm
not a lawyer and I wouldn't be able to pass upon this
myself. I do want just what the women want, and what
would help them. And I thought this was a measure
which would help them, this Equal Rights Amendment, but
I'll send up your draft to the drafting clerk who goes
over all these measures, and see what he thinks of it."

And so he said, without even looking at it, he sent
it up to the top floor of the building [where] the
whole floor is given to drafters who pass for the Senate
upon everything that's offered. They look into it from
every point of view. Its legality point of view, and
the history and anything that the senator may want to
know. So he said in a short time he sent it down and
said, "This is perfectly well drafted, and if it's what
we want in its purpose, the drafting is all right."

So he said, "I then just sent it up to the desk to
be read as an amendment and I really didn't know anything
about it. I hadn't the faintest idea that it would be
a   ,   this

Paul: there's lots of controversy and lots of debate and it's
        not such an easy thing to change a constitutional
        amendment that's been reported from the committee
        favorably. It never entered my head that it would go
        through." And he said, "To my great astonishment,
        people said, 'Why this was just a gift from heaven, this
        is just perfection.' And I suddenly found that my little
        amendment to the Amendment was passed and sent on the
        the House."

        And so he said, "Now when you tell me why you
        don't want it"--which we did--he said, "I really don't
        know what to do. "Because," he said, "I don't ever deal
        with any group but the official group that has to do
        with appropriations"--because Hayden was chairman of
        the Appropriations Committee. And he said, "If I began
        to deal with all individual people on appropriations, I
        would never get anywhere." So he said, "If something
        comes up related to Indians"--welfare of Indians, we'll
        say--"I call up or ask the advice in some way of the
        head of the Indian Bureau here in Washington, the official
        head appointed by the government. And they'd tell me,
        that's a good bill or a bad bill or we want this changed,
        and so I just accept it. I don't pretend to study it
        myself."

The Women's Bureau, a Hayden Ally

Paul: So now, he said, "When all this controversy begins to
        develop and Margaret Chase Smith, my only woman colleague
        and Mrs. St. George, the leader in the House of the Equal
        Rights Amendment forces, and you come, leading the Equal
        Rights Amendment forces on the outside of Congress, and
        you say you don't want this, the only way that I normally
        would proceed--and I have proceeded this time--I call
        up the head of the Women's Bureau and they are supposed
        to--I would always; that's my duty, I'm supposed to call
        up, I'm not supposed to make an investigation myself
        into the merits of all this thing, it's impossible to
        do. We make an appropriation for the Women's Bureau
        and we're in constant communication with them as the
        official group appointed by the labor secretary, so they
        seem to think that my amendment is just what they want."

        [Interruption.]

Paul: complete good will and good intention of Mr. Hayden.
But we were like Mr. Hayden; we didn't think anything
would come of this. We thought it would go over to
the House and just not get any further because a constitutional amendment isn't very easy to pass, and we
didn't know that this Hayden rider was going to make it
suddenly so easy. For the moment I went back to New
York where we were working at the United Nations, Elsie
Hill and a few of us on our little committee, and then
I discovered somehow or other that instead of its being
neglected, forgotten in the House, a very active campaign
was afoot to send it on to the states for ratification
because the Senate had acted with a big majority, and
we thought we heard a group of women were lobbying for
it.

So I was working in New York especially with our
New York state chairman, who lived at the moment in New
York. Mayor [John] Lindsay, who's now Mayor of New
York, was her nephew, and she was very familiar in many
ways with political work and an extremely good person,
in my opinion, extremely good chairman. So I told her
the situation, and she said, "Well, I will go down with
you. And together maybe we can do something to stop
this before it gets off to the states for ratification."

She had been in her young days a professional
dancer and had opened up in her home, which was then
in northern New York, a dancing school, and it was very
well established and very successful. And so after she
ceased to dance herself so much, she had made a great
success of teaching others to dance. So the only thing
she discovered when she went to Washington was that in
going around the halls of the Congress your feet is
the part of you that suffers. She said, "My precious
feet! that's the way I have earned my living." When
she married into the Lindsay family--she had had a
German name, [Annawelt?], and she was of German extrac-
tion and descent, it seems. So she bought herself some
shoes, which it seems the professional dancers use when
they're compelled in some way to have to walk some
distance. Simply enormous, I've never seen anything
like it in my life; maybe you know what this is, like
little boats. I'd never seen them, didn't know they
existed. But it seems very common among professional
dancers. So she got herself, or maybe she already
took down with her, these boots--not boots, but large
shoes [laughing], very enormous shoes. It protected
your fragile little feet, that had to be doing this
e) · · ·   _ . ,   ·   w (''ʱꞧ'' off

Paul: in the morning looking like a lovely young matron, but
when you saw her begin to walk, [laughter] your eyes
were glued to these enormous little ships she was
walking in. [Laughter.] So she became quite a figure
that everybody knew. The lady with the boots, [laughter]
with enormous boots. I don't know if everybody knew
they were for dancing purposes or what.

She started out faithfully every single morning
and she was charming and thoroughly convinced and
determined. She couldn't have been better. And we
started to do everything that you could possibly think
of to--I especially saw and was trying to get mainly
the leaders, the Republican leaders. The senator from
New York, Senator [Kenneth B.] Keating, who was, well,
was a very powerful senator in determining the program
that would come up. I'm not sure whether the Republicans
were in control or who was in control at that moment
of the House.

Fry: Let's see who's on the House Judiciary Committee.

Paul: I don't think it has to go to a committee when it goes
to one house. I'm not positive about that, but I don't
think it did have to go to committee.

Fry: It was introduced by Katherine St. George, but that
doesn't tell us which party was in control.

Paul: Well, at all events, we faithfully tried to see every
single man that we thought we could move, to say,
"Don't take any action on this. Congress is going to
adjourn in a very short time, and this is something
that ought not to be rushed through without a little
more study and so on. And we went especially to the
leaders. I remember going to the Republican leaders,
so I guess the Republicans were in control of the
House. But it might have been that we just did that
to get the Republican leaders and line up the Republicans, perhaps.

The Woman's Party vs. The Business and Professional Women

Paul: However it was, Mrs. St. George telephoned over one day
and said, "I want to ask the president of the Business
and Professional [Women], who lives out in Iowa, and
s⟨· · · · ⟩⟨· · · · · · · · · · · · · ⟩ ask

Paul: you (myself), and the president of the National Woman's
Party who lives out in Columbus." She said, "I've sent
her a telegram and also a telegram to the president of
the B and P, and ask you to meet about, say, two or
three days in the future, if you possibly can, in my
office, to discuss what we can do about this Hayden
rider."

She said, "A congressman comes to me, one of my
fellow congressmen and says, 'Will you tell me what the
situation is about this Equal Rights Amendment and what
you think we ought to do.' And he says, 'In the morning
bright and early comes somebody from the Business and
Professional and says, "We insist, we just insist, all
American women want this rider accepted with the great
vote it's had in the Senate and quickly passed in the
House and sent off for ratification."

'And then in the afternoon comes the lady with the
boots, the enormous boots that she wears, and she says,
"No, under no circumstances must this measure be allowed
to get to ratification until this rider is eliminated."
And they say, 'We just don't know what to do.'" And so
Mrs. St. George said, "And I don't know what to do, I
don't know what to do about this. I'm of course against
the rider, but I really don't know what on earth to do
with this situation," because of this Marjory Temple
that was being employed by the B and P--which is this
awful trouble with the B and P; they don't study--you
know what the B and P is?

Fry: Yes.

Paul: Because they don't really--as you keep saying--"do the
homework." It seems to me that they don't, ever.

So Mrs. Powell came down, our national chairman
from Columbus. She's a lawyer, very good, and their
B and P national chairman came down--I think they call
her the national president--came down from Des Moines.
She was in real estate or insurance, maybe both, an agent,
I suppose you say. And she was absorbed in her own
business and didn't know one single thing about it. And
trusted this lobbyist that they'd employed.

And another person, I think, went from the B and P
and I don't know who it was, don't remember. And I went
for the Woman's Party. So we had two and they had two.
And there we sat in Mrs. St. George's office maybe three

Paul: or four hours. And she told of the very great seriousness to our whole cause of having somebody who faithfully lobbied all day long because she was a labor
woman and she'd been employed by the B and P, and she
was in the name of the B and P and was getting her
salary from the B and P. And we had a person who went
equally all day long, that was Mrs. Lindsay, she wasn't
paid anything, she paid all her own expenses, but
nevertheless, she was just as though she had been. She
was out early in the morning and all day long she went.
So no wonder the men were perplexed and the leaders
were perplexed and everybody was perplexed. (I don't
think it was the [B and P] lobbyist who was present,
but it was somebody else working with her anyway.)
And I tried my best when I got down there, and so did
Mrs. Lindsay, to dissuade this lobbyist from going on
and doing it any longer, trying to show her.

Well, then we saw it was hopeless. She was employed to do it and she was going to do it. Or maybe
she was persuading her employers--persuading the B and
P leaders, perhaps. Finally I got up and said, "Well,
we mustn't take any more of Mrs. St. George's time,
because we don't seem [we're] ever going to come to an
agreement. The B and P say that they have almost the
number of votes, they're almost to the point of having
the vote taken in the House, and they know that they
will have within three or four weeks, that they will
have the total number, and nothing will cause them to
desist. And we say maybe we can't stop it, but nothing
is going to cause us to desist from trying to stop it.
And we never are going to come to an agreement." So we
got up and went out and left Mrs. St. George, who indicated
that she stood with us. She didn't make any bones about
that.

So when we got outside I remember we stood in the
hall for maybe another hour [laughing] going on with the
conversation, getting nowhere. And then we invited them
to come over to our headquarters in the afternoon and
let us try another session and have more people, perhaps,
on each, on their side. Because I know their lobbyist
wasn't there so it must have been the--I'm almost certain
she wasn't there--so we thought the lobbyist whom we had
to try to counteract ought to be there.

So they said they would come and they did. And I
remember our national treasurer, who hadn't been over
in the morning, Mrs. Elizabeth Forbes (she was one of
dog

Paul: that she was always being diverted by. Something or
other had to be done about her enormous poodle, you
know, one of these very thoroughbreds; so she sat
down right by the fire on her little stool, I remember.
Marguerite Rawalt whom you probably have heard about,
the first vice-president of the B and P, and it may
have been that she was over at the first meeting--I'm
not sure. But she sat there on the piano stool, I can
still see her sitting there on this piano stool right
next to the fire in our living room, and Mrs. Lindsay
and I of course were there. And Mrs. Powell on our side.
And then Helen Irwin who was the president of the B and
P, was a very nice person I thought. And we started
over again.

And then I remember Miss Marjory Temple, she said,
"Well, no matter what you say we're going to be able to
do this. We have practically all the votes now. And,"
she said, "if you hadn't come down," she said to Mrs.
Lindsay and to me, "if you hadn't come down here we'd
have had it off to the states by now. But you have put
this monkey wrench in by coming down here and holding
us up, by seeing all these different people. So we're
having some difficulty, but we're sure we have enough
votes to overcome it."

So, she gave me this flat statement, "Had you not
come, we would have had it on the way now." And we
began to see that we were making quite a good deal of
headway with Mrs. Irwin, their national president, who
really hadn't had the faintest idea of what was going
on in the name of the B and P. But I remember that
Mrs. Rawalt didn't once open her mouth from the beginning
to the end and sat on this piano stool listening to the
whole thing. And of course, she was the one in charge
in Washington, she was the first vice-chairman, and she
evidently hadn't informed Mrs. Irwin at all about the
seriousness of the situation and about the reasons for
not supporting the Hayden rider. So she was passively
at least supporting everything that this lobbyist said.

Well finally, it went on a long time, and I thought
it was producing some results because I could see very
clearly that Mrs. Irwin wasn't aware of what was being
done in the name of her organization and was quite
troubled when we began to say, "This is the long history
of this Amendment through all these years and years and
years, beginning back in 1878 when it was first introduced, and now we suddenly repudiate it." I said,
"-   .   .   , .   d

Paul: labored for it. Because this would be <u>in</u>equality
we'd write into the Constitution, not equality."

So suddenly Mrs. Forbes jumped up and said, "Oh,
my dog, I have to look after my dog, my poodle." And
she <u>always</u>--this always happened. [Laughing.] I don't
know whether it happened on purpose, she thought we'd
talked long enough or what. So then they all said, "Oh,
we didn't know it was so late. We certainly are tres-
passing on your time," (we'd served them tea and so on)
"And we'll just all leave right now." So I begged them
not to because I thought we were making such good
progress, but they really thought it was a signal from
Mrs. Forbes that they'd had enough, and so they departed
and we didn't see them again.

Well then, finding out how serious it was--they
were stronger than we had imagined they were--of course
we redoubled our efforts and they probably redoubled
theirs. And anyway we finally got enough of the leaders
to agree not to allow it to come up.

Fry: What leaders?

Paul: The leaders in the House. I remember Senator Keating
is the one I think of most. He was not senator then, he
was a House man then, over on the House side. I don't
remember [all] the different people. But we didn't
change the B and P, and we didn't change Senator Hayden
because he said, "I don't have anything to do with his.
I take my orders from the Department of Labor's Women's
Bureau."

But the only people we did succeed in changing
were people who had a good deal to do with when Congress
was adjourned and what the subjects were they would take
up before. Both sides, Republican and Democrat, we
worked just on them. And we did get enough of them to
agree not to bring it up, and it wasn't brought up. And
that session came to an end. At the end of that time,
pretty soon, Mrs. Irwin went out of office and a new
president was elected. And the new president was this
Miss Rawalt, that first vice-president.

So Miss Rawalt tells me now, I've seen her recently,
she said, "You know, I never was for the Hayden rider."
Well, I don't think much of that statement. I think she
was. She certainly gave every bit of the--she couldn't
be there in charge and have the lobbyist go out every
s '.   ' .,   _ :   _ _   .   )dy had

Paul: to be responsible for it. Certainly the first vice-
president must have been. But she said, "As soon as
I took office I dismissed this Marjory Temple." She
probably did, but I don't think that she--I think
that she _did_ give her support. She certainly gave her
support at this meeting by never speaking up and saying
a single word in defense of what we were arguing, but
apparently was giving all her support to this lobbyist,
Marjory Temple.

Well, now that's the Hayden rider as it started.
Now the next thing that happened was it was introduced
again, and again, and again and again and again and
again. In every Congress somebody put in the Hayden
rider, down to the last Congress. Always we had the
Hayden rider.

That's about the end of the Hayden rider, I guess.
We had to start, of course, then a campaign with all the
women's organizations over the country to educate them
on the Hayden rider: what it meant, what it would mean
if it went out to the states to ratification, what it
would mean if it got in the Constitution, and by the
end, there was no--one organization after another
finally joined us in opposing the rider.

Fry: Here in 1950 in your September-October issue of _Equal
Rights_ it says, "Members pledge congressional candidates
for the Equal Rights Amendment without the Hayden rider.
Support Senate friends who voted equality straight." I
wonder if also every two years you had this attempt to
get in members of Congress who would vote against the
Hayden rider.

Paul: Always.

National Organization for Women Enters

Paul: From the time it was introduced it was one of the
obstacles we had to overcome. And even as late as
1966, I guess it must have been, when the NOW [National
Organization for Women] organization was formed, this
Mrs. Betty Friedan, who's the national president and
formed it, at a meeting of the D.C. branch--

I had joined this, I told you I think, the moment
i   .   -   ,   '   ' ᴧ   -   ,   ' ·' I was

Paul: asked to join and I thought I ought to do it and I did,
thinking of <u>course</u> it would be for the Equal Rights
Amendment. And at this D.C. meeting, up got the chairman, Mrs. Friedan, and she said, "Now this is a new
era, and always when you get a new era, you must have,
you should have a new amendment to work for, and we
don't want to be bound down by the past and everything.
Let's get a new amendment, start out all fresh. And I
will appoint a committee to draw up a new amendment."
And so she said she would appoint, and she named a
person whom I have never seen and don't even remember
her name. It's a very peculiar name, she came from
some foreign country, wasn't born in this country, and
she had one of those Czech names or Lithuanian names,
very peculiar name. And so she was made one of the
three. One person was Mary Eastwood, whom I'd never
known, but she was put on this committee and she had
joined the NOW people. And one was, I think, Caruthers
Berger was a second but I'm not quite sure about that.
Caruthers Berger. She's one of our present--on our
national board. I think she was, but I'm not quite
sure. But I remember Mary Eastwood was. And I remember
this person with the queer name was. And the person
with the queer name immediately got up and said, "Well,
I'm very happy to go on this committee to draw a new
amendment. I, of course, am in the Women's Bureau and
I'm the one who's always sent from the Women's Bureau
down to Mr. Hayden, when we think he's going to weaken.
And I'm sent to make him stand firm and never deviate
from his opposition to the Equal Rights Amendment and
his support of the Hayden rider."

Fry: Did you jump to your feet?

Paul: I wasn't there. I didn't go to the meeting at all.
And so we had a firsthand statement anyway from the
person who was appointed to be the one to keep Senator
Hayden in line. And I went back--Mrs. Broy and I went
back together--several times to see Senator Hayden and
we always found he was stronger and stronger in saying,
"Well, I don't know what to do. You know how insistent
the Women's Bureau is that they just keep after me to
see that I always see that my amendment that they're so
pleased with is reintroduced and reintroduced and really
this--I just don't exactly know what to do about it.
It seems as though I have to do what the Women's Bureau
wants. And this is one thing that they want very much.
And I've never considered our position to pass on these
measures, with a slight change here,   nge
t r."

Paul: So we pretty soon found out what was happening:
that the Women's Bureau was really, actively, deter-
minedly trying to get this Equal Rights Amendment
weakened by putting the Hayden rider on so it wouldn't
be so much good if it ever did get through: in fact,
it'd be what they wanted. Because it was recognizing
the whole idea of a different standard for women.

Fry: Protective legislation and so forth.

Paul: Now the last great opposition we had with regard to the
Hayden rider finally made us think we would draft something that would incorporate the Hayden rider but make
it apply to both sexes. So we did. It said: "This
article shall not be construed to impair any rights,
benefits or exemptions now or hereafter conferred by
law equally upon both sexes." Instead of saying,
"--conferred by law upon persons of the female sex."
We just changed that.

Fry: Oh, [laughing] and suggested that for a rider?

Paul: No, we said, "If you have to have the rider"--we went
to Hayden and said, "If your obligation to the Women's
Bureau is such that you can't change this, that you
can't refuse your rider and can't withdraw your rider,
then make your rider apply, as you were talking about
doing, equally to men and women." And so we said, "We've
come here with a draft," and we showed it to him. "This
article shall not be construed to impair any benefits,
rights or exemptions, now or hereafter conferred by law
upon persons of the female sex," we say, "--now or
hereafter conferred by law equally upon both sexes."
Or, "equally without distinction as to sex," some such
word. "Without distinction as to sex" perhaps, I'm not
sure. So we said, "This is our idea. Will you accept
it?" And Senator Hayden said, "Well, I of course am
always telling you am not a lawyer, but I can't see
anything in the world that's the matter with that. And
of course we don't want any exemptions and so on deprived because of sex. It applies to both sexes." So
he said, "I'll send this up or I'll telephone this up
and ask the drafting clerk. The best drafting clerk up
there is the one from Sweden who's a very fine person
and thoroughly understands this point of view of equality
of sexes, and I'll call up and ask him to receive you."

         So we went up and talked to this man and said, "Now
this we think might be a way to unite everybody because
i+ ------:-? ---- - - - i- ---- -- --- -- :talitarians

Paul: and we don't see any reason why it wouldn't be accepted by everybody."

And so he said, "All right, I'll study it and I'll make a report in about a week." So he called up and told us he had made his report and sent it down to Senator Hayden, saying that as far as he could see, it couldn't be better drafted; it was drafted, as far as the wording we used, to express what we had in mind. If that was what Senator Hayden had in mind, he could go forward with it as far as the drafters were concerned. So Senator Hayden was prepared, I guess, to do it. He seemed to be.

And then we went to see him again and he said, "Well, you know, I've been called up by the Women's Bureau, and they say they want no change in the Hayden rider. It must be _just_ as they had drafted it," just as he had presented it in the beginning. We don't know who did that original drafting or whoever started this whole business. We've still never found out and Hayden never found out. So there we were, we were saddled with it.

Well, then, this Mrs. Peterson came into the picture. She was made the director of the Women's Bureau and assistant secretary of labor--given all authority in this whole field, what was done on anything, any measure like this. And she certainly couldn't have been more active in opposing it. So one night, I was telephoned to by a person in the Women's Bureau who had been very helpful to us, and what's her name? Catherine East, you may have heard of her. She's now the executive secretary of the Status of Women Commission, appointed by President Kennedy and later continued by President Nixon. The national executive director of that commission.

So she called me up and--I'd never seen her or met her, but I'd known by telephoning to her that she was always very cooperative and she seemed to be very friendly in the Women's Bureau and most of the people weren't. And so she said, "I'd like to come up and bring somebody to talk about this amendment." And the person she brought, although I'd never seen her, but she brought in Mary Eastwood, who was one of these three people appointed by Mrs. Friedan to draw up for NOW a new amendment because a new era required a new amendment [laughing]. So Mary Eastwood, the first time I ever saw rtment,

Paul: and she had a great deal to do because she prepared
any number of reports for the attorney general and she
thought that she'd been charged with this duty of being
one in three to draw up a new amendment, and she wanted
to come up and submit it to me. So I said, "Well, your
amendment may be much better, may be much better drafted
and a great improvement, but even if it is I don't want
to look at it, because," I said, "the one thing that we
have done is to get so many, many, many, many, many,
many congressmen pledged to the present amendment, and
so many senators pledged to it, and so many women's
organizations pledged to it, to change it now would be
a mistake, even if yours is better in wording, because
at least ours is worded well enough, we know, to accomplish what we are trying to accomplish by it. And
if I begin to discuss the points with you we'd never
get anywhere because I think no second amendment ought
to come into the picture now. We ought to build on our
present strength. We've practically enough people now
to take the vote," (which we found we did, because it
was just before the 1970 vote when we got it 350 to 15
in the House. And we knew that from the number of people
who had become sponsors). So Mary Eastwood said, "Well,
I will think this over," when I said, "I won't look at
it, you can take it back, I'm not going to see it. I
don't want to get into a discussion." And then finally
she said, "You know, I agree with you. I can see that
it would be a real way of defeating the whole Amendment
to discard everything that everybody had been for and
start fresh on a new version, just because Mrs. Friedan
says [laughing] a new era requires a new amendment."

I said, "I don't think it requires a new amendment
at all. We'd used the old one in the suffrage campaign,
we didn't change it in any possible way. We had the
same problem of people thinking they could write a
better one, and it's gone through and it's worked successfully and I think this will have the same luck if
we can stick together."

So Mary Eastwood became from that time on a very
stalwart supporter. And we had the other person,
whoever she was. So we had two on the committee of
three that stood for the old amendment. And then the
whole question was presented by the D.C. branch to the
national convention which met that year--

Fry: Of NOW?

Paul: N

Paul: convention. Mrs. Friedan presided and Marguerite
Rawalt was her assistant up in the front. And a terrific campaign was put on at that convention to discard
our Equal Rights Amendment altogether and put in a new
one, as Mrs. Friedan had proposed. But finally, we
won. A great many Woman's Party people had become
members of NOW, not on purpose, not on thinking they
would have any fight on the floor about this, but when
the fight came up, they all stood up and voted for the
Equal Rights Amendment as it was. And we captured the
NOW people. And since then it's been on their list
and they have--have--made us really, quite a lot of
trouble. [Laughing.]

Fry: [Laughing.] Maybe you were better off when they wanted
another amendment.

Paul: What they have done, you see, for instance, going to the
legislatures and insisting on talking all the time not
about equality for women but talking about these other
subjects, which gets the men all mixed up, and they
think that--

Fry: You mean, like abortion and--

Paul: Yes. Because this happens all the time, and I don't
know exactly [laughing] how to meet it. Well now, I
guess that's about the Hayden rider. You know
everything.

        When I was telling you about Mrs. Dorothy Greuning,
I was telling you about going out to meet with Mrs.
Peterson. That was the day that she changed.

1970-1971: VICTORY IN CONGRESS

Hayden and Anti-Draft Riders

Fry: So this brings us up to about 1970, is that right?
Alice, remember those riders that were put on it, I
guess, in 1971 in the House Judiciary Subcommittee
about exempting women from the draft? There was that
Hayden rider on it, and there was another to the effect
that this should not be construed to mean that women
should be subject to military duty.

Paul: Was that put in as an amendment? I don't remember.

Fry: Yes, that was one rider on it.

Paul: I don't remember anybody proposing that. It was never
put on, of course.

Fry: It never did make it out of the full Committee. The
reason it sticks in my mind is because I just happened
to be there in June of 1971 when it was voted out of
subcommittee, but--

Paul: Which committee?

Fry: House Judiciary Subcommittee, which Don Edwards headed.
And I remember I was so impressed with all of the ways
that you used to get that bill back into subcommittee
to be reconsidered and get those riders off.

　　　　I happened to arrive at Don Edwards' office just
as they got the bad news. It had passed by one vote in
the subcommittee, I believe, and to everyone's surprise.

Paul: Had it?

Fry:　　　　,　　　　·　　　　　　　　　　'　·　　· w﹍·﹍·﹍'　ʳ to be

Fry: either a tie, or lose completely. But it passed with
the riders by one vote. And then when it was reconsidered, I guess the riders were dropped and it went in
its pure form to the Committee. I wasn't on the scene
then when it went out of the full Committee. It took a
long time to get out of the whole Committee.

Paul: You know, we didn't want it to get out of the Committee
at all, you remember.

Fry: I remember you were trying to stop it. Because that
was the same as the Martha Griffiths-Bayh version too.

Paul: Yes, that's the reason we didn't want that to get out
of committee.
[End of Tape 17, Side B]

Objections to the Griffiths-Bayh Change in Wording

[Tape 18, Side A]

Paul: The last thing Bayh had proposed in 1970 when it went
through the House, he had proposed to amend the [ERA].
Remember he got up and gave a speech saying, "We can't
get the Equal Rights Amendment through the Senate in
the [form] it went through the House, and so I am
proposing to amend by substitution"--that means substitute a new one for the old one--"the insertion of
something in the Fourteenth Amendment," which was really
an amendment to the Fourteenth Amendment.

Fry: I remember that. Wasn't that in the fall? And Ted
Kennedy talked about doing it too--

Paul: And so then he said, "I will not ask for any vote on
it today or discussion of it today, but it will go over
to the lame duck session [late 1970] which is going to
meet in a month"--or something--"and then it will be
the first order of business." You may remember.

And so it was the first order of business, and up
got Mr. [Ted] Kennedy, who was then the Democratic
whip (not now, but he was then) and he said, "For
Senator Bayh, I wish to ask unanimous consent to postpone the first order of business, which is the equal
rights for women amendment substitute of Mr. Bayh's,
because of more pressing business now before us, and to
have it temporarily postponed." And then [we had] this
temporary postponement. We kept working all the time.

We had enough votes, you know, to carry the original

Paul: amendment as it had gone through the House. [There]
        wasn't any question about it. Mrs. Mesta, for instance,
        was so anxious to give some kind of a party for every-
        body to celebrate it--I guess you weren't there when
        all this happened--

Fry: No, I wasn't.

Paul: So one day she went up to the Senate and sent in her
        card and called Senator [Mike] Mansfield. Well, most
        people, of course, don't call the majority leader,
        [laughter] but she said that she had to make plans for
        some kind of a reception or dinner or party that she
        wanted to give to this whole Senate, now that they were
        going to pass it--it had just gone through the House
        [with a huge majority], and it looked as though it was
        going to go through the Senate. And I guess this was
        before the lame duck session, must have been before.
        Bayh got up and made his motion to substitute.

        And he asked for unanimous consent the night
        before. No, it was [Sam J.] Ervin who asked for
        unanimous consent the night before, to propose an
        amendment to the pending Equal Rights Amendment. And
        you know all you have to do to stop it is for one hand
        to go up and say, "I object." Then there isn't
        unanimous consent and that ends it. And that's what
        Bayh, who'd arrogated to himself the management of the
        whole campaign, should have done, but he didn't. And
        so--there were very few senators left, nearly everybody
        had gone home--and so the handful or more that were left
        said nothing and so whoever was presiding announced,
        "Well, by unanimous consent, Senator Ervin will be given
        the floor at eleven o'clock"--or some definite time that
        he'd asked for--"in the morning to present his amend-
        ment."

        And that's where all the trouble began. It was
        merely because Bayh, either intentionally or through
        negligence or whatever reason, didn't oppose it. It
        was so simple to prevent Ervin from ever getting the
        floor because you can't get the floor excepting by
        unanimous consent all out of order when he had no
        reason to be doing this.

        So Mrs. [Cecil] Broy, who was always a very great
        admirer of Mr. Bayh, one day said, "I just want you to
        not be so prejudiced against Mr. Bayh. I think you're
        all wrong on this. I think his heart is in this,
        trying to put the Amendment through, and I wish you'd

Paul: go and talk to Mr. [Mode?], who's his executive
director who's directing this whole campaign."

So to please her, I said I would. And I went with
her. She made the appointment. And so Mr. [Mode?]
began to say how strongly Mr. Bayh felt in support of
our measure and wanted it to go through but there were
all these difficulties and you had to be practical and
so on and this was the best that could be done. And I
said, "Well, will you just explain to me why in the
whole world--we didn't ask Mr. Bayh to be our leader,
we asked Mr. McCarthy to lead, and Bayh wanted to do
it and Mr. McCarthy stepped aside and let Bayh do it,
because he was chairman of the Judiciary Subcommittee
in the Senate. And so he just was representing us and
we couldn't help ourselves, apparently. And why, when
he was taking that responsibility, did he allow Mr.
Ervin to introduce his amendment--by unanimous consent
when all he had to do [to block it] was raise his hand?

Well, Mr. [Mode?] said, "Mr. Bayh wasn't there at
that moment and it was the fault of Mr. [probably Marlowe
W.] Cook." Well, I don't know whether Bayh was present
or not, but anyway he was in the city, he was available
to be present. And he should have been there minding
or have some faithful person there managing it.

Fry: That was before the last session?

Paul: That was before the lame duck session.

Then in the [1970] lame duck session when--I told
you--that Kennedy got up and said, "We'd like to temporarily postpone the Equal Rights Amendment" which was
a substitute, not our own amendment at all, but was a
substitute amendment that he had gotten--by unanimous
consent he had then gotten this through, and it wiped
out our amendment; there was no amendment left of ours.
And he was--his amendment was to change the Fourteenth
Amendment.

So when we were trying to have it brought up, we
thought, "Still we have a majority here pledged for the
real amendment, and by some way or other they can
certainly get rid of Mr. Bayh's substitute by voting it
down." Well then Mr. Bayh said, to all the women who
went to him, and all the NOW people--that's when they
began to make themselves, I thought, a supporting group
for Bayh and I thought they didn't understand what they
is if

Paul: you ever met her down there.

Fry: Yes, she was there when I was there.

Paul: Well, she was taking the lead with these people and I
don't think she paused long enough to know what on earth
it was she was doing. She was all for action, all for
activity, always saying, "We want action." That was
her [laughing]--no matter what the action was, she
seemed to want it. So Mr. Bayh would reply to everybody, "Well, never mind, the regular session's almost
here in January. Then we'll start fresh and I will
introduce the Amendment again," my--our original
amendment. So no one, I guess, was aware--and that was
excepting perhaps maybe Mrs. Rawalt, who worked with
him all the time--was aware of what he was doing. So
when he got up--I guess it was maybe a week or two before
we discovered that he'd changed the Amendment, because
the Amendment [itself] was intact and we didn't realize
that he'd changed the enforcement part.

Fry: Section Two.*

Paul: And at the same time had gotten Mrs. Griffiths to introduce the same [Bayh version], and almost everybody
thought it was the same [original version] in the House.

Fry: And I guess that was when I came to help lobby, in June,
1971. The House Judiciary Subcommittee staff told me
that the reason we should leave it alone as the Bayh-
Griffiths version was that the version had been agreed
on by the Senate supporters and the House supporters,
and it would work better because the conference committee,
then, would not have any problem.

Paul: You don't have a conference committee if they're
introduced the same [in both houses].

Fry: That's what they were saying: that they wanted to
avoid a conference committee, because they felt that--

Paul: They wanted to, naturally.

------

*The Bayh-Griffiths version referred to enforcement "by
Congress" and omitted "and the several states." A time
limit of seven years was also added for ratification.

Keeping it in Subcommittee

Paul: You know, I was the one who called you and asked you to come, do you remember?"* And I thought it was so vital that we get somebody that could have access at any moment to the chairman of that [sub]committee, because we were having--and you always have some difficulty in talking to a busy chairman. We thought if you could come you could probably keep him from allowing that bill in that form ever to get out of [subcommittee and] get into the hands of [Emanuel] Celler, because we knew if once it got over to Celler, he would rejoice and push it, which he [eventually] did of course. After it got out of his [Edwards'] we were pretty helpless because it had to go to Celler and he--

Fry: You're talking about Don Edwards as the chairman of the subcommittee, and Celler as the chairman of the full Committee.

Paul: So it had to go to Celler if it left Don Edwards. The only way we could [do it was to] keep it away from Celler. We knew that Celler would push through the Bayh amendment. That was the only way we could do it, was to keep it in the sub. And you know, we did keep it in the sub until after Labor Day, I think it was.

Fry: Yes, I was surprised at how long it stayed there. [Laughing.]

Paul: I know, but I mean it didn't stay there of its own. It stayed there by our getting enough people to keep it there, as you well know. You know that. It's the only way it could be done.

Fry: I didn't know it firsthand, because I had to return to California the first part of July [1971]. But I was quite sure that this was your work, when I read the reports.

Paul: I mean what you were starting, you see, to do, to try to keep it there, we did succeed. We did it by going to

---

*For the last week of June, 1971.

Paul: the Democratic leaders of the House because they could
have a great deal to decide what subjects were coming
up. And we persuaded them not to let this come up until
after Labor Day. And that gave us a good long time in
which to work.

Then we started in again to try to keep it from
getting out of Don Edwards' hands. And we didn't have
you there. We didn't have very good luck with Don
Edwards, you see, because none of us knew him personally.

And I went--I just worked morning, noon, and night,
all night and all day, trying to keep it from coming
up before Labor Day. And then I'd planned to go up to
this little cottage here, and I had this housekeeper
who went up with me, Mrs.--made life very easy when I
had her, until she just died, I told you--Mrs. Ewing.
And so as soon as we staved it off and it wasn't going
to come up until after Labor Day, that much was done,
then I came up here to try to get the house opened
again and see that it didn't go to destruction again by
being left alone.

Disagreement Within NWP

Paul: And when I went down [to Washington] after Labor Day,
as soon as I--I thought it was all fixed and the work
of keeping it from coming up would continue even if I
was not there. So when I went down, almost the first
thing I discovered was that our own headquarters group
were urging an immediate vote, that it be brought up
for a vote.

Fry: On that version, on the Bayh version?

Paul: And I remember Mrs. Longwell. One night I made an
appointment, just as soon as I got back almost, about
an article for the Swarthmore Alumni paper. Somebody
had come down and tried to write an article about the
whole equal rights movement and so on and she'd talked
to Mabel Vernon and to me as graduates. (She took the
alumni paper.) I think it was the only one she'd
talked to. And then she'd gone home and written the
article, and it was a very poor article. She probably
did her best, but in one or two interviews, you know
you can't learn very much about a movement, and she
than

Paul: she did.

So I'd rewritten--I'd first of all tried to get Mabel to correct this and Mabel didn't want to do it. So finally I said, "Well, I will do it," and when I started to do it, I thought, "The easiest thing is to write a new article." And I know when I did it and gave it to Mabel and Consuelo to work on also, Consuelo said, "Goodness, your article is a hundred times better than this one that she sent down to us. And certainly we can probably get her to use it." And then she said, "I'm not going to say it was a hundred times better; I think it's a thousand times better." Which shows you how awful her article was.

I changed it and said in my article--[pause] the topic was "Swarthmore and the Equal Rights Amendment," you see, that we were supposed to be writing about. So instead of having it just little dinky points, (it was no good at all, it really was a thousand times [laughing] worse than mine) I started with--said the first efforts made in the founding of Swarthmore was made when Lucretia Mott was one of the leaders of the feminist movement in our country and was on the committee that raised the money and turned the first piece of sod for the building of the college hall and so on. And [one] could identify our college with the whole movement beginning with Lucretia Mott when she was this great influence there, then on down to Amelia Walker, who was before my time and who'd become our national chairman and was continuing this work, exactly the same thing as Lucretia Mott had done. She was following Amelia Walker in these things you've been telling me. And then Mabel Vernon, and then myself, and then another person, Martha Moore, who'd been in prison with us, who'd been a Swarthmore graduate--just to show that this was a principle of the Quaker religion and that every one of these people had graduated Swarthmore or been at Swartmore, or had anything to do with Swarthmore, from Lucretia Mott down to our present time. Well, I thought that was a very good article [laughing]. But anyway, evidently the editor didn't think so.

So Mabel Vernon was more concerned about it than I was; I thought, well, we've done our best, we've given them all the facts and if they don't want it, all right. But she was very determined, so she phoned and said she'd come up, a day or two after I got back, and we'd go over together and see if together we couldn't take
'se

Paul: facts, and we did get them to use some of them.

So when Mabel arrived--and Consuelo came with her--almost the same moment came in Mrs. [Carol] Burris* and sat down beside us just as we're sitting here. And she--embraced me and was full of warm greetings and such. And I didn't know she was coming, had no idea why she was coming, and I'd never been particularly very much satisfied with what she was doing in our campaign. So I wanted to get on and get this Swarthmore thing done and was not too happy she came. And at the same moment in came [NWP chairman] Mrs. Longwell. And sat herself down--do you know all this?

Fry: No.

Paul: --and sat herself down--I don't want this recorded, this is just trifling gossip, I guess--so then Mrs. Longwell, I would say, was silent perhaps most of the evening. But for two hours, Mrs. Burris (and I know it was two hours because Mrs. Longwell said it was; she evidently timed it) for two hours Mrs. Burris delivered a speech and the speech was--gave nobody a chance to interrupt or say anything, and she said, "This is all fixed and all arranged that this vote is going to be taken in the House Judiciary Committee"--full committee. And this, you see, was just after the Labor Day extension was exhausted. We now were starting in again, had to make another extension, which I had thought they were all going to do, having won the first one.

She said, "We have gone there, we have just invaded Mr. Don Week's office and we're"--

Fry: You mean Don Edwards'?

Paul: "Don Edwards' office. We've surrounded it. We have people there every moment and everyone is saying, 'An immediate vote! We demand action! [Thumping table.] We're standing for action for now, right now. We are the NOW women, we went everything right away.'" Over and over she said, "This and this is what has got to happen. And we don't want you to come back and you've already started, we find you've started, you're already

---

*At this time, Burris was embarking on the development

Paul: at _work_ getting this thing postponed. You've talked
to this one and this one and this one and this one and
now everybody's upset and they think that it better
be postponed. We're here to see that you do not,
[thumping table again] and you _can_ not." This is the
way she talked. And so Miss Vernon would say, "Well,
what--" she would put in all kinds of questions. She
was very much impressed by Mrs. Burris and she didn't
have any of this uneasiness about her that I'd accumulated by seeing her work, because she didn't know
about it.

But her questions were all rather expressing
doubts, as to why she thought she'd get through the
Amendment we'd all stood for and so on, by this process
of having it taken up right now. And we'd had this
one victory and therefore--And [Mrs. Burris would say]
"It's impossible, you cannot do such a thing, you
cannot do it, you cannot have any effect on Mr.
Edwards, it's going to be done, it's all arranged,"
and so on.

And I really didn't do anything but sit and listen,
because I was hoping every minute she'd stop and get up
and go out. I didn't know why she'd come, why she was
making this speech to me. I'd never known her, you see,
very well. I just didn't know what it was all about.

And finally she went. And it was so late that
Miss Vernon said, "Well, I can't begin on the Swarthmore
article now at this late date, so we'll go home too."
So she got up and Consuelo went and Mrs. Longwell went.
I _did_ continue, you know, right afterwards, because I
thought we could probably do it by getting leaders of--
it was only a question of postponing, not of _doing_
anything, but of postponing. That's usually pretty
easy to accomplish because people are more ready to
postpone than they are to do something positive usually.

So I was proceeding happily [laughing] for maybe a
day, talking to the same people who had helped us to get
the first postponement, when in came Mrs. Longwell.
And she said,

"I understand that you're asking people to have
this postponed again. Well, how can you do such a
thing? You heard Mrs. Burris and Miss Vernon; they
both came here to urge you not to do this."

A . . . . " , ı . . .dn't.

Paul: She didn't know a single thing about this. Never heard
       of it."

           "Well," she said, "she came in the same time with
       Mrs. Burris."

           And I said, "I know very well she came at the
       same time, but I had an appointment with Miss Vernon.
       She and Consuelo came up about an article that we are
       somewhat responsible for in the Swarthmore magazine,
       and we had to do something about it. So she came. She
       happened to come exactly the same moment that you came
       and Mrs. Burris came, but she didn't come for the same
       purpose. She didn't know anything about what you were
       talking about. She didn't come to argue with me, as
       Mrs. Burris did."

           "Well, you heard Mrs. Burris. I think when Miss
       Vernon came at the same time, that was what she was
       trying to say to you, too." And, "You have no right,
       you have absolutely no right to come here. Here we've
       made this plan. We're sure we can achieve it. We can
       have a vote taken now, in the House Judiciary Committee."

           And I said, "Well, of course, I _know_ you can have
       it taken now. The hard thing is to see it is _not_ taken
       now. There is no difficulty about having it _taken_ now."

           So then, I finally said, "Well--I can see that--I
       don't know how you can possibly do this after the vote
       that the whole [NWP] council took not to have anything
       to do with this [Bayh] amendment. The whole council
       meeting before I went up to [Connecticut]--I put the
       motion myself and it went through unanimously." I
       said, "You all voted _not_ to do what you're now _doing_."

Fry: Oh yes, I remember that.

Paul: Well, you can't probably remember it because you
       weren't there.

Fry: I remember the report that the vote had been taken, at
       the time.

Paul: So, I said, "Well, you are all disregarding the vote
       that was taken, and you're the national chairman. And
       I don't know what to do. I don't want to start and make
       a difficulty for you as national chairman and to cause
       a division in the organization. So I think probably the
       ᵇᵉˢᵗ ᵗʰⁱ   ᶠ   ᵗ   ᵗ ᵏⁿᵒʷ ᵗ ᵐ ᵗ , ᵒt go

Paul: ahead and do just what you want, not to do anything
more. But I think it's a great mistake."

Alice Paul Drops Out

Paul: Well, I did withdraw. I didn't ask another person. I
didn't go forward with it at all. I just dropped out
of it.

And then they had the vote and of course they
voted out the [Bayh-]Griffiths measure. And now you
see, when Mrs. Longwell, when she sees the difficulty,
this very difficulty about the states' rights business
and so on down there in Alabama, she just gives up the
fight. You notice she said, "I'm leaving now"--

Fry: Oh, in her letter today.

Paul: Yes.

Fry: She said she thought she'd found a person there to
head up the fight.

Paul: I know, but we maybe find one woman or two or a thousand
women, but the thing is to stay when you undertake these
difficult things and get it done.

Fry: She said it was really very difficult.

Paul: She went down to do this, and she finds what we told
her all the difficulties there would be.

Fry: Well, you were there when it passed the House and the
Senate? Were you in Washington when it passed?

Paul: When it passed the House the second time? Yes. And
when it passed a second time, when it was introduced a
second time in this version, in the [Bayh-]Griffiths
version, we thought--I thought--we could possibly find
somebody who would have enough interest and enough power
to [substitute their previous vote on the original
version]. But it did come up [on the floor] when we
couldn't prevent it from coming up, which is what I had
hoped we could do. When it was certain to come up, I
thought we might find someone who would move to substitute their previous vote [for] the [original]
... ... r previous

Paul: vote. Because practically everybody who was going to
vote this time had voted for the other [original]
version. And it seemed to me if one person on the
floor could--

First of all, we knew we couldn't get Mrs.
Griffiths to do it. She would have been the logical
person--for her to say, "I would like to withdraw this
version in favor of the one you've all voted for." The
person who really took the greatest, I think, part in
trying to bring this to pass and to find somebody was
Mary Kennedy. And she found a man named Mr. Myers
who was a congressman who simply couldn't conceive
why, when they had voted one measure a few months ago,
they should suddenly be asked to vote another version
which--they had all thought the first version was right
or they wouldn't have voted for it. And why in the
world should they be asked to vote another one because
the Senate, a senator, had made this change over in
the Senate.

Well, so he undertook to take a poll of the whole
House and see if he could--maybe you know of this, his
name was Mr. Myers*--and see if he could accomplish
this. And there were several others, maybe a dozen
others, that had expressed themselves as willing to do
the same thing and to join with him. So when it came
to be the morning when the vote was to be taken, on the
Griffiths measure, I called up all the people--not all,
but a good many people who I thought might help. I
remember one I called, Mrs. [Florence P.] Dwyer of--you
remember her?

Fry: No, I only know she was an old faithful worker.
[Laughter.]

Paul: No, no, no. not an old worker; she was a congresswoman
from New Jersey, and one of the people who was the
strongest that we had in all of Congress for the Equal
Rights Amendment and a great co-worker with Mrs. St.
George and the other people who had brought it to this
stage.

And she said, "You know that you don't have to

*Probably John Thomas Y...., B.....'.. .. Virginia in
N

549

Paul: tell me any of this; I know it, maybe, better than you
do, the wisdom of keeping to the original amendment.
But," she said, "I wish to tell you this: that Mr.
Bayh has got it all tied up, and I won't take the time
to try to tell you all the details of what he's done,
but I know it's tied up. He's tied it up so there's
nothing that we can do in the House about it. And
while it seems unthinkable, he makes it seem plausible
and reasonable, and the people don't know enough or
they don't care enough about the little details to think
it's worth making too great a fight over." And she
said, "While I'm completely with you, there's no way
in which I can help, because I know it's hopeless. I
know what he's done and how he's done it." I don't
know what it was she knew, but she said, "It's an
impossible thing to undo now."

So then Mr. Myers called me up the morning it was
to come up. And he said, "Now I've taken a poll of the
whole House, pretty well, so I know what's happening."
And he said almost the same thing. He said, "I don't
think, as much as I'm for this, and I certainly don't
like to be announced, as I have been announced, as
wanting to go back to the original one and then not
carry it through, but I find it is all tied up. And I
don't know what at this late date I can do to change it."

And I said, "Well, if you can't, we wouldn't want
you to move to bring it up in the original form and then
have your motion defeated because it would be very bad
for us in every way. Now at least we can say this was
the sentiment, this was the way the people felt."

Fry: You had that overwhelming vote record on it in the House
the previous year.

Paul: Yes. And so I said, "Well, that's all right. We'll
understand if you think it's better not to do it."

And he said, "I think it's impossible to change it.
I don't know why it's impossible. But for some reason
or other it's been so consolidated, we can't do it."
So we lost it [the original version], you see.

I don't yet know how Bayh manages to do all these
things.

Fry: Well, maybe some day we can piece together the whole
story.

Paul: But I don't believe it's Bayh that's doing it, at all.
        I think that there's some master mind that's planning
        all these things and making use of Mr. Bayh.

Fry: Some interest group?

Paul: Some interest group perhaps. Somebody who wants its
        defeat, anyway. That's it. Is it time for you to go?

Fry: Yes, it is.

Paul: I think you are looking as though you are ready for bed.

        [Break. Tape off.]

COUP D'ETAT WITHIN THE WOMAN'S PARTY 1946-1947

Election Dispute in 1945

Fry: Now last night we ended by bringing the equal rights struggle up to date, and I thought that first priority this morning would be that 1945 challenge to the Woman's Party election that you said you wanted to be sure and tell me about before I left. I have some research here on that that might help.

Paul: Now what was the 1945 that you were talking about? What point was there in the 1945?

Fry: The challenge to the Woman's Party election. Remember that, when a group challenged the legality of an election?

Paul: I hadn't thought about putting that in at all. You think that's important?

Fry: You told me you wanted to put that in, at least I understood you to say that. Because you've already alluded to it a couple of times and you said, "Well, we'll talk about that later."

Paul: That of course was a very--it wasn't exactly a challenge to the election. Of course, we thought it was an effort of the Communist party to take over our organization, by bringing a lawsuit. You see, we were in the courts and it's all in the Equal Rights magazine where it will be [found] written up in the greatest detail and length.

Fry: I have that.

Paul: It was in--the person I think who signed most of those

Paul: articles was our national secretary, Mabel [E.]
Griswold, very very wonderful secretary we had then
[of Madison, Wisconsin]. An honorary unpaid secretary.
But you know, that's the time that the marshall appeared
at the door suddenly and Mrs. Emma Guffey Miller--I
guess I told you all that.

Fry: No, you didn't. We haven't talked about it.

Paul: Anyway, a suit was filed against us in the name of the
National Woman's Party against Emma Guffey Miller,*
we'll say, against this person on our national board.

Fry: Anita Pollitzer was the contested leader?

Paul: Well, against her, but it was a suit filed against
every person on the new board that had been elected.
A suit brought in the name of the National Woman's
Party and the first one that was served on anybody,
the complaint they call them, was served by a marshall
on Mrs. Emma Guffey Miller. She was rather a fairly
new person in our ranks but had gradually come to the
point where she was willing even to go--first she wasn't
even willing to be identified with us, and then finally
she came on the national board. One of the first things
that [laughing] happened after she came on the national
board--she was living up with her brother, Senator
Guffey, keeping house for him, her husband having died
and her children having grown up, she lived there with
him. And another sister lived with Senator Guffey.
Senator Guffey wasn't married. So, one night--they
lived fairly out in the suburbs--and a very, very snowy
night a marshall arrived and I think they had a Filipino
or a Japanese butler, and he went out to the door and
they handed him this complaint and he accepted it, of
course. He was really accepting it for Mrs. Miller; he
didn't know a single thing about what was happening. So
he came in [laughing] and with the paper, and therefore
she had been officially served with this complaint,
demanding of Mrs. Miller as one member of the national
board--the [so-called] National Woman's Party demanded
that Mrs. Miller hand over as one member of this board
that [according to the insurgents] was "pretending" to
be the board of the National Woman's Party, hand over
to the ["real"] National Woman's Party all property

_____

*﹍ ﹍ ﹍ ﹍ ﹍ ﹍ ﹍ ﹍ ﹍ ﹍ ﹍ itteewoman

Paul: rightfully belonging to the National Woman's Party.
        Everything in our investment and endowment fund, all
        our--everything in the bank, all our records, history,
        everything. And that's the first we knew about it.

Fry: It was? There wasn't anything that led up to this?

Paul: Well, we didn't know that they were going to bring a
        lawsuit. We knew that it was a lot of--we had a paid
        secretary named Caroline Lexow Babcock and she was our
        executive secretary.

            I just don't want this to go down in history any
        more than it has gone down.

Fry: Well, it needs to be explained because here's all the
        newspaper stories on it and--

Paul: Well, then you do know about it all.

Fry: I just got these clippings from Anita Pollitzer.

Paul: Oh, you did?

Fry: Yes, this was one of the things that she had preserved.
        I guess she had planned to put this in her write-up
        of the Woman's Party history, and so she asked me to
        get some copies made for her and I did.

Paul: What sort of thing is it then? Can you give me an
        idea of what kind of papers?

Fry: Christian Science Monitor, Washington Evening Star,
        Washington Post, New York Times, Baltimore News Post,
        and a Charleston, South Carolina, paper.*

Paul: Well, you know, it's very well she kept all that. I
        didn't know she had. Is that all she had on the subject?

Fry: Yes. You know where it was? It was folded up inside
        her copy of Inez Haynes Irwin's book, in a little
        plastic folder, and was being preserved there.

Paul: Well, did she tell you anything about it?

---

*C. An .

Fry: No, she couldn't tell me about it, Alice, because she
       wasn't able to talk that much. So she wanted me to take
       that, and I didn't want to take the originals because
       they were old and crumbly. So I made a Xerox for her
       and one for me.

Paul: Oh, you did. How wonderful.

Fry: So she got it, and now I have it.

Paul: That'll give the whole--

Fry: Well, it doesn't. All of these stories go something
       like "Anita Pollitzer, national chairman of the National
       Woman's Party, and other present incumbents are now the
       legal officers of the party."

Paul: That's after we won.

Fry: Yes. All of this is late November and early December,
       1947.

Paul: Well, that's when we won.

Fry: --which is the story of when you won. So what I need
       to know is what happened <u>before</u> that.

Paul: Well, you'll find it written up in great detail by an
       absolutely officially-speaking-for-us national secretary,
       Mabel Griswold, in the <u>Equal Rights</u> magazine.*

Fry: And I read that.

Paul: You see, the suit was filed, say, in February, 1947,
       and I know it was decided just before Thanksgiving
       because I remember thinking what an unhappy Thanksgiving
       we would have if it was decided against us. So you see
       it was a long, <u>long</u> trial going on and on and on and
       and on and on.

       Now I'll tell you the gist of it all.

       We discovered we didn't even know what was going
       on. We had this paid secretary and we discovered that

_____

*See <u>Equal Rights</u>, January-February, 1947, for a
chronology of previous four months' events.

Paul: she was going around the country, ostensibly to--she
was the executive secretary and was really in charge
of the campaign at that moment, under Miss Pollitzer
who was the national chairman. And whatever possessed
her to do this, we have no idea. But she was very much
more to the left than most of the people on the board,
herself. And she came up every day and worked at the
headquarters and then she would go off on trips connected with her work. And we discovered finally that
in these trips that she was taking, she was trying to
really organize an insurrection within the organization.
And it was unknown. I didn't know anything about it,
Anita [Pollitzer] didn't know anything about it.

But I went--you see, after this election had
occurred and Anita had been made the national chairman
[for two years] by this vote by mail [October, 1945],
I stayed on all the time to try to help her because
she was living up in New York. She had to come down
and leave her husband and make lots of changes in her
own life, which kept her away a little part of the
time. [Pause.]

Well, this agitation--exactly what, we never did
know what it was about--and I gained the impression
from the people I heard about and learned some things
about, was that Miss Pollitzer, who had been--it's
impossible to say how much the Woman's Party owed to
her and the woman movement owed to her. But of course,
she was pronouncedly Jewish and her grandfather was a
rabbi and she was from a long, long line of rabbis
and so on. And very--she wasn't a Jewess, you know, who
tried to conceal she was a Jewess, she was one that was
clearly very proud of her Jewish heritage. And her
family was certainly distinguished surgeons and doctors
in this country, at the very top of their profession.
And they'd been here a long time in the country.

Well, I don't know whether that was a cause--I don't
yet know, or have any real idea why this insurrection
broke out, and it was certainly largely directed against
me because I was identified completely with this Miss
Pollitzer. We had a nominating committee headed by
Mrs. Elizabeth Forbes, you remember, our national
treasurer. And she was pursued and hounded to have a
certain person named Dorothy Shipley Granger made the
new chairman and she didn't think--Mrs. Granger came
from Baltimore where Mrs. Forbes' family had lived a
long time, and she didn't--and I had been the temporary
chairman, and she didn't- - - - - - - - - - - - - -nan.

Paul: And Mrs. Forbes didn't want to put this--And very many
       other people were being proposed but the one person
       was very persistent in trying to be nominated was this
       Mrs. Granger. Well, Mrs. Forbes didn't want her--didn't
       think it was a wise selection.

       So they asked Mrs. Harvey [Anna Kelton] Wiley,
       who had been a previous chairman and was beloved by
       everybody and trusted by everybody. Mrs. Wiley had
       been, I think for maybe two terms, the national chair-
       man. And she was having a lot of difficulty that her
       son had gotten into--different things and she had
       personal problems and so on--so that she wanted to lay
       down the burden of being the chairman. And all the
       time she'd been chairman, she'd been the editor--

       [End of Tape 18, Side A]

       [Tape 18, Side B]

Paul: When Mrs. Wiley refused--just the chairmanship, she
       didn't refuse anything else--but she didn't want to
       continue to have to edit the paper. She just wanted
       to have more leisure for her family and for herself and
       her own things.

       So then they asked Anita Pollitzer, and Anita
       Pollitzer said, "Well, if Mrs. Wiley will take it I
       will support her and work for her and assist her and so
       on, as I've always helped the chairman, whoever the
       chairman is. If she absolutely will _not_ take it and
       can't be persuaded to take it, then I will take it."

       So [1945] Mrs. Forbes got out this ballot by mail,
       which we'd never done before but still all the organiza-
       tions nearly in the country were doing it, and practically
       everybody voted for the ticket that was presented by the
       nominating committee, which was Miss Pollitzer and her
       general board; there was not much change on the board.
       And so she was considered elected and she began to serve
       as chairman.

       And then, prior to this election, while it was
       going on, we'll say in the month perhaps that the
       people had to get back their ballots, in that period,
       Mrs. Wiley was prevailed upon by somebody, we don't
       know how it happened. Mrs. Wiley was that kind of a
       person: people always said, "Well, the last person who
       talks to Mrs. Wiley always has Mrs. Wiley's agreement."
       S   was,

Paul: although this was all formal and open, and out in the
open entirely with the nominating committee--the refusal
of Mrs. Wiley, there was no question about it--whoever
the last person was and whatever their motive was, we
don't know. But suddenly Mrs. Wiley was prevailed upon
by somebody to announce she would be a candidate for the
presidency, for the chairmanship.

And so her name was put up by whatever this little
group was that was in existence, though we hadn't known
it was in existence, and sent to all the membership.
Submitting Mrs. Wiley's name. Well, had Mrs. Wiley's
name been submitted in the very beginning, of course,
she would have gone out on the official ballot sent by
the nominating committee. But since the nominating
committee sent Miss Pollitzer's name out, then this had
to go from--in an informal way. Now they rejoiced to
say that Mrs. Wiley, who had been such a gallant soldier
in this movement, had allowed her name to be put up, and
a letter was sent by whoever these people were--and I
think that's all in the Equal Rights magazine there,
who sent this out--I don't know, I don't remember.
And so only, well, a scattering response came in from
people who hadn't already voted for Anita, saying that
they would support Mrs. Wiley.

So we had two candidates as it turned out, and Mrs.
Wiley had just a tiny little group. But of course had
[she] been [the nominee] in the beginning, she would
have had [the vote of] everybody, because she would
have been on the special ballot, and there was no
question that everybody in the whole organization was
grateful to her for all she'd done and full of trust
and confidence in what she would do. But I think they
had the same feeling for Anita. I never knew anybody
in the country--all over the world where she went, she
left friends and admirers, and people certainly had
great trust in her. How on earth this came to be, I
haven't the faintest, the faintest idea.

While all this was happening, one day Anita
Pollitzer and I went over to see Mrs. Emma Guffey
Miller, who had recently more or less joined us and we
knew didn't know anything, and we thought anybody who's
trying to make this defection will certainly go to Mrs.
Miller. And she was one of the great assets that we
had when she finally came because they were a power in
the Democratic party, being the national committeewoman
for the Democratic party. So we had a really, a very
g(.   ,   ing

Paul: Mrs. Miller's real support.

So we went to see her and I remember so vividly, we sat there and talked to Mrs. Miller, told her the whole situation, and she said, "Well, I don't of course know very much about anything yet, but I certainly know Miss Pollitzer and have worked with her and I'll support her completely and absolutely, you can count on me."

And it was a good thing we did go because pretty soon they began on Mrs. Miller, but she didn't waver.

And then, suddenly, which we didn't know they were going to do, they filed a suit, this group. And when you'd say, who were they, well, they'd say, "We're the National Woman's Party." And it was most extraordinarily mysterious. [Laughing.] And so poor Mrs. Miller, whom we just wanted to join our ranks in every possible way, suddenly one night had this disgrace (to poor Senator Guffey, [laughing] and to Mrs. Miller the national committeewoman) to receive a complaint brought in by their Japanese or their Chinese or whatever the man was--Filipino or something--and giving it to Mrs. Miller. Here is an officer serving you with this paper, ordering you to surrender all the money and everything that you're holding from the Woman's Party "illegally and willfully" and so on. So you know it was a great shock [laughing]--terrible shock to Mrs. Miller. And then we discovered they were going to serve everybody. So we closed the headquarters.

[Interruption.]

I remember there was one member of our board, Dr. Florence Armstrong, who was working in the government and so she lived out in Alexandria, I guess it was, just outside of Washington. And so she invited everybody who was on the national board, as many as they wanted to come, to her small little house that she had. She lived there all by herself. And she invited them to come whenever they came to Washington, not at the headquarters because they might suddenly be served with this paper, but to stay out there with her.

And so I went out, when I went down to Washington, I went out and stayed with her. And our first vice-chairman, Mrs. Clara Snell Wolfe, went out and stayed there the same time I did. So we had this sort of
might be

Paul: And then we just closed the headquarters itself,
as far as the door went; we had a tiny little staff of
very few people. We made it clear that they mustn't
open the door to anybody at this moment, because it
would be probably trying to serve a paper on somebody
who was there. What did they turn around and do?
[Laughing.] Serve the papers on the stenographers and
on the bookkeeper, and I think the houseman, sort of
like Charlie,* somebody who had--everybody at the headquarters was suddenly served with these papers.

Fry: They did open the door.

Paul: Well, but they didn't open the door to let anybody who
was on the board be served. We never <u>dreamed</u> that they
would be serving the papers on all the people who had
no official connection except they happened to be
employed there for the moment. But they all were very
good sports. They all [laughing], I think, were sort
of thrilled at being part of the whole war that seemed
to be arising.

And so since I wasn't there and they didn't know I
was there, I was served (and I didn't know about it for
a long, long time) by what they call publication, by
putting a notice in the paper, where I was living up in
Vermont. So my little Vermont paper had this very same
complaint. I guess nobody every saw it up there and I
didn't know it was there until, I guess the whole lawsuit was over before I ever discovered that I'd been
served by publication. Guess it was a matter that got
in the courts--must have been brought up how each one
of us had been legally served.

So then we asked Burnita Shelton Matthews, who'd
been so long doing all our legal work for us, if she
would act as our representative. We had no lawyer. Of
course, we had George Gordon Battle in the past, but
that was all on the legal part of the wording of the
Amendment and so on, and on getting the headquarters.
I don't know whether he'd died before this occurred or
not. I guess he had probably. So we didn't think about
anybody but Burnita.

---

*Alice Paul's carpenter/handy man who had been taking
care of her Ridgefield cottage and lake property for over
fifteen years--since he was a boy.

Defectors

Anna Kelton Wiley

Paul: And she said that she didn't want to take the case--
she'd now become quite an independent lawyer and trying
to build up and succeeding pretty well in building up
her own law office--because two of the people that were
on the side that brought the suit were connected too
closely with her. One was Mrs. Harvey Wiley and again
it was the last person who talked to her. How on earth
she ever got into this is past human understanding.
It's impossible to think anybody as good, really as
fundamentally good a woman as Mrs. Harvey Wiley could
have let herself be used, but she did. And as one of
the people who was in the suit against us. The second
one was the national treasurer, Miss Laura [M.] Berrien
and the third one was the national secretary, Mrs. [Dr.]
Margaret Sebree. Well, these people were really Woman's
Party people. Now we don't know yet what happened to
them. And the fourth one was Doris Stevens.

Fry: That one is surprising!

Paul: So we don't know, maybe in reading it back in this Equal
Rights because I've never read the account since. I
know that Mabel Griswold wrote it and I knew it would be
all right, but we don't know what made them do it. But
I think it was some personal grievance probably on
each one's part. Excepting I don't think Mrs. Wiley
ever had any grievance, but I think she'd gotten herself
put up as the rival to Miss Pollitzer and somehow or
other she was persuaded to join in this suit.

Doris Stevens

Paul: With regard to Miss Stevens, we did know--we knew pretty
well what had happened. You see, when Mrs. Belmont's
will was up for probate, Miss Stevens got a lawyer
whose name was Frank Wallace [?] or Walsh [?] if you've
ever heard of him, but he was a very well known lawyer
and he'd been very, very, very strong in helping the
Woman's Party through the years. So we knew him very
well. And Doris knew him in that way. So she got him

Paul: to represent her in contesting the will. Do you know all these things?

Fry: No, I've never heard this before.

Paul: You'll find it, I think, all in the <u>Equal Rights</u> magazine if you read it. But anyway, this is what happened: He sent his son, Frank Walsh sent his son, when he took the case for Doris, and he only knew Doris because he'd met Doris through the rest of us, through our knowing and working with Mr. Walsh, and so of course he accepted her as one of our people when she asked him to represent her in contesting the will of Mrs. Belmont. She was a very convincing and plausible person and she succeeded somehow in getting him. But he sent his son around the country, which was the first that I knew anything about it, because different people phoned me and said, "Well, Frank Walsh's son has just been here and he's bringing this suit to contest Mrs. Belmont's will and the ground that he's contesting it on is that you have used undue influence"--<u>I</u> had used undue influence to have Mrs. Belmont not leave any money to Doris Stevens! Well, and I remember one person after another said, "Well, this is the most extraordinary visit I've just had from Mr. Frank Walsh's son wanting me to come down and testify at the probate hearing that I know that you had the confidence of Mrs. Belmont and that you prevailed upon her not to leave any money to Doris Stevens."

Well, nobody was more surprised [laughing] than I, and finally the day of the probate court's hearing of this will occurred in New York, a certain day. And I was called up very early the next morning by Mrs. Belmont's secretary, who'd been over there with Mrs. Belmont for some years and her sister had gone to prison with us, and the whole family had always supported us, and then we had helped to get this position for this young girl, named Young, Mary Young, I think she was. (Anyway, she was a Miss Young, and I think she was Mary Young.) She'd stayed over with Mrs. Belmont say a year or two and had a very good position as a secretary, very well paid. And so she called me up, and I knew her of course, pretty well, not very well, but knew her, and had always encouraged Mrs. Belmont to keep this young girl and she lived and had a very interesting experience there and was well paid. In France, this all was.

A . · ·   ell you,

Paul: I came down on the night train and I've just gotten
into the station, and I want to telephone to you about
the trial yesterday, before the probate judge." And
she said, "You know, your name was the name that was
presented to the judge as the person who had influenced
Mrs. Belmont, and therefore they wanted the will set
aside so that Doris could have her rightful inheritance.
So," she said, "I wish to tell you that when the trial
opened, Mr. Walsh announced that his son had made this
survey of all parts of the country of people who'd be
apt to know what was going on in the world of Woman's
Party people, and he said, he comes back with a report
that not one person whom they interviewed had ever
heard me make a derogatory remark. (And you know I
certainly am not up to making derogatory remarks about
anybody. I think I'm not very likely to.) She said,
"No one had ever heard of such a thing, that they'd
always heard when you talked about Mrs. Stevens of
this tribute you always gave to her great organizing
ability and her courage and her vision, and you went
out of your way always to build her up." So they all
reported, "We don't know what this means, we can't
imagine that Miss Paul would ever say anything like
this to Mrs. Belmont. We knew she had no such ideas
about it."

So Mr. Walsh said, according to Mary Young, she
said Mr. Walsh announced, "We are changing our--paper"--
whatever it's called that you present to a probate
court--"We wish to change it and to omit the name of
Miss Paul as the person who had influenced Mrs. Belmont
because we can't find any evidence to substantiate this.
We were told this was the case and we wish to change
our"--legal document--whatever it's called--"and substitute the name of Elsa Maxwell. We believe that she
was the person who caused Mrs. Belmont to leave out
Mrs. Stevens' name from the people she would be leaving
her money to." So poor Elsa Maxwell had no notice of
this--you know who Elsa Maxwell was, don't you?

Fry: Wasn't she a columnist, a writer--

Paul: No, she was a great friend of Mrs. Belmont's and one
who Mrs. Belmont helped a great deal and she was an
American girl--not a girl exactly, she was an older
person by the time we knew her. But we first knew her
when she wrote a little play during the suffrage campaign, a little play to be used as propaganda, for
suffrage. And Mrs. Belmont--maybe this is the first

563

Paul: was persuaded by Elsa Maxwell to put on this little
play and finance it to help the suffrage movement.
That's the first time I ever met her.

And then she got to know Mrs. Belmont and other
people, a great many people, and she went over to live
in France and lived there the rest of her life, I guess,
and she lived her--she called it a profession--her way
was to arrange parties for Americans who came over and
invite people who were celebrities and they were wanting
to meet celebrities, wanting to come back having met
somebody and established some connection, whether they
were for professional reasons, or business reasons, or
just their own pleasure, I don't know. But she had a
genius, almost. She was very musical, very talented
in all ways, and she knew theatrical people, knew music
people and so on.

Well, Elsa Maxwell among other people got to know
Mrs. Belmont pretty well, <u>very</u> well, and would get Mrs.
Belmont to come to give some social glamour to the
parties that she--Elsa Maxwell--would give. So she
also was invited by Mrs. Belmont a good many times, I
guess, to come up to her own home for lunch or for
dinner. And it seems that, unfortunately, [Elsa was a
guest at her chateau] the day that Mrs. Belmont had
changed her will. She did have Doris's name in her
will originally, for some small sum apparently, and
she did change it. She had it changed by--as all this
came out in the probate as the result of Mr. Walsh's
researches, and Doris's researches--she'd had a lawyer
who lived in Malesherbes [?], which is very close to
where Mrs. Belmont--it was the biggest little town in
France nearest to where the chateau of Mrs. Belmont
was. This lawyer came out from Malesherbes and changed
the will and omitted Doris's name. And unfortunately
it happened that poor Elsa Maxwell, certainly knowing
nothing about this, had happened to be the guest of
Mrs. Belmont at her chateau. Thank heaven I was in
America [laughing], I wasn't there this day or it
might have all happened and I might never have known
about it. But this was the ill fate of poor Elsa
Maxwell. She happened to be there.

Therefore Mr. Walsh said, "Well, it's perfectly
clear <u>somebody</u> got Mrs. Belmont under their control
mentally and got her name taken out, and it must have
been Elsa Maxwell because who else was there?" [Laugh-
ing.] So poor Elsa Maxwell's name was the one that was
y Mary

Paul: Young.) So she said, "Your name never got up there to
be considered. It was only Elsa Maxwell's name and
she wasn't here, she'd known nothing about her name
going to be presented."

So what happened at this court was that the family
of Mrs. Belmont, her daughter and her two sons, were
persuaded themselves, they were convinced, that the
best thing to do with a person like Miss Stevens, who
was so determined on getting some money, was to make a
settlement out of court. And this I was told by Mrs.
Belmont's own lawyer, this Mr. Battle, because Mr.
Battle had been there looking after the estate and the
children. So he told me this, and he said, "I can't
remember whether it was $5,000 or $10,000." But he
said, "Anyway, they bought her off, saying 'We don't
want our mother's name dragged through the courts,
lots of newspaper articles and so on. We want the
whole thing forgotten, and we want to get rid of this
person as fast as we can.'" So they gave her whatever
it was--$5,000 or $10,000. I suppose that was the sum,
that's what he told me anyway--that he couldn't remember, but he thought it was one or the other.

Well, in the interval before this court proceeding
which finished it up occurred, apparently when the will
was first made known to the public, Doris had helped
and she'd worked with me because we tried to make really
an event of the burial of Mrs. Belmont, because she had
asked me once when I was over in France, she said, "I've
written out directions as to how I would like my funeral
to be conducted." And she said, "Any man who's been
in the public eye and been of service to the country,
when he dies there's a public ceremony, the government
has it or something like that." And she said, "Excepting
what you have done to try to have some tributes paid
to women after their death, by having meetings in the
capital as we did with Inez Milholland and other people,
nobody ever pays any attention to the death of a woman
who has made a great gift to her country in the way of
working for some reform. Especially reform for women,
I've never heard of anybody," she said. "Excepting
what you have done in the capital."

So, she said, "I've written it out, what I want
done for me." And she gave it to me in France, and
she said, "Take this down and give it to my lawyer,
Mr. Battle, when he gets back to America and make certain
that this is carried out." And she said, "If you don't
c   ,   r   n't,

Paul: then I won't have it done, because I don't know of
anybody else who will do it."

So I was entrusted with this, and when I came
back that time, from that trip to Europe, I know that I
saw Doris. And I think she invited me to spend the
night with her when I got back. She was married then
to Dudley Field Malone. So I did spend the night and I
told her the next morning I was going down to see Mr.
Battle to take Mrs. Belmont's instructions about how she
wanted her funeral and so on conducted.

Well, I think that she must have thought that I
also took the instructions about what the will was to
contain. That's all I could imagine. But I didn't
know anything about her will or ever speak to her about
her will.

And so Mr. Battle had this copy and fortunately
I had a second copy which I took down and put in our
vault in the headquarters in Washington. So we carried
all these instructions out and we had a funeral which
was--well, unusual in that we had all around the whole
church--it was in St. Thomas--we had young girls standing with purple, white and gold banners; we had right
up in front Mrs. Hilles and one of the DuPonts, sitting
beside her, two people one on each side of the coffin.
And so the Woman's Party just did all the spectacular
things that she had demanded as well as we could.

And Doris took part in it, of course, and helped
because she was always such a good organizer. And I
remember she and I sat together in the very front pew
and then walked out behind the coffin and so on together.
It showed that until this time there was nothing in
Doris's mind but friendship for everybody. And I suppose she was still thinking that I'd taken over the will
and had it put in Mr. Battle's possession and that she
was going to be one of the heirs. Which I had never
heard of--that idea.

So, then, shortly after the funeral--and I had
gone back to Washington and Doris was up in her home
with her husband at Croton-on-Hudson where she was
living--a newspaper article came forth in Washington--I
hope it's one that Anita preserved--but with a great
streamer across, I think it was the <u>Washington Star</u>,
saying, "Doris Stevens Accuses Alice Paul of Having
Alienated Mrs. Belmont's Affections"--and so on--
"A   .   ont to

Paul: cancel all her promised bequests to Doris." Well,
         maybe she made a promised bequest, I don't know. Doris
         never told me, Mrs. Belmont never told me. I didn't
         even know there was such a thing.

         And I remember I was immediately called up by the
         Star or by the other papers perhaps, and said, "Well,
         what is the truth about this charge?" Whole enormous
         page of what I'd done to Doris! I said, "Well, Doris
         has always been somebody we in the Woman's Party
         greatly honored and respected. We don't know of any
         change in her position. We don't know anything about
         this whatsoever." And I said, "I don't know anything
         about Mrs. Belmont's will, what it contains."

         You see, it had contained a gift, the only time
         she mentions in her will, a gift of $100,000, not to me,
         not to any individual, but $100,000 to the National
         Woman's Party to carry on the work in which she had
         been doing as president, something like that. That's
         all there was. And Doris charged that she had been
         promised $50,000, which was a big gift. Well, maybe
         she had, and maybe she hadn't. I have no way on earth
         of knowing. It's quite possible of course that Mrs.
         Belmont, knowing how much Doris was doing, and $50,00
         would have been very little for Mrs. Belmont, maybe
         she did once have it in her mind to do this, and maybe
         she once told Doris; but certainly I didn't alienate
         [laughing] or get Mrs. Belmont to change her mind.

         Doris said I was so anxious to get the money for
         the Woman's Party that I persuaded her to give the
         Woman's Party the $100,000. Well, I didn't. I'm glad
         she did, but I don't think that I caused it. I think
         Mrs. Belmont, being president, so it was a natural
         thing for her to have done. It would have seemed very
         unnatural if she hadn't done it. I would really think
         she would normally have given more than $100,000.

Fry: Yes, I'm surprised it was that small.

Paul: But that's the way the whole trouble with Doris started.
         So when she came down to Washington, I tried to talk
         to her, and I said, "You know, Doris, this is all some-
         thing that I know nothing about; I had nothing to do
         with Mrs. Belmont's will and never discussed it or
         mentioned it. I did nothing to get this $100,000, or
         nothing to deprive you of what you say was $50,000
         that she promised to you."

Paul: But she was just like an iceberg, and from that
          time on, she was always like an iceberg to me. And
          wouldn't come anywhere, not if she could help it, ever
          have a thing to do with me or with any of the people
          that'd been her colleagues in the Woman's Party, because
          of this terrible injustice she thought had been done
          to her. Money seemed to mean so much to her, so much
          more than it did to most of us, that we could hardly
          conceive of her attitude, and not refusing to believe
          this.

          [Interruption.]

          [About the] attitude of Doris. I think that some
          group in the country, just as I think there's some
          group--and I don't have any idea really what this group
          is--but anybody who wanted to make use of the Woman's
          Party--because at that time we had, I think, a great
          deal more public prestige because we were about the only
          group that was associated with the suffrage victory.
          There was almost no rival that was working. Of course
          there was only the old National American, and they'd
          practically stopped because of the war.

          So we were generally respected as a group that--I
          can see that anyone who wanted to capture a group of
          women--they probably would want to take part in the
          Woman's Party. So in doing this they would naturally
          go after the disaffected people, and try to use those
          disaffected people to get other people so there was
          enough to make a little showing.

          So it was some group that did it. And the only
          group that we could think of was the Communist group.
          You always think of the Communist group; maybe it
          wasn't the Communist group, maybe it was some other
          group. But it was somebody, because we discovered
          when this lawsuit was finally filed against us and the
          complaints were being made and served on all these
          individual people, that none of us ever suspected, we
          found they had been using our headquarters and had a
          series of meetings with apparently very well paid
          stenographic--I don't know what you would call it--firm,
          group, that was going in and taking these elaborate
          minutes in great detail the way they do at big corpora-
          tions and so on. And we found these meetings were
          going on in our library. We didn't know they were
          going on. And it was all done sort of under cover
          until the minutes were read in the trial. First time

Fry: What was the group?

Paul: The group that filed the lawsuit. They called them-
         selves the Woman's Party. So they'd been having
         National Woman's Party meetings, and the name National
         Woman's Party, that Miss Pollitzer never knew anything
         about, I never knew anything about. None of us knew
         that--if we ever knew people were meeting there, well,
         we thought people were meeting on [laughing] something
         in the library, I guess.

         So finally in the court they read, we'll say,
         [minutes of] September, October, November, December,
         these meetings and what they had voted to do and so
         on. All written up so they'd be--and here they got
         the Dean Acheson's law firm, and of course he'd been
         assistant secretary of state, I think he'd been even
         secretary of state, I'm not sure. And they had a trial
         lawyer--well, he's a famous trial lawyer. I don't
         remember, I guess I'll probably think of this name but
         I've forgotten what it was--but he was the trial lawyer
         of the Dean Acheson law firm. And then they had another
         man. (All this will be in that Miss Griswold's article,
         the names of these different lawyers.) And then they
         had the lawyer who prepared all the cases for the Dean
         Acheson law firm. And he was the one who'd been up here
         in our headquarters conducting this series of meetings.
         And all these minutes were there--it was all brought
         out in the court by that side, this group. So ap-
         parently Doris, who was not I think at that moment on
         our national board--I'm sure she didn't originate it,
         I'm sure she was made use of by some group, knowing
         here was a person who was publicly dissatisfied and
         didn't hesitate on all occasions to say this great
         injustice had been done to her and so on (which was a
         very strange way to act, of course, but she certainly
         did it).

         Laura M. Berrien

Paul: Now this Miss Berrien, who was our national treasurer,
         we don't know what happened to her, because she and
         Doris had been at swords' points for a long time, and
         every time that we would, which we normally did, we
         gave some honor at every meeting to Doris and had her
         preside or had her speak or do something, and Miss
         Berrien was always being quite disagreeable about it

Paul: and said we were giving all this honor and so on to Doris. They were not friends at all. But somehow or other they formed a coalition at this moment, and whether Doris knew things about Miss Berrien and threatened her, we don't know. We don't know what happened. Miss Berrien, being our national treasurer, was in a very bad position for us, to have her joining this group.

And Dr. Sebree, who was the secretary, she was new. She was a government worker and was in peril over her position or would be when the husband and wife couldn't both serve and so on. Somehow or other, I think while Mrs. Wiley was chairman and they were getting appeals from this Dr. Sebree to help in the campaign against that economy act [in the thirties], not allowing two people in the same family to have a salary from the government. She had a high position in the government and I guess probably from [that experience in that campaign] she was put on the board by Mrs. Wiley, who was a very thrifty person and had an idea that by having a [national secretary we could save money]. We'd always had an honorary secretary and often she wasn't much good at taking notes and so on. She had an idea that by taking somebody employed in the government who was a member of the Woman's Party and putting her in as the national secretary, they would have all their correspondence and minutes and so on costing less than we were having. So she wasn't exactly important; she was just an ordinary government worker who was able to type and so on. She was the secretary.

So we understood what was the matter with Doris, we understood the secretary all right--it didn't make much difference about her, and we understood Mrs. Wiley, we knew it was a passing moment, that she had let her name be used, being agreeable to people, and say, "Well, all right, you can use my name," and then she didn't realize what she'd done, I guess. But the last person, Miss Berrien, I never have known. Miss Berrien had sort of personal difficulties. I think her brother was in prison for having some kind of dishonesty, I don't know exactly what. And she was the sort of person that it's perfectly possible that whatever group that was using Doris would have found something that might have been difficult for Miss Berrien.

But at all events she also had a grievance. When
                                                                    e suffrage

Paul: campaign at all and we'd never heard of her, Laura
Berrien. But she had graduated in law and was working
in the--I guess the Bureau of Internal Revenue. Anyway
something to do with taxation in the government. And
she came up and joined us after the suffrage victory
when many, many people who didn't help us during this
campaign, came in with the victory. She was one. She
was introduced to us by some of our lawyer members
because she herself belonged to the National Association
of Women Lawyers which was just springing up in the
District of Columbia. And she wanted very, very, very
much to get our help, thinking that we'd gotten the
vote, so we must be able to help people, to get our
help in getting her promoted, because she had the
lowest position almost that you could have in the bureau,
whatever this government bureau was that dealt with
taxation. And so we did happen to know pretty well the
person that had been called in by, I think it was
probably by Coolidge, but anyway one of the Presidents,
we'll say Coolidge, he was called in as an efficiency
expert. And now his wife was one of our members and a
very good and influential member. (Seems to me his name
was Brown; I'll probably remember his name when I try to
think about it.)

Anyway, through his wife, we saw a great deal of
this man, and just about this time he came up one day,
and we told him about Miss Berrien who had made this
appeal for promotion in the taxation department, and we
said, "Perhaps you as an efficiency expert could look
into it and see if you could get any advancement for
her."

"Oh," he said, "I certainly would be glad to do
that." He went down and met her and talked to her.

And within about two or three days she had quite a
big promotion. Because that was his business, what he
was employed to do. And he never, of course, would have
interviewed her or seen her or known about her, if we
hadn't asked him to do this. And so he would always
go to somebody through whom he worked, he didn't go
direct to the President to report, but he went to some
one person, and anyway he made the report and he got her
promoted right away.

So she was very enthusiastic and became a devoted
member of the Woman's Party, really working hard, and
finally we made her our national treasurer because we
th   'ernment,

Paul: she might be good for that.

And then in a little while, she came and she wanted another promotion. And so we succeeded in getting the second promotion, again through this Mr. Brown; we couldn't have done it otherwise.

And she went on until she'd had a promotion to the top place she could reach, beyond the civil service, and that came up now to being a judge of the tax court. And that I remember, because she really hounded me to get her promoted to being a tax judge on the taxation level of the highest court that passes on everything in matters of taxation. I don't know whether this was all in the Bureau of Internal Revenue or what it was in, but it was--

[End of Tape 18, Side B]

[Tape 19, Side A. May 13, 1973.]

Paul: Two days after our treasurer, who'd been our treasurer for some time--I think her name was Gladys [Houston] Greiner, at that moment the treasurer--but whoever the treasurer was, and someone else, I guess Miss Mabel Brissel, who was our secretary, went down to our bank where we'd banked since we came to Washington in 1913.

[Interruption.]

So--Mrs. Wiley was always so nice about doing everything she could for anybody--so she went down, she the proper person that Miss Berrien wanted us to [send to] interview about putting her name down as a candidate to be the first woman judge of the tax board. She came back--and I remember so vividly!--sort of dejected and sad.

She said, "Well, they told me that they have given us all the promotions we've asked for Miss Berrien, but they can't risk this tax board because that's a very vital place where decisions might wipe whole companies out of existence or do great injustice if they were in the hands of somebody who wasn't competent." And they said, "We must tell you she's not competent enough to be on the tax board. We can do these other things where there's somebody above her who will maybe correct things. So, we did about all we could think of doing for Miss Berrien but, rightly or wrongly, they were determined
                                                    to be

Paul: promoted to the tax board.

So then Miss Berrien turned from being an
enthusiastic supporter of the Woman's Party and all
its things, to think that we had just--well, she was
very personal about it. She felt as though we hadn't
been willing to make the effort. She kept saying,
"I'm perfectly sure if Miss Paul will go out and really
try that I could be on the tax board and I am going to
be on the tax board! I'm determined to be!" So then
she got us to try to get other people, you know, that
might get her on the tax board.

So we knew she had a great grievance because she
just felt we'd deliberately failed to do what we could
have done. We didn't. It wasn't that we deliberately
failed. We failed because I don't believe anybody
could have gotten her on the tax board then. There
had never been a woman. It was something that people
were very careful about, who was on the tax board. You
know what I'm talking about, don't you? The whole tax
board, the final thing that people are up against.

Fry: Yes, your last appeal.

Paul: So, we knew she had this grievance. But how in the
world she came to be allied so closely with Doris, who
also had a very different grievance--but they were.
So, that was the little group that formed. They were
four Woman's Party people. And they were having these
private meetings and planning this and this and this,
and it was then brought before the court, so there was
no question about it at the end.

But we were all surprised when we suddenly got
these complaints served against us. For instance, to
me, to turn over all this money I'm "willfully with-
holding" from the National Woman's Party. [Laughter.]
Well, can you imagine! We thought we were the National
Woman's Party and to suddenly have the Woman's Party
bring a suit!

The Defectors Call a Woman's Party Convention

Paul: So then they called a convention. We had scheduled a
convention that spring--1946, I suppose it was.

Fry: It was the spring of 1947 when they scheduled their convention, because I happened to see that _Equal Rights_ issue.

Paul: Oh, it was 1947 then. I thought it was '46.

Fry: Do you want me to run down this chronology for you?

Paul: Where is this all coming from?

Fry: The _Equal Rights_ statement to the membership.*

Paul: Oh. That's Miss Griswold's I've been talking about.

Fry: I think so, except this only concerns that convention. It doesn't really concern anything else.

Paul: It doesn't concern the day they filed the lawsuit?

Fry: No. It says: "The party is now faced with a situation which may best be described as a coup d'etat, an attempt by a few individuals within the party to seize power by unlawful means," and then it reviews the past four months' events. This is from the January/February, 1947 _Equal Rights_ magazine.

It says that: "On September 28, 1946, the national council voted in New York for the biennial convention to be held in Washington in January of '47."

Paul: Yes that's right. That was in '46, was it?

Fry: Yes. About a month later, another call for a biennial convention came from the _other_ group for it to be held on January 10, 11, and 12, which was a different date.

So in November, your executive council was summoned to meet on the 24th--

Paul: Of what month?

Fry: In November of '46. Your council also met on December 15. They changed the convention dates that you had previously set to April, 1947.

---

*ibid.

Paul: You mean _they_ changed it or we did?

Fry: _You_ did. You changed it to April.

Then you had another national council meeting in January to reaffirm the action, and that council expressed the strongest possible disapproval of the "rump convention" that was scheduled and the rump convention took place at the Mayflower Hotel. They went ahead and had their convention in January.

Paul: When was that?

Fry: January of '47. So, they did have their convention.

Paul: I remember about the convention, but I'm not sure about the dates. I mean, was this before or after our lawsuit? I think the lawsuit was in '46.

Fry: Your lawsuit was over in November of '47. So it was finished ten months after their convention.

Paul: It was over in '47, was it? I thought it was '46.

Fry: I get those middle years mixed up there after the war.

Paul: It was '47, then, when the lawsuit was over and we won. It was before Thanksgiving, I know that.

Fry: Yes. Apparently, you won on November 22, in the New York Times story.

Paul: I told you we were all thinking, "Will we have a happy Thanksgiving or not?" [Laughter.] Well, that was over then.

Now, when was the rump convention?

Fry: January 10 and 11, 1947, at the Mayflower.

Paul: Before the lawsuit?

Fry: Their convention was in January and the lawsuit was won by you in the following November.

Paul: I know the lawsuit was started--does it say there--it was started in February. The lawsuit must have been started, then, right after their convention I guess.

Fry:

Paul: About then.

Fry: Right.

[Interruption. Tape off.]

Paul: We had held this [council] meeting up in New York. It
was voted in, we'll say, December or something, to have
this convention. It was about the time when we had the
first suspicion that something was--all this building
up that was going on, you see, we didn't really know
about it.

[Exchange about warmth of cottage and opening the door.]

I remember this board meeting was held at the very
beautiful apartment of one of our New York members. A
very lovely person that she was. When the meeting
opened, we hadn't one bit of inkling or suspicion that
all this was going on. It's where we first discovered
it, at this board meeting. [Pause.]

I'll have to think back about who was at that board
meeting, but somebody that we never thought had any
particular--she was not one of the inside people who
was knowing about much, but she happened to be on the
national board. She began with some kind of a question-
ing attitude, and one or two people joined, and we saw
that something was afoot that we didn't understand. We
didn't understand why there should be any particular
debate about holding and fixing a date for a convention.

Anyway this person, whoever it was, just kept the
floor and kept going on in a way that was apparently
going to make it impossible to come to any decision
about anything. (I haven't thought about this, you
see, ever since we met and they did this, I guess.)

Fry: Do you want me to read the names to you?

Paul: Who were at that meeting in New York?

Fry: Who were on the board.

Paul: No, no, I know who they were. But who these were--
there were some people who were inside the movement
and some people who were on the board but who, for one
reason or another, they hadn't had time maybe to attend
meetings and such. I just seem to remember there was

Paul: It was so obviously filibustering of the meeting
that they recessed for lunch. We were near that women's
hotel called the Barbizon something-or-other, not the
Barbizon Plaza but a little Barbizon hotel. This
apartment was. And of course this lady couldn't entertain all these maybe thirty people at the board meeting.
So we all went out and got lunch at this place. But
the hostess asked me if I would stay there and be her
own personal guest for lunch. So, I didn't go to the
place where they all went for luncheon.

So when we reassembled--and our hostess wasn't on
the board; she was just being a nice hospitable member,
entertaining the board by giving her beautiful apartment. When we came back in the afternoon, quite a
number of our people didn't return. They'd said, "Well,
there's no use being at this meeting. We don't seem to
be able to discuss anything. We don't understand what
all this fuss is about." I remember our chairman from
Connecticut was a Dr. [Emily Dunning] Barringer.

She was, I believe, the first woman in America who
had ever been an intern in a hospital. She was one of
the leading women in the American Medical Association.
I think maybe she was their national president; if she
wasn't their national president, she was their leading
legislative person who came to Washington. She was one
of our board members because the American Medical had
been such loyal friends--

Fry: You mean the Women's Medical?

Paul: The American Women's Medical Association--because of
the fact that we'd helped them in opening the Armed
Service Medical Department to women doctors. They felt
that we really had accomplished that for them and had
aided them so much. The bill went through, you know,
giving women medical people the right to be in the armed
forces in the field of medicine and surgery and so on.

So she was a very prominent member and she said,
"You know how busy I am and how hard it is for me to
get down here to a board meeting, and I can't come to
a board meeting where there's just this apparent filibuster that's stopping our having any deliberations."
So she and quite a number of the most important people
refused to return to this extraordinary meeting.

Anita Pollitzer was conducting the meeting and she
r   '' ' ' ',.   ' '+ ''p''e anybody

Paul: else would have done any better because this group had come evidently determined to break it up.

I remember one of the people who came was Betty Gram Swing. You know about her, don't you?

Fry: I know who she is.

Paul: She said, "You know that Doris is the back of this whole thing. She's gotten all these people to come and get up and make all this dissent and so on." She said, "I've worked for Doris a long time and I know when anything's going wrong that this is what she's doing." Well, we didn't know what was going on. From what you tell me of the dates, it was before the trial began.

So anyway, in the afternoon, we saw a large number of our most stalwart people hadn't returned, and we saw that one by one people were getting up and announcing that they had to catch the last train home and they couldn't stay any longer. I saw pretty soon that what was going on was that they were going to get it down to where people who were really Woman's Party people were going to be outnumbered, and then they were going to vote whatever it was they wanted to vote [laughing]. We didn't know. So, I suddenly just arose and said, "Well, I'm not going to stay any longer in this meeting. I think it's--" whatever I said. And I walked out, and I didn't know what would happen.

But Mrs. Lloyd Williams, who was one of our most stalwart people and one of the most powerful women on the board, and about half the room got up and walked out, not knowing what on earth I was about, but they didn't want to be left alone. [Laughter.] So, they walked out one by one. The result was there wasn't any quorum.

What they were striving to do, I think, was to make it so impossible for the people who were really the heart and core of the Woman's Party to do anything by getting it down so we would be a minority and then they would vote whatever it was they were about. But we were so completely taken by surprise! We weren't prepared. We didn't know anything about it.

I remember Betty Gram Swing got up and walked right out behind me and Anita walked out behind me, so the chairman wasn't there. We all went out into another r·   ·   ·   ly just

Paul: departed and went home. But we knew that there wasn't
a quorum there and they couldn't do anything legally.

Well, then we started to get up this convention
we'd voted to have, and suddenly we found that the
Mayflower had a big sign up: "National Woman's Party
Convention," with some other date. We found that a
second paper had gone out to our whole membership saying the date of the convention was to be so-and-so,
[presumably] our Equal Rights magazine. The publisher,
who lived over in Baltimore, had called up Mrs. [Dora]
Ogle, who was our business manager and always sent
over all the material to him for the paper. (She didn't
edit it, but she sent it all over as the business
manager.) He called up to Mrs. Ogle and said,

"Some people have been in here to see me, whom I
don't know, with material that doesn't seem to me would
be coming from your office. Is it all right for me to
go ahead and print this?" This was changing the date of
the convention and things that Mrs. Ogle had never
heard of and hadn't sent.

"Well," she said, "No, I don't know who these
people could be. This isn't any material that the
Woman's Party is sending to you."

And he said, "Well, I thought not." And he said,
"So, I'm going to tell them I'll have nothing to do
with it and I won't print it. They want me to use your
regular letterhead, list of officers, and everything,
the whole format, and make it look exactly like the
issue that you've always gotten out. I don't know
what they're about, but I won't do it." Later, he
testified to all this at the trial.

Then they went to several other places in Baltimore,
and finally they got somebody who agreed to make a complete reproduction of our paper as far as masthead and
everything, but put in the contents that these few women,
whoever they were--we don't yet know who they were--who
went over to try to have this second call put in. And
it was printed, finally, this new edition which we didn't
know was coming out.

Very early one morning when Mrs. Ogle was down at
the switchboard, which we had then down in the basement
of our headquarters--she always went down and opened the
house up for us and started the switchboard and looked
w we were

Paul: ready to open for the day. So, she said, early that morning, Miss Stevens and Miss Berrien arrived--and maybe somebody else--in a car and had come in as members of the national board and said they wanted to look over the membership files, and had taken all our whole membership file out of the headquarters. She'd thought it was all right because we hadn't had the lawsuit and she didn't know any reason why the national board members shouldn't look at the membership, especially the national treasurer, if they wanted to see it. So, we suddenly didn't have a single membership card left in the headquarters, and it never came back. So that's what they were using to send out the notice of the change in the convention.

Well, they had their convention. And then I think we voted to have ours later because of all this confusion. They went ahead with it at the Mayflower.

They [Mayflower management] said well, Mrs. [Perle S.] Mesta, who lived at the Mayflower, had come and asked them to arrange for a convention. [I know] because when we first called up the Mayflower and said, "Well, why are you doing this? This is the Woman's Party headquarters speaking to you. We haven't planned any convention at all at this particular date."

And they'd said, "Well, Mrs. Mesta, who lives here, is one of your officers and she told us that the convention had been changed and this was the date and it was to be here in the Mayflower and we don't think we can take down the sign. That's what we've been told. We can't enter into some dissension you've had in your organization. We don't understand it."

So, Mrs. Mesta had done this in all good faith. They had gone to her, as we often did, and said, "Well, there's this and that that you can get at the Mayflower." So she just obligingly said, "Will you put up a sign having a convention this date?" She didn't have anything particular to do with any of this business and wasn't brought into it, as far as I know.

Well, then, when the convention occurred, we didn't know who went or anything about it. It was kept very secret and private. But later we learned from Miss Jessie Dell, whom we'd happened to get to know, being one of the three Civil Service commissioners--and she was a very loyal member of the Woman's Party because

we .   '   was

Paul: with and certainly the ones that got her her position.
So, she had been invited.

In the last period of Miss Dell, after Hoover came
in--she had been appointed by the man before Hoover.
That was Coolidge, I think. Then she had to be reappointed. So, our chairman at that time was Mrs. Florence
Bayard Hilles. She wanted to write a note to Hoover to
say we wanted to think the government for having made
Miss Dell a Civil Service commissioner and to say how
much we hoped he would reappoint her. When she got
this letter ready, I think she read it to our board.

Miss Berrien was present and Miss Berrien made a
great protest and said that Miss Dell had been a complete
failure, that she had nominated Miss Dell four years
before and caused her to take off in the beginning,
but that she would have no more connection with it
anyway. She thought we should not. She made a violent
protest against Miss Dell.

So the relationship then between Miss Dell and
Miss Berrien, who'd been the original person who had
told us about her--we didn't even know Miss Dell when
Miss Berrien brought her to our attention. There was a
very great estrangement between these two people
because, after Miss Berrien had gotten Miss Dell in,
she wanted Miss Dell to join in and make her a tax
judge. Miss Dell--well, whatever the reason was, she
did everything in the world she could for Miss Berrien,
but she didn't succeed in making her a tax judge. She
probably encountered the same resistance we did.

So Miss Dell said she was seated next to Miss
Berrien, who had been so very hard upon her and had
tried so hard to get her not reappointed by Hoover.
But Mrs. Hilles was a very strong character and she
said anyway, "I'm going to write this as national president. This is what I believe and I'm going to recommend
it." And the board also approved it, although Miss
Berrien voted against it. So, we did ask Hoover to
reappoint Miss Dell, and she was reappointed. She served
until Roosevelt came in, who would have nothing, of
course, of anybody from the Woman's Party.

But she was the only person we knew of who was at
that convention.* So, she described it to us. And she

*1)Minutes of meeting of insurgent group, January 11, 12, 26,
1947, led by Doris Stevens, held at Mayflower Hotel, Washing-
to:, D.C. Minutes of meeting of the National Council of
the National Woman's Party, January 9, 10, 11, 12, 1947, held
at Alva Belmont House, Washington, D.C.

Paul: went down and testified in the court about it. It was
a very tiny little group and almost nobody that anybody
in the Woman's Party had ever heard of. They were
just people they dragged in from anywhere. But they
did have the convention.

When we heard this convention was going on or was
about to go on, we telephoned to our board members and
our state chairmen all over the country to come down and
have a board meeting and see what on earth we ought to
do. That's the first formal time we took up the question. They did come from everywhere. A chairman came
all the way from Wyoming, for instance. Everybody made
a supreme effort to come, so it was a very big council
meeting.

Most of us, I think, were too casual about it, took
it too--didn't give enough credence to what was going
on. So, we'd always had a board meeting that was--until
the one up in New York, which was the preceding one
before this--we'd never had any discussion or dispute
or dissension at any board meeting from the time we
were formed in 1913 till the time this occurred.

This board meeting was, of course, perfectly
harmonious. They'd all come to see what they could do
to rescue the Woman's Party from the terrible calamity
that had occurred.

The Invasion of Belmont House Headquarters

Paul: The people, I guess, who were away from Washington were
more or less suspicious, because I can remember our first
vice-chairman at the time, Clara Snell Wolfe, from
Ohio. She had been a teacher in Oberlin, I guess--
well, her husband had been a teacher at Oberlin, a
professor, when Doris [Stevens] had first been discovered; she was evidently a very able and brilliant
young student. She became the state organizer for the
state of Ohio for suffrage after she graduated from
Oberlin. Mrs. Wolfe, having known her as a student
because she was one of her husband's students, told us
this was somebody she thought would be very, very
useful to the suffrage movement, way back in the fairly
early days, and that we ought to try to get her to come
and be a national organizer and not continue just as

Paul: down to Washington and help for a time so we could
       see what she was like and so on. So we <u>did</u> ask her to
       become a national organizer.

       But the person in our whole group, when this
       difficulty arose that Doris seemed to be more the
       center and core and guiding spirit of--[who was most
       suspicious and apprehensive was Mrs. Wolfe].

       [End of Tape 19, Side A]

       [Tape 19, Side B]

Paul: So, just to please her because we wanted to, we author-
       ized her to take any steps she thought necessary to
       employ anybody she thought necessary to protect the
       headquarters. I guess every one of us who voted thought
       "This was the wildest idea that Mrs. Wolfe's had, but
       it won't do any harm to <u>authorize</u> her." [Laughter.]

       So, she proceeded to telephone over to Baltimore.
       (It seems to me it was Burns, but it's hard to remem-
       ber names of these great detective firms. Whatever
       it was, it's in that report of Miss Griswold's, I'm
       sure.) So we gave her the authorization and she went
       forth and telephoned to them to send people over to
       guard the headquarters, physically guard the head-
       quarters from any [laughing] invasion from outsiders.

       So that night, when we concluded our meeting quite
       late, maybe twelve o'clock or something, all the people
       who lived nearby went off in their cars or whatever way
       they'd come and went home. The rest of us began to just
       clear up the headquarters and get ready to go to bed
       when--[pause] there came to the door some people demand-
       ing to come in and saying they were Woman's Party
       officers or something.

       So, the Burns detective--we'll say it was Burns--
       the man at the door, employed now at the request of Mrs.
       Wolfe, very courteously opened the door and admitted
       them. [Laughter.] The person who came in was Doris
       Stevens with one or two others. She, then, marched
       into the living room and started to have a meeting to--
       that they had now come to take over the headquarters.

       When this all happened, everybody went up to the
       next floor, to my bedroom. I remember Betty Gram Swing
       particularly in the big Congressional Room; and our
       ' 'r .' ., r. w   · · . , ' ' . . , .r ' . , .,' ' we'd

Paul: never met. This was the first time she'd ever come to
Washington and she was, my goodness, a most wonderful
woman! But we never would have discovered what wonderful women we had if we hadn't had this experience.
[Laughter.] She was a very devout Christian Scientist,
so she started to read in a loud voice, that she hoped
would go over the whole building, the Ninety-first
Psalm. And she read the Ninety-first Psalm repeatedly,
over and over, with great eloquence and great feeling,
and with great, complete belief that the Ninety-first
Psalm was going to be all that was necessary to meet
this extraordinary situation she'd come to. [Laughter.]
You know, most people who'd come way out from North
Dakota and who'd never been there before and they'd
found people coming in and holding a meeting to ask us
to immediately vacate the place and hand it over to the
National Woman's Party, duly elected at this little
rump convention [laughter]--this was the day of the
rump convention, you see; they'd been elected on that
day and they said, "We've arrived with Doris to take
over the headquarters in accordance with the vote from
our convention, the National Woman's Party convention."

You know, most people who had never had any personal
contact with us--and we hadn't with Mrs. Owens--I think
would have sort of stepped aside and said--that's what
Mrs. Mesta did--"I won't get into this controversy!"
But not Mrs. Owens! She just thought, "Well, now I've
been placed by heaven, I guess, right here in the midst
of this thing, to straighten it out." So, she began
on the Ninety-first Psalm and she kept it up until, I
think, two in the morning, always.

And then Mrs. [Elizabeth C.] Forbes and this Mrs.
[Miriam] Holden decided that they would protect the
people who were most under attack, who'd all gone upstairs. So they occupied the ground floor steps, sat
there together on the steps, and no human being, they
said, was going to get up those stairs unless we opened
up and let them go.

So people just arranged themselves [laughing]
wherever they thought they could meet this assault of
these people who said, under Doris--her little--only
two or three or four people, mainly--that they had come
up as the representatives of the National Woman's Party
to take it over officially. They were going to pass
some resolutions right then at the first meeting after
they began their regime. So they entered the drawing

Paul: Then, Ailey Edson [?], Anita [Pollitzer]'s husband,
           had gotten so aroused over this attack on his wife and
           so on [laughing] that he had come down to Washington to
           be there to see that everything went all right, though
           nobody anticipated any of this sort of thing. But he
           kept [in touch] via the phone and the phone was always
           ringing and people inquiring where their wives were
           [laughter] and wondering what was going on. Then he
           would come (Mrs. Forbes and Mrs. Holden would always
           allow him to walk up, so he would go up and make a
           report to us as to what was going on).

           So then, pretty soon--there was one member [Mrs.
           Hays] that we had, a very fine person, who had taken a
           room there. She was an older suffragist and [pause] I
           think she and her daughter had taken a room, maybe over
           in the annex or something. They hadn't been doing very
           much by that time, but later they became very strong
           members; but then they were just people who wanted--you
           know, we've always used the headquarters for anybody
           who was in any way in our movement who wanted to just
           be a clubhouse member and have a room. So they were
           there and knowing nothing about any of this.

           Doorbells kept ringing downstairs. So Mrs. Hays--
           she wasn't at our board meeting and was totally unaware
           of anything--went downstairs to answer this incessant
           pealing of the doorbell down in the basement, which
           normally people didn't use at night. (You know that
           door down there, the basement door.)

Fry: I've never been down there, but I know that there is an
           outside entrance, isn't there?

Paul: Yes. There'd be a door that opens into the entrance
           into the basement. We have several steps up to go into
           the second floor, which was always used for offices and
           that sort of thing always. That's where the offices
           were, always have been.

           So, she went only to stop the ringing of the
           doorbell, to be helpful, there being no maid or anybody
           else to open it at that hour of the night or any typist
           down there or anybody. She went down the steps, turned
           on the lights, and opened the door. And there were
           maybe twenty or such, some big group, that had come up
           from the convention. They said they'd come up under
           Miss Stevens' direction and leadership, but they'd come
           in a different taxi or a different mode of travel, and
           t   se,

Paul: really welcomed them and said come in, she was sure
        everybody would be very happy they'd at last arrived.
        [Laughter.] Or something equivalent.

        So, they did come up. All this was reported by
        Anita's husband when he arrived up the stairs. They
        did come up, but the door was--let me see. The door
        that goes from that long hallway as you first walk in
        by the Burns detectives had been closed. So, when the
        people walked up from the steps down below, that door,
        when you come up from the steps down below, opens out
        into a little place we use for a dining room, you know.

Fry: In California we'd call it a lanai. It's an enclosed
        back porch, sort of.

Paul: Yes. This stairway comes up and normally you just
        walked into the chairman's office at the front hall
        door, but that door had been closed by the Burns
        detectives. So, when they got up to the top of the
        steps, all they could do was to walk out to the kitchen
        end of the house, which they did. Then they walked
        from the kitchen into that back office. You know the
        back office where we keep all the membership files and
        so on?

Fry: Yes. And that's next to your dining room, isn't it?

Paul: Well, no. It's next to the kitchen.

Fry: Doesn't that back office connect?

Paul: When you walk out of the back office, you walk into
        where we have the ironing board and all those things.
        It's connected with the kitchen. Anybody who wants to
        press her dress walks out there and presses her dress.
        It's next to the kitchen. Then, outside of the kitchen
        and outside of the place where the ironing board is is
        the place where we have our meals, as you remember.

        Well, they walked out and couldn't get into where
        they were trying to get, where we all were. And that
        [kitchen route] goes out to the library.

        So when the meeting was over there was nobody out
        in the library they could do anything with; that was
        over and closed and most of the people had gone home--
        practically all had gone home who lived in the neighbor-
        hood. Betty Gram Swing was staying with her sister, who

Paul: lived there, Alice Gram; she would have gone home in a
few minutes, but all this happened before she had time
to get away, so she was there with us at the beginning
of the night. I don't know when she finally left.

But these people--say around twenty, and they were
not particularly Woman's Party people; I never ever
knew the name of any of them, so I don't know who they
were--they walked out into the kitchen and then into the
next little room where, as I say, our ironing board and
that sort of thing is. And then, here was the door
leading into the office, and that door was securely
closed.

So what did they do? They **battered** at that door
until the door fell down, and then they walked **over** the
door into the office. Then they were in full possession
of everything.

But they couldn't get upstairs because of Mrs.
Holden and Mrs. Forbes [laughter], who were both so
distinctly very good sports, but they were also extremely
dignified and calm and very, very, very refined type of
people that you would hardly start in to move, especially
to fight with them. [Laughter.] So, they sat there and
all they did was to sit and nobody could pass them but
somebody like Ailey Edson or somebody whom we wanted to
come up.

So here they were, so they went in and joined Doris.
So they had quite a nice--they said--meeting of the
National Woman's Party to draw up these resolutions.
So they drew them up and then they addressed the resolutions to Anita, as the national chairman, from the
National Woman's Party: "We demand now that you surrender the headquarters tonight--we've arranged tonight
to take them over formally, and we want all the documents
and the treasurer's reports and your safe deposit boxes
and keys" and so on.

Then they had nobody to give them to because Anita
was upstairs. Then I think they addressed it to me a
being one of the chief conspirators in this terrible
thing of illegally taking over the National Woman's Party.
I just don't know how many people they addressed. It
may have been addressed to everybody. But one by one,
these resolutions were being brought up to us from somebody down below.

Now, I   a   do i   ay, "Well, we'll

Paul: allow Mr. Edson to carry them up or we'll allow somebody
[laughter], but you can't come up." This went on, we'll
say, till two o'clock. They met in their room sending
up resolutions and we sat upstairs, all hearing the
Ninety-first Psalm over and over and over again, coming
from across the hall, [laughter] and just not knowing
what to do. We really didn't know what on earth to do.

Fry: What was the private guard doing all this time?

Paul: The Burns detective men? By this time, they knew they
weren't to let any more people in and they didn't.
That's the reason these people had to go down and get
in the other way. But they were doing their very best.
It seems to me that Mrs. Wolfe stayed down there. I'm
not quite certain. I think after Doris had been let
in--see, we left all the guardianship to Mrs. Wolfe,
because these were her men that she had summoned and
she'd arranged everything with them, and certainly she
did do it efficiently. But after Doris had come in with
her two or three people in the beginning, before the
other people arrived, her whole contingent she was to
have had, you see, came later and got in down below when
they couldn't get in above.

But immediately, when this happened--the Burns
people let in the first [laughter] people they were
supposed to keep out--I remember Mrs. Wolfe went to
the door while she was trying to get it explained to
them that they must not let any more people in, and
she put her arm through something that was on that
front door at the time to keep it closed. These other
people, who hadn't gotten in in the beginning, were
trying to get in from the outside and they were pushing and it broke her arm. I remember that well. But
she finally got things in order and got these Burns
people to understand what they were to do. [Laughter.]
But she did break her arm in that happening, as it
turned out.

In all events, some policemen, anyway, arrived
because Mrs. Wolfe had not only arranged to get the
Burns people, but she'd gone around to the precinct
[station] and somebody who shared her apprehension also
went with her. I think it was Mrs. Holden who went
with her; I'm sure because Mrs. Holden was also very
much with Mrs. Wolfe for making a strong defense of the
building and so on. So, the police had said, "Now if
you need us and you find that there is some danger and
so on, telephone."

Paul: So, somebody--I guess it was probably Ailey Edson--
telephoned, anyway, to the police, or else they came
just to make sure. In all events, the police appeared.
The few people we had down on the floor, including Mrs.
Wolfe who, I guess, was still down there, evidently
said, "Well, we certainly do need you, (and so on) and
these people here in the living room who are having this
meeting, they're the ones that we have been warning you
about that we thought might come and try and take over
this building."

Then the police went in there, and they [the
insurgents] said, "Well, we've had this meeting and the
National Woman's Party has elected us as a group to
come up and take over the headquarters. We hope you'll
get these people there that are sitting on the steps
and the people upstairs out, because we've come officially
to take over."

So, then the police just didn't know what to do.
So, they said, "Well, we'll have to call up for more
instructions. We don't understand this situation."
[Laughter.] So, the police then were calling up for
further instructions as to whom they were to eject
[laughter] and whom they were to protect. They said,
"Here, everybody says she's a Woman's Party person and
that we're to eject somebody else. Then we go to that
person and she says, 'Oh, I'm the National Woman's
Party. You must eject--.'" [Laughter.]

Fry: Eject the others! [Laughter.]

Paul: So, they were at the phone inquiring. Suddenly, the
sirens began to sound. If you've ever stayed there,
you know how often the sirens, going up to Faculty
Hospital, right up on Eighth Street above us, you know,
come with a tremendous amount of noise. So, the sirens
all began to make a great noise,and they were taking
some people--

Fry: Oh, how nice! Here's tea. [Tea is brought in.] Just
what we need! [Small break.]

The sirens were going. The ambulance happened--

Paul: Anyway, the police were there making all this inquiry
and the people in Doris's group, I suppose, were all
down on that floor with no one knowing what was going
on. They heard the sirens, and they thought it was
the police in phoning for aid. That's what they said,

Paul: anyway. They thought, "Here these police, instead of doing what we asked them to do, they're bringing in aid."

       And when the sirens came--so, they began to come out in the hall one by one, tiptoeing, tiptoeing, out and down the front steps, as fast as they could get out of the building. So, we suddenly--heaven maybe granted the prayers of Mrs. Owens. [Laughter.]

Fry: There was that Ninety-first Psalm working! [Laughter.]

Paul: She was persuaded that heaven had come to our rescue. Whatever it was, suddenly the whole group tiptoed out as silently as they could, as quickly as they could, making no motion at all. I believe one of them went out the front window in the living room. They all got out somehow or other. I suppose they had some taxis or some cars of their own or something. Off they went.

       We, then, continued to have the Burns detectives, maybe a month or two months, always there, and the house practically barricaded, because at this meeting that we had had we saw that we had to get a lawyer, that this had gotten beyond us, and that they would probably go to [court] against us, because they were apparently threatening to do so.

       So, Miss [Burnita] Matthews had said, "I will send you somebody that has an office in my own personal suite, in my offices. She's not connected with my firm, but I know her very well. I will send her up and let you see if you would like to engage her to be your lawyer because I can't do it because I have this relationship with Miss Berrien." (In the meantime, Miss Berrien had joined Miss Matthews' own law firm, so it was Matthews and Berrien.) "So," she said, "You can see I'm not in a position to do it, and Mrs. Wiley's one of my clients," and so on. "But," she said, "You can trust this person I will send you. In my opinion, she's very, very good, and her name is Olive Lacey."

       Well, she was another gift from heaven. We never could have had a better lawyer. It would be impossible because we were up against the great law firm of Dean Acheson.

Fry: Goodness yes.

Paul: And this great trial lawyer. I remember when we were trying to get a lawyer before this night, Anita Pollitzer

Paul: had gone to see Burton K. Wheeler. I think I've told
you that before. You know, Senator Wheeler.

Fry: Yes.

Paul: The one who was the running mate of La Follette's for
the presidency. He and his wife were personal friends
of a great many of us. Maud Younger, for instance,
constantly used the little apartment and little house
which she bought next to the headquarters when she
entertained people, she had parties at which she would
practically always have the Wheelers come.

So, we went to Wheeler (Miss Pollitzer was the one
who went to him) and he said, "I can't possibly take
this case. I have nothing out in that field of law at
all. But I'm certainly sorry to hear that Dean Acheson's
firm is doing this because they have one of the greatest
trial lawyers in America. And for you to be up against
that trial lawyer, you've got to have somebody that--my
goodness!--would be able to help you out of this situation. But," he said, "I know that you have to go forward and fight this case because you have been entrusted
by your organization with really a very valuable property
and your investment and endowment fund has quite a large
sum of money and you absolutely have to do it. Otherwise, any member could bring a suit that you'd been
negligent in your duties. And you would be negligent
in your duties if you didn't defend this property that
you're now in charge of."

So, we thought then we certainly were up against
it and we'd have to get somebody. We had nobody to rely
on but Mrs. Matthews, who guaranteed this [Lacey] would
be a good person. But certainly, when she took it,
she felt she was so completely inadequate to meet the
people on the other side. But she was the kind of person who would devote all of her time, not just get a
little scrap of assistant lawyers who came in. But she
just sort of took in--she must have abandoned every
other case she had. She just said this she had to give
all her time to, she had to meet very great adversaries.

She would work with us all day when she wasn't in
the court and all night if necessary until she was
familiar with every single detail. We worked very hard
at accumulating all the books and things we could, giving
her all the chronology of everything. I sat down beside
her, next to her, through the whole trial, and we just
(. ' . ' 1. , ' ' arr e(out.

Paul: Well, that night we engaged her, that night when we met just before the invasion by our opponents. She told us, "Of course, I think, in the law, to be in possession of a place is nine-tenths of the victory and you are now in possession of all the things that somebody else is trying to get from you in the way of records and your bank account and your investments and so on and the building itself." So, she said, "I think you have to keep on with the Burns detectives so that nobody else can get in. Now, it's clear that you are the possessors of all these things and I think the court will be impressed by that and that somebody else is trying to take it from you. We don't know who is trying to take it, but somebody's trying to take it from you," because we knew it wasn't any of these individual women, most of whom we didn't even know their names and they had no connection with us at all.

So, from that time on, for, say, two months or three months, our headquarters was protected by the Burns detectives, whom we paid, and nobody came there but the--maybe some people were still living there as having rented a room, but not any of our workers or any of our officers went in the place.

Well, I guess that's the end of that.

Its Effect on the ERA Campaign

Fry: Could I ask you about--?

Paul: You'd better ask me quickly now, since your plane's going to leave so soon, any quick points that you need, and I won't discuss them at length.

Fry: All right. Did this affect your work for the Amendment?

Paul: Yes, terribly.

Fry: The Equal Rights magazine that I read on this said that this was the time when, for the first time in the history of the Amendment, "we are able to go to an incoming Congress with favorable committee reports from both Senate and House Judiciary Committees. We are on the brink of victory and a Woman's Joint Legislative Committee has been formed under the chairmanship of Nina Horton Avery," and so forth.

Fry: So, it was just at this very crucial time, I guess,
         when it happened.

Paul: I wanted to say that these opponents, whoever they were,
         they were doing just what I feel is happening at the
         present moment: The problem you have with the people
         that you're dealing with--and you know that somebody
         else is [behind them]--that you're dealing with some
         unknown force.

         For instance, they tied up our investment and
         endowment fund. Most of our women were too unfamiliar
         with all these things to know how to tie us all up. So,
         here we had all this money that we had struggled so hard
         to accumulate, we'll say $250,000 or something. They
         tied it up so that, since it was not certain that we
         were the Woman's Party, therefore the treasurer couldn't
         send any money to us or to anybody else. It was just
         all tied up. So, we didn't have any income whatsoever.

         [End of Tape 19, Side B]

         [Tape 20, Side A. May 13, 1973.]

Paul: I don't know whether it was two days or not, but
         shortly after the invasion, perhaps the next day, our
         treasurer and someone with her--for your sake, I'd say
         it was probably Miss [inaudible] because she was the
         secretary. They went down to the bank to say, "We think
         this is perfectly useless and unnecessary, but we're
         bringing you a resolution adopted at our board meeting,"
         (which was the night of the invasion, this board meeting
         had been meeting all day nearly; I told you about it--
         They came from all over the country.)

         They had passed a resolution at the request of
         Mrs. Wolfe, the same one that was always so full of the
         belief that things would be beyond our expectation in
         difficulty. The resolution had been adopted saying
         that they wished to state that the officer entitled
         to sign such and so on was the treasurer and no one
         else, because Mrs. Wolfe [had] said, "You don't know
         what they'll do. They'll go down and try to take all
         the money we have in the bank."

         So, they saw the vice-president and he said, "Oh
         well, you're too late. They have already been here.
         Somebody's come down saying she was the newly-elected
         treasurer (elected at the rump convention) and the new
         secretary came with a resolution authorizing them to

Paul: take everything out of the bank account," just what
Mrs. Wolfe had foreseen. They [at the bank had] said,
"Well, we have dealt with the Woman's Party now a
great many years and we know them very, very well. If
you have been duly elected, all right, we'd like to see
the seal of the organization attached to anything that
we honor. Will you just have it properly sealed?"

They said, "Goodness me! We didn't bring the
seal. We'll go off and get the seal."

So, Mrs. Matthews called up and I answered the
phone and--I told you Miss Berrien had been taken in
by Mrs. Matthews as her [law] partner. She said, "Miss
Berrien is here, of course, in my office, and she wants
the seal, the Woman's Party seal." And she said, "I
said, 'I can't give you the Woman's Party seal. I've
always been the Woman's Party lawyer and have always
kept the seal here.'"

So, Miss Berrien said, "Well, I have to have it."
Why she was having to have it was to get out the money
from our bank account! The bank wouldn't give it without
the seal, you see.

So thank heaven, you see, [laughing] how we were
protected by heaven anyway, so many times. Mrs. Matthews
said, "I'm going to take the seal up to the headquarters
and give it to you personally and I'm not going to have
it in this office and have any danger of somebody taking
it out. I told Miss Berrien I'm not going to keep in
here any longer, I will not allow her to take it or to
touch it, and I'm going to go right up and give it to
you personally."

So she did. We kept the seal and we still have the
seal. So they couldn't get the money out.

But we, then, drew the money all out ourselves
because we couldn't live in this situation, we thought.
of constantly having this thing occur. One of our
members, a very good and faithful one we had over in
Baltimore, said that she would take it all over and put
it in her personal account, so that nobody could possibly get it out of her personal account, and keep it
until all this trouble was over, which she did.

So, we had a hard time then to exist. We had no
bank account in Washington, and we had no access to our
l·. ··· ·   · · ·   ·   ·   enough

Paul: money among ourselves to just keep going. By each one
of us paying all that she possibly could, we continued
to bring out the magazine, pay the printer, and keep
the organization at least alive.

When you say, "Did it injure the campaign?", well,
it certainly did because we had to curtail everything
we could curtail, and we had a very hard time to survive. Of course, they thought we wouldn't survive.
By cutting it all off, whoever these people were, they
thought we couldn't continue the magazine, we couldn't
continue to communicate with our members, we couldn't
continue to function.

Fry: Am I wrong, Alice? I got some very scratchy telephone
notes once when you and I were talking--you were here
and I was in California--I thought you said Alma Lutz
was one person who was in with the insurgents. Is
that wrong?

Paul: Well, I wouldn't exactly say that. She was a newcomer.
We'd never known her in the suffrage campaign, you see.
[Pause.] I don't know--I've never known her very well.
I don't know her yet very well. [Pause.] But I think
I would say that she sympathized with them.

Fry: I see.

Paul: She wasn't in a position to--she didn't take any active
part in it.

Fry: Yes, I see. I guess what you were telling me was that
she did not stand wholeheartedly with you, then.

Paul: Our only connection at that time with her was that she
shared an apartment in Boston, where she lived, and a
home out in wherever it is that they live in New York
state somewhere with a fellow Christian Scientist. Miss
Marian May, who was the chairman of our investment and
endowment fund committee and a very prominent Christian
Scientist, got in touch with these two people because
they were also Christian Scientists and she was the
chairman, you see. Marian May was the chairman. One
of these two people was the treasurer.

That was one reason that they'd had an investment
counselor from Boston so the treasurer could be in
touch with the investment counselor. So, when all this
thing was sort of brewing, long before it got to the
stages I've been recounting and any of those things

Paul: happening, Miss May had tried to--First of all, the
people on the other side, Doris Stevens had gone personally to Miss May to try to get her completely in _her_
group. I know that we had a headquarters up in New
York and I was going in from here into this New York
headquarters and using that all the time and paying part
of the rent for it for our world committee.

So, Miss May said to me one day, "Well, Doris
Stevens has been to see me and she says you're in a
terrible jam."

I said, "Am I? Well, what's the jam about? I don't
know what you--."

So, she began to tell me all these things that Doris
was saying, and I just said,

"Well, I don't know really anything about it at
all."

So, she said, "Well, now I'm going to see what we
can do about this investment and endowment fund in case
there's any attack made on that."

So, she communicated with both Alma Lutz, because
they were together, and her treasurer up in Boston. She
said something like this: "Our endowment fund is in need
of protection." Something that she said Christian Scientists would understand; she told me she sent this
telegram. And they began saying, well, they thought
that probably there was some justice to this question.
(I can't remember what on earth it was all about, really.)
But finally, Marian May sent them a telegram and said,
"I don't think that you _are_ Christian Scientists or you
would arise to the defense of this thing which is so
vital to carrying on this movement," and so on.

So, they then called a meeting of the investment
and endowment fund committee in New York. Mrs. [Margaret
C.?] Williams, who was on the investment and endowment
fund committee and always was one of the pillars of
strength financially in our movement, asked me if I would
go to the meeting. (When I'd gone to Europe, I'd resigned from the committee and said, "I can't be on this
committee when I'm going to be over in Europe so much."
So I thought. So, I wasn't any longer on the committee.
So, Mrs. Williams said, "Will you come up to New York and
be at this meeting? It will be a very crucial meeting.")

Paul: This was in the offing before all these things had happened, months and months before, I guess. So, I did go up to New York and went down to be at the meeting. When I got there, Mrs. Williams, since she was on the inside, said she would like to move that I be invited to come into the meeting because I'd really founded the investment and endowment fund committee and been on it at the beginning, had always been on it, and had probably been the person who'd gotten most of the money that they had in it. So she said, "I want Miss Paul to be here answering questions and to speak up for me because I'm not very familiar with anything."

        So, they thereupon voted that I could not be allowed to go in. So, I sat out in the hall [laughter] all the time, expecting to be called in. But the treasurer, who was fairly new to us and had never been in the suffrage campaign at all--she had come in fairly recently into the movement--had been put on this committee because she was working in the field of investment up in Boston, I believe. So, I didn't get in. I couldn't go in. Alma Lutz was there with Margaret Smith, and of course was supporting her in the position that was taken. I think it was only just complete ignorance of new people who'd been entrusted with money and not knowing exactly what to do.

        But the people who'd been with us longer, it was very rare we had anybody defect; I don't know if we had anybody, who'd ever been in the Woman's Party any length of time. So, I've always felt, and probably still, that Alma Lutz, you see, wasn't in the suffrage campaign at all and we knew nothing about her, had never heard of her. When she did come in, we made her chairman of our editor committee, and at that she was good because she wrote well and she was conscientious. I didn't mean to speak in any way against her and I wouldn't say she was an insurgent.

Fry: Okay.

SECTION V: OTHER ACCOMPLISHMENTS

INTERNATIONAL TREATIES FOR EQUALITY

<u>Work with Bedia Afnan on the Third Committee, the United Nations</u>

Fry: One of these newspaper items about the defection says
         that one of the issues of the Doris Stevens group was
         that the Woman's Party was formed to work for suffrage
         and the Equal Rights Amendment and that it was spending
         too much of its time and energy in the international
         field.

Paul: Oh, is that so?

Fry: Yes. Were you aware of this complaint at the time?
         Do you think that that's a correct assessment by the
         newspaper?

Paul: Well, I mean, maybe Doris said--you said Doris Stevens
         thought I was doing too much time [in the international
         field]--

Fry: Yes.

Paul: Well, you see, in 1938, at our national convention in
         Detroit, it was voted that the National Woman's Party
         would take steps to form a world committee, of which
         the National Woman's Party would become a member, like
         other world committees which were in existence in
         almost all organizations. We were incorporated at a
         meeting in Washington. Sometime I will give you a
         photograph, if I can find it, of all the people, our
         whole national board, in fact, was there incorporating
         this world committee.

         We elected Lady Pethick-Lawrence of England to be
         our world president or chairman or whatever we called

Paul: her, and we started it formally in our own headquarters
        in Washington as the result of the vote taken by the
        convention out in Detroit. So, I think it was a complete-
        ly authorized part and a very important part of the
        campaign that we were undertaking.

        You see, as I told you first, we did it with just
        this international committee going to conferences where
        our government was represented. And then I just gave
        for quite a long time all of my time to building it up.

Fry: Yes. That brings us to another topic--the inclusion
        of the equal rights clause in the international Covenant
        on Human Rights that the United Nations was creating.

Paul: Yes, that's one thing we did. That was 1945.

Fry: Forty-five? No, this was later.

Paul: That's when Sara Bard Field helped us, you know.

Fry: Your efforts to get equality according to sex put in the
        Preamble of the U.N. Charter.

Paul: That was '45. Well, the Preamble <u>was</u> the United Nations
        Charter, really. In the Preamble, they told what it
        was to do. The Preamble, you know, begins: "We, affirm-
        ing faith in the worth and dignity of the human person,
        the equal rights of men and women, of nations great and
        small, we now hereby assemble,"--or launch or begin or
        whatever they said--"this United Nations." And then I
        gave you all the different little points that were put
        in in that sheet. You have it.

Fry: Yes. And then, in 1951, the General Assembly was to
        vote on sex equality, to include it in the Covenant on
        Human Rights, at Flushing Meadows, New York.

Paul: Wait a minute. In the Covenant of Human Rights?

Fry: Yes.

Paul: You mean there was some treaty on human rights?

Fry: That's right.

Paul: Well, the first treaty that was proposed was the treaty
        on--I think the first one proposes that they have an
        international treaty on nationality of women and that

Paul: the person who proposed that--[pause]. I think the
first one was nationality. Anyway, we got a series of
treaties through. One of them was the Nationality
Treaty. That's that one thing I wanted to get you
with all those dates of those treaties. I'll have to
mail it to you, I guess.

Fry: That would help if we could get it all put together.
By going through the Equal Rights magazine, too, we
might be able to cull this out.

Paul: Anyway, we had this thing that was gotten out by our
New York City committee, and it gives the dates of each
one of those treaties.

Fry: This one seemed to me to be especially broad.

Paul: I believe the nationality one was the first, or perhaps
it was--[pause] well, I can't say about that one. They
called them "covenants" and they were just treaties.
All those that had to do with the rights of women came
to the Status of Women Commission, and you know we
created the Status of Women Commission completely.

Fry: Yes.

Paul: And had it made finally a full commission through
Governor Weinard [?]. From that time on, till I went
down to try to help the national headquarters and I
stopped working at the United Nations, we worked with
very great success with that Status of Women Commission.
But I really deserted that field over trying to save
the Woman's Party from the [Carl] Hayden rider [to the
Equal Rights Amendment].

Fry: In 1950 on November 14, there was the woman from Iraq,
Madame Bedia Afnan, who was the one that submitted the
amendment for "an explicit recognition of the equality
of men and women on related rights."

Paul: Yes. But, you know, she was the person we got. Elsie
Hill and I got her to do that.

Fry: I wondered if you did.

Paul: Yes. I mean, she was the person whom we worked through
at that particular time. You see, every day Elsie Hill
and I drove down to Lake Success, where they [the U.N.]
were meeting there. Now, what year was that?

Fry: This is 1950.

Paul: And that's the year that we started in with our Hayden
         rider trouble, and I left to go down [to Washington]
         and work on that, unfortunately. But what happened was
         that we had this circle of women and men, mainly men,
         from all of these countries on what was the Third Com-
         mittee, I think it was always called.

Fry: Yes. The January-February Equal Rights tells the vote
         of the Third Committee. They voted for it 34 to 0 on
         that date, November 14, 1950.

Paul: Whichever one of these various treaties it was, I can't
         remember, but we'd gotten it anyway to the Status of
         Women Commission and then it went up to the Third Commit-
         tee. On the Third Committee, we didn't seem to have
         anybody willing to champion it and it might have been
         killed. I suppose at that time Mrs. Roosevelt was
         probably still there, I'm not sure. But in all events,
         we didn't have any friend.

         I remember Elsie Hill happened--As we went in
         every day, we would take the same seats. I think this
         is when we were out at Lake Success still. We were
         right behind, she and I, but she was the person who
         did all this business, right behind this girl from Iraq.
         Iraq didn't have any voting rights for women anyway.
         So, Elsie was this outgoing type. Wherever she was,
         she always began to talk and make friends and chat away.
         So, she became quite a warm friend of Madame Afnan.
         Then, when we needed to have this proposed, we asked
         Madame Afnan to do it, and so she did.

         I remember first of all she had to call up the head
         of her delegation and he said, "But women don't vote in
         Iraq. It will put us in a very preposterous position if
         you will be the leader of this in the Assembly of the
         United Nations. No, no, no. You couldn't do that." So
         she came back and said her chief wouldn't let her do it.

         So, then we said, "Well, why don't you go back and
         say that the world doesn't know very much about Iraq."
         And all the things that she was always telling us, which
         were mostly--Let me see--I'll have to think up those
         things about Iraq. It seems to me it was the country
         where the ten commandments were given. Anyway, it was
         a long history of the wonderful, marvelous things about
         Iraq.

Paul: The last time that I was up there to the United Nations and I asked her right away to come over and have dinner, she came. And for the first time she was not very warm. [Interruption.] She seemed sort of anxious to terminate the dinner and not to stay very long and she was totally different.

I finally said, "You know, I have a different feeling about being with you today from other times because we've always been so of the same opinion and so on. Is there anything that I've done to offend you?"

She said, "Oh, no, no. Oh, no, no," and so on. After a little while, I kept persisting and I said, "I have a feeling that there's something that's happened that you're not pleased with. Is it something I've done, or that somebody's done, or what is the matter?"

And she said, "Well, I'll tell you. [Pause.] The first person who came in and"-- Goodness, but this is so confidential, you know. You can't put these things down. So make a mark it's not to be transcribed. She said, "When Truman took over the presidency, the first person who came to see him"--it seems to me his name was Ben Gurion, but she told me the name--she said, "Your country's gone over to the Jews, and I am an Arab from an Arab country. I feel I'm dealing with a hostile group now here.

"Well," I said, "I don't take any part in that struggle and I don't know anything about that struggle. It's not anything that ought to disturb our relationship in working here at the United Nations." So she finally calmed down and I guess that was the [end of that].

Paul: I said, "We have learned, Miss Hill and I, all
about Iraq from you. It's <u>incredible</u>, what you've told
us about the history of Iraq. But the <u>world</u> doesn't
know it, and why don't you just get up and take this
leadership and have the world know that Iraq has not only
this glorious past, but it's now a leader in the whole
new world of the emancipation of women. Talk about the
advertising that you can give to this country, your
country, and the good light in which you could make it
appear before the world. See what reaction you get from
your chief."

           So, she came back and said, "You know, this was a
most good idea you gave me because he's very much impressed and he thinks this will all be to the glory and
honor of Iraq for me to do this. So, he said, 'Go
ahead, do it.'" So, she became our chief.

           And I remember that she was superb because of the
way she worked. She went to every single man and stopped
at his desk and talked with him. She told me, "Now,
when I went to Saudi Arabia, I don't believe anybody
in this committee could have gotten Saudi Arabia to
sponsor this treaty that you have if I hadn't gone,
because he knows that I'm of his world and they welcome
me. But if anybody just from what they think is the
other kind of a world [laughter] comes in, you couldn't
get anywhere." So she turned out to be just superb.

           I got to know her extremely well, and again and
again she came over and had dinner with me at the Women's
University Club where I lived. I was a member and lived
there always at the time I was with the United Nations.

Paul: But then I went on down myself and began to work
again in Washington. In the last few years, you see,
I've just deserted it completely and just let it be
quiescent because I thought my main purpose in coming
up here [to Connecticut] was to think I'd again go
into the United Nations and build up again the committee
and all the good feeling we'd gotten among all these
women from other countries.

    That's what I really want to do next. I don't
want to spend any more time going down over the details,
excepting I can see the ratification probably--I've got
to put off the United Nations work until we win or lose
that campaign. Because, you see, when I came up here
that's what I said to all the people there on our board,
"Now I'm going back to work on this [international]
committee that was formed by the National Woman's Party,
and I took the main part in getting it successfully
started over in Europe and successfully started in this
country. Now, I've just"--

[End of Tape 20, Side A]

[Tape 20, Side B]

Blocks to U.S. Ratification of Treaties

Bogotá

Paul: --said, "Well, we'd like to go in when you start it again
on the American end of that."

Fry: May I ask you a very stupid question about this Covenant
on Human Rights? It was passed by the General Assembly
on December 4, 1950. Now, the last I heard about that
was that the United States had not yet ratified that.
Has our country ever done this?

Paul: You know, the first time that this whole thing came up
was at Bogotá, whatever the year was. What was the year
of that? Do you know? That was the Conference of
American Republics.

Fry: Was that after Montevideo?

Paul: y⁺ , ᵛ ᶠ⁻·ᴛ. A ' '.1.

Fry: Wait a minute. I've got it right here somewhere. [Looks through notes.] I think it was around '47ish.

Paul: I think it was around '41.

Fry: Do you?

Paul: Well, I think it was in the forties anyway.

Fry: Yes. [Reading notes.] The World Woman's Party was first created in 1938--

Paul: Thirty-eight at Detroit, it was authorized. It was incorporated the next year in 1939.

Fry: And you had the dedication of headquarters in Geneva, Switzerland, on August 18, 1939. In December of 1941 you were at work organizing the North American chapter. In July of that year, they had given you a big, big dinner in Philadelphia.

Paul: No. I returned from Europe in '41 because--I wasn't busy about this business at all. I returned from Geneva because we were getting into the war.

Fry: I know.

Paul: I went up to my little cottage here, and I was asked to go down to a Philadelphia meeting. It wasn't to organize anything. It was just to be speeches, and I was one of the speakers. That's all there was to that.

Fry: Oh. Well, in the Equal Rights magazine it was written up as one of the largest dinners ever given for the National Woman's Party, in Philadelphia.

Paul: Well, it may have been, but it wasn't a dinner for anything--

Fry: And in Alice Paul's honor. [Laughter.]

Paul: It was nothing but a dinner at which I was one of the speakers.

Fry: [Looks through notes.] Here we go. May 2, 1948, was the Ninth International Conference of American States at Bogotá.

Paul: All right. Well, now wait. Let me just get this into . . . . Mrs.

Paul: Miller went over; of course it was a Democratic President
then.

Fry: Which Miller is that?

Paul: Emma Guffey Miller. She went over to try to get Muna
Lee sent as a member of the delegation so we'd have a
woman on the inside, and she was. She was appointed
by--it must have been Truman, I imagine. Forty-eight.
Who was President in '48?

Fry: Truman.

Paul: It's wonderful the way you know these dates and these
Presidents.

Fry: But I flounder the whole time!

Paul: I think it's marvelous! Well, I thought it must be
Truman, for Mrs. Miller to have gone. Truman agreed,
and he appointed her to be in the inside of our delegation going down to this Conference of American Republics.
Then Mrs. Walker--perhaps Mrs. Walker was our national
president at that time, I'm not sure--Amelia Walker.
But she went down on her own to be there for the conference, representing the National Woman's Party and she
paid her own expenses, I think, and went down. Of
course the government paid for Muna Lee. So, we had
two people there.

Now, at that conference--you see, we had always
pressed for this equal rights treaty. So, we went down
in support of an equal rights treaty, complete equal
rights in all fields, like the Equal Rights Amendment.
Muna Lee undertook to press it from the inside and
Amelia Walker from the outside, and it was adopted. It
was called the Treaty on Equal and Civil Rights, I
think.

The first treaty was on the nationality of women
at Montevideo and the second treaty that came from the
Conference of American Republics was this one at Bogotá,
which was called an Equal and Civil Rights Treaty, I
think. It was to cover all rights, civil rights.

Fry: "Political rights" was the article that I read, "treaty
giving political rights to women," in Equal Rights.

Paul: No, but that wasn't right.

Fry: Here's the quotation of the title: "The Inter-American
       Convention on the Granting of Political Rights to Women."

Paul: But there was another one at the same conference which
       was on--the political rights one was one we <u>had</u> gotten
       through. We got it through with the United Nations.
       But this <u>civil</u> rights one went beyond political rights,
       and that's one that we couldn't sign because we didn't
       yet have it in our own country. We had political rights
       all right.

           That's the time that the first Castro insurrection
       really started, you know, and broke up the conference.

Fry: I wondered what happened because it mentioned the madness
       of riot and the flames in the city.

Paul: Yes, it was. And it was the group that finally took
       over Cuba. Castro was there, and it was the beginning
       of that movement.

Fry: Were you in danger at any time?

Paul: I wasn't down there.

Fry: You didn't go to that one?

Paul: No one went for us except Amelia Walker and Muna Lee
       [?]. So, immediately when this disturbance occurred and
       practically broke up the conference, Muna Lee and all
       the other American delegates, I guess <u>all</u> of them, were
       removed by our country from any further participation.
       But Amelia Walker stayed on because she was independent
       and representing nobody but the Woman's Party. She had
       personal friends there that she lived with whom she'd
       known over the years, I guess. So she stayed on till
       the very end.

           It's my very dim recollection, but I have it in
       this one little leaflet that I have to get for you, that
       at that one, the real one we were after, which was the
       <u>new</u> one of complete equality for the American republics
       including the United States, was called the <u>civil</u> rights
       treaty. Of course, we couldn't sign that. That's one
       of the arguments we've been using ever since: that the
       other countries could sign this treaty, the other countries
       that went to Bogotá, but we couldn't because, of course,
       you can't sign a treaty for something which--maybe you
       <u>could</u> do it, but you wouldn't be apt to do it--if you
                                                      is we

Paul: couldn't in the beginning sign the Montevideo one. We
had to put through the nationality law [in the United
States] in the morning and sign it [the treaty] in
the afternoon, as you know. [We've not yet] put through
the [ERA] ratification, I mean, so we've never had the
one from Bogotá for our country for [treaty] ratification
because we haven't yet gotten the Amendment through.
That's the outline of it. I'm glad you told me about
the date so I'll get the date straight.

That's one of the terrible things, that we've
been held up so long with our [ERA]--you see, '48, and
then in '50 came the Hayden rider, that long fight that
women have themselves been responsible for.

Fry: Is it passage of the Equal Rights Amendment that is
holding up the signing of that treaty?

Paul: Well, we can't sign the treaty for complete legal
equality when we don't yet have it in our own country,
quite apart from the Equal Rights Amendment. We don't
have in many, many fields yet complete equality.

Fry: Is the problem the same with our ratification of the
Human Rights Covenant of the United Nations?

Paul: I'm not sure when you say--I mean, I'd have to look what
that treaty is that you're talking about (as I explained
before) the human rights one. The only one that I can
remember was the time that we had--and I'm not sure
whether the equality section was put in that one--because
I was there in the gallery when it was being discussed
in the Human Rights Commission.

The United Nations: Eleanor Roosevelt and the Human Rights Commission Vs. the Status of Women

Paul: We had been striving to get the delegate from India or
the delegate from Chile (both were with us) on that Human
Rights Commission, which was presided over by Mrs.
Roosevelt as you know, to get them to add to the treaty
as it was drawn, making it include equality for women.

The one that I'm thinking about was a rather vague
one that was being proposed on general human rights, and
we wanted (Are you listening to me?)

Fry: Yes!

Paul: --to have specifically put in equal rights for <u>women</u>.
I remember going to the Indian delegation and she said,
"Well, I don't know really what to do about it." Then
I ended up going to the Chilean one and she said, "All
right, I'll move it." So, she moved that they add the
word "sex" so it would include women, whatever form it
was in. It wasn't certain that it was not going to be
a general one on human rights but not mentioning the
equality of the sexes. Sexes are already in the Constitution and so on. We thought this must be included
in words so that nobody would misinterpret it.

Anyway, when Madame Figaroa, who was the delegate
from Chile, got up and proposed this--she's now over,
you know, in the International Labor Organization in
Chile at Geneva. Well, Madame Figaroa did propose it,
and Mrs. Roosevelt <u>staunchly</u> and very vigorously
opposed it.

Then this went on for some days and the newspaper
people--I think one paper came forth saying it was such
a strange thing for Mrs. Roosevelt to be opposing this.
We were trying to get people that we thought might
influence her to stop opposing it. So, she arose at
this meeting and I think she was chairman at the time,
but she may not have been chairman. Anyway, she was
the one who was opposing it.

And she said, "Well, I wish to make clear I'm being
criticized. I find in the press I'm being criticized
for opposing the equal rights for women section being
added to this as proposed by Figaroa from Chile. I want
to state that at all events, I have withdrawn my opposition to the equal rights for women amendment."

This was a very, of course, <u>important</u> declaration.
Anita Pollitzer was sitting beside me--I think I've told
you all this--and she rushed down and got a copy of it.

Fry: Yes, you did.

Paul: And that was the time when the hostility of Mrs.
Roosevelt to the Amendment was publicly withdrawn.
But it was forced as a defense to the people criticizing
her because she was opposing putting it in the World
Covenant on the grounds, I think, that the World Covenant
should be more general and just talk about general human

Paul: You see, on those grounds, she'd opposed having
the whole subcommittee ever established. And then when
we did get established against her will and her opposition in London by our delegation led by Lady Pethick-
Lawrence over there, she then--that was the opposition
to having it anything but a subcommittee. First of all,
she [voiced] opposition to having it brought up at all.
She said the commission should have the right to take
up all things in the field of discrimination and just be
trusted to deal with human rights and not have a special
committee. We wanted a special commission. So, at last
they compromised and put in a subcommission. Then we
had to have this fight in this country, for us led by
Mr. Weinard, to raise the subcommission to a full commission. So that way we got a full Commission on Status
of Women, with full commission rank.

So then, Mrs. Roosevelt went on with her Human
Rights Commission idea and I think I vaguely remember
that the treaty they were calling the Covenant on Human
Rights was not specifically including women. About then
I came down to Washington and I don't know what happened
afterwards.

Fry: Now, just a minute. I may be able to find that--we're
getting to the end of the publication of Equal Rights
magazine here. [Looks through Equal Rights issues.]

Paul: It ended in '53. That was a great calamity that ended.

Fry: Yes. It will always be a calamity too for historians.
[Laughter.]

Paul: Well, we did have a great many bulletins, and I think
maybe I could get all these bulletins together.

Fry: "At the end of 1950, the United Nations Assembly had
adopted a momentous directive to the Commission on Human
Rights." That was what Madame Afnan introduced. "It
directs that there be written into the World Bill of
Rights the ideal so long held by the National Woman's
Party and the World Woman's Party. This Assembly resolution, formally approved December 4, 1950, read: 'The
General Assembly decides to include in the draft Covenant
on Human Rights an explicit recognition of the equality
of men and women.'" [Read from Equal Rights magazine.]

Paul: Well, now that's what Mrs. Roosevelt, in the commission
stage, was speaking against, you see, what she was trying to keep out.

Fry: I see. Then you had a deputation after that to Sir
       Ramaswami Mudeliar of India, a member of the United
       Nations Economic and Social Council.

Paul: Yes. He led us in the--"Medalia," he called himself.
       Sir Ramaswami Mudeliar. He was the chairman presiding.
       I don't know whether I told you about this, but he was
       the chairman at the Third Committee Subcommittee on
       dealing with this particular covenant. I told you Mrs.
       Roosevelt attended every session in the beginning. We
       were trying to have the subject brought up of Human
       Rights Commission not being the sole group to deal with
       it but having the Status of Women Commission made equal.
       I remember so well that this Ramaswami Mudeliar pre-
       sided and day by day we would go down and stay till late
       at night there at the meetings of this particular sub-
       committee. And never would our subject come up.

            Finally, one day Mrs. Roosevelt announced that she
       could attend no more meetings, that she had engagements
       to speak or do something or other and she couldn't be
       present thereafter. So the next meeting, Sir Ramaswami
       Mudeliar brought up the question of making this sub-
       committee into a full committee and giving it all the
       rights under the Status of Women Commission, that the
       Human Rights [Commission] had. He had evidently done
       it purposefully, but we didn't realize he was doing it
       purposefully, and to wait until Mrs. Roosevelt was no
       longer there to make any opposition.

            So then, the man got up from the United States
       saying, "I'm speaking for Governor Weinard. He isn't
       present tonight. We didn't know this subject was coming
       up tonight. But my instructions say that whenever it
       does come up, the United States delegation strongly
       supports the raising of the Status of Women Commission
       to a full commission." Then, all over the little group
       that was on the committee, the men got up and supported
       us and it went through right away. Then we became the
       Status of Women Commission, equal to the Human Rights
       Commission. What was the date of whatever Mudeliar was
       doing?

Fry: This was in 1951 when "a deputation was sought to obtain
       Sir Ramaswami Mudeliar's support for the continuation of
       the Status of Women Commission, of which he had been one
       of the chief architects." [Read from Equal Rights.]

Paul: Who wrote that article?

Fry: This is by Mamie Sidney Meisen in the January/February
         1952 Equal Rights.

Paul: Yes, she's one of our best writers, but I think she
         made a mistake. It wasn't to continue the commission.
         It was to raise the commission to the status of a full
         commission.

Fry: Well, that may have happened a little bit earlier.

Paul: What I've just told you about?

Fry: Yes.

Paul: Because this was the real fight, you see. Mrs.
         Roosevelt would come in and make the report, which
         she did, for the Human Rights Commission and leave out
         everything that had happened on the Status of Women
         Commission. We probably couldn't get a hearing becuuse
         she had to present the case always to the Economic and
         Social Council. So, we first had to change the status
         of it so that the Status of Women Commission could make
         the report for complete equality.

Fry: Yes, I understand that.

Paul: And in the Human Rights Commission, she was trying to
         keep this pending treaty from recognizing at all this
         equality.

Fry: Well, this is a review of 1951 in the international
         field, and she sees one of the milestones being on May
         14 when "the Status of Women Commission approved at Lake
         Success a convention on the political rights of women
         with a Magna Carta." [Read from Equal Rights.] And she
         says that the Status of Women Commission had approved
         the principle of the year before.

Paul: Now I'm beginning to remember this. I remember it all
         now.

Fry: And then there were some sessions in Paris.

Paul: I couldn't remember whether we got through a political
         rights too. We did get through a political rights treaty
         and we got through an equal nationality treaty. The two
         of them got through.

Fry: Well, apparently, then, this was the big victory. "In
         Paris of May, 1951, the Commission on Human Rights adopted

Fry: Article 31 of the draft Covenant on Human Rights. This was in obedience to the December 4, 1950, directive from the Assembly. Here in a few words is summed up the result of centuries-long struggle by women. Article 31 reads: 'The states, parties to the covenant, recognize the equal rights of men and women to the enjoyment of all economic, social, and cultural rights and particularly of those set forth in this covenant.'...Women were at last within sight of the goal of the recognition of full equality in the covenant." [Read from *Equal Rights*.]

Now, there were three other articles on the status of women that had been incorporated earlier, which you may remember having worked for. One is Article 1, which says, "Each state party hereto undertakes to respect and ensure to all individuals within its territory and subject to its jurisdiction the rights recognized in this covenant without distinction of any kind such as... sex." Then, Article 12 is: "Everyone shall have the right to recognition everywhere as a person before the law." Article 17 says, "All are equal before the law. All shall be accorded equal protection of the law without distinction on any grounds such as...sex."

Paul: That makes me think about Mrs. Meisen [?], you know. She became so terribly ill. I saw her just before I came up here and she said she no longer could work in the government she was so ill, but she said, "I think I can start back and begin to write again, some articles." If I can ever get down there and start again, she's a person I could appeal to. This makes me remember about her. She was so very good, and she had this gift for writing.

Fry: The first council meeting of the World Woman's Party to be held in Europe since the war went on at the time she was writing this article, which was January of 1952. Did you go to that, Alice?

Paul: What does she say about that?

Fry: She says, "As we write this article in January, 1952, there is now taking place in Paris the first council meeting of the World Woman's Party to be held in Europe since the war." [Read from *Equal Rights*.]

Paul: Well, what does she say about it?

Fry: [Leafs through magazine.] She mentions the international
ıe says

Fry: that "this is scheduled to be the last year of work by the United Nations on the drafting of the Covenant of Human Rights." [Read from Equal Rights.] So there's a great deal of work yet to be done, is what she means. She says, "These are the last heights, but they must be scaled...No account of this work could close without grateful mention of the work of Alice Paul, the founder to the World Woman's Party."

Paul: Now, who says this?

Fry: Still Mrs. Meisen. She also says Lady Pethick-Lawrence is president of the World Woman's Party. That's all.

Paul: It's a great loss we didn't continue that paper.

        You see, everything that Mrs. Meisen wrote--she was employed, you know, in Senator Hayden's office, and she would come across and get the material which I always gave her. I don't know that anybody else ever dealt with her or ever knew her very well. So whatever she wrote she must have written because I gave her; but I don't have any belief that there ever was a meeting held in Paris. So, I don't understand that. I don't think that meeting was ever held after I came home.

        Let me see. You say that was after the war was over, though.

Fry: Yes.

Paul: All these people, so many of them, lost their lives in one way or another in the World War. Everything, everything was wiped out that we'd done.

Fry: You mean at your headquarters there?

Paul: [End of Tape 20, Side B]

        [Tape 21, Side A. May 13, 1973.]

        Of course, in that part of the world it was everything; there was nothing but the war.

        And then you see Lady Pethick-Lawrence died, and I know that we had a great deal in the Equal Rights magazines about Lady Pethick-Lawrence's death and what she'd done and so on, a great deal. Did you come across that?

Fry: There was a tribute to Lady Pethick-Lawrence in that; I

Fry: couldn't tell whether it was because of her death or not, but I don't think so because she calls her the president in here.

Paul: I'm getting all mixed up and I've got to go through these Equal Rights and sort it out again because I don't know just when--I knew I was in Washington when Lady Pethick-Lawrence died, and I saw to it that we had about two issues that gave a great deal of tribute to her. I remember Ann Carter was at that time the editor of the paper.

Fry: [Looks at magazine.] Virginia Star Freedom is editor at this time.

Paul: The last issue--who was the editor then?

Fry: Dr. Florence Armstrong.

Paul: She was the last editor?

Fry: I'm not sure; this is the September/October/November/ December issue of 1953. In here you wrote a statement on the vote from the Senate, so you were here in the United States, I guess.

Paul: Well, I know when I was here. I came back in '41.

Fry: No, wait. I'm sorry. They're reprinting a statement you wrote in 1950 here. Well, I think that all of this is available, too, in the records of the committees and the commissions of the United Nations.

Paul: Well, you ask me some things that I can remember, then, because I can't remember--I know that after I came back to--maybe a meeting was projected to be in Paris, but I don't think a meeting was ever held. I mean if it had been held, it seems to me I would have known about it. And I think that [inaudible] perhaps received a note from somebody saying, "We want to try to have a meeting," and I must have given all this to Mrs. Meisen and not, perhaps, supervised the article she wrote. Because I don't think this meeting occurred. I know that I didn't go to Europe again after 1941 and just because of being so wrapped up in the work in this country. I didn't try to do it. I knew I couldn't do both.

Fry: For a while there in 1948, Alice Morgan Wright was the World Woman's Party's observer at the United Nations
. She

Fry: writes this report back. I'm looking at one now in the
       January/February/ March, 1949, <u>Equal Rights</u>.

Paul: What was she observing?

Fry: The General Assembly of the United Nations, that fall
       of 1948.

Paul: Oh yes. She was very good. Now she's completely just
       lost all--lost her mind, really.

Fry: What a tragedy, for a person to be so able, and--

Paul: So wonderful she was, so wonderful. She has a lawyer.
       She had quite a great deal of money and her great, deep
       interest was in the protection of animals. Edith Good--
       whom you may know, just died a few months ago, I guess,
       maybe a year ago--she and Edith Good went to Smith
       together and they continued friendships all their lives.
       They both worked in this movement of ours.

       Alice Morgan Wright continued, I think, to live
       in the home that she'd always been in and she'd inherited--
       but her secretary told us that she just didn't know any-
       thing at all, didn't recognize anybody or know anything.
       So, so sad! [Pause.]

Fry: Well, I can ask you a few of these other smaller
       questions first to clear up some things, Alice.

Paul: Yes, go ahead.

"SIDESHOWS" OF THE NATIONAL WOMAN'S PARTY

National Recovery Act Code in the Thirties

Fry: I thought you might have some other comments to make on the National Recovery Act Code hearings because, according to my notes on that, the Woman's Party in the thirties had someone at all of those hearings.

Paul: Yes.

Fry: And there were over two hundred codes in all and I guess they had a hearing for each code or something. But, at any rate, the Equal Rights magazine--

Paul: But I told you we had all these what somebody's called "sideshows."

Fry: That was your term, yes. [Laughter.]

Paul: Did I say those were sideshows?

Fry: Yes. [Laughter.]

Paul: Anyway, that was one of them; it was only just because you almost had to see that somebody was there. But you knew that the only way to do it was to make it [women's rights] a fundamental part of the Constitution. Whatever we did would be changed pretty soon by some other code.

Fry: So that all of this activity, you knew, was not any permanent advance. Is that what you mean?

Paul: Well, I mean we didn't pay very much attention to it, except to have somebody go down and register our protests.

Fry: Yes. It was reported in Equal Rights at that time that

Fry: the NRA Code was a <u>model</u> code for equality for women,
       at least at first. Later on that may not have been
       true.

Paul: Whatever it was, some of the things were good and some
       of the things were bad. But we were trying to get the
       idea that the whole system of <u>law</u> must be changed by
       having as a basis the equality program rather than the
       subjection-of-women program. Anything that came up, we
       tried to give a little helping hand to make it look
       better, but I must say we didn't devote much time to
       these.

Fry: I see. Let me see whose name I have here for that.
       [Looks through papers.] I guess it's Maud Younger
       who was attending all of those hearings.

Paul: She would have been a very good person to go. She
       probably did. She felt the same way I felt about it.

       You know, the League of Women Voters always were
       different with this because they said, "Specific bills
       for specific ills." And they seemed to glory in all
       these specific ills just to apply a specific bill. We
       thought you must change the basis, the <u>whole inequality
       basis</u> of our law, of our whole legal system; and you can
       <u>only</u> do it by doing it from the very top, which is the
       Constitution.

       So I remember we always went to those, but that was
       a sort of a little dull duty we thought you had to do.

Sex Equality in the 1964 Civil Rights Act

Fry: Well, another little sideshow that last night when we
       were planning our interview we said we wanted to be sure
       and cover was the 1964 Civil Rights Act. Sex equality
       was put in that with the efforts of a Woman's Party.

Paul: Yes. And the efforts of nobody else. No other woman's
       organization helped us.

Fry: Do you have time to tell us--

Paul: It came up, you know, as a--a long series of these civil
       acts were coming up, with people working in civil rights.
       [Pa ...]

Paul: You see, the Negro movement and so on, which was
furthering--all the people that worked with the Negro
movement did not want to have sex included. They said
no because, again, "This is the Negro's hour." You
probably remember all this.

Fry: Yes.

Paul: About two years before the Civil Rights Act of 1964
there was another effort to get through a Civil Rights
Act. It wasn't till '64, till Attorney General [Robert]
Kennedy had sent this draft to the Judiciary, drawn up
in the attorney general's office and wanting it passed
as it was without a change of a syllable, that it seemed
to be on the way to having a nationwide act on the subject passed. That's the first time we really devoted
any great attention to it.

You see, this was '64, so you wouldn't have it, I
guess, in [Equal Rights magazine]. We would have it in
all these little information bulletins and so on that
we've gotten out. I'd better try to assemble those as
soon as I possibly can, order and send them to you, I
guess.

Fry: That would be good.

Paul: Because I can remember that before this came up as an
act that we really knew was going to be probably on the
statute books, it was introduced in Congress [probably
1962?] by the same people who were working for equal
civil rights for Negroes, an act which was to prevent
all discrimination in any way in the economic field--I
think it was limited to some field like that; I believe
it was--on the grounds of race, color, religion, and
country of origin, and not sex.

We asked Congressman [Gordon L.] McDonough of
California, who was the congressman that Dr. Mary
Sinclair Crawford had been chairman of his campaign
committee and had worked very hard for his election.
So she said, "Anything you want done, I think you'll
always find Congressman McDonough will be willing to
introduce the measures and so on." So, we asked him
if he would offer an amendment putting sex to this
"there should be no discrimination," we'll say, "in
economic fields." (It wasn't that, but it was something
on that order.)

s called

Paul: up by Mrs. McDonough. She was almost hysterical over
the phone and she said, "I've just been called by Mr.
Clarence"--I think it's Clarence [M.] Mitchell [Jr.]--
the legislative director of the NAACP [National Association for the Advancement of Colored People], and he
demands that my husband withdraw this proposed addition
of the word 'sex.'" And she said, "My husband isn't
here and I can't locate him." (She was working in her
husband's office; Mrs. McDonough was a regular secretary
in the office.) She said, "I'm so terrified of the
reprisals that will come against my husband from the
NAACP if we don't do it that I want you to call Mr.
Mitchell and say that my husband was not the author of
this idea--he merely did it--that you were the person
who was responsible for this and you called him and
asked him to do this, and out of politeness and so on
he did it." She said, "I really think he's going out
to try and have my husband defeated."

I said, "Well, I'm certainly perfectly willing
to say that we of the Woman's Party asked your husband
and that it was our concern, it wasn't his; but he was
very much in accord and he introduced it. But I don't
think I ought to do that without asking him. I really
think I ought not to interfere this way. He may not
want me to call Mr. Mitchell and say this."

So, she didn't think so. She said, "I know that
something has to be done. Since I can't locate him or
get any idea where he will be, and Mr. Mitchell's
pressing me so, I thought this was the best way out."

So, I said, "Well, let's leave it and see if I can
get your husband and find out what I ought to do in his
opinion."

A little bit later, she called up, maybe in the
afternoon, cooing like a dove [laughter] and happy and
tranquil. She said, "My goodness! I'm glad you didn't
call up Mr. Mitchell because when I got my husband he
said, 'Well, I certainly know what I want to do. I
wanted to introduce this; I don't want anybody to think
that I would introduce a thing and then withdraw the
thing; I certainly stand by it and I believe in it and
I accept all responsibility for it and don't want anybody
else to try to bail me out and don't want to hear anything more about placating this Mr. Mitchell.'"

Well, after all, he was defeated. Whether he was

Paul: defeated by the Negro people or not, I don't know, but
he was defeated. But he was a very gallant person in
standing up for us and he spoke for us on the floor
when this debate was on. I know I have the Congressional
Records of this period, which I could certainly get and
send to you.

Fry: Okay.

Paul: Then it was a limited application. I don't remember
whether sex was retained or wasn't retained that he
was trying to put in. But it wasn't anything very
fundamental. It was just some little phase of the
fight that the Negroes were making.

Then, when this one [1964] came along on the
presidential scale, being demanded by the President and
being drawn up by the President's brother, a great many
of our members felt, "Well, you mustn't take up these
side things so often." But I felt this we must take
up, absolutely must take up.

What happened was that it was sent from the
attorney general's office to Mr. [Emanuel] Celler,
chairman of the [House] Judiciary [Committee] at the
time and an opponent of ours. A note was sent and
reached all the men on the Committee--of the judiciary--
about, we'll say, ten at night or something, from the
chairman, giving a draft of this Civil Rights Act and
saying that, "This will come before the Committee tomorrow morning at ten o'clock and we will dispose of it
then and send it on to the floor."

So it happened just that way. The minority report,
which was presented from the Committee to the floor,
stated this thought: that the men had not received any
notice of it till ten o'clock the night before--we'll
say ten--no time to study a long and complicated bill
with many sections, many "titles," they called it. We
were concerned with Title VII, which was the one adding
the word "sex." That was the one on employment. We
were concerned with putting in the word "sex." There
was [also] a section on education. Of course, we wanted
to put it in all of them, but the one we started work on
first was employment as perhaps the most fundamental,
and we never got beyond that. There was a section on
education, a section on grants from the federal government in aid of anything--in every one of them, we wanted
to have "sex" put in.

Paul: So, according to the minority report, the men
arrived the next morning, not having had time to study
it. Mr. Celler arose and said, "I will allow myself
one minute to speak for this measure"--or two minutes,
perhaps--"and I will allow the ranking man on the Republican side the same amount of time to express any views
he may have. We will have no debate, no discussion,
and no questions. But we are going to send it straight
on to the House to vote on in the form in which it
arrived from the attorney general's office, with no
changes permitted." So, they registered the strongest
possible opposition.

Men got up on the other side--not on Celler's
side, Republicans or Democrats on the Committee--and
said, "Well, we want to know about this point and this
point and this point."

"No discussion is to be permitted. No debate is
to be held. No questions are to be asked. I [Celler]
of the Democrats, Mr. McCulloch for the Republicans,
we each have the same amount of time to express ourselves and then we will vote."

They had enough people lined up with the administration. Of course, this was the way the Kennedy administration, I guess, acted usually. They just voted it out
in the form in which it came from the attorney general's
office--it had arrived there [in the same form] before
to the Judiciary Committee. So, they had no chance to
do anything about it.

Well, we held then a meeting of our national
board. Mrs. Emma Guffey Miller was then president and
a Democrat, of course, and presided. We passed a resolution saying, "This is not a civil rights act; it's a
civil wrongs act as far as women are concerned." We
sent this protest to everybody that normally would
profess to pay any attention to us, in the House and
in the Senate and in the White House and so on. We
appointed someone to go over and try to find someone
who would represent us on the floor of the House when
this came up. It was to come up pretty soon after
Christmas. Our meeting was in December.

Anita Pollitzer agreed to go over while we were
having our meeting and talk to Catherine [Dean Barnes]
May, whom we thought might be the woman who would make
the biggest fight for us on the floor, because Miss St.

Paul: George was no longer there in Congress. She'd gone out, had been defeated.

So, Miss Pollitzer came back saying, "Mrs. May said, 'Yes indeed. I'll be very happy to take this matter up and make the fight on the floor to put sex in.'" Because, you see, we'd said, "Try to put 'sex' in; put a general amendment that in all sections 'sex' should be included among the groups protected by the Civil Rights Act, some general one." So, she said, "Well, we'll work it out some way or other, but I'll get this thing done, I assure you." So, we left thinking that we had that pledge [from Congresswoman May].

Then Mrs. Miller sent a request to the White House to be allowed to bring a delegation to protest to the President about the form in which this bill was drafted with the complete exclusion of women from it--race, color, religion, country of origin, and nothing on sex, in any of these discriminatory sections that were being taken up for the protection of Negroes against discrimination. So, then she departed right after the meeting to her son's home up in Greenwich, Connecticut, where she was going to spend Christmas. Then I think she went up after that to visit her son in Massachusetts and then was coming back some time in January.

So, pretty soon I was called on the phone by one of the President's secretaries [pause] the woman who was there so long, whoever she was. She said, "I'm calling up for Mr."--let's see--"Kennedy to say that"--[pause].

Fry: You mean for the President or for the attorney general?

Paul: No, for the President. It must have been for the President. [She said,] "I'd like to speak to Mrs. Miller."

I said, "Well, she's gone up to Connecticut," and so on.

"Well," his secretary said, "He wants to say that the President would be pleased to receive you after Mrs. Miller's return." [Pause.] And I think he said that he would receive us in Mrs. Kennedy's apartment in the White House, or that Mrs. Kennedy would be pleased to receive us, I guess it must have been, and that the President would come in and discuss Mrs. Miller's

Paul: telegram. Or something like that.

So, I sent word up to Mrs. Miller of this reply. Then, when Mrs. Miller came back in January, the first thing she did was to call up and say, "I want to make arrangements now for this interview." The secretary who she asked for, the one who had called me, wasn't available and wasn't there, and Mrs. Miller kept calling again and again and again and again for maybe a month, and never could make any arrangement about having the interview take place.

Then, in February I think it was, about the first week of February, it was due to come up in the House. We had somebody call all the different women's organizations and say, "This measure is coming up and we are hoping that you'll help in trying to get 'sex' included because it seems as though it will be enacted and be the law for the country. If only race, color, religion, and country of origin are protected in the Civil Rights Act, it would certainly be a backward step for women and have very serious, probably, practical consequences."

I remember we got one woman in the B and P [Business and Professional Women] to call their organization and they said, "Well, this is something that we could not do without a national convention and we won't have a national convention for perhaps another year." And each one, every one, refused to go on record or enter into this fight. We couldn't get anybody to agree.

I think it was then that Mrs. May called up and said that she had promised to do this, but she now found that the whole thing was so sewed up by the Judiciary Committee and the President and so on that she didn't--

[End of Tape 21, Side A]

[Tape 21, Side B]

Paul: We were defeated.

Fry: It was sewed up by whom?

Paul: By Mrs. May, the one who we had asked to take our lead.

Fry: And she said it had been so sewn up by whom?

Paul: Well, by whoever was running the Civil Rights Act. She

Paul: said, "The President's committed, the attorney general's
        committed, and the Judiciary is commited. From the
        inside, I can see that I can't do this. We have about
        forty people that I had <u>counted</u> on, that I thought would
        join me in putting in a general, sweeping inclusion of
        equality for women throughout. They always <u>have</u> worked
        with me. We always have worked together on all these
        reforms, but each one has assured me that they don't
        think this can be done. It would injure the Equal
        Rights Amendment if we should try this and fail and I
        don't see any possibility. If I can't get these sixty
        people I always work with to work with me, whom else
        can I get? I can't do it."

        So, then we started in to try to get somebody
        else. I remember we went to Mrs. [Martha] Griffiths and
        she didn't want to do it. I went over personally to
        talk to--tried to--to Katherine St. George, but she
        wasn't in and the person in her office said, "Well, I
        know Mrs. St. George would approve and want to do this,
        but whether she can do it or not, I don't know. But
        she'll call you or I'll call you when she comes back."
        And the person did call, not Mrs. St. George but this
        secretary, and said, "Well, Mrs. St. George thinks that
        she's not the person to do this. She's, of course,
        against this whole act. Everybody knows she is, and if
        she starts to do it, they'll say, 'Oh, well, you're not
        trying to help women. You're trying to kill this act.'"

Fry: May I straighten out a point? A while ago you said that
        you asked Catherine May because Mrs. St. George was no
        longer there. I thought you meant she was no longer
        in Congress.

Paul: Yes, I did--and now you tell me that she was. Because
        I know that I went myself to Mrs. St. George's office,
        so she had to be there. But why we asked Mrs. May, I
        don't know.

Fry: All right.

Paul: She'd been a friend, but I don't know why. Normally,
        I would have talked to Katherine St. George. I really
        can't answer that point, why we didn't. I just took for
        granted that she wasn't, but I know she was now because
        I know I went to ask her myself. Mrs. Broy and I went
        together.

        Then we went to Judge Howard Smith, who was chair-

Paul: sponsor of ours. And he said just what Mrs. St. George said. He said, "You know, this is an awful act. We never should enact such a thing as this. They'll all say that I'm trying to use this to defeat the act itself. I'm not a good sponsor for you at all. I'll handicap you. Of course, I'm for you and would like to do it, but I don't think I am"--just exactly what Mrs. St. George said.

I remember he said, "You ask Martha." That was Mrs. Griffiths. We said, "Well, we have asked Martha. I haven't personally, but somebody's gone to her, and she doesn't want to do it and I don't think she will do it."

Then, when Mrs. St. George's office telephoned, "No, she'd reflected and she didn't want to do it," we went back again and asked Judge Smith. We said, "The time is almost here and we have to have somebody who can be heard and attention will be paid to." He was chairman of the Rules Committee and in a powerful position in the House.

So, he said, "All right. I will agree to do it, but I want to tell you that I'm not the best person you could have. But I will do my best." And then he said, "I think of all the sections to begin on and the best way to do it is to do it when you get to the employment section. Perhaps that's the most important of all. There shouldn't be discrimination in the field of employment based on sex. Really, we will take them one by one by one and we'll begin with Section I, which is the right to vote. You don't need it in that because you already have the right to vote." And then he went down it and said, "Let's begin here and we'll see what we can do."

So, then came the morning when it was all to come up and begin the debate. Mrs. May called me on the phone and she said, "I want to talk again about this amendment, because you asked me at the beginning to put it in, and I've been again canvassing the situation and I find there's no possibility that you can get sex in. There's no possibility that it could be done and it will terribly injure the Equal Rights Amendment if you try and fail. So, I think the wise thing to do, and I make this plea to you, don't let it be introduced."

So, I said, "Well, I think myself that we ought to

Paul: introduce it even if we <u>are</u> defeated. I don't think
we should let an act like this that affects employment
of women and everything else of women in the whole
country go through. When these people are all <u>specifically</u>
protected--race, color, religion, and country of origin--
women <u>should</u> be in this. And we just have to risk it.
We have to take risks all the time and I think we'd
better take this risk."

Then, when this debate began, suddenly a new man
that we had never thought of asking, Mr. [John] Dowdy
of Texas, arose and, with the very first section that
came up--whatever it was, not voting rights, but the
next one--proposed that they add to the words "race,
color, religion, and country of origin," "<u>sex</u>."

Fry: And you hadn't talked to him?

Paul: No. He was an obscure man as far as we knew. We didn't
know him. We hadn't met him.

Fry: Did you ever find out why he did that?

Paul: Yes, we did find out; but we didn't know then. So,
whatever that first section was, we'll say--there's one
on public accomodations? Isn't there something? I've
forgotten what that first section was. Anyway, when he
said, "And now I move that we add the word 'sex.'"
Well, this had been very well organized by, I suppose,
the attorney general's office so that everybody was supposed to let it go through exactly in the form in which
they had presented it. So I remember a howl went up
all over the room, "No!" So they voted down adding the
word "sex." They just howled him down; they wouldn't
let him speak.

So the next day, we didn't still know who this Mr.
Dowdy was. We were delighted somebody had wanted to
bring it up but we were pretty much worried when we saw
that he was howled down and not even allowed to <u>speak</u>
on the word "sex." So, we knew somebody had been at
work organizing a very strong resistance, and still we
were only the Woman's Party and nobody else, excepting
one lady who had come up from Texas, one recruit we had
who belonged to the B and P. [Pause.] I'll have to
think up what her name was.

But what had happened was that she, in her own
right, had various unjust treatment on the ground of
] .   .   , I think

Paul: it was, a dental student. I think it was dental. Maybe
it was a physician, but I think he was studying as a
dentist. He was still in the dental--we'll say dental--
school and so, in order to make it possible for him to
graduate, since they had almost no money, she opened a
sort of little boarding house where she took students
who were also going to this dental school. She even
gave them all their meals and did everything to make
this a financial success. And she did, through a struggle, put her husband through this, we'll say, dental
school.

Then he opened an office, and in almost no time
he fell in love with his secretary and just went off
and left his wife. She had probably been supporting
herself in some way before she'd started to do this with
her husband, but she had a time of very great trouble
just to exist, and she was existing by becoming, I think,
a secretary or typist or something.

she was so impressed with the injustice of which
she seemed to have no redress in any way that she went
up to New York and got a position, I believe, in some
office in New York to support herself. Then she thought
she would start to join in and see if she could get anybody to join with her to see if she could get some law
through Congress that women wouldn't suffer as she had
suffered. So, she wrote, I think, to every senator and
gave an outline of what had happened to her and asked
if they would help her in some way to get some action
by Congress. She didn't know anything about what Congress
did, you see. She was very untutored in all this.

I think her first name was Hedy [?] and maybe I'll
think of her second name. I'm not quite sure, but I
think so. I know I have it here in my little telephone
book because recently I had a note from the government
saying, "This Hedy Somebody down in Texas has asked for
an inquiry as to whether you have received some letters
she's been sending you."

Well, at this moment, when she wrote to, I believe,
the entire Senate, she got an answer, she said, from only
one senator, Dirksen. She said it was such a very friendly and sympathetic answer, wanting of course to help her.
He said, "The best thing for you to do is to come down
to Washington and go to the National Woman's Party.
They're working all the time on this thing."

When she

Paul: went down, she went to his office and she saw him and
he was as sympathetic as his letter had been. He said,
"I just don't know that I can do anything. Just walk
across the street and there's the Woman's Party and
they'll help you." So, I remember she came in unan-
nounced and everything and I was having lunch all by
myself, sitting there at the table in the chairman's
office, when in she walked and said Senator Dirksen
said that she might come over and help.

I said, "Well, you've certainly come at a wonderful
moment. This is just when this Civil Rights Act is
being voted on, being ready to be voted on, being discussed on the floor, and we can give you a room and let
you stay here if you wish it."

"Well," she said, "I've already found a very cheap
room right here in the neighborhood, but I will come
over and help and begin right away. Tell me what to do."

I said, "Well, what do you belong to? Any woman's
organization?"

She said, "Yes, the B and P down in Texas," which
seems to be her permanent home where she comes from.

So, I said, "All right. Go to the phone and call
them up and tell them that this is now on the floor and
is going to be voted on in the next week. They probably
will spend the whole week on the vote. Try to persuade
them to help."

She came back and with this tale: "No. They say
they will wait for a national convention. They couldn't
possibly take any action on something as quickly as
this. But," she said, "I'll go just for myself."

So, she went over and she talked to everybody she
could get to listen to her in the House as they came
in and as they went out the door. She didn't know anything but to tell them this was a very important thing.
Then she sat up in the gallery and listened to it and
she threw her whole being into it. I think she really
was a big, big, big help. She felt so earnestly about
it. And, of course it was so simple. Each little
section was simple, guaranteeing to race, color, religion,
and country of origin.

Well, then each day, second day, third day, fourth
got to

Paul: know him and we called up this Mr. Dowdy. I remember
Caruthers Berger came up one night to help. She came
up every night. I don't know whether you know her.
She was with the Department of Labor in the legal
department; she was a young woman lawyer. She just
came up like this Mrs. Hedy Somebody as soon as she
left her office and would work the whole evening on
whatever she could.

So I said, "Well, I think the best thing to do,
since this is coming up tomorrow," whatever the next
thing was, "and Mr. Dowdy doesn't know very much, we
can see he just knows the general idea that women
should be protected." This was the field of education.
And I said, "Now, a report has just been issued from the
legislature of Virginia showing that educational opportunities are being denied on the grounds of sex in Virginia
just because they don't have the facilities."

This report showed that [pause] well, an enormous
number of girls, maybe up in the thousands, had applied
for college education and had no place they could go.
It was so impossible to believe! The figures were so
enormous! I remember calling up Mrs. Butler Franklin,
who lives where the Mary Washington College is down in
Fredericksburg, and I said, "You've had a great deal to
do with the Mary Washington College. Do you think it's
possible in the state of Virginia that 12,000 girls
were turned down,"--whatever that figure was--"who
wanted to go to college and they weren't allowed to?"

She said, "I'm sure of it because I know Mary
Washington turned down such an enormous number last
year. We just get almost no money from the state for
our Mary Washington part of the University of Virginia,
and there was no way we could do it. We couldn't take
them." And this really probably is true what this
report shows, issued by the legislature--well, by the
government of Virginia, whatever bureau it is; I don't
know. It was a governmental, anyway, report.

So, I said to Caruthers Berger, "Just get that
report out and tell these harrowing things about Virginia
and show this is a sample of why we must have equal
educational opportunities for women students." So,
she worked, that whole evening and got all the facts
down, and she was writing these briefs for the government every single day, so she could do it pretty rapidly. She would even type herself and mimeograph herself.

Paul: So, she came back with this pretty late at night and put it in form so we could take it over to Dowdy.

So somebody went over at the crack of dawn almost, as soon as the offices were open, to get Dowdy and said, "Now, when you make the speech today, show all the facts to support it and maybe they won't howl you down if you begin on something factual like this." So, I don't know who went over, but whoever went over, Dowdy grasped it with joy and alacrity and said he would certainly present this.

So, he did and it's in the <u>Congressional Record</u>. (I probably have these <u>Congressional Records</u> of that fight. I know I kept them in Washington. Whether I have them up here or not, I don't know.) So, he got up to make his same remark that "I want to amend this by adding 'sex.'" And he succeeded in making his speech, being howled down when they could, just when he stopped to have the vote taken. But he was certainly howled down again.

But anyway it was all incorporated in the <u>Congressional Record</u>, everything that Caruthers Berger had prepared the night before. So, by this time, we regarded him as an ally and began to consult with him. He said, "Of course, I'm not succeeding in helping you, but at least I get the subject before [them], which seems to be all I can do."

We said, "When we get to employment, which is the Seventh Title, we think that nobody will howl down the chairman of the Rules Committee. His own colleagues will never do that. We believe it will be really presented, and you can start in then with all the facts you've accumulated and help."

So, when we got there to Title VII, Judge Howard Smith, who was the chairman of the Rules, got up. Of course he was highly respected on the floor, being the chairman of one of the most powerful committees, and was the Democrat. I think Dowdy was a Republican. I'm not sure though. I <u>think</u> he was.*

---

*John Dowdy was a Democrat from the Seventh District of Texas.

Paul: So the chairman immediately recognized Judge Howard
Smith, and he said, "Now, I have been sitting here for
this whole week and haven't said a word, and many other
people have been sitting here this whole week and haven't
said a word for different changes they think ought to be
made in this Civil Rights Act. We're given no opportunity
whatsoever. We're not recognized. I was recognized,
but we were not recognized when we wanted to bring up
our protests. I want to protest about the way this
whole Civil Rights Act is being put through," and so
on. Mr. Celler [Smith?] didn't say anything about he
was talking about equal rights for women.

      So Mr. Celler said, "Well, of course everybody
wishes to hear immediately anything that you wish to
say, Judge Smith, and we want you to have every opportunity to say anything you have at heart. We are
unaware of anybody feeling that he has not been allowed
to present his views, and will you just take the floor."
And he was welcomed and given all possible attention.

      He said, "Well, my purpose in rising is to make
one specific amendment to this Civil Rights Act. I'm
taking just the present one before us, Title VII, that
says 'race, color, religion, sex, and country of origin,'"
(or something or other; he put it in some way) "And I
want to speak to it."

      So, he had the floor and he spoke to it very brief-
ly. Then Mr. Celler got up and spoke, as chairman of
the Judiciary, against it. He read something from the
Women's Bureau, the director being this Mrs. Esther
Peterson. He brought her name into it. He said, "Here
we have an official statement from the Women's Bureau,
representing the American women, and she says this is
not the time or the place to begin to bring in the
question of sex, discrimination on the grounds of sex."
Then he told all why he thought it wasn't a--(I certainly must get this for you if you don't have it, this
very historic debate).

      So other people got up and supported Judge Smith.
Among others, practically every woman whom we had
labored with got up and made a splendid speech. I've
given you the one from Mrs. Griffiths, which now she's
extremely proud of and had made into a public document
and we had it reprinted. That's when we had it reprinted, I guess, or maybe the one I gave you she had
reprinted. But it says at the top: "Not printed at

Paul: Mrs. May spoke, and I don't think quite all but practically every woman in the House spoke in support of Judge Smith's additions, although they had refused to take the leadership and to do it when we asked them. Then, the one and only woman, I think, who didn't speak for us was Mrs. [Edith] Green of Oregon. [Pause.]

Fry: Do you know why?

Paul: Then a great deal of lobbying was going on right on the floor. Mr. Celler was managing it and also getting up and speaking and answering points and so on in the debate. Then when Mr. Celler was at the point, apparently, of exhaustion, he had James Roosevelt and Mrs. Green--I think perhaps they were the only two; they're the only two I remember--who would alternate, so that one would sort of take the floor and manage the opposition side, the Judiciary Committee side. And he walked up and down the aisles speaking to person after person after person and saying, "You understand, the administration is in back of this. The attorney general's office has prepared this. It's the desire of the administration this go through and it should not be changed," and so on.

All this lobbying was going on up and down the aisles. Mrs. Green was one of Mr. Celler's aides. So she not only didn't speak for us. She was actively doing all she could against us. I'm sure she didn't _speak_ against it, but she spoke to the _men_ against it, from all the reports that were given to us.

Then came the time for the vote. And someone--I suppose Judge Smith, but I don't know--asked that they have roll call--what do you call it--I've forgotten what the name is. It's when you march down the aisle. All the pro's march on one side and all the other side march to the other--two columns. Whatever that's called. It's not very commonly used, but whatever it was, they demanded this.

So, Mr. Celler headed the administration side and marched down the aisle and Mrs. Green marched with him in his. Our side was led by Judge Smith. He marched down and all the women (excepting Mrs. Green) marched down there behind him.

I didn't go over, but Mrs. Broy went and she was very--she said she used to go year after year when her
h   .   pretty

Paul: well familiar with everything and she knew the people
       by sight. She came back and gave a very good report.
       We really were prepared for defeat, especially after
       Mrs. May said she'd taken this careful poll and there
       was no possible chance of doing it. I think that the
       day that she called up and said not to let it go through
       to a vote was the day when Judge Smith had promised to
       bring it up. I think it wasn't the beginning, because
       in the beginning she said, "You couldn't do it." Then
       the second time, I believe it was the day it was to
       come up for a vote on Title VII that she said again
       she'd taken the poll and again she knew we couldn't
       carry it and again it would do so much harm and not to
       let Judge Smith go forward with it. Well, then, we
       sort of were prepared for defeat.

            Mrs. Broy came back and I remember she came in,
       she threw her arms around me, and she said, "All the
       years I've been up in the gallery, I've never, never,
       never, never, never seen such enthusiasm as was registered
       when we won! We won and put it through and put 'sex'
       in." She said, "So, the people themselves who have
       been so terribly articulate against us really weren't
       voicing what they felt because the people applauded
       and applauded and applauded and applauded when it was
       announced from the chair that Judge Smith's amendment
       had carried."

Fry: You mean by the gallery or downstairs on the floor?

Paul: By the men on the floor. This is what Mrs. Broy
       said. She said, "I've witnessed so many debates, so
       many victories. But I never saw the whole floor rise
       up and applaud a victory the way they applauded today."

Fry: Now, let me ask you one minor point here. Was it this
       lady, Hedy Someone from Texas, who saw Congressman
       Dowdy, do you think, and talked to him?

Paul: No, no.

Fry: Oh that wasn't the connection, then.

Paul: No, but she--if you get these reports of the Congres-
       sional Record, and I'm sure it was in some of these
       bulletins we got out--Goodness, we did fail in not keep-
       ing the magazine going! Sometimes you get to the point
       of raising more money and you can't possibly stand it
       that it's so hard! Anyway the price of paper went up

Paul: and the price of printing went up and these things.
Then we dropped the paper, I think I've told you, when
Mrs. Ernestine Powell became chairman and suddenly she
had all these difficulties with her son, who was being
arrested day after day for riding without a permit in a
car and all these things, she was just so harassed.
And then he finally developed some kind of tumor in the
brain and he died. But she had more than any mother
almost could possibly bear and was working all the time
in her husband's law office. She was quite good.

So, she just said, "I give it up. I cannot possibly raise the money to go on with this paper." So,
we just gave it up.

Fry: Well, I just wondered if you did find out afterwards
what--

Paul: Well, I wanted to say, from the gallery, this Mrs. Hedy
Somebody--[laughter] I'm almost sure she was Hedy. You
see, she was as innocent as a babe.

[End of Tape 21, Side B]

[Tape 22, Side A]

Fry: Nineteen sixty-four was the year of the presidential
election.

Paul: And I remember reading the Democratic platform that was
issued to all voters, you know, every four years. And
one of the achievements they put down was getting through
the Civil Rights Act of 1964, with all they'd done for
women by preventing all discrimination hereafter in
employment. Of course, we never got beyond this because
Title VII was near the end of the titles.

And one woman got up. [Pause.] Anyway, and said
she had an amendment she wanted to present, which was
to cover all titles. After we'd had the victory in
Title VII (I have to think of who this woman was) which
was what we wanted to have done in the beginning, and
that seemed to Judge Smith and everybody that we wouldn't
get anywhere if we didn't take one specific title and
try it out there.

So she got up [pause] I think it was Mrs. [Frances
P.] Bolton--because I know she was a woman we had never
dealt with very much, and she was--I think it was, but

Paul: I can look this up and make sure. Mrs. Bolton was--she
had a Negro man--she was a _very_ good person, but she
certainly never got to the stage, it seemed to me, where
she was very independent in her way of deciding what to
do.

Fry: Wasn't she from Ohio?

Paul: Yes. And she was one of the _wealthiest_ women in Congress. And there was no doubt about her feeling of
wanting to champion the rights of women. But she could
afford to have a very elaborate office, and there was
one Negro, you always had to encounter this Negro--
whether he was her chief secretary or not, I don't
know--who seemed to be guiding, _we_ thought, taking too
much control over what she did. We just felt, "Oh, if
we could only get Mrs. Bolton to sit down and really
listen to somebody who could help her a little bit in
deciding what to do."

Well anyway, she arose, and this was certainly a
very good thing she was trying to do. And so Mr. Celler
was very polite and said, to the "Gracious lady" or
somebody and so on, "Of course, she really probably
doesn't understand that this is a subject that should
be brought up at the very _end_ of the debate, because
now [her idea] would be applying to _all_ [titles], and
this is not the point to bring this up."

So she said, "Oh, thank you very much for giving
me this help."

And then someone got up, and we'll say it was Judge
Smith but I'm not sure, and said, "Well, I rather question whether this advice from the chairman of the Judiciary
Committee should be followed, because I think when we
get to the end there will be no opportunity, because in
the end we'll probably be on technical details, and there
won't be anything to amend. I think this ought to be
considered," or something, and it was very right what
he said.

But Mrs. Bolton had already thanked Mr. Celler
for the good advice she got from him. So after the
next two or three titles--however many there were--then
came the windup, which was more or less a summary. But
there was nothing to amend in it. And so then she got
up as she'd been advised to do by [Mr. Celler], and
[what happened was] just exactly what this other person
[said, w' ' ' ' ' ' ' ' r, .d .i. '' .,. . d in

Paul: warning her because she'd followed Mr. Celler's advice. She tried again to have it cover everything, and then they said, "But there's nothing here to amend. There's no way you can amend this; it's all on technical points." It had to be amending race, color, or national origin, you see, and there was no race, color, etc. in it, by the last titles.

So that effort didn't succeed.

Well then, at the end of the whole thing, which was concluded that week. (I think our vote was taken on Friday, and maybe they voted Saturday. They finished it up, anyway.) And on Monday they were to have the final reading, because it had been section by section by section--all the votes had been on individual titles. And the whole completed thing had to be voted as a whole.

So Mr. Dowdy on Sunday--I remember so well this point--called me up and said, "I have received a telegram from" [pause] (I guess it was) "national association of university women"--it was from some woman's organization. [Pause.]

Fry: You mean the AAUW [American Association of University Women]?

Paul: Yes. [Pause.] It seems to me it must have been from them. He said, "--asking me to try to have the word 'sex' eliminated in the final reading, when the whole thing will be adopted as a whole." And he said, "I don't know if they are criticizing me very much for having taken this part; perhaps it's gone to every member of the House. But anyway, I've got it."

And I said, "Well, we don't know how it happened, and we want to say as far as our organization is concerned, we're entirely behind you in what you've done and are grateful to you, and we hope you won't hear from any more people wanting to eliminate it, because we had thought it was done now."

But he said, "No, you see it isn't done. Whoever is managing that campaign is now starting in on another campaign, which I just wanted to let you know about, which could very easily be done when they vote on accepting the whole Civil Rights Act. It just could be taken out again."

Paul: So then we had <u>that</u> great anxiety. And when it was
taken up again as a whole on Monday, it went through as
a whole and was not taken out. So whatever effort was
made by this group--I'm just telling you this so you can
see what a great force we had against us, whoever it
was. And the thing that they were always doing was
saying, "Of course, we're not against, you know, but we
don't want to imperil any forward steps that are being
made in the defense of the Negro by this. This is the
Negro's hour. The whole thing is <u>for</u> the Negroes, what
the administration is trying to do for the Negroes.
And you're just complicating it by insisting on putting
in 'sex.'"

            Well, then in the enforcement section, they created
the Equal Opportunity Commission to enforce it. And we
started right in, sent a delegation before they were even
organized, when one of the Roosevelts was made the temporary chairman, led by Mrs. [Emma Guffey] Miller again
as our president, to ask for the enforcement of this
particular section, just to show we were back of it and
watching over it and so on. And the Roosevelt [James]
said that he was only temporarily there; they would have
a permanent chairman.

            Well, pretty soon the permanent chairman was ap-
pointed. And for a long time we didn't get much enforcement, any real--well, we could say we got no enforcement.
Because people would apply discrimination against the
Negro, and immediately it was forwarded to the attorney
general's office to be acted upon. But women would go
themselves or we would go for them, and never never a
single case, as long as I was there, got into the attorney
general's office.

            Women were always told, "Well, you file a lawsuit."
And some did file lawsuits, but as far as getting the
Equal Opportunity Commission to help, by the time that
I left anyway, we hadn't succeeded.

            You see, in the suffrage campaign, I was there all
the time and I could tell from the beginning to the
end. But these times when I went down and then left
when a thing was accomplished, I don't feel that I'm as
much in touch with it, especially since we didn't have
the record in our paper.

Fry: Well, that was a good narrative that tied everything
together, which can be pieced--

Paul: You mean this particular thing.

Fry: Yes.

Paul: Well, I stayed on until that was finished, you see, until we got the civil rights thing. Then I always came back again, trying to do something at the United Nations. That was '64, about eight years ago.

Appointment of Jessie Dell to the Civil Service Commission

Fry: Would you like to tell about how the Civil Service commissioner was appointed?

Paul: Which one?

Fry: The Civil Service Commission appointment of Jessie Dell.

Paul: That's all been written up in the Equal Rights magazine. Since we have so little time, you can get all of that from there.

Fry: One thing we haven't mentioned--

Paul: She was appointed by--let me see--[pause]. Yes, she's the one I'm sure that was appointed by Coolidge. The only difference of opinion among our own organization about her was when she wouldn't help Miss Berrien be the tax judge.

Fry: But that was later.

Paul: That was when Hoover came in. That was her second appointment. She was appointed the first time by Coolidge, the second time by Hoover, and we were the people who put her name up. Previously, right after the vote had been given to women, Wilson appointed a woman, Mrs. Helen Clem Gardner, to be the first woman on a Civil Service Commission. But that was sort of an honorary thing that she had, and it wasn't very long that she was in. And then women began to complain a great deal about their treatment in Civil Service, many thousands of women all over the country were complaining and saying they had no one to speak for them as a commissioner. So it became something they began to

Paul: And then a good many people came to us from what
we called the [National Woman's Party] government
workers' council. This was the time we formed all these
councils. Miss Isabel Kendig formed them, and one of
the most prominent and flourishing ones was the government workers' council because they did have a real grievance they felt, which made them glad to join somebody
that was going to protest for them. They didn't have
to make themselves unpopular by protesting, but the
government workers' council they welcomed. It was one
that flourished and became very big and prosperous. And
so they wanted us to take up getting a woman commissioner
from the ranks, who would know what women were suffering
and would not regard it a political thing and think only
of what she was going to get out of it, but would really
seriously try to get for women the definite things they
wanted.

        So we agreed to do it. And then we didn't know
any particular woman, and there was Miss Berrien, who'd
just joined our ranks. She was a government workers'
councilwoman herself, because she was in the government
(the Bureau of Internal Revenue, I think it was, as I
said). And so she presented the name of Miss Dell, whom
she knew personally and she thought she would be a very
good person for the position, and she had been dismissed.
It was a period of economy, when they were not only having other regulations that were harmful to women but
were dismissing a good many of them. But she'd gotten
to quite a high position in the government, therefore
had quite a high salary, I guess, and she'd been over in
Europe quite a great deal during the war doing something
or other for the government. And nobody seemed to question her ability or her character or anything; excepting
in the general cutting down of high positions for women,
she was eliminated.

        So, we found that the government workers' council
would help and that all the people connected with it
were all for her. There was no opposition to her personally. So then we did agree to try to get her in. I
don't know exactly, when you say how it was done--[pause]
but anyway, somehow or other we got her name up to the
President, and he appointed her. And the second time we
merely wrote a letter to Hoover, and he reappointed her.

Fry: There were some notes in the Equal Rights magazine--

Paul: I remember it was a long campaign, because I can remember
        (.   ,   .   w   i me up to ur head-

Paul: quarters and we'd discuss what could be done next. I
          think we just did what you normally have to do, to get
          a good many people--

Fry: To write letters?

Paul: No, I don't think to write letters, but to [pause] well,
          people who were somehow influential with Coolidge to--I
          don't think there was ever any opposition from Coolidge;
          [it was] just that it didn't come too easily. And
          after her nomination had been made she had to be con-
          firmed. And I know when she was nominated we wanted to
          get up a dinner and so on in celebration. And she said,
          "Oh, no, no, don't do it until I get confirmed, because
          I don't know whether there's any chance I can get
          confirmed."

          So then we had a long campaign again, where we
          perhaps helped more easily, by trying to show there was
          such support for her among the people who had to--
          probably the Judiciary Committee, who had to approve
          her nomination. And then when it was all accomplished
          and it was finally done and she was confirmed, and there
          was no question she was going to be the first woman
          commissioner who'd ever been in the ranks (a little bit
          different from the one who'd had it as a personal
          political plum for her because she'd supported Mr.
          Wilson in some way or other) we then did have a very
          big dinner at one of the hotels. And she turned out
          to be very good.

Appointment of First Woman Diplomat

Paul: Every one of the women that we have supported has
          turned out, in my opinion, to be very good for the
          nation. Perhaps the best one of all has been [Federal
          Judge] Burnita [Matthews]. She's been extraordinarily
          good in a very difficult place. And then this first
          girl that we ever helped with, this Lucille Atchison I
          told you about, who was appointed to go to Zurich and
          stayed there until she married. She was successful in
          every way.

Fry: She was the first one in the diplomatic corps, is that
          accurate?

Paul: v .   ~   · · ·   perators

Paul: perhaps, and so on; women had gone over to be a typist with some one of the men, but she was appointed on her own as a representative or our country and assigned to Zurich. And as far as I know, she made a very good record and was in every way a credit, and she was really appointed with almost no difficulty at all by us--no difficulty on our part. I don't know how much difficulty she had before.

We had on our board--I think on our board, anyway I guess she was a national officer--one of the people who was very close to Harding because her husband had been one of the biggest men in the political life of Ohio. And this person, whose name I'll get for you--a very, very wealthy family, extremely wealthy family, so they evidently contributed a great deal to the Republican campaign.

So, when this girl from Ohio was struggling along to get somewhere in the diplomatic world and not meeting any success, we asked Mrs. whoever-she-was to talk to Harding about her and she did, and she was just appointed right away. We happened to have this connection with a person who could do it.

Women Physicians Allowed in the Army

Fry: The other sideshow that we haven't really talked about is that of changing the military rules during World War II to allow women doctors in as well as men. This was at a time when the armed services needed doctors.

Paul: Well, by the Second World War so many women had good training, that they felt they could apply to be in the armed service. When there was a general appeal to everybody to do what they could, you know, for the war, a great many women in the American Medical, a very considerable number (I don't know how many) volunteered as surgeons or as doctors in some such capacity. And they went wherever they were supposed to go for their training and so on, and then there came the question of the first pay they would receive. And the comptroller general gave a ruling that he had no authority to pay them, and he had no authority to have anybody serve without pay. And so all these doctors and so on were sent home; they couldn't stay.

Fry: Oh, I didn't know that.

Paul: You didn't? Well, then the first thing that we knew, a
       little committee came down from the American Medical
       [Women's Association] headed by the person who became
       later our state chairman up here in Connecticut, Dr.
       [Emily Dunning] Barringer. The president at that time
       was a Dr. Ratterman, but the person who was in charge
       of the whole effort to get women into the armed service
       was a committee headed by Dr. Barringer.

            So Dr. Ratterman, Dr. Barringer, and other doctors
       arrived and told us this situation and asked if we would
       help them in trying to get a law passed by Congress
       authorizing the payment of women physicians and surgeons.
       The law as it existed didn't forbid it, but there never
       had <u>been</u> a woman. And he said, "I don't see any precedent
       for doing this and any law enabling me to do it, and
       while they don't say it <u>must</u> be males, it's always <u>been</u>
       males and I feel I might violate the law and get in a
       great deal of trouble if I paid the checks without some
       authorization from Congress."

            So we said, "All right. We'll do everything we
       possibly can (And I was there at this little meeting)
       to help them have a hearing." And I remember their
       legislative person sitting there on that sofa in that
       window in the living room, and she said, "You know, I
       was entrusted with getting this thing done, and I have
       to report to you that I have completely failed." And
       she said, "I don't know how to put a law through Con-
       gress." And she said, "I was told that the way you do
       is to go through an agency. If you want to publish a
       book, you go to some book agency, and some agent who
       gets your book published. If you want to put a law
       through Congress, there's an agency for that." And she
       said, "You have to pay this agency," I think she said,
       "about $500," or some sum. "So I collected from the
       women doctors, and I went to New York, not knowing how
       to do it, but I'd been asked to do it by the American
       Women's Medical Association.

            And so I phoned an agency that puts bills in Con-
       gress. And this man said to me, "I will get your bill in
       for you, and you won't have to pay the man who puts it
       in. He's not supposed to have any money for it. But
       you pay the agency. And then all the legal work that
       always results from putting a bill in, you give to this
       congressman's <u>law</u> office. And he can take the money from

Paul: his law work that he does for you, but you don't pay
him directly. So that's the status of it."

She said, "Now I have gone back to the man, and
I'm taking him the rest of the money that he wants
and paid him, and he says I'm not to pay the congressman, but that the congressman he's gotten was so-and-so.
And that now I can pay to his law office all the money
that he needs for carrying it on."

And I said, "Well, that's not the way, of course,
you get that bill through Congress at all. You don't
go to an agent, you go straight to the congressman and
you ask him to do it and he does it, and he doesn't
charge you anything for doing it if he believes in what
you're doing."

So they said all right, as many of them as they
could would stay down there and help in the lobbying and
help with the hearing and help with all if it, if we
would go over with them every day and introduce them to
the congressmen and explain it, which we did. Everybody
turned out and was doing lobbying, like Maud Younger,
and went over day after day and introduced them until
they built up a movement, and finally, the bill went
through.

[Tape off.]

Paul: --They've become the staunchest supporters of the Equal
Rights Amendment.

Fry: The women's medical association?

Paul: The American Medical Women's Association. Whatever
else happened with any other woman's organization, we
always could depend on them. Then, as I said, when we
started to form this women's Joint [?] [Congressional
Committee?] they of course came; we just knew they
always would. And when we had a very hard time to form
it and to get the women to cooperate in working together--

[Interruption--tape off.]

I wish I could think of this man that they asked
to introduce the bill for them. I only wish Dr.
Ratterman were living so I could call her up and ask
her all these things.

Fry: You may think of that by the time the transcript gets

Fry: back to you, and you can fill it in.

Paul: Well, I can look it up in <u>Equal Rights</u> and so can you.
          Because it was in that period, you see, that we had the
          <u>Equal Rights</u> magazine. [Tape off.] [Anyhow, her work
          with that agency, the only point was,] nothing came of
          that, it was money thrown away.

Fry: [Laughing.] I think that's illegal.

Paul: And he turned out to be a man that--whoever he was, he
          was the last man in the world we would have selected.
          [Laughing.]

Fry: He must have been well-heeled if that's the way he
          operated. [Laughing.]

Appointment of Burnita Matthews, First Woman Federal Judge

Fry: --What was it that India Edwards did and what was it that
          Emma Guffey Miller did about Burnita Matthews' appoint-
          ment for judge?

Paul: Wasn't it taken down when I told you?

Fry: No, I was just sitting in there eating dinner.

Paul: Well, I can say this: when it was learned that there
          was the thought of the possibility of appointing a
          woman as a federal judge, there never having been a woman
          federal judge in America, the Woman's Party officially
          presented the name of Burnita Shelton Matthews for this
          appointment. And Dr. Agnes Wells, then chairman of the
          Woman's Party, national chairman, and I went down to
          the White House--no, we went down to the national Demo-
          cratic headquarters and presented Burnita's name to
          Mrs. India Edwards, director of women's activities for
          the Democratic party. And when we explained that Mrs.
          Matthews was a member of the Republican Women's Club,
          although not a particularly active person in any
          partisan politics, Mrs. Edwards said, "There's no use
          in even discussing her. I know nothing about her, and
          I couldn't possibly bring up her name because this is
          one of the biggest "plums," as we call it, that can
          be given to any woman, and certainly the Democratic

Paul: National Committee would never back me in appointing a Republican woman." So she said they wouldn't even discuss it or hear anything about it.

And then we thought the only person perhaps who could change the situation would be Mrs. Emma Guffey Miller, who was <u>dean</u> at the time of the women on the Democratic National Committee. And so we asked Mrs. Miller if she would join in in presenting the name of Mrs. Matthews. And she said she quite agreed with Mrs. Edwards; this was unthinkable, to give a position of this importance to a Republican.

And so, after much thought and many conferences and so on, Mrs. Miller finally said that she had thought this over and she felt that this is not a political appointment in any way for a political position. It was a position for which the only thing to be thought about was whether a person would be the most competent woman, make the best record for women that could be found, regardless of what her party was. And she said she would change her mind, and would go down and tell India Edwards she'd changed her mind and thought that the Democratic women and the Democratic National Committee <u>would</u> back this appointment, because as far as she could see, Burnita had better qualifications than any other woman we could think of who had legal training.

Fry: What do you mean, "After much thought, she changed her mind"? I think you're leaving out the role of the Woman's Party here.

Paul: Well, it was really much thought on Mrs. Miller's part, really, much thought on whether she should be confined to a Democrat because of her party relationship. She decided that it was a position in which the only thing one <u>should</u> consider would be one's qualifications, because it was such an <u>important</u> position to be a federal judge, and it didn't make much difference <u>what</u> you thought about Republican policy or Democratic policy.

Fry: Oh, I thought you had meetings with her during this period.

Paul: Well, of course; we all discussed it constantly.

So Mrs. Miller <u>did</u> go down and see India Edwards and told her she'd reached this conclusion and she t . . . . y . . . . . .ratic National

Paul: Committee and all the Democratic women because of the
        unusual qualifications she thought Burnita had, among
        all the possible women who could be appointed--could be
        appointed because of their qualifications in the legal
        field.

        So then Mrs. Edwards said, "Well, if this is your
        wish and you are willing to be quoted as the person who
        nominates Mrs. Matthews for this position, I'll go and
        ask the President to appoint her." And she did go in
        and she came out and said Yes, that President Truman
        said, "I've left it to you to choose the woman. I will
        appoint her." And he appointed her. And I think that
        but for Mrs. Miller's action on this point, she would
        never have been appointed.

Fry: It would seem unlikely, being a Republican woman.

Paul: Well, I mean in view of the fact that the decision had
        been made on her nomination when Dr. Wells and I had
        first presented it. They had taken the position, "We
        won't even consider her name. We won't submit it, won't
        consider it."

        And of course, Burnita's candidacy had been sup-
        ported and endorsed by a great many women's organizations
        all over the country, but I don't think it had very
        much influence on the final outcome.

Fry: I believe she said [in her interview] she had spent a
        lot of time and effort getting many, many endorsements
        and letters written in and things like that. That was
        this woman she employed--

Paul: Miss Ann Goodby had been employed by Mrs. Matthews
        personally to line up as much support as she could among
        women's organizations.

Fry: I saw some letters in the Anne Martin Collection in The
        Bancroft Library that were written by Mabel Vernon, who
        was apparently helping to get letters written in support
        of the appointment too. So, there was an enormous
        amount of effort that went into this.

        How long did this go on, do you think? I just
        wondered how long it takes to appoint a federal judge
        when it's an unconventional appointment like the first
        woman or something. Would you say two years or three
        years, or about how long do you know that this took?

Paul: [Pause.] I don't know about that.

Fry: Of course, I don't know what you'd start counting from; do you start counting from the first time the Woman's Party mentioned that we need women federal judges, or do you start counting from the time that a specific vacancy occurred?

Paul: Well, a vacancy had occurred and there was the question of filling this vacancy, and of course, women were beginning to agitate for several appointments of women. It was becoming politically important to do it.

Fry: Alice, when I was in Washington there was that vacancy on the Supreme Court and I was staying at the Woman's Party headquarters, and there was a lot of talk about maybe a woman from Pennsylvania and another woman from somewhere else was being seriously considered. And then I left and I never did hear what happened. A woman was not appointed.

Paul: Nixon had announced he was going to appoint a woman.

Fry: We had high hopes, but Harry A. Blackmun was appointed ultimately. Weren't you making a few phone calls?

Paul: Of course, we would like to have, and I thought and still do think--[interruption] I thought that Burnita would still be the best person for the Supreme Court. And I've talked to her about it a good many times and she always says she's past the age limit where she thinks they would appoint her. Of course, she could be appointed; there isn't anything in the law that says she cannot be above a certain age. But she says she thinks that they won't appoint her because of her age. I don't know how old she is, I've forgotten. Anyway, she did resign [retire]--about two years ago, I would think--from being a federal judge, and she's able to get her pension and get everything else now.

Fry: You mean retire, but she's still working--

Paul: But when she resigned, there was such a backlog of work that they gave her some special title (I've forgotten what it is), to continue, not as a federal judge, but she's still doing the work of a federal judge, doing exactly the same work and trying to help get caught up. So she still goes down and stays there all day and does exactly the same thing. If you want to call her, I 't ...'' l w 't 'h~ ~ ~r', ~nd there she

Paul: is in her chambers, with her clerk and everything else as always. And so she says a person who's resigned and withdrawn herself, she doesn't think any President would do it. But when you think of the women whose names have been presented, there certainly doesn't seem to be anybody who would compare with Burnita in preparation, in character, in qualifications, and so on.

The only reason I'm liking to talk about Mrs. [Emma Guffey] Miller, I think it's so very important that people themselves know--and for some reason I don't think Burnita ever did realize--how much she was helped in getting this position. At times I think almost everybody I know is so apt to think that through her own unusual gifts, and so on, that this has come to her through her own merit, while practically never do I know of a case where I think it's come through her own merit.

Fry: No, I think that's a law of politics: [laughing] it's not the merit, but it's whom you know. Isn't that the way it works?

Paul: Well, women (maybe men too) are so apt to think, "Well, I'm unusual. You see what I've done." They always see what they have done, "How wonderful it's been. I've been a success. Why do you clamor for more opportinities and so on for women? Look what I've arrived at." Almost always. Not that I've ever heard Burnita say that, but I think she really thinks that [and] hasn't the faintest idea of how hard it was to get her in, and how really very much she owed to Mrs. Miller. How unusual for a woman who's the dean of all the women on the National Democratic Committee to buck a whole committee and a whole thought of the Democratic party that "this is a plum that must go to a woman who ought to be rewarded in our party."

So, it just shows what an unusual woman Mrs. Miller was.

Fry: Yes.

That is a typical argument, isn't it, Alice, about the Equal Rights Amendment--that women who are in a position to really help feel that there isn't much need for the ERA because after all, they've made it. [Pause.]

[Interruption.]

Paul: ⁚ ⁚, ᴛ · · ᐧ · · ⁚   ı of an

Paul: argument. I don't think it's any argument against the
        Equal Rights Amendment. To open all opportunities and
        make it absolutely equal for every person regardless
        of sex, is all we're doing. But I do think that the
        women who happen to succeed because perhaps .they're
        more aggressive, or whatever it may be, are very prone
        to rather exaggerate their own good points, I think,
        [laughing] when you hear them talk and they say, "Oh,
        look at all I've done."

Transcribers: Frances Berges
                Marilyn White
Final Typist: Ann Weinstock

APPENDIX

APPENDIX TABLE OF CONTENTS

NATIONAL WOMAN'S PARTY

NATIONAL HEADQUARTERS LAFAYETTE SQUARE
WASHINGTON, D C

NATIONAL EXECUTIVE COMMITTEE
MISS ANNE MARTIN Nevada Chairman
MRS PHOEBE HEARST California 1st Vice Chairman
JUDGE MARY A BARTELME Illinois 2D Vice Chairman
MISS MABEL VERNON Nevada Secretary
DR MARGARET LONG Colorado Treasurer
MISS ALICE PAUL New Jersey Ex Officio

CAMPAIGN HEADQUARTERS: MICHIGAN BOULEVARD BLDG., CHICAGO.

October 19, 1916.

Miss Anne Martin,
153 North Virginia Street,
Reno, Nevada.

Dear Miss Martin:

I have been so busy that I have not had time to write you. I have asked Mrs. White to write and hope she has kept you informed of how things are going during this hectic week that I have been here.

Mrs. Colvin, our Minnesota state chairman, arrived here this week and is helping us with our demonstration during Wilson's visit. She leaves tomorrow for Kansas and will remain there until after election. She could not go far away from home and wanted to go either to Kansas or Illinois, so I thought she ought to go to Kansas because Miss Morey does not feel able to get up the Milholland meetings alone.

Mrs. Nelson Whittemore arrived yesterday and will remain until after the election. She cannot go to any other state than Illinois as she does not want to go any further away from home. She will remain here speaking over the state.

Miss Caroline Katzenstein arrived this week and will leave tomorrow after our demonstration for Montana, remaining there until after election, helping Miss Burns in the press work for that state.

Mrs. Whitehouse, our Maine state chairman, is also here and leaves after our demonstration for Wyoming, where she will help Miss Loss until after the election, following Mrs. Field who is giving a week to Wyoming.

Mrs. Field, on leaving Wyoming, goes to Oregon until the 30th and spends the rest of her time in Southern California. She wanted to spend the last two weeks in her two home states.

We have with us now Frances F., Mrs. Mildred Gilbert. ... Miss

(Miss Martin, page 2)

Stevens found her. I have not seen her.

As you will see by the reports, Miss Milholland's meetings
in Wyoming, Idaho, Oregon, Washington and Montana have been
extremely successful. I have not received reports from the
other states.

According to all reports, Illinois also is going Democratic.
The Republican headquarters informed Mr. Gardner that they had
given up hope of the state and are not inclined to make a fight
for Hughes, though they expect to carry the state ticket. The
Republicans have apparently counted upon Illinois as absolutely
safe until about three weeks ago, when their canvass showed a
decided sweep of the state for Wilson,—so decided that they
did not seem to think it could be counteracted. The local
Republicans are apparently not interested in counteracting it
and the national headquarters does not seem to be making any
effort to do so.

We will do all that we can here during the next weeks, but
our task is, of course, very difficult.

Mrs. Brooke is holding a constant series of street meetings
during the day and evening, speaking as much as she can herself
and having others speak between the times that she holds the
meetings. We have a decorated tally-ho going over the city
all the time with our slogans calling on the woman voters to
vote against Wilson.

Miss Elder sits at the desk all day arranging opportunities
for speakers to go to clubs and all other gatherings we can find
over the state, and Mrs. Gardner and Mrs. Whittemore are taking
these meetings, in addition to quite a number of local speakers
whom we have enrolled. Mrs. Gardner is going next into Mr.
Cannon's district.

Miss Arnold is helping on the mass meeting for Inez Milholland at the Blackstone Theatre the Sunday before election.

Mrs. Sippy is concentrating on her effort to get two
workers for each of the twenty-one polling booths in Chicago
for election day. We are also doing this in the suburbs and in
the different parts of the state, as far as we can do so, when
we are able to get in touch with local women who will take the
responsibility for this work.

We have a number (I think, about a dozen) of banners across
the street in Chicago urging the women to vote against Wilson,
have been in a number of places over the state in addition
to ...

(... ....t'., . . 2)

th. (t...t, .   .stic ..r..'. .urty.' .. .... ti. ..h.ve
..o o.ded .n . kin. . . .r....noe ..lt .. .. . .tc.

We h.ve h.. v.r. excellent pres. reports this week, so I
fe.l much encour.ged .bo.t that. I .o hope you .ill let us know
.bout the work .n .ov..a. .e h.ve received n. reports for the
Suff..gi.t for . fortni.ht .t least.

.ping that you .re not too .orn out by this camp.ign, which,
.ccor.in. to the pre.. clippings I h.ve been re..in. from .ev.da,
seems to be .oing wonderfully in your st.te .t le.st, I am

                    Very sincerely yours,

                            .h..irman,
                    .ongres.ional Union.

AP/G.

Congressional Union for Woman Suffrage

Woman's Party Convention

1004 Stevens Building

Telephone Randolph 1094

CHICAGO, ILL.

NATIONAL EXECUTIVE COMMITTEE

MISS ALICE PAUL, N J Chairman
MISS LUCY BURNS N Y Vice-Chairman

MRS O H P BELMONT, N Y	MRS. WILLIAM KENT, Cal
MRS JOHN W. BRANNAN N Y	MRS LAWRENCE LEWIS, Pa
MRS GILSON GARDNER D C	MISS ANNE MARTIN Nev.
MRS DONALD R HOOKER Md	

September 19, 1916.

Dear Organizer:

I want to suggest that in your press work and speeches you make it very clear that we are asking the women voters to vote against Mr. Wilson and the Senatorial and Congressional candidates of the Democratic Party. I find in looking through out press clippings that they frequently state that we are holding meetings and trying to arouse interest in the National Suffrage Amendment, but that nothing whatever is said about voting against President Wilson and the Democratic national candidates.

I think we can not be too explicit in telling the people just what we are asking them to do at election time. We will, of course, arouse more antagonism by this course than we would by vague generalizations, and the result undoubtedly will be that people will resign. However, a direct and vigorous attack will achieve much greater results in the election than will a more conciliatory policy. If we are consistently aggressive in our attack it will probably result in the Democratic papers beginning to criticize and attack us, in return, on the suffrage issue. If we can only get the matter taken up by the Democratic and Republican papers as one of the burning issues of the campaign in the suffrage states, we will have achieved one of the main objects of our campaign. What we want to do, of course, above all other things is to make the National Suffrage Amendment one of the election issues. We can help attain this, I think, only by a positive and aggressive stand in our speaking and in our press work.

Very sincerely yours

Alice Paul

Chairman.

The Woman's Party Song.

The walls that hold us from our on-ward sweeping, Walls bar-ring wo-men e-ver from the reaping, These walls must fall. Standing togeth-er, wo-men shall take Their lives in their own keep-ing.

Horizons wider, wider, ending never,
Horizons beckoning, whither and wheresoever,
Horizons call, enter and conquer
The wider world, ever and forever.

Words by Josephine Nestor Cassidy
Music from ... woman's ... Washington

THE MARCH OF THE WOMEN.

ETHEL SMYTH, Mus Doc

2

Long, long—we in the past
    Cowered in dread from the light of heaven,
Strong, strong—stand we at last,
    Fearless in faith and sight new-given.
Strength with its beauty, Life with its duty,
    (Hear the voice, oh hear and obey!)
These, these—beckon us on!
Open your eyes to the blaze of day.

3

Comrades—ye who have dared
    First in the battle to strive and sorrow!
Scorned, spurned—nought have ye cared,
    Rising your eyes to a wider morrow.
Ways that are weary, days that are dreary,
    Toil and pain by faith ye have borne;
Hail, hail—victors ye stand,
    Wearing the wreath that the brave have worn

4

Life, strife—these two are one,
    Naught can ye win but by faith and daring
On, on—that ye have done
    But for the work of to-day preparing
Firm in reliance, laugh a defiance,
    (Laugh in hope, for sure is the end),
March, march—many as one,
    Shoulder to shoulder and friend to friend

THE NATIONAL WOMAN'S PARTY

Object

THE National Woman's Party is a non-partisan organization of women formed to complete freedom for women in all fields. It is open to all women who will put the woman's freedom before the interests of any party.

Founded

Founded in 1913, as a temporary body, to secure an amendment to the National Constitution enfranchising women.

Reorganized

Reorganized in 1921, after the winning of suffrage, as a permanent association to secure the removal of all the remaining forms of the subjection of women.

Principles of the Woman's Party

The objects of the Woman's Party are given in its *Declaration of Principles,* based upon the Equal Rights program drawn up by Lucretia Mott and Elizabeth Cady Stanton, at the first Equal Rights convention, at Seneca Falls in 1848. Of the original Equal Rights demand of 1848, only one point, suffrage, has been completely won in the United States. The remainder of the 1848 program constitutes, in substance, the program of the Woman's Party today. The Declaration of Principles of the Woman's Party, adopted at a national conference of its officers and leaders in 1922, is as follows:

Memorial Statue of Pioneers, Elizabeth Cady Stanton, Susan B. Anthony, and Lucretia Mott, placed by the Woman's Party in the crypt of the National Capitol.

—*Adelaide Johnson, Sculptor.*

DECLARATION OF PRINCIPLES

WHEREAS, Women today, although enfranchised, are still in every way subordinate to men before the law, in government, in education, in opportunities, in the professions, in the church, in industry, and in the home.

BE IT RESOLVED, That as a part of our campaign to remove all forms of the subjection of women, we shall work for the following immediate objects:

THAT women shall no longer be regarded and shall no longer regard themselves as inferior to men, but the equality of the sexes shall be recognized.

THAT women shall no longer be the governed half of society, but shall participate equally with men in the direction of life.

THAT women shall no longer be denied equal educational opportunities with men, but the same opportunities shall be given to both sexes in all schools, colleges and universities which are supported in any way by public funds.

THAT women shall no longer be barred from any occupation, but every occupation open to men shall be open to women, and restrictions upon the hours, conditions, and remuneration of labor shall apply alike to both sexes.

THAT women shall no longer be discriminated against in the legal, the medical, the teaching, or any other profession, but the same opportunities shall be given to women as to men in training for professions and in the practice of these professions.

THAT women shall no longer be discriminated against in inheritance laws, but men and women shall have the same right to inherit property.

THAT the identity of the wife shall no longer be merged in that of her husband, but the wife shall retain her separate identity after marriage and be able to contract with her husband concerning the marriage relationship.

THAT a women shall no longer be required by law or custom to assume the name of her husband upon marriage, but shall have the same right as a man to retain her own name after marriage

THAT the wife shall no longer be considered as ... ted by the husband, but their mutual ... to the family maintenance shall be ...

THAT the headship of the family shall no longer be in the husband alone, but shall be ... the husband and wife.

THAT the husband shall no longer own his ... ices, but these shall belong to her alone ... ase of any free person

THAT the husband shall no longer own his w... nings, but these shall belong to her ...

THAT the husband shall no longer own or ... wife's property, but it shall belong to be ... led by her alone.

THAT the husband shall no longer control th... property of his wife and himself, but th... nd and wife shall have equal control of the ... property

THAT women shall no longer be discriminated against in civil and government service, but shall have the same right as men to authority, appointment, advancement and pay in the executive, the legislative, and the judicial branches of the government service

THAT women shall no longer be discriminated against in the foreign trade, consular and diplomatic service, but women as well as men shall represent our country in foreign lands

THAT women shall no longer receive less pay than men for the same work, but shall receive equal compensation for equal work in public and private employment

THAT women shall no longer be barred from the priesthood or ministry, or any position of authority in the church, but equally with men shall participate in ecclesiastical offices and dignities

THAT a double moral standard shall no longer exist, but one code shall obtain for both men and women

THAT exploitation of the sex of women shall no longer exist, but women shall have the same right to the control of their persons as have men

THAT women shall no longer be discriminated against in treatment of sex diseases and in punishment of sex offenses, but men and women shall be treated in the same way for sex diseases and sex offenses.

THAT women shall no longer be deprived of the right of trial by a jury of their peers, but jury service shall be open to women as to men.

THAT the husband shall no longer obtain divorce more easily than the wife, but the wife shall have the right to obtain divorce on the same grounds as the husband

THAT the husband shall no longer have a greater right to make contracts than the wife, but a wife shall have equal right with her husband to make contracts

THAT married women shall no longer be denied the right to choose their own citizenship, but shall have the same independent choice of citizenship as is possessed by their husbands.

THAT women shall no longer be discriminated against in the economic world because of marriage, but shall have the same treatment in the economic world after marriage as have men

THAT the father shall no longer have the paramount right to the care and custody of the child, to the guardianship of its estate, and to the control of its education, religion, services and earnings, but these rights shall be shared equally by the father and mother in the case of all children, whether born within or without the marriage ceremony

THAT no form of the Common Law or Civil Law disabilities of women shall longer exist, but women shall be equal with men before the law.

IN SHORT—THAT WOMAN SHALL NO LONGER BE IN ANY FORM OF SUBJECTION TO MAN IN LAW OR IN CUSTOM, BUT SHALL IN EVERY WAY BE ON AN EQUAL PLANE IN RIGHTS, AS SHE HAS ALWAYS BEEN AND WILL CONTINUE TO BE IN RESPONSIBILITIES AND OBLIGATIONS

LEADERS OF THE NATIONAL WOMAN'S PARTY

Like the first pioneers in the emancipation of women, the leaders of the National Woman's Party face, and must ever face, in certain quarters, ridicule, virulent opposition, misrepresentation and worst of all, misunderstanding from the very misguided women who would benefit most from equality before the law They with their many helpers face great appreciation also

The gallant and dauntless leaders, who have kept flying the banner of equality before the law for men and women, are herewith presented as historical figures in an unselfish quest for justice and the advancement of the welfare of the human race

NATIONAL CHAIRMEN OF THE
NATIONAL WOMAN'S PARTY

1913-1921	Alice Paul, N J
1921-1933	Alva E Belmont N Y (*National President*)
1921-192	Elsie Hill Conn
1921-1927	Edith Houghton Hooker, Md
1927-1930	Jane Norman Smith, N Y
1930-1943	Anna Kelton Wiley, D C
1933 (Jan-Nov)	Florence Bayard Hilles, Del
1943-1934	Sarah T Colvin Minn
1934-1936	Florence Bayard Hilles, Del
1936-1939	Sarah Thompson Pell N Y
1939-1942	Anna Kelton Wiley, D C
1942-194	Alice Paul N J

THE WASHINGTON DAILY NEWS MONDAY, JANUARY 20, 1947

Just to Keep the Record Straight

FOR those who can't quite remember which is which in the National Women's Party, this contingent is best described as the "ins." They're shown in session at the Alva Belmont House, 144 B-st ne, where they met to scout all this talk about a NWP "convention" at the Mayflower last week which elected its own officers. The Mayflower branch branded those in office now as

The National Council, National Women's Party, Meeting January 9, 10, 11, 12, 1947 at National Headquarters to Discuss the Emergency Confronting the Organization.

Left to Right, Front Row. Mrs Arthur C Holden, New York City, Miss Mabel E Griswold, Wisconsin State Chairman and Secretary of National Council, Miss Alice Paul, past National Chairman and founder of National Woman's Party, Mrs Marie Moore Forrest, D C, 3rd Vice-Chairman, Mrs Emma Guffey Miller, Pa., Congressional Chairman, Miss Anita Pollitzer, S C, National Chairman, Mrs Clara Snell Wolfe, Ohio, 1st Vice-Chairman, Mrs Lloyd Williams, Conn, 2nd Vice-Chairman, Miss Gladys Houston Greiner, Md, Treasurer, Mrs Lucia Hanna Hadley, Ind.

Standing Miss Florence E Kennard, Md., Assistant to Treasurer, Mrs. Theodora Forbes, Md ; Mrs Mary E Owens North Dakota State Chairman, Mrs Meta Grace Koebler, Alabama State Chairman, Mrs Helen Vanderburg, Iowa State Chairman; Miss Cecil Norton Broy, Va, Political Chairman, Mrs Mary A Murray, N Y, Chairman, Industrial Council,

Present at the meeting but not in photograph Miss Mary C Kennedy, Indiana State Chairman, Dr Alma Jane Speer, D C, Mrs. Grace Cook Kurz, N Y, Organization Chairman; Mrs Betty Gram Swing, Conn, Northeast Regional Chairman.

These are samples of press notices which carried the judge's decision

EVENING STAR, Washin
SATURDAY, NOVEMBER 22 1947.

Miss Pollitzer Faction Ruled Legal Officers Of Women's Party

A list of officers, headed by Miss Anita Pollitzer of New York, was recognized as the legal slate of the National Women's Party by Justice James M Proctor of District Court yesterday.

Justice Proctor yesterday ruled against the plaintiffs who had sought to establish the legality of the slate elected last January in the Mayflower Hotel and headed by Mrs John L Whitehurst of Baltimore

Justice Proctor had taken the case under advisement on November 13 after a lengthy hearing. The jurist ruled the Mayflower Hotel convention was called illegally At the same time, he held that a convention slated by the Pollitzer group for the Mayflower later the same month was properly called This convention was postponed to April, however.

The April convention also was canceled because of the controversy within the party.

Besides Miss Pollitzer, the others declared legal officers of the party include Mrs Clara Snell Wolfe, Columbus Ohio first vice chairman Mrs Margaret C Williams, Ken, Corn second vice chairman, Mrs Randolph Keith Forrest, Washington third vice chairman Miss Mabel E Griswold Madison Wis secretary, and Miss Gladys Greiner Baltimore treasurer

Miss Olive Lacey was chief counsel for the Pollitzer group

Justice Proctor s decision gives the Pollitzer group authority to remain, in control of the party s headquarters in the 100 block of B street NE

BALTIMORE AMERICAN
Sunday, Nov. 23, 1917—

Mrs. Whitehurst "Washes Hands" Of Women's Council

Mrs John L Whitehurst, whose election as chairman of the National Woman's Party was declared invalid by a Federal judge in Washington yesterday, declared last night she had "washed her hands" of that organization months ago

The Baltimore woman president of the Maryland Women's Council and past president of the General Federation of Women's Clubs, explained

"I never attended a meeting of the organization and have not been connected with it for months in any way at all "

COURT RULING.

Her explanation followed action of Federal Judge James M Proctor, who ruled that a national council meeting of the National Woman's Party, called last January, was illegal

It was at this meeting that a convention at which Mrs Whitehurst was elected was called

Judge Proctor ruled that the convention and the election also were illegal.

N. Y. WOMAN CHAIRMAN.

The decision left Miss Anita Pollitzer of New York City, the legal national chairman of the Woman's Party

Mrs Whitehurst said she did not attend the convention which elected her

She said

" At the time I was approached to become chairman there were two conflicting groups within the organization

" When I found the groups were irreconcilable, I dropped out "

The Baltimore News Post
Saturday Nov 22, 1947—

Women's Unit Election Held Invalid

Miss Anita Pollitzer of New York city is the legal national chairman of the National Woman's Party and the convention which elected Mrs John L Whitehurst of Baltimore to that office was illegal according to a decision by Judge James M Proctor, U S District Court, Washington D C

The decision stated further that a national council meeting called last January was illegal It was at this meeting that a convention was called and Mrs Whitehurst subsequently was elected chair-

The group, headed by Mrs Whitehurst, was represented by Dean Acheson, former Under Secretary of State The case has been in court for the past five weeks

Maryland members of the National Council declared to be the legal council are Mrs Amelia Himes Walker, Mrs Theodore Forbes Mrs Florence Laynor Wheatley, Mrs Virginia Starr, Mrs Alice Mann Kaisaudolian, Miss Gladys Houston Greiner and Miss Florence Elizabeth Kennard

Approximately 350 Maryland women are members of the National Woman's Party, which numbers 7 000 members throughout the United States.

Equal Rights 'Rebels' Ask Equal Rights

By a Staff Correspondent of
The Christian Science Monitor

Washington

The National Woman's Party long-time champion of equal rights for women, is having a little problem of equal rights among women

An insurgent group has broken off from the organization and is attempting to wrest the control of the Party, its headquarters, and its funds from the present incumbents

The rebel group even went so far recently as to stage an invasion by force into the Party headquarters the Alva Felmont House on Capitol Hill from which they were persuaded to withdraw only after arrival of the police

Mrs Belmont, wealthy patron of the Party, who bequeathed to it her home, also left it ample funds for operation

'Rebels' Seek Control

Control of these were sought by the dissidents The bank, however, scenting trouble within the ranks, checked authorized signatures and refused to honor the claim of the new applicants.

All this came about as the Party councils met in national session at the Belmont House last week, while the insurgents flounced off to a meeting of their own at the Mayflower Hotel and elected new Party officers The incumbents deny the 'legality' of these elections

The split has developed over interpretation of the purpose and scope of the Party

The insurgents claim that the Party's only legitimate function is the promotion of the Equal Rights Amendment and that it has no authority to dabble in the international field

Opposite Viewpoint

The incumbents headed by the Party's National Chairman, Miss Anita Pollitzer and Party founder, Miss Alice Paul, take the broader view that while the Party's main concern is passage of the amendment its interests appropriately include international aspects of equal rights for women as well

---

THE WASHINGTON POST
Saturday, November 22, 1947

Miss Pollitzer Ruled Leader Of National Woman's Party

Miss Anita Pollitzer national chairman of the National Woman's Party and other present incumbents are the legal officers of the party, Associate Justice James M Proctor ruled in District Court yesterday

The ruling climaxed a lengthy legal battle between the incumbents and an insurgent group known as the "Mayflower" faction over elective offices

The "Mayflower" group had elected Mrs John L Whitehurst of Baltimore as the chairman at a convention of the group held last January.

Proctor ruled that the meeting which resulted in the selection of the Whitehurst slate was illegal and in the nature of a "rump" parliament.

The decision meant that the group of officers headed by Miss Pollitzer remains in control of the party headquarters at the Alva Belmont Mansion, 144 B st, ne

Besides Miss Pollitzer, other officers are: Clara S. Wolfe, Columbus, Ohio, 1st vice-president, Margaret C Williams, Kent Conn, 2d vice president; Mrs Randolph Keith Forrest, 1319 34th st nw, 3d vice president, Mabel E. Griswold, Madison, Wisc, secretary; and Gladys Houston Greiner of Baltimore, treasurer.

Miss Olive Lacey was chief counsel for the Pollitzer slate. Spencer Gordon represented the insurgents

---

December 2, 1947

THE CAPITAL TIMES   WISCONSIN

Rules Women's Group Officers Legally Named

A slate of officers, including Mabel E Griswold, Madison, secretary, was held to be the legal officials of the National Woman's party by Associate Justice James I Proctor in a decision in district court at Washington, D C, Nov 21.

The group of officers held legal by the court was headed by Miss Anita Pollitzer, party chairman

The ruling climaxed a lengthy legal battle between the incumbents and an insurgent group known as the "Mayflower" faction

Miss Pollitzer and the present officers were elected in 1945 Miss Griswold was named secretary last June to replace the former secretary who went over to the insurgent group

The "Mayflower" group elected Mrs. John L Whitehurst, Baltimore, Md, as chairman at a convention of the group last January

Justice Proctor ruled that the meeting which resulted in the selection of the Whitehurst slate was illegal " the nature of a "rump" parliament

The National Woman's party, with headquarters at Washington, D C., was organized by Miss Alice Paul in 1913 to work for women's suffrage, Miss Paul is now president of the World Woman's club The organization is now working for complete legal equality for women.

Confidential ?   Oct.12,1945.   mt. avy

De r Anne: [illegible]

For the first time in the history of the NWP a large group of officers
felt they would have to avail themselves of the existing constitutional
machinery of the party to call a Council meeting to right long-standing
wrongs. You will have received the for al call. Can you not combine
a visit east with attendance at the October 27th meeting? Many feel
your prestige, coolness, sense of fair dealing, remoten ss from the
scene where cliques have been permitted to flourish, will make your
presence a strong aid toward getting justice and resolution of the crisis.

Briefly this is the situation and my part in it. I was minding my own
business when a few months ago, I began to get one SOS after another
from unhappy officers. Would I, a life member, a long-time "loyalist",
not listen to their griefs and help? Reluctantly, stop by step, I was
drawn in and heard their stories. What came across my desk should give
pause even to Miss Paul, as consciously striving for immortality as ever
one did!

Little in the situation would be new to you. At the base lie Miss Paul's
habits of governing with which you are familiar. Those habits have become
more pronounced with the years; her deceits less guarded. There is this
difference: Whereas heretofore, Miss Paul was able to kill off many good
feminists, one by one, this time it isn't so easy. Instead of departing
one by one from the scene to nurse their wounds, the dissidents are acting
together and mean to clean things up if they can. They want to save the
party from ruin with the consequent loss to the whole feminist movement.
Miss Paul has lost of the allegiance to and confidence in her of such
devoted women as Mrs. Wiley, Laura Berrien, Alva Lutz, Nora Barney, who
with the Congressional Chairman, Finance Chairman and many State Chairmen,
voted against her wishes, violently spoken by her, at the Sept.Council
meeting. ?

Last year's election -by-mail in lieu of a convention, seems to have
solidified the disaffection for one reason and another. Anita is merely
the unfortunate puppet, Miss Paul, the target. Action took the form of
asking the Council to approve a request, initiated by the Eastern Regional
Conference last June, that a national convention be called in Washington
this year. There has been no convention since 1942. The Council approved
a convention- compromised on next Jan - over the bitter opposition of
Miss Paul and after, according to all reports, she had insulted the
proponents of a convention,heaped abuse on them, shouted,"Who are these
people?"..."They don't do any work"..."I have to raise all the money"...
etc etc.Finally when she moved to table a motion, proposing to set up a
cttee there and then to organize the details of the convention, and her
motion was lost, she ordered her remnant of forces to walk- out, " to
prevent a quorum" and broke up the meeting! The insulted and abused
women are not disposed to take this lying down.

The Oct. meeting will endeavor to get fair cttees- not stacked ones- for
the convention. All State Chair men at the meeting with the exception of
Ohio and Conn, plus written approvals from some of the Western ones,
were pro-convention. The bulk of the party membership and the majority
in the meeting should have prevailed. We believe it will next meeting.

Don't you feel moved to give a hand to those who seek to recover the
rights they once voted away to one who has cruelly abused their tolerance?
If these women can't make good a fight for their rights within the organization
which they have all labored to build and which belongs to all members, not
to one, how in the world can they ever hope to persuade the community
they are fit to fight for the rights of all women? A few months ago some

wanted to bolt and start a schism. I advised against it for 2 reasons: 1.
Martin Luthers are rare and I don't see one among us at our age. 2. The NWP
no matter how battered by Miss Paul and despite its meager gains, is still
the spearhead of the conscious, organized feminist movement in this country.
It can be revived more easily and fruitfully, I believe, than a " third
party" can be brought to life.

What do you say? My affectionate regards to you and high hopes of seeing you
soon again in our midst- say October 27th.

Doris. (Stevens)

From Smithsonian, November 1972

By Lynne Cheney

How Alice Paul became the most militant feminist of them all

*She marched through a gauntlet of derision
and helped win the vote for women
Now she still fights on for equal rights*

Mabel Vernon was there, lecturing the younger women who gathered around her, using the same rhetorical techniques to educate them that she once used on anti-suffrage crowds Hazel Hunkins Hallinan was there, looking remarkably young at 82 Yes, she confessed, she had once scaled the White House fence and set protest fires among President Wilson's trees

A tea in Washington, D C , had brought the onetime suffragists together, a late afternoon tea at the Alva Belmont House, the historic headquarters of the National Woman's Party Feminists of all ages and persuasions crowded into the headquarters, which, with its antiques and statues and paintings, is a kind of shrine to the first stages of the women's movement

One feminist, perhaps the Woman's Party's most important member, was absent Alice Paul, the most militant of the suffragists, the woman who more than anyone created and shaped the Woman's Party, had told me earlier that she wouldn't be coming

Appearing at tea parties has never really been Alice Paul's style For the more than 60 years that she has been in the women's movement, Miss Paul has been organizing, planning, usually moving behind the scenes, leaving the limelight and frivolity to others She was not at all anxious to have me write about her "Write about the National Woman's Party," she commanded brusquely. Only after I expressed interest in

Free lancer Ly·· (·   .   ·
in Literature" . ι.   ,·   '

working for ratification of the equal rights amendment did she agree to talk to me at any length "I thought it was just for an article," she said "If you can help, maybe we can make some sort of arrangement "

Having invested her lifetime in securing equality for women, and with the passage of the 19th Amendment to her credit, Alice Paul is still at work on the proposed 27th—the one that makes discrimination based on sex unconstitutional Approved by Congress, the amendment becomes law on the affirmative decision of three fourths of the state legislatures In September, Pennsylvania became the 21st state to ratify.

I soon found that the "arrangement" Miss Paul mentioned did not include much talk about the past. She would rather discuss getting the equal rights amendment ratified in Wyoming than recall the suffrage struggle And conversations with Alice Paul go where she wants them to "Why in the world would anyone want to know about that in 1972?" she responded to one historical question And to another You know the answer to that as well as I do, or else you haven't read any of the books '

At 87, Alice Paul is tiny and her hair has turned gray, but she is not a sweet little gray-haired lady And though old pictures show her as a fragile, delicately pretty girl, she seldom played the role Her dictatorial ways are as legendary as her stubborn persistence

Yet along with bruising egos, she arouses great admiration The intensity of her lifelong dedication to equal rights for women is awe inspiring One woman who knew her during the suffrage campaign believed that Alice Paul had made a vow not to think about anything except suffrage until the federal amendment had been achieved And then, after almost 50 years
··f·h·i··f·········h·······ndment, Miss
anything but
spoken to the

point of rudeness," as William L. O'Neill says in his book, *Everyone Was Brave*, it's because she has no time for anything unless it will advance the cause of women's rights—and that includes tact.

Yet Alice Paul, during the suffrage campaign, had an uncanny ability to draw people to her, to get them to respond the way she wanted. In January 1913, the 28-year-old Quaker-born PhD took over chairmanship of the National American Woman Suffrage Association's Congressional Committee, which was practically defunct. NAWSA's annual budget for Congressional action was $10. Within eight years, the dark-haired, blue-eyed woman had raised $750,000 and enrolled 50,000 members in the National Woman's Party. More than that, national attention had been attracted to the woman's suffrage amendment, which had been languishing in Congress since 1878. Alice Paul helped convert a President, a Congress and a nation into supporting that amendment.

She started by organizing a parade: floats and 5,000 marching women—the touch of pageantry that was to characterize events that Alice Paul put together. Leading the parade astride a white horse was beautiful Inez Milholland in white cossack suit, white kid boots and pale blue cloak. General Rosalie Jones marched with her band of women who had walked to Washington, D.C., from New York. The parade was on March 3, 1913, the day before Wilson's inauguration. This probably explains the crowd of half a million—and their rowdiness. One drunk came close to being run over

when he almost fell under a float. Others tried to climb aboard. Crowds surged into the streets, breaking the restraining ropes. The police, claimed the marchers, were of little help. A Congressman's wife reported that a policeman had shouted at her, "If my wife were where you are I'd break her head."

No woman was seriously hurt, but they had an issue nonetheless. A Senate investigation followed, keeping the affair—and the suffrage amendment—alive in the public mind for weeks.

For the next few years, Alice Paul led her forces in quieter warfare. Lobbyists sought to get the suffrage amendment out of committees and onto the floor. On one Valentine's Day, members of the House Rules Committee were favored with suffrage valentines (see page 98).

In 1914, after breaking with the National American Woman Suffrage Association, Miss Paul's group organized a campaign against Democrats in the nine states where women had gained the vote through state action. Alice Paul theorized that the party in power should be held responsible for the lack of a federal suffrage amendment, and their control of the Presidency and Congress made the Democrats the party in power. Two years later, Alice Paul directed the party's campaign against Woodrow Wilson.

On January 9, 1917, he received 300 women who brought him resolutions commemorating Inez Milholland Boissevain, the young herald of the 1913 parade who had recently died. He seemed distinctly cold to the deputation. Perhaps he had not expected it to turn into an-

other lobbying session, or he may have been piqued that the spokeswoman for the group should quote Charles Evans Hughes, the candidate he had defeated in 1916. At any rate, Alice Paul was left with the impression that the President would not be receiving any more Woman's Party deputations for suffrage. "So," she says today, "we decided to send him a perpetual deputation." The next day, January 10, 1917, she led a group of 12 women to the White House with banners demanding that Wilson back suffrage.

Like the March 1913 parade, the picketing had an air of pageantry about it. Day after day, the women made their ceremonial march to the White House gates, carrying the Woman's Party's purple, white and gold colors as well as the lettered banners demanding suffrage. "We always tried to make our lines as beautiful as we could and our banners were really beautiful," Alice recalled.

Standing outside the White House gates in winter twilight, the women were aware of the picture they made—tricolor banners contrasting with the black grillwork of the fence and the bare branches of the trees. And then on spring mornings hyacinths, azaleas and forsythia on the White House lawns repeated the purple, white and gold of the banners.

But the entry of the United States into World War I broke up these patterns and inspired the Woman's Party to militancy. Picketers' slogans became increasingly pointed, increasingly unpatriotic to some eyes. When a Russian delegation visited the White House on June 20, 1917, the pickets carried a banner declaring in

Clad in brown and carrying pilgrim staffs, suffragists march from New York to Washington in 1913.

part: "WE THE WOMEN OF AMERICA TELL YOU THAT AMERICA IS NOT A DEMOCRACY. TWENTY MILLION WOMEN ARE DENIED THE RIGHT TO VOTE." That was too much for one man in the gathering crowd; he tore the banner down. Next day an irate woman ripped a banner that read, "DEMOCRACY SHOULD BEGIN AT HOME."

The following day, police began arresting pickets, but that, of course, did not dissuade Alice Paul and the Woman's Party. Before the suffrage amendment passed, there were some 500 arrests and 168 women served prison sentences, mostly for "obstructing traffic."

From the District Jail and the Occoquan Workhouse, the women reported food full of weevils and worms, cells full of rats and roaches. They were put to work painting latrines and sewing with the other prisoners. At one point, a group in Occoquan testified that prison authorities physically assaulted them, twisted their arms, dragged and threw them around. Prison authorities in the District of Columbia workhouse, on the other hand, claimed that suffragists attacked *them*, falling upon the acting superintendent, matron and three male guards.

Imprisoned pickets demanded to be treated as political prisoners. When ignored, they went on hunger strikes. It was a trick Alice Paul had learned in England—along with one of the consequences of hunger striking: force feeding (SMITHSONIAN, July 1970). "They ran a tube through the nose into the stomach," Hazel Hunkins Hallinan explains. "And you mustn't think of the nice soft rubber

Alice in her youth: tiny, fragile, pretty—and tough as nails.

tubing they have today." Rose Winslow, in jail with Alice Paul, smuggled notes to friends: "The same doctor feeds us both. . . . Don't let them tell you we take this well. Miss Paul vomits much. I do, too . . . ." When the women still refused to eat, prison authorities moved Alice Paul to a psychopathic ward.

Late in November 1917, however, she and the other pickets were released. Someone had apparently realized that making martyrs out of them was no way to quell the movement. The Woman's Party was already sending speakers, especially recently jailed women, throughout the country. Early in December 1917, at a mass meeting held to honor released pickets. more than $86,000 was raised.

On January 9, 1918, Woodrow Wilson declared himself in favor of a federal suffrage amendment. The fact that his declaration came exactly one year after the Inez Milholland deputation had visited him suggested that militant tactics had worked. So the party turned to them again to prod Wilson toward doing more for the suffrage amendment. In September, they ceremoniously burned the President's words in Lafayette Park. Many suffragists, most notably Carrie Chapman Catt and her National American Woman Suffrage Association, believed that suffrage was finally achieved in 1920 in spite of, rather than because of, Alice Paul's militant strategy.

In a peaceful mood, militants sent valentines to key government leaders.

pickets and hunger

strikes, especially with the country at war, Carrie Catt's group disavowed militancy and erected a two-block-long billboard on New York City's upper Fifth Avenue dissociating themselves from it. While the Woman's Party was harassing Wilson, Mrs. Catt's organization—with quite different tactics—was gently persuading him to see the light. Perhaps the two groups, without consciously cooperating, served to convince the President. Even Mrs. Catt couldn't deny that Alice Paul's early tactics brought needed attention to the federal amendment. It had not even been debated in Congress for 26 years.

In Alice Paul's eyes, suffrage was not the whole war. There were other battles to be fought. "It is incredible to me that any woman should consider the fight for full equality won," she said in 1920. She and her party began in 1923 to work for the passage of an equal rights amendment. It would be 49 years before this would get by both houses of Congress, and during that time Alice Paul earned three law degrees besides lobbying to have the equal rights principle recognized by the League of Nations and included in the United Nations preamble.

"Equal rights has been a harder fight than suffrage," she now admits. "The difference is that the equal rights amendment would take something away from the groups that opposed us." From the time it was first proposed, the equal rights amendment's most bitter opponents have been groups such as the National Consumers League and the YWCA that have worked to achieve legislation protecting women from "hard" labor and long hours.

"One by one the organizations have come over," Miss Paul notes. Last May the League of Women Voters—the group founded by the National American Woman Suffrage Association even before suffrage was won—authorized local leagues to work for equal rights ratification.

But it has been a long struggle, one in which the old dramatic tactics seem to have had little effect. In 1959, flares were lighted in front of the Alva Belmont House to burn until the amendment passed Congress. But the flames died out long before approval.

A new movement, women's liberation, seems to have done for equal rights what Miss Paul's group did for suffrage. "Well, I don't care what people think," Alice Paul said when I pointed this out. "They do stand for many things we don't stand for," she added, mentioning abortion and the desegregation of men's clubs. "They aren't concentrated on a single measure like we are."

The Alva Belmont House, where Miss Paul spends much of her time, seems to have had its character molded by her single-minded intensity, perhaps fittingly, since she has saved the house from government plans to raze it for a parking lot. Although the years have taken their toll on the house (one of the oldest on Capitol Hill), there is a grandeur about it and its handsome antiques, many of which are directly related to the women's movement. Here stands Susan B. Anthony's desk, Elizabeth Cady Stanton's chair. Paintings and busts of suffragists line a front hall lit by a red-and-gold Victorian fanlight. At the far end, a purple-and-gold banner demands suffrage for the women of the United States.

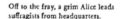
Off to the fray, a grim Alice leads suffragists from headquarters.

From Smithsonian, November 1972

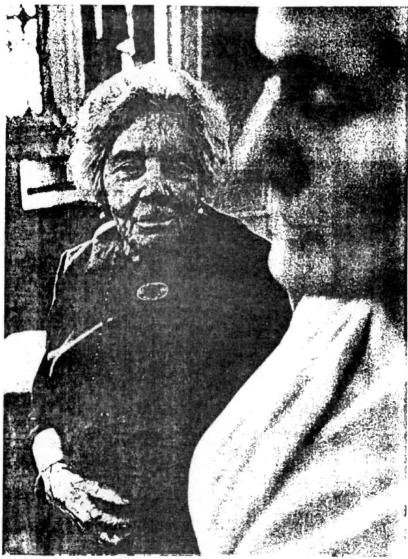

Alice Paul, bes
is, at 87, still ac

INDEX - Alice Paul

General Federation of Women's Clubs:
    support for Equal Rights Amendment, 440-441
George, Lloyd, 50
Gildersleeve, Dr. Virginia, 286
Gillette, Frederick, 328, 353
Gillette, Emma, 66, 67, 99-100, 308
Goodby, Ann, 645
Gore, Louise, 390-392, 463
Gram, Alice, 195, 348-349, 356-357
Gram, Betty, 194-195, 253, 348-349, 577, 582
Green, Edith, 631
Green, Rena Maverick, 111
Greuning, Dorothy, 138, 496-499
Greuning, Ernest, 138-139, 495
Grey, Sir Edward, 52-54
Griffiths, Martha, 540, 548, 630
Griswold, Mabel E., 552, 554, 560, 568, 573, 582
Guffey, Joseph F., 517

Hale, Matthew, 379
Harding, Warren G., 491-492, 640
Harper, Ida Husted, 90, 350, 352, 353
Harrison, Cary, 289
Havemeyer, Mrs. H. O., 260
Hayden, Carl, 518-524, 529, 531-533
Hayden rider to Equal Rights Amendment, 518-535, 599-600
Hazard, Mrs. Dora, 227, 228
Hearst, Phoebe, 245-246, 317
Hearst, William Randolph, 245-246
Heitman, _____ , Mrs. 503-505
Hepburn, Mrs. Thomas, 122-123, 330
Hill, Elsie, 71-75, 83, 92, 118, 132-133, 163, 204, 243, 256-257,
    262, 265-266, 277, 354, 357, 458-459, 487, 524, 599-601
Hilles, Mrs. Florence Bayard, 141, 193, 210-211, 222, 233-234,
    245, 252-253, 565
Hodgson, James D., 500
Holden, Miriam, 583-587
Hooker, Mrs. Donald, 110, 211, 257, 307, 315, 322, 325, 330, 493
Hoover, Herbert, 422, 424, 478, 490, 580, 637-638
Hopkins, Alison [Mrs. J. A. H.], 210- 211, 219, 222, 223-224, 452
Hopkins, J. A. H., 235, 452
Howe, Mrs. Frederick, 215, 218
Hughes, Charles Evans, 155-156, 370
Hunkins, Hazel, 161, 175, 243, 344-346
Hurlburt, Julia, 222

Ingham, Mary H., 222
Inter-American Commission on Women, 418-425 passim, 468-470, 494
International Council of Women, 207, 466-470
International Woman Suffrage Alliance, 203-207, 258, 359-360,
    46 4+1

Jamison, Maud, 217, 221
Johnson, Adelaide, 351
Joliffe, Frances, 149
Jones, Andreus Aristides, 298, 363-366, 373
Jones, Wesley L., 331-332, 363-366

Katzenstein, Carolyn, 61, 161, 220, 393
Kellerman-Reed, Ivy, 307
Kelley, Florence, 406, 409-412, 429
Kendig, Isabel [Mrs. Howard Gill], 433-435, 638
Kennedy, Edward [Ted], 537, 539
Kennedy, Mary, 199, 516, 548
Kennedy, Robert, 617
Kent, Mrs. William, 64-71 passim, 80, 97, 101, 105-107, 173,
    193, 210-211, 245, 296-297, 301, 308-317 passim, 328, 347-
    348, 443
Kent, William, 80, 347-348
Kerr, Mina, 181
Kincaid, Mrs. B. R., 222
King, Dr. Cora Smith, 115-116
Knowland, Mary A., 240
Knowland, Joseph, 151
Koontz, Elizabeth Duncan, 499

Labor Department. See Women's Bureau
Lacey, Olive, 589-591
Laidlaw, Mrs. James Lee, 176
Laughlin, Gail, 338, 475-482, 503
Lawrence, Pethick, 49
Lawrence, Lady Pethick, 38, 48, 597, 608, 612-613
League of Women Voters, 182-183, 258, 405, 616
Lee, Muna, 604-605
Leonard, Margie, 498
Leslie, Mrs. Frank, 201, 204-207
Lewis, Mrs. Lawrence, 63, 65, 91, 105, 154, 180, 190, 211,
    227, 245, 250, 253-255, 262, 313, 354, 393
Lewis, William Draper, 255
Lewis, Shippen, 255
Lindsay, Mrs.____, 524-529
Littleboy, Anna, 40
Lloyd, Georgia, 199
Lloyd, Lola Maverick, 131
Lockwood, Belva, 71
Lockwood, Mary Marsh, 183
Lodge, Sir Oliver, 32-34
Longwell, Mrs. ____, 276-277, 542-547 passim
Lutz, Alma, 594-596

McCarthy, Eugene, 471-472, 539
McCormick, Mrs. Medill, 102-103, 106, 310-314
McCormick, M... .... , ..., .., -.

Pound, Roscoe, 266, 269, 458
Powell, Ernestine Breisch, 516, 526, 633
Price, Nina Broderick, 459
Protective Labor Laws, 183, 411-413, 476-482, 519. See also
    Equal Rights Amendment, Women's Bureau
Putnam, Mabel, 472

Rankin, Jeannette, 161, 174-177, 185-187, 212, 237-238, 298,
    326
Rawalt, Marguerite, 528-530, 535, 540
Reid, Mrs. Ogden, 359
Reyes, Consuelo, 121, 146, 185, 216, 496-497, 544-545
Reynean, Mrs. Paul, 222
Reynolds, Mrs. A. Scott, 395
Rhondda, Lady Margaret, 205-206
Robinson, Alice Gram. See Gram, Alice
Rogers, Elizabeth S. (Mrs. John), 76, 124-125, 166-170, 223, 337
Rogers, Dr. John, 167-170
Roosevelt, Eleanor, 489-498, 606-610
Roosevelt, Franklin D., 4-8, 493, 580
Roosevelt, James, 631, 636
Roosevelt, Theodore, 154, 369-370
Rosenwald, Mrs. Julius, 163

Saboroden, Nina, 179
St. George, Katherine, 158, 520-527, 623-624
Sanger, Margaret, 494
Sayre, Pearl Mitchell, 385-387, 388-389
Scott, Dr. James Brown, 424, 468
Sebree, Dr. Margaret, 560, 569
Seneca Falls Resolutions, 264-265, 459. See also National Woman's
    Party
Sewall, May Wright, 467
Shafroth-Palmer Bill, 103, 104, 109, 111-113, 123, 156, 159,
    312-318, 324, 369
Shaw, Dr. Anna Howard, 75- 93, 95-96, 102, 105, 317, 325, 350
Sherman, _____, [Senator], 247
Sherwin, Ella, 435
Smith, Mrs. Clarence, 467-468, 489
Smith, Judge Howard, 623-637 passim
Smith, Margaret, 3
Smith. Margaret Chase, 520-523, 596
Smuts, Jan Christian, 286-287
Stanton, Elizabeth Cady, 94, 351, 512-513
Steinem, Gloria, 196
Stevens, Doris, 111, 160, 204, 211, 222-223, 330, 360, 420-423,
    479, 560-568, 572, 577, 579, 581-597 passim
Stevens, Frank, 201
Stimson, Henry Lewis, 76-80
Stimson, Mrs. Henry Lewis, 76

Amelia R. Fry

Graduated from the University of Oklahoma, B.A. in
psychology and English, M.A. in educational psychology
and English, University of Illinois; additional work,
University of Chicago, California State University
at Hayward.

Instructor, freshman English at University of Illinois
and at Hiram College. Reporter, suburban daily newspaper,
1966-67.

Interviewer, Regional Oral History Office, 1959--;
conducted interview series on University history,
woman suffrage, the history of conservation and forestry,
public administration and politics. Director, Earl
Warren Era Oral History Project, documenting govern-
mental/political history of California 1925-1953;
director, Goodwin Knight-Edmund G. Brown Era Project.

Author of articles in professional and popular journals,
instructor, summer Oral History Institute, University of
Vermont, 1975, 1976, and oral history workshops for
Oral History Association and historical agencies;
consultant to other oral history projects; oral history
editor, Journal of Library History, 1969-1974; secretary,
the Oral History Association, 1970-1973.

CPSIA information can be obtained
at www.ICGtesting.com
Printed in the USA
LVHW022329301221
707417LV00002B/10